THE ECONOMICS OF EUROPEAN INTEGRATION

THE ECONOMICS OF EUROPEAN INTEGRATION
THEORY, PRACTICE, POLICY
Second Edition

WILLEM MOLLE

Dartmouth
Aldershot • Brookfield USA • Singapore • Sydney

Published by
Dartmouth Publishing Company Limited
Gower House
Croft Road
Aldershot
Hants GU11 3HR
England

Dartmouth Publishing Company
Old Post Road
Brookfield
Vermont 05036
USA

First published 1990
Reprinted 1991, 1992
Second edition 1994

British Library Cataloguing in Publication Data
Molle, W. T. M.
  Economics of European Integration: Theory,
  Practice, Policy. – 2Rev.ed
  I. Title
  337.142

Library of Congress Cataloging-in-Publication Data
Molle, Willem.
    The economics of European integration: theory, practice, policy /
  Willem Molle. — 2nd rev. ed.
      p.   cm.
  Includes bibliographical references and index.
    ISBN 1-85521-498-9. — ISBN 1-85521-506-3 (pbk.)
    1. European Economic Community.   2. Europe—Economic
  integration—History.   3. Monetary policy—European Economic
  Community
  countries.   I. Title.
  HC241.2.M58   1994
  337.1'42—dc20   94-11914
                                                                      CIP

ISBN 1-85521-498-9
    1-85521-506-3 (pbk)

Printed and bound in Great Britain by
Biddles Ltd, Guildford and King's Lynn

CONTENTS

PART VI   CONCLUSION

ANNEXES

List of Tables

List of Figures

Acknowledgements

In writing this book I have been supported by many. In particular I wish to thank students and colleagues. The book's present form owes much to students at the various universities where I have lectured, particularly in Maastricht and Rotterdam, but also at universities in Shanghai, Paris and Lyons for example, where I have been a guest lecturer. My students' critical comments on the text have resulted in this adapted version, which is better suited to students' needs. Many colleagues, too numerous to list here, have helped me by correcting errors in the text and by making suggestions for including new material or presenting the existing material in a different way. Their expertise in their own fields has made it possible for me to cover areas far beyond the territory I could possibly have hoped to become an expert in myself.

I thank them all for their help and encouragement. Needless to say, all remaining errors and shortcomings are my responsibility.

PART I
GENERAL ISSUES

1 Introduction

Definition of the subject matter

Progressive integration has been one of the most characteristic aspects of economic development in the last few decades, worldwide and in Europe, where it has found expression notably in the European Community (EC), now European Union (EU). The EU has had a direct and profound influence on the economy of member states and third countries.

Much has been written about European economic integration. In the 1950s and 1960s, the discussion on economic integration was concentrated on international economic relations, as witness the specialised books on the subject from that period. In the 1970s and 1980s, the idea of economic integration quickly spread to the economics of the industrial sector branches (agriculture, energy, manufacturing, services, transport) and to such aspects as market regulation, macro-economic equilibrium, monetary control, regional equilibrium or social welfare. In all those fields, the body of specialised literature is growing very rapidly.

To *students of the economic integration process per se* this literature is inconvenient because it is addressed to sector specialists rather than integration 'specialists'. And because sub-disciplines have been slow to share their experiences and results with others, the overall significance of European economic integration is difficult to get hold of. Yet this is exactly what is increasingly needed. As economic integration touches ever more areas of society, more and more people are confronted by the bewildering complexity of the functioning of the EU, and look for a systematic analysis.

This book attempts to come to their help by offering a text that aims to:

- place the wide variety of issues in a robust conceptual structure;

- integrate theoretical developments with the results of empirical research and of policy analysis;
- explain the logic of the dynamic processes;
- describe the structural features of the European economy;
- depict the 'historical' developments so as to give a sound basis for the understanding of the present situation and the likely future development.

The book is based mostly on the results of theoretical and empirical studies of a large number of colleagues, and to some extent also on original research by the author.

Organisation of the material

The book is divided into six parts. **Part I** treats three themes. The first is the fundamental concepts that will be used in this book, such as the definition of integration, the distinction of stages and so on. The second is an historical overview of the process of integration, which makes it easier to understand the present dynamics. The third is the objective, the institutional set-up and the regulating capacity of the European Union.

Part II is devoted entirely to the first stage of integration. A theoretical treatment of product market integration will introduce this part, followed by separate chapters on goods and services. The chapter on goods is fairly elaborate as a vast literature makes it possible to draw up a very detailed picture. The opposite situation prevails for services; here a lack of relevant data and operational concepts preclude an analysis of the same depth and detail.

Part III examines the second stage of integration that deals with the liberalisation of the markets for production factors. It is structured in a similar way to the first. A chapter on the theoretical basis is followed by separate chapters on labour and capital, in which the results of empirical studies are set in the framework of the dynamic development of the European policy regimes for both production factors.

The integration of markets of products and of production factors permits entrepreneurs to make their operations more efficient. The way enterprise responds to the opportunities created by integration is of much interest. These more micro-economic aspects will be given due attention in **Part IV**, with separate chapters for each of the broad sectors of economic activity. The breakdown into sectors is based, on the one hand, on the famous Clark (1957)/Chenery (1960)/Kuznets (1966) triad and, on the other hand, on the differences in EU policy regime. This leads to a division into five main sectors: agriculture, manufacturing, energy, services and transport. We will describe the EU policies for each of the five sectors, together with the sectors' development under conditions of integration, referring, wherever useful, to theoretical notions specific to the sector concerned.

The first important question adressed in **Part V** is how the integrating European market economy has to be regulated, and what type of economic order and policy set-up will lead to the best outcome in terms of economic growth of welfare. The next question to be addressed is the policy regime that the EC has developed to deal with the problems of an integrating economic area. For the discussion of these two matters a division has been made along the lines of the most widely accepted distinction of socio-economic policy fields. We may recall that the well-known Musgravian (Musgrave and Musgrave, 1989) triad covers allocation (market functioning), stabilisation (macro and monetary policies) and redistribution (that is, cohesion policies); it is the one we will adopt here also. In view of the growing international identity of the EU, external relations will receive attention in a separate chapter. In each of the four chapters in this part, theoretical and policy elements will be mixed with the results of empirical economic research.

Part VI contains an evaluation of the results presented in Parts II to V, together with a short presentation of the prospects for the future development of the European integration process.

Specification of the readership

The book addresses primarily two groups of readers. First, it addresses the increasing numbers of students who are following courses on European integration: in this book they will find a general introduction to the dynamics of economic integration, covering in a systematic and coherent way the areas that are most relevant, ranging from agriculture to trade, monetary matters and cohesion. It also addresses students of economics specialising in specific fields, such as industrial economics, international economic relations, and monetary and financial economics, who find themselves increasingly confronted by the European dimension of their specialisation. In this book they will find a general framework for the study of their own special area. The material of the book has been organised and presented to allow fruitful study of individual subjects without having to go through the complete text. To facilitate deeper and more complete study starting from this text, ample references to more specific literature are given.

Second, it is written for all those interested in the economic aspects of European integration in the widest sense, including the increasing number of people who in their professional activities are faced with questions as to the organisation and functioning of the European economy (researchers, consultants, journalists). To facilitate their access to the material, the book has been written in such a way that only a basic knowledge of economics is needed; the use of mathematics has been reduced to a minimum. Only basic knowledge of linear equations and their graphical representation and the essentials of regression analysis is required to understand the whole text.

Constant update

A difficulty encountered in writing about the EU is that the text needs continuous adjustment and updating. Indeed in the past the EU policy environment and the response of firms and individuals have shown a remarkable dynamism. Recently some really dramatic changes have occurred. One is the upheaval in Central and Eastern Europe leading to the integration of the German Democratic Republic into the Federal Republic of Germany. Another is the decision to realise an economic and monetary union by the end of the century. In the near future new, although probably less dramatic, changes are likely to occur. This second revised edition comes, therefore, only a few years after the publication of the first.

The present edition differs from the previous one in that it:

- covers new developments as to deepening of the EU, such as the completion of the internal market and the setting up of the Economic and Monetary Union;
- addresses the widening of the EU (for example, the accession of the EFTA countries and the association of the Central and Eastern European countries);
- updates with figures for recent years the series of data that highlight the long-term trends and indicate the structural factors in the integration process;
- gives additional references to the latest literature on the various subjects.

2 Basic Concepts and Structures

Introduction

For a proper understanding of the details of the process of economic integration as described in the subsequent chapters, it is essential to know a few fundamental elements that we will present in this chapter.

To start we will give a set of definitions and indicate the objectives that integration pursues. We will thereby define the three elements that, as the title indicates, are central to this book: economics, European and integration. In a subsequent section we will make a basic distinction between the integration of markets and of policy. The former relates to the taking away of barriers to movement of products and production factors between member states, the latter to the setting up of common policies for the union. We also define the stages that mark the progress of economic integration.

Next we will go a little deeper into markets, specifying the objectives and instruments of market integration, and the dynamics of its development. The different aspects of policy integration will then be examined. We will describe the dynamics of the process leading towards increased involvement of union institutions in policy matters; the areas these policies cover, the criteria that can be applied to settle the debate over competences between national and union governments and the type of instrument that is used for progressive policy integration. A short summary will complete this chapter.

Three fundamental concepts

Integration

The expression 'economic integration' covers a variety of notions. It may refer to the absorption of a company in a larger concern. It may have a spatial aspect, for instance if it refers to the integration of regional economies in a national one. In this book, the expression is always used with respect to international economic relations. The *definition* of integration that is used here is the gradual elimination of economic frontiers between independent states; as a result the economies of these states end up functioning as one entity.

Economic integration is not an *objective* in itself, but serves higher objectives, both of an economic and of a political nature.

- Economic welfare. The prosperity of all participating countries is enhanced through specialisation of production and through cooperation in policy making, the two basic elements of economic integration.
- Peace. When countries become dependent upon each other as a result of economic integration this reduces the chance of armed conflicts between them.[1]
- Democracy. If participation in a group that brings benefits through integration is made conditional on the existence of a parliamentary form of democracy, it is less likely that attempts to overthrow this system of government in a member country will stand much chance of success.
- Human rights. In much the same way, the respect for human rights may be safeguarded if this is set as a precondition for participation in a scheme for economic integration.

In this book we will not go further into the last three objectives, which are of a political nature; we will henceforth concentrate on the economic objective.[2]

The term economic integration can be interpreted in two senses. In a dynamic sense, it is the process whereby economic frontiers between member states are gradually eliminated (that is to say, whereby national discrimination is abolished), with the formerly separate national economic entities gradually merging into a larger whole. In a static sense, it is the situation in which national components of a larger economy are no longer separated by economic frontiers but function together as an entity. The dynamic interpretation is the more usual, and the one to be used in this book. Of course, the static meaning of the expression will apply in full once the integration process has passed through its stages and reached its object.

Economics

As to economics, three elements will recur throughout the book. We will analyse and describe:

- theoretical principles: we will present a selection of theory most relevant to explaining the dynamics of economic processes associated with the integration of (segments of) the economy;
- empirical facts: we will describe how the various segments of the European economy have evolved under conditions of integration, using selected long-term statistical series on the one hand,[3] and drawing lessons from case studies of earlier developments on the other;
- public policy: we will discuss how the EU and national governments influence the economic process with policy measures.

We will not undertake an attempt to unite the dispersed elements of theory in one integrate framework of theoretical concepts of economic integration, neither will we assemble the empirical evidence, nor group together the discussion of all public policy issues. On the contrary, while dealing with different aspects of integration we will combine a brief theoretical treatment with an analytical description and with the relevant elements of policy of the subject at hand.

In all parts of the book we will finally evaluate the results of the integration processes in economic terms. To measure advantages and disadvantages of integration, use will be made of the well known concepts of welfare economics (see, among others, Mishan, 1982).

Europe

The word 'European' refers in principle to the whole geographical entity of Europe, but in practice Western Europe will be the focus of this book. Indeed the dynamism of the integration processes there was much greater than in the 'centrally planned' economic systems of Central and Eastern Europe. The European Union (EU), extended since its foundation from six to nine, then to ten and twelve states, and open for further enlargement, constitutes the core of Western Europe. (For reasons of simplicity we will henceforth use the term European Union (EU) to indicate for the whole period of analysis and irrespective of the prevailing precise legal situation both the group of member states and the policy system drawn up on the basis of the various treaties.)

European integration is not an isolated process: it takes place in a world in which international relations are more and more interwoven. Therefore we must keep an eye on *external aspects*. Speaking of labour market integration, for instance, we will discuss not only internal migration within the EU, but also migration from and to third countries, distinguishing between other Western European countries, Eastern Europe and other countries. We will give an overview of all these external aspects in Chapter 19.

Stages

Main elements

Consideration of economic integration is generally divided into two parts. The first applies to the integration of the *markets*, of goods and services, on the one hand, and of production factors (labour, capital, entrepreneurship) on the other. The second concerns *policy*. In an economy which leaves production and distribution entirely to the market, the elimination of obstacles to the movement of goods and production factors among countries would suffice to achieve full economic integration. Not so in modern economies, which are almost invariably of the mixed type, the government frequently intervening in the economy to pursue a number of political objectives (such as an equitable income distribution).

The integration of markets (products and production factors) and the integration of different areas of economic policy follow in practice a sequence through a hierarchy of forms. We can describe these stages of integration as follows.

Markets

Goods and services   Progression may be summarised as follows:

- Free-trade area (FTA). All trade impediments such as import duties and quantitative restrictions are abolished among partners. Internal goods traffic is then free, but each country can apply its own customs tariff with respect to third countries. To avoid trade deflection (goods entering the FTA through the country with the lowest external tariff) internationally traded goods must be accompanied by so-called 'certificates of origin', indicating in which country the good has been manufactured. This enables customs officers at frontiers between member countries with different outer tariffs to determine whether duties or levies are still due (on goods originating from a third country) or whether the merchandise originates from another member state and can therefore be imported duty-free.
- Incomplete customs union (ICU). As in the free-trade area, obstacles to the free traffic of goods among partner countries are removed. Moreover one common external tariff is agreed upon, which does away with the certificates of origin at internal borders. Once a good has been admitted anywhere in the customs union, it may circulate freely. However, with respect to some categories of goods and services, barriers continue to exist.
- Customs union (CU). All obstacles to internal free movement

are abolished without exception as to category of product or type of barrier. A common external tariff is implemented.

Production factors Two stages may be identified:

- Incomplete common market (ICM). Its first building-block is a (incomplete) customs union. Moreover there is internal free movement of significant segments of labour and capital. Various options as to the relation with third countries may be chosen: different national regulations (comparable to the FTA) or a common regulation (comparable to the CU). Combinations of common policies (for instance for labour) and national policies (for example for capital) *vis-à-vis* third countries are possible.
- Common market (CM). This consists of (1) an internal market: that is, fully free internal movement of products (goods and services) and of production factors (labour and capital); and (2) common external regulation for both products and production factors (so this definition encompasses a CU).

Policy

Economic There are three manifestations of integration of economic policy:

- Economic union (EU) implies not only a common market but also a high degree of coordination or even unification of the most important areas of economic policy; as a minimum these comprise those that are associated with the CM, such as market regulation, competition and industrial structure; next come those that are related to the MU, such as macro-economic and monetary policies; and finally there are those that refer to the more social aspects, like redistribution policies and social and environmental policies. Towards third countries common policies are pursued on trade, production factors, economic sectors, monetary stability and so on.
- Monetary union (MU). The currencies of the member states are linked through irrevocably fixed exchange rates and are fully convertible, or one common currency circulates in all member states. Capital movements within the union are free.
- Economic and monetary union (EMU) combines the characteristics of the economic and the monetary union. The latter implies quite a high degree of coordination of macro-economic and budget policies. In view of the close interweaving of monetary and macro policies, integration evolves mostly simultaneously for both policy fields.

Other   Two further aspects of integration policy should be considered:

- Political union (PU). Integration is extended beyond the realm of economics to encompass such fields as anti-crime policy (police) and foreign policy, eventually including security policy.
- Full union (FU) implies the complete unification of the economies involved, and a common policy on many important matters. For example, social security and income tax are likely to come within the competence of the union. The same holds true for macro-economic and stabilisation policy; this implies a budget of sufficient size to be effective as an instrument of these policies. The situation is then virtually the same as that within one country. Hence some form of a confederation or federation will then be chosen.

Theory and practice

The definitions of the stages given here are the ones that are now most commonly applied. The transitions between them are fluent and cannot always be clearly defined.[4] The first stages, FTA, CU and CM, seem to refer to market integration in a classical laisser-faire setting, the higher stages (EU, MU, FU) to policy integration. In practice, however, the former three stages are unlikely to stabilise without some form of policy integration as well (for instance, safety regulations for a FTA, commercial policy for a CU, or social and monetary policies for a CM). So, between a customs union and full integration, a variety of practical solutions for concrete integration problems are likely to occur.

The various stages are not only different as to their economic significance, they are so too as to their institutional consequences. In general we may say that the institutional demands to be fulfilled are higher, the higher the stage of integration. The stages of integration just sketched have two characteristics in common: (1) they abolish discrimination among actors from partner economies (internal goal); (2) they thereby maintain or introduce some form of discrimination with respect to actors from economies of third countries (external goal).

Market integration

Objectives and areas

Free movement of goods and services is the basic element of economic integration. The free exchange of goods promises a positive effect on the prosperity of all concerned. It permits consumers to choose the cheapest good, generally widens the choice, and creates the conditions for further gain through economies of scale and so on (see Chapter 5).

Free movement of production factors can be seen as another basic element of economic integration. One argument for it is that it permits optimum allocation of labour and capital. Sometimes certain production factors are missing from a place where otherwise production would be most economical. To overcome this problem, entrepreneurs are apt to shift their capital from places of low return to those which are more promising. The same is true of labour: employees will migrate to regions where their labour is more needed and therefore better rewarded. A second argument is that an enlarged market of production factors favours new production possibilities which in turn permit new, more modern or more efficient uses of production factors (new forms of credit, new occupations and so on).

Dynamics

The obvious welfare gains from the liberalisation of product markets are a good economic reason for starting integration. However integration schemes tend to follow a political logic rather than an economic one. The political reasons for beginning integration at the goods market are that:

- a lasting coalition between sectors demanding protection, and sectors and consumers demanding cheap imports is hard to accomplish;
- substitute instruments (such as industrial policy, non-tariff barriers and administrative procedures) can be used to intervene in the economic process;
- vital political issues like growth policy and income redistribution are guaranteed to remain within national jurisdiction.

The choice of production factors as the object of the second stage in the integration process is partly based on the economic advantages that spring from such integration. But here, too, we have to consider the political logic. The integration of labour markets seems to be the obvious choice in periods of a general shortage of labour (for instance the EU in the 1960s – see Chapter 9). A tangle of national regulations on wages, social security and so on, seems to leave politicians sufficient opportunities for practical intervention at the national level for them to accept general principles at the European level. With capital market integration the issue of direct investments seems straightforward; many politicians may hope to attract new foreign investment in that way. For other capital movements the willingness to integrate is less obvious because integration would imply giving up the control of sensitive macro-economic instruments.

Instruments

Market integration can proceed without much demand on institutions and policy making. It will in general suffice to liberalise (that is, deregulate) with measures of the 'Thou shalt not' type. The taking away of barriers was termed 'negative integration' by Tinbergen (1954). Such measures can in general be easily and clearly defined, and once laid down in treaties are binding on governments, companies and private persons. There is little need for a permanent decision-making machinery. The respecting of these measures is a matter of law; any actor may appeal to the courts if infringements damage his interest.

Policy integration

Objectives

In all European countries there has been progressive government intervention in economic life. This is based on the role of the state to enhance economic welfare by correcting imperfections of markets and so on. The objectives and forms of regulations diverge among countries owing to differences in preferences (traditions, institutions and so on). As a result of the considerable international interwovenness, the policy of one country has effects in another. If objectives of two governments are inconsistent, the policy of one country will frustrate that of the other. Policy integration may bring economic benefits as its leads to the recovery of effectiveness in policy making. It will also take away the extra cost of compliance for companies that operate internationally under a multitude of different national regulations. Therefore, as the economic integration progresses, the national regulating systems will gradually be integrated.

The **aim** of policy integration (termed 'positive integration' by Tinbergen, 1954) is the creation of a common policy framework that creates equal conditions for the functioning of the integrated parts of the economy. Common policies require common institutions. These need to be stronger, the higher the complications of the various policy stages: preparation, formulation and implementation. Policy integration is often based on vaguely defined obligations requiring public institutions to take action. Such obligations leave ample room for interpretation as to scope and timing. They may, moreover, be reversed if the policy environment changes.

Policy integration, even if beneficial from an economic point of view, may be difficult because of the interests of the polity and of the bureaucracy of the member states. National politicians are likely to be the more unwilling to give up their intervention power the more such elements as employment or budgetary policies (referring to expenditure on schools and subsidies, as well as revenues from taxes) are involved. Moreover national civil servants tend to uphold their way of operating interventional schemes as the most efficient and, since their very existence depends on complicated sets of rules, many of them will be hardly inclined to cooperate in the creation of a harmonised or common policy. Thus the conditions for common policies in fields like social protection or monetary expansion will not readily be met – let alone the conditions for the integration of policies that touch the very heart of a nation's sovereignty, like defence.

Dynamics

By their very dynamics, the lower forms of integration tend to bring forth more advanced forms. In the (neo)functionalist theory of integration this phenomenon is called 'spill-over'.[5] A few examples may be illuminating.

Customs union Impulses to policy integration come from both the external and internal dimension of the free movement of products. Externally the setting of a common external tariff and its regular adjustment to changed circumstances call for a common trade policy. Moreover negotiations with third countries can be conducted to greater advantage by the customs union acting as an entity than by each member state on its own. Internally tariffs and quotas appear to be easier to abolish than non-tariff obstacles, such as higher taxes on foreign goods than on domestic ones (wine against beer), technical norms (allegedly meant to safeguard workers and consumers, but actually supporting the country's own production), priority to national companies for (government) orders, and so on. To remove such obstacles, regulations must be harmonised in such widely divergent fields as taxation and safety, regulations which are often deeply rooted in the countries' legal, institutional and social structure.

For the internal market to function properly, measures are also needed to prevent competition distortion. Competition can be limited by companies (agreements) as well as governments (state support, export subsidies and so on). Hence the need for a common competition policy, with rules for private and public sectors. Such a policy affects other areas as well: equal competitive conditions for companies require a degree of harmonisation of consumer policy (concerning responsibility, for instance) and also of environmental policy (avoiding unnecessary costs; pollution abatement).

Common market   The establishment of free movement of productive factors also gives strong impulses towards the coordination of policy. Free movement of workers requires in practice the mutual recognition of diplomas or certificates of professional proficiency. Measures of social security must be harmonised lest different claims for sickness, accident, old-age and other benefits should in practice make a mockery of the free movement. Free movement of capital necessitates the elimination of some administrative obstacles, such as exchange control, and legal ones, such as company laws. In the fiscal sphere, too, some adjustment will be necessary to prevent capital flowing to states with a favourable tax regime. Finally the mobility of capital demands the adjustment of monetary policies (rates of exchange, interest and so on) to diminish economic disturbances caused by speculation. In principle, capital is more mobile than labour. The creation of a common market may lead to concentrated investments in certain regions, and growing unemployment in others. Such situations call for measures of common social and regional policy.

Economic and monetary union   The pursuit of the objectives of an EMU means that integration extends into different policy areas. The most important objective is the stimulation of economic growth. One way to do so is to lower transaction cost for firms by introducing a single currency. Another way is to conduct a research and technology policy which encourages innovation and thus the creation of new sales prospects. Any national measures to that effect must be coordinated to avoid similar, or even conflicting, developments at different places. Another way is to foster favourable and stable conditions. As the free movement of goods and factors renders the economies of member states more mutually dependent, economic or fiscal measures taken by one member state become more likely to affect all others, perhaps conflicting with their policy. Because member states no longer have authority to counteract such disturbances by measures of trade policy, they may resort to budgetary and monetary instruments. To prevent an escalation of such measures in all countries, which again would make for disturbances, coordination of the macro-economic and monetary policies of member states becomes imperative.

Political union Finally economic integration favours integration in other areas from political motives, economics and politics being in many ways interwoven: a good example is external relations. To enforce their interest *vis-à-vis* third countries, member countries could be induced to coordinate not only their common trade policies but their foreign policies and their defence policies as well. Thus economic integration may pave the way to political integration.

Areas

Overlooking these tendencies towards a gradual increase in the number of fields of policy integration, one has the impression of a fairly heterogeneous bunch of issues. To bring some order to this we will use the breakdown of public policy into three functions (Buchanan, 1968; Musgrave and Musgrave, 1989), to which we have added a fourth dimension:

- allocation of resources, requiring mainly micro-economic policy instruments aiming at the efficient use of resources, this function comprises all policies aiming at the proper functioning of the internal market;
- stabilisation, requiring mainly macro-economic and monetary policy instruments to attain such objectives as high growth rates, price stability and full employment;
- redistribution of income, requiring policies that aim to ensure that different social groups (social policy) and regional groups have a fair share in the benefits of integration should the market mechanisms fail to achieve an equitable outcome;
- external relations: at each stage of integration the union has to define itself *vis-à-vis* the third world through commercial policies in a customs union up to defence in a full union.

If the first two policies are essential to gather the full benefit of integration, the third is indispensable to gain the necessary political support from all participants in an integration scheme and the fourth to establish an international identity.

The distinction between allocational efficiency, macro-economic stability, redistributive equity and external identity, so neat in theory, is often blurred in practice in the process of political bargaining. Indeed instruments devised to serve policies in one area are often adapted under political pressure to serve other purposes as well. A good example is allocational efficiency. The instrument of guaranteed prices, introduced to make agricultural markets function properly (see Chapter 11), can easily be used also for redistribution purposes. Another example is the use of the instruments for the regulation of financial markets to control credit in the framework of stabilisation policies. A final example is state aids for the restructuring of industries that in practice may become an instrument for permanent subsidisation of certain sectors, in order to enhance their 'competitiveness' on external markets. The general rule can be formulated that original objectives are often lost sight of as policies, including common policies, develop.

As combinations of policies, for instance trade and structural policies (Klein, 1985), are often made for specific sectors, for such sectors different sets of objectives and combinations of instruments from the four policy areas can be observed. This may lead to a situation where some sectors are exposed to external and internal competition without receiving subsidies (allocation) or transfers (redistribution), while other sectors are sheltered from external and internal competition by generous subsidies, with considerable redistributive effects.

Subsidiarity

Which criteria are to be used to decide, at any point in the evolution of an integration scheme, whether certain policy areas should be integrated or not? This question is not specific to integration schemes; any state, be it a unitary or a federal, has to decide on the best way to distribute competences over the various layers of government. Most authors who have written about this problem, in economics notably the school of fiscal federalism,[6] have come to the conclusion that in general decisions have to be taken at the lowest level of government feasible. This is now generally called the principle of subsidiarity.[7]

The economic theories of optimal distribution of powers over different layers of government take efficiency as the main criterion. The starting-point is that a policy executed at the lowest level of government is thought most efficient because: (1) differences in needs, and in preferences and so on, will be better taken into account, participation will be higher and implementation cost lower; and (2) innovation and experiment will be given more latitude. Competition between jurisdictions will then sort out the best combinations of providing public goods and imposing taxes.

Competences should be handed over to the next higher level of government, for example from a nation to the union, for four main reasons (see, among others, Tinbergen, 1954; Oates, 1972; MacDougall, 1977):

- Transaction costs. The diversity of rules in a decentralised system may make it costly for private actors like firms and owners of production factors to know what the best options are. A higher level of competence may bring more uniformity, hence more transparency and lower cost.
- Economies of scale. For the production of public goods and policies there exists an optimal scale much in the same way as for private goods and services. Policy competences should be given to the layer that can provide the lowest cost given the level of output. An example is monetary policy, which is better organised by a union central bank than by a loose coordination of independent local central banks.
- Externalities. There are cases where outsiders, that is non-residents, may benefit from or have to bear the cost of actions of a specific jurisdiction. For example, if the pollution of a firm in country A is carried by the wind to country B, country B incurs high environmental cost, while country A has the economic benefits. In such cases the matter needs to be dealt with by a higher authority. If not, the spill-over of important cost or benefit elements to other areas will lead to inefficiencies, that is to, respectively, an over- or under-supply of public goods (such as clean air). As integration advances, spill-over effects are likely to increase in importance and hence more competences need to be transferred to the union level.
- Credibility. In many cases countries have a stimulus to enter into cooperative solutions for common policies (common advantage) but may also have a stimulus to break them (free-rider). Although the choice of the latter is diminished by the fear of retaliation, many may be seduced into selecting this option for short-term policy reasons. The market which experiences this will put little faith in the effectiveness of cooperative policies. So the better solution in these cases is to hand over the competence to the union level.

There is a difficult trade-off between the advantages and disadvantages of centralisation or, in our context, of further policy integration. In theory it would be possible to calculate for each area of policy making in each stage of integration whether a further step would be beneficial or not. However, as many of the cost and benefits involved are rather intangible in nature, it will not always be possible to come up with a complete economic evaluation. Hence the decision will often be based on political motives, taking into account the economic trade-off.

In practice that will lead to a situation whereby the union is responsible for certain matters, the member states for other matters and that there will be a very large number of policy matters where they have to come together to exercise authority jointly. One might call this 'cooperative federalism' (Casella and Frey, 1992). An example of a policy measure that brings economic advantages of integration, but puts in jeopardy certain national social objectives, may illustrate this. The harmonisation of taxes is considered necessary to the undisturbed movement of capital in the integration area. However, that may bring about a shift from direct to indirect taxes in some countries, so that the tax system can no longer be used to lessen income inequality. Whether the positive effects outweigh the drawbacks is not sure. So the union and the member states may come to the essentially political decision not to centralise fully the competence in matters of taxes, but to share the responsibility, limiting integration to the coordination of those aspects of the tax system that impinge most on allocational efficiency. Similar political trade-offs, but with different outcomes in terms of integration, exist over a wide range of matters of public concern, leading to a large variety of practical solutions to integration problems.

Instruments

All forms of integration require permanent agreements among participating states with respect to procedures to arrive at resolutions and to the implementation of rules. In other words, they call for partners to agree on the rules of the game. For an efficient policy integration, common institutions (international organisations) are created.

All forms of integration diminish the freedom of action of the member states' policy makers. The higher the form of integration, the greater the restrictions on and loss of national competences and the more power will be transferred from national to union institutions. The following hierarchy of policy cooperation is usually adopted:

- *Information*: partners agree to inform one another about the aims and instruments of the policies they (intend to) pursue. This information may be used by partners to change their policy to achieve a more coherent set of policies. However partners reserve full freedom to act as they think fit, and the national competence is virtually unaltered.
- *Consultation*: partners agree that they are obliged not only to inform but also to seek the opinion and advice of others about the policies they intend to execute. In mutual analysis and discussion of proposals the coherence is actively promoted.

Although formally the sovereignty of national governments remains intact, in practice their competences are affected.

- *Coordination* goes beyond this, because it commits partners to agreement on the (sets of) actions needed to accomplish a coherent policy for the group. If common goals are fixed, some authors prefer the term 'cooperation'. Coordination often means the adaptation of regulations to make sure that they are consistent internationally (for example, the social security rights of migrant labour). It may involve the harmonisation (that is, the limitation of the diversity) of national laws and administrative rules. It may lead to convergence of the target variables of policy (such as the reduction of the differences in national inflation rates). Although agreements reached by coordination may not always be enforceable (no sanctions), they nevertheless limit the scope and type of policy actions nations may undertake, and hence imply limitation of national competences.

- *Unification*: either the abolition of national instruments (and their replacement with union instruments for the whole area) or the adoption of identical instruments for all partners. Here the national competence to choose instruments is abolished.

Relation between stages and instruments

There is a certain relation between the stages of integration and the instruments of policy integration mentioned in the previous section, in the sense that, in the early stages, the less binding instruments of integration will be applied. On the way to a common allocation policy, member states may begin by consulting one another with respect to certain elements (systems of value-added tax, the structure of tariffs, for example), to end up with the full unification of value-added tax rates and so on. Between the two stages, harmonisation may be practised. Parallels can be found in external policy, where a free trade area may start with consultations on the level of the external tariff, may next review the advantages of harmonisation of the structure of tariffs and may end up with unification by the adoption of a common external tariff, which turns the free trade area into a customs union.

Another option is the distinction within one policy area between cases calling for integration and others for which partner-state competences are maintained. Examples are the fixing of a common external tariff while maintaining partner competence with respect to quotas *vis-à-vis* third countries. So long as the balance between gains and losses of a particular transfer of competence remains doubtful, the lower degrees of integration, like consultation, are likely to be preferred, in line with the principle of subsidiarity. As soon as the benefits of further integration outweigh cost, the next higher degree of integration will be tried out.

Each successive degree of autonomy lost will make it harder for a member state to achieve the policy mix suited to its specific objectives. Therefore progress towards further integration depends on the clear proof that the gains from each individual step towards integration will outweigh the cost. Gains will come from steps towards common allocation, stabilisation and redistribution policies. Costs will come from the impossibility of meeting national preferences owing to a loss of autonomy, in terms of taxes, consumer protection, health and other matters. Therefore policy integration will vary in extent, nature and combination of elements of allocation, stabilisation, redistribution and external policies according to the prevailing practical political circumstances; there is no theoretical optimum blueprint for the intermediate states between the CM and the FU.

We can schematise the dynamics of integration as follows (see Figure 2.1). As one moves through the various stages of integration more and more competences of the member states will be handed

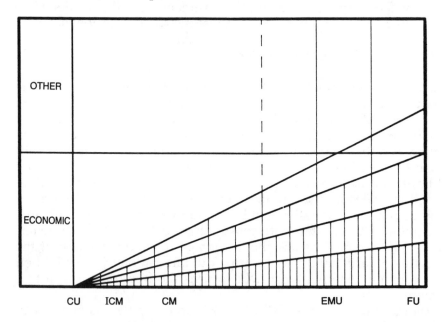

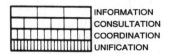

INFORMATION
CONSULTATION
COORDINATION
UNIFICATION

Figure 2.1   **Distribution of competences between nation and union in several stages of integration**

over to the union. First this applies only to economic areas, next also to non-economic ones (like culture, social, defence). Moreover, the intensity with which the union is involved will increase (from consultation to unification).

Summary and conclusions

- Economic integration is the gradual elimination of economic frontiers between partner countries. It is a dynamic process in which the economies of partner states become more and more interwoven.
- The main objectives of economic integration are of an economic nature: for example, higher growth, hence more prosperity. Other objectives are of a political nature: for example, the reduction of the chance of armed conflicts among partners.
- The main stages in the process of economic integration are the customs union, the common market, and the economic and monetary union, representing the integration of, progressively, the markets of goods and services, of production factors and, finally, of economic and other policies.
- Market integration is needed because it improves efficiency and hence welfare.
- Market integration is carried out by the removal of the numerous measures which impede the free movement of goods and production factors among member states.
- Policy integration is needed because the intervention of national governments in modern mixed open economies has lost its effectiveness.
- The main areas of policy that are subject to integration are those aimed at allocational efficiency, macro-economic stability, redistributional equity and external identity.
- The main instruments for policy integration are consultation and the coordination (harmonisation) or unification of government regulations; the higher forms of integration require more binding instruments.
- Neither the optimum mix of union and national measures nor the areas where further integration will be most beneficial can be determined a priori on theoretical grounds.

Notes

1   Empirical support for this statement is given, for example, by Polacheck (1980) who (using data for 30 countries in the 1958–67 period) showed that doubling

the trade between two countries leads to a 20 per cent decline in the frequency of hostilities. Hirsch (1981) suggests that countries feel obliged to adopt a peaceful attitude when a 'balance of prosperity' is created instead of a 'balance of deterrence'. Moreover other authors such as Buzan (1984) stress the importance of a liberal type of economic integration for peace (or international security). As a consequence the use of armed forces to improve welfare diminishes (Rosecrance, 1984). On the other hand, security (for example, NATO) stimulates economic integration (for example, EU, OECD).

2   The first objective has been central to all stages of the deepening and widening of European integration. The second objective has notably played a role in the early days of the setting up of the ECSC and the EEC. The third has played a major role in the second round of extension of the EU and will do so again in the next round of extension with Central and Eastern European countries (including Turkey).

3   Note that the statistics used here go up to the year 1990; they cover the area of the EU12 in that year; the effect of the extension of the EU following the reunification of Germany is not yet taken up. Neither are the effects of the extension of the EU with EFTA countries.

4   Many authors have used different definitions (for example, Tinbergen, 1954; Scitovsky, 1958). The definitions given here largely follow the classical work of Balassa (1961); other sources are the major reports preceding the various jumps that mark the European integration process, such as Spaak *et al.* (1956), Werner *et al.* (1970), MacDougall *et al.* (1977), Padoa-Schioppa *et al.* (1987) and Delors (1989). See also Pelkmans (1991). Note that the definitions given here are conceptual ones that do not always correspond to the setting up of concrete integration schemes (Balassa 1976). Note also that the various stages distinguished here can be split up further: see, for example, for the CM, Pelkmans (1986) and, for the MU, Gros (1989).

5   The explanation of the progress of integration is to be found in political rather than in economic factors. We therefore have to look to political science more than to economics. The economic arguments put forward here are akin to the political arguments put forward by the (neo)functionalist school of political science (Mitrany, 1966; Haas, 1958; see also Keohane and Hoffmann, 1991).

6   Again economics does not give the full explanation; the political science school that comes up with similar propositions for the explanation of the dynamics is 'federalism'. It takes a more normative approach to the problem than functionalism. Other theories of government like intergovernmentalism and supranationalism have not found their counterparts in the economic theory of integration. A political economy approach (Hirschmann, 1981) went some way to bridging the gap between economics and the political science of integration. All in all the theoretical basis for explaining the dynamics of economic integration is not yet very robust (Moravcsik, 1993). We will come back to this point in Chapter 20.

7   In the works of classical thinkers such as Mill and Proudhon, the most commonly used term was 'principle of federalism'. It lies at the basis of the constitutions of many federations like Germany, Switzerland and the USA. The papal encyclical *Quadragesimo Anno* (1931) introduced the term 'subsidiarity' that has since been most widely used (see also Wilke and Wallace, 1990). Note that the EU has also accepted the principle as a basis for its constitution. The Treaty of Maastricht, in specifying the tasks of the Community (part of the European Union), says in its art. 3B: 'The Community shall act within the limits of the powers conferred upon it by this Treaty and the objectives assigned to it therein. In areas which do not fall within its exclusive competence, the Community shall take action, in accordance with the principle of subsidiarity only if and in so far

as the objectives of the proposed action cannot be sufficiently achieved by the Member states and can therefore, by reason of the scale or effects of the proposed action, be better achieved by the Community. Any action by the Community shall not go beyond what is necessary to achieve the objectives of this Treaty.'

3 Short History

Introduction

Economic integration was defined in the previous chapter as a process of economic unification of national economies. The expression has become so current, especially with respect to Europe, that it gives the impression of a fundamental notion with a long historical background. Actually the term, or rather, its negative counterpart, 'economic disintegration', was used for the first time in 1930. In a positive sense the term does not occur until after the Second World War (Herbst, 1986). That the term is new does not mean that the process of economic integration and disintegration is also new. On the contrary, it has been going on all through modern European history.[1] Two factors (Pollard, 1981a) have always stimulated integration:

- *Technical progress.* Long-term economic development is determined by some autonomous factors, of which technology is the most important. Mechanisation and automation of the production process have completely changed production methods. Advances in energy technology, for instance, led to the replacement of human and animal power with steam and, later, with electricity. With respect to transport, horse-drawn vehicles gave way to railways and lorries. As a result, goods can now be produced and distributed cheaply in large numbers. But production in large series makes, first, exportation and, next, integration, imperative. The exchange of technical knowledge and capital also urges more economic integration.
- *Political idealism.* The conception of Europe as a separate entity, separate in particular from Asia, is very old (Chabod, 1961; Duroselle, 1965) and has been developed and deepened through the ages. Especially since the Middle Ages there has been virtually no period in which statesmen or philosophers did not point to the common European heritage and the necessity for

more 'political' unity in Europe. The arguments have become
louder as the national states became stronger. Notably since the
Second World War, economic integration has been appreciably
accelerated by political pressure.[2]

In the course of history, the weight of these two main elements of the
dynamics of European economic integration has constantly shifted.
Apart from these two there are other factors that have either a positive or a negative influence on the progress of integration. One negative factor is economic recession. One positive factor is institutional
development. Consequently there have been periods in which developments favoured integration, and others in which integration seemed
to stagnate or even to be reversed.

In the following sections we will describe the progress of economic
integration for five such periods. We will thereby concentrate on the
structural adaptations of the economy and the institutional arrangements that accompanied integration. The chapter will be concluded
by a brief summary.

Until 1815: a traditional world with little integration

From the Middle Ages to the French Revolution

In the early Middle Ages, the European economy was marked by a
great fragmentation of markets. The feudal system had made all
regions almost perfectly self-supporting. Under the influence of urban development in the 12th century, the system was adapted; in the
following centuries this tendency continued, bringing about an increased integration of markets of products and production factors.

The *movement of goods*, that is trade among regions and countries,
was slowly resumed (Pirenne, 1927). In the 16th and 17th centuries
trade expanded steadily but remained of limited scope, being mostly
concerned with luxury goods. There were three reasons for this:

- Countless obstacles: Tolls, different weights and measures and
  coins, staple rights and the privileges of merchant groups hindered trade between regions and cities of the European countries. These intra-national barriers were comparable to those
  that prevailed until recently between European states, for national frontiers then did not have the economic function they
  have now: tolls were levied at bridges, town gates, locks and so
  on, rather than at the national frontier. In the late Middle Ages,
  the citizens of all towns tried to obtain privileges so as to get
  around tolls and other trade obstacles. The resulting patch-
  work of privileges for various groups heralded in a way the

complex systems of trade discrimination by country groups that developed in the 19th and 20th centuries.

- Primitive means of transport: On land, everything had to be hauled by waggon and pack animal. Most tradesmen preferred the cheaper transport by water: sea or river. The fleets of river barges and sea-going vessels increased steadily, but the tonnages of the vessels remained small.
- Economic policy. The aim of mercantilist policy was, first, to be as much as possible self-sufficient and, next, to achieve the highest possible export surplus. To that end, goods trade among countries was limited by import levies, export embargoes (on strategic goods) and so on (Gomes, 1987). Evidently the arguments for old mercantilist and modern protectionist policies are much alike. With mercantilism, no greater internal integration was achieved, however, for local tolls continued to be levied on all goods, domestic or foreign.

The *movement of production factors* was also very gradually improved. The reasons differed for labour and capital:

- Labour movements used to be hampered because virtually the entire population, with the exception of the nobility and the clergy, was bound by law to a certain place (serfdom). Over the centuries, citizens fought for, and gained, the right to move and trade freely everywhere.
- Capital movements were in principle free. In practice, however, the transfer of money was much hindered by the defective monetary system and the limited means to convey money from one place to another. From an early date, money traffic consisted, not only of payments for commercial transactions, but also of money loans, mostly loans to princes to cover their military expenditure. Investments in transport infrastructure were mostly made and financed locally.

The innovations of the French Revolution

The French Revolution, a political event, was soon developed by the citizens, who became all-powerful, into an economic revolution, totally upsetting the 'feudal' economy. The following measures show clearly the essence of this revolution: *the integration of the regional and local economies into a national economy*:

- abolition of all rules impeding the free traffic of goods, instantly followed by the abolition of all seigneurial rights and serfdom;

- shift of customs duties to the outer frontiers;
- creation of quota systems and tariffs to protect national production;
- abolition of all privileges of companies and guilds, and of rules about the manner of production;
- introduction of a uniform system of weights and measures;
- introduction of new legal rules for trade;
- construction of new infrastructure.

Owing to the national character of these measures, at first economic integration increased internally but decreased externally. During the Napoleonic regime the above novelties were introduced all over the European sub-continent. Moreover the so-called 'continental system' was created, intended to make the continent independent of Britain. The ensuing selective international integration was the fruit of a politico-military concept rather than economic logic.

With the collapse of Napoleon's empire, the continental system broke down as well. Once more, British goods could be sold on the continent and, given Britain's technological leadership, a whole range of new industries on the continent had to be closed down. That put free trade, and international integration, in a bad light. On the other hand, measures like the removal of tolls, which had fostered economic integration at the national level, were found useful and were maintained practically everywhere in Europe.

Fading concept of Europe

The late Middle Ages can be characterised as a period during which the pan-European ideas of Empire and Papacy were fading more and more, giving way to a growing nationalism. The idea of a Europe acting as a unity receded into the background, to reappear only when the common heritage was under immediate threat from outside. In concrete terms, the threat came from the Turks, steadily encroaching upon Eastern Europe. To take a European stand against them was pleaded more than once, but only when the Turks threatened Vienna was collective action taken: the Turks were beaten by a European coalition. Internal threats to peace also inspired some advocates of a united Europe. They looked for a way to avoid the internal armed conflicts which constantly ravaged Europe. Out of the long range of illustrious men who devoted themselves to the creation of some type of European federal state, we will mention only Sully, Leibniz, Penn, Bentham, Kant, von Gentz and Saint Pierre. However all their plans came to nothing, and their worthy goals – avoiding the constant wars for the hegemony in Europe, frontiers or heritages, or trade privileges – failed to come about. The clearest evidence of that failure is found in the Napoleonic wars concluding this period.

1815–1870: progressive integration following the industrial revolution

Theory and policy

'Protection or free trade' had become the central theme of discussions between politicians and economists in many countries, and until the middle of the 19th century the free-traders were in the ascendency. The successful coalition of economists and politicians heralded a decisive stage in history (Pollard, 1981b):

> Unlike some earlier examples of freedom from frontier control it was not based on the technical inability to levy duties or on the insignificant quantity of traffic, but on the conscious decisions of modern governments to encourage the closer integration of European economic life by opening out the opportunities to international trade and competition'.

Total external trade increased rapidly (see Table 3.1). Intra-European trade in this period relied strongly on sectoral specialisation, itself the result of different technologies practised in different countries. At the end of the period international trade, migration and capital movement were practically free all over Europe.

In the period from 1815 to 1870, the progress of economic integration differed according to the initial situation of the European countries.

Unity Far-reaching integration was realised by the UK, which, with an open economy of long standing, was the first to accomplish a drastic industrial revolution. The ideas of free trade were given a theoretical foundation and a political shape. Great classical economists such as Smith, Ricardo and Mill emphasised in their work that free national and international trade would lead to the greatest possible prosperity. They paved the way for political aspirations towards free trade (Gomes, 1987). Obstacles to the free movement of goods, people and capital were increasingly felt as suffocating and were gradually removed. The UK, as the leader in industrial technology, initially prohibited the exportation of machinery and the emigration of skilled workers. Nevertheless, British craftsmen went to work in other countries of Europe, often using smuggled machinery. Because the prohibition could not be enforced, the UK abolished all legal barriers to the emigration of skilled workers in 1825 and of capital goods in 1842. It moved further towards free trade with the abolition of the Navigation Acts and the repeal of the Corn Laws.

Homogeneity   In areas such as Germany, Austria and Italy, where economic frontiers were dividing a space felt to be culturally united, economic integration spelled a way to political unity. For example, Germany tackled the problem of trade obstacles by means of the *Zollverein* (theoretically underpinned by the German economist, List). Under Prussian leadership a customs union was created in 1834 and gradually expanded. It involved the abolition of all duties at inner borders, and a duty levied on the outer frontier which was low for 'European' and high for colonial goods. Gradually more and more states in central and southern Germany joined this union. The rapid industrialisation which commenced in Germany during this period contributed much to the success of this type of integration, and was itself stimulated again by progressive integration.

Diversity   It is interesting to see that integration was progressing even among countries that were clearly independent from one another. Most European countries adopted more liberal external policies.

Table 3.1   Some indicators of European economic development, 1810–70

Indicator	1810	1830	1850	1870
Gross National Product per head (index 1900 = 100)	47	53	62	79
Industrial production (index 1900 = 100)	n.a.	20	33	51
Production of pig iron (MT/y)	1	2	4	10
Production of coal (MT/y)	20	29	67	180
Share of exports in GNP (%)	3	4	7	11
Share of foreign investment in GNP (%)	—	1	2	3
Railway track (× 1,000 km)	—	—	24	105

n.a. = not available.
Source: Bairoch (1976).

Technology and diplomacy

While integration was clearly stimulated by the industrialisation, founded on technological innovation (see, for example, Mathias and Davis, 1991) and by the ensuing fast economic growth, the rapid industrialisation marking most West European countries in this period (see Figure 3.1) was in turn fostered by the progressive integration. Indeed, the application of modern technology made further specialisation not only possible but also desirable (see Table 3.1).

A second important component of the 'natural techno-economic process' is the means of transport and communication and in particular the railways. The tremendous accumulation of capital required for the construction of railways was sometimes warranted only if transport nodes and feeding points were also internationally connected; moreover, to be feasible, railway transport had to be liberalised to a high degree. River transport, too, was liberalised: the new, larger steamships called for flexible exploitation. Successive international agreements ensured free navigation on the Rhine (Central Committee for Rhine Navigation, 1815, and Mannheim Treaty, 1868), the Danube, the Scheldt and so on.

Monetary integration was also attempted in this period (Bartel, 1974). Many of the large states of Western Europe had already reached a considerable degree of internal monetary integration (as early as the 13th century, Saint Louis, King of France, introduced one single coin, the ECU, for his entire kingdom!). After the Napoleonic wars, practically every country had developed its own national currency system. International monetary cooperation was set up by the German (Holtfrerich, 1989) and Italian (Sannucci, 1989) states before unification. International monetary integration without political integration was attempted by the Latin Monetary Union, which was based on the French franc and to which the Belgian, Swiss, Italian and later the Greek and Spanish currencies were joined. All these systems suffered from the lack of mechanisms obliging the participants to practise consultation and cooperation. These experiences show that a monetary union seems to have to go hand-in-hand with political union if it is to be successful (see also Hamada, 1985).

The form in which integration was expressed varied over the years. International integration had always been a more or less factual process partly consolidated in bilateral agreements. This continued in the period under discussion, for instance with the famous Cobden–Chevalier free-trade Treaty of 1860, which gave French industry access to cheaper and better coal and iron from Britain. It was copied by many other countries for similar matters. Its importance lies in its unconditional most-favoured-nation clause, which had considerable implications for Europe-wide tariff reductions. These treaties were drawn

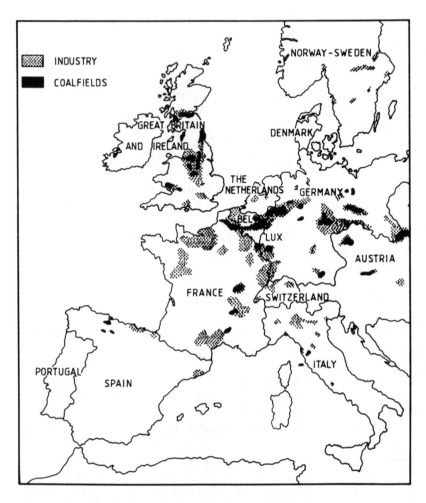

Figure 3.1   European industry around 1870

up and implemented through the usual diplomatic channels, no permanent bodies being created for the purpose. Postal services and telecommunication are noteworthy exceptions; only for them was the need for positive integration already so great at the time as to warrant the setting up of an international organisation.

Monarchist ideologies and socialist utopia

In the period after the Napoleonic wars, three widely different initiatives were taken towards lasting peace in Europe.

- *Monarchist and anti-revolutionary.* The Holy Alliance was a bond of heads of state whose objective was to prevent revolutionary troubles in and wars between, European states. To that end, the monarchs consulted regularly with one another, and in some instances decided to act collectively. It was a 19th-century variant of what would now be called a federal Europe. The Holy Alliance made but little impact; the system fell apart after some time through internal conflicts and for lack of a strong institutional organisation.
- *Philosophical and visionary.* From a utopian analysis of the developing industrial society, Saint-Simon concluded that the political organisation should be left to representatives of trade and industry, in particular manufacturing industry and banks. In his view, for a satisfactory development, a peaceful international community in Europe was an absolute condition. Saint-Simon's ideas and their elaboration by the Saint-Simonists were not translated into action and made little impact at the time.
- *Republican and democratic.* The most important representative of a movement aiming to accomplish in Europe a fraternal collaboration of free peoples (Giovine Europa) was probably Manzini, the theorist of Italian unity. The movement did not have much of an impact.

Other suggestions by intellectuals for some form of political integration (almost invariably involving economic integration) in Europe hardly found any response at the time either.

1870–1914: stagnating integration

Depression and protectionism

The long period of growth came to a sudden end around 1870, in a depression which has been compared to the Great Depression of the 1930s. Many governments responded to it in a protectionist fashion. The French–German war and the Italian struggle for unity had completely upset the situation. The powers demanding more protection for economic reasons were reinforced by a desire for autarky of mostly political and military inspiration. As a result, in many places attempts were made to curtail the existing freedoms of trade and traffic of production factors; straight tariff and subsidy wars were fought between some countries (see peak around 1890 in Figure 3.2). Having become far better organised than before, national states found themselves in a better position to impose taxes and customs duties, regulate their social affairs and pursue a protectionist, nationalist policy.

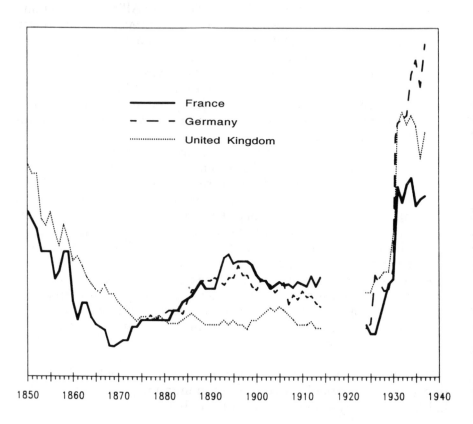

Figure 3.2   Evolution of British, French and German average tariff rates of protection, 1850–1938

Note: Reliable data for the years during and immediately after the First World War are not available.
Source: Messerlin and Becuwe (1986).

Trade in goods developed slowly, but it increased at the same rate as production, which indicates that protectionist inclinations did slow down, but not reverse economic integration (see Table 3.2, row 5). Indeed some countries soon found out that complete autarky was an illusion, given the international specialisation which had developed. Not different natural endowment, but far-reaching sectoral specialisation had become the main reason for goods trade, a specialisation based on economies of scale and technological leadership. Improved transport techniques (leading, among other things, to lower freight rates) also made for continued economic integration in Europe; the

Table 3.2 Some indicators of European economic development, 1870–1910

Indicator	1870	1880	1890	1900	1910
Gross National Product per head (index 1900 = 100)	79	80	85	100	110
Industrial production (index 1900 = 100)	51	61	77	100	136
Production of pig iron (MT/y)	10	14	17	25	37
Coal production (MT/y)	180	217	328	438	574
Share of exports in GNP (%)	11	13	13	11	13
Share of foreign investment in GNP (%)	3	4	4	4	5
Ocean freight rates (index 1900 = 100)	212	180	127	100	83
Railway track (× 1,000 km)	105	169	225	292	351

Source: Bairoch (1976).

railway and canal networks proliferated during this period (see Table 3.2). However, in the construction of infrastructure, nationalist tendencies were becoming more and more manifest.

Movement of production factors, that is, of workers and capital, also remained free to a large extent during this period.

Labour International migration mainly involved seasonal workers. Several thousands of Italians were employed in France, Germany and Austria. Some hundreds of thousands of Poles went to Germany every year, as did quite a number of other East Europeans. Many of them were employed in manufacturing industry, the mining industry or the construction trade, but many also filled the jobs in agriculture left open by the urbanising rural population. Many specialised labourers tended to move from country to country to operate special machines in regions and countries starting up new industrial projects.

Capital During this period the financial sector developed quickly (Cassis, 1991). Europe became the banker of the world. Its total stock of foreign investment rose significantly to reach, in 1913, a level that exceeded its GDP. Annual flows amounted to more than 5 per cent of GDP in 1913. About a quarter of outgoing capital was oriented towards other European countries, one-quarter to the USA and half to the rest of the world. Banking organised itself internationally to engage in large investment projects: railways in Russia, textile factories in Silesia, and also government loans. As a consequence, the total foreign investment of European countries increased (Table 3.2).

The monetary relations of all major industrialised countries were governed by the automatic rules of the gold standard. The combination of free movement of goods, labour and capital with fixed exchange rates was achieved by abstaining from an independent monetary policy (Hawtrey, 1947; Bordo and Schwartz, 1984).

The European idea

In the last part of the 19th century, there were hardly any movements to promote the idea of a united Europe. Though not typically European, an important anti-nationalist movement should perhaps be pointed out, the Socialist International. This movement suggested that the popular masses had nothing to gain either from an armed conflict or from economic conflicts among capitalists of various countries. Successive versions of the Socialist International proved unable, however, to translate suggestions into a clear plan of action, let alone make the plan operational. Once more, the self-interest of national 'sections' proved the main obstacle to practical internationalisation.

The almost complete lack of utopias and proposals for concrete actions for the unity of Europe should not make us forget that most Europeans at the time under consideration continued to take the cultural unity of their part of the world more or less for granted. In spite of wide differences among nations, neither literary and artistic trends nor great spiritual movements were confined to any one nation; they were part of one common European cultural world (Duroselle, 1987) – a conception which in economics, and especially politics, was still a long way off.

International organisation and coordination

At the turn of the century, forms of integrated policy (positive integration), were practised for the first time, international institutions being founded for the purpose. This was the logical outcome of increased government intervention in the economy, combined with intensified international exchange. Not surprisingly, this policy integration concerned only areas directly connected with international trade or conditions of international competition.

- *Transport.* The technical standardisation of railway equipment was mainly due to the British system of measures being adopted by most states. The coordination of other elements, such as the exchange of rolling stock, the treatment of goods, time schedules and so on, was accomplished in international committees.

- *Post and telecommunication.* Among the first international organisations were the International Telecommunication Union (1865) and the Universal Postal Union (1874). Both were established to harmonise internationally all national regulations with respect to rates, procedures, infrastructure (cables) and so on. The harmonisation has contributed much to the rapid growth of PTT traffic.
- *Agriculture and fishery.* Several attempts were made at international coordination and regulation; a first, limited success was the regulation of trade in sugar (premiums being abolished). An effort was made to achieve one European tariff for foodstuffs, to protect European producers against competition, on the European market, from new producer countries.
- *Social policies.* Efforts towards integration were inspired largely by the fear that the improvement of social services and work conditions in one country would put that country at a competitive disadvantage. Much later, after the First World War, the problem was the subject of discussion at various conferences, which finally led to the creation of the International Labour Office. The abolition of slavery was among the first steps towards social policy integration: in 1890, a General Act against Slavery was signed.

Some hesitant steps were taken to bring about some coordination in other areas by diplomatic deals, but the pressure of the techno-economic circumstances was not so strong here. These hesitant attempts were, for the most part, not very successful and they will therefore not be elaborated upon here.

1914–1945: disintegration

The First World War and the peace treaty

With the outbreak of the First World War, every country started to practise autarky: they reasoned that to depend economically on foreign countries makes a country vulnerable in military terms. The result was a process of disintegration. This had its effects both on markets and on policy.

- *Markets.* The first victim was international trade, which showed a steep drop, due to government intervention. The next was production factors, their movement being more and more curtailed. Under the pressure of conscription, among other things, the free movement of individuals collapsed completely. Capital was more and more contained within national borders by a multitude of national rules. The international loans concluded during this period were concerned exclusively with the assistance of one government by another.

- *Policy*. The state began to interfere intensively with trade and industry, organising them for purposes of war. Because the control was strictly national, a coordinated international policy was practically impossible. Even within a bloc, integration was shunned for fear of disloyalty of allied states. Any agreements concluded between the members of each bloc covered only restricted areas. For instance, during the First World War the Allies only coordinated the use of shipping tonnage, and made some attempt at specialising production (Monnet, 1976).

The Peace Treaty of Versailles consolidated the disintegration. The central theme of this treaty was the nations' right to self-determination. On that basis, many new states were formed in Europe, which instantly began to quarrel about frontiers, debts, minorities and so on. The result was a great length of new frontiers (some 11,000 km) with corresponding customs barriers. To support the autonomy of the national economies, most barriers were made sky-high (see 1930–40 period in Figure 3.2). Thus the industry and transport structures were forced to adapt themselves to a multitude of small territories. Factories were built at uneconomic locations, railways rerouted, and so on.

The period between the two world wars

After the First World War some countries (notably Germany) were left with enormous debts, leading to serious balance-of-payment difficulties. These were aggravated by low prices and diminishing sales prospects on export markets. Under such circumstances, non-competitive companies, traditionally in favour of protection, grasped their chance, and the enormous unemployment consolidated the protectionist tendencies. This movement spread quickly through Europe and, as a consequence, imports were reduced to almost half the pre-war level; this in turn led to a decrease in exports as well (as illustrated by Table 3.3). An even greater decrease befell international capital movements, which fell back to about one-fifth of their pre-war level.

The disadvantages of the economic disintegration were increasingly recognised and attempts were undertaken to reintegrate the economies of certain groups of states.

Table 3.3 **Some indicators of European* economic development, 1913–38**

Indicator	1913	1920	1930	1938
Gross National Product per head (index 1938 = 100)	n.a.	73	89	100
Industrial production (index 1938 = 100)	n.a.	61	86	100
Production of pig iron (MT/y)	39	21	36	38
Coal production (MT/y)	498	392	480	481
Share of exports in GNP (%)	16	9	9	6
Share of foreign investment in GNP	5	n.a.	1	1
Railway track (× 1,000 km)	193	189	197	199

* Only present EC12 countries.
n.a. = not available.
Source: calculated on the basis of figures given in OECD (1964), Bairoch (1976), Mitchell (1981).

- *Markets.* The plan to unite in a customs union the old Habsburg states failed (Ponteroso Conference), as did a worldwide free-trade scheme in which 29 states agreed to abolish all trade restrictions within six months and never impose them again (Conference of Geneva, 1927).
- *Policy.* The League of Nations, founded by the Allies, came into operation in 1920; its object was to maintain peace in Europe. The League developed some activity in economic and social affairs (among others it created the ILO, the International Labour Organisation). However, all those initiatives hardly made an impact. In this period of general disintegration only one example of positive integration can be mentioned. The Bank for International Payments, a joint venture of the central banks in Europe, was founded in 1930 to facilitate payments, quite a feat in a period of great monetary disorder (inflation, devaluation race, downfall of the gold standard, etc.).

In the 1920s a slight improvement on some points raised hopes for a period of more intensive integration. However, as Table 3.3 indicates, during the 1920s average dependency on external trade remained virtually stable. Even that comparatively modest integration was curtailed by the depression of the 1930s. Again there was a sharp effect on both markets and policy integration.

- *Markets.* The United States' introduction of the very high Smoot–Hawley tariff in 1930 sparked off a further wave of protectionist measures in Europe, leading to tariffs of unprecedented height (see Figure 3.2) and the multiplication of the number of quotas.
- *Policy.* The most important area of disintegration was monetary policy. The gold standard, which had not worked very well during this period, collapsed (the UK left in 1931; other countries soon followed). A period of currency competition ensued, one devaluation following upon the other. All attempts to solve the crisis by international agreements failed. In other fields, too, policy integration decreased. To overcome the depression, states began to intervene even more than before in the economy, and Keynes (1936) furnished the theoretical foundation. National solutions (armament, infrastructure works) to the unemployment problem were governed by national circumstances, and once more the economy was often made subservient to military objectives.

The idea of a united Europe

During and between the two world wars, short-term economic thinking (the fight against unemployment) and strategic–military thinking (autarky was believed to be safer than integration) were dominant; however some enlightened spirits began to see that nationalism only breeds economic problems and is a permanent threat to peace. The best known attempt of this period to solve the problem in a European perspective was the Pan Europe Movement, led by Coudenhove-Calergi. Although this movement aroused considerable interest, it shared with comparable activities the weakness of keeping rather aloof from the political reality of the time and being too utopian.

Initiatives towards European unity taken by leading statesmen seemed more promising, in principle. There was, for instance, the plan for a European federation which Briand, French prime minister in 1930, after consultation with the German foreign minister, Stresemann, submitted to the League of Nations. The scheme was well received, but support was soon found to be very superficial. It failed to stir the masses in any nation; nationalism had sunk too deeply in the consciousness of the average citizen. Even such weak attempts were heard of less and less in the 1930s, when fascist movements were organising themselves along blatantly nationalist lines, more and more straining international relations, and finally even trying to impose the hegemony of the Axis powers on Europe by military force. Hardly a situation to foster a true European vision.

1945 to the present: a new upsurge of integration

Europe and world policy

The Second World War brought about a measure of integration. On the side of the Axis powers it was achieved by enlisting the economies of territories occupied by Germany in the German war efforts. The integration concerned not only products (agricultural as well as industrial): production factors were forcefully integrated as well (*Arbeitzeinsatz*, war loans). On the side of the Allies some integration could also be perceived: once more, production and means of transport were to some extent normalised for the sake of the war effort. The integration efforts hardly touched the other sectors of the economy, however.

The terrors of war inspired attempts to improve the post-war relations among nations by creating a number of international organisations, only the most important of which are briefly dealt with here:

- United Nations (UNO). The lesson from the experience with the League of Nations was that all large countries would have to be members of the central organisation, in this case the United Nations. A range of other specialised agencies was founded as well.
- World Bank (IRBD) and International Monetary Fund (IMF). The combined task of these organisations was to ensure well regulated international monetary relations (Conference of Bretton Woods). That meant fixed exchange rates between currencies. Countries that through temporary balance-of-payment problems found it hard to maintain these fixed exchange rates could obtain hard-currency loans. Since its creation, the IMF has expanded its scope and has become the place for coordination and consultation in the international monetary sphere.
- General Agreement on Tariffs and Trade (GATT). This organisation's task is to stimulate free trade. One important instrument against the occurrence of trade disputes is the so-called 'most-favoured nation' clause, according to which any favourable tariff which two countries accord to each other is essentially valid for all other participants in the General Agreement. The GATT has accomplished a considerable worldwide tariff decrease; many non-tariff impediments have been eliminated as well.

Integration, which had come to a halt during the war, was gradually re-established during this period. First, there was a move towards free trade, and next towards convertibility of currencies and free capital movements, with exchange rates pegged to the dollar. The monetary and macro-economic coordination schemes of the IMF and OECD (see below) could not cope with the emerging inconsistencies, and in the 1970s the Bretton Woods system collapsed. The experiences of the period led to the conclusion (Padoa-Schioppa *et al.*, 1987) that free movement of goods and capital cannot be combined with pegged exchange rates and independent macro-economic policy making of member countries.

After the Allied victory, Europe was cut in two. If at first the spheres of influence of the western Allies and the Soviet Union were not precisely delimited, soon afterwards the outbreak of the Cold War, the revolutions in some East European countries and the refusal of Russia and its confederates to accept Marshall Aid led to the very sharp dividing line which went by the name of the Iron Curtain. Economic integration of European countries from the western bloc with those from the eastern bloc was thus excluded for a long time. The only platform where 'integration' of East and West was still a point of discussion was the Economic Commission for Europe (ECE), a regional organisation of the United Nations. Its role has been very modest, however. Any further integration has proceeded within each separate bloc. Some integration of the economies of Eastern Europe has taken place in the framework of the Council of Mutual Economic Assistance (CMEA or Comecon), a different organisation from that chosen in the West (Kozma, 1982; Pinder, 1986). We will concentrate henceforth on Western Europe.

The pursuit of European unity

Already during the Second World War, the pursuit of intensive economic integration was put on a political–idealistic footing. Especially in circles of the Resistance the conviction was growing that nationalism was at the roots of the disaster which fascism had wrought in Europe and that, therefore, Europe should be rebuilt in a sphere of increased international integration, especially in economic terms. The Ventotene Manifest published in 1941 by personalities grouped around Spinelli is perhaps the best known of the ideas fostered by the Resistance. It led more or less directly to the Geneva Declaration of 1944, which confirmed the principles of an Atlantic Charter and proposed a federal solution for the whole of Europe (including Eastern Europe). For the first time the sentiments initially expressed by some members of the Resistance appeared to be attractive to large groups of people. A whole series of initiatives for European integration were fostered by these sentiments, many of which found active support from leading politicians in all West European countries. The first result was the creation of the Council of Europe, and the Union Parlementaire Européenne was the second.

Many groups continued to submit proposals and to campaign for a more far-reaching European unity. The movements varied widely in objective and organisation. International pacifism, European federalism and economic functionalism were joined, however, into one European Movement (Lipgens *et al.*, 1982). The generally felt need for economic integration soon generated a favourable climate to create, with American support, the OECD (see next section).

A limited set of countries pushed towards further integration. The UK appeared to set greater store by an Empire than a European orientation, and the British gradually withdrew from initiatives towards greater European integration. However continental nations continued to strive for closer cooperation. This is not surprising, as most initiatives were inspired by the hope of eliminating forever the potential war threat posed by French and German differences. That political aim was to be achieved, not through unrealistic plans for complete political union, but through a strategy of gradual integration of certain functions (for example, Haas, 1958; Mitrany, 1966). These could then later be followed by other functions. The first function chosen was of an economic nature, which seemed the most practical as very good economic reasons were pushing in that direction.[3]

This needed to be accompanied by the setting up of institutions in order to safeguard the durability of the integration scheme. There has been considerable debate, about the degree to which national governments needed to transfer powers to these organisations, between advocates of two concepts: (1) an *intergovernmental* organisation, characterised by a small secretariat, and where the representatives of the national governments take decisions by unanimity; and (2) a *supranational* organisation, with an organ that independently executes policies and prepares decisions, and where the representatives of national governments may take decisions by majority rule. The plan launched on 9 May 1950, by the French foreign minister Schuman, and inspired by Monnet, to join together the French and German basic industries under a High Authority was based on a functional and supranational approach. The road Europe took at that moment towards economic and political integration, and has followed since, consisted in the creation of a factual solidarity based on practical realisations.

The functional character appears in the choice of one sector, in this case the strategic sectors of coal (the major form of energy) and steel (the basic material). The supranational character appears in the setting up of the organisation of the European Coal and Steel Community (ECSC), to which much of the national authority was transferred. The success was due to the heavy support the plan received from leading politicians (including Adenauer and de Gasperi). After the successful creation of the ECSC, new initiatives were taken to extend the functions to be integrated beyond economics into fields such as defence and foreign policy. However the ratification of the treaties of the European Defence Community (EDC) and the European Political Community (EPC) eventually miscarried in the French parliament. The pressure of the Europeans was then once more brought to bear on the economic function. This resulted in 1958 (after the Spaak report and the Messina Conference) in the establishment, on a supranational basis, of the European Economic Community (Jansen and De Vree, 1985).

What were the reasons for this success, where other attempts had failed? In the past, voices pleading integration had hardly found any response. Now that all nations were feeling the chafing scars of war, these voices had at last gained sufficient political weight to be heard. Moreover the basis for further integration had been enlarged as the social differences among European countries had gradually become less outspoken, a development that gained momentum in the post-war decades (Kaelble, 1986).

European organisations

The ravages of war made it clear that Europe's only chance of survival lay in progressive economic integration. To that end some important multinational agreements were concluded and some international bodies, widely different in structure and authority, were created (see, for instance, Palmer, Lambert *et al.*, 1968; Van Meerhaeghe, 1992). Examples are the Council of Europe, concerned in particular with cultural affairs and human rights, and the West European Union, mainly occupied with defence. Four others deal more specifically with economic integration.

The Benelux Economic Union (1944), which joins together the Netherlands, Belgium and Luxemburg, has a long history. Unsuccessful attempts at creating a Benelux customs union had already been made in 1919 and 1932. The present agreement provides for a customs union as well as an economic union. The customs union took a relatively short time to realise; the economic union is still being worked at. The importance of the Benelux lies in particular in the opportunity it gives to gain experience in certain forms of integration, an experience with has proved useful for the establishment and extension of the European Community.

The *Organisation for European Economic Cooperation* (OEEC) (1948), later reorganised to become the OECD, was created to administer Marshall Aid. To prevent the tremendous currency deficit of the

European nations from disrupting international trade and payments, the European Payment Union was established. It undertook the clearance of bilateral currency surpluses and deficits, and provided credit facilities. The OEEC aimed for trade liberalisation by the elimination of all manner of obstacles. The OEEC further provided for some coordination of national policies, for instance at the macro-economic level and with respect to manufacturing industry and energy, constituting a clear, albeit light, form of positive integration. The type of organisation chosen, namely, full inter-government collaboration with a modest secretariat, seemed to many European nations too limited and too weak to foster further economic integration. These nations kept looking for other ways to consolidate the integration. The OEEC was extended and relaunched in 1961 under the new name of Organisation for Economic Cooperation and Development (OECD); at present it comprises the entire industrialised western world (Western Europe, the United States, Canada, Australia, New Zealand and Japan).

The *European Community* (EC) foundations were laid in 1952 when the Treaty of Paris created the European Coal and Steel Community (ECSC). Its objective was to withdraw the French and German basic industries from the national authority and place them under a European High Authority. Besides France and Germany, the Benelux countries and Italy joined the pact. The UK, having serious reservations about its supranational character, kept aloof. The sectoral limitation of the ECSC was felt to be a serious practical handicap, and a fuller economic integration was aimed at. It was achieved in 1958 when the European Economic Community (EEC) was created (again on a supranational basis) by the Treaty of Rome. The member states were the same six mentioned above, the UK again keeping apart. With the EEC, European integration reached a decisive stage in its development, for the Treaty of Rome set ambitious goals. In that same year, 1958, the same countries also founded the European Atomic Energy Community (EAEC or Euratom). Since then the EC has extended both its membership and its competences (see next section).

The *European Free Trade Association* (EFTA) was created in 1959 in Stockholm, under the leadership of the UK, by the remaining nations of Western Europe. While recognising the advantages of further integration, these countries could not, for different reasons, accept the objectives and the organisation of the Community. The objectives of EFTA were far less than those of the EC, only a free trade zone being established. The institutional organisation of EFTA was no other than the usual intergovernmental structure of most international organisations. Over the decades it became clear to a number of EFTA members that their interest would be better served by joining the EC. Some of them actually left EFTA. Practically all present EFTA members have now applied for EC membership. Their accession to the EC is facilitated by the 'European Economic Area' (EEA), a pact signed and ratified in 1992 merging the EC and the EFTA into one single market.

From European Community to European Union

The legal foundation of the European Community consist of the three treaties of the ECSC, the EEC and the EAEC. Right from the start of the latter two organisations, two of its institutions (Parliament and the Court of Justice) assumed responsibilities for the three organisations. In the 1960s, the executive bodies (Commission and Council) of the ECSC, the EEC and the EAEC were merged as well. From that moment one institutional structure was in operation for the three separate legal entities. Of these three, the EEC has come to occupy a paramount place. Its treaty has been constantly adapted to cope with the new constitutional needs of the dynamics of the European integration process. For example, the Single Act of 1987 provided among other things for further market and policy integration. The Maastricht Treaty formalises the colloquial name European Community (Article 1) and creates the European Union. The latter encompasses (apart from the EC) cooperation of member states in matters of foreign and security policy and justice and home affairs. (We use henceforth the term 'European Union', which also includes the EC.)

Deepening   The EU has gradually extended its field of activity and intensified its involvement in already existing common policy areas. The first objective of the EEC Treaty (Article 3) was to create a Customs Union and an incomplete Common Market. The next was to create an Economic Union by setting up common policies and to coordinate many national policies. Market integration made rapid progress in the 1960s and the beginning of the 1970s; a customs union was indeed quickly realised for most of the sectors of the economy. Similar results were obtained for major parts of the labour and capital markets. Policy integration made headway, for example with the setting up of a common agricultural and a common trade policy. The economic crisis of the middle of the 1970s and early 1980s brought the integration process practically to a halt. When the negative effects of this situation became evident, a new impulse was given with the successful completion of the internal (common) market by 1992. Over the years a gradual extension of policy integration took place, based on agreements on new objectives. At some points an acceleration of this process took place. The Single Act codified the objectives of environmental protection and regional development and brought European Political Cooperation (on international diplomacy matters) into the Community framework (Article 30). The Maastricht Treaty provides notably for an Economic and Monetary Union and for more social protection. Moreover the Treaty extends the integration process into a number of non-economic fields, such as home affairs, defence and foreign policy and European citizenship.

Widening The number of member countries of the EU has gradually been increased (see Figure 3.3). This was the result of the success of the EU in the realisation of its objectives. When other European countries realised that they had no part in these advantages, they decided to apply for EU membership. In 1972, the UK, Denmark and Ireland left the EFTA to join the EC. In 1981, Greece was admitted, followed in 1986 by Spain and Portugal. Most of the remaining countries of the EFTA have applied for membership, and negotiations are under way. Recently the geographical perspective of the EU has been further widened by the collapse of the system of central planning in the countries of Central and Eastern Europe. The former GDR was taken into the EU when it was united with the Federal Republic of Germany in 1990. Moreover a number of Central and Eastern European countries have applied for membership and others have indicated they will do so in the near future.

The EU has shown a remarkable dynamism. As a matter of fact its velocity of integration exceeds the speed with which other integration schemes have proceeded (for example, France, Switzerland, the USA). Unfortunately the causes of this success are not yet well understood (Tinbergen, 1991).

Summary and conclusions

- Economic integration of Europe has been not so much an objective as a by-product of technological progress, on the one hand, and aspirations to political unity, on the other.
- Technical and economic factors (for instance large-scale production attended by mechanisation and automation, and the development of new means of transport such as trains and lorries) were the principal stimulus to progressive economic integration in Europe.
- Political and idealistic motives for European unity were strongly inspired by the need for peace. Their influence on practical economic integration remained slight, however. Indeed, not until after the Second World War did the European idea become really effective.
- Not only can integration cease to make progress, it can also,

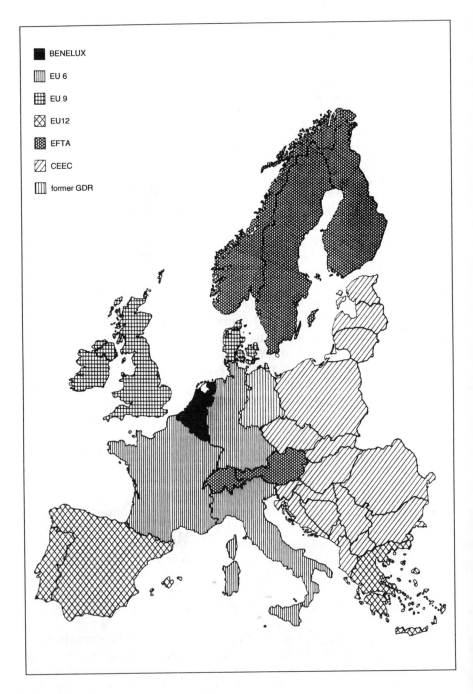

Figure 3.3   Gradual extension of the membership of the European Union

once achieved, be reversed. Especially in times of economic depression and decline, the forces arguing against integration tend to become stronger and harder to resist.

- Integration of goods and factor markets and of macro-economic and monetary policy making is most effective under strict rules and in a strong institutional setting.
- From a multitude of institutions dealing with economic integration the European Union has emerged as the most dynamic. It has extended both its fields of activity and its geographical coverage.

Notes

1 The organisation of the subject matter of this chapter has been largely borrowed from Pollard (1981a); the paragraphs concerning the 'ideology' of European unification lean in particular on the standard volume by Brugmans (1970).
2 For a description of the changes in the perceptions of Europe in history, see A. Rijksbaron *et al.* (eds) (1987).
3 See Machlup (1977) for a review of the contributions to the thinking on integration of historians (ch. 5), political economists (ch. 6), statesmen, men of affairs and men of letters (ch. 7), committee members and organisation staff (ch. 8) and economic theorists (ch. 9).

4 Institutions

Introduction

Economic integration is dependent on the legal framework that is set for it. In general one can say that strong institutions are a necessary condition for the stability of the schemes and for the internal dynamics. The main components (ECSC, EEC, Euratom) of the European Union have, right from the start, been endowed with strong institutions. The institutional set-up of the EU is rather original. On the one hand, it has traits of an international organisation, as the member states have kept their sovereignty and competence in essential areas. The member states are represented in the Council of Ministers; as in all traditional intergovernmental international organisations, this is the dominant institution where final decisions are made. On the other hand, the European Union has also some obvious traits of a federal union. It has developed its *own system of laws* and its institutions exercise a *clearly defined authority* in an increasing number of areas. European law, being instantly and equally applicable in all member states, is neither national nor international; it is often called supranational. EU institutions are endowed with powers largely exceeding those of an intergovernmental international organisation like the OECD (with only a general secretariat to assist the ministers at their task), but falling short of those of a strong federal government (the USA).

In this chapter we will give the essential aspects of the development of the EU system that are useful for the understanding of many of the issues dealt with in later chapters. In the next section we will present the various institutions and the original way in which they relate to each other. We will thereby refer in broad terms to their present competences.[1] Four of these institutions that form the backbone of the system merit fuller treatment, and we will describe in some detail the composition, procedures, tasks and competences of each.

The complex way in which the law- and decision-making machinery functions will then be examined. We will indicate briefly the different legal forms in use, the diversity of the decision-making processes and the dynamics of the system. Finally a section will be devoted to the budget, describing briefly the structure of expenditure and receipts and the way budgetary powers are executed, and a summary section with some conclusions will round off the chapter.

Institutional framework

Major and other institutions

The four most important institutions are the Commission (or, for the ECSC, the High Authority), the Council, Parliament (formally called the Assembly) and the Court of Justice. Until 1967 the three Communities (ECSC, EEC and Euratom) had separate executive bodies (Commissions and Councils); the two other institutions (Parliament and Court) had decided to act for all three Communities. In 1967, a new treaty merged the executive bodies of the three Communities as well.[2] Alongside these four, a fifth body has been promoted to the rank of official institution by the Treaty on European Union (TEU) (Maastricht Treaty): the Court of Auditors (Article 4 TEU). Table 4.1. gives a schematic representation of the institutional system of the European Union.

Table 4.1   The institutional system

Council	Commission	Parliament	Court of Justice	Court of Auditors
12 national ministers (or heads of government)	17 members	567 members	13 judges 6 advocates general	12 members
European Central Bank	*European Investment Bank*	*Economic Social Committee*	*Committee of Regions (CR)*	
11 members	12 governors 22 directors	189 members	189 members	

Some other institutions exist (Article 4a and 4b TEU) that need some brief introduction.

The Court of Auditors (ECA)   This body examines the accounts of the Community, to determine not only whether all revenue has been received and all expenditure incurred in a lawful manner, but also whether the financial management has been sound (Article 188 abc).

The Economic and Social Committee   The ESC, composed of representatives of employees and employers, professionals and consumers, advises the Commission and the Council on their policy plans (Articles 193–197).

The Committee of the Regions   The CR also acts in an advisory capacity to Commission and Council on matters regarding local authorities and regional interests (Article 198 abc).[3]

The European System of Central Banks (ESCB) and the *European Central Bank (ECB)*   These have the task of maintaining price stability. To that end the ESCB/ECB define and implement the monetary policy of the EC. Moreover, they support the general economic policies of the Community (Article 109 a).

The European Investment Bank   The EIB grants credits to business companies and governments notably for projects of common interest to several member states that are of such a nature or size that they cannot be entirely financed by one state. Moreover, the EIB can finance projects in less developed regions (Article 198).

Division of power under different regimes

The European Union, as set up by the TEU, has two main components:

- The European Community, that inherits the 'acquis communautaire' of the EEC, the ECSC and Euratom. Its field of action is complemented by new policy matters, such as monetary union. The Community regime involves all institutions mentioned in the previous section (Titles II, III and IV).
- New provision for common foreign and security policy (Title V) and justice and home affairs (Title VI). For these matters a purely intergovernmental regime exists that practically involves only the Council (with limited roles for Commission and Parliament).

For Community matters the division of competences over institutions follows to a large extent the usual division of powers existing in national states. The legislation lies with Parliament, execution with the Commission and judication with the Court. The Council occupies a special position in the institutional framework. It has both important executive and legislative powers. For the first function it shares powers with the Commission, for the second with the Parliament. The rules for Community matters are as follows.

Execution   Commission and Council are jointly responsible for (1) coordinating national policies; (2) issuing regulations and directives and taking decisions in the policy areas foreseen in the treaties; (3) giving form and substance to Community policy wherever the treaties have not done so; and (4) supervising the observation of the treaties and the implementation of decisions. In practice, there is some division of work; the Council coordinates and determines the strategy to be adopted, while the Commission takes care of daily operations and controls and supervises the observation of the treaties. The difference is one of emphasis only, for the Commission helps to prepare Council decisions, and often consults the Council or the representatives of the national governments on the execution of its tasks. Indeed Council and Commission perform their duties in constant consultation.

Legislation   Contrary to many national parliaments, the European Parliament (EP) has limited legislative power. In some matters it has only an advisory role; final decisions lie with the Council. In others it has the power of co-decision, which means that Council and Parliament have to come to an agreement in order to put legislation into effect.

The Commission

The Commission consists of 17 members, appointed, after mutual consultation, by the governments of the member states for a four-year period. The largest countries (Germany, France, the UK, Italy and Spain) appoint two members each, the smaller ones (Belgium, Denmark, The Netherlands, Ireland, Portugal, Greece and Luxemburg) one each. The members are chosen on the grounds of their 'general competence', and their independence must be beyond doubt. Although one member acts as president and six others are vice-presidents, all members have in principle the same powers, none being subordinate to any of the others. Decisions are made by majority vote.

Once appointed, the members of the Commission have a European responsibility; that is to say, they must not set themselves up as national representatives. For that reason, a member state cannot call 'its' Commissioner to account, or withdraw him. Nor can the Commission as a whole be dismissed by the Council of Ministers. However the Commission is accountable to the European Parliament, and can be forced to resign as a body only by a motion of censure of the Parliament. In that event, the governments of the member states must appoint a new Commission (it has never happened yet).

To perform its task, the Commission has at its disposal an international staff (informally called the Eurocracy), for the greater part established in Brussels. At the beginning of the 1990s, a total of some 17,000 officials were employed in the Commission's services, many of them engaged in translation work. Each member of the Commission is responsible for one policy sector or, in more concrete terms, for the work of one or more Directorates General (comparable to national ministerial departments). In the course of time the role of the president of the Commission as the representative of this institution and as the person responsible for the consistency of the actions of the various commissioners has greatly increased.

The Commission is assisted in its many tasks by a large number of specialist committees. Some (300) of them have an advisory role; that is, they must be consulted before the drafting of EC legislation. Others (100) have a regulatory or management role. These committees are mainly composed of representatives of member states and of professional and corporatist groups.

The Commission occupies a special position in the system of the Union. It has very extensive powers in Community matters. On the other hand, for foreign and defence policy, and home and justice affairs, it has a limited role of initiative and support in preparation and execution (the Council will keep the Commission 'fully associated' to its work in this area (Articles 79 and K4)). In Community matters, however, its role is not to be compared to that of the secretariat of other intergovernmental institutions, which can only prepare decisions and implement them by delegation of authority of the representatives of member states. Nor can the Commission be compared to the government of a sovereign member state, which has full executive power, whereas the Commission shares its powers with the Council of Ministers.

The major tasks of the Commission are the initiation of actions, the execution of its policies, the implementation of the budget and finally the enforcement of the laws:

Initiation of actions The Commission has the right of initiative, it develops new policies, proposes new regulations, directives and decisions. To fulfil its role effectively, the Commission is represented in the meetings of the Council and COREPER (see next section). The role of initiator is a highly important one, for it is that role which enables the Commission to safeguard the Community interest against the national interests dominating the Council. Admittedly the

Commission is not the sole actor here. Indeed the European Council (of heads of government) has reserved to itself the initiating of major new developments.

Execution of policies   Some of the Commission's executive powers have been bestowed on it by the treaties; these include the customs union, the fight against monopolies and competition distortion due to government support. Other powers are transferred to the Commission by the Council. Indeed nearly all Council decisions contain articles which call for implementation by the Commission. However the Council tends to take a rather narrow view of the executive tasks to be entrusted to the Commission. In some cases it ties up the Commission in its executive task with some form of consultation, for instance with the so-called 'management committees', composed of national experts (on, for instance, agricultural markets or harmonisation). A proposal of the Commission agreed to by the majority of the management committee need not be submitted to the Council and can be carried out immediately. Commission proposals not accepted by the management committee have to be submitted to the Council, which then decides by qualified majority.

Implementation of the budget   This includes the operations of the so-called 'structural funds' (Agricultural, Regional, Social and Development Funds). The Commission is also authorised to raise loans to finance investments in energy, industry and infrastructure projects envisaged to help realise certain policy objectives.

Enforcement of the laws   The Commission supervises the correct implementation of treaties and decisions. The authority to gather information was bestowed on it in the treaties. When the Commission finds, through an inquiry, that a company, individual or member state has violated the EC rules, it invites that company, individual or member state to explain its behaviour. If no satisfactory explanation is given, the member state or individual will be invited to stop the violation. In some cases a fine is imposed. Should that prove ineffective, the Commission will institute legal proceedings before the Court. Here too the role of the Commission as guardian of the Community interest is manifest.

The Council

The Council consists of one representative minister of the government of each of the member states. The composition of the Council varies with the matter in hand. In general, the Council consists of the

Ministers of Foreign Affairs of the 12 member states, but it may also consist of the Ministers of Agriculture or Transport or Finance. The Council of Ministers meets as often as it considers necessary, mostly in Brussels, sometimes in Luxemburg, often in any other convenient city of a member state.

The member states take the presidency in turns, for six months each, in alphabetical order. The president of the Council takes responsibility for the progress of the work of the Council. In order to safeguard the necessary continuity a troika is formed in which the past, present and future president coordinate the timing of consultations, negotiations and decisions.

On a number of subjects the Council decides with unanimity (on defence and home affairs, for example). On most subjects it decides with a qualified majority. Depending on the size of the countries, the representatives have different numbers of votes. The total number of votes is 76; they are distributed as follows (Article 148):

10: Germany, France, Italy and the UK;
 8: Spain;
 5: The Netherlands, Belgium, Greece, Portugal;
 3: Denmark, Ireland;
 2: Luxemburg.

A proposal of the Commission must be supported by a qualified majority of at least 54 votes in the Council to be accepted; in some cases these 54 votes must come from at least eight member states. In the past, unanimity was often tried for by persevering with the negotiations for as long as necessary to find a compromise acceptable to all. Naturally such a procedure slowed down decision making a great deal, and was not conducive to transparent and consistent outcomes. The Single European Act established that many decisions about the internal market, regional policy, and research and technology could be taken by qualified majority. The TEU has further enlarged the area of majority voting.[4]

The ministers on the Council are accountable to their national parliament and not to the EP. There is, however, a dialogue between the two bodies: during sessions of the EP time is reserved for a debate between the EP and the Council on topical subjects.

Since 1975 there have been regular meetings of the European Council, which is composed of heads of government (and head of state for France) (Bulmer and Wessels, 1986). These 'summits' (in which the president and vice-president of the Commission and the foreign ministers also participate) take place at least twice a year. The European Council's role is to give direction to EU policy making. It sets the broad guidelines and determines new stages (for example, cohesion, environment, single market, EMU).

The Council has a separate staff of European officials who prepare the meetings. It is a small staff compared to that of the Commission. Important in the preparatory work is the Committee of Permanent Representatives, often indicated by the French abbreviation of COREPER. This Committee meets every week in task-oriented workgroups, in which civil servants of national departments also take part. COREPER deals with the Commission's proposals. If COREPER is agreeable to the proposal, the Council's final decision is no more than a formality. If not, the proposal is further negotiated in the complete Council of Ministers.

According to the treaties, the Council has three different roles to play in execution and legislation:

Community matters   To coordinate the various economic policies of the member states. The Council has the 'power to take decisions'; in other words, the Council has the final say in Community legislation. In some cases it has to share this power with the EP (see next section).

External matters   To regulate the European Union's relations with other countries by treaties. In actual fact, it is mostly the Commission which acts as negotiator by the mandate given to it by the Council; the final decision is the Council's. For some treaties it needs the approval of the EP.

Other matters   To execute the specific tasks common to intergovernmental cooperation in matters such as foreign affairs, security, justice and home affairs.

The European Parliament

The members of the European Parliament (EP) are elected directly for a term of five years. In most countries the election proceeds by proportional representation. There are 567 members. After reunification Germany is by far the largest country; it has 99 seats. Other large countries, like the UK and France, have 87 members each; a medium-size country like The Netherlands has 31 members, and small countries, like Ireland, 15. Each member has one vote. The Parliament elects from its members a president and a number of vice-presidents, who together constitute the 'Bureau', the executive body responsible for the agenda, competence of committees, and so on.

From the start, EP members have grouped themselves not by national delegations, but along party-political lines (Social Democrats,

Christian Democrats, Liberals, and so on). The preliminary work of the Parliament is carried on in the parliamentary committees, which may be standing or temporary, general or special. From their members, the committees choose rapporteurs, who report on subjects to be treated in the full Parliament. Most reports contain a draft resolution, to be voted on by the full EP.

The seat of the Parliament is a bone of contention. The secretariat, the Parliament's own clerical staff, is established in Luxemburg. The Parliament's plenary sessions (during one week of every month) are mostly held in Strasbourg, while the Committees most often meet in Brussels. The situation is very inefficient and expensive. A majority of EP members would prefer to conduct all its activities in Brussels, but there are still legal obstacles to this.

In the past the competences of the EP remained far below those of most national parliaments (see Van Schendelen, 1984). Therefore the EP has striven constantly to extend its authority, on the argument that only the European Parliament can make up for the democratic gaps in EU decision making (the Council of Ministers is not accountable to the European Parliament, while each individual Minister tries to circumvent accountability to his national parliament on the argument that the negotiations in the EU obliged him to act as he did). The tasks and competences of the EP have been extended gradually. In Community matters the competences of the EP are now very wide. In matters added by the TEU (foreign and defence policy; home and justice affairs) on the contrary, the competences are limited; the Council consults the EP on the main aspects and basic choices and keeps the EP informed (Articles 77 and C6). The EP competences refer to four areas: (1) decision making (legislation), (2) budget, (3) policy, and (4) control. The role of the EP varies greatly among the four; even within each area a differentiation of competences of the EP exists.

Legislation Four different procedures exist: consultation, cooperation, co-decision and assent. The EP initially had only an advisory capacity. It discussed the proposals of the Commission and drew up a report, which was submitted to Commission and Council. This advisory role still applies to many social policy matters. The cooperation procedure was introduced by the Single European Act (SEA). Here the position of the EP is strengthened, as the Council can reject amendments of the EP only unanimously. If the Council wanted to go against the advice of the EP about Commission proposals with important financial implications, reconciliation of the different standpoints is attempted. The field in which this procedure applied had been extended by the TEU to cover not only internal market aspects but also matters like transport, competition, environment, development aid and some aspects of social policy. The third procedure (introduced by the TEU) gives the EP the right of co-decision. This applies to matters related to the internal market (formerly cooperation) framework programmes for the environment, technology and transport. Finally, assent by parliamentary approval (practically an EP veto) is required (since the SEA) for the conclusion of treaties and for extension of the Community. Its field of application has been extended by the TEU to cover now matters such as outline measures for cohesion, for European citizenship and so on.

Budget The competence of the EP is quite extensive. It can accept the complete budget or reject it. It has different powers regarding the various parts of the budget. With regard to expenditure necessarily resulting from the Treaty ('obligatory' expenditure) it can only propose modifications within the total expenditure set. With regard to other expenditure, however, it can amend the draft budget.

Policy The EP can influence the scope of EU activities; it is entitled to ask for existing policies to be extended or amended and for new ones to be initiated.

Control The powers of the EP are limited, the major aspect of control being that the Commission has to account to the EP for its actions. It does so in answer to spoken or written questions, and in the discussion of its annual General Report. In the extreme, the EP can force the Commission to resign by a motion of censure. The Council is not accountable to the EP, but the two bodies are in continuous dialogue.

Court of Justice

The Court's task is related to Community matters. It has no task in the four areas that the TEU has added (foreign, defence, justice, home). The ECJ has to ensure the proper and consistent interpretation and application of European law. It concerns both the treaties and the derived legislation, that is to say, all regulations, directives and decisions (see next section). The treaties have established an original legal order. Rights are conferred and obligations imposed directly on citizens and authorities of member states by European law; member states do not need to intervene for these provisions to take effect. On the other hand, citizens can appeal to European rules in national courts. The consistent application of European law in all member states evidently called for a supreme body to settle conflicts; this task was entrusted to the European Court of Justice. The national judge is subordinated to the European Court of Justice.

The Court's composition consists of 13 judges and six advocates general. Judges and advocates general are appointed by member state governments, by mutual agreement, for a period of six years. They must satisfy the requirements valid in their own country for the fulfilment of the highest judicial offices. They must be entirely independent and cannot be dismissed.

When a question is put before the Court, the procedure is as follows. First, an advocate general is appointed to prepare the decision of the Court. He analyses the matter and relates the facts to the relevant legal rules. He then publicly draws his independent and impartial conclusions, which form the basis for the consultations and judgement of the Court. Actually the Court has no legal or police staff of its own; it relies on the goodwill of all member states involved for the enforcement of its ruling. The judgement of the Court is directly applicable in all member states.

Who has access to the European Court? Member states and EU institutions (Council, Commission and Parliament) have unlimited access. Natural and legal persons (companies, for instance) have only limited access; they may initiate proceedings in disputes relating to such acts, or the failure to act or give compensation, of the Commission and the Council as affect their interests directly. In a national lawsuit, too, judgement may depend on relevant European law. Individuals can request a national judge who is not sure about the interpretation of European law to demand, before pronouncing judgement, a 'preliminary ruling' from the European Court of Justice (Article 177). In the past, there was a very rapid increase in the matters regulated by the EU. In line with this, the number of cases brought before the ECJ increased rapidly too (see Table 20.3). To cope with the workload of relatively less important matters, the Court of First Instance was created (Article 168 a), attached to the Court of Justice. It deals with cases that particularly concern private citizens and/or business (competition, anti-dumping, coal and steel, compensation proceedings and so on). Its verdicts are subject to a right of appeal in the ECJ.

The subject matters brought before the Court were concentrated in the main areas of European policy making. The action of the Court has been very important in maintaining dynamism in the process of European integration. For example, the Court has repudiated, in many judgements, any form of protectionism with respect to free movement of goods and services within the EU, and in this way the realisation of the internal market has been safeguarded. The same holds for the preservation of undistorted competition; the many disputes between the Commission (which can act against violations of fair competition, imposing fines if necessary) and companies who disagree and have submitted their case to the Court have given rise to a very extensive jurisprudence.

The proceedings before the Court fall into three categories:

- Failure to fulfil an obligation. For example, if the Commission thinks a member state is not honouring its obligations, it may ask the ECJ to make it comply with the European law.
- Annulment, directed against binding acts of the EU. It may be sought by an EU institution and, in the case of an EU decision concerning him personally, by a natural or legal person.
- Failure to act: means of penalising inactivity on the part of the Commission or Council in cases where they infringe the treaties by not acting.

Laws and rules, decision making

Legal instruments

In order to carry out its tasks, the EU makes regulations, issues directives, takes decisions, makes recommendations or delivers opinions (Article 189).[5]

- A regulation is general in its application; it is binding in its entirety and directly applicable in all member states. This means that national legislation, if existent, is overruled by regulations; indeed, European law takes precedence over national law. The national governments have no right or need to take action once a matter has been settled by a European regulation, for it is automatically valid in all member states.
- A directive is binding, as to the result to be achieved, upon each member state to which it is addressed, but leaves the national authorities the choice of form and methods. So, to implement directives, action of member states is needed in the form of national laws and decrees.
- A decision is binding in its entirety upon those to whom it is addressed.
- Recommendations and opinions have no binding force.

The process of legislation

Decisions about regulations and directives are made by a procedure that differs according to the matter in hand. They differ in the degree of supranationality that the member states were willing to accept. In each area of activity the role of the various institutions differs. The Treaty on the European Union defines two regimes for the fields in which the union will be active:

- *Community*. Decision taking in general implies qualified major- ity voting in the Council, and important roles for the other institutions.
- *Other*. Two new 'pillars' of competences have been created, one for foreign and defence policy, and one for justice and home affairs. In these two fields a traditional intergovernmental deci- sion-making structure will prevail (that is, unanimity in the Council; with a very limited role for some other institutions).

For deciding on Community matters, four regimes exist, again de- pending on the matter in hand. They differ notably in the role played by the European Parliament (see previous section). Two (cooperation and co-decision) are very involved, so we will only present here a very schematic view of the common features of the legislative pro- cess (Figure 4.1) in which the differences in the involvement of the various institutions according to the applicable regime have not been represented. The process can be described in broad terms as follows:

1 Preparation

- The Commission elaborates a planned proposal with the help of its staff; to that end work discussions are often held with committees of national experts.
- The Commission presents its opinions and outlines its planned strategy in communications to the Council and the Parliament.
- The Council and the Parliament communicate their reactions to the Commission; the Commission revises its plans, establishes its proposal and submits it to the Council and to Parliament in the shape of draft regulations or directives.

2 First reading (consultation)

- The proposal is discussed in the Economic and Social Commit- tee, in the Committee of Regions, and in the Parliament.
- ESC, CR, EP, Council and Commission form their opinions.

3 Second reading (negotiation)

- The Council's decision on the proposal is prepared by the Com- mittee of permanent representatives (COREPER). Most of the work is done in workgroups composed of national officials, created for the purpose, in which officials of the Commission are always represented. Any amendments proposed will be submitted by the COREPER to the Council, together with the ESC and EP positions and recommendations.

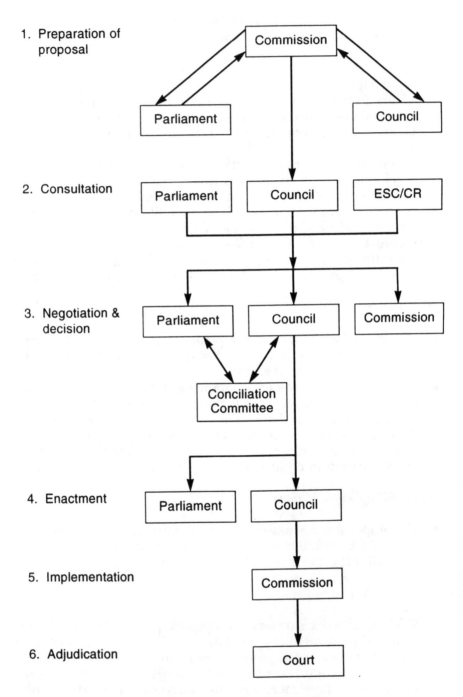

Figure 4.1   A schematic view of the legislative process (Community matters)

- The European Parliament discusses the Commission proposals, the Council's position and, in cases where it has competences in the matter in hand (cooperation, co-decision), negotiates with the Council in the framework of a Conciliation Committee (Article 189b).
- The Commission participates in this stage by adapting proposals, intermediating and so on.

4 Enactment

- Depending on the procedure followed, the Council decides about enactment (cooperation) or it elaborates a 'joint text', agreed upon both by the Council and the Parliament (co-decision).
- The regulation, directive and so on is enacted by publication in the *Official Journal*.

The practice

The decision-making processes of the EU are complex. They have determined the dynamics of the integration process as to speed and form. The EU instutional set-up is very conducive to international cooperation. In general national governments have an incentive to cooperate where policy coordination increases their control over domestic policy outcomes, in the sense that they create new options for policy. International organisations increase the efficiency of the multinational bargaining that leads to policy cooperation. The EU institutional set-up in general and the qualified majority voting in the Council in particular do represent very efficient forms for reducing the transaction costs of reaching cooperative agreements. Moreover, by using a two-level strategy, that is by simultaneously playing both the EU and the national political game, the governments of member states can use the legitimacy of the EU to overrule domestic lobbies, or to mobilise domestic coalitions in favour of agreements reached at the European level (Moravcsik, 1993).

The speed of decision making has in the past been slowed down for several reasons:

- Subjects. In a simple economy negative integration would suffice. However the EU deepened its policy integration at the moment when each of the members had set up a welfare state with government intervention in many areas. Positive integration was made a lot harder by the differences in models adopted by the various member states.
- Size. The increase in the number of actors that followed from

the widening of the EU from six to nine and to 12 and the increased diversity of interests of its members make negotiations more complicated.

- Detail. There was a tendency to lay down in the European law not only the general principles but also most technical details. National officials have been insistent on this point (hence many delays in COREPER), because their main concern was national acceptance and the consistency of national policy.

To speed up the decision-making process of the Council (for it is there that most stagnation occurred) two changes had to be made. The first was the extension of the fields in which the Council votes with qualified majority; the second was to put the emphasis on general principles rather than on details. This has proved to be very successful. Notwithstanding the complexity of the process, a huge amount of legislation has been adopted.

A geographical differentiation is often necessary to arrive at decisions, in cases where progress can only be made by abandoning the idea of equal forms for all member states in favour of a set-up which permits different roles for different countries: this was the solution adopted for the European Monetary System, for the European Monetary Union and for the social chapter of the Treaty on European Union. This gives rise to expressions such as 'two-speed Europe'.

The sectoral segmentation of the decision-making process (Faber and Breyer, 1980) tends to lead to unequal progress for different policy areas. The expert Council (of agriculture, for example) cooperates with the expert member of the Commission, seconded by his expert Directorate General, the expert Committee of the EP and with expert committees of national civil servants, after hearing experts from lobby groups. In some areas this leads quickly to results, while in other fields blockages may occur that are very difficult to remove. With such a decision-making structure it is hardly surprising that integration has developed in widely divergent forms and to varying degrees in different areas (as we shall see in the next chapters), notwithstanding the efforts of the Commission and the European Council to maintain as much consistency and unity as possible.[6]

Lobby groups

European decision making involves not only the EU institutions described earlier, but many more (see, for example, Keohane and Hoffmann, 1991). These range from national ministries via government agencies to industry associations, professional organisations and individual firms. They generally act as lobby groups. Lobbying is best defined as the informal exchange of information in order to try to influence the decisions of public authorities (Van Schendelen, 1993). With the growth of EU powers, firms, organisations, regions and so on increasingly realised that the EU could have a considerable influence on their vital interests. They realised that they should try in turn to influence EU decision making so as to make sure that their interests would be taken into account. Indeed EU lobbying has increased considerably, for different reasons:

- Growing regulatory authority: the areas in which the EU has acquired authority have gradually increased (including the internal market, economic and monetary union). Moreover the areas in which the Council decides with qualified majority have been stepped up considerably, which implies that national interest groups could no longer count on 'their' national representations to block decisions that would harm their interests. To safeguard these interests it became necessary to try and influence all the stages of the European decision-making process.
- Discretion over spending considerable funds: the increased attention that the EU gives to aspects of economic and social cohesion has given rise to a considerable European redistribution from rich to poor regions. Being eligible for EU structural funds can make a big financial difference for a local authority infrastructure development. The same is true for a firm that may be eligible for funding of part of its research and development under a EU programme.

These developments have led to the increase in both the number and size of lobby groups in Brussels (see Table 20.3). Recently the growth of these groups has been very spectacular as a result of the internal market programme, the EMU and the growing complexity of the EU machinery. Indeed a recent estimate (Anderson and Eliassen, 1991) suggests there are up to 3,000 lobby organisations and almost 10,000 lobbyists.

Budget

General

The cost of international institutions is almost invariably paid from member states' contributions, each country paying a fixed percentage of total expenses. Most international organisations only incur staff and household expenses, larger outlays for special programmes being taken care of by those member states wanting to participate.

With the European Union, things are different, on two essential counts. On the expenditure side, the EU has the cost of the large programmes it executes. On the receipts side, the EU has had its own resources. These are pre-federal traits. Nevertheless the budget of the EU cannot be compared to that of a national state, for the following reasons:

Allocation   With the relatively limited budget divided among a long list of programmes in different fields, only limited influence can be exerted on the economy in specific areas, by subsidies to certain branches of industry, infrastructural development, medical care, and so on. The only exception is agriculture, which devours huge sums.

Stabilisation   The budget is not an instrument of macro-economic policy. Indeed, Article 199 of the EEC Treaty reads explicitly: 'The revenues and expenditure shown in the budget shall be in balance.' That means that the EU's macro-economic policy stretches only to the coordination of the corresponding policies conducted by the member states. Moreover the total weight of the EU budget (a little over 1 per cent of EU Gross Domestic Product, against some 40 per cent of GDP in some member states, total EU budget being about 2 per cent of national budgets) is too low for an effective macro policy.

Redistribution   Although the expenses on regional and social policies have increased considerably over the past years, both in absolute and in relative terms, the redistributive power of the EU budget is very limited if compared to national budgets (which include income tax and social security payments).

Receipts

The EU has its own funds, but, unlike most federal and confederal structures, the EU cannot itself levy taxes, as it has no fiscal sovereignty. Its revenues consist essentially of EU claims on fiscal and para-fiscal levies and other receipts of the member states.
  The EU's own resources consist mainly of the following (the figures mentioned are shares in total receipts, based on 1993 budget figures):

- *Customs duties* (22 per cent) are levied from products imported from outside the EU. The member state levying these duties will often be the one most favourably situated for importation into Europe, which is not necessarily the one for which the goods are destined (think, for instance, of German imports through the Dutch port of Rotterdam). In such a case, to allocate the duties to one member state seems unjust, so, from

1971, they have flowed into the EU treasury. They have decreased over time as external tariffs of the EU have been lowered continuously (see Chapters 6 and19).

- *Agricultural levies and contributions* (2 per cent). Special types of import levies are the variable agricultural duties levied at the outer frontiers of the EU to adjust the price level of imported produce to EU prices. Duties and contributions are levied from internal EU produce as well, to control production and thus limit the need for financing from the Agricultural Fund. Once more, logically these levies accumulate to the EU. The levies have also tended to decrease as the EU has become increasingly a net exporter of agricultural produce (see Chapter 11).
- *Value-added tax* (55 per cent). A uniform basis has been established for value-added tax in all member states. A fixed percentage (at present 1.4) has to be transferred to the EU. Value-added tax was introduced in 1960 to replace fixed national contributions. Because the importance of the other two items decreases, the share of VAT perforce increases (Chapter 16).
- *GDP-related income* (21 per cent). Since 1988 each member state pays a certain percentage of its GDP to the EU budget; this percentage is fixed every year. Through this mechanism the contributions to the EU budget tend to take better relative wealth levels of each member into account, thereby limiting the need for redistributive measures on the expenditure side.

Expenditures

In the past, the total EU budget has shown a substantial real increase. It was needed primarily to cope with the expansion of the existing policy area (agriculture) and the introduction of new ones (cohesion, for instance). In the 1993 budget, the expenses totalled about 70,000 million ECU. This may increase to some 80,000 million ECU by the year 2000. The major categories are (the figures mentioned show percentage of total outlay and are based on 1993 budget figures):

- *Agriculture and fishery* (53 per cent). This category used to absorb a very large portion (two-thirds) of the total budget, mainly through the European Agricultural Fund's outlays for guaranteed prices. Because of the way decisions are made, these outlays are very difficult to control effectively (Chapter 11).
- *Structural adaptation* (32 per cent). Expenditures to reinforce social and economic cohesion have assumed increasing weight over the years. Much of the outlay is financed from the so-called 'structural funds' (European Regional Development Fund, Social Fund and the new Cohesion Fund) (Chapter 18).

- *Internal* (5 per cent). The programmes of major policy fields like energy, manufacturing industry, transport and research fall into this category. No large funds have been created; the amounts are spent directly on programmes (Chapters 12 to 15).
- *External* (5 per cent). Under this heading falls expenditure for development aid. In addition the European Development Fund (EDF) grants credits to developing countries (Chapter 19).
- *Running costs* (5 per cent) consist of cost of staff, offices, travel, and so on.

The procedure

The budget is established by an involved procedure,[7] the main steps of which, in Community matters, are as follows:

1   *First reading*

- The Commission establishes a preliminary draft budget, taking into account the guidelines of the Council and the Parliament, and submits it to the Council of Ministers.
- The Council goes into consultation about the preliminary draft, amends it if necessary and turns it into a draft budget (acting by qualified majority). The draft is then sent to the European Parliament.
- The Parliament discusses the draft budget. It can only propose modification to the Council as far as the so-called 'compulsory expenditure' is concerned: that is to say, expenses springing from the legal commitments of the EU towards third parties (farmers enjoying guaranteed prices, developing countries with which cooperation agreements are in force, and so on). The European Parliament can amend the budget as regards so-called 'non-compulsory expenditure': that is to say, outlays associated with, for instance, regional development. (At the onset of the budget procedure, the Commission computes the maximum percentage by which such categories of outlay may increase from one year to another.)

2   *Second reading*

- The Council of Ministers receives the draft budget with proposals and amendments for a second reading. It must reach a qualified majority to adopt or reject the amendments and modifications proposed by the Parliament. The Council is fully competent to reject EP modifications with respect to compulsory outlays. Decisions on that score are final. If it rejects the amendments with respect to non-compulsory expenditure, the draft budget is again forwarded to Parliament, together with a report on the deliberations.

- Parliament deals with the second reading of the budget. It may reinstate the amendments rejected by the Council, acting by majority of the members and three-fifths of the votes cast. At the end of the second reading the Parliament may reject the budget (which happened for the first time with the 1980 budget and again with the 1985 budget).
- To avoid such conflicts, smooth the procedures and take the increasing influence of Parliament into consideration, a conciliation procedure between Parliament, Council and Commission has developed.

3 Adoption

- After a final round of negotiations between Council and Parliament, in which the Council decides on compulsory and Parliament on non-compulsory expenditure, the president of the European Parliament signs the budget, thus formalising its adoption.

Major issues

The budget procedure is subject to continuous criticism. There are four major points on which improvements are sought.

Responsibility   There is a bicephalous budget authority, vested in the Council of Ministers and in the European Parliament. The Commission is involved only in the proposition of a draft budget. Conflicts that result from this situation are now largely resolved in the so-called 'consultation procedure'. The Parliament tries to have the final responsibility in budget matters.

Discipline   Many decisions bearing on expenses are made in a fragmented way, by specialised Councils of Ministers (for instance, of agriculture). Moreover some decisions of the Commission entail expenses. Many expense categories (such as the Agricultural Guarantee Fund) depend on market and monetary developments. The Council of Ministers draws up the framework for the budget but cannot make sure that other decision making is consistent with it. That task has now been entrusted to the Commission; the Treaty forbids the Commission to make proposals or take implementation measures that entail expenses that cannot be financed within the limits set by the Council (Article 201a).

Equity The contribution to and the receipts from the budget are not in equilibrium for each member state. Some are net contributors, others net beneficiaries. This is felt to be acceptable in so far as rich member states fall into the first and poor member states into the second category.

Controls The execution of many European policies demands the participation of member states, which makes the control function of the budget difficult to accomplish. The European Court of Auditors, charged with the control of expenditure and revenues and endowed with powers of investigation with regard to EU institutions as well as national administrative bodies, reports every year on the most important deficiencies, amongst them fraud. To remove their causes has proved extremely difficult, but should be improved in future by specific measures (Article 209 a).

Summary and conclusions

- The EU has created an original legal system; its law is instantly and equally applicable in all member states.
- A strong institutional set-up safeguards the continuous development of the integration process.
- The usual division of powers in a state is partly to be found in the EU in the sense that, for Community matters, legislation is with Parliament, execution with the Commission and judication with the Court. The Council does not fit very well in this scheme as it has both important legislative and executive powers.
- Decision-making procedures in the EU are rather involved and differ according to subject area. In the past this has led to some sluggishness, but recently means have been found to provide an efficient and rapid decision-making procedure.
- The budget of the EU is relatively small. It increasingly serves redistribution purposes. The EU has its own financial means.

Notes

1 These competences have developed gradually; we will not refer to that evolution here, but come back to some relevant aspects of it in various chapters dealing with specific subjects.

2 Although institutions were merged, treaties were not. Indeed the merged bodies have continued to act according to the legal rules and procedures valid for the individual communities, as the matter in hand required. That situation has long been considered unsatisfactory, and plans have been made to merge the treaties into one, with a single set of legal rules. The new Treaty on European

Union, the Maastricht Treaty, goes a long way in integrating the various legal set-ups. It encompasses not only the realms of the existing three Communities, but also a much intensified integration of foreign and security policy. References to the various articles of these treaties in this and subsequent chapters are to the EEC Treaty (for example, Article 85.1) unless otherwise specified (for example, Article 4 TEU).

3   The predecessor of this institution was the Advisory Committee on Regional and Local Authorities set up by the Commission to take into account the views of regions, for example on the execution of the regional policy. The stronger institutional set-up of the regional representation is a consequence of the growing importance of sub-national government through decentralisation in many member states.

4   For an economic analysis of voting rules, see Mueller (1989), especially page 105.

5   These are the terms used by the EEC and Euratom; we will disregard the slightly different terms used by the ECSC for practically the same notions.

6   How serious the damage to consistency could be is illustrated by the outcomes of past negotiations concerning agriculture. In the 1970s and early 1980s, decisions have repeatedly gone against the principles of the EC, violating the unity of the market, exploding the financial frameworks and jeopardising the integration reached in other areas (monetary, for example). Even a kind of legal restraint imposed by the ministers of finance on the agricultural ministers met with no success.

7   For a thorough treatment, see Strasser (1982) and, for a succinct one, CEC (1986d); Isaacs (1986) is also interesting in this respect.

PART II
CUSTOMS UNION

5   Customs Union Theory

Introduction

The theory of integration of product markets is relatively recent (Machlup, 1977). It is based on international trade theory. Classical economists occupied themselves quite frequently with the problems of free trade (Ricardo) and also with preferential trade agreements, and the creation of the German *Zollverein* in the 19th century gave rise to a theoretical debate on the advantages and disadvantages of protection (List, 'infant industries'); still the subject of economic integration remained embedded in a more general economic analysis. International economic integration actually only became a separate object of economic thinking after the Second World War (Viner, 1950). Since then, the literature on the subject has accumulated, not least because the post-war integration processes greatly stimulated profound theoretical studies (Tovias, 1991).

The customs union represents a special case of (internal) free trade and (external) protection. So, to provide the fundamentals of the analysis of the effects of a customs union, this chapter sets out to explain (with neoclassical partial and general equilibrium models) the major principles of trade theory.

Next, we will go into the short-term effects that can be expected from the formation of a customs union. In spite of the relevance, in terms of economic theory, of the distinction between free trade area (FTA) and customs union (CU) (Robson, 1988) we will focus on the latter, the former not having, after all, counted for much in Europe. To explain in essence the static welfare effects of customs union formation,[1] we will compare the customs union with a situation of free trade and with a situation of protection. We will also consider some refinements which in the abundant literature have been added to the basic theme.

Finally, we will deal with the long-term effects of a customs union. This development of the theory started in the mid-1960s and gave attention to aspects such as intra-industry trade, economies of scale, imperfect competition, changes in production, organisation and marketing techniques, and finally non-tariff barriers. The welfare effects of integration of goods markets appear to be in the long run appreciably higher than those of the short run.

A short section in which the major features of these developments will be recalled, will complete the chapter.

Free trade versus protection

International trade leads to more welfare

The theory of international trade has developed largely from the relatively simple case of two countries (A and B) each producing two products (x and y), with two production factors, labour (l) and capital (c). Initially, the countries are two closed economies. The availability of production factors is different in the two countries, which implies different production costs (comparative cost theory). The upper part of Figure 5.1 represents the situation for both country A (left-hand side) and country B (right-hand side). The concave curves, from the origin's point of view, are the so-called 'production-possibility' or 'transformation' curves, reproducing for either country the combined quantities of goods x and y that can be produced with the available quantities of production factors. The curves are different for the two countries owing to differences in availability of production factors and technology. The convex curves are the indifference curves of the collective consumers in either country; they represent the combinations of goods x and y that yield equal utility. We assume that the indifference curves of the two countries are dissimilar (on account of different climates, for instance). In either country, production and consumption will take place where the indifference and transformation curves touch. The price ratios of the goods, given by the tangents α and β, are evidently different for the two countries.

Now suppose the two countries enter into trade relations, each country specialising in the production of that commodity for which it needs the smallest relative input of production factors. Specialisation will continue until the price ratios in both countries have become identical (tangent γ). In country A, production will shift from point I to point H owing to more of y and less of x being produced, and in country B from I' to H' because production shifts from y to x. That such trade increases welfare follows from the indifference curves. Thanks to trade and the changed price ratios, the two curves no longer need to have a point of tangency (touching point) in both

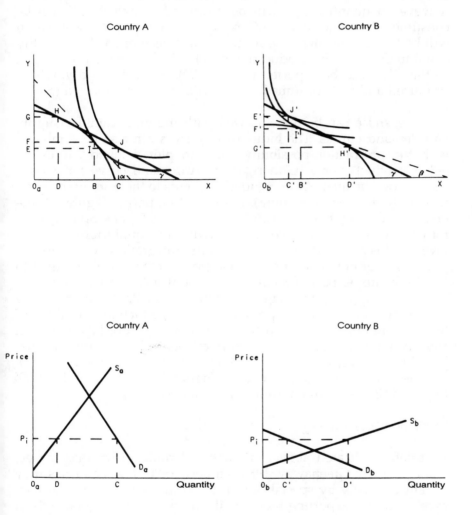

Figure 5.1   Advantages of international trade

countries, and either country can reach a higher indifference curve touching the common price-ratio tangent γ.

We can now indicate each country's production and trade as follows. In country A, a quantity equal to O_aD of good x will be produced domestically, and a quantity equal to DC imported. Of good y, however, a quantity O_aG will be produced, of which OE will be consumed domestically and EG exported. In country B, the situation will be the reverse: once the frontiers have been opened, a quantity equal to O_bD' will be produced and only O_bC' consumed of good x, so that $C'D'$ can be exported ($C'D' = CD$), while of good y, OG' is produced and OE' consumed, so that $G'E'$ must be imported ($E'G' = EG$).

The exercise can be done as well with the more familiar supply and demand curves. The indifference curves can also be combined with the production-possibility curve to plot demand curves for either product x or y (Lindert, 1986). A demand curve for good x shows how the quantity demanded responds to the price of the good (generally downward-sloping). In the bottom part of Figure 5.1, the demand curves (D_a and D_b) and supply curves (S_a and S_b) of good x for countries A and B have been drawn. The equilibrium situation given in this part of the figure occurs after integration, with a price p_i prevailing for both countries. At that price, demand is O_aC (equal to O_aC in the upper part of Figure 5.1) in country A, and O_bC' (equal to O_bC' in the upper part of Figure 5.1) in country B. In country A, the supply of good x by home producers is O_aD, which implies that DC has to be imported (equal to DC in the upper part of Figure 5.1). In country B producers are much more efficient (the S_b curve runs below the S_a curve) and at price p_i they are prepared to supply O_bD' (equals O_bD' of the upper part of Figure 5.1). The quantity $C'D'$ (equal to CD) is exported from country B to country A.

The trade effects of a tariff

As briefly indicated above, international trade theory has it (see, among others, Greenaway, 1983; Lindert, 1986) that countries may benefit mutually by specialising in the commodities at which they excel, and also exporting them, while importing those goods which they could produce only at relatively high costs, leaving their production to other nations. That implies that, theoretically, on certain assumptions, prosperity would be greatest if trade were free the world over. In practice, however, world economy is not based on general free trade. On the contrary, most countries have raised barriers in the shape of tariffs, quotas and so on. The establishment of tariffs affects production patterns and trade flows; a simple diagram (Figure 5.2), derived from partial-equilibrium analysis, may illustrate

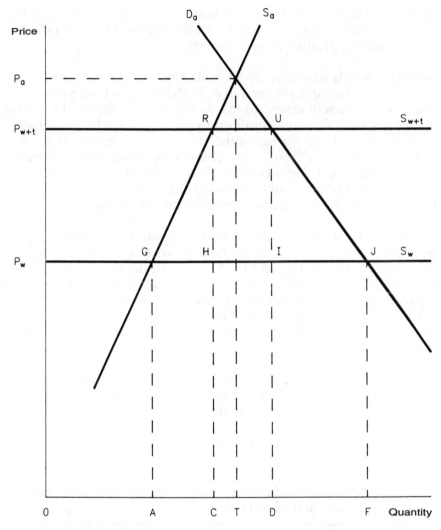

Figure 5.2   Trade effects of a tariff

them. The diagram contains first of all the traditional supply and demand curves of a given product in country A. The demand curve D_a of the home country (A) is combined with the country's supply curve S_a.

We now assume, besides country A, a country W representing the free world market. We further assume a fully elastic supply on the world market, at a price of p_w. The assumption of a fully elastic supply implies that this price is unaffected by changes in the supply or demand of country A. In Figure 5.2, S_w is the curve of world supply. For country A, we can envisage a situation of autarky, of free trade, or of protection. Let us consider the effects of each situation on price, demand, production and imports.

Autarky   In this situation suppliers in A have a 100 per cent market share; they cover total demand in A. In that case, in which country A remains completely closed to the world market, the world market price p_w is far below the equilibrium price p_a. To achieve isolation, country A needs to operate either a system of import bans or a prohibitive tariff of at least p_a-p_w. This demonstrates that the producers of country A are less efficient than producers in the rest of the world beyond point G; in other words, country A has no comparative advantage for the production of the good in question.

Free trade   If, on the contrary, country A pursues a policy of openness, the price in A is equal to the low world market price p_w; the domestic supply is limited to OA, but both demand (OF) and imports ($AF = GJ$) from the world are considerably higher than in the autarky case. In other words, the market has expanded (to OF); the market share of supplies of home producers has decreased (to $OA:OF$) and the market share of imports has increased (from zero to $AF:OF$).

Protection   Should country A establish a customs tariff t, then national production in A (and hence the market share of A suppliers), national consumption and imports (and hence the market share of 'world' suppliers) will stabilise somewhere between the two extremes of autarky and free trade. The effects are summarised in Table 5.1.

Table 5.1   Effects of various forms of protection on trade and production of country A

	Autarky	Free trade	Protection
Domestic price	p_a	p_w	p_{w+t}
Domestic demand	OT	OF	OD
Domestic production	OT	OA	OC
Imports	—	AF	CD

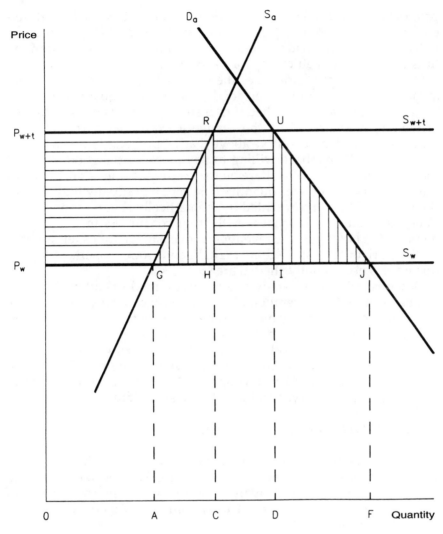

Figure 5.3   Welfare effects of a tariff, country A

Welfare effects of the introduction of a tariff

In economic terms, free trade is preferable, the introduction of tariffs having two adverse effects. Figure 5.3, and the examples given in the previous section on free trade and protection, illustrate this. On the producer side, the introduction of a tariff by country A, which had practised free trade before, causes a loss. In the protected economy, goods are produced at a cost (p_{w+t}) higher than would have been necessary with free trade (p_w). The waste involved in the use of production factors (*GH*) which could be put to better use (cost difference *HR*) elsewhere is represented by the vertically shaded triangle *GRH*. Contrary to a widely held belief, an increase in production can thus entail a loss in efficiency for the economy as a whole.

On the consumer side, too, there are additional costs: the consumer pays more for the same goods, and the total quantity of goods at his disposal has diminished (*OD* instead of *OF*). The resulting loss of welfare is measured by the change in consumer surplus, or the area below the demand curve above market prices. (Some consumers would indeed have been willing to pay more for the good.) The net (or deadweight) loss of welfare on the consumer side is calculated as the total effect of a lower quantity (*IJ*) times a gradually higher price (half of *IU*). This is represented by the vertically shaded triangle *IUJ*. There is a redistribution of wealth from consumers to the government, as the latter gets the revenues from customs duties represented by the horizontally shaded area *HRUI*, and from consumers to producers: the horizontally shaded area $p_w p_{w+t} RG$.

Obviously the above analysis for one commodity and one country can be extended to several goods and several countries. Because the introduction of a tariff by one country is mostly followed by countermeasures by others, the negative welfare effects will be felt in many countries. That the introduction of a tariff works out negative for overall welfare can also be illustrated with the help of Figure 5.1; indeed, as trade diminishes, countries A and B are forced back to lower indifference curves and thus to lower welfare.

Welfare effects of quantitative restrictions

A quantitative restriction (QR) has in many respects the same welfare effects as a tariff. Under a system of QR, importers are given licences to import a given quantity of goods. On the assumption of full competition, the effects of quantitative restriction can be explained from Figure 5.4.

With free trade, demand would have been *OF* at a price p_w and an imported quantity of *AF*. Restriction of the latter to *CD* = *RU* will entail a diminished demand, and a market equilibrium in country A at a price of *p* and a domestic production of *OC*. As after the introduction of a tariff, that domestic production increases from *OA* to *OC* and consumption drops from *OF* to *OD*. From the diagram, this QR is in that respect equivalent to a tariff of *t*, which is why a QR (*CD*) is expressed as tariff equivalent (*t*). There is, however, an important element which makes a tariff in general preferable to a quota, if protection is needed at all: in the case of a QR (to, say, *RU*) the government does not have the benefits which would accrue from a tariff (*HRUI*). At best, the amount involved flows to domestic com-

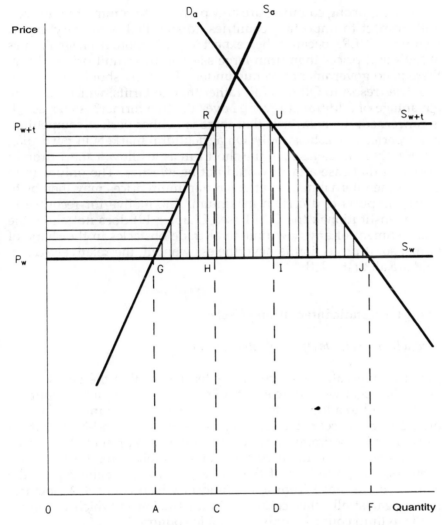

Figure 5.4   Welfare effects of quantitative restrictions, country A

panies (importers), but it may also accrue as profit to the foreign manufacturers. The only way open to the government to prevent the diversion of welfare from domestic consumers to foreign producers would be to sell the licences by auction. If not, the total welfare loss to country A from the QR are the two triangles *GRH* and *IUJ* and the rectangle *HRUI*, together vertically shaded. There is again a redistribution effect of $p_w p_{w+t} RG$ from domestic consumers to domestic producers.

Some exporting countries are now prepared to commit themselves, with respect to importing countries, to so-called 'voluntary export restraints' (VER), because they expect to profit more from small sales at high unit prices than from large sales at lower unit prices. Again there is no government revenue under VER. Why should importing countries resort to QR or VER, rather than to tariffs, which have the advantage of additional revenue over the two former? As far as QR is concerned, the answer is that there is neither perfect competition nor a perfectly elastic supply. On agricultural markets in particular, the supply is so inelastic in the short run as to allow a sheer drop in prices; in that case a tariff would not be effective. The only way to protect the internal market at given minimum prices may then be to restrict imports to a certain maximum. The motive for recourse to VER is institutional: the GATT (see Chapter 19) does not allow the establishment of any new unilateral trade obstacles in the shape of tariffs; so, if protection is nevertheless wanted, the relatively costly VER are all that is left.

Short-term static integration effects

Production and trade effects of altered tariffs

Classical international trade theory teaches us that the best way to avoid the negative welfare effects of protection is for all the countries of the world to adopt perfect free trade. However countries, finding progress on that score too slow, try to adopt as a second-best strategy a geographically limited form of free trade, as represented by a customs union. Recall that a customs union implies free trade among partners, but protection of the entire union against the rest of the world. So we move from a situation in which country A operates tariffs against all other countries to a situation in which it applies tariffs to third countries only and not to country B.

The theory of customs unions relates to the gains and losses incurred by the establishment of such unions. These include, first, the static short-term gains from specialisation referred to in the preceding section. The preceding sections may have given the impression that the introduction of a CU maintaining a tariff wall lower than the average of the ones existing before would be unambiguously advantageous to the members and the world as a whole. However we will demonstrate that this is too simplistic a view and that both positive and negative effects occur. In economic terms the creation of the CU is warranted only if the former outweigh the latter. In political terms it is feasible only if the advantages and disadvantages are fairly distributed among partners.

The effects of a customs union between countries A and B are best studied by making a distinction between trade creation, trade diversion (Viner, 1950) and trade expansion (Meade, 1955). We can explain these effects as follows:

- *Trade creation* will occur when trade between partners A and B increases. In country A, demand will shift from the expensive protected domestic product to the cheaper product from the partner country, implying a shift from a less efficient to a more efficient producer.
- *Trade diversion* will occur when imports from the efficient or cheap producer 'world market' are replaced by imports from a higher cost (or less efficient) producer, namely, the 'partner country'. That country's products can be sold more cheaply in country A than world market production, because the CU imposes a protective tariff on imports from W, while leaving imports from the partner country free.
- *Trade expansion* will occur because the lower market price in A stimulates total domestic demand, which will be satisfied by foreign trade (either from the partner or the world market).

For a better understanding of the nature and volume of these three effects, let us take a close look at Figure 5.5, which gives the situation for country A on the left-hand side and for country B on the right. We assume that the supply from producers in the rest of the world is fully elastic at a price level p_w. The corresponding supply is represented in the diagrams by the horizontal line S_w. Assume that, as a high-cost producer, country A enables its industry to capture part of the home market by introducing a fairly high tariff. Country B, on the contrary, produces at rather low costs, and needs only a low tariff to make sure that its producers can cover the entire internal demand. Assume now that countries A and B form a customs union which establishes a common outer tariff t^*, the average of the tariffs of countries A and B. Once the customs union is established, supply and demand in the area will settle at a price p_{cu}. Now, country A will buy all its imports (BE) from the partner country, p_{cu} being lower than p_{w+t^*}. Production in country A will be O_aB. Country B, for its part, produces the quantity O_bE', of which $B'E'$ (equal to BE) in excess of its home demand (O_bB'); B exports this quantity to the partner country.

What, then, are the trade effects of the creation of this customs union? The effects differ according to the initial situation (see Table 5.2). Let us take the two cases of protection and free trade of the previous section as examples.

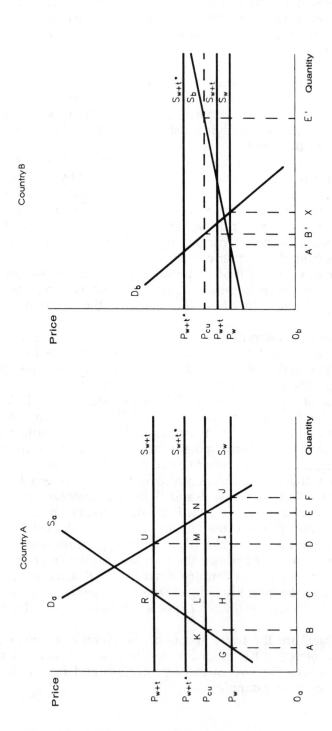

Figure 5.5 Trade and production effects of a customs union, countries A and B

Country A. If protection marks the initial situation of country A, a positive development occurs. A new trade flow (*BE*) occurs between partners, of which *CD* is trade diversion; it replaces the imports that used to come from other countries in the world. Trade creation is *BC* and trade expansion *DE*. On balance, trade has increased in our example (*BC* + *DE* being larger than *CD*), and international specialisation has intensified accordingly. Starting from free trade for country A, a negative development occurs. Trade actually diminishes by *AB* on the producer side and by *EF* on the consumer side. Moreover *BE* is diverted from the lower-cost world producer to the high-cost partner country.

Country B. Starting from free trade, the introduction of a common tariff stops the trade that existed between B and W, which implies negative trade creation (–*A'B'*) and expansion (–*B'X*) as less efficient home producers take over from more efficient world producers. Starting from a situation of protection in B, a customs union does not give rise to trade effects (but for the exports *B'E'*), as there were no imports from the world anyway.

Table 5.2   Trade effects of a customs union, countries A and B

Effect	Starting situation			
	Free trade		Protection	
	A	B	A	B
Creation	–AB	–A'B'	BC	*
Expansion	–EF	–B'X	DE	B'E'
Diversion	BE	*	CD	*

*   not applicable.

Welfare effects of altered tariffs

What are the advantages and disadvantages ensuing from the customs union and the tariff? On the one hand, trade diversion tends to make production less rational, which is a disadvantage. On the other hand, trade creation and trade expansion make production more efficient, which is advantageous. To get an idea of the magnitude of the effects, consider Figure 5.6, starting from protectionism. We assume that the price for the customs union is p_{cu}.

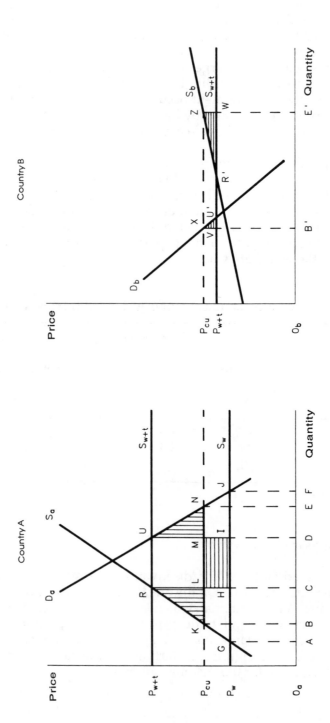

Figure 5.6 Welfare effects of a (trade-diverting) customs union

92

Country A. The advantages on the production side (trade creation *BC*) are represented by the triangle *KRL*. This indicates that the saving on production cost equals, on average, half the difference in costs between home production and that in country B ($p_{w+t} - p_{cu}$), leaving economic resources available for other purposes. On the consumption side (trade expansion equal to *DE*) the advantages are represented by the triangle *MUN*. The disadvantages for country A are represented by the square *HLMI*. For the amount of trade equal to *CD* which has been diverted, production inputs have been higher than necessary. In our example the establishment of a customs union produces a net advantage for country A.

Country B. The disadvantages are on the consumer as well as the producer side. The consumer gets less quantity for more money; his loss is indicated by the horizontally shaded little triangle *VXU'*. On the producer side, there is a production loss indicated by the horizontally shaded triangle *R'ZW*. The producers in B will of course enjoy a net gain.

Alternative cases can be imagined in which the profits or the losses are heavier. If, for instance, the only effect is trade expansion, there will be larger net advantages, as can be shown by a slight variation of the former example. Assume the supply curve of country B is equal to that of the world. The effects of a customs union between countries A and B will be positive, in fact the reverse of the negative ones found for country A passing from free trade to protectionism (Figure 5.5). By varying the differences between p_{cu} and p_w and the gradient of the supply and demand curves, the reader can work out other examples, to arrive finally at the point where the trade diversion exceeds trade expansion, so that the establishment of a customs union produces a net disadvantage to the world as a whole.

The present examples refer to only one product. To judge the economic desirability of a customs union by its static effects, the profits and losses for all products involved need to be calculated, under consideration of the specific circumstances obtaining for each.

Trade and welfare effects of the removal of non-tariff barriers

Apart from tariffs there are many other means to protect the domestic market against competition from abroad. These are generally called non-tariff barriers (NTBs). Among them we find such diverse things as quantitative restrictions and cost-increasing testing procedures (see Chapter 6).

While a customs union does away with all quantitative restrictions among member states, they can be maintained with respect to third countries. The effects of a customs union with tariffs and quantitative restrictions are different from those of a customs union with only tariffs. Starting from the same example as before, we will describe the developments for country A. Suppose in Figure 5.7 there is a question of a tariff equal to $p_{w+t} - p_w$, and of a NTB n, equivalent to a quantitative restriction of $CD = RU$. For defining the effects of a CU that takes away internal tariffs, two cases can be distinguished, depending on the exporting country to which initially all licences had been granted.

- Country B had all licences. The effect of a CU between A and B is then that the tariff for partner producers is taken away; as a consequence country B crowds out country A, implying a trade

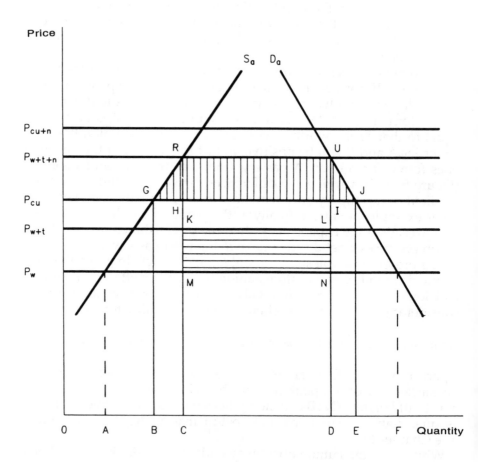

Figure 5.7   The effects of tariff and non-tariff barriers on imports

creation of *BC* and a trade expansion of *DE*. *CD*, too, continues to be supplied by B (no trade diversion), but at lower prices.

- Country W had all licences. Because after the establishment of a customs union there remains a price difference between country A and the world market, failing further agreements of a common policy of the customs union with respect to country W a quantity *CD* will continue to be imported into country A from the world market. The effect will again be a trade expansion and trade creation equal to *BC* + *DE* (no trade diversion *CD*).

Evidently the welfare effects of abolishing quantitative restrictions differ from those caused by tariff elimination. The advantages *KRL* and *MUN* (from Figure 5.6) obtain in both cases. The disadvantage *HLMI* does not accrue in the latter case, while in the former it represents a transfer of income; loss of quota rents earned by local importers and gain to local consumers.

The elimination of different cost-increasing non-tariff barriers, such as testing and certification requirements and cumbersome customs procedures,[2] has only recently won attention (under the impulse of the EC 1992 programme). The removal of such barriers among the members of a customs union leads to trade diversion from third to partner countries, but that is welfare-increasing (Pelkmans and Winters, 1988). Much depends on the sequence of measures; if member countries of a customs union proceed first to the internal abolition of tariffs without doing away with the internal non-tariff barriers, and next proceed to the taking away of these barriers (as was the case for the EC), then trade diversion from third to partner countries may be welfare-reducing because the revenue that was previously generated by the tariff is lost (Sapir, 1989). The argument can be illustrated with the help of Figure 5.7. For a member country of a customs union, this figure shows domestic demand and supply (D_a and S_a). Imports are available under free trade at p_w from the rest of the world and at p_{cu} from the rest of the customs union. All foreign supplies are subject to a cost-increasing NTB n. In addition, a tariff t is imposed on all imports from the rest of the world. Initially the domestic price is P_{w+t+n}. Domestic consumption and production are *OD* and *OC*, respectively and imports *RU* entirely from the rest of the world.

When also the NTB is removed between customs union members, the domestic price falls to p_{cu}, domestic consumption and production becomes *OB* and *OE* and imports *BE* come now entirely from partner countries. These imports replace some domestic supplies *BC* (trade creation) and all previous cheaper imports from the rest of the world *RU* (diversion). The welfare effects are similar to those described in Figure 5.4, in that the vertically shaded area *GRUJ* is a net gain of consumer and producer surpluses. However in this case government revenue falls by the area *MKLN*. The net effect (that is, the difference between *GRUJ* and *MKLN*) depends on the slopes of the curves, the level of *t* and *n* and may consequently be positive or negative.

The incidence of positive and negative effects

Various factors influence the occurrence of positive and negative effects of a CU.

- *The production structure.* Two countries can be complementary or competitive. Viner (1950) pointed out that, with complementary production structures, most probably the two countries have already specialised to a high degree in specific types of commodity along sectoral lines; in that case the advantages of a customs union cannot be very important (for example, one country specialising in metal and chemicals, the other in food and textiles). If, on the contrary, the production of either country is a potential competitor of the other, specialisation along the lines of inter-industry trade, that is specialisation within the same sector in the products which either country can make best and cheapest, is probable and the advantages are likely to be relatively important (as with, for example, jeans and T shirts; or with even greater specialisation between cars of different makes).
- *The size of the union.* The more numerous and the larger the countries participating in the CU, that is, the larger its share in total world trade, the better the prospects for division of labour and the smaller the risk of trade diversion (Viner, 1950; Meade, 1955; Tinbergen, 1959).
- *The level of the tariffs.* As the initial tariffs of the trade partners are higher, the attendant inefficiencies will be worse and the welfare effects of the abolition of tariffs greater (Viner, 1950; Meade, 1955). On the other hand, the introduction of high common external tariffs against third countries will reduce the positive effect.
- *Transport and transaction costs.* The increased trade has to be realised physically, for which efficient transport is required. Failing that, the transport costs will replace the tariffs as an obstacle to further specialisation. For that reason, customs unions tend to be concluded between contiguous countries (Balassa, 1961). The remark about transport costs applies also to time-consuming clerical procedures at the frontier, and probably as well to the linguistic differences in Europe which tend

to make transaction costs between linguistic areas higher than within such areas.

- *Flexibility*. The advantages are greater as both countries can respond more flexibly to new prospects. The reverse also applies: the advantages are smaller if production bottlenecks prevent the full accomplishment of advanced specialisation and the corresponding reallocation of production. We will come back to this point when discussing the long-term restructuring effects, also called dynamic effects.

Terms of trade

So far we have mostly assumed a fully elastic supply function in countries B and W. That may be realistic if a small country A forms a customs union with a large country B, leaving a still larger world market W, but makes no sense for a customs union of several large countries, confronting a relatively small world market. In this latter case a group of countries can grasp benefits for itself by liberalising intra-group trade and discriminating against extra-group trade.

Indeed importing countries united in a customs union can enforce lower supply prices on the world market (for instance, by trade restrictions or bargaining power). In this way they may improve the terms of trade (defined here as export price divided by import price) for the customs union.[3] This is illustrated by Figure 5.8, where D_{cu} is the customs union's demand curve and S_{cu} its supply curve. The rest of the world supplies at price p_w any quantity demanded. The customs union now introduces a tariff t. That takes the price from p_w to p_{w+t} and domestic supply from OA to OC. As demand falls from OF to OD, foreign suppliers are confronted with a decrease in their export volume from AF to CD. To prevent such a considerable loss of exports, the third country producers will cut their prices to p_{w*}, which means they keep an export volume of BE. The customs union can import much more cheaply than before; on the assumption of constant prices for its exports, the customs union lands a net gain; its welfare from improved terms of trade is the rectangle $KHIL$, which has to be set against the two triangles GMH and INJ.

This positive net effect for members of the customs union is much larger than the net effects described up to now with fixed infinite supply elasticities from all external producers.[4] It is also larger than the effects that can be obtained by partner countries by full worldwide liberalisation of trade. So the formation of a customs union will for many countries be a rational choice, notably for smaller countries that lack market power.

On politico-economic grounds, a large customs union is in a better position to substantiate its trade policy towards the outer world and

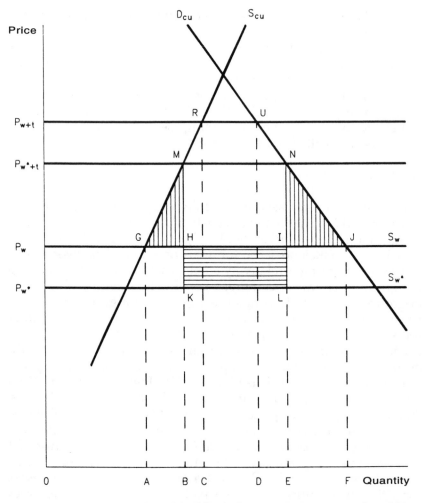

Figure 5.8   Terms-of-trade effect of a common external tariff

to improve its terms of trade than the individual countries. Customs unions can therefore be expected to shape their strategic trade policy in such a way as to set a common external tariff that is higher than the average of the member tariffs. The increase in the members' welfare would then be accompanied by a loss in non-members' welfare (Petith, 1977).

Evaluation

The short-term effects of the creation of a customs union on member countries and third countries depend on initial situation, level of tariff and so on. However, for a number of nations to conclude a customs union, a profit must accrue to each of the would-be partners or, if not, compensation must be given to the country that stands to lose. But even in a country which on balance would benefit, to tip the scales towards the decision to engage in the formation of a customs union, those who hope to profit from it must be politically stronger than those who fear they may suffer from it.

We have seen that the effects of a customs union can in principle be computed. In practice there are many difficulties, however. To draw a complete picture of the whole economy of all member states and third countries necessitates the calculation and netting out of the various effects for a virtually infinite number of cases (goods with different elasticities of supply and demand, different tariffs, and hence different ex-ante production and imports).

A more fundamental problem with partial analysis of trade policy measures is that changes in tariffs alter the structure of the economy and hence the demand for production factors; this in turn may change the amount producers are prepared to pay for employing them (Corden, 1972a). This argument can be illustrated as follows. Suppose the export sector of country A is labour-intensive and the import sector capital-intensive; the liberalisation of trade will induce larger imports of capital-intensive goods, so that the scarce capital production factor will be set free in A. The supply of capital remaining equal, this means that capital becomes cheap and labour scarce and thus expensive. In the end, imports may thus cause an equalisation of the relative cost of production (see Chapter 8 on the common market).

Finally, we must keep the lack of realism in mind: indeed the restrictive assumptions on which many of the approaches presented rely seldom hold in practice.[5] On goods markets, perfect competition is disturbed by cartels; adjustment processes are not without cost; factors are to some extent mobile across national frontiers, and not completely mobile within them; unemployment will arise through imperfections, and so on. In sum, a better, more dynamic general equilibrium approach has to be looked for.

Long-term restructuring effects

Some distinctions

Besides the factors discussed in the previous section, there are others which are recurrent in the discussion of the advantages and disadvantages of a customs union; some have called them 'dynamic effects' (Balassa, 1961). We prefer the term 'restructuring effects'. They occur because firms, workers and government do not just sit back but react to the new situation and adapt the structure of production and the economy. On the one hand, firms faced with increased competition will try to lower their costs to stay in the market. On the other, the extended market allows large-scale production at lower average cost. These two effects are very important and will be analysed in some detail. Some other effects (internal to the company, such as size, or external to the company, such as the industrial environment) are much less developed theoretically and empirically and will be referred to only in passing. Still others, such as the possible negative effects of regional concentration of production, or the (un)employment effects on certain groups of the labour force, will not be discussed here. We should keep in mind, however, that a customs union may entail an important restructuring of the economies of the member countries, a process which cannot always be carried through without incurring significant adaptation costs. On the whole, however, the long-term benefits, to be described hereafter, are considered to outweigh by far the short-term costs. For that reason, the groups incurring these costs are given compensation (see Chapter 18, on redistribution) to facilitate the restructuring.

Increased competition and efficiency

In the 1950s, most people in Europe were convinced that the limited competition prevailing in some countries caused production to be less efficiently organised than it could be, or, to put it otherwise, that the input was higher than would be required for efficient production. The expectation was that the inefficiency would be overcome in a common market. It is the same argument which has lately been used to justify the entry of Spain and Portugal into the EC.

With the help of Figures 5.9 and 5.10 we can demonstrate how improved technical efficiency due to increased competition can have a welfare effect, exceeding many times the limited static effect – two small triangles – we analysed in the previous section. The first step in the analysis of the effects on trade and welfare can be illustrated with Figure 5.9, which reproduces the market for good x in country A. Curves S_a and D_a represent, as in Figure 5.5, supply and demand in country A itself. Supply from the world, fully elastic, is once more denoted by S_w. A change has occurred in the representation of the supply from country B; it is not indicated by a curve S_b here, but combined with supply S_a and incorporated in curve S_{cu}, which is valid for the entire customs union. The diagram has been drawn in such a way that the tariff t_2 is just sufficient to avoid any imports from the world market (S_{cu} cuts through N). Now suppose that before the CU was established, country A operated a tariff of t_3. After

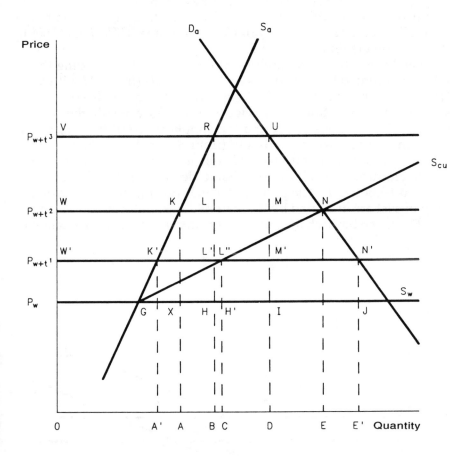

Figure 5.9   **Effects of tariffs and improved technical efficiency, account being taken of the customs union supply curve, country A**

creation of the customs union, the common external tariff will be set at t_2, and further lowering of this common outer tariff to t_1 is envisaged. Let us consider the static effects of this customs union; according to the model given in Figure 5.6, the lowering of the initial tariff from t_3 to t_2 would mean that total demand in A is now satisfied by supply from the customs union. This implies a trade-creation effect of *KRL* and a trade-expansion effect of *MUN*, against a trade-diversion effect of *HLMI*. As the area of the latter is about equal in size to the combined areas of *KRL* and *MUN*, this customs union would be about welfare-neutral. Reducing the tariff further to t_1, triggering off an import quantity $A'C$ from the partner country and CE' from the world market, would be highly welfare-creating, as the combined areas $K'RL'$ and $M'UN'$ clearly outweigh the area $XK'L'H'$ ($A'C$ being the trade diversion from W to B).

Now this is not the whole story. Manufacturers in A, finding themselves confronted by a great loss of sales markets (from OB with tariff t_3 to OA' with tariff t_1), rather than accept the loss will accomplish savings on production costs (Figure 5.10). As a result the supply curve of A will move down and the supply curve of the entire customs union will drop accordingly (from S^1_{cu} to S^2_{cu} in Figure 5.10). We have assumed[6] that it dropped sufficiently to permit the customs union producers to satisfy total home demand in the CU under a tariff protection of t_1. The production and consumption effects of this drop in cost are indicated by the shift of the equilibrium point from F to I. To see the basic change in welfare effects, consider the change in

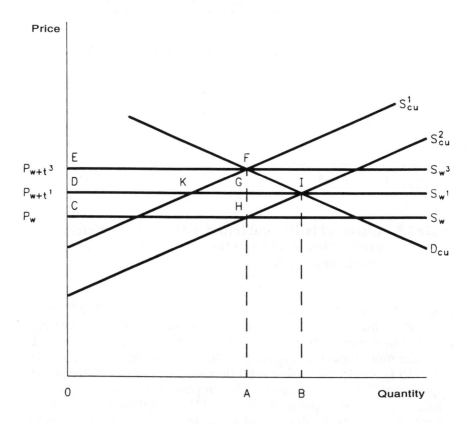

Figure 5.10   Advantages of improved (technical) efficiency

cost of production of the initial quantity from *OE* to *OD* that producers have realised under the pressure of stronger competition.[7] The
cost reduction is equal to *DEFG*. This is a net positive effect and not,
as in the earlier static examples, a redistribution effect of *DEFK* and a
new effect of *KFG*.

Economies of scale

An establishment which can produce larger quantities more cheaply
than smaller ones, and is constrained in its outlets by a market of
limited size, would profit from the extension of the market, for instance by a customs union (Corden, 1972a). Figure 5.11 can help us to
analyse the effect of 'economies of scale'. In this figure, D_a and D_b are
the (identical) demand curves for countries A and B, and D_{cu} their
common demand curve. S_w is the world supply curve; once more we
assume a perfectly elastic supply. Contrary to the demand curves,
the supply curves are not the same for countries A and B, country A
producing, on average, at higher cost than country B. In both countries the cost decreases as the production increases in volume (definition of 'economy of scale').

We can again analyse trade effects for situations of free trade,
protection and integration.

- Free trade appears to be the most advantageous option: at price
  p_w, countries A (left-hand upper part of Figure 5.11) and B
  (right-hand upper part of Figure 5.11) both import their total
  demand (*OQ* for either) from the world market.
- Protection has drawbacks for welfare. If countries A and B both
  close their markets, in other words adopt a policy of autarky,
  country A consumes *OL* at price p_a, country B consumes *OM* at
  price p_b. Evidently, to prevent the national producer from making monopolist profits in this case, the tariffs must not be higher
  than $(p_a - p_w)$ for country A or higher than $(p_b - p_w)$ for country B
  (see the discussion of 'made-to-measure tariffs' in Corden,
  1972a). The total demand in countries A and B would be O_aL +
  O_bM, appreciably less than the $O_aQ + O_bQ$ in the case of free
  trade.
- Integration, through the formation of a customs union between
  countries A and B, has different effects depending on the choice
  of the common external trade policy it wants to adopt. Suppose
  that this customs union decides to close its own market to competitors from the rest of the world. Evidently in that case, represented in the left-hand bottom part of Figure 5.11, demand in
  the union could be $O_{cu}R$ at a price of p_{cu} and a customs tariff of
  $p_{cu} - p_w$. The implication is that country A would take care of the

entire production, production in country B being discontinued. The effects of trade creation, diversion and expansion of this CU are in line with the definitions given earlier, albeit that account has to be taken of the slope of the supply curves.

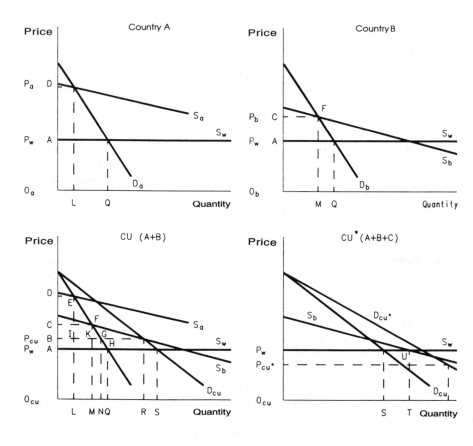

Figure 5.11   Economies of scale in production for individual countries A and B and for customs unions of A and B and of A, B and C

What are the welfare effects of the customs union of A and B that protects itself against external competition by a tariff of $p_{cu} - p_w$ in comparison with a state of autarky of both country A and country B and with a state of free trade in a situation of economies of scale? (See Table 5.3 for an overview.) Compared to the case of autarky, consumption in country A becomes ON instead of OL, an advantage equal to $BDEG$. Part of it, namely $BDEI$, is the cost-cutting effect of the 'economies of scale', equalling trade creation O_aL; the other part, the triangle IEG, is trade expansion (LN). For country B, consumption becomes ON instead of OM; the advantage is $BCFG$, of which $BCFK$ represents the cost-cutting effect, which equals trade expansion (MN). This example shows once more that, to promote trade between partner countries, an external tariff has to be set which just protects the most efficient producer. Compared to free trade, the customs union produces for both countries A and B a negative trade contraction of NQ and a trade diversion of $O_{cu}N$.

For the customs union to be an advantageous alternative to overall free trade, the prices of the world producers must be equal to or higher than those of country B. That would be so if a third high-cost country C with a domestic market at least the size of ST joined the customs union (the case depicted in the right-hand bottom part of Figure 5.11). The considerable advantage of such a large market achieved by the customs union is that it enhances the international competitiveness of the union. Indeed this enlarged customs union enables the producer in country B to diminish his costs so as to deliver the good at price p_{cu}^*. As this price is below p_w, he can start to export his product to the world market. This will permit the customs union to abolish the tariff $p_{cu} - p_w$, which leads to a further trade expansion and creation in both countries A and B.[8]

Do 'economies of scale', as described above, justify the creation of a customs union? That depends in the end on the net effects for the union as a whole, and the distribution of benefits and cost over

Table 5.3 Trade and production effects of a customs union under conditions of economies of scale (countries A and B)

| | Initial situation | | | |
| | Free trade | | Autarky | |
	A	B	A	B
Creation	*	*	O_aL	*
Expansion	$-NQ$	$-NQ$	LN	MN
Diversion	$O_{cu}N$	$O_{cu}N$	*	*

* not applicable.

partners. In our example, a customs union seems favourable on balance. However the losing partner A is likely to demand compensation in terms of money transfers from country B, or to try and achieve a better starting-point than country B for other products, so that their manufacture can be concentrated in country A.

Imperfect competition may change the distribution of the effects over the customs union partner and third countries. If the supply curve of third country producers is not fully elastic, but also subject to increased returns, the decrease in third country exports to the CU due to the increase in the internal competitiveness of customs union producers depicted in Figure 5.11 will lead to an increase in the cost level of these producers and hence a further loss of their competitiveness on third markets (Venables, 1987).

Advantages of scope and growth

Next to the advantages of market integration discussed up to now (which are internal to the establishment) there are three advantages that rather affect the whole company. These apply to the company's size, its growth rate and its learning curve. They are all rather difficult to grasp and quantify in empirical studies. Still, a brief description of them based on many micro-studies may suffice to make the point.

The average *size of companies* may increase after the establishment of a customs union because the extension of the market will induce many firms to merge with others for a stronger collective market position. Production may become more efficient because large companies tend to be more efficient than smaller ones (represented by a lower supply curve in the graphs presented; for example, B versus A in Figure 5.11). There are various reasons for these relatively low cost levels. For one thing, large companies are stronger negotiators than smaller ones, and therefore able to make better deals when purchasing raw materials and intermediary products. They also have easier access to capital and pay relatively less interest. For another thing, they tend to need relatively less manpower because they can, more easily than small companies, shift their staff from one department to another. With respect to their environment and the public authorities (subsidies), large companies have a stronger position than small ones. Large companies are more often in a position to mobilise the ressources required for innovation. Finally they are better able than small companies to build up stable market positions, also in export countries. However, these advantages are far from decisive. A small company is often able to respond more flexibly to new market needs, needs less overheads (no bureaucracy), is better equipped to motivate the staff, and so on. Moreover new needs tend to be recognised sooner by small than by large companies.

The *growth rate* of companies tends to have a positive effect on efficiency. On the one hand, growing companies tend to have the most up-to-date machinery; in addition, their workforce performs better because in growing companies the adaptation of staff is smoother and the atmosphere tends to be more innovative than in companies with a more established pattern. On the other hand, growing companies tend to be unsure about the prospects on entirely new markets, and growth is often paid for dearly. The growth effects of a customs union may be enhanced if companies innovate in the manner described here.

Finally there is the *learning curve*, indicating that companies learn to produce more efficiently by the actual production of greater quantities. Indeed practice is thought to be the best teacher of how to make things, how to organise production, and so on. Learning by doing is different from economies of scale, in that the latter give the curve a downward slope, while the former tends to lower the entire curve over the course of time. The first company to produce great quantities will learn so much that it will outrace the others in cutting costs, and thus gain a profit. To the extent that a customs union creates a market in which a company is able to proceed fast along a learning curve, production can be made cheaper in the union than in a separate member country. The effects for the whole economy are akin to the ones shown in Figure 5.9 on technical progress.

The points mentioned in this section and in the previous one have an important bearing on the choice of the level of external trade protection by the customs union. In a world of increasing returns and learning effects, so called 'first mover' advantages are essential. The temptation for a government is then to intervene and to make sure that domestic companies arrive as soon as possible at the position of producer B in Figure 5.11, so that it can outrace producer A on the union market. A competition policy at the union level should prevent any such action distorting fair competition. At the union level, however, this situation may lead to a 'common strategic trade policy' (Krugman, 1986, 1991). Action is taken at the union level to bring firms into the position of producer B in the enlarged customs union (see right-hand bottom side of Figure 5.11). Since the internal market is larger, the strategic trade policy at the level of the union is more effective than at the national level. However there will be many conflicts between member countries as to which activities to promote, and between the union and third countries as to the degree to which such support schemes are allowed (see for instance the discussion between the EC and the USA over European support of Airbus).

Other effects

It has been argued (among others by Balassa, 1961) that the industrial interwovenness of an economy can have a positive effect on total efficiency. When a customs union puts a company in a better position, the positive influence is not confined to that company, but extends to all suppliers and buyers. For instance, a successful product innovation may stimulate the suppliers of machines to innovate their production processes, and the suppliers of intermediate products for machines to design better parts. Thus, starting from some key producers, the positive effect propagates through the whole economy. That effect will, of course, be the greater, the better the various parts of the economy are equipped to respond to the impulse.

Another argument is that technical progress is consolidated by the integration of markets. Stimulated by increased competition, companies will be on the lookout for new producers and new production methods. The enlarged market will also foster the exchange of technical know-how. The ensuing enhanced dynamics will in the end stimulate economic growth.

An argument in favour of the creation of a customs union is that it gives smaller countries a sort of guarantee against world market price uncertainty (Fries, 1984). Of course the validity of this argument depends on the level of protection the union gives its members, and the level of uncertainty that prevails on the internal market.

Evaluation and dynamics

There are a large number of trade barriers that should be removed in a customs union. Moreover the degree and form of external protection has to be determined. Depending on the initial situation (protection, autarky), the structure (relative factor endowments or technology), the measures taken (tariffs and NTB) and the reaction of competitors, both the trade and welfare effects may be quite different. That not only influences the size of the effects but may even change the net effect from positive to negative. So the policy makers may wish to fine-tune the blend of measures and the timing so as to arrive at optimal effects. However in view of the uncertainties involved, this may be very difficult to do, so the other solution is likely to be across-the-board internal liberalisation. There is an obvious political dimension to the decision to create a customs union, as some sectors of the economy will suffer while others will benefit. In order to get to agreement among partners and realise the economically desirable trade creation (with losses for non-competitive groups) it may be necessary to accept some politically vital trade diversion (Sapir, 1989).

The effects of the creation of a customs union through the removal of internal barriers to trade may be synoptically represented as in Figure 5.12. As tariffs, quotas and other non-tariff barriers are eliminated, competition increases and domestic producers have to reduce their price to the level of producers in partner countries. The first implication is for them to give up economic rents in the form of excess profits. If the resulting cost P_2 is not yet competitive, they will reduce such inefficiencies as overstaffing, excess overheads and so on. As the price goes down to P_3, the demand increases to Q_3, which may induce new investment. The process of increased competition will induce mergers and exits of firms, which in turn will entail economies of scale, learning effects and technological progress that bring prices down to P_4, permitting demand to increase further to Q_4.

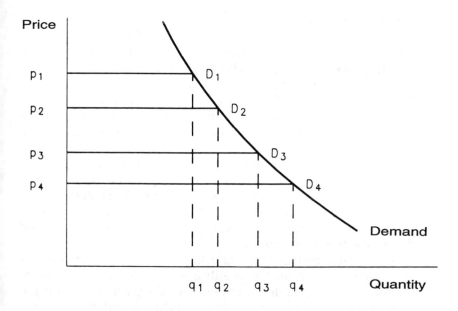

Figure 5.12   Effects of eliminating trade barriers in a customs union

Consumers gain from these price reductions (area $P_1D_1P_4D_4$) as they obtain more goods at lower prices. Producers offset the loss with cost reductions. The total welfare gain to the economy is $P_2D_2P_4D_4$ as the excess profits $P_1D_1P_2D_2$ are transferred from producers to consumers. The final gain may be even greater if producers become so efficient

(P_4) that they are able to export to third countries. That conclusion rests on the assumption that no member country has a comparative advantage in all products over other member countries, and that redundant resources are re-employed.

The dynamics of customs unions go in the direction of increased membership because (1) the increased weight of the group in international negotiations facilitates the improvement of the terms of trade; (2) the size of the market will permit more firms to attain their optimal level and hence their lowest cost. However, that effect may be greatest for firms in new member countries, and irrelevant for many firms already in the CU and producing at optimal levels (Venables, 1987). So the effects of further enlargement of a large customs union with a number of smaller candidate members may not be very great for the union (Tovias, 1978).

Summary and conclusions

- The creation of a customs union has some positive and some negative (welfare) effects. The creation of a customs union is justified if the former exceed the latter.
- The global welfare effects of a customs union formation are uncertain and so are its distributional effects, both between the union and the rest of the world and between members of the union.
- As regards the short-term effects, which may concern the consumer as well as the producer and the government, the analysis has shown that (on certain assumptions) the customs union is the more positive as the production structures are more competitive, the economy is larger, the initial tariffs are higher and the transaction costs lower.
- The long-term restructuring effects offer better reasons for creating a customs union. Competition and economies of scale are the most important effects; among the others are larger companies, growth rate, learning curve and industrial interwovenness. The latter effects are hard to define and even harder to quantify.

Notes

1 Students unfamiliar with welfare analysis are referred to Part II of Mishan (1982) for a succinct and clear introduction to concepts and methods.
2 Another important NTB is discriminatory government procurement. For the effects of the removal of such NTB, see Tovias (1990).

3   Terms of trade effects have been analysed by several authors (for a review see Tovias, 1991). Their models focused on the distribution of the advantages to member and non-member countries under different assumptions as to level of external tariff, size of countries, transfer possibility and so on.

4   The example given in the figure 5.8 above is not a realistic one. The supply curve of the world producers, for example, will in practice be upward-sloping. For a realistic analysis, the present simple illustration does not suffice, and a wide range of differently shaped supply and demand curves have to be reviewed, which makes the analysis rather complicated. Moreover substitution effects and income effects due to alterations in the differential prices of imported (tariff-burdened) and exported goods must also be taken into account. We will not go into the literature on the subject, extensive though it is, because the general conclusion must be that no satisfactory method has as yet been developed for a proper analysis of the problem (Wonnacott and Wonnacott, 1981; Tovias, 1991) and that, therefore, general statements on the effects of the customs union on trade and price formation between member countries and with third countries are out of the question.

5   Attempts have also been made to extend the 3×2 case (three countries, two commodities) to a 3×3 case (three commodities) with a high- and a low-tariff import good (Lloyd, 1982) or an *n* commodity case (for example, Berglas, 1979). The results of these exercises are very indeterminate; and all attempts at improvement failed to produce clear-cut results.

6   More involved cases can be worked out, specifying what happens to the income from tariffs of both countries A and B. However here it suffices to show specifically the welfare effect of the cost reduction.

7   The discussion in this section presupposes that competition is not reduced by collusive practices of firms. For this assumption to hold, competition policies have to complement economic integration. However in the presence of economies of large-scale production (see next section) leading to monopolistic situations in the customs union, domestic competition policy may not be sufficient to reap the benefits of integration, and a worldwide competition policy may be required (Jacquemin and Sapir, 1991).

8   In the 1970s and 1980s the argument of economies of scale was related increasingly to the theory of inter-industry trade; see Chapter 6 on goods and Chapter 12 on industry. It was also related to imperfect competition and its effects on external relations; see Chapter 19.

6 Goods

Introduction

The centrepiece of most integration schemes is the integration of goods markets. In the previous chapter we described in a theoretical way how markets evolve when barriers to movement are torn down. In this chapter we will describe the way in which the EC has realised the integration of the markets for manufactured goods of its member countries.

Before we embark on the main discussion we will give in a first section some basic concepts: advantages of integration, defining and specifying barriers and reasons for protection. Next we will turn our attention to the way the EU has regulated the free movement of goods between its member states. We will also pay some attention to its external relations in terms of goods trade, although the main discussion of this point will be presented in Chapter 19.

The main body of the chapter will be devoted to a close analysis of the changes in the geographical as well as the product structure of the internal and external trade of the EU under the influence of integration. Having thus dealt with the quantity aspect of trade, we will next turn to the price aspect, finding out whether or not prices have converged under the pressure of integration.

Finally we will present a selection from the literature dealing with the way liberalised goods movements in Europe affect welfare and economic growth. As usual, the chapter will be rounded off with some conclusions and a summary.

Some basic concepts

Advantages

Fully integrated goods markets imply a situation of free trade among member states. As we have seen in the previous chapter, countries aim for free international trade because they expect economic advantages from it:

- more production and more prosperity through better allocation of production factors, each country specialising in the products for which it has a comparative advantage;
- more efficient production thanks to scale economies and keener competition;
- improved 'terms of trade' (price level of imported goods with respect to exported goods) for the whole group in respect of the rest of the world.

Integration of goods markets implies first of all the removal of (all) impediments to free intra-union goods trade. In modern mixed economies such negative integration is not sufficient, however. For the market to function adequately, there must be common rules for competition on the internal market and for trade with third countries.

We recall that the free trade area has been defined before as a situation where there are no factors impeding the free internal movement of goods within the area. If the area adopts a common external protection regime, we speak of a customs union.

Obstacles to free trade

The trade-impeding factors fall into two categories, tariffs and so called 'non-tariff barriers', or NTBs.[1] They can be described as follows:

- Tariffs, or customs duties or import duties are sums levied on imports of goods, making the goods more expensive on the internal market. Such levies may be based on value or quantity. They may be in fixed percentages or variable amounts according to the price level aspired to domestically.
- Levies of similar effect are import levies disguised as administrative costs, storage costs or test costs imposed by the customs, and so on.
- Quantitative restrictions (QR) are ceilings put on the volume of imports of a certain good allowed into a country in a certain period (quota), sometimes expressed in money values. A special type is the so-called 'tariff quota', which is the maximum quantity which may be imported at a certain tariff, all quantities beyond that coming under a higher tariff.
- Currency restrictions mean that no foreign currency is made available to enable importers to pay for goods bought abroad.
- Other non-tariff impediments are all those measures or situa-

tions (such as fiscal treatment, legal regulations, safety norms, state monopolies or public tenders) which ensure a country's own products' preferential treatment over foreign products on the domestic market.

Motives for obstacles

Obstacles to free trade are mostly meant to protect a country's own trade and industry against competition from abroad, and therefore come under the heading of protection. Protection can be combined with free trade. A customs union, for instance, impedes trade with outside countries by imposing a common external tariff and/or other protectionist measures, while leaving internal trade free.

Like individual countries, a customs union may hope to benefit from protection against third countries, that is, from import restrictions. From the extensive literature we have distilled the following arguments for such measures:

- Strategic independence. In times of war and supply shortages, a country should not depend on unreliable sources in other countries as far as strategic goods are concerned.
- Nurturing so-called 'infant industries'. The idea is that young companies and sectors which are not yet competitive should be sheltered in infancy in order for them to develop into adult companies holding their own in international competition.
- Defence against dumping. The healthy industrial structure of an economy may be spoiled when foreign goods are dumped on the market at prices below the cost in the country of origin. Even if the action is temporary, the economy may be weakened beyond its capacity to recover.
- Defence against social dumping. If wages in the exporting country do not match productivity, the labour factor is said to be exploited; importation from such a country is held by some to uphold such practices and is therefore not permissible.
- Boosting employment. If the production factors in the union are not fully occupied, protection can turn local demand towards domestic goods, so that more labour is put to work and social costs are avoided.
- Diversification of the economic structure. Countries specialising in one or a few products tend to be very vulnerable; problems of marketing such products lead to instant loss of virtually all income from abroad. This argument applies to small developing countries rather than to large industrialised states.
- Easing balance-of-payment problems. Import restrictions reduce the amount to be paid abroad, which helps to avoid

adjustments of the industrial structure and accompanying social costs and societal friction (caused by wage reduction, restrictive policies, and so on).

Pleas for export restriction have also been heard. The underlying ideas vary considerably. The arguments most frequently heard are the following:

- Strategically important goods must not fall into the hands of other nations; this is true not only of military goods (weapons) but also of incorporated knowledge (computers) or systems.
- Export of raw materials means the consolidation of a colonial situation; it is hoped that a levy on exports will increase the domestic entrepreneurs' inclination to process the materials themselves. If not, then at any rate the revenues can be used to stimulate other productions.
- If exported goods disrupt foreign markets, the importing country may be induced to take protective measures against the product and a series of other products; rather than risk that, a nation may accept a 'voluntary' restriction of the exports of that one product.

In continuation of the discussion of the previous chapter, it should be pointed out that most arguments for protection do not hold water: protection in general has a negative effect on prosperity.[2]

EU regime

Treaty

The principle of the free movement of goods within the EU is expressed in the Treaty of the European Economic Community (Article 9) in the following words:

> The Community shall be based upon a Customs Union, which shall cover all trade in goods and which shall involve the prohibition between member states of customs duties on imports and exports and of all charges having equivalent effect ...

By this definition, the freedom of movement within the EU extends to goods from third countries for which, in the importing member state, the administrative conditions have been met, and the (common) customs tariffs, or measures of equal effect, settled by the importing member state (Article 10). Exceptions to that general rule require extraordinary procedures (Article 115), to which no government is entitled on its own discretion.

- *Import duties and levies* of equal effect in force between member states were to be abolished according to a strict schedule (Articles 12–17). Thanks to the favourable economic climate that schedule could even be speeded up. A year and a half earlier than foreseen in the Treaty, namely, in July 1968, the last internal tariffs among the original six member states were eliminated.
- *Quantitative restrictions and measures of equal effect* (import: Article 30; export: Article 34) among member states were also eliminated before the end of the transition period, that is, before 1969. Quotas for manufactured products had already been completely abolished by December 1961.

The three states that joined in 1972 (the UK, Ireland and Denmark) and the three others that joined in the 1980s (Spain, Portugal and Greece) have abolished all quotas and tariffs in intra-EU trade after a transition period of several years.

Regulations and directives, programmes

The creation of a customs union means first the abolition of all tariffs and quantitative restrictions between the different member states. However that is not enough to liberalise trade internally. The non-tariff barriers may be as important hindrances to internal free goods trade as are tariffs. A number of these NTBs (like the practice of the railways in some countries of applying high rates for imported goods and low rates for exported goods) were abolished in the 1960s, partly under the impulse of the Commission's action programmes, partly as the result of verdicts of the Court of Justice. Many NTBs proved very difficult to remove as they were closely related to national regulations set up to pursue important objectives of public policy. Examples include the differences between member states in levels and structure of indirect taxation (as on tobacco and liquor), in the technical standards set for the protection of the worker, the consumer and the general public (for example, for pharmaceuticals), in consequence of the external policy (national quotas for textile products), in national industry-oriented government procurement policies (such as those on telecommunications, computers and defence equipment) and in the administrative stipulations for such diverse matters as statistics and crime.

In the early 1980s the negative aspects of the remaining NTBs, which caused a fragmentation of important segments of the European market for goods, became increasingly apparent. The white paper on the completion of the internal market (CEC, 1985d) proposed doing away with all these remaining barriers by 1992 by abolishing the controls at the internal frontiers. The so-called 'Single Act' (CEC, 1986a) laid down these objectives in a treaty and gave increased powers to the institutions of the EU to pass all necessary legislation. A huge number of regulations and directives have since been adopted, with the result that by now the single market for goods is practically completed (see also Chapters 12 and 16).

External situation

The Treaty of Rome established a customs union; in line with the definition of the customs union (Chapter 2) the Treaty (Article 9) obliges the member states of the EU to adopt 'a common customs tariff in their relations with third countries'. At the end of the transition period, the common external tariff (CET) came into force.[3] For the CET the arithmetical average of the duties applied in the various countries was to be taken as the basis (Article 19). The national tariffs were gradually adjusted to that CET as the mutual tariffs were broken down. France and Italy in particular had to adjust themselves to freer trade, while the other member states had to introduce more protection against third countries.

The level and structure of the CET have been adapted several times under the influence of a drive for worldwide liberalisation of trade relations. This has taken place in the framework of negotiations on tariffs and quotas of the General Agreement on Tariffs and Trade (GATT) (the so-called 'Dillon round' of 1960–62, the 'Kennedy round' of 1964–7, the 'Tokyo round' of 1973–9 and the 'Uruguay round' that was completed in 1993). The reduction was entirely in line with the policy laid down in the Treaty (Article 110), to the effect that the EU wishes 'to contribute in the common interest to the harmonious development of world trade, the progressive abolition of restrictions on international trade, and the lowering of customs tariffs'.

Apart from the general negotiations mentioned, the EU has negotiated trade privileges with certain groups of countries with which it wants to keep up special relations. The most advanced agreement is the Free Trade Treaty with the other countries in Western Europe, being part of EFTA. Furthermore agreements have been made to allow other groups of states privileges in their access to the EU market (Chapter 19, dealing with the EU's external policy, will discuss these agreements in some detail).

The CET system, that is to say, the system of tariffs (in value percentages) and quotas, applies in general to all manufactured products. However the external protection of the agricultural market of the EU is ruled by a separate system of variable levies on imports and subsidies on exports (export restitutions) for variable quantities of produce (Chapter 11 will explain the details of that system).

Trade patterns

Relative importance of total foreign trade

International goods trade is essential to the economies of EU member states, as is illustrated by the figures of Table 6.1, representing the relative importance of goods trade in gross domestic product.[4] First, the table shows that a country's participation in international goods trade depends on the size of its economy. For large countries, the

Table 6.1   Percentage share of goods imports and exports[a] in total GDP of member states (current prices), 1960–90

	1960		1970		1980		1990	
	imp.	exp.	imp.	exp.	imp.	exp.	imp.	exp.
Germany	15	16	16	18	21	22	24	27
France	11	11	14	13	19	17	21	19
Italy[b]	13	10	15	13	24	22	17	16
Netherlands	42	37	43	38	46	43	50	50
Belgium/Lux	37	34	45	45	50	59	68	64
UK	16	14	18	16	25	22	23	19
Ireland	35	23	41	28	66	47	53	61
Denmark	28	23	27	21	28	22	25	27
Spain	11	5	13	7	13	9	18	13
Portugal	19	10	24	11	27	15	45	30
Greece	17	5	21	7	27	13	31	13
EU12 (average)[c]	15	14	18	17	25	23	29	28
Intra[c]	5	5	8	8	12	12	17	17
Extra[c]	9	9	10	9	12	11	12	11

[a]   The exports of goods comprise all (national or nationalised) goods carried permanently, free or against payment, from a country's economic territory abroad; for imports a similar definition applies.

[b]   Upward correction of GDP in the mid-1980s.

[c]   On the assumption that the EU consists of 12 member states in all years.

Source: Eurostat; *National Accounts 1960–79, 1983* (totals); *Basic Statistics*; *Trade Statistics; External Trade; Statistical Yearbook* (several years), Luxemburg.

value of goods trade (average of imports and exports, including intra-EU trade) amounts to about one-fifth of their GDP, while for smaller countries with an open economy (The Netherlands, Belgium and Ireland) the percentage rises to some two-thirds. Second, it shows that the internationalisation of the economy depends also on the level of development; that is evident from the low ratios for low-income countries like Greece (moreover historically weak in goods trade, having always applied itself to the export of services) and Spain and Portugal. Finally the figures show very clearly that, in 30 years, the international integration of the economies of the EU member states by the exchange of goods has constantly increased; on average it has doubled (from about 14 to about 28). This is due mostly to the integration between member states; over the period, intra-EU trade increased threefold.

The integration of the EU as a whole in the world economy has also increased (from 9 to 12 per cent) but less than the intra-EU integration. The orientation of trade changed over the period under discussion. In 1960, trade was relatively more oriented towards third countries than to the countries that are now part of the EU12. In 1990, this situation was reversed; in line with theoretical expectations, integration has led to intra-EU trade now clearly outweighing extra-EU trade.

The openness with respect to third countries is much higher for the EU than for the other major trade partners in the world, the USA and Japan. However the gap between the EU and the USA has almost closed over the past decades, the USA having switched from a relatively autarkic economy connected to its large size to an economy that is more dependent on the rest of the world as a result of the liberalisation of trade, the globalisation of production and intensified specialisation. For the smaller Japanese economy, one would have expected a degree of openness higher than those of the EU and the USA. The opposite is true, however, and the trend is towards a further decrease in openness. This is notably due to the very low level of imports into Japan (CEC, 1992a).

Internal trade among member states of the EU

The member states of the EU trade more among themselves than with third countries. We know from Chapter 5 that the creation of a customs union may divert, or create, trade flows. Despite measures taken to prevent large-scale shifts (EFTA/EU custom tariff agreements), trade-creating and trade-diverting effects were experienced at the moments of the formation and enlargement of the EU. Table 6.2 gives an illustration.

Table 6.2 Percentage shares of EU in total commodity imports and exports of (future) member states, 1960–90

Country	1960[a] imp.	1960[a] exp.	1970[a] imp.	1970[a] exp.	1972[b] imp.	1972[b] exp.	1978/79[b] imp.	1978/79[b] exp.	1980[c] imp.	1980[c] exp.	1990[c] imp.	1990[c] exp.
Germany	31	32	44	41	54	47	50	48	49	51	54	54
France	32	34	49	49	56	56	51	53	52	55	65	63
Italy	29	31	41	43	49	50	45	49	46	52	58	58
Netherlands	49	48	56	62	62	74	57	73	55	74	60	77
Belgium/Lux	51	53	59	69	71	74	69	73	62	73	71	75
UK	15	17	29	22	32	30	41	42	41	45	51	53
Ireland	11	8	17	12	69	78	75	78	75	76	71	75
Denmark	39	29	33	23	45	43	50	49	50	52	54	52
Spain	26	38	33	36	42	46	36	48	31	52	59	68
Portugal	38	22	33	18	46	47	42	57	45	59	69	74
Greece	38	31	40	46	55	52	44	49	41	48	64	64
EU12	36	38	45	47	54	55	50	54	49	56	59	61

[a] Exports to, and imports from, the six original member states of the EU, also for new member states.
[b] Exports to, and imports from, the EU extended to nine members; also for Greece.
[c] All 12 member states.

Source: Eurostat, *Basic Statistics of the Community; External Trade; Statistical Yearbook* (various years) Luxemburg.

Since 1960, for all six original member states, the EU share in exports as well as imports rose. Trade among the six original EU member states between 1958 and 1972 (the year of the extension with the UK, Ireland and Denmark) had increased ninefold, while goods trade with the rest of the world grew by a factor of three. Evidently in the same period the importance of the EU as a trade partner increased with respect to two of the three new member states (trade with Denmark declined).

After 1972, the year of the first enlargement, the picture changed somewhat. The trade of the six original member states with the three new ones increased very fast between 1972 and 1978, but their trade with third countries grew even faster in the same period, as appears from a slight decline in the ratios of the original six between 1972 and 1978 (effect of the first oil crisis). As could be expected, in the period from 1972 to 1979 the EU became more important to the UK, Denmark and Ireland. For the candidate members, Greece, Spain and Portugal, however, the relative importance of the EU to their foreign trade remained fairly constant during the 1960s and 1970s. The sudden rise in their EU shares observed between 1970 and 1972 is merely a statistical artefact, reflecting the effect of the joining of the UK, Denmark and Ireland, states with which the three southern countries already had close trade relations.

For the period since 1978 the figures show that, in practically all member states, the share of EU imports has declined. This is the effect of the second oil crisis causing a fast rise in the costs of energy imports from outside the EU. However a development of increased integration of member countries in the EU economy can also be observed, as is evidenced by the figures of the last two columns of Table 6.2 (notably as regards the three new Mediterranean member states) and by a more detailed analysis of manufacturing imports by product (Jacquemin and Sapir, 1988).

In the EU12, intra-EU trade accounts for an average of 60 per cent of the total; the percentage showed a clear rise up to the first oil crisis, was fairly stable in the 1970s, and increased again in the 1980s.

Geographical pattern of internal trade

The geographical structure of internal trade in the present EU of 12 member states is marked by large flows between some pairs of countries and much smaller flows among others (Table 6.3). By far the largest trade partner (accounting for almost one-quarter of the total) on the import as well as the export side is Germany. This country is the largest exporter to the markets of all EU member states. It is, moreover, the largest importer from all countries except Spain and Ireland.

Table 6.3   Intra-EU trade (million ECU), by country, 1990

From \ to	GER	FRA	ITA	NETH	B/L	UK	IRL	DEN	SPA	POR	GRE	EU12
Germany	.	40	30	26	22	27	1	6	11	3	3	169
France	32	.	20	8	15	16	1	1	10	2	1	106
Italy	25	22	.	4	4	9	1	1	7	2	2	77
Netherlands	32	13	8	.	18	13	1	2	3	1	1	92
Bel/Lux	22	20	7	14	.	8	—	1	2	1	—	75
UK	18	14	7	8	8	.	8	2	5	1	1	72
Ireland	2	2	1	1	1	6	.	—	1	—	—	14
Denmark	6	2	1	1	1	3	—	.	1	—	—	15
Spain	6	9	4	2	1	4	—	—	.	3	—	29
Portugal	2	2	1	1	—	2	—	—	2	.	—	10
Greece	2	1	1	—	—	1	—	—	—	—	.	5
EU12	147	125	80	65	70	89	12	13	42	13	8	664

Source: Eurostat, *External Trade; Statistical Yearbook*, several years, Luxemburg.

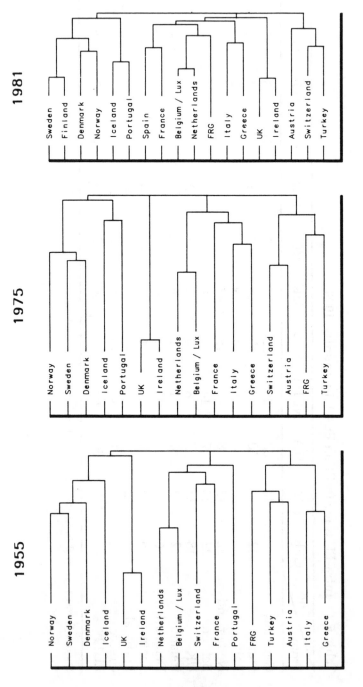

Figure 6.1 Clustering of European countries by trade pattern

Source: Peschel (1985).

On the trade balances of all member states, the exports to and imports from the other members are of the same order of magnitude and fairly equilibrated. The same (approximate balance of imports and exports) is largely true even of the bilateral trade flows, as appears from a pair-wise comparison of columns and rows.

Has the integration process changed the trade orientation of the member states? Peschel (1985) has analysed this with the help of a linkage procedure clustering the OECD countries by their trade orientation in three reference years. In Figure 6.1 the joining of the lines shows which countries are integrated the closest with each other (the combinations evolving on the left-hand side of each of the three diagrams), and which are only slightly integrated with each other (combinations on the right-hand side of each of the three diagrams). So the further to the left the clustering occurs, the higher the degree of integration. The picture for 1955 shows that the pre-EU situation predicted neither the formation of the EU6 (Italy, Germany, France and the Benelux belonging to different blocs) nor that of EFTA (whose member countries also belonged to different clusters). Actual integration did not change that picture very fast: by 1975 the nucleus of the EU (though without Germany) shows up in the diagram, but EFTA had not yet emerged. Only in 1981 did trade figures begin to reflect the institutional arrangements: the central cluster of the figure is indeed made up of the member states of EU9, to which Greece and Spain were already associated but from which Denmark was still keeping apart.

External trade of the EU, by partner

The EU12 is the world's largest trade partner. Over the past 30 years, exports and imports of the EU (without intra-EU trade) amounted to some 20 per cent of total world exports and imports; so trade of the EU has increased at about the same pace as total world trade.

Table 6.4 shows the relative importance of EU trade with groups of third countries (without intra-EU trade). From the figures given, the first conclusion is that this relative interest has been quite stable over time for almost every group of countries. Next we see that the trade relations are much closer with one group than with others. Trade intensity depends on a number of factors, such as attraction (highly developed economies) and friction (distance or barriers) (see also the next section). Let us look briefly at the different categories.

Paramount among trade partners of the EU12 are the countries in the western industrialised world. Within that group, the small bloc of countries that form EFTA hold a large and increasing share, which can be explained by their high income level, their small distance from the EU and the absence of trade barriers (the EU has concluded

Table 6.4   Geographical distribution (in percentages) by groups of countries, of extra-EU12 trade in goods, 1960–90

Country (group)	Imports				Exports			
	1960	1970	1980	1990	1960	1970	1980	1990
Industrialised	51	54	46	60	51	58	50	60
EFTA	15	16	17	25	22	25	26	27
USA	20	22	17	18	14	17	13	18
Japan	1	3	5	10	1	3	2	5
Rest of OECD	15	13	7	7	14	13	9	10
Third world	42	39	46	31	42	33	42	32
Mediterranean	7	8	8	8	12	9	11	11
ACP	10	8	6	4	9	7	6	4
OPEC	13	14	23	9	10	8	16	8
Latin America	9	7	6	6	8	7	6	5
Asean	3	2	3	4	3	2	3	4
Former centrally planned	7	7	8	9	7	9	8	8

Source: Eurostat.

a free trade arrangement with these countries). The figures for the USA and Japan reflect the changes in economic power of the two countries.

The developing countries have a more modest and a decreasing share. Within that group the associated African (ACP) countries and Latin America lose ground, the ACP notwithstanding their privileged access to the EU market, while the Asean countries gain market share. The position of OPEC improved dramatically as a result of the increases in oil prices of the late 1970s, but has been eroded since with the fall in oil prices.

The formerly centrally planned economies account for only a small portion (just under 10 per cent). This reflects to a large extent a deliberate choice by their governments to keep trade with the West to a minimum. About ten years ago that strategy was hesitantly changed. At present the former East bloc countries are all clearly in favour of openness, a tendency that is reflected in quite a sizeable trade increase (not shown in Table 6.4).

The relative importance of each group depends on, among other things, the trade barriers, hence on integration, so in Chapter 19 we will discuss in detail the policy pursued by the EU with respect to each individual group.

External EU trade, by commodity groups

The type of commodity internationally traded by the EU12 has changed quite significantly in the period of the past 30 years (Table 6.5). The structure of EU import trade reflects the traditional dependence of Europe on other parts of the world for its raw materials and energy supply. The two oil crises led to a steep increase in the money value of energy imports by 1980 and hence of that item's share in total imports (see Chapter 13). However by 1990 that effect had been expunged. The share of the other raw materials has markedly diminished, mainly as a result of reduced prices on the world market and increased efficiency.

Table 6.5   Distribution of EU12's foreign trade by commodity group, in percentages, 1960–90

Commodity group	Imports		Exports	
	1960	1990	1960	1990
Food, drink, tobacco	25	8	9	7
Energy products	16	15	4	3
Raw materials	26	8	4	2
Chemicals	4	7	10	12
Machinery, transport equipment	10	28	37	40
Other manufactured products	17	29	33	31
Miscellaneous	2	5	3	5
Total	100	100	100	100

Source: Eurostat; various statistics; *External trade; Statistical Yearbook,* various years, Luxemburg.

On the export side, manufactured products, with machinery and transport equipment in the lead, are observed to account for about three-quarters of total exports, a share which has increased over time.

A major shift in the pattern concerns agricultural produce. Although agricultural imports increased considerably in the period analysed, their relative share dropped steeply, and by 1990 was on a level with exports. That development is closely tied up with the common agricultural policy, to be described in Chapter 11.

Competitive position of the EU on the international market

Is the pattern of specialisation reproduced in Table 6.5 also indicative of the sectors for which the EU is most competitive on international markets? Indeed the EU is generally considered strongest in capital-intensive industries (where wage costs are less relevant) and in knowledge-intensive products (for which other countries do not always have the qualified labour); however other countries have specialised in those sectors as well. For that reason the EU has repeatedly analysed its competitive position, especially in comparison with the USA and Japan. These studies focus on the sectors of technologically advanced products. The index used is the ratio between two shares, on the one hand the share of exports of technologically advanced products in a country's total exports, and on the other hand the share of that country's (or the EU's) total exports in total OECD trade. Table 6.6 surveys the results of that analysis. From the figures, the EU appears to have been since 1970 on a lower level than its two competitors, Japan and the USA, and its relative position has weakened further over the years. Japan in particular has consolidated its position very rapidly.[5]

Table 6.6   **Specialisation index of export trade in high-value technological products, 1963–83 (OECD = 100)**

	1963	1970	1980	1983
EU	1.01	0.94	0.86	0.82
USA	1.27	1.28	1.27	1.26
Japan	0.72	1.07	1.30	1.36

Source: CEC, 1982a; *European Economy*, September 1985, p. 108.

The EU used to specialise rather in medium technology products and to hold a neutral position in low technology products (OECD, 1987a). For the products of the former categories (motor vehicles, wireless and television sets, office machinery, other machinery) the competitive position of the EU on its own market has been gradually eroded (Jacquemin and Sapir, 1988). This erosion continued in the 1980s; the export–import ratio for high-tech products declined from 1.1 in 1982 to 0.8 in 1990 (CEC, 1993b) – a ratio in excess of unity reflects a trade surplus, a ratio of less than unity a deficit. There are many who believe that the deterioration of the EU's position is due to structural weaknesses of its manufacturing industry, which used to be confronted by a segmented home market. To remedy that situation, two types of action were taken: an industrial policy specifically aimed at stimulating innovation (see Chapter 12) and a policy focusing on market conditions (see Chapter 16 on the programme for completing the internal market by 1992).

Explanation of spatial trade patterns

Some 'traditional' approaches to goods-market integration

Trade theory puts a heavy accent on comparative advantage. In practice, the concept is rather difficult to work with, however. Prices and availability of factors are not easy to integrate in our framework with export and import structures. The suggestion has been made (Balassa, 1977) first to analyse the so-called 'revealed comparative advantage' (RCA) with the help of an index dividing a country's share in the exports of a given commodity category by its share in the combined exports of a group of countries, and then relate that ratio to relative cost (compare the figures in Tables 6.6 and 6.7). However systematically relating these RCA indices for the EU to explanatory factors proves too difficult.

Trade patterns may also be influenced by trade impediments. Among these we find structural factors as well as government and private distortions. Tariffs occupy a preponderant place in integration theory (Chapter 5). Distance has also been cited in that respect. Distance-bridging transport has a clear effect on aggregate trade flows (Linnemann, 1966; Aitken, 1973). This is also the case in the EU on the disaggregate level of manufacturing industries (Bröcker, 1984). We will come back to the effects of integration through tariff cuts in the last part of this chapter. In recent times the study of goods trade has tended to focus on other aspects, highlighting the role of industrial organisation (see Chapter 12), technology and so on. However, to the author's knowledge, no systematic studies have been made explaining the trade pattern from trade impediments other than tariffs and transport.

Intra-industry specialisation

Contrary to what some had expected, the further opening up of the national markets for manufactured goods by the integration schemes of the EU and EFTA and the liberalisation in GATT has not produced specialisation among countries along the lines of traditional trade theory, according to which one country specialised in one good, for instance steel, and the other in other goods, for instance port wines, on the basis of comparative advantages. On the contrary, at the beginning of the 1960s it became clear that the specialisation occurred *within sectors*, with, for example, both countries producing cars, but of different types. 'The more similar the demand structures of two countries, the more intensive potentially the trade between these two countries' (Linder, 1961). Trade liberalisation in Europe was in fact accompanied by increases in the extent of intra-industry trade (IIT) among the countries in question (Balassa, 1966, 1975).[6]

The process of IIT in the course of European integration is illustrated by Table 6.7 (established by Sapir, 1992). The development over time of the index figures shows that in all countries and throughout the 1958–87 period, IIT was on the increase.[7]

Table 6.7   **Intra-industry trade as a percentage of total intra-EU trade for member countries, 1958–87**

Country	1958[a]	1963[a]	1970[a]	1970[b]	1980[b]	1987[b]
Germany	47	57	67	73	78	76
France	61	68	73	76	83	83
Italy	42	48	59	63	55	57
Netherlands	50	57	64	67	73	76
Belgium/L	54	60	66	69	70	77
United Kingdom	—	—	—	74	81	77
Denmark	—	—	—	41	52	57
Ireland	—	—	—	36	61	62
Spain	—	—	—	35	57	64
Portugal	—	—	—	23	32	37
Greece	—	—	—	22	24	31

[a]   Computed with EU6 trade data.
[b]   Computed with EU12 trade data.
Sources: Balassa (1975) for columns 1, 2 and 3, and Buigues *et al.* (1990) for columns 4, 5 and 6.

Several factors can explain intra-industry trade. The first is scale economies; if there is much product differentiation and a wide range of products, each country will produce only a limited subset (such as the trade in cars produced in different European countries). Technology is another factor; if R&D produces a rapid turnover of products protected by patents, each country will specialise in different segments of the market (pharmaceutical products are a case in point). Moreover the strategies of multinational companies lead to flows of intermediary goods among plants (for example, parts and components of cars) and the delivery of final goods in their distribution systems (Caves, 1982).

Now is a growth of IIT also due to integration? A set of studies would suggest so. In the 1959–80 period, intra-EU, intra-industry trade grew more rapidly than total EU intra-industry trade (Greenaway, 1987). In addition, the level of IIT in Western Europe was shown to be positively influenced by the factors just cited and negatively by increasing distance and differences in culture (Balassa and Bauwens, 1988).

Technology

Modern theory of trade tends to look towards technological and industrial factors for the explanation of trade patterns. The idea is that the level of innovation determines the quality of the product, which in turn determines its competitive position on external markets. This leads to specialisation: some countries specialise in high-tech goods, others in low-tech goods; the latter are generally believed to create less value added.

Within the EU, countries show a wide variation in innovation efforts, the pattern being that R&D per head is highest in the richer countries and very low in the poorer ones. It would be interesting to verify whether that pattern is reflected in the internal trade patterns. An empirical study directly testing that hypothesis has not yet been made, however.

An attempt to explain for a range of products the trade shares held by the wider circle of OECD member states (Soete, 1987) by such explanatory variables as a country's innovative capacity (country's patents in the USA), factor proportions (gross fixed capital formation divided by employment) and, of course, a distance variable indicated a significant role of the technology variable. Better explanations still seem a long way off (Cheng, 1983; Dosi and Soete, 1988).

Price differences

Measuring differences

The degree of integration can be measured not only by the growth in the exchange of goods but also by the degree of convergence reached by their prices in the various countries of the EU. Under the law of one price, undistorted markets would result in completely equal prices, and trade would reflect the location of demand and the location of the lowest-cost producers. However, owing to transport costs, collusion practices, tariffs and so on, prices do differ from one (sub-)market to another. A comparison (Glejser, 1972) of the prices of a fairly well-defined product set before (1958) and after (1970) the creation of the EU was not very conclusive; out of 36 cases, 15 showed a tendency towards greater disparity and 21 a tendency towards convergence.

To compare price levels in different countries has always been a hazardous undertaking. To be meaningful, such a comparison should be made between products which are not only available in all the countries surveyed, but also representative of all the national (and regional!) consumption patterns. The size of the EU and the many differences in historical origins within its borders give rise to a great variety of consumption patterns. From a series of comparable and comprehensive sets of price data for the EU9, we have selected those headings of consumer and equipment goods that are broadly representative of final demand in tradeable goods. Some of the price differences among countries spring from the differences in taxes, in particular value-added tax and excises. The comparisons have therefore been made for prices inclusive and exclusive of taxes. For an idea of the magnitude of the price differences among countries and their development through time, coefficients of variation have been calculated; Table 6.8 gives the results.

Table 6.8   Price dispersion (coefficient of variation) in the EU9, by product group, 1975–85

Category		Without taxes			Taxes included		
		1975	1980	1985	1975	1980	1985
1.1	Food	16.4	15.3	14.4	19.2	18.0	17.3
1.2	Food products subject to excise duty	19.0	21.2	17.0	31.3	38.3	32.7
1.3	Textiles, clothing, footwear	13.7	16.4	12.9	15.8	17.8	13.5
1.4	Durable consumer goods	12.4	13.9	12.3	17.7	17.7	17.4
1.5	Other consumer goods	21.3	21.4	19.3	21.8	20.0	20.1
1	Total consumer goods	16.3	17.1	15.2	20.5	20.9	19.4
2	Equipment goods	13.7	13.8	12.4	13.7	13.8	12.4

Source: Eurostat; Emerson *et al.*, 1988, p. 120.

Price levels evidently differed appreciably from one member state to another, more so for consumer goods than for investment goods. Indirect taxes, which in the period of study varied considerably among countries for the same product, were responsible for about one-quarter of the total price differences. Note that the composite calculation method used reduces the gap considerably; the absolute price differences between maximum and minimum prices are far greater. In 1985, for example, the dispersion of car prices net of tax was 14 per cent, but the absolute difference between countries at either end of the scale (Denmark and the UK) was 35 per cent; for refrigerators the dispersion was 10 per cent and the highest absolute difference (between Italy and France) 39 per cent.

The dispersion of prices widened between 1975 and 1980, but narrowed enough between 1980 and 1985 to cancel out the increase previously recorded, with the result that for all products the coefficients were lower in 1985 than in 1975. As the exchange-rate turbulence at the turn of the decade may have distorted the picture for 1980, we will look only at the 1975 and 1985 indicators. The conclusion is that, in that period, prices in the EU tended to converge.

Causes of price differences

Differences in prices among EU countries are due to different factors. One has already been mentioned in the previous section, namely, the differences in indirect taxes. However, even net of indirect taxes, prices differ considerably. Taxes and excises do influence the price net of taxes (for example, cars in Denmark: Chapters 12 and 16). Indeed for consumer goods the table shows that for items normally subject to excise duties prices tend to differ more than for other items.

More detailed material, not reproduced in Table 6.8, reveals larger differences for certain goods, such as boilers and transport equipment. An interesting observation is that these goods belong to the categories of products that are mainly purchased by the public sector and which show sizeable differences in technical regulation or standard, in other words, categories for which trade is subject to non-tariff barriers. Moreover, in those sectors where there are non-tariff barriers, price dispersion has tended to increase in the period 1975–85 (+ 5 per cent), while narrowing appreciably in the sectors more open to EU competition (– 24 per cent).

These are indications that tax differences and non-tariff barriers need to be removed to achieve further integration (see Chapter 16). However even after their removal numerous factors will continue to cause price differences between countries as well as, indeed, within each country. That is the case of, for example, transport costs on account of different distribution networks, of quality on account of regional and cultural differences in taste and of margins on account of differences in competitive pressures. However these factors do not justify the differences observed in Table 6.8; indeed an analysis applied to a specific sample of products (Emerson *et al.*, 1988) showed the price dispersion within Germany to be half that in the EU, indicating a large potential for further price convergence in the EU.

Welfare effects

Effects on member countries

One of the most common indicators with which to measure the effect of integration is the intensity of trade among partners (see Table 6.3). However growing mutual involvement of that kind cannot be considered a good sign of the progress in integration as the indicator captures a large number of other effects as well (Lloyd, 1992). More sophisticated methods have been developed to analyse the trade and welfare effects of progressive integration (Waelbroeck, 1976). These methods build on the theoretical considerations set out in Chapter 5; they are essentially an exercise in completing the accounting frameworks with data about, for instance, cost differences, supply and demand elasticities, trade flows, tariffs and consumption by good category in the countries participating in the customs union. At the time of the creation and successive enlargements of the EU, various attempts were made along these lines.[8]

To calculate the trade effects, a legion of methodological problems had to be overcome and methods varying in sophistication have been applied.[9] For the first period of the EU6, from 1955 to 1969, the period of eliminating high tariffs, some estimates amounted to a doubling of trade in comparison to a situation without EU. The first enlargement has been estimated to produce a 50 per cent rise in trade between the UK and the EU. The effect of the second enlargement, which entailed the abolition of low tariffs only, was estimated to be not more than a 5 to 10 per cent increase of EU–Spain trade. A survey of the results of computations of the trade effects of the creation of the EU in the 1960s and 1970s (Mayes, 1978) showed that trade creation has amounted to between 10 and 30 per cent of total EU imports of manufactured goods. Trade diversion is on the whole estimated much lower, at between 2 and 15 per cent. Agriculture is an exception to the general picture; considerable trade diversion occurred for this sector.

The next step is the calculation of income effects. The scarce empirical studies (Verdoorn, 1952; Johnson, 1958; Miller and Spencer,

1977; Balassa, 1975) found the income effects of the dismantling of tariffs to be slight, in the order of magnitude of less than 1 per cent of GNP. The studies cited have a number of drawbacks. Many use simplified methods to avoid data problems. Most studies, moreover, confine themselves to manufactured goods, leaving agriculture largely out of account. Finally, and this is a major objection, none of these studies has properly come to grips with such dynamic effects of goods-market integration as economies of scale, efficiency or learning by doing. The dissatisfaction with the static models stimulated work along new lines.

In some (Marques-Mendes, 1986a, 1986b) a macro model is used to calculate the effects of changes in trade and in terms of trade. The percentage growth of GDP actually observed can be split into a part due to the EU and a residual part. The effects of the EU6 appear to be quite substantial, particularly for the smaller countries (which is in line with the suggestions made by Petith, 1977), much larger anyway than the effects calculated by the Vinerian type of study discussed earlier. The effects of the EU9 present quite a different picture. Of course the period differs from the preceding one in many respects. At the start of the EU9 most tariffs were lower than at the time of creation of the EU6; besides, a profound need for economic restructuring was recognised, energy prices were on a steep increase, trade balances were adversely affected and 'new protectionism' was becoming generally accepted.[10]

In others, micro economic studies were made, better suited to deal with the dynamic effects. One (Owen, 1983) estimated that the effects of the opening of the European markets in the 1960s on increased competition, economies of scale and restructuring of firms have increased prosperity with some 40 to 100 per cent of the additional trade involved, or some 5 per cent of GDP.

Effect of the EU Customs Union on trade with third countries

The formation of a customs union also affects the patterns of trade with third countries. The taking away of the internal barriers in the EU has been a catalyst for the reduction of external barriers as well (Hufbauer, 1990; Messerlin, 1992).

The effects of the formation of the EU6 on trade with third countries differ by good category (Sellekaerts, 1973; Balassa, 1975). Particularly large positive trade-creation effects occurred for machinery, transport equipment and fuels, and negative ones for food, chemicals, and other manufactures. The EU formation caused a significant trade gain for associated less developed countries, and somewhat lesser positive trade effects for the UK and the USA. By contrast, net trade-diversion effects occurred for the other developed countries and the centrally planned economies; very small negative effects could be observed for the other EFTA and other LDC groups.

The effects of the first enlargement on trade partners (Kreinin, 1973) were found to be largely trade-diverting; they were heaviest for the group of other developed countries (approximately 20 per cent) and somewhat less heavy for the LDC (approximately 15 per cent). The effects of the completion of the internal market for goods on the trade partners of the EU were very diverse. For the group of EFTA countries the analyses (Haaland, 1990; Norman, 1991; Lundberg, 1992) all indicate significant increases of EU/EFTA trade, notably of the inter-industry type, going hand-in-hand with substantial welfare gains. For the group of LDCs the conclusion of an overview of studies (Koekkoek *et al.*, 1990) is that 'the trade effects of 1992 vis-à-vis developing countries are more likely to be positive than negative'. There are, however, important differences between countries (LDCs, NICs). The effects of a further enlargement of the EU with EFTA countries (in other words of the European Economic Area) on third countries were found to be very positive for all trade areas of the world (Haaland and Norman, 1992). The magnitude of the effects is different for different countries: highest for EFTA, average for the EU and small for third countries.

Summary and conclusions

- The integration of the economies of EU countries through the exchange of goods has greatly increased in the period 1950–90 and their mutual involvement has increased more than their involvement with third countries.
- Specialisation took the form not so much of each country concentrating on a specific sector, but of specialisation within sectors (intra-industry trade).
- The prices of most goods tended to converge, in line with theoretical expectations.
- Trade creation has on the whole been considerably greater than trade diversion; on balance, the EU appears to have contributed clearly to the efficient allocation of production factors in the world.
- Where the EU was externally open (manufacturing), the welfare effects were positive; where it was externally protected (for example, agriculture) the effects were negative.
- Integration has entailed only limited static welfare effects; the great advantages of the EU have been found in the improvement of the terms of trade, the reduction of costs and economies of scale.

Notes

1   Non-tariff barriers are very common, because international agreements forbid countries to have recourse to tariffs. The negative effects are similar to those of tariffs; see, for instance, Krauss (1979); Greenaway (1983). For a more thorough treatment of voluntary export restraints (VERs), see Jones (1984).

2   The arguments for protection and the (lack of) economic basis for them have been extensively studied in the literature. We refer here only to the authoritative work of Corden (1971, 1974), the handbook by Caves and Jones (1984), the case studies by Meyer (1973), the political economy approach of Frey (1985), the inventory of the OECD (1985c) and the European study of new protectionism by Page (1981).

3   The introduction of a CET is insufficient to guarantee the efficient working of the customs union. For that purpose, the customs procedures as well as the practices of separate customs administrations have to be harmonised as much as possible. In line with the Treaty obligation (Article 27 EEC) the member states have proceeded, before the end of the transition period, to the approximation of their legal and administrative customs regulations. This applies to uniform ways of establishing the customs value (on which to apply the tariff), uniform rules for verifying the 'origin of goods' (relevant to the tariff, because different agreements have been made with different groups of countries), rules about the collection of money at the frontier or at inland offices, rules with respect to processing trade (relevant to the free importation of goods to be re-exported after processing) and so on.

4   Naturally one should keep in mind that the goods trade is given at production value and GDP value added. On the other hand, GDP also comprises some activities which do not enter into the international commercial circuit. For lack of basic data, the ratio has not been corrected for these influences.

5   That result is confirmed once more by a study by Rollet (1984), who defines a category of products 'mastering technology', products at the frontier of technology development, with a very high R&D content (computers, telecommunication, robots and so on), and another category of investment goods which are at the crossroads of different production systems; see also Maillet and Rollet (1986).

6   The question of how to measure and explain IIT has received much attention in the literature (see among others, Grubel and Lloyd, 1975; Tharakan, 1983; Greenaway and Milner, 1986; Kol, 1988).

7   Similar results for the EU in Greenaway (1987). Information for EFTA countries shows the same tendency, but at a lower level; for CMEA the indices are lower (Drabeck and Greenaway, 1984). The EU results are also corroborated by Bergstrand (1983), who calculated IIT indexes for the years from 1965 to 1976 for the four large EU countries; he found that, on average, in three-quarters of the sectors he analysed IIT had increased, sometimes considerably (30–50 per cent).

8   For a brief review of methods and outcomes, we will borrow from the surveys made by, in particular, Verdoorn and Schwartz (1972), Balassa (1975), Mayes (1978) and El-Agraa and Jones (1981).

9   See, for example, Krauss (1968); Williamson and Bottrill (1971); Resnick and Truman (1975); Balassa (1975); Miller and Spencer (1977), Petith (1977), Viaene (1982), Grinols (1984), Winters (1985) and Jacquemin and Sapir (1983). Note that many of the methods and definitions used by these authors are not directly compatible with the theoretical conception of the CU of Chapter 5. However a discussion of the details would lead us too far off the main road.

10   In later chapters we will take up the other effects of integration, such as mobile production factors and/or common policies. For instance, the effect of stable exchange rates on the volume of trade will be taken up in Chapter 17, on monetary policy.

7 Services

Introduction

Over the last decades the importance of services in international trade relations has increased dramatically. This applies both to intra-EU trade and to trade of the EU with the rest of the world. The major causal factors of this trend are (1) the growing contribution of the sector to domestic growth and welfare, and (2) the benefits certain countries were able to draw from the liberalisation of their national service markets. So the discussion that follows is well warranted.

Like the previous chapter the present one will go first into a few basic concepts; although in many aspects services can be thought of as comparable to goods, they nevertheless reveal some specific characteristics that call for preliminary elucidation. Next we will consider the EU regime. This is of particular relevance because the EU has played a crucial role in the process of both internal (internal market programme) and external (GATT round) liberalisation of trade in services.

The specific patterns of trade in services will be described in the next section with the help of statistical series, detailing the structure by area and by branch of activity. Although less well documented than trade in goods, trade in services can now be described adequately. This is not the case with prices, or with the welfare effects of service trade, so we can only devote very short sections to each of these problems. The chapter will be concluded by a short summary of the main findings.

Basic concepts

Forms of integration

The integration of service markets proceeds in ways that are in agreement with the characteristics of this sector. Following Bhagwati (1987a) and others, we distinguish three types of international transaction. We will consider service markets to be integrated if the following obtain:

- Consumers of one country can move freely to producers in another country to receive the service offered. Personal services (such as staying at a seaside resort) and retail services (such as Dutch people shopping in Paris) are cases in point.
- Producers of one country can move freely to a foreign country to provide their services there. Managing a construction site, or a plumber fixing a problem in a house across the border, are cases in point.
- In cases where no spatial move of either producer or consumer is needed because the service is rendered through trans-border flows of information, integration is considered to exist if a consumer in country A is free to contract a service (for instance an insurance policy) with a company in country B.

A fourth type is sometimes distinguished, 'establishment-based trade'. It occurs when service providers create a permanent subsidiary in the importing country in order to produce and sell the service, parts of which will have to be imported (compare direct investment (DI) induced trade in goods!).[1] There is quite a difference between the liberalisation of the setting up of an establishment and of cross-border provision of services. The former maintains the coexistence of different national regulations, whereas the latter implies a direct competition between the various services produced under divergent rules.

The transaction costs involved in international service trade are often considerable, and not all services are susceptible to economies of scale. Hence, even without restrictions, services tend to be traded less than goods. The proximity of the supplier to the customer being of crucial importance for many services, the creation of a foreign establishment by a direct investment is a solution that is more often chosen for services than for goods. However, as technological progress in telecommunications lowers the transaction costs, integration according to one of the three models described may be expected to intensify, particularly for the third category of transactions.

Advantages

The standard arguments for the integration of service markets are similar to the ones used for goods (see survey in Messerlin, 1993, and Chapter 5):

- Comparative advantages of countries determine international specialisation patterns, and higher international specialisation raises the efficiency of resource allocation and hence income. In other words, consumers will have more choice and the products produced and consumed will be better matched.

- Economies of scale and scope will be better exploited (for instance in banking through spreading risks).

As with goods, the liberalisation of international trade in services alone does not suffice to integrate markets. Most of these markets have been regulated for several reasons (to protect consumers, for example) and a certain degree of harmonisation of the rules is necessary to avoid distortions. In much the same way, competition rules must be enforced and the relations to third countries defined.

Obstacles

The obstacles to free trade in services are fairly comparable to those to goods trade.[2] However, as the value of a border-crossing service is harder to control than that of a good, tariffs are seldom practised, and restrictions on the trade in services are mostly of the non-tariff type. Moreover, because the provision of some types of service across the border involves direct investments, a set of restrictions to entry of markets is relevant too.

Trade in services can be hampered by the following instruments:

- quantitative restriction, notably on domestic consumption[3] (for instance, advertising, air transport);
- shares of markets reserved for home producers (for example, for movies);
- subsidies (for instance, in construction);
- government procurement (for instance, construction, data processing);
- currency controls on transfers to foreign countries for services provided;
- restrictions on the qualifications of manpower required to perform certain services (legal, medical);
- technical requirements for capital goods (transport, for example);
- customs valuation problems for goods required to perform services (for instance, plumbers' tools).

Entry restrictions on a profession or restrictions on setting up in business are the second category of barriers. These can take the following forms:

- restrictions on the right of foreign firms to set up or take over subsidiary companies;
- exclusion of foreign firms from certain types of activity;
- discriminatory performance requirements;
- selective taxation;
- restrictions on the transfer of profits.

Motives for obstacles

Most of the obstacles are allegedly drawn up to *protect consumers*. A few examples from different sectors may illustrate this.

- In banking and insurance, regulation serves to limit the risk of insolvency through surveillance of private operators by (semi-) public organisations (central banks, among others). Since foreign suppliers are hard to control, access to the national market is barred to them.
- In air transport, the safety of the passenger is the main concern. Standards are accompanied by mutual import controls in the form of landing rights.
- In communication and energy (electricity), services are regulated to protect consumers from unfair pricing by a 'natural' monopolist.
- In medical services, the interests of the patient are protected by the enforcement of standards for the qualifications of personnel (medical doctors and so on).

Although the arguments for consumer protection are valid, they do not necessarily have to lead to trade protection; indeed other policy measures can be devised with the same effect for the safety and health of consumers while leaving international competition free.

Many other obstacles overtly aim at *protecting national companies*. There are several reasons to do so:

- strategic importance: an example is maritime transport, where international trade is restricted by a complex system of cargo reservation; a national merchant navy is thought to be necessary in times of war to provide the country with essential goods;
- economic policy: the control of macro-economic policy (through the banking system);
- enhancing the national prestige (civil aviation);
- control of key technologies (telecommunication);
- safeguarding cultural values (movies, television).

However, even if consumer protection is the official reason for this protectionist regulation, in practice the real reason is often that domestic firms want to be sheltered from international competition.

EU regime

Treaty

The Treaty of Rome is fairly brief on services. It reflects awareness of the wide variety in products of the service branches. The general definition of services (Article 60) reads: 'activities normally provided for remuneration in so far as they are not governed by the provisions relating to freedom of movement for goods, capital and persons'. They include in particular activities of an industrial or commercial nature and those of craftsmen and professions. For all these activities the Treaty stipulates two freedoms:

- to provide services (Article 59a): a company of member country A can provide services in member country B without having an office there;
- to set up an establishment: that is, companies (or persons) of country A wishing to set up an establishment (that is, a legal entity with, in general, premises, staff and so on) in member country B, are free to do so under the same conditions as are laid down for the nationals of the country of establishment (Article 52).

There are a few exceptions to this general freedom:

- activities which are connected with the exercise of official authority are excluded completely;
- medical and pharmaceutical professions: here liberalisation depends on coordination of the conditions for their exercise in various member states;
- transport services are governed by another title of the Treaty;
- banking and insurance services: as they are closely connected with movements of capital, their liberalisation will be effected in step with the progressive liberalisation of capital.

So one can say that the Treaty considers that services and goods can be subjected to the same type of general rules for liberalisation of markets; this irrespective of whether the service is provided by cross-border trade or by establishment.

Liberalisation by the Court of Justice

In the lengthy negotiations carried on to substantiate the freedom to provide services, the equivalence of qualifications proved one difficult point, another being the way in which governments had organised certain markets (or sanctioned private groups to organise and protect them). The general result was that some foreign penetration through subsidiaries had occurred in several service markets, but that very little progress towards liberalisation via cross-border trade had been made. Conflicts occurred between countries and cross-border operators. The country where the service was delivered claimed the right to supervise that service or subject it to licensing. The cross-border operator maintained that compliance with the rules of his home country was sufficient. In a set of famous rulings in such conflicts the Court of Justice has clarified the meaning of freedom of services, first, by pointing out the direct application of Article 59 in matters of services, thus confirming that national rules discriminating by nationality are null and void, and second, by extending to services the basic principles that had governed its decision in the famous 'Cassis de Dijon' case (see Chapter 16). In this and similar cases the Court ruled that a service lawfully provided in one member country can in principle also be freely provided in another member state.

The common element in the rulings was the consideration that governments have to demonstrate clear reasons of 'public interest' before imposing requirements on a foreign trader over and above those fulfilled to receive a permit from his home authorities, or duplicating qualification checks already performed at home. When applying these principles to insurance, for example, governments may regulate to make sure that individual private consumers do not get confused by the (lack of) coverage from an insurance policy imported from abroad. On the other hand, corporate clients of insurance companies need less regulation of this type because they are often very competent buyers.

The Court has also clarified the role of competition on service markets by ruling that the relevant EC rules apply fully to the service sector. This regards both firms that set prices (such as airlines) and governments that influence quantities (for example, public procurement).

Harmonisation and liberalisation efforts of the Commission

The ruling of the Court has in principle liberalised all services connected with agriculture, manufacturing, craft and trade (commerce). But in its verdicts the Court indicated that there should be a balance between liberalisation and harmonisation. The Commission has worked on liberalisation/harmonisation programmes for several service sectors. Two examples may give an idea of this process.

- In *professional services* (lawyers and auditors, engineers and so on), strong national corporations either had themselves regulated the profession (allegedly in the interest of the consumer) or were subject to detailed government regulation concerning both the access to the profession and the type of products supplied. The instrument used to regulate access is the specification of qualification requirements (diplomas, for instance). The EU has been working on directives for the liberalisation and harmonisation of such requirements and the mutual recognition of diplomas, but for a long time progress has been extremely slow and cumbersome and, apart from a framework directive on the recognition of university degrees, little has been achieved (Pertek, 1992).
- *Financial services* (banking and insurance) are regulated on a national basis to permit prudential control of the soundness of the undertakings to make sure that they will be able, for instance, to pay the client at the moment a life insurance comes to term. The harmonisation of these rules has been extremely involved, but has finally been realised in the form of several Banking Directives.

However the Commission has found that this process was too slow and, when successful, ran the risk of leading towards too detailed European regulation. So, while proposing the liberalisation neccessary for the completion of the internal market in services, a new approach was followed. This approach consists of three elements: first, free service delivery, through either cross-border trade or the setting up of an establishment; second, a 'single licence' system with mutual recognition: that is, service providers operating under the licence of member state A can work in member state B, the latter recognising the quality of member state A's surveillance system; and third, a minimum of EU-wide harmonisation in the form of common EU rules on the crucial features of the behaviour of service providers, on the one hand, and on the control system of member states, on the other.

External situation

Contrary to the situation for goods, the Treaty is silent as to the organisation of an external policy in matters of services. Article 59 merely stipulates that the Council may extend the freedom to provide services to nationals of third countries who are *established* within the EU. Now the external regime for a large number of services was in fact not a common one, but a set of national ones, each country having regulated the industry on a national basis and maintaining an external regime both *vis-à-vis* EU partners and other countries to protect its industries from foreign competition.

Two factors have changed this situation recently: first, the pursuit of an internal market in services has considerably changed the outlook for the external regime; second, in the framework of the GATT the EU has worked on the GATS, the General Agreement on Trade in Services. This agreement sets rules and creates a framework for basic fair trading principles such as non-discrimination. Individual signatories, among them the EU, pledge market opening in a wide range of service branches. For some branches special provisions have been made, as for financial services, telecommunications and sea and air transport.

GATS is not of the same inspiration as the single market. The latter tries to do away with all remaining barriers in one go, and to create a new competitive situation. The former has listed the present barriers, evaluated the problems they create, has drawn up an inventory of the potentional for liberalisation by each of the negotiating partners, and finally has worked out an agreement on a reduction of protection. The more partial and segmented approach of GATS is the result of the great diversity of preferences of the national governments that take part in the GATT negotiations.

It will be some time before a consistent external regime for services is set up by the EU from these rather dispersed elements.

Trade patterns[4]

Relative importance of trade in services

Services are to an increasing extent traded internationally. For the period 1960–80 we can only analyse the trends with data on 'invisibles' that encompass, besides services, such items as income from investment. The trend these figures reveal is very common among all EU member countries and shows that service trade has an increased share in GDP. From the comparison of Table 7.1 with Table 6.1, which gave the same information for goods, the transactions in services appear to be relatively small (less than one-quarter of those in goods). In relative terms, the growth of international service transactions seems to have followed that of goods integration; measured as a percentage of GDP it doubled in the 1960–90 period. For service integration the pace seems to have decreased over the last decade, but this does not yet reflect the influence of the internal and external liberalisation programmes. The internal market programme started in 1985, while the worldwide drive for liberalisation of trade in services got off the ground only in 1993 with the GATS agreement. So in future we may expect a relatively faster growth of intra-EU trade than that of extra-EU trade in services. Two indicators show that this is exactly what is happening. The first is the share of intra-EU trade in total trade by country; for most member countries this indicator decreased somewhat in the first half of the 1980s, while it increased in the second half, to more than compensate for the earlier decrease. The second indicator is the intra-EU trade share in total trade by branch; it did indeed go up for most service branches in the course of the second half of the 1980s (Messerlin, 1993). We have to be careful in attributing this latter phenomenon to the single market programme, because it may also reflect an increased effectiveness of member states' protection against non-EU service providers.

If we compare the growth of intra-EU cross-border trade of services with that of goods, we see that the increase of the latter category has been much faster. One explanation for this phenomenon is that in services the internationalisation process has proceeded much more

Table 7.1 **Percentage share of service imports and exports in total GDP of member states (current prices), 1980–90**

Country	1980		1990	
	import	export	import	export
Germany	6	4	6	4
France	5	6	5	6
Italy	4	4	4	4
Netherlands	10	10	11	11
Belgium/Lux.	12	13	15	15
UK	4	6	4	5
Denmark	7	9	10	11
Ireland	10	6	9	6
Spain	2	5	3	6
Portugal	5	8	6	9
Greece	4	11	5	13
EU12	5	6	5	6
Intra	3	3	3	3
Extra	2	3	2	3

Source: Eurostat: *International trade in services, EUR12*, Luxemburg, 1993.

by establishment-based competition, rather than in terms of cross-border trade-based competition (Messerlin, 1993).

Main trading partners

The EU had a surplus on its balance of trade in services over the whole 1980–90 period (Table 7.1). This surplus is, however, a relatively small percentage of total trade in services (figures in Table 7.1 exaggerate the difference, as the result of rounding). The exports and imports of total services by the EU are not only fairly balanced for the total extra-EU trade, but they are also very balanced for the various (groups of) trading partners (see Table 7.2), notably in view of the statistical error margin.

Table 7.2   Geographical distribution (in percentages) by groups of countries, of extra-EU trade in services, 1980–90

Country group	1980		1990	
	imports	exports	imports	exports
Industrialised	65	57	69	68
EFTA	25	19	24	24
USA	30	28	33	31
Japan	2	3	4	6
Other	8	7	8	7
Third world	31	39	27	29
ACP	10	16	5	8
OPEC	6	9	5	6
Other	15	14	17	15
Other (ex-state trading)	4	4	4	3
Total	100	100	100	100

Source: Eurostat, *Geographical breakdown of current account, EUR12,* 1980–90, Luxemburg, 1993; some estimates.

The large surplus the EU had in 1980 with the third world (notably ACP countries) has disappeared since and the same is true for its deficit with EFTA. The similarity in the patterns of exports and imports is typical for services; it does not appear for other types of current account transactions.

The table also shows that the EU trade in services is geared very much more to the industrialised countries than to developing countries (the same structure that obtains for goods: see Table 6.4). The main trading partner for the EU in services is the USA (much larger than for goods). The paramount place of the USA in EU services trade can be explained by the weight of its economy and the importance services have in its branch structure. Exchanges with the EU have, moreover, been enhanced in the past decade by the drop in the cost of transport, of telecommunications and of information processing (the latter, for example, by 65 per cent between 1975 and 1985). EFTA is second for services, while it occupied the first place for goods because of the free trade arrangement with the EU and its geographical proximity. Its relatively low weight and the persistence of trade barriers in services explain the difference between its position in goods and in services.

Trade in services by branch

The structure of the external trade in services by sector of activity (see Table 7.3) has remained fairly stable over the past decade.

Transport and tourism are by far the most important items in terms of exports as well as imports. The EU has a net surplus on its balance of trade in services, largely owing to tourism; indeed the EU accounts for a large share (25 per cent) of total world tourist receipts and always attracts more foreign tourists than it sends (a difference, more or less, of 15 million a year). The countries that attract most non-EU tourists are Spain, France and Italy.

For the rest, the surplus is notably due to good performances by the sectors of construction and financial services. The latter is largely attributable to the very competitive UK banks and insurance companies. The surplus of the branch of business services (engineering, software, accounting, management consulting) would appear to indicate a strong competitiveness of these branches on world markets. Unfortunately the diversity of this sector places a constraint on the further analysis of this branch. A negative balance exists for audio-visual services and software, where the USA has a very strong competitive edge. For other services, including services related to transport, commerce, technology and intra-firm transactions, the EU situation is fairly balanced.

Price differences

The comparison over time and space of prices for typical services is a rather complicated operation. In the past a few attempts have been

Table 7.3   **Extra-EU trade in services, by branch (milliard ECU), 1980–90**

Category	1980		1990	
	exports	imports	exports	imports
Transport	27.6	24.8	45.8	44.2
Sea freight	11.4	11.2	15.4	16.6
Air freight	1.3	0.6	2.7	1.5
Air passenger	4.9	3.6	9.9	8.6
Other	10.0	9.4	17.8	17.5
Travel and tourism	13.9	13.1	34.0	28.6
Other	31.2	22.0	54.9	43.0
Construction	6.3	2.8	6.3	3.1
Merchanting	4.4	4.6	7.3	8.5
Banking & insurance	3.3	2.3	10.7	6.4
Business	7.9	4.2	11.1	8.1
Communication	1.1	1.0	2.3	2.5
Films, TV	0.3	0.4	0.9	1.4
Other	7.9	6.7	16.3	13.0
Total	72.7	59.9	134.7	115.8

Source: Eurostat, *International trade in services, 1980–1989*, Luxemburg, 1993.

made for specific products, but these did not produce any conclusive results. Attempts for broader categories (see, for example Table 20.2) did not provide a clear picture either, so we have no way of checking whether the integration process in service markets has brought price convergence or not. The scanty evidence that is available does not run counter, however, to the general assumption that the lack of integration that has characterised service markets until recently tended to maintain price differences, while the recent liberalisation programmes in many branches led to further price convergence.

Welfare effects

There are no empirical studies that permit us to evaluate the trade, let alone the welfare effects of decreased protection, in services. The reason for this is that the conceptual and statistical basis for such studies is very weak. For example, the estimation of 'ad valorem' equivalents of existing restrictions in services is very difficult, and hence the economic cost of these restrictions can generally not be established. This is contrary to the case of goods, where welfare cost of protection and welfare benefits of liberalisation have been estimated on several occasions. However there is a growing demand for such assessments, coming from the increased weight of services in the EU economy.

For a large part the argument that trade liberalisation leads to positive welfare effects rests on the assumption of increased (potential) competition. It is here that some caution is needed. Indeed, in many cases where liberalisation went hand-in-hand with deregulation, an initial period of enhanced competition was followed by a period of concentration of firms, leading to a situation of limited oligopolistic competition. So a prudent policy of regulation and of enforcement of competition rules is needed (see Chapter 16).

Summary and conclusions

- Until recently many service markets have been protected from foreign competition by a variety of instruments; often the official reason was the protection of the consumer, but in practice the consumer has often borne a high cost while the producer has mostly profited.
- International trade of services is relatively limited. This is partly due to protection. It is also partly due to the need for proximity of producers and consumers that induces firms which undertake internationalisation to prefer the setting up of an establishment in the country to cross-border trade.
- The EU has liberalised the internal trade in services; this has been accompanied by a mutual recognition of home country supervision and a minimal set of EU regulations.
- The effects of liberalisation have started to become visible in terms of increases in cross-border trade and direct investment; however the deficient data situation precludes as yet any conclusion as to price convergence and positive welfare effects.

Notes

1 This is different from trade in goods where DI-based production is not considered to be part of the liberalisation of goods but of capital flows.
2 A detailed description of these trade barriers is given in OECD (1981b, 1983a, 1984a, 1985b, 1986a).
3 These measures are favoured by many policy makers, for several reasons. First, they are particularly well suited to being applied in times of economic downturn, to increase the effectiveness of stabilisation policies. Next, their protectionist impact is independent of substitution between foreign and domestic produc-

ers. Finally, their enforcement is often done through the involvement of agencies in which domestic producers are represented.

4   To measure trade in services is quite a complicated proposition. For a service incorporated in an information carrier, for instance a consultancy report, the international transaction can in principle be recorded the moment the report passes the frontier. In cases where either the consumer (a student who studies abroad) or the producer (a professor who teaches abroad) travels from one country to another the transaction is difficult to register. To overcome such difficulties, most international service transactions are registered only at the moment the payment is made (through the records of the central banks). The criterion for the international export of a service is then that it be paid for by a person resident or a company established in a country other than the home country of the producer. As a consequence of these recording problems most statistics on trade in services are very deficient. Consistent series over a long time-period are not available. For this reason we have to limit ourselves here to relatively short series, generally covering the period 1980–90 only.

PART III
COMMON MARKET

8 Common Market Theory

Introduction

If the obstacles to free movement among partners are removed, not only for goods and services, but also for production factors, the stage of a common market (CM) is reached. In this chapter we will discuss the theoretical basis for this stage of integration. We will deal not only with the liberalisation of factor markets as such, but also with the interrelation of the goods and factor markets that is typical of the common market.

The reason to strive for a common market is the hope that the freedom of capital and labour to move from activities with a low marginal product to those with a higher one will lead to a more efficient allocation. The next section will discuss to what extent the integration of factor markets helps to equalise factor returns and to create and distribute wealth. Economic integration does not always proceed by the stages sketched in Chapter 2. In practice this means that trade impediments may persist where international capital and labour markets are already partly integrated. Goods markets and factor markets influence each other in many ways, and consequently the integration of one market affects that of others. How this mutual influencing operates, and how the removal of barriers to either goods or factor movements affects welfare, will be discussed next.

The abstract nature of neoclassical theory is not very well suited to grasping the reality of a world in which entrepreneurial skills and technological innovation vary among nations and the functioning of many markets is far from perfect. So the next step will be to present elements of a theory of international production likely to explain the intricacies of the common market better than the loose strands of thought so far developed on the integration of separate markets for goods and production factors. The chapter will be rounded off as usual with a brief summary and some conclusions.

Integration of factor markets, disregard of goods movements

Movement and movement cost, price convergence

The effects of the integration of factor markets can be illustrated by comparing situations without and with migration of labour (Lindert, 1986). That is done in Figure 8.1, where the upper part of the graph indicates the situation without, and the bottom part the situation with migration. We have assumed that the world consists of two countries, A and B; the situation for A is depicted on the left-hand side, that for B on the right-hand side. The situation on the labour market is given by the upward-sloping curves S_a and S_b representing labour supply, and the downward-sloping curves D_a and D_b representing demand for labour. Together they determine the price of labour (wages) and the number of workers employed.[1]

In the non-integrated situation, in which the labour markets of countries A and B are separate, that is, without migration (upper part of Figure 8.1), the supply and demand conditions in country A lead to high wages and those in country B to low wages. Two national labour markets with such different wage levels can be kept separate only by dint of control measures, for instance 'permits' or restricted access to professions (see next chapter).

In the integrated situation such barriers are removed (bottom part of Figure 8.1). Now workers of country B will move to country A where they earn a higher income. As movement entails costs, both in economic and psychological terms, this will not lead to the complete equalisation of wages. We assume these costs to be equal to C. The inflow of migrant labour into country A pushes the wages down, which leads to a lower quantity supplied domestically (O_aM) and a higher quantity demanded domestically (O_aN). The difference (MN) indicates the number of migrants from country B in country A. In country B the opposite occurs: the higher wages lead to a lower quantity demanded (O_bP) and an increased quantity supplied (O_bQ); the difference PQ indicates the number of migrants from country B to country A. The number of out-migrants of country B (PQ) is of course just equal to the demand for foreign labour created in country A (MN). The new curves of domestic labour S_{a+m} and S_{b-m} demonstrate the consequences.

The welfare effects of the migration caused by the joining of markets are also illustrated by Figure 8.1. They are fairly intricate and apply to both workers and employers in country A and country B (for a review, see Table 8.1).

Workers from country A lose area *JEKF* because their wages are forced down. (For that reason, many trade unions in developed countries are against immigration.) On the other hand, workers remain-

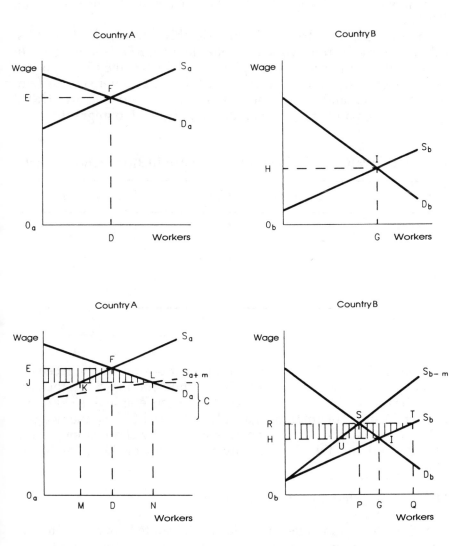

Figure 8.1   Integration of factor markets, price convergence

ing in country B gain from out-migration; there is less competition for jobs, which raises the wage rate from O_bH to O_bR. The gain is the producer surplus above the new supply curve (*HRSU*). The migrants also gain: they earn a higher income in A than they would have in B. However account should be taken of cost factor C. So the gain is the area above the old supply curve S_b and below the new one S_{b-m} (*USTI*).

Employers in country A gain considerably: the area *JEFK* is redistributed to them from workers, while the area *KFL* is a net gain. In country B, on the contrary, employers are losers: they have to pay higher wages and hence lose profits. Of their consumer surplus (employers are demanders of labour!) they have to hand over area *HRSU* to workers remaining in the country, and area *USI* to migrants.

Table 8.1   Welfare effects of integrated production factor markets

Category	Country	Gains	Losses
Workers	A	*	*JEFK*
	B	*HRSU*	*
	B to A	*USTI*	*
Employers	A	*JEFL*	*
	B	*	*HRSI*

* not applicable

Countries A and B are clearly in different positions. The receiving country A has a net gain (*KFL*). The sending country B, on the contrary, has a net loss *USI* (difference between employers' loss and workers' gain). The migrants gain also: *USI* and *STI*. So the net gain to the world is *KFL* and *STI*; the distribution of welfare among countries depends on the allocation over countries of the gains to migrants.

Movement of factors, full price equalisation

That the integration of factor markets will lead to better allocation of capital and labour can also be illustrated by a somewhat different neoclassical static two-country diagram (again, there is no influence from the rest of the world). In Figure 8.2, the horizontal axis gives the stock of capital (or alternatively labour). The sloping curves *AD* and *BE* indicate the level of production that can be obtained at each size of input of capital (or alternatively labour) assuming a certain input of the complementary production factor. The curves of country B mirror those of country A, so that one picture describes the effects of integration on both countries (see Grubel, 1981). The effects of integration of markets for production factors (on the assumption that goods markets are not integrated) can now be illustrated by comparing the situation in which there are barriers to movement, with that of integration, in which these barriers have been removed.

We will first consider the situation in which the capital markets of countries A and B are completely separated (upper part of Figure 8.2); in other words, where capital is fully immobile between nations.[2] The vertical axis gives the price of capital; with perfect competition on the national markets, this price is equal to the marginal product of capital. The horizontal axis gives the supply of capital (O_aO_b, indicating the total stock of capital at the disposal of the two countries), demand of capital and supply of labour being given. Country A has a relatively abundant capital supply, hence a low interest rate; in country B capital is scarcer and hence the interest rate higher. The differential is ED. The downward-sloping curves for both country A and country B indicate that the marginal product of capital is lower as the capital stock is greater; with a given capital stock (K) in both countries (O_aC for A and O_bC for B) the price of capital is given for either: r_a for A and r_b for B. We assume there is no unemployment. From this picture the distribution of income can be derived. Total output is O_aADC for country A and O_bCEB for country B (the total production realised at all points on the horizontal axis; it consists of two components: capital income and labour income). Capital income (measured by the quantity of its input times the marginal product of capital at the point where the market is in equilibrium) corresponds to the rectangle O_ar_aDC in country A, and to the rectangle O_bCEr_b in country B. The triangles r_aAD and EBr_b represent labour income in countries A and B, respectively.

What happens when the two countries integrate their national capital markets? The lower part of Figure 8.2 illustrates the effects of the removal of obstacles. Owners of capital will now move their capital from the country where it earns a relatively low income (A) to the one where interest is higher (B). On the assumption of equal risks and uncertainty for foreign and domestic assets and of no other costs being involved, this will lead to upward pressure on interests in A (smaller supply of capital) and downward pressure in B (greater supply of capital). In the end it will bring about the full equalisation of return on capital in both countries at level r_{cm} (representing the marginal productivity of capital in the common market). The capital stock of A declines while that of B increases by the amount GC, equal to A's net foreign asset. So country A will specialise in savings and country B in investment.

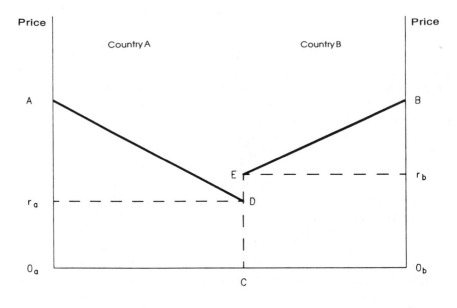

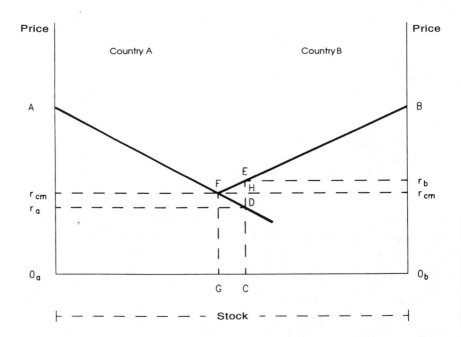

Figure 8.2   Integration of factor markets, price equalisation

The same approach can be followed for labour-market integration. In the lower part of Figure 8.2, *r* represents wages; they may differ in the two countries because of different endowments with qualified labour and barriers to migration between the two countries. If the latter are taken away, a number *GC* of workers will move from country A to country B, attracted by the higher wages there. The movement will equalise wages in the two countries.

Even if there are no differences in factor prices between the two countries, the removal of controls is likely to favour a better allocation of ressources. On capital markets, different liquidity preferences in the two countries will cause the importation of long-term capital and the exporting of short-term capital in A, and the reverse in B. On labour markets, the different qualifications may lead to migration of certain categories of active persons from A to B, while other professional categories may want to move from B to A.

Welfare effects

The integration of the two markets does not only lead to equal prices, but also has important welfare effects, which are different for different groups and hence lead to distributional disputes. (For an overview of these effects, see Table 8.2)

Total welfare will increase for both countries by the following process. The net domestic product of country A declines by *GFDC*; its net national product, composed of the domestic part O_aAFG and the investment income earned abroad, *GFHC*, increases by *FHD*. The net domestic product of B increases by *GFEC*. As *GFHC* must be paid to A, the net gain for B is the triangle *FEH*. The total net gain arising from the better allocation of capital through integration corresponds for both countries to the triangle *FED* (*FHD* in A and *FEH* in B).

The distribution of income between the main functional categories (wage income versus capital income) changes when the factor markets are integrated. In country A the part of total income that accrues to labour is reduced in favour of the part that accrues to capital owners (by $r_a r_{cm}FD$), whereas in B the share of labour increases at the expense of owners of capital (by $FEr_b r_{cm}$). This explains why trade unions tend to welcome incoming investment, but are opposed to domestic investment abroad, even if it leads to a higher aggregate income. Of course that effect will come about only if markets function properly; that is, if the wages are adjusted downward. If not, the result may be more unemployment, leading to reduced production, which the growth of capital income may fail to compensate in the short run.

Integration is bound to change government revenue springing from the taxation of international capital. If country B taxes foreign assets, a proportion of the area *GFHC* remains in B. If it exceeds the net gain of A (the triangle *FHD*), country A will suffer a net loss from opening up its capital market while country B had not done so completely (Grubel, 1974).

The welfare effects of labour migration are similar to those of capital movement. On the assumption that the migration is not permanent, the migrants will transfer a labour income *GFHC* to their home country, creating a net gain of *FHD* for country A and *FEH* for country B. Bear in mind, however, that the division of revenues resulting from labour movement may not run fully parallel to that of capital; since labour will incur subsistence cost while staying abroad, the remittances will be less than *GFHC*, and may even become so small as to offset the gain *FHD* for country A, the emigration country.

Table 8.2   Effects of the integration of production factor markets

Indicator	Country			
	Segmented markets		Common markets	
	A	B	A	B
Stock (cap.lab.)	O_aC	O_bC	O_aG	O_bG
Price (int.wage)	r_a	r_b	r_{cm}	r_{cm}
Income (first factor)	O_ar_aDC	O_bCEr_b	$O_ar_{cm}FG$	O_bGFr_{cm}
Income (second factor)	r_aAD	EBr_b	$r_{cm}AF$	FBr_{cm}
Net domestic product	O_aADC	O_bCEB	O_aAFG	O_bGFB
Net national product	O_aADC	O_bCEB	O_aAFHC	O_bBEFHC
Net gains	—	—	FHD	FEH

The removal of internal constraints and its effects on the balance of payments and welfare

In the previous section we assumed full employment, at the national level, of the two production factors, labour and capital. However that assumption is unlikely to be fulfilled in reality. In small segmented markets specialised labour will be hard put to it to find sufficient demand for its services, or the necessary capital with which to complement prevailing technological know-how. So in small segmented markets both the supply of and the demand for factors of production may be constrained, with negative effects on production and welfare. By taking away controls on the international movement of labour and capital, both supply and demand can assert themselves, and an efficient allocation of all specialised factors of production will come about.

The 'trade' and welfare effects of removing the constraints on, for example, the capital market, are illustrated in the upper part of Figure 8.3, which gives the supply and demand curves for capital. The supply of capital comes from savers, its demand from investors. Controls on capital imports and exports are making the capital market of country A inefficient. The financial products provided by the banking sector in A being inadequate, potential investors and savers refuse transactions, which implies that some capital remains idle; this is indicated in the figure by AB (given demand), investment and hence savings being limited to the amount OA. The price for the investor, or the borrowing rate, is OI, and the lending rate for savers is OG. The spread between the two, GI or FD, is the margin taken by banks for their intermediate role. This margin can be that high because banks are protected from foreign competition. This creates a 'monopoly', permitting banks to earn a monopoly rent of GIDF (quantity OA times the margin GI). Assume now that controls on international capital movements are abolished and thus all inefficiencies in the markets removed. Fear of new entrants from abroad taking away profitable markets will induce banks in the home country to propose new products, better adapted to the wishes of both savers and investors. This will bring additional supply and demand on the market. Let us assume provisionally that the resulting rate of interest (OH) is just equal to the interest rate abroad. Both savings and investment will now expand to OB. There is an important gain to society as a whole. First investors increase their 'consumer surplus' by the area HIDC. Next savers increase their 'producer rent' by the area GHCF. Of their monopoly rent GIDF, banks lose HIDE to investors and GHEF to savers. This leaves a net gain to society equal to the triangle FDC.

The effects of partial liberalisation are different. Under such conditions, the liberalisation of financial markets is unlikely just to balance out home supply and demand at the prevailing world-market price. The lower part of Figure 8.3 represents the situation where the world interest rate OH is lower than the domestic equilibrium rate without international exchange. Now controls may affect only capital outflows, leaving inflows free, or alternatively, may affect only capital imports, leaving exports free. Let us analyse the effects of either case on the situation $r_w < r_h$.

In a situation of free outflow and controlled inflow, savers will take the opportunity of getting higher returns on the foreign market (OH) than on the domestic market (OG), and expand their supply to OJ. Under this pressure, domestic banks will have to diminish their

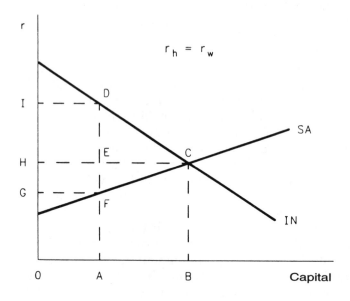

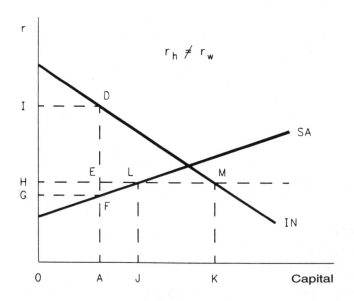

Figure 8.3   Welfare effect of capital market integration through deregulation

margins from *GI* (=*FD*) to *HI* (or *ED*) to acquire the necessary capital (*OA*) for making the transaction with the domestic investors. The remaining supply *AJ* is invested abroad (either directly by savers or indirectly by banks). This will give rise to an inflow of interest payments equal to the area *AELJ*. The 'rent' of savers increases by the area *GHLF*, of which *GHEF* is gained at the expense (transfer) of the banking sector's monopoly rent, and *FEL* is the net welfare gain to society.

In the situation of free inflows and controlled outflows, the same reasoning applies. In the closed domestic market, investment was constrained by savings to *OA*. In the new situation, foreigners will acquire equity (portfolio investment) or companies (direct investment) and get higher returns than on the world market. That inflow will take total investment up to *OK* instead of *OA*, the quantity *AK* being imported, which entails payment of interest on foreign debt corresponding to the area *AEMK*. Investors find their 'surplus' increased by the area *HIDM*, of which *HIDE* is at the expense of monopoly 'rents' of financial intermediaries (that is, a transfer), and the triangle *EDM* is the net welfare gain.

In Chapter 5 we found that, contrary to popular belief, welfare may improve if a good is produced less at home and imported more from abroad, provided that the resources set free are used to produce other goods for which the country has a comparative advantage, thus offsetting the negative balance-of-payment effect. Failing that, total growth will be constrained by the balance of payments. In much the same way, we find that a liberalised capital market has positive effects on economic growth (welfare effects) despite an initial deterioration of the balance of payments (from the equilibrium in the upper part of Figure 8.3 to the deficit of *JLMK* in the lower part of Figure 8.3. However, if the imported capital is used to create production units, the output of exportables may expand, compensating for the deficit in interest payments.

Other effects

In the foregoing we have shown some welfare effects of liberalising international capital and labour movements. There are other effects, which we will not discuss in detail, but which nevertheless call for some attention.

For one thing, factor-market integration may ease the *restructuring* that will follow the liberalisation of trade in a customs union. Indeed new combinations of production factors may often prove impossible with the capital and labour available nationally (by sub-category), and therefore the common market may speed up the realisation of the dynamic effects of the CU.

For another, there are *external effects* of internal liberalisation, which tend to differ according to the initial situation with respect to external factor movements. The effects of creation and diversion of trade (Chapter 5) can find their counterparts in effects of creation and diversion of labour or capital movements. Figure 8.3 could indeed be developed in the same way as Figure 5.2 to demonstrate these effects, an exercise well warranted, as the creation of a CM might be bad for world efficiency if a union between countries A and B diverted production factors from third countries. However for practical reasons we will refrain from going into the matter. As most countries initially restrict labour movements to all third countries alike, the net effect of the liberalisation of labour movement among partner countries is very unlikely to have such an effect. For capital the possibility of diversion seems unlikely, as countries with free movement of capital will not easily accept the introduction of a control system discriminating between partners and third countries.

The *dynamic effects* of the integration of factor markets (compare goods markets in Chapter 5) will stem from enhancing competition between financial organisations, boosting their economies of scale and raising the quality of their products. Of course the banking industry in countries with very protected capital markets will suffer from liberalisation, but on the other hand all the activities that use financial products will gain. The gains will be small for multinationals but large for borrowers who until now had no access to foreign markets. The advantages accumulating to governments borrowing in protected markets are likely to diminish as investors find substitutes for domestic government bonds abroad. Finally the reduced gap between the interest paid by borrowers and the interest received by lenders means that both categories benefit from liberalisation, both investment and savings are stimulated, and better conditions are created for future growth. As the dynamic effects of the CM are very poorly worked out in theoretical terms, we will not go into the matter further.

Finally there may be an effect of *spatial concentration*. At advanced levels of development of financial markets, not only are excess demand and excess supply being transferred from local markets to a financial centre, but borrowers and lenders on local markets may decide to move their whole activity there (Kindleberger, 1987). The effects are shown in Figure 8.4.

The situation before integration is given in the upper part of Figure 8.4. The top graph gives supply (S_l) and demand (D_l) in the small local market with a high price. The middle graph gives the supply (S_{ce}) and demand (D_{ce}) in the large central market with a low equilibrium price. The bottom graph gives the situation after integration of the local and central markets; the central market has taken over all

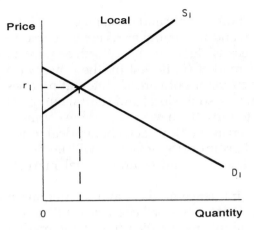

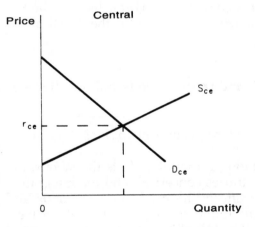

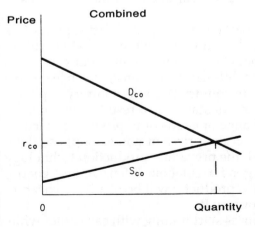

Figure 8.4   Demand and supply of capital transferred from small (local) markets to a large (central) one

activity from the local market (both supply and demand). After integration, savers of both the local and the central areas are prepared to accept a lower rate of return because they will henceforth acquire an asset in a wider, more liquid market (indicated by the downward shift in the combined supply curve of both areas). Integration does not change the curve of borrowers, so the local and central curves of demand have been added up to form the new curve for the common market D_{co}. Borrowers of both areas will thus get a better deal in the central market. The new equilibrium price of capital will lie below the price prevailing on both the local and central capital markets before integration.

This may have considerable influence on the way the integration of capital markets takes shape. Relatively small countries will almost always find it more profitable to integrate with a third large market than with each other, for such a combined market is likely to be less efficient than the external one (see Chapter 10 for the practical relevance of this observation).

Interrelations between goods and factor markets and the effects of barriers to movement

Are goods and factor movements substitutes or complements?

The creation of a customs union profoundly affects the labour and capital markets in the two countries concerned, and the integration of production-factor markets affects the production of goods and thus trade. The close relations found to exist between them have induced economists to study the mutual impact of the two forms of integration.

The integration of goods markets may equalise factor prices (see Chipman, 1965/66). Suppose there are two countries that are differently endowed with the production factors, labour and capital. In country A labour is abundant while capital is scarce, which leads to a relatively low price of labour. In country B, on the contrary, capital is abundantly available but labour is scarce; as a result capital is relatively cheap. There is no exchange of goods or of production factors. This situation has an impact on the prices of goods. Suppose there are two products x and y. With the prevailing production technology (identical in both countries) good x is labour-intensive and good y capital-intensive; consequently, product x will be relatively cheap in country A and product y in country B.

Suppose now the two countries start trading with each other while the production factors remain immobile internationally. According to comparative-cost theory, country A will then export good x and country B good y. The trade relations thus created will affect the production structure of both countries. On the assumption of full internal mobility of production factors, the hope of profit from trade will induce producers in either country to shift resources to the production of the good for which they have a comparative advantage. So country A will curtail the production of good y and divert the production factors thus set free to sector x, expanding it and enabling it to export part of its output. In country B, on the other hand, the production of good y is expanded at the expense of good x.

From the above theoretical exercise it follows that there is a relation of *substitution* between goods and factor movements (Mundell, 1957). This occurs in two ways:

- *Movement of goods substitutes for the movement of production factors.* The change in the production structure entails a change in the demand for production factors, which will in turn lead to a change in relative prices. An amount of capital becomes available in country A as the production of good y is reduced; given the technology, relatively small switches in the amount of capital may boost the production of good x considerably. On the assumption of full competition on factor markets (an unlikely assumption, especially when wages are at stake), in country A capital will become cheaper and labour more expensive, while in country B the opposite occurs. So in both countries the relatively high factor prices will go down and the relatively low ones up, and in certain conditions complete equalisation of factor prices may even be achieved. In that case, there would be no more incentive for labour and capital to move from one country to another. In other words, the creation of a customs union would dispense with the need to create a common market; trade is a substitute for factor movement.
- *Factor movements substitute for goods trade.* The movement of production factors will alter the relative scarcities of the two production factors in countries A and B, and thus equalise their prices. This will in turn reduce the cost differences between the two countries in the production of goods x and y, thus removing the stimulus to trade in these goods.

However interesting its results, the theory just described is not very helpful for practical purposes (Hufbauer, 1968) since its assumptions rarely hold in practice: markets are not characterised by perfect competition, factors are not perfectly mobile, countries are differently endowed with natural resources, and so on. Thus the substitution relationship has been questioned too (Markusen, 1983). A relation of *complementarity* may occur in two ways:

- *Factor movements lead to trade.* One case in point in capital mobility is international direct investments of the optimal location type that engender goods trade. A case of labour mobility is the differences in tastes of migrants that may lead to a demand by the host country for goods that are typical of the home country of the migrant.
- *Trade leads to factor movement.* If there are economies of scale in production, countries may specialise in that good (for example, aircraft). Increase in the export of that industry may boost the price of the factor with specific skills that are exclusively used in production for export. If countries had equal factor prices before trade, the liberalisation of goods trade may thus lead to factor price differences that in turn will trigger factor movements.

Welfare effects of various types of trade impediments under conditions of capital mobility

If goods and factor movements are substitutes, the question arises whether it is better to integrate goods markets or factor markets; in other words, the question is how to achieve the optimum mix of goods, services, capital and labour movement. Theoretical work on this issue is scarce, and mostly concerned with the relations between third-world and developed countries (Bhagwati, 1987b). In western countries the answers tend to be politically tinged. As migration of labour is considered socially undesirable, most governments would prefer the movement of goods and of capital to take care of the equalisation of prices on goods and factor markets. And as the free movement of capital is closely bound up with macro-economic policy making, for which governments are reluctant to give up autonomy, goods trade will in general be preferred to capital movement.[3]

However some theoretical indications for the optimum choice can be distilled from the effects of trade barriers on welfare, if the analysis described in Chapter 5 is extended to a situation in which capital is free to move from one country to the other (Neary, 1987). The partial-equilibrium diagram of Figure 5.2 is therefore complemented with a supply curve of goods that comes within reach when investors (such as industrialists) can use foreign capital. In Figure 8.5, the curves D_a, S_w, S_{w+t} and S_a represent, respectively, home demand, world supply without and with a tariff t, and home supply without capital mobility. S_{cm} is the curve representing the supply of country A on the assumption that capital can be imported. To facilitate the comparison of several situations this curve passes through point G (where free trade obtains). This common market supply curve is more elastic than that of home supply, as producers can now use better combinations of capital and labour, which lowers production cost.

Now capital mobility has different welfare effects for tariffs, quantitative restrictions (QR) and voluntary export restraints (VER).

- *Tariff.* Consumers suffer a welfare loss of *IUJ* due to the introduction of a tariff *t* (compare Figure 5.2), which is equal in both integrated and non-integrated capital markets. However on the producer side the welfare loss from a tariff increases from the triangle *GRH* without capital mobility to the much larger triangle *GR'H'* with capital mobility (see also Neary and Ruane, 1984). In the same operation the government revenue decreases from *HRUI* to *H'R'UI.*
- *Quota.* Introduction of a quantitative restriction of the size *RU* raises the price to the level p_{w+t} when the capital markets are segmented, but only to p_i in a situation with capital mobility.

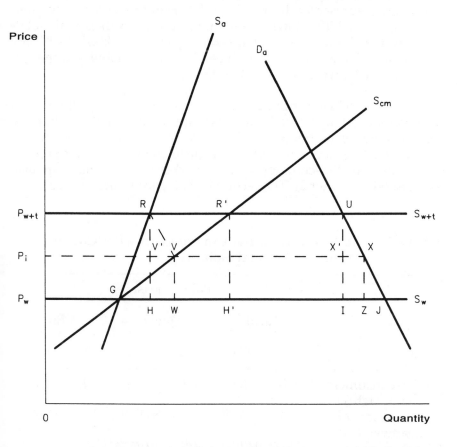

Figure 8.5   Welfare effects of trade impediments with and without capital-market integration

This is illustrated by the figure: by drawing a line parallel to D_a through R, intersecting S_{cm} at point V, we apply the same quota ($VX = WZ$ equals RU) but arrive at a much lower domestic price p_i. We assume that the quota rights are sold by a system of auctioneering to foreign producers; with capital mobility the government revenue is $WVXZ$, which in the present case is of the same order of magnitude as the revenue the government would get from a tariff under conditions of capital mobility. The welfare cost of a QR under a common market is the total of the areas GVW and ZXJ, the loss suffered by consumers being far below the cost of a tariff (the difference being $IUXZ$), while to producers the cost (with the present S_{cm} curve) remains about the same (area GRH being approximately equal to area GVW).

- VER. When a voluntary export restraint is applied, the assumption regarding the government revenue no longer holds. The 'rent' represented by rectangle $HRUI$ in the situation without capital mobility flows to foreign producers. With capital mobility, the loss to the domestic economy is only $WVXZ$. As $WVXZ$ equals $HV'X'I$, the gain induced by capital mobility is the difference between the two: $V'RUX'$.

The first conclusion from the above analysis (of which the results are summarised in Table 8.3 – see also Figure 8.5) is that to introduce capital mobility without abolishing the tariffs spells a loss to the economy, which is one reason why a customs union should precede the creation of the common capital market (a view that was also expressed in Chapter 2). The second is that, once tariffs are abolished

Table 8.3   Effects of various trade instruments with (CM) and without (CU) capital mobility

	Policy measures					
	Tariff		Quota		VER	
Category	CU	CM	CU	CM	CU	CM
Loss to consumers (deadweight)	IUJ	IUJ	IUJ	ZXJ	IUJ	ZXJ
Loss to producers (deadweight)	GRH	$GR'H'$	GRH	GVW	GRH	GVW
Government revenue	$HRUI$	$H'R'UI$	$HRUI$	$WVXZ$	—	—

and capital is made mobile, the cost of applying quotas and VERs is much reduced (which may explain in part why these trade instruments have been so popular under the conditions prevailing in the 1980s).

Effects on the international distribution of factor returns of removing trade impediments after integration of the capital market

In a previous section we have seen that partial liberalisation of capital markets may precede the liberalisation of goods (commodity) markets. If under these conditions two countries enter into a customs union, the welfare effects are more complicated than the ones described in Chapter 5. 'There are additional gains and losses for the host country which arise from the change in rents earned by foreign companies and that imply a redistribution of income between the latter and the host country. In case of an importable commodity produced by foreign firms where price falls after integration, the host country will gain from the reduction in foreign company rents and vice versa' (Tironi, 1982). Figure 8.6 (which is very similar to Figure 5.2) illustrates the point for the following two cases.

Foreign profit diversion (FPD) We assume that the whole production in A of good x is realised in the plants created in A by direct investments of foreign firms. Previous to the customs union the production is OC, determined by the world market price plus tariff (p_{w+t}). If a customs union is formed, with a fully elastic supply from B, the production in A will go down to OB, and quantity BE will be imported from country B. Recall that the creation of a customs union creates a net welfare gain of MUN on the consumer side and of KRL on the producer side. However there is an additional gain for country A of $AFRK$, because this amount (which we assume was previously a remittance of foreign profits of country A to country B, or, in welfare economic terms, a rent paid to companies from country B producing in A) is now transformed into an indigenous consumer surplus. Evidently the effect is the same when more countries are involved and the line AN is no longer p_b but becomes p_{cm}.

Foreign profit creation (FPC) A similar reasoning can be applied to the case where country A is the most efficient producer. Assume the presence of foreign firms in country A that produce at the price OA. Creation of a customs union with a country B that until now has had a very high price level and very high protection implies that a customs tariff for the whole union is set at AF and that the new price for the customs union as a whole becomes OF. The welfare effects will be those of the case analysed in Chapter 5 as one of protectionism. However, with the presence of foreign firms, an additional loss is incurred on top of the traditional negative welfare effects of *KRL* and *MUN*. It springs from the part of the consumer surplus *AFRK* that is transformed into additional rents earned by the foreign producer in A and thus transferred abroad.

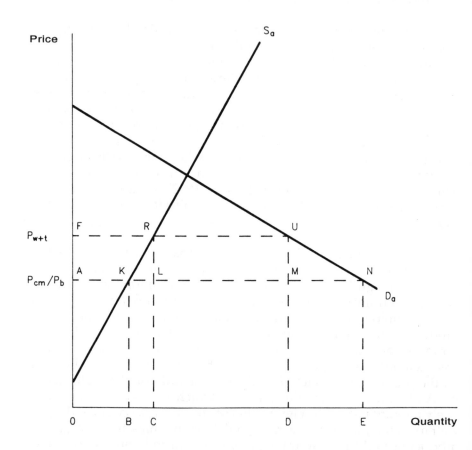

Figure 8.6   Effects on factor earning under partial integration of goods and capital markets

The significance of these effects for the advantages of the formation of a customs union depends critically on the origin of the foreign capital. Should the capitalists of the partner country B be the investors in A, then the negative FPC effect for country A will be compensated by a net positive effect of the same size for country B; the inverse would apply to the FPD effect. In both cases, however, the problem is only one of distribution of wealth, not of net gains of integration. The situation is different, however, if the investment in A is owned by capitalists of a third country, when the FPC effect will become a net loss for the customs union as a whole, and the FPD effect a net welfare gain.

Different forms of capital movement with free trade and protection

The theory of international capital is not a sufficient base for a study of the effects of a common market on capital movements. The reason is that very often international capital transactions are not made as portfolio transactions, but in the form of direct investments (DI). Typically direct investments are internal to the company involved but external to both countries where they operate. DI mostly involve the transfer not only of capital but also of other resources, such as technological know-how, management and marketing skills. Now it is the expected return on the total of the transferred resources rather than on the capital per se that is the rationale for firms to engage in direct foreign investment. Several approaches have been tried to explain DI (Carson, 1982) welded together into an eclectic approach that has provided a fertile basis for further analysis (Dunning, 1979). The principal hypothesis of that approach is that a firm will engage in foreign direct investment if three conditions are satisfied:

- it possesses net ownership advantage *vis-à-vis* firms of other nationalities in serving particular markets. These ownership advantages largely take the form of the possession of intangible assets – a technological lead, for instance – which are, at least for a period of time, exclusive or specific to the firm possessing them;
- on the assumption that the previous condition is satisfied, it must then be more beneficial to the company possessing these advantages to internalise its advantages through an extension of its own activities than to externalise them through licensing and similar contracts with foreign firms;
- once these conditions are satisfied, it must be profitable for the firm to utilise these advantages in conjunction with at least some factor inputs (including natural resources) outside its home country; otherwise foreign markets would be served entirely by exports and domestic markets by domestic production.

Assume that capital movement for direct investment is free between two countries; the type of DI will vary according to whether or not trade in goods is free as well (Dunning, 1980; de Jong, 1981, among others). We can distinguish two types of foreign direct investments dependent on the situation with respect to goods trade:

- *Protection.* If country A operates trade impediments, firms from B that want to export to A need a comparative advantage superior to the level of the tariff equivalent of country A's trade barrier. This advantage may be based on superior production technology, on the exclusive right to use a patent for the product, or, more generally, on better management or entrepreneurial skills. Exporting firms of country B who judge their advantage real but inferior to the tariff, and firms of B unwilling to have their profit margin taxed away by the tariff, will consider setting up production in country A. This necessitates a direct investment of country B in country A. Many governments are keen to attract such direct investment to further their country's development. Firms in B will invest in A to be able to serve the markets of A. Such investments (often called 'tariff-jumping' investments) are based on product differentiation and tend to be substitutes for trade.
- *Free trade.* Many firms following a strategy of growing through product specialisation opt for operation on several markets, wanting to export to foreign markets from their home base. However this may not always prove the optimum solution, as production in other countries may be less costly. Within the market area, a location will be chosen for each plant that is optimal in view of the prevailing market conditions and other locational determinants such as transport cost, taxes and so on. To cash in on the advantages of international division of labour within the firm (such as scale economies and use of factors in different countries), the type of direct investment that could be called 'optimum location seeking' will then be preferred. After production is started, international trade will develop. Some countries will specialise in one good, other countries in others. Often the direction of the investment is contrary to the direction of trade; that is, the export of capital goes hand-in-hand with the importation of goods, and vice versa.

The abolition of tariffs is not a sufficient reason to stop the first type of direct investment. Indeed even in a customs union other barriers may persist that are equally important impediments to trade; these may include poor access to government contracts or the obligation to comply with national technical norms that compel firms to keep in close contact with national authorities (see Chapters 2 and 16). In some cases the type of foreign direct investment that actually occurs is difficult to tell from the observed pattern. On the one hand, firms may have production facilities in a series of countries to jump trade impediments in those countries. On the other hand, they may do the same in a situation of free trade because consumer tastes vary among countries, and technical factors do not push towards production on a very large scale.

Capital movements under conditions of integration

The creation of a common market implies the liberalisation of capital movement, including foreign direct investments. The pattern and magnitude of direct investment flows depend on the characteristics of a country. The more the firms in a country show entrepreneurial competitiveness (related to ownership advantages) the higher will be outward DI, as these firms will want to cash in on their advantages by investing abroad. The higher the locational attractiveness of a country, the higher the inward DI, as firms will have advantages in producing there rather than elsewhere (Sleuwaegen, 1987).

The DI flows will be affected by integration, as the different measures of goods and factor market integration affect firms in member and third countries in a different way (Yannopoulos, 1990) and hence will lead to different strategic responses of firms to their new production environment.

- *Intra-union*. The creation of a common market by the liberalisation of goods and factor movements leads to a restructuring of the economies of the partner countries and to an increase in trade. This is partly based on the static trade creation and expansion effects and mainly on the dynamic effects of economies of scale and innovation. This increased specialisation entails a profound reorganisation and rationalisation of production and obliges firms to redefine their international investment strategies. The combined effect of the opening of goods markets and of capital markets will lead to an increase in DI of the optimal location type. The pattern of these increased DI flows will be determined by the combination of entrepreneurial and locational advantages of each country for each activity under new conditions of integrated markets.
- *Extra-union*. The trade diversion effect of the customs union formation will induce foreign producers that experience a loss in their export market to start production within the union (tariff jumping). Other third country producers may want to exploit the dynamic growth effects caused by integration and decide to set up activities within the union (in other words, integration has enhanced the locational attractiveness of the union). In both cases incoming DI increases, while imports

decrease. This does not mean that external trade decreases too, as the union producers may have gained competitiveness on world markets and start exporting (compare Figure 5.11). The effect of market integration on outgoing direct investment is not certain. On the one hand, one may expect an increase, as the growth effects of integration may permit many union firms to obtain new entrepreneurial (ownership) advantages that they will want to exploit in third countries. If the relative position of a location in a union country deteriorates relative to a third country, an increase in DI may follow. If, on the contrary, the union performs better than third countries, a decrease of outgoing union DI may be the result.

So it is not possible a priori to say whether trade and DI are substitutes or complements.

Towards a theory of international production

Interrelations between goods and factor movements

International trade and international movement of production factors, at least of capital, should not be considered in isolation, as they tend to be different reflections of the spatial organisation of the production process by private firms. The pattern is shaped by such factors as prevailing technology (which provides the potential for economies of scale), availability and price of factors of production at different locations, the location of demand and the structure of markets, and corporate organisation (see, among others, Helpman and Krugman, 1985; Rugman, 1982).

An interesting model permitting the combination of some of these elements in a simplified view of the international economy is based on the *product life-cycle theory*. This theory distinguishes four stages in the life of each product: (1) introduction, (2) expansion, (3) saturation, and (4) decline. At each stage in this cycle, the companies that produce them show differences in size, profitability and so on; the markets are differently structured and competition takes on different forms; and the division between capital, labour inputs and returns also displays wide variation. A schematic view constructed from indications in the work of various authors is given in Table 8.4.

Many elements of this framework are relevant to the process of integration. A common market may speed up innovation and enforce changes in industrial structure (see Chapter 12); it may sharpen competition (see Chapter 16) and thus lead to economies of scale, cost reductions, product improvement and a better export potential (see Chapter 5). New producers are potential competitors on the mass markets, and by innovation and imitation they will speed up the passage through the life-cycle described above.

But it is the bottom part of the table that indicates how the use of differentiated production factors and the location of production and trade take shape internationally. The continuous process is set going by a technical change inspiring the development of a new product. At the first stage of its development this product will need close contact with existing customers, located in developed countries. At the second stage, it will still require special skills to produce and a strong market potential to sell; this means that the production will be located in developed areas where it generates a high value added and sustains high wages. At the maturity stage, margins will fall and, to cut costs, the production will be relocated to areas where wages are lower. The richer countries will change over to new products that are still at an earlier stage of development.

Here again a common market is likely to influence the process. First, the larger market will offer prospects to specialist producers who would not have been viable in smaller, nationally segmented markets. Next it presents a sufficient diversity in production environments, thereby offering better opportunities for the location of firms in the course of the expansion and saturation stages. Finally it makes it possible to find locations to accommodate within its territory the production of articles at the final stage of their life-cycle, and thus postpone the moment of delocation of these activities to third (-world) countries.

Divergence or convergence in development?

The distribution of welfare among the different partners in an integration scheme is an issue of overriding political importance. The objective is in general to stimulate poor countries to catch up with the richer ones. The question whether integration of product and factor markets does contribute to this objective is therefore of particular relevance. Now the answer to that question is not clear; there are theoretical arguments that plead for and others that plead against.

- *Convergence.* The neoclassical and Heckscher–Ohlin–Samuelson models lead to the conclusion that factor returns (that is, interests and wages) tend to converge when markets are opened up after the creation of a customs union and a common market (see Figure 8.2). However the outcome of such models depends on many assumptions, the most important probably being that markets function properly and that there are no impediments to movements. The model based on the life-cycle of the product

Table 8.4   **Characteristics of companies during the life-cycle of a product**

	Introduction	Expansion
Sales	Small	Fast growth
Products	Very diversified	Few competing concepts
Innovation	Very high product innovation	High product innovation Increasing attention to process innovation
Structure	Few suppliers in separate markets, joint ventures, innovation, monopolies	New entrants Deconcentration, licensing
Competition	By adapting products to needs of specific clients, pioneering	Imitative improvement Price competition
Profit/loss	Initial losses; also incidental profits	Considerable profits
Jobs	Little employment, highly qualified	Fast-growing number of jobs, decreasing qualifications
Capital/ labour ratio	Labour-intensive processes	Intensification of capital input
Location of production	Developed (central) areas	Intermediate areas
Markets	Regional and national markets	Increase of exports; growing imports from partner countries

Saturation	Fall
Slow growth	Stagnation and decline
Standardised	Only brands different
Low product innovation, accent on process innovation	Absence of innovation
Strong tendencies towards concentration and oligopolies, concerted practices, mergers	Restructuring cartels; diversification through takeovers of young firms in markets with good prospects; splitting up of firms
Product differentiation High promotion cost	Cut-throat competition, rationalising Collusion
Decreasing profits	Increasing number of companies with loss
Beginning decline in job numbers, simplification of tasks	Large-scale reductions in jobs
Large-scale investment in capital-intensive processes	Reduction of labour through closure of the most labour-intensive plants
Low-cost areas	Third-world countries
High interpenetration of markets; third-country competition on home markets	High pressure of imports from third world

may also lead to convergence between the levels of development of different areas in the common market. It comes about by the gradual absorption of skills and know-how in areas benefiting from direct investment to develop production at the middle stages of a product's life-cycle. This permits them to develop gradually their own research and innovation and to upgrade the quality of the production, at the same time increasing the capacity of their productive system to sustain high wages and high profits.

- *Divergence* may occur as the effect of an initial imbalance that causes cumulation when coupled with investment behaviour based on, for example, a technology lead and labour movement based on career potential (Myrdal, 1956, 1957; Vernon, 1966; Hirsch, 1974). This may be illustrated with the help of Figure 8.2. The *AFD* and *BEF* curves, being about equal at the outset, may shift under dynamic conditions (see also Figure 18.1). If the environment in country A is better for growth, as the result, for example, of a higher input in technological innovation than in country B, the curve *AFD* may shift upwards while the *BEF* curve remains where it is. The expectation of a continuation of this trend may lead to a situation where the expected returns on labour and capital are higher in A than in B and consequently where labour and capital may start to flow from B to A. This, in turn, may lead to further dynamic effects.

This effect of cumulative causation towards divergence with both capital and labour movements can be illustrated with a two-country, two-product case (Krugman, 1979). The two composite commodities are 'New' with a high value added, and 'Old' with a low value added; the two countries are: 'North', which is rich, and 'South', which is poor. Capital is mobile and labour is not.

Figure 8.7 shows how the capital stock of these two countries is allocated; the situation for North is on the left-hand side of the graph, and that for South on the right-hand side. The curve D_s shows the marginal product of capital in the South, which is also the demand for capital. D_n shows the marginal product of capital in the North, measured in terms of old goods at some given relative price of new goods. At that relative price, the equilibrium return on capital is r_2 with a stock of capital K_s in the South and K_n in the North (K_n+K_s being the total stock of capital). Now if technical progress leads to the birth of a new good and that new good is much in demand so that the demand for old goods drops, the relative price of new goods rises. The marginal product of capital in the North increases, which can be illustrated by the shift in the curve D_n to $D_{n'}$. As a consequence, the return of capital rises to r_1, and capital moves from South to North ($K_{n'}>K_n$; $K_{s'}<K_s$; $K_{n'}+K_{s'} = K_n+K_s$). This has consequences for factor prices. The income of northern workers relative to southern workers rises, for two reasons. For one thing, the rising relative price of the goods they produce sustains higher wages and, for another, their real wage in terms of output rises because of the reallocation of capital. Southern wages, on the contrary, fall.

The lesson from this is that the technological change in country North triggers off a capital inflow. The rents of the North's monopoly on new goods are collected by the immobile factor of production: labour. So technological change under these conditions equalises the returns on the mobile factor (capital) while increasing the inequality of the immobile factors (labour).

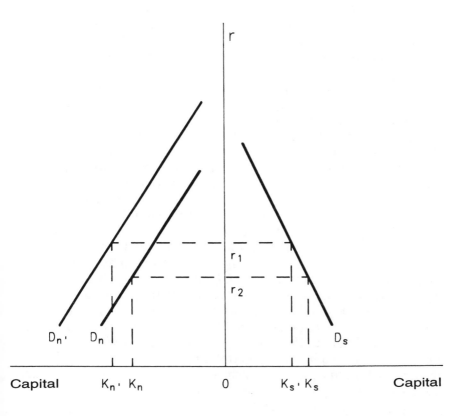

Figure 8.7   **Allocation of the capital stock to countries under conditions of technological dominance**

Selective labour mobility

In the previous sections we have seen the critical importance of the life-cycle for a number of phenomena in the international division of production. Presumably the firms operating in 'Northern' countries in sectors losing their comparative advantage would give up their production and transfer it to lower-wage countries. However parts of the labour force and management may seek to avoid the adaptation cost that is involved, and demand protection against goods imports. If that option is difficult to realise because of international agreements, firms will try to counter lower-price imports in other ways. The most common option is then to cut cost domestically, an option that is feasible only if labour can be imported and effectively paid lower wages than those prevailing in other sections of the industry. That can indeed be achieved by allowing the selective inmigration of foreign workers.

In Figure 8.8 (adapted from Bhagwati, 1982) *OS* represents the real wages of the domestic labour in country A, which is threatened by low-cost competition from outside. *OL* represents the lower, fixed real wages at which foreign labour can be imported to execute the parts of the production process that have lost their comparative advantage. *SHR* is the marginal product curve of the labour that is permitted to immigrate (immigration quota *OJ*) given the input of domestic capital and qualified labour. The output in country A is then *SHJO*, of which only *OLHJ* accrues to foreign workers and the rest, *LSH*, to domestic capitalists. The latter effect makes the policy welfare-improving to the labour-importing country.

So we can conclude that, if the internal labour market can be effectively segmented, capitalists and the unions of the remaining domestic labour of the industry in question will bring pressure to bear on the government to import labour and thus postpone the restructuring of the sector and its relocation to other countries. In view of the net welfare gain of *LSH*, governments will be inclined to accept such a policy for economic reasons (being pushed in the same direction for electoral reasons as well). However, as the product progresses into later stages of the life-cycle, competition from foreign producers is likely to increase, rendering the cost reduction that was made possible by a liberal immigration policy insufficient to keep up the production in country A. Industrialist pressure groups will then cry for protection, supported by both domestic and immigrant labour. After the discussion of the previous sections there is hardly any need to argue that the case for protectionist measures is very weak. Indeed, on top of the well-known welfare losses they would entail (Figure 5.2), a 'foreign-labour income-creation effect' would accrue,

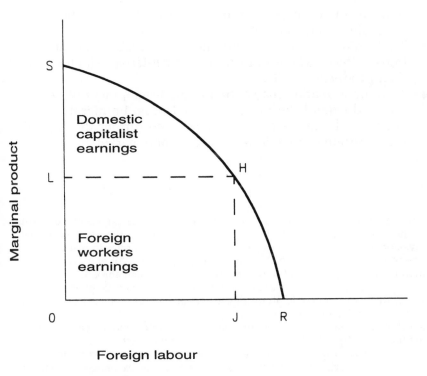

Figure 8.8 Labour import in sunset industries

similar to the foreign-profit creation effect that occurs when capital is owned by foreigners.

Summary and conclusions

- Integration of national labour and capital markets leads to net welfare gains for the participating countries.
- Under certain conditions the integration of goods markets does away with the need for the integration of factor markets, but these conditions are seldom fulfilled.
- Integration of goods markets should precede the integration of capital markets; indeed the costs of protection of goods markets by tariffs and other instruments are much higher under conditions of free capital flows than under conditions of segmented capital markets.
- The international movement of capital in the form of direct investment is a substitute for goods trade in the case of protec-

tion on goods markets, but will create trade in the case of
integrated goods markets.
- Trade, direct investment and migration of labour are all reflections of the decisions of firms as to the international location of
  their production units.
- A common market may enhance the development of new sectors and extend the presence of old ones. Immigration of labour may be resorted to to extend even further the economic
  life of certain productions in the common market.

Notes

1   The reasoning followed here for the movement of labour can easily be adapted
    to the movement of capital. It suffices to put savers in the place of workers,
    investors in the place of employers, and to read interest rates in place of wages.
    The interpretation of the cost difference may be in terms of extra cost of infor-
    mation (markets, taxes and so on) incurred on investment abroad.
2   A list of instruments that may be used to separate markets is given in Chapter
    10; in this case one could think of the use of control or of a foreign capital
    interest tax in B equal to ED $(= r_b - r_a)$.
3   Recall that a major argument for controls on capital movements is not the
    regulation of capital markets, but the stabilisation of exchange rates. However
    this motive for capital controls cannot be upheld, as the instrument is not
    efficient in achieving the objectives; in the long run the exchange rate will have
    to adjust to the basic economic variables (see Chapter 17). A number of other
    arguments for capital controls are based on the need to deal with externalities
    due to market failures and (foreign) government interference (see, among oth-
    ers, Claassen and Wyplosz, 1982). The welfare effects of these controls coupled
    to goods market controls depend on many factors. However such complications
    tend to lose their relevance if all partner countries dismantle their controls, as is
    the case in a common market.

9 Labour

Introduction

Under certain conditions, the creation of a common market entails movements of labour which in turn have a levelling effect on the price of labour (the wages). In this chapter we will describe in some detail how these two phenomena have taken shape in practice with the integration of the labour markets of the EU member countries.

We will start the discussion with the presentation of a few basic concepts, such as the definition and specification of movement and of barriers to movement and the forms and advantages of integration. Next we will devote a section to regulation. Each country has tried to regulate the labour market with a complex whole of national legislation and administrative rules and practices and multinational or bilateral agreements. The EU has first of all ensured unrestricted migration for work reasons within its border to nationals of member states. Next it has gradually increased its regulating of aspects of social policy that influence the functioning of labour markets. We will deal at some length with the regulatory role of the EU in these matters, because without that knowledge the working of the European labour market is hard to grasp.

The exchange of labour among member states through international migration is the subject of the following section.[1] Although labour is much less mobile than goods and capital, labour migration is an important phenomenon. In Western Europe, labour has always been on the move (see, for instance, Winsemius, 1939; Lannes, 1956); the movements were often inspired by political motives.[2] Migration for economic reasons is distinguished from politically induced migration, in that it is voluntary and often intended to be temporary. In this section we will give the results of studies that have tried to explain movements of labour to and in the EU.

Next we will turn to the development of the price of labour under the influence of integration, examining how far wages in the member states of the EU have actually adjusted to the new conditions. We will see that factor prices have indeed converged but that several factors have been at work to prevent the complete elimination of wage differences among member countries of the EU. An evaluation of the welfare effects and a brief summary of the main findings conclude the chapter.

Some basic concepts

Forms of integration

There is free international movement of employed persons if (1) nationals of one member state may unrestrictedly look for and accept a job in another; and (2) self-employed people from one member state are free to settle in another member state to exert their profession or activity.

There are as yet no generally accepted notions to capture the various *forms* in which the labour market may be integrated, but here, too, a distinction can be made along the lines of free trade area and customs union made in Chapter 2. In both a free labour movement area (FLMA) and a labour market union (LMU), employed persons are free to accept a job in any of the partner countries. However, in the FLMA, participant countries are free to establish their own conditions with respect to third countries, while in the LMU that competence is transferred to the union. In the former case, therefore, employed persons from third countries admitted to one member state would not automatically have the right to move freely into other member states. With the fully integrated labour markets in a union, this last limitation does not exist. Full labour market integration means, indeed, that among partner countries (all) restrictions are abolished. But to achieve real integration, measures of positive integration are needed as well. Such positive integration will mostly be realised by coordinating labour market and employment policies, as well as social policies and taxes.

Advantages of integration

The advantages (see previous chapter) hoped for from the free movements of labour (that is to say, the integration of labour markets) depend on the type of exchange chosen. In general terms, the following advantages are expected from permanent migration:

- for supply of labour (employed persons) a better chance to capitalise on their specific qualities;

- for those demanding labour, better possibilities of choosing a technology with an optimum capital/labour ratio from the management point of view;
- levelling of differences in production cost as far as they were due to the compartmentalisation of the labour market.

In the case of temporary migration a distinction must be made between advantages to the emigration country and those to the immigration country (Scott, 1967; Kindleberger *et al.*, 1979; MacMillan, 1982).

- Emigration countries expect three major advantages: (1) to ease their unemployment situation (and lower the budgetary cost of unemployment benefits); (2) to ease their budget and balance-of-payments problems through remittances; and (3) to improve the quality of the labour force (return migrants having acquired skills abroad).
- Immigration countries hope to gain a direct production effect: by adding foreign workers with skills that are scarce to their own manpower in places where investments require it, they are able to make the most of their own capital stock and indigenous manpower. Sometimes the advantages are manifest only in times of cyclical highs, but they may also be of a more structural nature. Immigration may also have a redistributive welfare effect: the larger labour supply lowers the wage rate of the indigenous labour force; the additional income is shared by capital and foreign labour (Chapter 8). Moreover the pressure on inflation is diminished because of relaxation of labour scarcity.

The profitable effects of international migration may well be distributed unevenly between sending and receiving countries. In politics, the voices pleading restriction are often louder than those pleading full freedom. The outcome is often free movement of labour within a common market, but a policy of restriction towards third countries. This is the more likely as the common market is supplemented by some form of redistribution mechanism which could offset the potential negative effects of emigration for the less developed member countries (Chapter 18).

Restrictions

To control the international exchange of labour, most governments use permits as a tool (comparable to quantitative restrictions in the exchange of goods), forbidding all immigration without a permit.

The permit may be accompanied by all kinds of restriction, sometimes defined so sharply that in practice no immigration is feasible. The mere abolition of such permits does not mean that factor markets are integrated. There are, indeed, several ways to impede migration of workers; they can be divided into the following categories:

- Access to functions and professions. This can be limited by direct conditions stipulating, for instance, that foreign nationals cannot be lawyers. It can also be done in a subtler way, as with the setting of professional demands which foreigners cannot satisfy (for instance because foreign certificates are not recognised); or by making public labour exchange services accessible to a country's own nationals only.
- Accommodation conditions. To accept a job, a person must have accommodation. A residence permit for foreigners can be refused or made hard to get. Restrictions can also be imposed on obtaining residential accommodation or schooling for children, and so on.
- Financial disadvantages. These can be created, for instance, by imposing higher taxes, or charging premiums for social security without granting rights to benefits. Finally the transfer of earnings can be restricted (foreign currency).

Motives for impediments

Opponents of the free movement of the production factor, labour, raise certain arguments, which are mostly directed against immigration. The following arguments against immigration are frequently heard:

- pressure on wages: at equal demand, additional supply leads to lower prices;
- increase in unemployment: demand remaining the same, additional supply expels existing supply;
- rise in government expenditure: because foreigners often need costlier social provisions (education and housing, for instance) and make more demands on social security than nationals;
- societal disruption: cultural differences tend to disturb the social equilibrium;
- regional disparities: labour tends to move to concentrations of economic activities;
- balance of payments deterioration: via increased invisible imports (remittances);
- high cost of recruitment and travel.

On the other hand, arguments are also raised against emigration, such as:

- loss of human capital essential to the development of the economy;
- depopulation of certain regions, causing waste of societal capital;
- opportunity cost of forgone output.

Developed countries rarely inhibit emigration, but for developing countries there may be valid arguments to do so.

EU regime

Treaty

The Treaty of the European Economic Community forbids (Article 7) any discrimination on the grounds of nationality. This means that nationals of other member states shall in principle receive the same treatment on the labour market as a state's own nationals. The treaty works out the principle of non-discrimination differently for employed persons and persons practising an activity on their own account and responsibility.

- *Workers* are persons performing work in an employment situation against payment. 'The freedom of movement shall entail the abolition of any discrimination based on nationality between workers of the member states as regards employment, remuneration and other conditions of work and employment' (Articles 48 ff).
- *Self-employed*, or *independent* persons are those who exercise an economic activity in their own interest and on their own responsibility. Member state nationals have the right to set up businesses abroad (agencies, branches or subsidiaries) and the right to take up and pursue activities as self-employed persons and to set up and manage undertakings in a member state, on the same conditions as those laid down for its own nationals by the law of the country where the establishment is effected (Articles 52 ff).

The rules of the Treaty as regards non-discrimination can be specified as follows.

- *Sectors of activity.* All sectors of the economy are affected, with one exception: 'this freedom shall not apply to employment in the public sector (Article 48.3) and activities which in that state are connected, even occasionally, with the exercise of official authority' (Article 55). Given the prominent place which the government now occupies in the economy of many member states, manifest in the large shares of workers with a civil servant or equivalent status in total employment, large portions of the labour market could thus be excluded from free migration. However the Court of Justice has pronounced clearly in several verdicts that such an interpretation would be contrary to the intention of the Treaty. The Court has laid down that the notion of 'public sector' must be understood narrowly, as comprising exclusively those positions and tasks which imply direct or indirect involvement in the exercise of public authority, or functions which concern the general interests of the state and in particular its internal and external safety.
- *Member countries.* Non-discrimination (Article 48) does not mean that wages in the different member countries have to be equal, but that there shall be no difference in the remuneration of workers of different nationalities working in the same establishment and country. Before the Treaty of Rome was drafted, there had been a discussion about the need to harmonise wages and the other elements of manpower cost firms have to pay (such as social security contributions, holidays and fringe benefits) prior to the internal liberalisation of labour movements. Most of those participating in the debate did not recognise such a need, however. The basic idea of the founding fathers was that wages were to be determined in the process of national bargaining between trade unions and employers.
- *Sexes.* The Treaty stipulates that men and women are to receive equal pay for equal work (Article 119). However this principle departed from the practice in many member states. It was not strictly needed to ensure the proper functioning of the common labour market, so its introduction in the Treaty represented in a sense a first step in setting up common principles for social policy.

The Treaty makes a distinction between the situations during and after the so-called 'transition' period, which was to end on 1 January 1970. Some verdicts of the Court have made it clear that, since that date, the anti-discrimination clause does apply in full and can be appealed to directly before the national judge. The EEC Treaty also obliges the member states to cooperate in such matters as social security, work conditions, health and safety conditions and so on.

(Articles 117–118), so as to create the conditions for a good functioning of the labour market.

Regulations, directives, verdicts and programmes

The rights of movement of workers, and of establishment of independents, have no meaning unless accompanied by some other rights. In the course of the transition period, several regulations (directly applicable in the member states) were issued by the Council to give substance to the general stipulations (Articles 48 to 54). They concern a variety of matters.

General applicability   Discrimination is forbidden not only to the public authorities of member states, but also to companies, institutions and so on, and to private employers (Regulation 1612/68). This means that all stipulations in collective or individual labour contracts as to conditions, remuneration, dismissal and so on, are null and void by force of law if they contain elements which are discriminating against workers from other member states.

Priority   Member states must pass on to the labour exchanges of other member states vacancies and applications (Article 49a and 49d; Regulation 1612/68). The Commission has recently made new proposals to improve the working of SEDOC (European system for the international clearance of vacancies and applications for employment) (CEC, 1992b).

Access   Elimination of illegal discriminatory regulations subjecting immigrants from other member states to higher taxation, claims of caution money, certificates of solvency or of good conduct, criteria for admission, for the obtaining of licences to join professional or sectoral organisations with or without ruling authority, and so on.

Social security   To prevent the loss of claims while moving to another country, principles have been laid down (Regulation 1408/71) and guidelines set (CEC, 1992c) purporting to prevent discrimination in matters of benefits (such as for sickness) of migrating workers in respect of non-migrating colleagues, and to prevent the collection of double premiums as well as the payment of double benefits with respect to the same period of insurance.[3]

Move and stay   The right to move to and stay freely in another member state (Directives 68/360 and 73/148) applies not only to the worker (employed or independent) moving to another country, but also to his or her spouse, children and family members. The right to stay is not forfeit, in principle, after the professional activity or employment have ended. A closely related right is that to housing, which also exists for workers, the self-employed and their families. It concerns the right to either rent or purchase a dwelling. For independent workers, the right to purchase land and buildings for the purpose of setting up in business is relevant.[4]

Payments and capital transactions   Without the possibility of one's money crossing frontiers for investments and payments and for repatriating profits and transferring wages, the principle of free movement of workers would be completely eroded.

Professional education   The right to education (general and professional) and to retraining applies to foreign workers and independents in the same way as for nationals of the receiving country. These rights also apply to the children of foreign workers (for example, the apprentice system).

Mutual recognition of diplomas   On the one hand, education is generally looked upon as a typical national concern, and the Treaty does not provide for cooperation on that front. On the other hand, free movement cannot be realised without mutual recognition of qualifications for jobs and professions, so much work has been done in that area (for example, Directive 85/432 for pharmacy, Directive 89/48 on higher education).

Wages

Neither the (original and amended) Treaty nor the relevant regulations and directives contain rules about wages. This implies that the remuneration discrepancies that exist among countries are accepted; indeed wages remain a matter of concern of national contractual parties. Wage differences are due to several types of differences between EU countries, such as industrial structure, productivity and supply factors. Moreover institutions are different, and so are the attitudes of trade unions and of employers' organisations, the legal frameworks in which they operate and their respective bargaining strengths (Seidel, 1983; Ferner and Hyman, 1992; CEC, 1967).

In the future the EU may have some influence on wage formation. The legal base for this has been developed in the framework of the building up of a 'Social Europe' (Article 118, adapted by the Single Act and the Social Chapter in the Maastricht Treaty). Now, if management and labour so desire, their 'dialogue' (in other words negotiations) may lead to contractual relations. Up to now this framework has only been used for labour-related matters. Notably the employers' organisations shy away from the idea of Europe-wide constraints on their operations; they have no intention whatsoever of being involved in too many matters, and have flatly refused to deal with wages as such.

The argument is that Europe-wide wage formation will lead to inflexibilities and regional unemployment. Indeed, in many European countries, the drive of labour unions towards nationwide bargaining has made regional differences in wages disappear and thus widened the regional differences in unemployment. As the same tendency would manifest itself on the European scale, most parties involved (trade unions, employers organisations and governments) in high- and low-wage countries agree that wage formation should for some time remain a national issue.

Present situation

The application of the fundamental principles of the free movement of salaried workers and of the free establishment of independents, laid down in the Treaty and interpreted by the Court, coupled with the efforts at harmonisation of related issues by the Commission, have had as a result that, by the end of the transition period (1970), a free market for labour had been realised for most activities. However, for a large number of professions, problems continued to exist springing from different qualifications required for access to their practice in different countries (see Chapters 14 and 15). Other activities, too, continued to encounter difficulties in actual practice. Some of these difficulties can be explained by deeply rooted cultural differences, others are of a legal or administrative nature.

The Commission has tried to reduce the remaining obstacles as much as possible by further harmonisation of the rules. This was given impetus by the programme for the completion of the internal market that created a completely free internal labour market by 1992 (see Chapter 16). This was based on the Single European Act of 1987 that defines the internal market as an area without internal frontiers in which free movement of goods, services, workers and capital is ensured.

The Schengen Treaty of 1985 tried to accelerate the process of extending the freedom of movement from workers to all persons. For a group of continental EU countries this Treaty laid down very detailed rules about controls at the outer frontiers, about visa obligations, about cooperation between police and the courts of member states and so on. The group has subsequently been enlarged by Southern member states. Many of these rules have now been further developed as administrative cooperations. One should bear in mind that these rules do not change the fundamental rights, but only their mode of application.

The Maastricht Treaty, by introducing the concept of citizenship of the union, specifies (Article 8a) that 'every citizen of the union shall have the right to move and reside freely within the territory of the member states'. This, too, has still to be elaborated and is unlikely to change the fundamental rights already existing.

Third countries

The notions of free trade area and customs union can be transferred from goods trade to the movements of production factors, in particular as regards the frontiers between the EU and third countries. While the Treaty clearly lays down a preferential regime for member states as far as goods trade is concerned, it is far less outspoken as to free movement of persons. Neither do the regulations and directives implementing the Treaty give unequivocal rules about the treatment of nationals of third countries (CEC, 1979a). Moreover the situation differs for workers and self-employed persons. The various legal rules can be interpreted as follows in economic terms:

Workers   The priority of workers from other EU member states is implied rather than prescribed, so that member states may extend certain advantages to workers from third countries. For the latter, the advantages are restricted to the member state involved; the other member states are not obliged to apply them as well.

Independents   The right to establish is confined to natural persons who are nationals of a member state. Nationals of third countries are excluded; they are subject to the rules each individual member state cares to issue. The fact that they are established in one member state does not give them the right to establish in other member states. The right to establish in the entire EU does apply to persons who are nationals of a member state but are still residing outside the EU. The right to establish also applies to workers with an EU nationality who want to set up in business in another member state.

Apparently, as far as the movements of active persons are concerned, the EU resembles a free trade area rather than a customs union. Obviously such a situation is difficult to maintain as physical frontiers are abolished (see Chapter 16); for that reason attempts are made to work out a common admission policy for workers and independents (and other non-active immigrants) from third countries. However, as neither the Single Act nor the Treaty on the European Union, nor any international organisation[5] regulates these points, there is little legal basis, with the consequence that the matter is still left to the discretion of the member states (see Chapter 19).

International exchange of labour (migration)

The six original member states (1958–73)

In the first decade after the Second World War, international migration of labour in Western Europe had been on a small scale. In the 1950s, Italy provided about half the supply of migrant labour, while Switzerland and France were the greatest demanders. Moreover France received significant numbers of immigrants from North Africa. By the end of the 1950s, the situation was changing. Germany started to recruit foreign labour, at first mainly from Italy.

From 1958 onward, the free movement of labour among the six original member states was gradually introduced. In the period between 1958 and 1973 the labour market was tight in all member states except Italy. That was one reason why the number of foreign workers (that is to say, workers originating from one member state and staying in another) remained, in general, limited. Only Italians migrated north in numbers (Table 9.1). However the recruitment of hundreds of thousands of Italians was not sufficient to provide the economies of the 'northern' member states with enough labour, so these countries soon extended their recruiting efforts outside the EU. That immigration enabled the EU to keep activities within its borders which otherwise would have had to relocate outside the EU (entailing outward direct investment flows) (see Chapter 10). Owing to this growing inflow of workers from third countries, the relative share of member countries, in particular Italy, in the inflow was reduced. Other reasons for this drop were the growth of the Italian economy and the reduction of intra-EU wage differences.

Table 9.1   Foreign workers[a] in the EU6 (first work licences[b]), 1958–73

	1958–61	1962–65	1966–69	1970–73
Total (000s)	273	595	565	751
of which EC (%)	60	36	30	26
of which Italy (%)	49	32	26	21

[a]   Algerians in France not counted.
[b]   In 1968, abolished for workers from EC countries.
Source: KEG, DGXV, *Beschäftigung ausländischer Arbeitnehmer* (V264/76-D), several years, Brussels.

The size of the migration flows was actually much larger than indicated by the figures of Table 9.1. Indeed most work licences were valid for a short period only. The holders of such licences, mostly unmarried, unskilled workers, used to arrive at workplaces in Western Europe, stay for a period of two years, and then return to their home country. Around 1970, nearly one million migrants entered the EU, but about the same number returned home. Taking into account migration to other European countries, such as Sweden and Switzerland, and to a lesser extent the UK, we observe in Western Europe, in that period, a yearly gross migration of between two and three million people. In the flows, cyclical patterns can be perceived (Kayser, 1972; Moulaert and Derykere, 1982).

Much of the migration described here was so-called 'organised' migration through recruitment bureaus of the host countries established in the countries of origin. These bureaus often took upon themselves the organisation of transport, medical checks and housing. This means that the size and direction of the flows was ultimately determined by policy. Figure 9.1 shows the principal bilateral recruitment agreements existing at the end of 1973, and hence gives an idea of the direction of migrant flows around 1973. It also shows that at the time Western Europe and the southern and eastern flanks of the Mediterranean indeed formed one large market for unskilled labour.

In the period 1960–73, foreign labour was essential to the economy of European receiving countries. In the original six member states the number of foreigners on the labour market rose between 1960 and 1973 from approximately two million to nearly five million (Table 9.2).[6] The detailed national data show that between 1960 and 1973 the number of foreign workers rose in particular in Germany (by some two million); therefore that country accounts for most of the rise in the number of foreign workers in the entire EU over that period. If we relate the number of foreign workers to the size of the total labour force, we find that in 1970 in five of the six member states (Italy being the exception) an average 7 per cent of total labour supply came from third countries, against 3 to 4 per cent in 1960. For certain sectors the dependency was actually much greater; in particular the metal industry, construction and some service sectors (catering) attracted much foreign labour in this period (Bhagwati *et al.*, 1984).

The first enlargement (1973–81).

In 1973 the UK, Ireland and Denmark became members and from that year onward the free mutual exchange of workers could be extended across the nine member states. Let us see what the situation was at that moment with respect to the interpenetration of labour

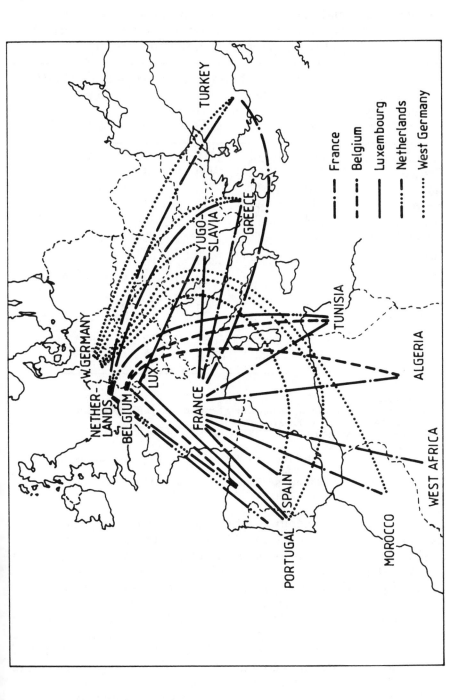

Figure 9.1   Bilateral recruitment agreements, end of 1973

Table 9.2   **Estimate of the number of foreign workers in the member states, 1960–73, and their relative importance (%) in the labour market of the host country**

	Absolute figures (000s)			Percentage of labour force		
	1960[a]	1970[a]	1973[b]	1960[a]	1970[a]	1973[b]
Germany	461	1727	2519	2	6	11
France	1294	1584	1900	6	8	11
Italy	20	30	55	—	—	—
Netherlands	47	134	121	1	3	3
Belgium	170	257	211	5	7	7
Luxemburg	20	27	43	16	21	35
EU6	2012	3759	4849	3	5	7
UK	1233	1815	1751	5	7	7
Ireland	1	2	2	—	—	—
Denmark[c]	15	30	36	1	1	2
EU9	3261	5606	6638	3	6	8
EU12[d]	3300	5600	6600	3	5	6

a   Labour force.
b   Dependent workers.
c   Given the free movement of labour existing between Denmark and Sweden, Norway and Finland, these figures have to be corrected upward.
d   Estimates for total: intra + extra EU12. Figures are rounded. Figures for Spain, Portugal and Greece are very low.
Source: 1960 and 1970: United Nations (1979, p. 324). For Italy, Denmark and Ireland: national statistics and estimates.
1973: KEG, *Beschäftigung ausländischer Arbeitnehmer,* various years, Brussels.

markets of the nine member states. The degree of integration of the EU labour markets in 1973 was still quite modest (3 per cent).

Three types of labour exchange among EU member states can be distinguished. The first refers to a hard core of workers stationed abroad by multinational companies and international organisations, or working as border commuters. The second type refers to emigrated Italians, already discussed in detail in the previous section (about one million). The third type refers to Irish emigrants (almost half a million of them), traditionally destined for the UK; that kind of emigration had already been regulated by bilateral agreement before 1973 (Böhning, 1972; Sexton, *et al.,* 1991).

The workers from third countries in the nine member states can be split into three groups (Table 9.3):

- *Greece, Spain and Portugal.* The destinations of their emigrants show very clear patterns: practically all Portuguese were staying in France, most Spaniards in France but also some in Germany; by far the most Greeks were employed in Germany, a very small proportion in the UK. Emigration was highly important to these three countries. In 1973, 19 per cent of the labour force of Portugal, 9 per cent of the Greek and more than 4 per cent of the Spanish were employed in the EU9.[7] Salt (1976) mentions that migrants had transferred to their home country sums that equalled 24 per cent of imports for Greece, 9 per cent for Spain, and as much as 37 per cent for Portugal.
- *Other Mediterranean countries.* Turkey and Yugoslavia were important emigration countries in 1973 (each accounting for 0.6 million emigrants). Workers from these countries were employed almost exclusively in Germany (Turks to a lesser degree in The Netherlands). Emigrants from North West Africa (Algeria, Morocco and Tunisia) were rather selective as to their destination, being oriented almost entirely to France and to some extent to the Benelux.[8]
- *Other countries.* A small proportion of this group were citizens of third countries who work for multinational companies or international organisations (Americans, Japanese and other nationalities). Another limited part of this group was formed by foreign workers from Central and West African countries. The

Table 9.3 Total number of foreign workers (millions) in the EU12, by country of origin, and % shares in total labour force, 1973–90

	Area	1973	1980	1990
Intra-EU	EU9	1.8	1.5	1.1
	EU + 3	1.4	1.0	0.9
	Total EU12	3.2	2.5	2.0
Extra-EU	Mediterranean	2.0	1.9	2.0
	Other	1.4	1.5	1.9
	Total of third countries	3.4	3.4	3.9
Total	World	6.6	5.9	5.9
Per cent share in	Intra+Extra–EU12	6	5	5
total labour force	Extra–EU12	3	3	3

Sources: KEG, *Beschäftigung ausländischer Arbeitnehmer*, 1975 and 1982, Brussels; OECD, 1992; see also Eurostat 1985, 1987.

main body was formed by the approximately one million foreigners staying in the UK. Most immigrants into the UK come from Commonwealth countries. For many of them the status of foreigners, in the legal sense, is far less clear than for other immigrants. For that reason, the figure of about one million Commonwealth immigrants resident in the UK should be looked upon as merely indicative.

The first enlargement in 1973 coincided more or less with a changed attitude to migration, and with the end of a long period of stable growth in Western Europe. The changed economic situation in the host countries led to a drop in GDP; many companies got into difficulties and the tension on the labour market rapidly diminished. These economic factors were reinforced by socio-cultural ones. The concentration of foreign labour in certain areas invoked feelings of *Ueberfremdung*, of being swamped by foreigners.

Governments of immigration countries started to pursue restrictive admission policies *vis-à-vis* citizens of non-EU countries (Hammar, 1985) and actively to stimulate return migration (Böhning, 1979), introducing measures of four types (Lebon and Falchi, 1980): (1) return premium to the person involved; (2) aid for setting up in business to person involved; (3) subsidies for professional training to the home country; (4) development aid to projects to home country. Moreover schemes were developed to stimulate the assimilation or improve the integration of workers settled more permanently (that is, whose families were resident in the host country) (Council of Europe 1980, 1983; Castles and Kosack, 1985; Edye, 1987, CEC, 1985a).

The developments and measures described above have led to a drop in the number of migrant workers. This decline varied in size for different groups of country of origin, depending on the degree of integration (Table 9.3):

- *EU partners*. The figures indicate an integration effect; that is to say, migration diminishes as free trade grows.[9] For instance, on balance, 200,000 Italians working in other member states returned home in the 1970s once free trade among the EU countries had led to accelerated growth, more employment opportunities and better wages in their home country. Other countries too – such as Belgium and the Netherlands – registered a drop in the number of citizens employed in another EU member country. It is also possible that, in times of economic depression, both workers and employers tend to prefer their own labour market. The increasing number of British employed abroad in the 1970s may have been the initial effect of the UK workers' progressive integration in the common labour market, clearly helped along by economic (push factor) motives; moreover, given the widespread knowledge of the English language, the 'social distances' may well be shorter for English workers than for workers from other member states.

- *The three new member states.* The steep drop in the number of workers from Greece, Spain and Portugal employed in the rest of the present EU can be attributed to changes in admission policy in the receiving countries. Total return migration amounted to almost half a million (about 200,000 Spaniards, 100,000 Portuguese and 150,000 Greeks).

- *Other Mediterranean countries.* Here the restrictive policies have had less effect. Between 1973 and 1980, the numbers of Yugoslavians had decreased considerably, but those of North Africans and Turks had increased.

- *Third countries.* The doubtful measurement of the remaining group (UK) does not permit a clear-cut conclusion.

The spatial patterns of European international migration have been subjected to studies using different approaches; some were mostly theoretical (for example, Mueller, 1980), others concentrated on the motives of individual migrants and employers (for instance, OECD, 1978), yet others focused on phenomena well known from interregional migration analysis (for instance, Klaassen and Drewe, 1973; Heijke and Klaassen, 1979). A model combining elements from these studies with factors suggested by integration theory, international sociology and modern political economics (Molle and Van Mourik, 1988, 1989b) confirmed that international migration to and in Western Europe is influenced to a large extent by push factors – low earnings and the lack of job opportunities in the sending country; pull factors – availability of jobs and better pay in the host countries; friction factors – cost of movement, cultural differences between LECs and LICs; and finally immigration-restricting measures in receiving countries. Less straightforward is the outcome with respect to the hypotheses concerning degrees of integration (capital markets and goods trade). Other empirical investigations show that there is no clear correlation between the movement of goods and of people (OECD, 1992). The available evidence when viewed in the light of the debate on substitution v. complementarity (Chapter 8) suggests three things: first, that in Western Europe labour movements have to some extent been a substitute for goods movements (low-skilled labour maintaining certain productions in high-wage countries); second, that the movement of goods and capital has been a substitute for labour movement (low migration, high trade flows; see also direct investment, Chapter 10); third, no evidence of complementarity has been found.

Second enlargement and the opening up of Eastern Europe (1982–92)

The second enlargement with the addition of the three Mediterranean countries coincided with a new impetus to European economic growth given by the internal market programme. The economic restructuring of the most advanced member countries that ensued diminished the pull factors for migration, as the demand for low-skilled jobs declined. Moreover the access to the EU markets and the increased confidence of both domestic and foreign investors in the three new member countries (see next chapter) diminished the push factors: the large increase in investment and an accelerated growth of GDP increased domestic employment opportunities and wages. Consequently migration from the traditional emigration countries decreased considerably. In some of these countries, such as Italy, the opposite even started to occur: immigration of low-skilled labour from third countries (CEC, 1991b). Table 9.3 indicates that the number of immigrant labourers from third countries into the whole EU has increased in the last decade. The causes of this increase differ within sub-groups:

- *Third countries of the Mediterranean basin.* These countries have continued their sending of people and hence workers to the EU. Return migration, notwithstanding policy measures, remained low. On the contrary, again notwithstanding policy measures, immigration continued, mainly in the form of family reunion and illegal entrance. The main explanatory factor of this development is the push factor: low income and low employment possibilities due to a very dynamic population growth and a lagging economic growth in the home countries.
- *Other third countries.* The developing countries of Latin America, Asia and sub-Saharan Africa have started to send people to the EU in significant numbers. Although often occurring officially on political grounds, this increasing migration appears in practice to be motivated by economic reasons, or a combination of both.
- *Central and Eastern Europe.* These economies are going through a painful adjustment process, from a regime of central planning to that of market orientation. In that process large numbers of workers are made redundant, many of them highly skilled. The wage differential being very large and the prospects of a quick improvement in that situation being limited (Molle, de Koning and Zandvliet, 1992), many decide to use the various possibilities of entrance into the EU and try to find a job there.

These migratory flows are very different from the ones that prevailed in the 1960s, for several reasons. First, they concern more sending and more receiving countries over a much wider geographical area. Second, migrants often go to the tertiary sector instead of the secondary one; large numbers of migrants tend even to enter the informal, sometimes even illegal, labour market (Pugliese, 1992). Third, the causes of migration tend to become more complex (intertwining of political, security and economic factors) leading to increased pressure. Finally, the conditions for integration in the LIC have deteriorated (job opportunities and social integration). As a consequence voices are growing loud in the call to severely limit immigration into the EC (Böhning, 1993; OECD, 1993; Siebert, 1994).

Wage structures, convergence or divergence?

International differences in wages

There are wide differences in average wages among the countries of the EU. On the whole they are highly similar to the international differences in GDP (see Table 18.2), with mostly high figures for the countries in Northern Europe, and low ones for the Mediterranean states. Here we are interested not so much in the absolute differences as in their development in the course of the integration process. Economic theory offers elements for theses of decreasing as well as increasing differences in wages among countries.

The *convergence school* concludes that mobility of labour will level out any differences in wages. In this line of thinking the international integration of goods markets, reflected by increasing trade, leads to the equalisation of factor income, wages and interest rates (see Chapter 8). Some early analyses of the effects of European integration (Meyer and Willgerodt, 1956; Fisher, 1966; Butler, 1967) did indeed show a certain convergence of wage levels.

The *divergence school* maintains that the conditions for equalisation mostly do not obtain. Movement of labour tends to be restricted by factors like spatial and cultural distance and by institutional factors. Even in a customs union, trade can be impeded by collusive practices, transport costs, multinational firms monopolising new technology, and so on. The technological advance of certain countries implies that they will always select the new products with high value added as soon as they come on the market, abandoning products as soon as their value added drops and no longer sustains high wages. Thus the wage gap that accompanies the technology gap is not only perpetuated but even accentuated. The liberalisation of European goods and factor markets was thought to have such an agglomeration effect (Giersch, 1949; Seers *et al.*, 1979, 1980).

Rigorous testing of the alternative views used to be very difficult because of deficient data (Tovias, 1982; Gremmen, 1985; van Mourik, 1987). However, for the founder countries of the EU, a considerable degree of international convergence of wages was found for the 1964–89 period (van Mourik, 1989, 1993). This convergence is primarily due to Italy's catching up with its partners in terms of productivity.

Industrial and occupational structure

There are several reasons for the limited convergence of wage levels. One is the imperfect factor mobility among countries; an idea of the relatively limited migration among the member countries of the EU has indeed been given in the previous section. That lack of mobility is not only an international phenomenon; it does obtain also among sectors of activity and among occupational groups. Impediments to movement are many and manifold; they encompass personal choice, capacities and discrimination. Personal choice is reflected in the different amenities going with certain jobs, which may offset pay differences, and in the unwillingness of certain persons to pay for the retraining required to move to a better occupation, or to change their place of residence. The capacity factor shows up in the personal qualities (intelligence, skill and so on) needed for certain jobs and limiting the number of possible entrants. Movements may also be impeded by opaque markets and by the high cost of gathering information. Finally differences in pay may spring from restrictive practices based for instance on trade union power or on government regulations issued under pressure of certain groups. Open discrimination is shown by employers refusing to employ, for example, people of a certain race, gender or religion.

The industrial structure of wages is very similar in the different European countries, despite large differences among them in trade union practice, availability of manpower, relative importance of the sector in the total economy and so on (Butler, 1967; Bouteiller, 1971; Saunders and Marsden, 1981).[10] That similarity is due to branches having the same characteristics as to skill, sex, capital/labour ratio, firm size and so on in different countries (Vassille, 1989). Moreover the structure is remarkably stable through time because the determinant factors are stable through time (Lebergott, 1947; Reder, 1962; OECD, 1965, 1985c). Although over time the ranking of industries tends to remain the same, there seems to be a slight tendency of convergence towards the mean.

The occupational structure of wages shows the same features of similarity and stability as the industrial structure, despite differences in demand for and supply of different grades of labour, different values and cultures, and different intervention by the government

(UN/ECE, 1967; Phelps-Brown, 1977). The reason is that in all countries occupations requiring more education, experience and skill, or carrying more responsibility, are more highly paid than others. The stability is due not only to the persistence of those structural characteristics, but also to the heavy weight of tradition, which determines the notions of the hierarchy of wages and the principles of fair pay, and causes relics from the past to be long preserved (Phelps-Brown, 1977).

Equal pay for equal work: gender

One of the main policy objectives (Article 119) is that member states shall ensure that men and women shall receive equal pay for equal work. However, when the deadline came in 1970, almost nothing had been done to end discrimination. Member states had such difficulty in reaching a consensus on the specific actions needed because strong forces were at work to maintain existing practices (UN/ECE, 1980, Ch. 4). Then the Court of Justice (in the famous Defrenne Case of 1976) declared Article 119 directly applicable.

The gap between the principle of equal pay for equal work and the 1972 practice was still very wide (Saunders and Marsden, 1981). On average, the hourly earnings of women were about a quarter lower than those of men (Table 9.4, column 1). Now such differences are not necessarily due to discrimination; they also spring from men and women doing different work, explained by factors such as less skill, lack of seniority, inappropriate age and more part-time work (Table 9.4, column 2; Kottis, 1985).

The men–women wage differential decreased over the period 1950–83 (Schippers and Siegers, 1986). Action of the Commission and rulings of the Court have since 1970 taken away the discriminatory

Table 9.4   Female–male earnings differential (ratio) 1972, EU6

Country	Actual ratio	Expected ratio	Unexplained differential
Germany	0.72	0.85	0.13
France	0.75	0.92	0.17
Italy	0.81	0.96	0.15
Netherlands	0.71	0.71	0.00
Belgium	0.74	0.95	0.21
Luxemburg	0.59	0.73	0.14

Source: Kottis (1985).

elements in the differences in pay between men and women. Moreover in all member countries supplementary action was needed to help women overcome the handicaps which affect their work characteristics unfavourably.

Welfare effects

The welfare effects of European labour market integration (set out succinctly in theoretical terms in the second section of this chapter) are different for LICs and LECs. The magnitude of these effects (resulting from a set of empirical studies) is equally different for both groups.

For a *labour-importing country* the benefits and costs present themselves in the form of static and dynamic effects. The static direct production effect relates to the increase in GNP as a result of the employment of immigrant workers. Case studies indicate that these effects are limited; in France, for example, immigrant workers, forming about 7 per cent of the French wage-earning labour force, contributed about 5 per cent of French GNP in 1971 (MacMillan, 1982). The contribution of migration to the economic growth of EU countries amounted on average to only 0.05 per cent (Askari, 1974). The static distribution effect concerns the shift of income between categories. As the more abundant labour supply lowers the wage rate of the indigenous labour force, the extra output is shared by domestic capital and foreign labour. Returns to capital therefore rise. For France, the magnitude of that effect was calculated at between 1.2 and 2.2 per cent of GNP in 1971 (MacMillan, 1982). The dynamic effects of labour migration to LICs are less well known (Böhning and Maillat, 1974), but some think that labour immigration, by taking away certain bottlenecks in the economy, has led to a permanently higher growth rate of GNP (UN/ECE, 1977). Some negative aspects have also been pointed out. One of these is the presumably high cost of social services for immigrants (schools and so on). However there is no evidence that active immigrants' demands on social (security) and public services (schools, hospitals and so on) exceed their contributions, rather than the contrary (Blitz, 1977; Bourguignon *et al.*, 1977; Löffelholz, 1992; SER, 1992). Negative aspects of migration are that it has prevented the economies of the LICs from adjusting structurally to the new world conditions in comparative advantages. On balance, however, labour-importing countries seem to have benefited from immigration.[11]

For a *labour-exporting country*, too, the emigration of part of its labour force has both significant advantages and costs. Although long-term growth may not be impaired by out-migration of unskilled workers, it is different for the outflow of skilled workers (Sexton *et al.*, 1991). One advantage of emigration is that unemployment decreases, but the loss of manpower it implies has not been as beneficial to LECs as might be expected, as a substantial proportion of the emigrants have received more education than the average workers in the LECs. Secondly, emigrants are supposed to have increased skill on their return but the enhanced quality of human capital has had little positive effect on the economies of LECs. On the one hand, the inability of LECs to offer sufficient employment opportunities to returning skilled workers has led to a net loss of skilled labour. On the other hand, returning migrants are generally disinclined to accept low-status jobs and frequently set up 'unprofitable' service trades (Papadimetriou, 1978). Migrants' remittances count as a possible third positive effect of labour export. They amount to a considerable proportion of the LECs' GNP and in the short run constitute a very convenient means of financing deficits on the balance of trade. The long-run effects of remittances on the LECs' economy are limited, however, because on the whole they have been used for investment in houses and consumption purposes rather than for productive capital formation (Keely and Tran, 1989). The increased consumption they have made possible has caused substantial price and wage increases and contributed to the misallocation of resources in LECs. And sometimes they have led to an overvalued currency. The transfer of savings, which also seemed promising, has proved rather disappointing in terms of investments in the emigration country, for too much money has been invested for purposes that are not directly productive. Interesting from a theoretical point of view, but difficult to implement, are proposals to introduce an emigration tax (Bhagwati, 1987b) and to transfer financial means to LECs through an 'International Labour Compensatory Facility' (for example, Kennedy Brenner, 1979).

Summary and conclusions

- Politically the EU holds as a fundamental principle that nobody must be forced to submit to the socio-cultural and legal adjustments involved in international migration within Europe, and that ideally everyone should find sufficient work in his own country. Thus, unlike the situation on goods markets, the further integration is not meant to entail large migration flows.
- The degree of interpenetration of EU labour markets (number of foreigners divided by the total number of employed) is less than 2 per cent. This suggests that goods and capital movements have largely been substitutes for labour movements.

- Intra-EU migration will remain limited because of the reduction of wage differentials, the decrease in the demand for low-skilled workers, the taking away of barriers to goods, services and capital movement and cultural differences.
- The fairly wide wage discrepancies prevailing among EU member states in 1960 have decreased considerably since, which is in line with expectations fostered by the convergence school.
- Occupational and industrial wage structures are very similar in the various member countries, and change only very gradually.
- Most migration comes from third countries. The welfare effects of these movements are not clear. An EU policy in this matter is needed.

Notes

1   The definition of movement of labour refers to persons residing and working outside their home country; frontier-zone workers are therefore generally excluded. Although they also reflect the integration of labour markets, their motives are different from those of actual migrants. The coordination of policies of national states towards such frontier workers presents particular problems, which for lack of space we cannot discuss here. Those interested in the phenomenon may be referred to the works of Aubrey (1984) and Ricq (1983).

2   The migration wave just after the Second World War comes immediately to mind; more recent examples of 'political' migration are the repatriation of French people from North Africa and of Portuguese citizens from Angola and Mozambique, while very recently emigration from the war-ridden former Yugoslavia is a case in point.

3   Benefits can be enjoyed in any country, irrespective of where they have been acquired; in other words, a worker who has long been employed in a foreign country can have his social security benefits transferred to his country of origin when he returns there. Recently proposals have been made to extend this to all insured people, not only workers (CEC, 1992c).

4   The right to move and stay within the EU has been extended to students (Directive 90/366) and pensioned people (Directive 90/365) and other non-active persons (Directive 90/364). The TEU has practically extended the free movement to all Union citizens; they can all now move freely but, in case of sickness or lack of financial means, they cannot fall back on the social security system of their host country.

5   International organisations, such as the International Labour Organisation (ILO), the OECD and the Council of Europe have each assumed a coordinating role; however, this is by no means comparable to the competences of an organisation like GATT in the field of trade.

6   In interpreting these data, keep in mind that they should be corrected upwards because of the considerable clandestine migration going on. Some estimated illegal migration at that moment at certainly no less than 10 per cent.

7   These national figures obscure even higher figures for certain regions: in some regions of Portugal, up to half the male labour force appeared to have emigrated to North Europe in 1973. In interpreting these data one should moreover keep in mind that all three countries are traditional emigration countries

for other destinations than the EU: Iberians particularly to South America, Greeks to Australia and the USA (UN, 1980; Bernard, 1978).

8   The volume of the North African presence in the EU around 1973 is probably incorrectly reproduced in the table, owing to the fact that at one time Algerians were admitted to France without working or residence permit. Some observers estimate the number of employed North Africans resident in France during this period at more than one million.

9   Very few authors have tried to test this hypothesis quantitatively, although the subject has been debated for a long time (see, for instance, Meyer and Willgerodt, 1956; Mihailovic, 1976).

10   It was even similar in the liberal Western and the centrally planned Eastern European systems (for example, Redor, 1992).

11   This is also the experience of the USA, as noted in the studies of Simon (1989) and USDL (1989).

10 Capital

Introduction

Capital markets reveal many special characteristics that cause their integration to differ in practice profoundly from the way other markets are integrated, notwithstanding the basic theoretical similarity to, for example, labour market integration (as we described in Chapter 8). To prepare this difficult ground we will start with a short description of the basic concepts of integration of capital markets, including of course the various barriers to movement, the advantages and so on. Next a brief sketch of the European regulatory environment in which capital liberalisation proceeds will be given.

The remainder of the chapter will be a description of the changes in the structure of international capital market transactions by private enterprises. We make a distinction between direct investment and long-term loans,[1] first examining the former. The main objective of direct investment is to acquire control of, say, a company, which can be done either through equity transactions or through direct capital participation. Patterns and volume of direct investment in Europe have been profoundly influenced by integration.

Next we go into the present patterns of other international capital movements from and to the EU, discussing two important indicators of the degree of integration, namely, the volume of international transactions and the equalisation of interest; that is, of the price of capital. A short section on the welfare effects of capital market integration and a brief summary of the findings complete the chapter.

Some basic concepts

Forms of integration

The movement of the production factor 'capital' can be considered free if entrepreneurs can satisfy their need for capital, and investors

213

can offer their disposable capital, in the country where conditions are most favourable for them.

Once more a parallel can be drawn with free trade areas and customs unions. A free-capital movement area (FCMA) would then be a zone within which capital can move freely, each state making its own rules with respect to third countries. In a capital market union (CMU), on the contrary, there would be a common policy concerning the union's financial relations with third countries.

The integration of capital markets can be defined first of all as the removing of constraints on foreign exchange, of discriminatory tax measures and of other obstacles. This is the so-called 'negative integration'. Since capital is highly mobile and apt to go where the returns are highest, positive integration will also be needed; that is, the integration of capital markets by coordinating or harmonising the rules which govern their organisation and functioning, such as prudential regulations for bank credit, payments, and so on. Given the interwovenness of the capital market with monetary policy, a certain integration of monetary policy, and coordination of the monetary relations with third countries, would be implied.

Advantages of integration

Integration of capital markets is aspired to (see also Chapter 8) because it:

- diminishes the risk of disturbances such as tend to occur in small markets;
- increases the supply of capital, because better investing prospects mobilise additional savings, the investor being free to choose the combination most favourable to him in terms of return, solidity and liquidity;
- enables those who are in need of capital to raise larger amounts in forms better tailored to their specific needs;
- makes for equal production conditions and thus fewer disturbances of competition in the common market.

Impediments

We can distinguish three groups of instruments to restrict the importation and exportation of capital (whether or not speculative), (compare Woolly, 1974).

Market-oriented instruments   These resemble tariffs in goods trade, as they influence the price of capital:

- split-currency markets, with a more (or less) favourable rate of exchange for current payments than for capital transactions;
- lower (even negative) interests on foreign deposits, caused by taxes on interest or deposits, or otherwise.

Administrative and legal instruments   These instruments are comparable to quantitative restrictions and non-tariff barriers:

- securities: trade may be impeded by reserving the right to hold stocks and bonds to persons or institutions of a given nationality and restricting non-residents' purchases of domestic securities; moreover restrictions may be placed on domestic investment and pension funds investments in foreign securities;
- bank deposits may be hindered by a ceiling on deposits kept by foreigners or, alternatively, by restrictions on residents' deposits in foreign countries.

Other instruments   These may include the following:

- currency restrictions on certain transactions, the authorities allotting only limited amounts of foreign currency for given capital transactions;
- taxes or levies on the acquirement of foreign currency, tax withheld on foreign investment, or heavier taxes on foreign profits than on domestic ones;
- profits and interests transfers may be hindered by an obligation to reinvest in the host country all profits made with foreign capital, and by committing exporters to return as soon as possible (for instance, within five years) any capital drained off abroad.

Motives for impediments

Arguments for restricting capital movements are based mostly on the disadvantages associated with long-term capital drain-offs (Cairncross, 1973; Swoboda, 1976). The most frequently heard reasons for governments to feel they should impede the *exporting* of capital are the following:

- The bloodstream of the national economy. Capital drain-offs will reinforce the economies of other countries to the detriment of the country's own economy (for instance there is less domestic investment, so the government receives less tax on the ensuing revenue). Moreover the government often wishes to reserve to itself the national capital market.

- Loss of currency reserves. This jeopardises the ability to meet other international obligations; this is particularly relevant when the balance of payment is in disequilibrium and authorities are trying to prevent changes in the exchange rate.
- Internal equilibrium – an argument mainly associated with the price of capital. A large outflow of capital may compel a high rate of interest when a low rate would be recommendable for the development of the national economy.
- External equilibrium. Capital outflow may lead to currency devaluation even though the rate of exchange as such is not unbalanced. In that way, the nation might be forced into more expensive imports and imported inflation.

Rather paradoxically, arguments are also raised against the *importing* of capital, such as the following:

- Capital is power; therefore capital in foreign hands means loss of authority over one's own economy.
- Disturbance of the internal and external equilibrium: a large inflow of capital may entail a lower rate of interest than the monetary authorities think adequate for internal equilibrium; capital inflow may thus prohibit a scarce-money policy with reasonable interest rates. To avoid such an inflow, the authorities may consider upward adaptation of the rate of exchange; however that weakens the export position.

Finally there are arguments pleading against *both the importing and the exporting* of capital:

- Disturbance. We have already pointed out the disturbances that may be the result of exporting short-term capital. Capital imports can be disturbing because they are often of a speculative nature, that is anticipating changes in the rates of interest and/or the exchange rates of currency.
- Perversity: free movement of long-term capital does not lead to optimum allocation, but to concentration in countries with a large market where capital is already in abundant supply, while states with smaller markets are deprived of capital.

The welfare effects of capital restrictions are rather complicated (see, among others, Phylaktis and Wood, 1984). To give a simple 'yes' or 'no', on economic considerations, to the restriction of international capital flows is not possible from an economic point of view. Anyway the experience with controls has shown them in the long run to be ineffective instruments for preventing structural adjustments to the balance of payments. The arguments for fighting speculative capital movements, on the contrary, are on the whole economically sound, but for that purpose other instruments may be more effective (see Chapter 17, on monetary policy).

EU regime

Treaty

The liberty of capital movement is laid down in the Treaty of Rome (Articles 67 to 72). The most important stipulation is that member states 'shall abolish between themselves all restrictions on the movement of capital belonging to persons resident in member states and any discrimination based on the nationality or on the place of residence of the parties or of the place where such capital[2] is invested.'

However, while the Treaty decrees a far-reaching freedom of movement for goods and a fair degree of freedom for services and labour, with respect to capital the freedom of movement is limited. Indeed *capital discrimination needs to be abolished only to the extent necessary to ensure the proper functioning of the Common Market* (Article 67). That restriction, consciously introduced by the member states, indicates that member states did not aspire to fully free movement of capital as an object in itself. The reason is that member states dared not give up the right to influence the capital flow, because it is one of the few instruments available to them for the effective control of internal macro-economic and monetary developments (OECD, 1979, 1982c). Moreover full freedom of capital movement is hard to reconcile with the selectivity implicit in the measures of fiscal policy, investment stimulations and so on of many member states. As a consequence, the provisions for freedom of capital are not directly applicable, unlike those for goods and labour. Indeed, the Treaty does *not* enjoin upon the Community the creation of a veritable European capital market.

The Treaty permits the following *restrictions* of capital movement:

- 'Domestic rules governing the capital market and the credit system' may be applied by member states but only in a non-discriminating way; in other words, member states must treat residents of other EU nationalities on the same footing as their own residents (Article 68.2).
- 'Loans for the direct or indirect financing of a member state or of its regional or local authorities shall not be issued or placed in other member states unless the states concerned have reached agreement thereon' (Article 68.3).

- 'If movements of capital lead to disturbances in the functioning of the capital market' the Commission after consultation with the Monetary Committee may authorise member states to undo the liberalisation introduced since the creation of the EU (Article 73).
- Balance of payments problems may justify capital movement restrictions (Articles 108 and 109).

The last point to be made (Article 71) is that member states have committed themselves to the readiness to *go beyond the degree of liberalisation* of capital movements prescribed by the Treaty, in so far as their economic situation, in particular the situation of their balance of payments, so permits. Indeed efforts made towards the progressive liberalisation of capital movements have been made ever since the EU was founded, but up to 1987 they did not result in agreements reaching beyond the stipulations of the Treaty.

Directives of 1960–62

With respect to capital movements as well, the Treaty is a framework agreement, setting out some general principles to be complemented later by further rules. Such rules were drawn up at an early date (1960–62) in the shape of two directives, which distinguish three groups of transactions by the degree of liberalisation:

- *Fully free*. This category encompassed such transactions as direct investment (making capital available for an establishment abroad), the purchase of real estate, short- and medium-term trade credits, personal transactions like repatriation of earnings and former investments, and the acquisition by non-residents of quoted stocks in another member state. The liberalisation of this group rested on the direct connection with the free movement of goods (short- and medium-term trade credits), of employees and self-employed (personal transactions) and the right to free establishment (direct investments and investments through participation in capital stock).
- *Partly free*. This group comprised the issue and placing of shares listed on the stock market of a member state other than the one where the placing body resides; the acquisition of non-quoted shares by those not resident in the same country; shares in investment funds; and finally long-term trade credits. For this group, capital movement was only partly liberalised.
- *No obligation to liberalise* existed with respect to such short-term transactions as the purchase of treasury bonds and other capital stocks and the opening of bank accounts by non-residents.

The reason why the principle of free movement was not applied to these transactions is that they may be of a speculative nature and therefore a cause of disturbance. Full and irrevocable liberalisation of these transactions could not be achieved while certain conditions were not fulfilled.

So the EU was at its start rather an incomplete common market, the situation on the capital market resembling a free trade area for selected products on the goods market rather than an encompassing customs union. In the mid-1960s, a team of experts reported on the prospects of further liberalisation and integration of markets (Segré *et al.*, 1966). Between 1966 and 1986 many concrete proposals were made, but in practice nothing was achieved. The causes are involved but in the main associated with the conviction of many governments that restricting capital movement is an essential instrument for an effective monetary policy.

Progress in deregulation and liberalisation

Although the integration of financial markets by EU regulations ceased to progress in the 1960s (Philip, 1978), actual integration has not stopped since. On the contrary, member states (Germany, The Netherlands, Belgium and the UK) have proceeded with the liberalisation, not only for transactions with partners, but also for transactions with third countries. Others, like France and Italy, went on controlling many capital movements (by virtue of Article 73) in spite of partial liberalisation. The same was true for the countries which considered themselves in transition (since joining), such as Greece, Spain and Portugal.

Many and varied have been the proposals made to improve the European capital market (for example, Verrijn Stuart *et al.*, 1965; Segré *et al.*, 1966). In the 1980s, the attitude towards international capital transactions shifted gradually but significantly (Lamfalussy, 1981) in favour of deregulation and liberalisation. What factors brought this change about? First, the improvement in the external position. The improvement of the balance-of-payments position of many European countries permitted them to abandon capital controls. Second, the poor efficiency of the external regulation. Governments had realised that restrictions on capital movement often just delay structural adaptations of the economy that will be necessary anyway in the end and may become more costly if put off. Controls that seemed effective in the short run generally had to be intensified and extended to related fields to counteract the evasive behaviour of economic actors. Moreover the costs related to such restrictive regulations as the salaries of those involved in controls both in the public and private sector had become more evident (OECD, 1980, 1982a). A third factor was a general tendency to deregulate national financial markets. The progressive abolition of restrictions on credit expansion by quotas or the compulsion placed on financial institutions to invest in public bonds was stimulated by the experience in many countries with the negative effects of distortions created by such intervention of the public sector in the market. Another important consideration in that respect was the increased internationalisation of the financial sector and the trade in financial services that permitted financial actors to evade many of these regulations (see Chapter 14). This has led to the introduction of new financial techniques that produced products better adapted to borrowers' and lenders' needs. Fourth was technological innovation. The telematics revolution has greatly reduced the information and transaction costs of the financial sector. Information on financial markets anywhere in the world is now instantly available anywhere else. Standardised electronic transactions are, moreover, cheaper than those involving lots of paper work. A final factor was competition from largely unregulated Euromarkets. To avoid the problem of regulated home financial markets, a large unregulated international financial market had developed that proved increasingly efficient in coping with investors' and borrowers' needs.

Recent measures for liberalisation

Inspired by the worldwide trend to liberalise capital markets and by the will to complete the internal market (Chapter 16) also for capital (CEC, 1986e) the EC decided to realise a free European capital market by 1992 (June 1988 directive). Capital movements between member countries are now fully liberalised (with a possibility of exception for Greece and Portugal up to 1995). The Maastricht Treaty has codified the free movement of capital (Article 73b) in the following words: 'Within the framework of the provisions set out in this chapter, all restrictions on the movement of capital between member states and between member states and third countries shall be prohibited.'

The freedom of movement between member states can be negatively influenced by differences in taxes on capital, differences in obligations for financial institutions, and so on. The new treaty (Article 73d) permits member states to maintain such regulations that differentiate between 'tax payers who are not in the same situation with respect to their place of residence or the place where the capital is invested'. Moreover member states are allowed 'to take all requisite measures to prevent infringements of national law and regulations in particular in the field of taxation and of the prudential supervision of financial institutions or to lay down procedures for the declaration of capital movements for purposes of administrative or statistical information or to take measures which are justified on grounds of public policy or public security'. Examples of the latter may be tax evasion and consumer protection.

Improving the conditions for a proper functioning of European financial markets; harmonisation

To be effective, capital market integration cannot be limited to removing barriers; it also needs transparent markets and conditions enabling investors and creditors to be informed about the quality of foreign financial products. The plan for the completion of the internal capital market contains action programmes to improve these conditions, of which three stand out as particularly important.

Taxes Differences in tax levels may distort the market as they may induce investors to locate in countries which offer the highest tax-adjusted profit rates (OECD, 1991). This applies notably to corporate taxes and to taxes on the revenues of capital (deposits, for example). We will come back to this point in Chapter 16.

Company law Direct investors (for a takeover), investors in stock (for portfolio purposes) and subscribers to foreign companies' loans want to be able to judge the solvency and profitability of the company in question. A series of directives on company law (in accordance with Article 54) have been adopted and more are in preparation. They concern the obligation to publish annual accounts according to certain specifications, minimum capital requirements, the qualifications of company auditors, national and international mergers, and the creation of a European company. These directives guarantee that certain minimum rules are respected by all companies. The EU rules are stricter for companies listed on the stock exchange than for others. The directives establishing them concern the minimum requirements for listing, the information to be given with the application for listing (prospectus) and after admission (half-yearly reports). Other directives of interest concern the issue of prospectuses, insider trading and public takeover bids.

Financial intermediaries A saver who places his deposit with a foreign bank wants to be reasonably sure that the bank is trustworthy, and the same is true of an investor in so-called 'open-end' funds. The directive of 1977 ('European Banking Law') lays down uniform criteria for admission to the banking trade and for the prudential control of banks in all member countries. Other directives determine the information banks have to give in their annual reports, the definition of the term 'own funds', and the application of common solvency and liquidity ratios, and even the specification of certain financial products (mortgages, for instance). Harmonisation has not always been easy, owing to differences in the legal status of certain intermediaries, different traditions of prudential control and deep-rooted differences in culture (such as the opposition between the British view of finance as an independent industry and that of some continental countries of finance as an activity that should be placed at the service of the real economy).

External situation

The attempts made by the European Commission to liberalise capital movements in Europe are in line with more general efforts in the same direction made by other international bodies. At the world level, the International Monetary Fund (IMF) is the framework for such efforts. The IMF's primary aim is the greatest possible freedom to settle all current payments associated with the free movement of goods and services. Indeed the Bretton Woods Agreement (by which the IMF was founded) only provides for a very limited liberalisation of capital movement. At the level of the industrialised world it is the Organisation for Economic Cooperation and Development (OECD) that has declared free capital movement an objective of its actions. After a thorough study of the specific aspects of national markets (OECD, 1968), the so-called 'Code of Liberalisation of Capital Movements' (OECD, 1982b) was agreed upon. This code divides capital transactions into a number of categories for which different degrees of freedom are envisaged.

The external policy of the European Union with respect to capital movements has changed over time. The Treaty of Rome does not set an objective for capital movements with third countries. Unlike the case for goods (where the Treaty establishes as a basic principle 'the greatest possible freedom' with respect to traffic with third countries), the Treaty only urges member states to coordinate their capital movements with third countries (see Chapter 19).

The Maastricht Treaty has, however, installed a very clear principle for the common policy in matters of capital movement with third countries. Indeed the principle is that external movements need to be fully free, like internal movement. The reason is that many countries that had liberalised their capital transactions 'erga omnes' (with respect to all other countries, partners and third countries alike) while a common European policy did not yet exist were not prepared to reintroduce restrictions towards third countries under a new common policy.

The policy of openness to third countries is not one of laisser-faire, though. Indeed according to the new treaty the EU may regulate 'the movement of capital to or from third countries involving direct investment (including investment in real estate establishment), the provision of financial services or the admission of securities to capital markets' (Article 73c). The EU may even adopt restrictions on the freedom of capital movement with third countries if in exceptional circumstances movements of capital 'threaten to cause serious difficulties for the operation of the Economic and Monetary Union' (Article 73f). And it will promote the adoption of liberal policies by third countries as well, so as to obtain symmetry in its external relations.

Direct investments

Relative position

An international direct investment (DI) is made when a company in one country transfers capital to another country to create or take over an establishment there which it wants to control.[3] DI of some significance are a relatively recent phenomenon: it is since the 1960s that DI has rapidly gained importance. To give an example: the total stock of foreign direct investments in OECD countries grew in the 1960s by some 13 per cent a year, a percentage equal to that of the growth of international trade. Between 1967 and 1977, DI grew faster and clearly outpaced trade growth. This tendency was accentuated in the 1980s: while worldwide trade grew by some 10 per cent a year, DI grew by almost 30 per cent. Growth was particularly fast in the second half of the 1980s; under the influence of the recession, DI has fallen back in the early 1990s. Most DI (80 per cent) finds its origin in one of the three major areas of the world (USA, Japan, EU). Two-thirds of the flows apply to manufacturing and one third to services; the latter share is growing.

The geographical pattern of the flows of DI from and to the EU reveals some interesting characteristics (see Table 10.1). Contrary to what one would expect from their relative levels of integration, the DI interactions between the EU and third countries are larger than those among the member countries themselves. Despite the increased trade and policy integration within the EU (Chapters 6, 16 and 19) DI flows with third countries grew much faster in the 1970s and early 1980s than those among EU countries. However, from the middle of the 1980s, that situation changed; apparently the internal market programme stimulated intra-EU DI growth. Extra-EU DI is very important in relative terms; indeed, by the end of the 1980s, the EU had become by far the largest outward investor in the world. This reflects a double strategy on the part of many European firms that consists of

Table 10.1   **Direct foreign investment flows of EU12 by major partner, 1969–88 (billion current ECU)**

Origin or destination	1969–73		1974–78		1979–83		1984–88	
	I	E	I	E	I	E	I	E
EU12	8	8	13	13	20	20	55	55
World	14	13	20	28	29	58	45	116
USA	7	2	9	9	13	31	10	83
Japan	—	—	—	—	1	1	4	1
EFTA	—	—	—	—	n.a.	n.a.	19	6
As a % of GFCF*								
EDIE	0.9		0.8		0.8		1.6	
(FDIE+EDIF):2	1.4		1.5		1.7		2.3	

I = inflow into the EU.
E = outflow from the EU.
*   five-year averages.
GFCF = Gross Fixed Capital Formation; EDIE = European Direct Investment in Europe; FDIE = Foreign Direct Investment in Europe; EDIF = European Direct Investment Abroad.
Source: Eurostat, several issues of *Balance of Payments* (some estimates).

a rationalisation of their operations within the EU and the setting up of a network worldwide.

The sectoral pattern of outward DI shows that manufacturing and services have equal shares, some 40 per cent, the remaining 20 per cent being taken up by energy. Inward DI shows a completely different pattern; here some two-thirds go to services and one-third to manufacturing, so that energy is hardly significant. Within both outward and inward DI the dominant branch is financial services. The structure of intra-EU DI strongly resembles the picture of incoming DI in the EU, with services again accounting for nearly two-thirds.

The relative share of foreign direct investment in total investment (Gross Fixed Capital Formation: GFCF) is small. DI flows within the EU (EDIE) accounted for no more than 1 per cent in the 1970s. That figure increased sharply in the mid-1980s as a consequence of increased integration. External DI flows (FDIE and EDIF), while not much larger, did also show a clear growth, which was, however, smaller than the growth of intra-EU flows.

External position

The role of the EU in international DI has changed with time: a net recipient in the 1950s and 1960s, the EU proceeded to a balanced situation around 1970, and since then has increasingly accentuated its role as a net direct investor, to become the largest direct investor in the world. The main explanation is the increased availability of funds and the growing capacity of EU firms to organise international production. The pattern of DI flows is dominated by the flows between countries of the industrialised world. The relations with other groups of countries, such as third-world countries, are less important in quantitative terms.

The structure of *inward* DI has for a long time been dominated by the USA; recently some other players have also come on the scene.

- *USA.* Direct investment flows from the USA to the EU in the 1960s and 1970s sprang mostly from American companies, which capitalised on their ownership advantage in technology and management by conquering a portion of the growing European market. Because that market was liberalised internally and protected externally, local production (that implies direct investment) was preferred to exporting from existing production facilities in the USA. In the terms of Chapter 8, this DI was of the 'tariff-jumping' type. The export of capital was all the easier because during this period the USA had a strong currency and no balance-of-payment problems. Many authors have tried to assess the effect of the creation of the EU on US direct investment in Europe (USDIE). This effect is visible in the differential development of US direct investment in the UK (before it joined the EU) and in the countries on the continent that were EU members. In the 1950–58 period, the growth rate of US DI was almost equal in both areas. Between 1958 and 1973 the UK growth rate was half the EU's; after 1973 the two rates became equal again (Whichart, 1981). The first econometric analyses (Scaperlanda, 1967; d'Arge, 1969; Scaperlanda and Mauer, 1969) showed considerable doubt about a possible effect of European external trade protection on the pattern of USDIE; they stressed the importance of the access to the EU market. However later analyses (for instance, Schmitz, 1970; Schmitz and Bieri, 1972; Lunn, 1980) showed that the tariff jumping (the external tariff) and the global diversification strategy (market size) were both important determinants. In recent years USDIE has been of limited size. US firms have concentrated on consolidating, rationalising and expanding their European operations (Graham, 1992).
- *EFTA.* After a slow start, this group of countries is now the leading direct investor in the EU. In recent years the wish of many EFTA industrial and service groups to take part in the

internal market has led to further EFTA investments in the EU countries, many by takeovers.

- *Other*. Among the other countries that are now large direct investors in the EU we find that Japan has recently come up very quickly. The reasons for Japanese firms' participation are diversified (Thomsen and Nicolaides, 1991; Ozawa, 1992): we find the localisation strategy based on leads in the product and production technology, on economics of scope and on product differentiation. Other factors are financial strength, the 1992 programme and fears of a protectionist stand by the EU. Some of the newly industrialising countries like Korea have begun following the same strategy as Japan.

The structure of *outward* DI is quite different.

- *USA*. The US has become the main destination (Sleuwaegen, 1987). This European DI in the US (EDIUS) springs from the wish of many European companies to profit from the possibilities offered by the American market for the development of a product at the 'growth stage', when the European market was still too fragmented. Now many European entrepreneurs believe they need a foothold in the three main centres of the world: EU, USA, Japan (see, for instance, OECD, 1987c). The first European companies to follow that strategy were based in countries without balance-of-payment problems that relaxed or abolished capital market controls with respect to third countries at an early date. First among these countries was the UK, followed by Germany and The Netherlands. Now other EU countries have joined in as well (France, for example). This has resulted in a rapid increase in EDIUS (Graham, 1992).
- *Japan*. The importance of Japan as a destination for European DI is still very limited.
- *Other*. This is a very diversified group, among which are many developing countries. In recent years the share of this group has increased rapidly as a consequence of the growing involvement of EU firms in the countries of Central and Eastern Europe.

Intra-European direct investments

Internal direct investment flows have been completely free in the EU since the 1970s. On theoretical grounds we may expect that direct investments will increase as soon as companies become convinced of the advantages of selecting optimum locations within an enlarged market area (the 'free trade' type of Chapter 8). In line with this, direct investments by companies from one of the original six member states in other member states than their home country (EDIE) increased very fast in the 1966–70 period (by some 63 per cent in four years: Pelkmans, 1983). That finding is corroborated by the observation that in the same period the number of subsidiary companies of multinationals in the EU rose from 340 to 774 (Francko, 1976). In the period 1970–83 double-digit percentage growth continued. However the real boom for EDIE came after 1985, when EDIE doubled about every two years under the impetus of the 1992 programme. This is again in line with the optimum location hypothesis, as the taking away of the many remaining non-tariff barriers has a similar effect to the taking away of tariffs. An analysis of the importance of DI in the total European economy shows fairly low values (Table 10.1). This low percentage in terms of flows does obscure the fact that the accumulation of such DI over the years now makes for considerable percentages of production of each of the EU countries controlled by firms from other EU (or third) countries. Increasingly this no longer applies exclusively to large multinationals but also to small and medium-sized companies.

The flows of DI among EU countries (EDIE) show a regular pattern (see Table 10.2 for 1985–9; the same picture holds for earlier periods). One observes, first, that there is a considerable interpenetration of the major markets. Other evidence (Cantwell and Randaccio, 1992) shows that this is of an inter-industry type; for example, manufacturers of country A invest in country B, and vice versa. Much of this investment is, moreover, of the type of parts of the production and distribution network of multinational companies (MNC). Next one observes that the poorer member states, Greece, Ireland, Spain and Portugal, are net importers of capital, while the richer countries Germany, France and the Netherlands, are net exporters of capital. The UK and Italy have a balanced situation. It is very clear that the structure of the flows is dominated by the relations between the countries in the core of the EU (some 75 per cent). The flows between the poorer member states are almost negligible.

These patterns are highly illustrative of the European integration process. They indicate that there is a net flow of capital towards the less developed EU countries; in other words, they confirm that jobs are indeed going to the people, although formerly people also used to go where the jobs were (see previous chapter). The accession of Spain and Portugal to the EU (CEC, 1988a) has accelerated the present trend for them; both countries have attracted a growing flow of DI, of which most came from the EU (Petrochilos, 1989; Buckley and Artisien, 1987; Durán-Herrera, 1992; Simões, 1992). Apparently the concentration effects which the divergence school had feared (Chapter 8) have not materialised in the recent period. The patterns also

Table 10.2   Direct investment flows between the member countries of the European Union (in billion ECU), 1985–9

From \ to	GER	FRA	ITA	NETH	B/L	UK	DEN	IRL	SPA	POR	GRE	EU12
Germany	–	2.2	1.3	1.5	1.6	2.5	0.1	0.6	2.5	0.2	0.2	12.6
France	1.8	–	2.5	2.1	4.4	4.4	0.3	0.3	2.2	0.2	0.2	18.4
Italy	0.5	1.7	–	1.2	0.9	0.6	0.0	0.0	0.7	0.0	0.0	5.7
Neth	1.3	2.2	1.2	–	2.0	4.4	0.1	0.2	1.0	0.1	0.1	12.6
Bel/Lux	1.0	1.6	-0.6	1.7	–	1.9	0.0	0.1	0.4	0.1	0.0	6.3
UK	1.1	4.4	1.8	2.6	0.7	–	-0.1	0.5	3.3	0.7	0.1	15.1
Denmark	0.3	0.3	0.0	0.4	0.1	0.6	–	0.0	0.1	0.0	0.0	1.8
Ireland	0.0	0.0	0.0	0.2	0.0	0.3	0.0	–	0.0	0.0	0.0	0.7
Spain	0.2	0.2	0.2	0.2	0.2	0.2	0.0	0.0	–	0.3	0.0	1.4
Portugal	0.0	0.0	0.0	0.0	0.0	0.0	0.0	0.0	0.1	–	0.0	0.1
Greece	0.0	0.0	0.0	0.0	0.0	0.0	0.0	0.0	0.0	0.0	–	0.0
EU12	6.2	12.6	6.5	9.8	9.9	15.0	0.4	1.7	10.3	1.7	0.6	74.6

Note: Columns and rows do not always add up due to rounding.
Source: Based on Eurostat, *European Community Direct Investment 1984–1989*, 1992, Luxemburg, and a number of unpublished sources.

suggest that there is a complementarity between goods and capital movements, whereas there is rather a substitution between capital and labour movements (Chapters 8 and 9).

An explanation of the pattern of these EDIE flows reveals several determinant factors (Morsink and Molle, 1991). The financial strength of a country proves very important: the largest EDIE flows occur when the origin country shows a net financial resource and the receiving country a high borrowing requirement. Moreover the ownership advantage is important (high R&D leads to high outward DI, and vice versa). Integration stimulates DI; for practically all pairs of countries with very little trade, DI was non-existent. This highlights the fact that EDIE is of the optimum-location rather than the tariff-jumping type (Chapter 8). Moreover the exchange rate risks proved a negative factor, which means that monetary integration, creating stable exchange rates, is likely to influence the EDIE flows positively. Finally both geographical and cultural distance were found to be relevant resistance factors, and differences in the return on capital are also an important determining factor (Mortensen, 1992).

Direct investment through takeovers

Companies that have decided to expand production and/or distribution in other countries than their own have a choice between creating a new subsidiary company or taking over an existing foreign company. The latter strategy has the advantage of immediate access to markets whose specific characteristics are known to the management. Such a takeover often takes the form of a (public) offer to buy all existing shares. This does not make the operation a portfolio investment (see next section) because the essential motive for the transaction is to obtain control of the company.

While by the EU regulations this type of DI transaction is completely free in principle, in practice it is not. In many countries (legal) measures (like the possibility of issuing preferential shares that limit the power of other shareholders) or the involvement of banks or the state in the capital protect companies from such takeovers. The fact that some member states have a free market for companies (the UK, for one) while in others (Germany, France) it is restricted or closed, clearly illustrates that the integration of capital markets in the EU is not complete.

The different national regimes have important consequences for the strategy of firms. This is revealed by the performance of the 20 companies of each country that between 1979 and 1988 showed the fastest growth of turnover (sales) and profitability (Table 10.3). Evidently companies under a 'liberal' regime (UK, USA) were forced to maximise profits, whereas companies in countries like Germany could systematically aim at market power through maximising their sales. They were free to follow that strategy because their management was not threatened by potential bidders wanting to make a profit by increasing the firm's value by discontinuing its less profitable activities. The efforts of the EU to create a truly free capital market in Europe, where all national differences in shelter from takeovers would disappear, are not yet very advanced. Hence the national differences in firms' profit and growth figures have not yet flattened out.

Table 10.3   Growth and profitability (%), 1979–88

Country	Growth of sales	Tax-adjusted profit rate
Germany (FRG)	80	4
France	51	4
Netherlands	53	5
UK	45	9
USA	48	10
Japan	190	4

Source: De Jong (1989).

Long- and short-term loans

Quantity exchanged

The development of capital market integration might ideally be measured by the size of the loans that were contracted between savers and investors in different countries, much in the same way as the development of the goods market integration is measured by the trade in goods between different countries. Unfortunately there is no good statistical record of such transactions.[4] The analysis of the deficient figures on international capital transactions (IMF or Eurostat balance of payments statistics) reveals three aspects: first, a considerable volatility over time of both portfolio and other categories of investment; second, a substitutability between these two categories, as large decreases of one often go hand-in-hand with equally large increases of the other; third, an impressive magnitude that increases considerably over the medium term; flows of the size of considerable percentages of GDP are increasingly common.

Contrary to what we found for direct investment, the time and geographical pattern of these recorded flows does not show much relation to economic fundamentals. These conclusions do not change even after the putting of the largest and politically most sensitive parts (short-term capital) into the perspective of trade flows (see Table 10.4). So we have to look for other explanations.

Table 10.4   European capital flows: short-term capital

	Capital flows as percentage of trade, averages			Intra-industry index, averages		
	1982–3	1984–5	1986–8	1982–3	1984–5	1986–8
Germany	1	5	6	48	53	30
France	2	4	10	46	90	99
Italy	7	8	4	90	98	89
Netherlands	2	4	7	n.a.	87	89
Belgium/Lux	8	54	51	86	96	97
UK	26	16	31	90	82	92
Denmark	7	13	10	90	98	82
Ireland	5	2	5	72	43	82
Spain	2	3	6	56	57	52
Portugal	2	2	3	43	n.a.	86
Greece	2	5	1	n.a.	n.a.	n.a.

Note: The ratio of capital flows to international trade is the sum of the absolute value of asset and liability flows over the sum of imports and exports times 100. The index of intra-industry trade is 1 minus the absolute value of the difference between asset and liability flows over the sum of these assets and liabilities times 100.

Source: Eurostat (taken from Gros and Thygesen, 1992).

Have capital controls been at the root of such differences? This question, particularly relevant for integration studies, may be answered by comparing the size of the flows of the countries that have practised such controls with the figures for countries that had a liberalist regime. In the former category fall France and Italy; their controls were stringent in the period 1982–3, slightly relaxed in the period 1984–5 and gradually abandoned thereafter. In the latter category we find a country like Germany. The pattern one would expect – flows in countries with controls smaller than in countries without – is not found reflected in the figures of the left-hand part of Table 10.4. This suggests the conclusion that capital controls were not very effective. Now controls were mostly meant to restrict capital outflows. That means that we would expect the outflow to be smaller than the inflow for countries practising controls. However the 'intra-industry index of capital flows' (given in the right-hand part of Table 10.4) shows that in and out flows were more equilibrated for France and Italy than for Germany. This seems to corroborate the conclusion as to the lack of effectiveness of such controls (Gros and Thygesen, 1992).

Euromarket

The integration of long-term and short-term capital markets in the EU had made very little headway until recently owing to the restrictions imposed on capital movements by a number of member countries. Failing the integration by direct dealing between member countries, a different type of integration has developed in which both countries deal with a third party (see Chapter 8) (transfer from local to central markets). This has been done through the so-called 'Euromarkets', a misleading term because it actually refers to off-shore capital markets falling outside the control of any monetary authority. These markets, almost non-existent in the early 1960s, have developed very quickly since, actually tenfold every decade (Johnston, 1983; Kane, 1982) (Table 10.5).

Table 10.5   Growth of international markets (milliard US $) (liabilities), 1960–90

	1960	1970	1980	1990
Currency	1	73	851	n.a.
Bond	0	3	23	229

Source: BIS, *Annual reports*; OECD, *Financial Market Trends*; IMF, *International Capital Markets*, various issues.

The *bond* market concerns long-term bonds with denominations other than the currency of the country where they are issued. Better efficiency has made the Eurobond markets more competitive for many issues than national capital markets. The success of Eurobonds was based on an inconsistency in regulation: governments tended to limit the access of foreign issuers of bonds to their national markets, but their control of domestic investors purchasing foreign bonds was less stringent or non-effective. So banking firms active in international investments could bypass national restrictions by issuing bonds and similar debt instruments. Eurobond borrowers range from international institutions and multinational companies to national and municipal governments.

The *currency* market is the short-term equivalent of the Eurobond market. It thrives on the difference in interest levels on deposits: lower than national ones for borrowers and higher than national ones to lenders (Levi, 1981; Dufey and Giddy, 1981; Clarke and Pulay, 1978). Hence their explosive growth (recent figures not available).

Although little is known about the origin and destination of capital on these markets, the Bank for International Settlements (BIS) estimates that Western Europe in the 1980s held a share of some 40 per cent in total demand. Regrettably there is no way to assess the transactions between European countries, interesting though they are from the integration point of view. Most transactions on the bond and currency markets are denominated in US dollars. The ECU (see Chapter 17) is the third currency after the dollar and the yen.

Interest rate parity

A second way to measure the integration of financial markets is by studying the equalisation of prices. In practice this is the movement towards parity of interest rates for comparable financial products in different national markets. A distinction is thereby made between assets with a short- and with a long-term maturity. Differences in interest rates between countries stem mostly from two causes: first, there is the difference between supply and demand, a factor that should disappear with the taking away of barriers to international financial transactions in the framework of the integration of capital markets; second, there is the inflation differential (related to the likely change in exchange rates: see Chapter 17), a factor that should only disappear with monetary union. In addition, there is a set of factors such as the quality of the debtor, the differences in reserve requirements of financial intermediaries, fiscal regime, transaction costs in thick or thin markets, and so on.

The development of both short- and long-term national interest rates[5] over the period 1960–90 shows marked differences by group of countries and by sub-period (Figure 10.1). For the short-term rates, a certain tendency of convergence can be observed for the period up to 1973. The monetary unrest that was created by the first and the second oil crises increased the divergence again. Since the mid-1980s convergence has set in again. Note that after 1980 the level of divergence was much less for the five core countries of the Exchange Rate Mechanism (ERM) of the European Monetary System (EMS) (see Chapter 17) than for the other EU countries that observed less strict rules as to their monetary cooperation. For long-term rates, the effects of the developments described are cushioned, but do indicate clearly the reduction in divergence, again most pronounced for the core countries of the EMS.

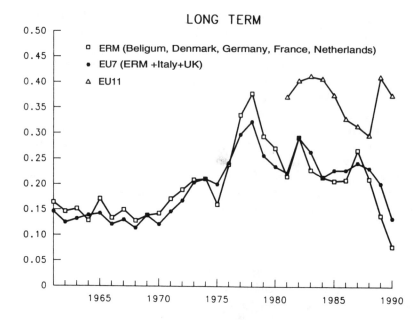

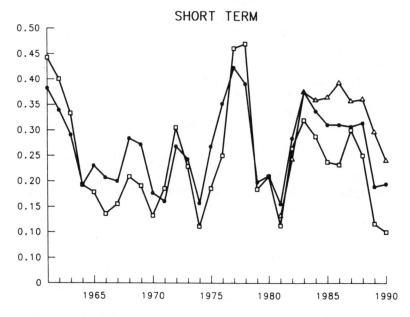

Figure 10.1   Divergence* of interest rates between groups of member countries, 1960–90

*   unweighted coefficient of variation.
Source: Mortensen (1992).

With increasing capital liberalisation, there also exists an increasingly close relation between the interest rates on Euromarkets and national markets. However there are still many imperfections, illustrated for the Eurocurrency markets by the differences in speed with which the two markets adapt to changes in environment (Thorton, 1992).

Welfare effects

The empirical evidence on the 'trade' and welfare effects of the integration of European capital markets is very thin. This may be due to the absence of a clear-cut objective; indeed the markets of EU countries were to be only partly integrated among themselves, and the attitudes of EU member countries towards world integration were very different. Let us briefly review the situation with respect to the three main categories.

The few studies that have analysed the effects of free internal flows of European direct investment have been limited to the employment effects in both source and destination countries. The latter seem invariably to have benefited from DI. The effect on the former varies from negative, when exports from the home bases are replaced, to positive, when the penetration into a foreign market actually increases home employment (Buckley and Artisien, 1987). To our knowledge, no European studies have been carried out on the welfare effects of DI (for example, on profit diversion; see Chapter 8).

An estimate of the welfare effects of the integration of short-term and long-term capital markets made along the theoretical path indicated by Figure 8.1 resulted for the EU as a whole in a benefit of 1,500 million ECU (Price Waterhouse, 1988).

Summary and conclusions

- The objective of European capital market integration was fairly limited and for a long time remained practically restricted to direct investment; only lately has complete internal and external freedom of capital movements been installed.
- Direct investment in the EU has expanded considerably. The intra-EU pattern of DI shows a net flow from the richer (northern) member states towards the poorer (southern) member states, which should lead to more convergence of wealth levels (Chapter 18).
- Long-term and short-term loans were for a long time controlled on segmented markets. An alternative to European integra-

tion has developed with the growth of the practically unregulated off-shore markets. With increasing liberalisation, the national markets in the EU countries have tended to align with
these 'world' markets.
- The welfare effects of the integration of European capital markets are unknown as far as DI and portfolio investment are
concerned. However, for short-term and long-term loans, it
was shown that considerable benefits can be gained through
integration.

Notes

1   An indicator of integration that groups both direct investment and portfolio
investment is income received from investment abroad. Balance of payments
figures show that these have increased rapidly over the past decades (see Table
20.1).
2   Capital and payment are both financial transactions and are therefore often
treated together. Free movement of goods, persons and services presupposes, as
we have seen, freedom of payments for such transactions. Such payments are
completely free (Article 106 of the Treaty). This freedom cannot be revoked by
any member state. Equally free (Article 67, second paragraph) are 'all current
payments connected with the movement of capital between Member States'
(that is, payments of interest and dividends), with the proviso, however, that
member states have the right to check whether such operations are not capital
transactions in disguise.
3.   Or in the IMF definition: 'an investment that is made to acquire a lasting interest
in an enterprise operating in an economy other than that of the investor; the
investor's purpose being to have an effective voice in the management of the
enterprise'.
4   An attempt has been made to bypass this difficulty by using the balance between national savings and investment, assuming that there is more integration
the less the correlation between domestic investment and savings in a set of
countries (Feldstein and Horioka, 1980). The empirical testing of this approach
proved beset with such difficulties that the approach was considered less suitable for measuring the progress of financial integration (Lemmen and Eijffinger,
1992). So one has to work with other indicators.
5   Three price criteria are generally used (Frankel, 1989) for measuring the degree
of capital market integration. It is perfect if there is parity of uncovered nominal
interest rate (UNIR), covered nominal interest rate (CNIR) and real interest rate
(RIR). *Covered interest parity* has been analysed by Van den Bergh *et al.* (1987),
who estimated the interdependence between the development of short-term
interest on Euromarkets and internal markets. The results for the 1970s show
very little integration. In the 1980s, on the contrary, the markets of Germany, the
UK, the Netherlands and Belgium became highly integrated, whereas the integration of the Italian and French market remained poor.
   Real interest rates (RIR) parity among countries for the short term has not been
found in any empirical study. Mishkin (1984a, 1984b), who studied seven OECD
countries, found neither equality at one point in time nor short-term RIR to
move similarly through time. Mark (1985a, 1985b) came to the same conclusion

after incorporating taxation effects. These results were confirmed by Gaab *et al.* (1986), Caramazza (1987).

Long-term real interest rates on international markets are much less documented than short-term ones. One reason is that comparable financial instruments on Euro and domestic capital markets are hard to find. Following Fukao and Hanazaki (1987), we have estimated the significance of real interest rate differentials between Germany and five other EC countries. We have made a distinction between the pre-crisis period (1963–73), with low inflation and fixed exchange rates, the 1973–79 period, when monetary disturbances occurred and capital controls abounded, the 1980–86 period, when international capital movement controls were abandoned or relaxed in many countries, and the period 1987–91, when these trends gained momentum. The analysis shows that in the first period only small differentials occurred (index 94). In the second period the differences were fairly large, in particular for the UK and Italy (index 81). After the relaxation of capital controls, the differences became very small (index 92 in 1980–86).

Nominal interest rates have converged as inflation differentials disappeared under the rigour of the European Monetary System (see Chapter 17). See, for the quantitative results of some of these indicators (for example, Van den Bergh *et al.*, 1987), Table 20.2.

PART IV
SECTORS OF ACTIVITY

11 Agriculture

Introduction

The integration of the markets for goods generally refers implicitly only to manufactured goods. However the advantages of integration do apply to the integration of agricultural produce markets too. Notwithstanding this, agriculture is in many integration schemes excluded from the free traffic of goods (for example, EFTA). The reason is that national governments have often regulated agriculture strongly to protect farmers and pursue other social objectives (such as maintaining the viability of small family business) or spatial planning objectives (such as maintaining a specific regional balance). The political resistance to change is such that it has been deemed preferable to forgo the advantages of integration.

These factors also played a role when the EU was founded. However the EU has decided to integrate agricultural markets on theoretical as well as political grounds. The theoretical motive was the strong association of the agricultural sector with the rest of the economy; differential prices for agricultural produce, affecting the cost of raw materials as well as labour cost (through food prices), lead to differential costs in other sectors and may thus disturb competition. The political motive was that, as a counterweight to the prospects the common market opened to German manufacturing industry, equivalent chances had to be created for French agriculture.

In the first section below we will discuss in detail the principles of EU agricultural policy. The next section will give a summary description of the development of the agricultural sector under conditions of integration, detailing production levels, trade, production structure, concentration of firms and so on.

The system chosen for the EU is neither the only one feasible nor the best one from an economic point of view. To grasp the workings of EU and alternative systems, we will then dwell on some theoretical aspects and on that basis describe the welfare effects of alternative systems. The disadvantages of some characteristics of the EU regime will then stand out clearly.

To round off the chapter, some observations will be made about the options for lowering the costs of the present policy and the possibilities for improvement of the Common Agricultural Policy (CAP).

EU regime

Treaty

The Treaty of Rome states that the common market encompasses all agricultural products and that for good performance and development of the common market a common agricultural policy must be pursued (Article 3). That policy has been accomplished in the course of the transition period (that is, between 1958 and 1970) according to the Treaty obligations (Article 40).

The objectives of the Common Agricultural Policy (CAP) (Article 39) are:

- to increase agricultural productivity by promoting technical progress and the optimum use of production factors;
- to ensure a fair standard of living to the agricultural community by increasing their per capita income;
- to stabilise markets;
- to assure the availability of supplies;
- to ensure reasonable consumer prices.

The editors of the Treaty, realising that objectives were to some extent conflicting owing to the conflicting interests of consumers and producers, tried to give some indication of priority by the order of the points of Article 39. From the position of points 1 and 2, to improve the income prospects of the producers is clearly the primary aim.

The Treaty (Article 40) orders the EU to elaborate the CAP and gives some instructions on how to set about it: a conference of expert representatives of the member states was to be convened to plot the main lines of such a policy. That conference was held in Stresa in 1958; two kinds of policy were found necessary:

- *market control policy* (including the following three elements of the Treaty):
    - market regulation, comprising an intervening body, competition rules and rules for foreign trade;

- price policy, consisting in the setting of minimum prices by criteria which are as objective as possible;
- a fund to pay guaranteed prices (guarantee);
- *structural policy*;
  - production factors;
  - production conditions;
  - involving a fund for financing this policy at the EU level.

The results of the Stresa conference enabled the Commission to submit the first drafts fairly soon, and as early as 1960 the Council could on that basis issue the first regulations. In the course of the years these have been followed by untold regulations, directives and decisions, too detailed to go into here. The new member states have subsequently adopted these.

Policy of market control

Many countries have established a policy of market control for agricultural products. The reason is that agricultural markets have more difficulty in getting to equilibrium than manufactured goods markets, and the social consequences of disequilibria were thought unacceptable. The causes for disequilibria are as follows. On the demand side, agricultural products are vital necessities and so have a very low price elasticity. On the supply side, the vagaries of the weather may cause large fluctuations in production volume. Coupled with inelastic demand, this leads to large price fluctuations. The very many suppliers, by reacting simultaneously to price signals, may boost fluctuations even further. So governments often regulate prices and quantities in a detailed way.

The common European policy of market control is based on three principles, important enough to be discussed in detail:

- *Unity of the market* implies, first, the completely free internal traffic of agricultural products (that is to say, no customs tariffs, quotas and so on). Given the special structure of agriculture, it also implies a common organisation setting one price for the whole market and using in all member states the same intervention instruments to regulate the market. One important instrument is the protection of the outer frontiers; another is the guaranteed sale of the domestic production of some major products at the set price. Unity of the market also implies mutual adjustment across the whole EU of national instructions with respect to health control, veterinary care and so on, and supervision to prevent certain, mostly national, measures from distorting competition.

- *Priority for EU's own products.* The needs of the market are in the first instance provided for by European production; only if that is insufficient will imports be resorted to.[1] Should the world market price be above the EU price, then the system provides for a subsidy to be paid on imports to avoid upward pressure on the internal price level, and for a levy to be imposed on exports, to prevent the EU production from seeping away abroad.
- *Financial solidarity* among member states. A policy of market control yields (levies) as well as costs money (restitutions, storage costs and so on). All yields are paid into the European Agricultural Guidance and Guarantee Fund, Guarantee Division (EAGGF) whatever the member state collecting them; all costs are paid from that Fund, no matter what member state the amounts flow to. Because in general the returns from levies on agricultural produce are not sufficient to finance all costs, the European Agricultural Fund has to be fed as well from the EU's other own financial means (see Chapter 4).

The issue of a common market regulation does not imply that it is the same for all products. The three most important types of systems of market control are the following:

- A guarantee scheme and intervention prices when the world market is screened off. This scheme applies to by far the greater part of production (more than 70 per cent), namely cereals, sugar and dairy products. This type of scheme guarantees a minimum price at which intervention agencies will buy up any domestic supply, the quantities involved being stored and sold when the market situation is favourable. There are broadly similar market schemes for pork, fruit and vegetables, and table wine, but they put the emphasis on storage and processing support rather than on an automatic sales guarantee at fixed prices.
- Limited free price formation with the world market screened off. This type of scheme has been introduced for about a quarter of the products, in particular for certain kinds of fruit and vegetables, flowers, eggs and poultry meat. These products do not count as basic foods and often have a short production cycle, which is why guarantee prices are not judged necessary and constraining the imports by levies and restrictions is thought sufficient.
- Bonuses based on the quantity produced. For some other products, for instance those for which international agreements allow no protection at the border, a system of subsidies on the

value of the produce is sometimes applied. Such a system allows domestic production to be maintained at high producer costs, consumer prices being kept low nevertheless. It is applied, for instance, to oilseeds. Producers of olive oil, too, are given support in proportion to their production volumes. In other cases, subsidies by hectare, number of cattle and so on are offered. Together these schemes do not account for more than 5 per cent of the total production value of EU agriculture.

From the above, the pivot of most market regulations is the *intervention price*. Since among the objectives of agricultural policy farmers' income has pride of place, it is hardly surprising that intervention prices are mostly set as high as possible. The yearly price setting by the Council, on the proposal of the Commission and after consultation of the European Parliament, has long been the main event of European decision making. This remained so after the new plan of MacSharry (the European Commissioner for Agriculture) had been adopted by the Council; this plan foresees a considerable lowering of the guarantee prices and puts more weight on income support systems to farmers (see subsequent section).

The day-to-day implementation of agricultural policy is in the hands of the Commission, but in practice carried on in committees in which representatives of the Commission and member states confer. If the Commission decides according to the committee's opinion, the measure becomes valid at once; otherwise it has to be submitted to the Council for consideration.

In the prescribed system, one price prevails throughout the market for a given product in the whole EU. The EU not having a currency of its own, the price must first be expressed in the ECU (European Currency Unit) and next recalculated in the various national currencies. This means that changes in the rate of exchange may cause the price suddenly to rise for farmers in the devaluating country and drop for farmers in the revaluating country. To cushion such changes, the so-called 'Monetary Compensatory Amounts' (MCA) were introduced: a system of levies and restitutions on the interior frontiers, serving to eliminate the effects of sudden price differences on the market, but having the effect of breaking the unity of the common market. This system has been discontinued, however.

Structural policy

If the EU policy of market control was worked out rather rapidly, things were different as far as structural policy was concerned. Given the pluriform production conditions and national regulations, until the early 1970s the Commission practically confined itself to some coordination of the member states' structural policies. Still a limited number of schemes deemed of common interest by the Council were financed by the Guidance Division of the European Agricultural Fund.

The impulse towards a genuine European structural policy for agriculture was given by the so-called 'Mansholt Plan' (CEC, 1968). Some relevant decisions were made around 1972, and from then on this policy has been gradually extended. At present it comprises three main elements: support to management, improvement of trade channels for agricultural produce and reduction of regional differences. As is evident from the word 'structure', the long-term aim of structural policy is to enhance the productivity of agricultural enterprise, an aim that derives directly from the first objective of agricultural policy (Article 39).

Support to management means first of all supporting investments aimed at technical progress, interest subsidies and investment subsidies being the instruments wielded. Improving educational and training possibilities for agricultural workers is another form of support. Rational management is stimulated by support to senior owners of marginal establishments willing to close shop, and infrastructural measures such as improvement of the water economy, reallotment schemes and so on. Finally quite a network of consulting agencies has been built up, able to give advice on widely diverging matters associated with conducting a business.

Improving the often complicated structure of sales channels and processing of agricultural products is indispensable to a well-functioning agricultural sector. In that connection, dairy factories, slaughterhouses, packing establishments for fruit and vegetables, wine-bottling establishments, auction rooms, cold-storage warehouses and so on, fulfil important roles besides the trade proper. Therefore EU structural policy provides for EU subsidies to such establishments for improving their performance. Furthermore the EU can make funds available for producer groups ('cooperations') with a view to reinforcing the farmer's position in his negotiations with customers.

The structure of agriculture differs greatly between areas of the EU, which is evident from the large regional discrepancies in productivity. The agricultural productivity of weak regions cannot be improved by the simple expedient of stimulating the outflow of workers, for these regions mostly have not much to offer in the way of alternative activities. For that reason the EU may sometimes introduce supporting measures, provided they fit in with other regional actions in the framework of an integrated development programme. (This point will be taken up in Chapter 18.)

The EU measures sketched above are not the only ones to be taken to improve the European agricultural structure; indeed the EU's policy is merely complementary, the main responsibility being still with the member states, as is apparent from a comparison of expenditures incurred by the EU and the national budgets.

The costs of the European structural policy are paid from the EAGGF, Guidance Division. In practice this often means that the EAGGF finances a certain proportion of a programme's total costs. That proportion is on average small in so-called 'strong' areas, but may be as much as 50 or 65 per cent in so-called 'weak' areas. The Guidance Division has for some time been spending considerable sums, especially in comparison to the expenditures of the EU for other sectors.

Sketch of the sector

The sector as a whole

From the fact that agricultural policy is the EU's most elaborate policy area and has always been the focus of interest, one might presume that this sector is the most important in the EU economy. That is not true, however. Admittedly in the past agriculture used to be the most important sector of the economy, but gradually industry and, later, services have developed, reducing agriculture to a relatively modest position. Table 11.1 shows the steep drop in the relative significance of agriculture in the EU economy over a period of 40 years.

Table 11.1   Percentage share of agriculture in total GDP and total employment of the EU12, 1950–90

Indicator	1950	1960	1970	1980	1990
GDP	12	8	6	4	3
Employment	30	21	13	10	7

Sources: GDP: Eurostat, *National Accounts*, various years; Molle *et al.* (1980). Employment: 1950–70, Molle *et al.* (1980); 1970–90, OECD, *Labour Force Statistics*, various years.

At the moment, less than 3 per cent of total GDP is produced by the agricultural sector, with only 7 per cent of total active population of the EU still employed in agriculture, figures which in 1950 were still four times as high. In the 1950s the shares of agriculture differed widely among the countries of Europe. While in Italy, France and other Mediterranean countries such as Spain, Portugal and Greece the sector was still very important, in the UK it was very modest. The differences, though still there, have shrunk in the course of time.

The main cause of the relative reduction of the agricultural share in the economy is the low income elasticity for food products. Indeed, as incomes rise, people tend to spend a smaller portion on food. Typical income elasticities in the EU are between 0.1 and 0.3 only, and for some products elasticity is even negative (see, for example, Hill and Ingersent, 1982). Because the cost of food is increasingly made up of such industrial activities as processing, packaging and presentation, the share of agricultural products in the economy is even smaller than the elasticities seem to imply.

Sub-sectors

The broad sector of agriculture hitherto referred to falls into some important branches: (1) arable farming (cereals); (2) livestock farming (meat, milk, dairy products); (3) horticulture (vegetables, fruit, flowers and so on); (4) viniculture; (5) forestry (timber); and finally (6) fishery.[2] Each of them can be sub-divided into product groups. Table 11.2 indicates their relative importance and the stability of the shares of the groups through time.

Table 11.2   Percentage share of some selected product groups in the total production value of agriculture

Product		1974	1980	1990
1	Cereals (mainly wheat)	12	12	11
2.1	Dairy (mainly milk)	19	19	18
2.2	Meat (mainly beef and pork)	31	32	30
3	Vegetables, fruit, olives	13	14	15
4	Wine	4	5	6
5	Other	21	18	20

Source: CEG, *De Toestand van de Landbouw in de Gemeenschap* (The state of agriculture in the Community), Brussels, various years, 1974–80 EU9; 1990 EU12.

Size of farms

The structure of the agricultural market is characterised by almost perfect competition on the side of supply. Table 11.3 gives an indication of the number of suppliers, in this case the number of farms. The picture is not complete, very small holdings (often run as side activities) not being included.

National and EU measures to improve the structure were among the causes of a rapid decline in the number of establishments in the past 25 years, by nearly 40 per cent. Table 11.3 also shows that small farms in particular have been closed down or taken over, or have had their land put to another use.[3] Agriculture in the countries of the original EU6 was dominated by smallholdings, while in the UK and Denmark there were more large farms. The share of small farms (between 1 and 10 ha) dropped by some 8 percentage points (of a shrinking total!) over the whole period. In the last few years the decline has been slowing down, owing to, among other things, the worsening prospects of employment outside agriculture. As a result of the developments described, in the EU10 the average farm size rose by more than half between 1960 and 1985.

Table 11.3   Development of the number and size of farms (agricultural establishments) (EU10)[a]

	1960	1970	1980	1987
Number of holdings larger than 1 ha (thousands)	8 100	6 600	5 500	5 000
Share of holdings smaller than 10 ha in total area of holdings of over 1 ha (%)	70	66	63	62
Average size of holdings (ha)	11	14	16	17
Area per worker (ha)	6	8	10	13

[a]   no comparable figures available for EU12 for whole period; more recent figures not available either.

Source: Eurostat, *Yearbook of Agricultural Statistics*, various years; *Statistical Yearbook*, various years; some estimates.

A second indicator of structural change is the number of persons by hectare of cultivated land. In the past 25 years the area of land cultivated by farms of more than 1 ha has hardly changed: there has been a slight decline of about 5 per cent. Apart from small differences in definition, the decline in employment discussed in the previous section is therefore an adequate measure of the increase in the number of hectares cultivated by one agricultural worker. By a crude computation (total area of land cultivated in farms of over 1 ha divided by active population in agriculture), each person employed in agriculture in the EU10 corresponded to about 4 ha of cultivated land in 1950, and 13 ha in 1987; a very large but gradual increase.

There are large differences between the EC member countries in average farm size: in 1987, when in the EU12 50 per cent of the farms fell into the category from 1 to 5 ha, in Greece, Portugal and Italy the corresponding figure was still around 70. Moreover in these countries the average number of hectares per employed person was less than half of the EU average.

Productivity

Another indicator of the changing structure of agriculture is the degree of mechanisation. The number of tractors, for instance, has grown rather spectacularly. Account being taken of the contraction of cultivated land, in 1985 there appeared to be three times as many tractors for every 1000 ha of cultivated land than 25 years earlier. Total capital use would be the best indicator, but that is difficult to measure, so that we are forced to go by the overall effects.

An idea of productivity rises is given by Table 11.4, which shows how the average yields of certain agricultural products increased. With sugar-beets the rise in productivity is less than 1 per cent a year overall, with milk and potatoes somewhat less than 2 per cent; the rise of 3.5 per cent achieved by wheat was very high indeed. (For the other cereals the more modest increase of 2 per cent was registered.) All increases are mostly due to better varieties and the use of more fertilisers.

The above picture of the various structural characteristics of agriculture in the whole European Union conceals marked differences among member states. More detailed values of the various indicators by country reveal that the productivity in a country like Greece is poor beside that of northern member states like the Netherlands and Denmark. As far as certain crops are concerned, even Italy's productivity still remains below that of the EU average.

Table 11.4   Average yields of agricultural products

Product	1960	1970	1980	1990
Milk (kg/cow)	2 900	3 400	4 100	4 500
Wheat (100 kg/ha)	23	32	48	57
Sugar-beets (100 kg/ha)	400	420	450	540

Sources: LEI, Selected agri figures of the EC; Eurostat, *Land Use and Production 1980*; *Yearbook of Agricultural Statistics*, various years, 1960–80 EU10, 1990 EU12.

Market regulation and its effects

Unstable markets

Agricultural markets, as we pointed out earlier, tend to be rather unstable: demand is price-inelastic and so is supply in the short term. Farmers are small producers compared to the size of the market. They tend to react to price changes without taking account of the underlying demand and supply changes. An illustration of the inability of agricultural markets to achieve equilibrium is the so-called 'hog-cycle', which owes its name to the German economist Hanau, who was the first to analyse the phenomenon with respect to the pig market. Figure 11.1 presents the relevant supply and demand curves. Suppose a sudden rise in demand (from D_1 to D_2); supply fails to adjust (it takes some time for pigs to be born and become fit for slaughter).

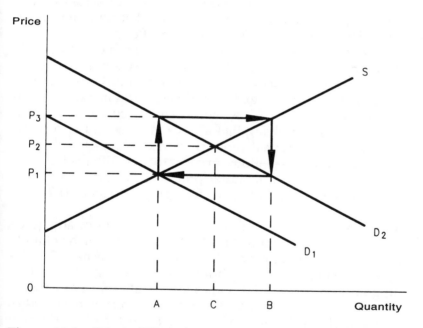

Figure 11.1   **Disequilibria in agricultural markets: hog cycle**

As a consequence, the price rises to p_3 instead of p_2, which would be the new equilibrium price at which the equilibrium quantity OC would be sold. Producers considering the high price p_3 to be the long-term measure will extend the supply of pigs from OA to OB. However demanders are not prepared to digest so much supply at that price, so that the price will drop to the p_1 level. Many producers now decide not to produce at this price; fewer pigs are raised, supply is after some time limited to OA, after which the cycle can start anew. In its pure form the cyclical movement only occurs if the gradients of the demand and supply curves are equal. If the gradient of the demand curve is steeper than that of the supply curve, the system is explosive, that is to say, it progressively removes itself from the equilibrium; if the supply curve has a steeper gradient than the demand curve, the system converges (cobweb theorem). The disequilibrium inherent in agricultural markets can give rise to heavy social costs, which is why many countries decided at quite an early date to introduce some kind of control of these markets.

Effects of various systems of market control; production, trade and welfare

There are two major systems of market control; both influence the price (through guarantees or subsidies, for example), sales (through market organisation) and the access to the market (through import constraints). They have very different welfare effects.

The first is the EU system of *guaranteed prices*; some features of it have already been pointed out in the previous section. The way this scheme of market control works and the effects it produces on various internal (national or EU)-guaranteed and world market prices is shown in Figure 11.2. Here S_{com} is the EU supply curve, which runs rather a level course, implying that a price increase causes a somewhat more than proportional production rise. D_{com} is the demand curve, drawn as rather precipitous, in concordance with the inelasticity of demand for most agricultural products. We can now distinguish four cases corresponding to the four prices in Figure 11.2.

- The price on the world market is p_1, at which price any quantity wanted can be obtained (fully elastic supply). In an entirely open economy, domestic production will now become OA, domestic demand OB, and a quantity AB will be imported, everything at the price p_1. The domestic agricultural production is low in that case; so are consumer prices. Government subsidies do not apply, so the taxpayer is not asked for a contribution (left-hand upper part of Figure 11.2).
- At a guaranteed price p_2, domestic production will rise to OC and demand drop to OD. On the quantity imported, CD, an import levy of $p_2 - p_1$ will be imposed to make prices on the world and EU markets equal. That yields $CD \times (p_2 - p_1)$ in tariff revenue, the shaded area $IMNT$ in right-hand upper part of Figure 11.2. The consumer is worse off: he consumes less at higher prices (consumer loss $ZXNK$, deadweight loss TNK).

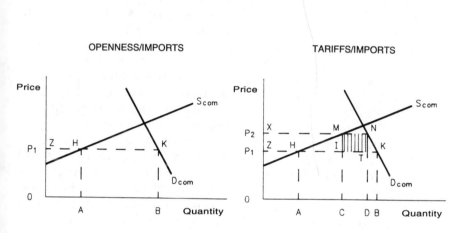

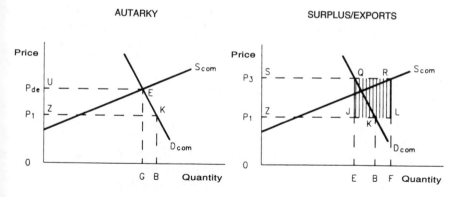

Figure 11.2 EC market-regulation system for major agricultural products (guarantee prices)

The farmer's gross return, achieved in one transaction, namely through selling to the intervention authority, will amount to $OXMC$. The area $ZXMH$ represents an extra producer rent transferred to farmers from consumers (HMI deadweight loss).

- The price is raised to p_{de}, which indicates the domestic equilibrium between supply and demand. It can be done without creating surpluses and without involving public budget expenses to be born finally by the taxpayer, albeit at a cost to consumers (left-hand lower part of Figure 11.2).

- At a price p_3, the situation changes profoundly, however. Demand will drop to OE, entailing an additional loss in consumer surplus as less product becomes available at higher prices. As supply rises to OF, market authorities find themselves compelled to buy up a quantity $OF - OE$ at price p_3. That quantity has to be sold on the world market, which implies an export subsidy (or 'restitution' in EC jargon) of the difference between the guaranteed price (or intervention price) p_3 and the world market price p_1. The amount is $JQRL$, which will be charged to the taxpayer. The gross return to the farmer, achieved in one transaction through selling of production to the intervention authority, will amount to $OSRF$ (right-hand lower part of Figure 11.2).

The second type of market regulation to be dealt with is the one that used to be applied, among other countries, in the UK, where it was known as the scheme of *deficiency payments*.[4] Slightly altered, it is also common within the EU in the form of 'bonus'. Figure 11.3 illustrates the working of this scheme, which leaves trade in agricultural produce free. Its special characteristic is that it dissociates the price that is paid by the consumer from the price that is calculated to determine the income of the producer.

- At a price p_1 (world market price) (upper part of Figure 11.3) demand will be OB and domestic production OA. The consumer enjoys high quantities OB at a low price and the government's (taxpayers') resources are not tapped.

- A country wanting to boost its own production will grant farmers a kind of subsidy by unit of produce (upper part of Figure 11.3). A subsidy of $p_2 - p_1$ will entail a domestic supply of OC and imports of CB. The price remains low for all consumers: p_1. The taxpayer contributes $ZXMI$. The farmer's gross return consists of two parts: the market part $OZIC$ and the subsidy part $ZXMI$. Even less costly is a system that is related not to the production volume but to the difference in cost and revenue. With such a system, based on information on production cost of groups of farms, producers in the *OA* range would not receive any subsidy, producers at point *C* the full subsidy $p_2 - p_1$, and producers in the *AC* range a subsidy that would be just sufficient to cover their cost. Costs to the government (taxpayer): the triangle *HMI*.

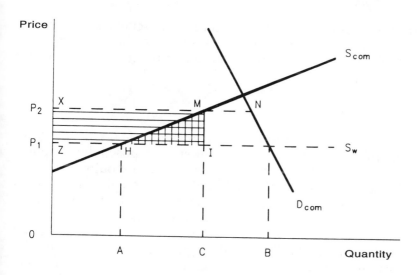

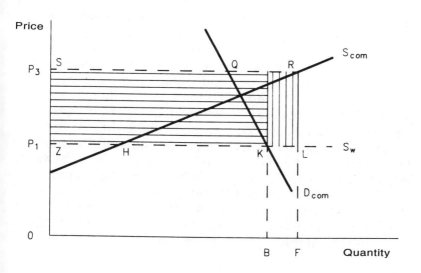

Figure 11.3   Alternative market regulation systems (deficiency payments)

- Because with this system farmers' income-support and price policies remain largely separate, a pressure strong enough to push up the price to p_3 (through subsidies in the order of magnitude of $p_3 - p_1$) is not likely to build up easily; should it happen nevertheless, then the subsidy would work out as a production subsidy for the *OB* part and as an export subsidy for the *BF* part (see lower part of Figure 11.3).

So it results from these examples that different schemes clearly have widely divergent welfare effects, dependent on the domestic price level and the differences between the domestic guaranteed and the world market prices.

Price policy and the consumer

Before 1964, the Common Agricultural Policy made no move toward common prices. In that year the Commission proposed the establishment of common price levels for cereals, pig meat, poultry meat and eggs. The negotiations with the Council were difficult, wheat prices being at the time much higher in Germany than in France and somewhere in between in other countries. Because of the German position, the EU price finally resulting was well above the average of all other countries. Later the Council also agreed on prices for fruits and vegetables and for some other important products. The complete price structure, with other cereal prices derived from the high wheat price, became effective in 1968. Because many animals are on a cereal diet, meat prices rose in proportion. Following that trend the EU adopted relatively high prices for other products as well.

EU prices were thus set well above world market level, as is illustrated by Table 11.5 for some selected products: on average EU prices appear to be almost double the world market ones. Moreover, over the years 1970–90, they have tended to depart further from world price levels. This does not mean, however, that European consumers pay twice as much for their food as they would without the CAP price system. As a matter of fact, prices on the world market are heavily influenced by the EU system that dumps goods on the world market, bringing down prices there. Should prices in Europe, and hence European production and exports, drop, those on the world market would probably recover to some extent, though not to anywhere near the EU level; even during the commodity price boom of 1973, many European prices remained well above world levels.

Table 11.5   EU agricultural prices (threshold) as a percentage of
world market prices (five-year averages)

Product	1970	1980	1990
Soft wheat	157*	147	156
Hard wheat	199	220	237
Barley	207	248	288
Maize	163	198	234
Sugar	261	185	252
Butter	133	136	151

* Not fully comparable to figures 1980–90.
Source: Own calculations based on Eurostat, *Yearbook of Agricultural Statistics*, various years.
AgriEurope, FAO.

Domestic production and world markets

Prices, increased to raise farmers' incomes, do not necessarily entail
external problems through subsidised exports; domestic prices can
rise to well above world market level (p_{de} versus p_1 in Figure 11.2)
without giving rise to surplus production (that is, production beyond OG).

The same idea can be expressed in the self-sufficiency ratio (SSR).
In Figure 11.2, at price p_1, domestic production is below the equilibrium levels of domestic supply and demand, so that the SSR is below
100. On the other hand, at price p_3, domestic production exceeds
domestic demand, and hence SSR is above 100. For the period from
1960 to 1990, Table 11.6 indicates the SSR for a set of important
products. Before the enlargement of 1973, the EU increased its self-
sufficiency for many products to a considerable degree, in some
cases by more than 100 per cent. The first enlargement entailed a
drop in self-sufficiency for the EU9, due mostly to the UK's position
as a large importer of many agricultural products. Since then, however, the production of practically all commodities has grown considerably. By 1984, the EU had again become a net exporter of many
of the products mentioned in the table. The extension of the EU to 12
countries did not affect this situation very much for, first, agriculture
is an important sector in these countries too, and, second, production
in the EU continued to grow beyond demand growth. Indeed raising
the internal prices to p_3 levels had obviously boosted production to
levels exceeding demand. A very important line had thus been
crossed. Instead of receiving an income from levies on imports, the
EU increasingly had to pay subsidies to exporters. The appearance of
the EU (as well as other countries) as a structural supplier on world

Table 11.6   Self-sufficiency ratio[a] of the European Union for some selected agricultural products, 1960–90[b] (index)

Product	1960	1973	1974	1981	1985	1990
Wheat	90	111	103	117	122	127
Rye	n.a.	105	94	103	112	109
Barley	84	113	106	114	133	131
Maize	64	67	58	66	84	77
Cereals, total	85	97	92	103	114	120
Rice	85	90	98	95	75	76
Potatoes	101	102	100	101	102	100
Sugar	104	116	91	135	125	n.a.
Vegetables	n.a.	97	93	97	107	106
Fresh fruit	n.a.	82	80	83	86	85
Citrus fruit	n.a.	41	42	43	74	70
Wine	89	101	99	102	104	112
Cheese	100	102	102	107	108	n.a.
Butter	101	118	101	120	129	n.a.
Powdered milk, unskimmed	139	191	208	411	348	n.a.
Powdered milk, skimmed	97	124	137	142	106	n.a.
Beef	92	85	92	105	106	101
Veal	n.a.	104	104	101	112	115
Pork	100	99	101	101	102	103
Poultry	93	100	103	109	105	104
Meat, total	95	92	96	102	101	102
Eggs	90	100	100	102	102	102
Oils and fats	n.a.	44	40	43	63	70

[a]   Bear in mind, in interpreting the SS rates of this table, that many of them are much too low, because the EU includes in demand the quantities which it has been forced to sell on the internal market to low-grade users and at special prices. Corrected for this unrealistic demand, the self-sufficiency ratio for powdered milk, for example, goes up from 130 to 470.

[b]   1960–73: EU6; 1974–81: EU9; 1985–90: EU12.

Sources: Eurostat, *Basic Community Statistics; Yearbook of Agricultural Statistics; Statistical Yearbook Agriculture; Supply Balances; Animal Production* and *Crop Production; Quarterly Statistics,* various issues, *De Toestand van de Landbouw in de Gemeenschap,* 1991.

markets, where prices tend to fluctuate strongly with changes in demand and supply, has had a downward effect on world market prices.

Besides internal problems, this causes grave external conflicts. Indeed other exporting countries are increasingly pushed out of existing markets owing to subsidised exports of the EU, or, if they manage to keep their hand in, have to be content with lower prices than they would have without the EU's 'dumping' activities. The predicament is serious, for the EU is in conflict not only with developed countries like the USA (about cereals, for example) but also with developing countries which depend very much on the revenues of their exports (of sugar, for example) to pay their imports (Hine, 1992). Thus the beneficial effects of EU development policy (see Chapter 19) are partly undone by the detrimental external effects of the CAP. On the other hand, an analysis, carried out by means of a very large multi-country multi-product model (Tims, 1987), has shown that the complete abolition of the EU protective system would favour the LDCs as a group only slightly. One reason is that, as soon as the EU stops dumping its surpluses on the world market, prices there are bound to rise, to the detriment of the many LDCs who are themselves importers of food.

Price policy and the taxpayer

As surpluses accumulate, the government and hence taxpayer is again asked for increasing contributions. With the EU realising net exports of many products over long time spans, import levies do not suffice to compensate for the cost of restitutions. Moreover, as every additional unit of export tends to have a negative effect on world market prices, the restitution needed per unit increases accordingly. The costs of stockholding are also steadily mounting. Table 11.7 illustrates the rapid increase in the budgetary cost of the CAP.

From the data underlying this table, the EU's total expenditure on agriculture indeed amounts to almost 1 per cent of total GNP in Europe. It rose very sharply between 1970 and 1985, doubling every

Table 11.7 Outlay (in 1,000 million ECU) on the European Guidance and Guarantee Fund for Agriculture, 1970–90*

		1970	1980	1990**
1	Guarantee	2.0	11.2	29.8
2	Guidance	—	0.4	1.8
3	EAGGF	2.0	11.6	31.6
4	Total budget	2.4	16.8	49.0
1	as a percentage of 3	97	96	94
3	as a percentage of 4	88	70	61

* Average figures for five-year periods around reference years.
** Budget 1991, 1992 and 1993.
Source: CEG, *De Toestand van de Landbouw in de Gemeenschap*, various years.

five years; recently a slowdown in growth can be seen, resulting from restrictive measures.[5]

The burden of the budget is shared 'equally' by the member states (see Chapter 4). The benefits of the CAP, however, tend to go to member states with a high national SSR (Strijker and De Veer, 1988). In some studies attempts have been made to measure these redistributional effects of the budget (Buckwell *et al.*, 1982; Koester, 1977; Rollo and Warwick, 1979). The group of states with low SSRs being relatively poor, large compensation amounts need to be paid out to them (for instance, to the UK), which upsets the budgetary balance of the EU. If market disequilibria in agriculture could be avoided, the distributional problems would be much easier to handle.

Conflicts and solutions

Problems and conflicts

The common agricultural policy has realised its objectives on many points. Markets have been stabilised (that is to say, supply has been ensured, if at rather high prices). Farmers' incomes increased in the period between 1969 and 1979 at about the same rate as the rest of the economy (they would probably have done so also without any policy, at higher social costs for this group but lower cost for consumer and taxpayer). Production has grown rapidly (by about 7 per cent between 1968 and 1973, by about 5 per cent since). On the other hand, there are enormous problems whose solution requires a thorough adjustment of the CAP, for the CAP objectives (Article 39) contain an inherent conflict. Indeed the attempt to keep up agricultural incomes by boosting the price levels has led to a large overproduction: surpluses which have to be stocked and for which special campaigns have to be conducted to sell them on EU or world markets.

Contrary to the political evaluation of the CAP just given, its *economic evaluation* shows many negative points. The first group of losers in the EU are the consumers, because they pay more for their products than necessary. A second group incurring welfare losses are the taxpayers. If consumers pay too much for products they need, taxpayers pay for production nobody really wants. A third group of losers are the third countries (in so far as they are net exporters), many of them developing countries. They are facing not only poorer possibilities of exporting to the EU, but also lower revenues from their sales to world markets because of dumping by the EU. There are, however, more negative points to be mentioned.

First, one result of the EU price policy is the misallocation of production factors. Agriculture and the industry producing inputs for it are using up resources that could have been better employed elsewhere. Biotechnological industries have difficulties developing, among other reasons because their input prices are too high (sugar, for instance). A considerable area of agricultural land which could have been used for other products (wood, for instance, which is in very short supply in the EU) or for nature reserves, is tied up in useless production. In some countries, the high product prices even led to the further extension of agricultural land at the expense of woodlands.

A final point to be made refers to the growth potential of the EU economy. The large claims agriculture makes on the budget frustrate the development of programmes for the industrial and service sectors. The common agricultural policy contributes to the compartmentalisation of the EU market (indeed the Monetary Compensatory Amounts broke the principle of unity of the market, but the programme for completing the internal market by 1992 (see Chapter 16) obliged the EU to discontinue this system).

The negative effects of the high prices on taxpayers, consumers and trade partners and the need to complete the internal market for agricultural products were good reasons for the CAP having to be reformed.

A revision of the CAP: different options

How did a policy for a major sector of the economy with considerable negative effects come to be elaborated in the first place? And how could a system so evidently incapable of correction be maintained for so long? These are points of particular interest to analyse. The answer to both questions is largely contained in the workings of the EU institutions (see Chapter 4) in general and the specialised Council of Agricultural Ministers in particular. Special interest groups have been able (supported by their power in elections) to force decisions and many observers were convinced that, to understand the CAP, its political rationale should be the primary consideration, its economic rationale being at best of secondary importance.[6]

The gigantic production surpluses have made it clear that the policy of market control can no longer be based on guaranteed unlimited sales at fixed prices for practically all products; such guarantees are particularly out of place for products for which the EU is already or will soon be more than one hundred per cent self-sufficient. Nor can the present structural policy, which tends to expand production by increasing productivity, be maintained. To cope with the problem on the European level, proposals have been made which are based on two major ideas.

The first type of proposals are *market-oriented*. They reserve the instrument of price policy for clearing the markets, maintaining some form of market regulation to stabilise prices (for example, Koester and Tangermann, 1976; Heidhues, Josling and Ritson *et al.*, 1978; Van Riemsdijk, 1972; Meester and Strijker, 1985; Tarditi, 1984).[7] Their evident advantage is that they would further efficient distribution of resources within Europe and between Europe and the rest of the world. Moreover they would diminish the costs of farmer-aid schemes to both consumer and taxpayer and would do away with the tensions between the EU and its trading partners. At the end of the 1980s the EU timidly set out on the road indicated by these proposals by introducing a system of so called 'stabilisers' (for example, for cereals and oil seeds). They imply an automatic reduction in the intervention price in cases where the production exceeds a certain ceiling. If this excess production continues the next year, a further reduction is applied, until market equilibrium is realised.

Proposals of the second type are more *interventionist*; they tend to maintain high prices while limiting production through production quotas or limited guarantees. Such schemes have now been adopted for milk and sugar (Petit *et al.*, 1987); they involve fixing maximum production levels for each country and, within each country, setting a maximum authorised production level for every farmer. The advantage of quota schemes is principally to reduce budget cost. This is illustrated by Figure 11.4. At an intervention price of p_3, production will be at OF and demand at OE, the difference between the two being exported with a subsidy of $p_3 - p_1$ (intervention price minus world market price) at a cost of $JQRL$ to the budget. Introducing a quota system that limits total quantity to OW for the whole of the EU limits the budget cost to $JQTU$ (horizontally shaded in Figure 11.4). It also eases the strain on external relations because the quantity exported to world markets is reduced by WF. However, under this quota system, the loss of consumer surplus remains at $ZSQK$ (the same as before in Figure 11.2), of which JQK is deadweight loss. The deadweight loss on the producer side diminishes by about $UYRL$; as some of the most inefficient producers will continue to produce their quota while some efficient producers have to cut down, the exact amount depends on the share each group has in the quota.[8]

Another interventionist way to regulate quantities is to limit the use of the production factor, land. One option considered is to pay the farmer for not using his land; crop-specific measures are a variation on the same theme. One such measure which has already been in operation for some time is that the area under viniculture is not allowed to expand. Although the proposals for interventionist schemes have some appeal to those who think in political terms, most economists reject them because of their serious disadvantages (Tangermann,

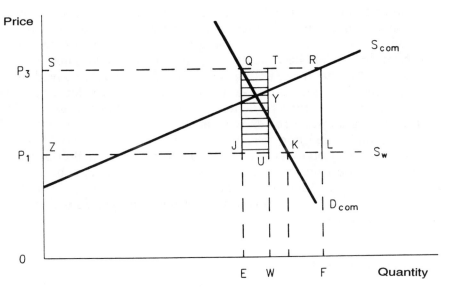

Figure 11.4   The effect of quotas

1984): they tend to fossilise existing market situations and block the entry of newcomers (such as that of Ireland and the UK into the dairy market). Moreover persistent high prices tend to put industries using the products as inputs (for instance sugar in biotechnology) at a disadvantage on world markets. Finally farms holding production authorisations may claim rents that are not economically justified.

Apart from these two major lines of attack, the EU is discussing a whole set of measures to improve the situation, among them premiums for voluntary production cuts and buying up farms to take agricultural land out of production. Measures of *structural policy* have to be revised as well, as the present policy tends to stimulate production in the long run. New measures of structural policy should aim at improving the quality of products rather than increasing productivity. Finding *alternative products* is the aim of a last group of measures. This is not an easy approach in general. One obvious solution is to increase the cultivation of products for which the EU is not self-sufficient, such as oil seeds and protein crops, but to that end the existing external trade relations would have to be revised. There is no such problem if, in particular, marginal holdings were to switch from agriculture to forestry, the EU being very short of wood and paper. Another possibility would be to put existing agricultural products to commercially sound alternative uses, for instance as inputs for manufacturing industries or for energy production; biomass especially comes to mind in that connection. This might be profitable, notably in countries which combine a weak agricultural structure with very poor domestic energy production. However from many studies it has become evident that for all such solutions to become operational the overall level of farm prices has to come down substantially. The recent decisions of the EU for transforming the CAP combine both market-oriented and interventionist measures. In broad lines, guarantee prices will increasingly be replaced by systems of product-tied bonuses. To get such bonuses farmers have to accept the obligation to reduce production capacity (cereals, oil seeds and so on). The rules are differentiated according to size of farms, type of region, products and so on. All in all, this is a very complicated set of regulations that could be termed 'interventionist' rather than 'market-oriented'.

Summary and conclusions

- While under the EU regime a liberal spirit predominates, in the sense that market forces are to take care of the orientation of production and the price mechanism is to play its full role, the sector of agriculture has been set apart and is in fact intensely regulated.
- Heavy pressure has been brought to bear by the farmers – the directly interested – to create mechanisms for the transfer of money from both consumers and taxpayers to themselves. The codification of rules in the Treaty of Rome makes it extremely difficult to realise on the political level what should be done on economic grounds.
- The restructuring of the CAP started with the decision of the Council (of April 1986) to stop the raising of agricultural guarantee prices and even to reduce some of them, together with its refusal to adopt more quota systems. However the adoption of the McSharry plan does not bring EU agricultural policy more in line with the EU principles for all sectors of economic activity; very many detailed interventions remain.

Notes

1 This does not mean that there is no important world-scale trade in agricultural produce. However within international organisations there have been hardly any attempts at international harmonising of the organisation of agricultural markets (production and trade). Admittedly international agreements have been drawn up for certain products, aiming at some control of their world markets, so liable to great fluctuations through speculations and other causes. Such con-

trol schemes tend to be specialist in their orientation – to one product – and weak in their institutional structure. The Food and Agriculture Organisation of the UN is concerned in particular with worldwide aspects of food supply. The OECD's concern (for example, OECD, 1987d) has been of a coordinating nature (exchange of information and cautious adjustment of policy). The GATT has recently formulated worldwide objectives for the liberalisation of trade in agricultural products.

2 The fishery policy of the EU has some very distinctive characteristics. Interested readers are referred to CEC (1985b), Farnell and Ellis (1984), Leigh (1984) and Wise (1984).

3 In the period 1970–80, the number of farms of between 10 and 20 ha also declined strongly in the EU9, while the number of between 20 and 50 ha remained the same and only that of establishments of more than 50 ha increased.

4 Such payments can be compared with production subsidies for industrial products, because they serve a protectionist aim: to increase home production. As farmers have taken them as income-support schemes instead of production-support schemes, the political debate is now transferred to income policies for farmers, although such schemes are practically non-existent for other socio-economic groups in Europe. For a detailed study of the effects of various schemes of income support to farmers, see OECD (1983b).

5 Relative expenditure on agriculture could go down as the EU has increasingly assumed new responsibilities that entail budgetary costs (regional policy, technology, environment and so on) that have increased the total budget outlays faster than outlays for agriculture.

6 For an analysis of the political economy of the CAP, see Pelkmans (1985).

7 Most of these proposals advocate the introduction of a series of new – national or European – instruments to attain other goals, such as subsidies to individual farmers threatened by too large a reduction of their income. Non-agricultural interest such as landscape preservation or maintaining the population in areas threatened by desertification are also considered.

8 The quota system is not always easy to implement. The EU has introduced a system whereby farmers receive less than the guaranteed price for excess quantities, the difference often being claimed in the form of levies. The solution seems practical only for products with a concentrated organisation of outlets.

12 Manufacturing

Introduction

The industrial sector is at the heart of most integration schemes as these tend to begin with the integration of the market for manufactured goods. However this negative integration is to be followed by positive integration. Indeed, given the importance of the industrial sector for the growth of the economy, most countries pursue a national industrial policy. As this may lead to distortions in the common market, a European framework is needed.

The way in which the EU has regulated both negative and positive industrial integration will be discussed in the next section,[1] after which we will first give a concise description of general industrial development under conditions of international integration (highlighting such aspects as specialisation, concentration and firm structure). Next we will describe the dynamics of some selected branches of industry at different stages of integration. We will do this with the help of three case studies (steel, a sector with which European industrial integration started, and two mature sectors, motor cars and white goods). In the final section we will recall briefly the most important features of the analysis.

EU regime

Market control policy; prices and quantities

The EEC Treaty does not envisage the regulating of the prices and quantities of the markets for industrial products: self-regulation through the free play of the market mechanism is the central principle. Although from time to time proposals have been made to give the Commission or the national states the authority to make such interventions, the practice has gone in a different direction. Price controls, where they still existed, were abandoned. There is of course some indirect influence of EU and national government on markets. One example is competition policy; both the ECSC and EEC treaties give ample power to the EU to prevent companies taking action affecting trade negatively within the EU or abusing dominant positions (Chapter 16). Another is external trade; foreign producers have access to the EU market, subject to the rules of the Common Commercial Policy (see Chapter 19). These permit different import levies being imposed for different products, which implies a certain element of price regulation. For certain products, quantitative restrictions can also be imposed on goods entering the Common Market from the outside.

The ECSC Treaty, however, permits a further-reaching market regulation policy for the steel sector. It introduced special rules for steel, allowing certain interventions in prices and quantities such as minimum prices, national production quotas, import restrictions and so on (Article 61). In the past the Commission used its competence in this respect to overcome the 1975–80 crisis in this sector. After declaring a state of 'manifest crisis', the Commission regulated directly both quantities and prices in the steel sector (by the power given it in Article 58). Quantities were controlled by introducing a system of production and supply quotas by country and by company for a large number of products. In setting the quotas, the position on the market as well as so-called 'restructuring aspects' for efficient companies were taken into account. Prices were directly set (by virtue of Article 60) through so-called 'price lists'. Not only producers but also traders were included in this system (Article 95). A close check was kept to ensure that the prices declared were indeed identical to the prices actually charged. Now that markets are back to normal, the system has been discontinued. It is unlikely that in the future these powers will be used again, as many negative side-effects have appeared.

Structural policy: legal bases and development

The Paris Treaty founding the European Coal and Steel Community instructs the EU to conduct a structural policy with respect to the steel sector. The Treaty has endowed the High Authority, now the European Commission, with ample powers for the preventive control of investments and financial support for projects improving the structure, and the issuing of social support measures in the case of restructuring of firms and plants (see Chapter 18).

The Rome Treaty founding the European Economic Community lays down the rules for the EU policy in matters of market structure for all other branches of manufacturing. While being explicit as to agricultural and transport policy, the Treaty nowhere mentions an industrial policy in the sense of setting the course for and stimulating structural development. At least some of the designers of the Treaty were of the opinion that such a policy was not called for: healthy competition would keep prices low for the consumer, ensure the suppliers' efficient use of production factors and guarantee the continuous improvement of the quality of the product. However, in due time, a mere competition policy was found insufficient to achieve certain desired changes, and a European structural policy for industry was contemplated (CEC, 1970; Toulemon and Flory, 1974) and slowly realised (Hall, 1986; Franzmeyer, 1982).

There are many motives for a structural industrial policy (see also Chapter 16).[2] Many national governments have indeed in the past pursued such policies, with different effectiveness. The European integration process has eroded the capacity of governments to further industrial development through state intervention. The common commercial policy has taken away the instrument of external protection; the European competition policy has done the same with instruments like state aids and government procurement, while the internal market policy took away the instruments of technical standards. The capacity for national industrial policies is further eroded by internationalisation and technical progress that leads to an increase in scale; indeed the scale of many new projects (as in aeronautics) is now such that it goes far beyond the capacities of one national state.

Those in favour of industrial policies have pleaded for recovering at a European level the capacity to intervene that had been lost at national level. Opposed to these were those who question the effectiveness of any industrial policy. For quite some time the EU has not been able to choose between these two opposing points of view. In the 1970s, the pressure of the old industries (like steel and textiles) confronted with restructuring led to some involvement of the EU. Much more success was gained in the 1980s by the growth industries (such as electronics and telecommunications) that were able to obtain support for the stimulation of technological innovation via large programmes financed by the EU.

However a constant controversy as to the justification of EU involvement in such programmes (for example, high definition television) remained. The Commission in its memorandum 'An Industrial Policy' (CEC, 1991d) mainly took the view of the non-interventionist, putting the accent on policies that create the good conditions for improving competitiveness (a good functioning of the internal market, a speeding up of the structural adaptation, and so on). However, in practice, there is still much of a sectoral policy with attention to 'key technology industries' on the one hand and to so-called 'sensitive' sectors on the other (shipbuilding, steel and so on).

Interesting in this respect is the Treaty on European Union, which states (Article 130) that the EU in cooperation with the member states shall ensure that the conditions for the competitiveness of European industry exist. This article suggests that this policy be non-interventionist, judging by the actions that are specified, although it does not seem to preclude an interventionist policy. However as, for the elaboration of such measures, a large consensus of member states is necessary, it is unlikely that the industrial policy of the EU will evolve in that direction.

Structural policy: instruments

To the EU, as to the individual member states, six instruments are effectively available (Rothwell and Zegveld, 1981). We shall briefly discuss how each of them is used by the European Community.

Exchange of economic and technical information is of great value to those committed to decisions at the government or the private level, particularly in a period of fast technical progress and much uncertainty about the external environment. Accelerated technological progress and changes in the international environment have made good insight into possible medium- and long-term developments not only more necessary, but also harder to achieve. The Commission is active in carrying out prognoses and pilot studies providing information as well as scientific and technical documentation. It favours direct consultation with representatives of industry and national governments in order to see, case by case, how far elements of a policy can be devised that are agreeable to all those involved.

Financial intervention is much preferred as an instrument for governments to deal with production structures, in the form of either direct support (subsidies or favourable loans) or tax relief. The treaties leave taxes as a national matter; on the other hand, they make it possible to give two main kinds of European financial support:

- Grants. For a long time budget funds reserved for structural, non-agricultural purposes used to be set aside for nuclear research. Later on, greater variety was introduced in favour of research in other areas. For some years the budget has also set aside funds for the financing of industrial programmes. Their common aim is to achieve real cooperation of companies, research laboratories and universities in various European countries. To avoid problems with European competition policy, all schemes address the so-called 'pre-competitive' stage of technical development. Afterwards each company is at liberty to exploit the common results to develop and market its own products.[3] The Treaty (Article 13 f to p) says that the EU and the

member states shall coordinate their policies in the field of research and technology development. To that end the EU has set up a multiannual framework programme.
- Loans. Although the EU's financial leeway in this area is still limited, the important thing is that the instrument exists legally and may gain force in future. Along with the operations of the Commission, the operations of the European Investment Bank (EIB) should be cited.

In sum, the EU's means for financial stimulation have become quite substantial; they are concentrated in the growth sectors (such as telecommunications).

Company regrouping means that large European companies can better face the competition of American and Japanese firms on internal as well as external markets. In the early days the EU (CEC, 1970) tried to help companies to acquire a sufficient size of operations by stimulating mergers. Now it considers that the safeguarding of liberal trade in an internal market is the best tool to promote such a larger scale (Schwalbach, 1988; Helg and Ranci, 1988).

Technical standards and norms counted in many EU countries as effective protection against competition by third parties. They were equally used to achieve certain social objectives, such as curbing pollution, and protection of consumers or people in employment. The EU has tried steadily to harmonise such norms at the European level to acquire competitiveness on a global scale. However, regulation at the EU level is but rarely used as an instrument to further innovation (as with car exhaust gas!).

Government procurement is frequently used to stimulate the development of certain products at the national level; especially in sectors of advanced technology, national suppliers have tended to receive preferential treatment. As far as such preference implies discrimination against products from other member states, it is obviously in conflict with the competition rules of the Common Market. The Commission has tried to keep the negative effects for Europe of its use at the national level within bounds. It has not yet achieved any effective application as an instrument of industrial policy at the European level, owing to the smallness of the EU budget.

Trade policy, too, can be put at the service of industrial policy, but the EU has but little scope. The Preamble to the EEC Treaty explicitly states the principle of an 'open-door policy' towards other countries: 'Desiring ... to contribute ... to the progressive abolition of restrictions on international trade ...'. However sectoral problems have constantly prevented full adherence to that principle. For one thing, agreements were concluded with trade partners for the voluntary restriction on the export of sensitive products; the multifibre agreement is a case in point. For another, higher import tariffs are sometimes introduced for a limited time, to enable European producers to improve their competitive position by building up a home market of their own. In recent years the so-called 'strategic trade policies' have again attracted much attention from politicians and academics. Although the EU practice contains elements of this, there is no deliberate industrial development-oriented external trade policy. (The last-mentioned instrument will be discussed in more detail in Chapter 19, on external relations.)

Sketch of the sector

Development of branches

Historically manufacturing industry grew out of craft, which in the beginning could hardly be separated from agriculture and trade. For a long time, manufacturing industry remained a relatively small sector. The great industrial revolution of the 18th and 19th centuries, involving thorough mechanisation and entailing scale enlargement and concentration, changed the picture drastically. In the first half of the 20th century, manufacturing industry grew into the most important sector in the economy of developed ('industrialised') countries, larger than agriculture and services.

In the post-war period, the manufacturing sector became one of considerable importance to the economy of the EU countries, as Table 12.1 shows. Although its relative importance has declined since 1970 in favour of the service sector, the manufacturing sector still accounts for almost one in four of all jobs in the EU, and almost a third of total wealth creation. The development of the totals of this large sector is the result of diverging developments of its constituent branches.[4]

Table 12.1   **Percentage share of manufacturing in total GDP and total employment (EU12), 1950–90**

	1950	1960	1970	1980	1990
GDP[a]	n.a.	40	36	33	27
Employment	29	32	33	28	23

[a]   Inclusive of mining, public utilities, energy (approximately 4%).
Sources: GDP: OECD, Eurostat: *National Account Statistics*, various years; Employment: 1950–70, NEI FLEUR data base; 1970–90, OECD, *Labour Force statistics*, various years.

The life-cycle of every product begins with an innovation, or rather an invention followed by an innovation (Schumpeter). These processes give rise to whole new groups of products, which frequently coincide with branches of manufacturing industry. The economy is therefore often divided into new or growth industries and stagnating ones. The result of these dynamic processes is that the importance of branches within total industry tends to vary considerably over time.[5]

A picture of the long-term growth and decline of manufacturing branches in the EU economy is given in Table 12.2 (presenting employment figures, the only indicator for which long time-series could be made comparable in some detail). The metal industry (ranging from basic metals to transport equipment) is by far the largest sector. The table also indicates that employment in all sectors of manufacturing industry has declined in absolute terms since 1970. Much can be explained by improved productivity:[6] in terms of production (gross value added) many sectors have at least remained stable or have grown.

Table 12.2   Employment (millions) in manufacturing, by branch (EU12), 1950–90

	1950	1960	1970	1980	1990
Food, beverages, tobacco	3.5	4.0	3.9	3.6	3.3
Textiles, clothing, footwear	8.0	7.5	6.4	4.7	3.5
Wood, furniture	2.3	2.2	2.1	2.0	1.6
Paper and printing	1.5	2.0	2.3	2.2	2.1
Chemicals and rubber	1.8	2.5	3.0	3.1	3.2
Non-metallic mineral products	1.4	1.7	1.8	1.6	1.6
Basic metals	1.6	2.1	2.1	1.8	1.2
Metal products	2.3	2.9	3.2	3.0	2.9
Non-electrical machinery	2.4	3.5	4.0	3.7	3.3
Electrical machinery	1.5	2.6	3.2	3.1	2.9
Transport equipment	3.0	4.0	4.8	4.6	3.5
Other	1.1	1.5	1.8	1.8	1.9
Total	30.4	36.5	38.6	35.2	31.0

Sources: NEI: FLEUR-data; Eurostat: various sources; estimates based on national statistics.

In some industries the drop in employment due to technical progress and competition from third world countries started early, especially in such traditional industries as textile and clothing, wood and furniture. Their share in total manufacturing employment fell between

1950 and 1990 by almost half. By contrast, chemicals and metal were obvious growth industries in the period 1950–80: their shares increased considerably. The figures are totals only and hide important developments at the sub-branch level (for example, growth of informatics and telecommunication equipment).

Size of European firms

Following the development of the world's largest manufacturing firms over the past decades, one is immediately struck by the dominance of American firms. In the world rankings, most European firms fall outside the top 20. Size is mostly measured by turnover (sales), but employment is another much used indicator. Ranked by employment, the largest European firms give the display shown in Table 12.3.

Table 12.3   The nine largest manufacturing[a] firms based in the EU12 (private ownership, worldwide employment, thousands), 1970–90

	Name	Country	1970	1990
1	Siemens	FR Germany	300	370
2	Daimler-Benz	FR Germany	150	370
3	Unilever	UK/NL	340	300
4	Fiat	Italy	190	300
5	Philips	Netherlands	370	270
6	Volkswagen	FR Germany	190	270
7	British American Tobacco	UK	150	220
8	Hoechst	FR Germany	150	170
9	Bayer	FR Germany	100	170

[a]   excluding financial trusts and energy.
Source: *Fortune*, several issues.

The table shows three interesting features:

- *Branch.* The largest firms are concentrated in very few branches: cars (3), chemicals (2), electric machinery (2) and food and tobacco (2).
- *Country.* Germany is very well represented on the list, with four firms; in relative terms that is also true of The Netherlands. However most member countries do not show up on the list at all.

- *Rank.* During the 1970–90 period, the composition of the list of the nine largest firms in the EU did not change. The rank of these nine did not change much either for quite some time. However in the last five years it was more or less revolutionised, as the result of, among other things, worldwide restructuring, and the dynamics of 1992.[7]

Specialisation, economies of scale, and location

The EU was conceived to bring about a better allocation of resources through specialisation and large-scale industrial production. Notably in manufacturing, economies of scale are very important (see, among others, Pratten, 1988) and, therefore, an analysis of the effects of the formation of the EU on production, direct investment and marketing is in order. See Table 12.4, which gives the differences in strategy and internal organisation of multi-product, multinational companies under different trade and direct investment regimes. A good example of a firm that has experienced these changes in environment is Philips, and we will now briefly describe how its strategy has evolved over time (Muntendam, 1987).

Table 12.4 **Production and trade patterns of multinational, multi-product companies under different trade regimes**

Trade regime	Location of production units for each product	Dominant part of firm
Free trade	one plant (usually home base)	production and export
Protectionism	numerous plants (one in each major national market)	national companies
Integration	limited number of plants (at good locations)	matrix of national and product organisations
Free internal market	one plant (optimal location)	international product divisions

Taking advantage of the liberalist trade environment from the first decade of the century, Philips rapidly increased its production of lightbulbs and set up an international sales organisation (compare row 1 of Table 12.4). The company moved into other products, such as radio sets and domestic appliances, and mainly cashed in on the internalisation advantage (see Chapter 8), guaranteeing the quality of its products through horizontal and vertical integration of other production stages. As early as 1910, Philips had established sales companies in 18 European countries, and eight more in other countries of the industrialised world. Most were supplied by the plants at the home base, Eindhoven, built for low-cost, large-scale production, and some by local production plants that Philips had acquired through mergers to strengthen its market position. Under such conditions the dominant parts of the firm are the production and export departments.

In the 1930s, the surge of protectionist measures taken by European governments (see Chapter 3) compelled the company to change its strategy thoroughly. It switched to the exploitation of ownership advantage and its direct investments became of the tariff-jumping type (see Chapter 8). First, assembly lines for each of the major products were set up in every individual country in whose market Philips was well established. This was soon followed by the creation of national Philips companies, which became responsible for the production and local marketing of all Philips products. Quite naturally these national companies, having to gear their production to local taste, also acquired some responsibility for product development and, needing to survive in their specific environments, also for the development of production technology. Conditions during and immediately after the Second World War only reinforced the system of geographically decentralised combined production and selling units.

When the formation of the EU in the 1960s opened up the markets, Philips once more drastically revised its strategy. Now the exploitation of locational advantages became the central element. First, national companies were forced to coordinate their production and export policies; for this coordination a matrix structure of multi-product national companies and international single-product divisions was formed. Next, they were integrated in a centralised international system based on product division. Factories in different countries producing one specific product for the national market were integrated in one system, production now geared to the international market being gradually concentrated in a single plant. This reflects a direct investment behaviour of the 'optimal location type' (see Chapter 8). The major plants, which used to produce a whole array of products, were now made to specialise in only one or two products. More recently, this European strategy of specialisation and product division has been extended all over the world for effective worldwide competition (Teulings, 1984).

Concentration

The creation of a large integrated market area like the EU will entail an increase in average firm size and a higher concentration in national and EU markets (Pryor, 1972; Scherer, 1974). There is evidence that this has indeed already happened. An early EU study (CEC, 1974) showed for the EU6 that in 1962, in 13 out of 46 sectors of activity, the four largest firms had a market share of over 50 per cent; by 1969, that number had gone up to 18 out of 46. In the same period the situation in the UK (not a member) did not change. Other measures, such as the top eight, 30 and so on, convey the same message: their share in total output increased significantly in the 1960–75 period (Jacquemin and De Jong, 1977; Locksey and Ward, 1979; de Jong, 1988).

The same is true for the top-50. After a hesitant start in the early 1960s, the 50 largest companies increased their shares in the output of the total manufacturing sector from 15 to 30 per cent between 1965 and 1980, accounting in 1980 for about one-fifth of the sector's total employment. The next-largest 50 accounted, in 1980, for another 10 per cent of jobs and 15 per cent of output (Geroski and Jacquemin, 1984). In the early 1980s the concentration of manufacturing seems to have been more or less stable. The 1992 process has had some influence on further concentration in manufacturing (sheltered sectors), although this is difficult to assess quantitatively.

An interesting question is how the large European manufacturing firms perform in comparison with their American and Japanese counterparts. The EU and the USA had comparable numbers of firms in *Fortune's* Top 100 (19 and 23, respectively), while Japan had only a few (Geroski and Jacquemin, 1984). Their relative performances, however, were very different. European firms compared poorly to their competitors; their outputs by employee and their profitability ratios were much lower then those of their American and Japanese sisters. This conclusion points to a significantly lower cohesiveness in European industrial and market structures, possible due to cultural, legal and political differences among the member countries of the EU. This situation has convinced decision makers of the necessity for the 1992 programme to do away with a large number of such barriers to better performance (see Chapter 16).

Case study 1: steel

Structure of the industry: no international integration of firms

Technological change has pushed the European steel industry towards operation on ever larger scales. For the years up to 1960, the exact magnitude of the development is hard to assess; the scanty information nevertheless permits the conclusion that the 1950s were marked by the disappearance of many small plants and firms. The development after 1960 (apart from very small plants producing less than 0.5 Mt/y) is given in Table 12.5, which clearly shows the tendency towards concentration of basic steel production in only a few, very large-scale plants.

Table 12.5   Estimated number of steel plants by size category (Mt/y) in the EU9, 1960–90

Capacity	1960	1970	1980	1990
0.5–2.0	56	62	30	24
2.0–5.0	7	15	24	25
over 5.0	—	1	9	4
Total	63	78	63	53

Source: Own estimates based on *Iron and Steel Works of the World*, several issues.

Continued technical progress in all parts of the industry in the period 1950–90 increased the necessity for concentration of firms. In the period up to the Second World War, concentration had taken the form of vertical integration (coal, iron ore, iron- and steelmaking, and metal working). Since then horizontal concentration has dominated the restructuring process. We can distinguish a few stages in this process.

At the beginning of the 1950s, the situation of the European steel industry was marked by the existence of a large number of firms, tending to be linked (via financial groups) to other firms in the same sector, located in the same region. There was hardly any international integration. Some Belgian capital had penetrated into companies of the Lorraine district; the Dutch blast-furnace company Hoogovens controlled the German firm of Hörder, and the Luxemburg and Saar industries were to some extent controlled by French and Belgian capital. International trade in iron and steel was limited. After the creation of the ECSC in 1952, competition soon made further concentration imperative.

In the 1960s concentration followed a regional pattern. Evidently such technical factors as economies of scale, transportation costs and labour force adaptations induced firms to join efforts with firms close by rather than with firms in other countries. From a low spatial level (Liège, Sambre and Dortmund, for example), the concentration movement was extended to operations on a larger scale. In France, the government stimulated the formation of the groups Usinor in the north and Sacilor in Lorraine; similar developments took place in the Ruhr area. Likewise, in Spain, Ensidesa regrouped firms in the Asturias, and Altos Hornos companies in the Viscaya district. Arbed integrated steel firms in the Luxemburg/Saar/Lorraine area into what became practically the only international steel company in Europe; later Estel merged the German Hoesch group with Dutch Hoogovens in another international regional grouping.

The next round of horizontal concentrations assumed a national dimension. In Italy, the large financial holding of the state (Finnsider/Ilva) assured a lively interest in the development of the national steel industry. In the UK, the nationalisation of the steel industry led to a concentration of three-quarters of national steelmaking capacity in British Steel. In Belgium, France and Germany the crisis of the mid-1970s induced the governments to step in with very substantial aid, given in exchange for a certain measure of control of the developments that invariably led to concentration on the national level. Usinor and Sacilor in France merged into a company covering almost the whole of national steel production (see Table 12.6). The international Estel group fell victim to nationalist pressure (the German Hoesch group was forced to participate in a 'German' restructuring). The tendency towards concentration of firms was accentuated by the restructuring measures of the years since 1980 and again by the crisis of the early 1990s. This remains, however, within national boundaries (for example, Krupp-Hoesch).

Notwithstanding this continuous process of horizontal merger, the concentration ratio in the EU as a whole is not very high. In 1990 the four largest companies accounted for about 40 per cent and the eight largest for about 53 per cent of total steel production. This is higher than in 1980, when the C4 stood at 31 and the C8 at 45 per cent (see also Oberender and Rüter, 1993). Table 12.6 gives an impression of the result of the process of growth and concentration.

Little integration of markets owing to public intervention

In the period of continuous growth between 1950 and 1974, capacity was expanded in line with demand. EC firms were competitive on the world scale (reflected in net exports; see Table 12.7). The process of adjusting to the enlarged competition triggered by the new large market resulted in increased intra-industry specialisation among European firms, with all countries developing certain product lines (Adler, 1970) and intra-EU trade gradually developing (Table 12.7).

In the period of economic crisis (1974–85) the total production of crude steel in what is now the EU12 dropped by 20 per cent (see Table 12.7). A considerable overcapacity (capacity-utilisation level in

Table 12.6   Largest EU12 steel producing firms with a crude steel output of over 3 Mt/y and national concentration ratios, 1980, 1990

Company	Country	Mt/y EU output		% of national production	
		1980	1990	1980	1990
Usinor	FR	9.2	⎫	40	⎫
Sacilor	FR	3.3	} 17.9	14	} 95
Sollac	FR	2.6	⎭	11	⎭
British Steel	UK	8.4	13.8	74	78
Ilva (Finnsider)	IT	13.7	11.5	52	45
Thyssen	FRG	12.4	11.1	28	29
Hoogovens	NL	5.0	5.2	94	96
Cockerill	B	3.5	⎫ 4.3	28	⎫ 38
Hainaut/Sambre	B	3.4	⎭	28	⎭
Peine Salzgitter	FRG	4.4	4.2	10	11
Hoesch	FRG	5.2	4.1	12	11
Ensidesa	SP	4.7	4.0	37	31
Sidmar	B	2.7	3.8	22	33
Arbed	LUX	4.6	3.6	100	100
Mannesman	FRG	4.3	3.6	10	9
Klöckner	FRG	4.8	3.4	11	9
Saar	FRG	3.2	3.1	7	8
Krupp	FRG	5.4	3.0	12	8
Total		100.8	96.6	71*	71*

*   percentage of EU12 market.
Source: International Iron and Steel Institute.

1980 approximately two-thirds) was the result, and the industry had to restructure in depth, closing down the older plants and laying off hundreds of thousands of employees. However, micro-economic as well as social factors spoke against the reduction. Given their very high fixed costs, firms were prepared to make drastic price cuts to stay in the market. When that strategy threatened to make some of them go bankrupt, governments moved in with subsidies to maintain employment. In the whole of the EU, these amounted to a total of some 50 milliard ECU for the 1979–86 period. They have led to the de facto nationalisation of large parts of the industry (in 1990 over 80 per cent in the UK, France and Denmark; over 60 per cent in Italy, Belgium and Luxemburg).

Table 12.7   Some characteristic data on the EU12 steel industry, 1950–90

	1950	1960	1974	1980	1990
Employment (000s)	n.a.	975	895	749	386
Capacity (effective (Mt/y))	n.a.	104	196	220	184
Crude-steel production (Mt/y)	49	99	168	141	137
Net exports (third countries) (Mt/y)	6	12	21	24	11
Consumption (Mt/y)	43	87	147	113	126
Intra-EU trade (Mt/y)	n.a.	9	27	29	47
Intra-EU trade as a percentage of consumption	n.a.	10	18	26	37

Source: OECD, *The Iron and Steel Industry; The Steel Market* and *Outlook,* various years; Eurostat, *Iron and Steel Yearbook,* various years.

Faced with this situation, the Commission has used its powers from the ECSC treaty to restructure the industry and stabilise markets. In the mid-1970s the Commission negotiated a programme of voluntary restriction of output by all producers. This was no longer sufficient when the second crisis occurred in the 1980s. Declaring a situation of manifest crisis (Articles 58 and 61), the Commission introduced a system of production quotas and minimum prices.[8] The practical implication was that the European market broke down into national markets, largely fed by national production (as witnessed by the stabilisation of intra-EU trade during this period). The economic appraisal of the crisis management of the EU is not very positive; adaptation has taken a very long time and welfare costs have been very high (Oberender and Rüter, 1993).

A normalisation of the situation occurred in the second half of the 1980s. Market integration was re-established gradually, one product group at a time, and was completed by the end of the decade. As a consequence of rationalisation and specialisation, integration of markets has increased (which means firms have become less oriented towards their home markets) (see Table 12.7).

By the end of the 1980s the industry had again been thrown into a crisis as a result of the changes in Eastern Europe. The extra cheap supply of Central and East European (CEEC) firms on both home and export markets of EU firms forced the latter into a new round of restructuring. This led to capacity reduction (a decrease of 20 to 40 per cent with respect to 1990 figures in view of the existing overcapacity; see Table 12.7) and the laying off of substantial parts of the workforce (about 50,000 to 100,000 after 1990). There have been voices pleading for a new regime of manifest crisis. However, in view of the results of the last experience, the Commission has no intention of heeding them. On the contrary, it is trying to arrive at an orderly process by the exchange of information between industrialists and a trusted representative of the Commission. This way of handling a restructuring process has proved its efficiency in the refinery sector (see Chapter 13).

For the immediate future, the rationalisation of the industry will lead to new rounds of concentration (notably in the FRG) but is likely to delay privatisation. The industry not having a tradition of international integration on the EU scale, it need not come as a surprise that there is as yet very little sign of future regroupings of EU and CEEC firms.

Case study 2: cars

Firm structure: little international integration of firms

In 1990, three of the nine largest European manufacturing firms were in the automotive sector (and five out of 12) (see Table 12.3). It shows the importance of economies of scale in that industry. Consequently the concentration of firms in European car manufacturing is fairly high. Between 1960 and 1990 the industry was dominated by five European 'volume' producers (Volkswagen, Peugeot, Renault, Fiat and, initially, British Leyland), two US multinationals (Ford and GM), (together taking up 76 per cent of the production in 1963 and some 90 per cent in 1990) and a number of high-performance specialists (Daimler-Benz, BMW and Volvo). Concentration has not advanced much further; from Table 12.8 we can calculate that the four largest producers accounted for about 50 per cent of total production in 1960 and about 60 per cent in 1990.

In the 1950s and early 1960s the European volume producers were national champions in the sense that most of their production facilities were concentrated in one country, were controlled by capital from their home country and very often enjoyed government support; standing up to international competition was often only possible with government assistance for restructuring of operations and development of new products. The European volume producers concentrated on family cars with idiosyncratic national styles, which meant that they were oriented towards their national markets.

In the late 1960s and 1970s, under the pressure of the US firms pursuing their concept of global industry, styles and technology converged into one rather homogeneous product, which can be sold both on national and foreign markets. More than before, attention was on minimising unit cost by large production series. In the face of increased competition, a tendency to concentrate along national lines prevailed (but for takeovers by US concerns), smaller firms being gradually absorbed by the larger ones. The only major attempt at an international takeover by a European firm (Citroën being acquired by Fiat) failed and, after considerable intervention by the French government, Citroën was finally merged with Peugeot.

In recent years a new group of players has come to the European market. Japanese car firms, which until now were satisfied with exporting to the EU, have started to build production and assembly facilities in the EU (Nissan since 1986, Toyota in 1992 and Honda in

Table 12.8 **Production in thousands of the largest European car manufacturers in the EU12 (by country producing over 100,000 cars a year in 1990)***

Country	Company	1960	1990
Germany	VW/Audi	740	1930
	GM (Opel)	330	1030
	Ford	190	590
	Daimler-Benz	200	570
	BMW	60	500
France	Renault	430	1320
	Citroën/Panhard	280	
	Peugeot/Talbot	190	1980
	Simca[a]	220	
Italy	Fiat (AR/Lancia)	690	1860
Belgium*	Ford	n.a.	310
Netherlands	Volvo	n.a.	120
UK	BMC–Rover	450	460
	Ford	340	330
	GM (Vauxhall)	130	250
	Rootes[a] (Peugeot)	120	120
	Nissan	—	160
Spain	VW/Seat	n.a.	470
	Renault	n.a.	250
	Ford	n.a.	330
	GM	n.a.	380
	Peugeot/Citroën	n.a.	260

[a] Merged first with Chrysler, later with Peugeot.
* Not included are the assembly plants in Belgium producing some 800,000 cars a year.
Source: *L'Argus de l'automobile*, various years; ACEA, *Autodata*.

1993, all in the UK) and to take shares in European companies, as with Mitsubishi (Netherlands). The total capacity of these plants by 1992 amounted to some 600,000 units and is expected to rise to 1 million by the end of the decade.

Table 12.8 gives an idea of the evolution of the production of the most important car manufacturers. The smaller producers, most of whom lost their independence in the past have been left out. The table indicates the shifts in European car making from the United Kingdom (where the industry is stagnating) initially to France, Germany and Italy and recently in particular to Spain, where many firms have established production facilities.

External trade structure

The overall position *vis-à-vis* the outside world is characterised by both substantial exports and imports (see Table 12.9). The export performance of the EU has stagnated since the 1970s, while its openness to producers from third countries has increased considerably since 1960.

Table 12.9   Production and consumption of, and external trade in, cars in the EU12 (millions), 1960–90*

	1960	1970	1980	1990
Production	4.8	10.2	11.4	13.2
Imports	n.a.	0.2	n.a.	1.7
of which, from Japan	(—)	(0.1)	(0.9)	(1.2)
Exports	1.1	1.8	n.a.	1.7
Consumption	3.7	8.5	10.3	12.2

*   Data on production, imports etc. are not fully consistent.
Source: As for Table 12.8; Owen (1983), Maillet (1977), Mueller (1981); additional estimates.

The European industry, while falling behind on export markets mostly in favour of the Japanese, has been able to retain much of its home market, thanks to important protectionist measures. However, against all kinds of impediment, the Japanese managed to capture as much as 13 per cent of the market in 1990, from a negligible beginning in the years when the EU was established.

Some member states have over a long period maintained protectionist measures against third country producers. Italy, for one, restricted its imports of Japanese cars to 2,300 a year, a quota dating from before the foundation of the EU. France has had, since 1977, a bilateral agreement with the Japanese government to restrict the Japanese share in the French market to 3 per cent. Finally British and Japanese associations of car manufacturers have voluntarily agreed to restrict the Japanese share to 10 to 11 per cent. Such VER (CEC, 1983a; OECD, 1987e) have led to physical checks of all cars at some intra-EC borders. These barriers have been removed in the framework of the 1992 programme. At the same time, an EC-wide arrangement with Japanese exporters has been made that runs to the end of the century. After that, external protection with QR will be lifted.

Intra-EU trade

The interpenetration of markets in the EU can be measured by the evolution of the shares of the three largest producers in total sales on their national home markets. This indicator has the advantage of taking into account both the growing openness of the EU countries to producers from other EU countries and producers from third countries (Owen, 1983). Table 12.10 shows the – foreseeable – considerable and consistent decrease of the indicator between 1960 and 1990 for the four largest member countries of the EU.[9]

Table 12.10   Shares (%) of the three largest national producers in home market sales, 1960–90

Country	Companies	1960	1970	1980	1990
Germany	VW, GM, Ford	79	66	59	54
France	Renault, Peugeot, Citroën	82	70	67	61
Italy	Fiat, AR, Lancia	90	72	63	53
UK	BL, GM, Ford	79	76	57	55

Source: *Tatsachen und Zahlen, Automotive News*, various years; ACEA, *Autodata*.

In the 1950s international trade in cars was low, as it was hampered by high tariffs (20 to 40 per cent), by the intervention of governments in car production, the difficulty of creating dealer networks abroad, and so on. Scale economies are very important in the car industry, probably even more so for parts than for final goods, so there is ample impetus for scale-driven exports. Indeed large producers can use their savings on cost to penetrate foreign markets. To stop such inroads into their home markets, producers of other countries are forced to take up exporting as well.

In the 1960s and 1970s this determined the intra-EU pattern of trade (Owen, 1983). The importance of scale economies in competitive markets (see Figure 5.11) is illustrated by the relative performance of French producers, which deteriorated every time their unit cost went out of line with that of their German competitors. The effect thereof in terms of change in market shares became larger the higher became the penetration of the two countries in each other's markets. Market integration progressed much in the 1960–80 period, but most firms remained national champions, as concentration followed largely national patterns (Fiat acquired Alpha Romeo and Lancia, Volkswagen acquired Auto Union, British Leyland resulted from a merger of UK companies, Citroën acquired Panhard and Peugeot Citroën).

Recently, owing to the effects of the 1992 programme (Salvatori, 1991) that removed a number of obstacles in the field of taxes, technical standards and import restrictions, interpenetration has been enhanced again. This factor, added to the creation of the European Economic Area (see Chapter 19), the transition of Central and Eastern European economies and increased Japanese imports, led to more international concentration: Volkswagen (Germany) acquired Seat (Spain) and Skoda (Czechoslovakia), Renault tried to make a deal with Volvo (Sweden) and Fiat (Italy) invested in FSM (Poland). In line with this, international specialisation increased; in order to cut cost, large parts of production were transferred to low-cost EU member countries (like Spain and Portugal) and even lower-cost Central and Eastern European countries.

The trade structure of the finished product hides the enormous specialisation and hence international trade in parts. Dicken (1986) gives the example of the Ford Escort model, the final assembly of which takes place in the UK and Germany, but whose parts are provided by factories in eight EU countries and four EFTA countries, as well as the USA, Canada and Japan. A highly developed European industry for components is an asset to the EU car industry (Salvatori, 1991; Bongardt, 1993).

Price effects of integration

Manufacturers by their control over dealers are able to fix different prices on different national markets. Appreciable differences between car prices have persisted for various reasons. Tax pressure leads to low net prices in Denmark: companies selling are forced to reduce pre-tax prices in a country with such a very heavy tax burden on cars (Murfin, 1985). High penetration of foreign cars leads to low prices in Greece and Belgium. Alignment with prices of the major national producer and a market protected by left-hand driving (few parallel imports) leads to high prices in the UK, where producers prefer greater benefits from limited sales volumes to higher market shares at lower prices (BEUC, 1982). Difference in taxes, import restraints (quota and VER) and a preference for domestic cars were confirmed as important determinants of price differences in recent studies (Gual, 1993). Transport cost differentials did not show up as an important factor. The Commission has tried to do away with this price discrimination between countries by favouring the possibility of parallel imports, with some success (BEUC, 1989, Rule 123/85). Exclusive rights for sales networks are accepted, but consumers have the right to go and buy a vehicle in any other EU country. Some small firms specialise in this trade. Car manufacturers have to accept normal obligations of guarantee and so on for these cars.

Case study 3: domestic appliances

Dynamics of trade and production: early integration of EC markets

The domestic appliance industry in general and the refrigerator industry in particular show in an interesting way how market integration sharpened competition, forcing European manufacturers to respond with progressive international specialisation (see Maillet, 1977; Mueller, 1981; Owen, 1983; Bianchi and Forlai, 1993). The manufacture of refrigerators has flourished greatly in the last four decades: from being a luxury item in the possession of only a few families, the product has become standard household equipment with a very high degree of penetration (practically one hundred per cent in the more highly developed West European countries).

The post-war period was characterised by stability, demand characterised by isolated national markets and supply by restricted national oligopolies. In the late 1950s, Italian industry, by combining some major innovations in the production and product technology with the standardisation of the product range of refrigerators, achieved enormous economies of scale. Considerable national concentration occurred in Italy in the early 1960s.

The 1960s were a period of great turbulence. The cost advantage achieved by mergers enabled the Italian producers to penetrate very quickly the markets of the other EU countries (whose markets had been opened) and even the market of the UK (which until 1973 was not an EU member). Table 12.11 gives an idea of the magnitude of the effect; by 1972 the Italians had captured over two-fifths of the German and British markets and two-thirds of the French.

Producers in the other European countries responded in three ways. Some tried to merge with other producers in their home countries to

Table 12.11 Production of and trade in refrigerators (1,000 units), 1958–72

	Germany 1958	Germany 1972	France 1958	France 1972	UK 1958	UK 1972	Italy 1958	Italy 1972
Production	1550	1700	580	500	360	1110	500	5400
Exports	n.a.	470	n.a.	50	n.a.	190	n.a.	3900
Imports	n.a.	870	8	890	n.a.	580	n.a.	30
from Italy	n.a.	710	n.a.	600	n.a.	n.a.	n.a.	—
Imports/consumption %	3	40	1	65	—	42	5	2

Source: Owen (1983), Maillet (1977), Mueller (1981), additional estimates.

form a company of the size required for successful competition. Others decided to give up the refrigerator market altogether, concentrating on other products. Others again stopped their domestic production but stayed in business by taking shares in Italian firms. The process was the same in all major European countries where companies had been shaken up by Italian competition. The French firms Thomson-Houston, Hotchkiss-Brandt and Claret merged to form Thomson-Brandt; firms like Frigidaire and Arthur Martin, who did not join in, had to withdraw. The German firms Bosch and Siemens merged, and so did AEG-Linde-BBC; again, several firms withdrew from the market. The UK was not at the time a member of the EU; in its protected market three domestic producers merged in the late 1960s to form BDA; others left the trade. Dutch Philips stopped its own production but took over Ignis, while AEG acquired a one-fifth stake in Zanussi. Still others continued only as commercial operators, leaving production to (Italian) large-scale producer firms. The three largest Italian producers (Ignis, Zanussi and Indesit) together accounted for more than three-quarters of Italian production by the mid-1970s. The additional sales thus realised enabled them to achieve further scale economies, and thus to displace (other) competitors.

A second period of stability (1972–82) occurred after this period of turbulence in the EU market, both in terms of products (decrease in growth) and competitive positions of firms. Firms used their mastering of national distribution channels to split production and commercial control. As a consequence price differences between EU countries developed. Since the early 1980s a new period of restructuring has started. Stagnating demand and increased capacities put a pressure on price. The 1992 programme was to take away barriers to access to foreign markets. A new wave of concentrations followed, in which the Swedish firm Electrolux took a leading role. As a consequence the share of the four largest companies (the C4 index for all domestic appliances) was raised from 20 in 1964 to 50 in 1976 and 60 in 1988.

Recently a similar development has been occurring on the world level, with some very large companies (Whirlpool, Electrolux) having taken over a number of competitors, competing for world markets (Bianchi and Forlai, 1993).

Summary and conclusions

- The EU industry has gone through a process of profound structural change. New sectors of activity have developed (electronics), older ones (shipbuilding) have faded out. This has caused the creation of many new jobs and new firms, on the one hand,

and the loss of many jobs and firms, on the other. It has also meant the relocation of activities within and outside the EU.

- The creation of the EU has not affected all sectors in the same way; some have responded quickly and are now characterised by firms with European dimensions and much intra-industry trade; others have been kept sheltered by various types of government intervention and are not much integrated, as witness the price differences among countries, the existence in certain sectors of national champions for which large parts of home markets are reserved and so on. This situation has recently changed as the execution of the internal market programme (1992) has torn down the remaining obstacles to free internal trade of goods and the free flow of production factors.

- As far as industrial policy is concerned, the attitude of the EU is fairly non-interventionist; market forces, regulated by competition policy, are supposed to take care of the process of change. However the EU does stimulate the renewal of industry by positive action in the field of innovation (R&D).

Notes

1   Manufacturing is also more or less regulated by the coordination efforts of other international organisations. The developed ('industrial') countries have formalised their international industrial cooperation in the OECD. Since its foundation, this organisation has carried out comparative studies, collected statistics of various sectors and compared national policies with respect to industry (and technology). The integration achieved in that way is limited, however. This is even more so for UNIDO (United Nations Industrial Development Organisation), which stimulates industrial development in third-world countries by exchanging information and supporting projects.

2   The reasons for adopting an industrial policy are, in general terms: to take away negative external effects, to make markets transparent and stable, to lower thresholds and reduce the financial risks of companies. To that end, young sectors are stimulated, the conditions of mature sectors guarded, and old sectors assisted in their restructuring.

3   Since 1986, three schemes have been in operation to stimulate the use of the principal new technologies: informatics, telecommunication and biotechnology. Besides these there is a scheme for rendering the results of all modern research applicable to all sectors, traditional ones included. The positive effect of the new approach induced the intensified continuation of efforts (CEC, 1989). We must not leave unmentioned in that connection the EUREKA programme, set in motion outside the EU framework, in which 18 countries participate. This research programme covers quite a number of subjects; its objectives and means are very much like the EU programmes mentioned above. Another matter worth mentioning is that some successful cooperative associations of industries in various member states have been accomplished (with the coordinated support of some governments) with the aim of making certain products ready for marketing. Airbus, the European consortium for the construction of civil aeroplanes,

is a well-known example; Ariane, a group of companies concerned with space travel, is another.

4 These branches are distinguished by their different products and production processes. Most of them can be clearly delimited, as with foodstuffs, electronics and furniture. With some modern activities, however, the differences are steadily becoming vaguer. A case in point is informatics, a sector comprising classical industrial production (such as cables and equipment for telecommunication), less classical industrial activities like the graphic arts, as well as a large number of traditional service sectors such as libraries, telecommunication and so on.

5 See, for a general discussion of the relation between sectoral growth, life-cycles and industrial policy, De Jong (1993).

6 The quantitative side of employment change hides the technological progress of the last few decades, which has radically changed the production apparatus and the qualifications of the workforce. The large numbers of 'blue collar' factory workers have been replaced more and more by the grey and white collars of those concerned with management, research, control, checking, sales and organisation, working in offices, showrooms and laboratories.

7 If the list was extended for 1990 to include all companies with over 170,000 employees and a sales figure of more than 20,000 million ECU, Renault, Peugeot and Alcatel/Alsthom would be added.

8 To complement these measures, the Commission also negotiated VERs with, among others, Japan and East European countries. It was in turn confronted by import restrictions on EU steel in the USA.

9 In each of the large countries given a home producer was present. That is not always the case for smaller member states. Hence the relative share of imports in the smaller countries was much greater than for the four larger countries. As Hocking (1980) has shown, the negative relation between the size of the home market and the volume of imports diminished in the 1960s, but still persisted to some extent into the mid-1970s, some 15 years after the formation of the EU.

13 Energy

Introduction

Energy is essential to economic development. Without it, most of the present production and welfare would not be possible. It is considered by many governments as a strategic good, and the control over energy supplies has always been a matter of concern for governments. In an integration scheme, the equal access to energy is of great economic importance; as energy is a major input in many other productions, non-integrated energy markets coupled with integrated goods markets would lead to distortions. It also has much political weight as the interdependency on strategic commodities may be the best guarantee for peace.

For precisely these two reasons the EU has from its very beginnings pursued the integration of energy markets. The regime it has created is described in the next section. It is a complicated one, because it needs to take account of the different ways in which all member states intervene in the energy markets and in the structure of the energy sector.[1]

The third section sketches the changes which in the 1950–90 period occurred in the consumption and production of energy in Europe. The fourth and fifth sections treat the integration of certain submarkets in some depth; oil and electricity have been chosen as examples. For both we will describe the development of production, trade and prices and the strategies of the major firms. Some conclusions will complete the chapter.

EU regime

Treaties

The EU energy policy is based on three different treaties, each containing rules for specific segments of the energy sector. The *European*

Coal and Steel Community (ECSC), was created in 1952. At that time, coal was still the most important energy source for Europe. The ECSC treaty mentions a number of objectives (Articles 2 and 3) of a market regulation and a structural policy for the coalmining sector. The High Authority's (now Commission's) first task concerns the adequate functioning of the market; it has to 'ensure an orderly supply to the Common Market; ensure that all comparably placed consumers in the Common Market have equal access to the sources of production; ensure the establishment of the lowest prices'. In principle, the EU gives free scope to competition to govern the market process. However, in times of 'manifest crisis' or scarcity, it can intervene either directly in the prices (Article 61) or through production quotas (Article 58) and international trade (Article 74); such intervention must be applied only if more indirect measures fail. The second task, to pursue a structural policy, is formulated by the treaty as follows: 'ensure the maintenance of conditions which will encourage undertakings to expand and improve their production potential'. To attain this objective, the ECSC draws up indicative programmes, appraises individual investment programmes, supports investments and research, and finally supports restructuring by appropriate measures (Articles 46 to 56).[2]

The *European Atomic Energy Community* (EAEC) (created in 1958) has no powers as to the regulation of the market; demand is free, and for the supply of ores, raw materials and fissionable material an EU monopoly has been given to an 'Agency' created for the purpose. The EAEC's main task is a structural–political one, in which we distinguish the following elements: to develop research (Articles 4–7) – it carries on extensive research programmes in its own EC research centres – to disperse knowledge (Articles 14–24), and to make investments (Articles 40 and 47). Apart from supporting and coordinating, the EAEC can also participate directly in investments.

The *European Economic Community* (EEC) was also created in 1958. Its treaty contains no specific stipulations for the energy sector; therefore the functioning of the (crude-)oil, (natural-)gas and electricity markets is left to supply and demand forces regulated by the general stipulations of the treaty, for example with respect to competition (Articles 85 and 86). No structural measures for these sectors have been provided for at all either.

Gradual development of policy

On the basis of the three treaties a more coherent energy policy has gradually been developed. Changes in the external situation have determined its different stages. We distinguish two periods: 1958–72 and 1973–90. In the early 1960s it was recognised that the situation in the energy field lacked balance. Since then, the Commission has submitted a series of proposals for a more coherent EC energy policy. The 1962 Memorandum on Energy Policy was followed in 1968 by a 'First Orientation to a Common Energy Policy', which reflected the fundamental problems of the EU energy position and established the principles of EU policy, namely to ensure supply at the lowest possible price, with due regard to the specific structure of the energy sector. A common market for energy products and coordination of the member states' energy policy were to be the means. This led to the decision of the European Council in 1972 to develop a coordinated energy policy.

The 1973 energy crisis showed that the EU was confronted by three major problems (CEC, 1981a):

- Insecurity of supply. The EU was dependent for a large part of its energy on foreign oil. The cutting of supplies was used as a weapon by some producers for strategic as well as economic reasons (d'Anarzit, 1982).
- Instability of prices. Fluctuations in the price of crude oil and the exchange rate to the dollar (see Figure 13.1) had caused huge disturbances of the European economy in general and the energy sector in particular.
- Disequilibrium on the balance of payments. Between 1973 and 1981, the oil bill of the EU had multiplied by eight (in dollars), despite a simultaneous decline of net imports by some 40 per cent.

The very divergent national responses to the crisis (virtually disintegrating the common energy market) made the EU painfully aware of the need for further action. This was reinforced by the second oil crisis of 1979. In a series of communications from the Commission to the Council, the former progressively worked out the objectives and implementation of its policy, a central element of which is the coordination of national policies, in order to render consistent the objectives and measures of energy policy as pursued by national governments. To coordinate the programmes of member states (Alting von Geusau, 1975; Lucas, 1977, 1985), the Commission organises periodical surveys of member states' energy policy schemes (for example, CEC, 1982c).[3]

In the course of the 1980s three new major developments shaped a new framework for EU energy policies. The first was the drive towards the completion of the internal market. Traditionally the markets for the different fuels are very heavily regulated on a national basis, and as a consequence the European market was very segmented. The new objective to create a competitive market with a

Figure 13.1   Import prices of energy

Source: CEC (1986f, 1992d).

pan-European regulatory framework implied a major restructuring of the sector. The second new development was the increased concern with the environment. Indeed one of the major causes of air pollution is the burning of energy sources with a high carbon content, so the objectives of the policies became more oriented towards the limitation of consumption, and towards less polluting sources (CEC, 1992c). The third development was the opening up of the Eastern European countries with very important energy reserves. A European energy charter has been signed between the EU and the CEEC to expand the trade in energy between the two areas. This has fundamentally changed the external dimension of the EU energy policies (CEC, 1992e).

The objectives of the Common Energy Policy are: (1) security of supply, (2) primacy of market forces, and (3) sustainable development (environment). The specific objectives of the EU energy policy first formulated in 1974 and subsequently confirmed (CEC, 1988b, 1992c, 1992d) can be summarised as follows:

- to diminish the ratio between the growth of energy consumption and the growth of GNP;
- to diminish oil consumption to some 40 per cent of total primary energy consumption; the share of solid fuels should be expanded;
- to reduce the share of oil and stimulate the use of solid fuels and nuclear energy in electricity generation; the share of hydrocarbons in total electricity production should be reduced to less than 15 per cent by 1995.

Many of these objectives have either been reached or are within reach in the near future. This is the result of cooperation within the EU, with the member states using short-term measures with a rather direct effect on the market, and longer-term measures of a more structural nature.

Market control: the short term

The Commission has laid down, in regulations and directives, rules for the intervention of member states in the market. An important impetus has come from the completion of the internal market for energy products, whereby the causes for the present distortions on the EU market for energy, such as differences in taxes on energy products, national monopolies, government interventions and protective national procurement, are taken away. The EU activity may be grouped under three headings:

Disturbances of supply   This applies especially to crude oil (d'Anarzit, 1982). To avoid the type of problem that occurred during the oil crisis, member states are committed to maintain minimum stocks of oil (equivalence of at least 90 days' consumption) and in times of supply problems to introduce a rationing scheme for these stocks. To ensure that member states help one another in such circumstances, the Commission can draw on certain executive powers.

Transparent markets   Member states are committed to inform and consult the Commission on the development of prices and domestic and foreign supplies in the different sub-markets (oil, gas and so on). For example, the conditions and prices of home deliveries, of imports and exports are published (Directive, 1990), and the market situation is discussed regularly on the basis of the Commission's quarterly reviews.

Access to markets   In the electricity and gas markets the monopoly power of the companies controlling the distribution networks bars the access of efficient producers to potential clients. The EU has realised some improvement (Transit Directives, 1990 and 1991) and has proposed a whole series of directives to complete the internal market for energy for these products too.

Structural policy: the long term

The objectives of the common energy policy (CEP) cannot be realised without a rather drastic restructuring of energy production, consumption and trade. The following measures of structural policy are in force in the framework of the CEP:

stimulating EU production
- nuclear energy (financing by EAEC);
- coalmining (ECSC financing and regulation);
- alternative (permanent and renewable) sources: subsidies to research projects and demonstration (ALTENER, JOULE and THERMIE programmes);

energy saving
- loans to manufacturing industries applying new technical procedures (programme SAVE).

Sketch of the sector

Employment and value added

Energy is a collective term for many types; a common distinction is that between primary and secondary energy. Primary energy springs from a variety of sources. Historically human and animal muscle power, wood, wind and water (tides and rivers) were important. In more modern times fossil fuels have come to the fore (coal, oil, gas). Since the Second World War, nuclear energy has developed fast. Recently other forms of energy have regained interest, in particular the so-called 'renewable resources', sun radiation and tidal energy, but also biomass and so on. Because primary energy sources are not always easy to use, they are converted into secondary ones, such as coke and gas from coal, petrol and liquefied petroleum gas (LPG) from crude oil. Some of these are converted a second time for the generation of electricity in coke- or oil-fired power stations.

The constituent branches of the energy sectors both of primary energy production (such as coalmining), and of secondary energy production and distribution (for example, electricity generation and oil refining) each count for less than 1 per cent of total employment, which means that the entire energy sector represents about 2 per cent of total employment. In terms of gross value added the percentage is about 3 per cent higher because of the relatively high productivity and the large contribution the sector makes to government revenue. Evidently the sector does not add up to a large part of total economic activity. If we have singled the sector out for separate treatment it is because the EU has decided to hammer out a common policy for energy in view of its strategic importance.

Total consumption of primary energy

The 1950–73 period was characterised by high and stable economic growth that caused total energy consumption[4] in the European Union to increase very fast too. In the 1950–60 period, average annual growth was 3.9 per cent; in the 1960–73 period, attaining even 5.2 per cent. The ratio between the increase of energy consumption and that of GNP (elasticity) was 0.8 in the 1950–60 period, and somewhat higher, 1.1, in the 1960–73 period. Another way to express this is with the help of the energy intensity index, that relates the consumption of energy to the level of GDP. In the period up to 1973 this index gradually crept up to 51.

The 1973–82 period started with some events which were to exert a strong effect on the entire consumption pattern. For one thing, the oil price, practically stable until then, rose almost fourfold. For another, the continuous supply of oil became uncertain as some oil exporters put an embargo on oil exports to certain consumer countries. An economic recession was the result, with, in 1975, the first decline of GNP since the Second World War. Energy consumption dropped as well: by some 7 per cent between 1973 and 1975. The high price of oil induced its replacement by other sources of energy, as well as measures to diminish consumption by energy saving. As a result, energy consumption rose but slightly between 1975 and 1979. Given a growth of the EU economy by approximately 1.5 per cent in the same period, the elasticity of energy consumption in respect of GNP appears to have dropped to 0.2. In 1979 there followed the second oil shock, again multiplying the oil prices by almost four. It was the main cause of a drop in energy consumption of some 10 per cent between 1979 and 1982, compared to a 1 per cent GDP increase. So, in that period, elasticity turned negative. The energy intensity index consequently dropped to 41 in 1983.

In the 1983–90 period, with prices of energy decreasing drastically, demand picked up again (by some 2 per cent a year). However, as GDP increased even faster (by some 3 per cent a year), the energy intensity index of the EU was able to decrease further, to reach 39 in 1990.

Consumption by primary energy source

Consumption has developed differently for the various primary energy sources, as Table 13.1 illustrates. Certain trends can be discerned throughout the period 1930–90, such as the fall in the share of coal, the rise and subsequent fall in the share of oil and the continuous rise of the shares of gas and electricity. The table shows that there is some differentiation between sub-periods. In the period 1930–39 almost the entire energy consumption was supplied by solid fuels, especially coal. In the period from 1950 to 1973, consumption switched fast from coal mostly to liquid fuels (crude oil), but also to (natural) gas and primary electricity, comprising hydraulic power and nuclear energy. The latter especially is progressing steadily. The downward trend for coal and the upward trend for oil reached a turning point in 1973. As a result of the considerable increase in oil prices and subsequent policy measures, the share of oil decreased from 1973 onward. The increase in gas and primary electricity continued all through the study period; the share of solid fuels was practically stable from 1973 onwards. Since 1985 there has been a steep fall in oil prices due to the breakdown of the OPEC cartel, which halted the decrease in the share of oil in total energy consumption in the EU.

Table 13.1　**Percentage shares of primary energy sources in total energy consumption (EU12, Mtoe), 1930–90**

	1930	1937	1950	1960	1973	1980	1990
Coal	95	90	83	63	23	23	21
Oil	4	8	14	31	61	51	45
Gas	—	—	—	2	11	15	19
Electricity	1	2	3	4	5	11	15
Total	100	100	100	100	100	100	100

Source: OECD, *Energy Statistics, Energy Balances, Oil Statistics*, various years; OECD (1966, 1973).

The determinant factors behind the substitution of one energy source for another are costs, consumer convenience and availability; of course, the latter two can also be translated into costs. The most important substitution has been that of oil for coal. This did not come as a surprise, since their relative prices had diverged steadily from 1950 to 1973. While high labour costs of production and transport made coal more and more expensive, the consumption prices of oil could be reduced thanks to its capital-intensive production and the economies of scale achieved in production and transport (Eurostat, 1974).

The steady rise in the share of gas in total consumption has been due in particular to its convenient use in many installations and to the fact that it is more and more produced in the consumption areas. Finally the share of primary electricity is steadily growing. The cost of electricity generated in thermal power stations, and the wish to be independent of primary-energy imports, have stimulated the development of hydro- and nuclear energy. The quantities obtained in practice from other primary sources, such as wood, wind, sun and animal force, are negligible at the moment; their limited availability and the high costs and/or great inconvenience to consumers have been the main delaying factors.

Conversion of primary into secondary energy

Primary energy sources are not always convenient to users, which is why they are converted into secondary ones. *To convert energy costs energy.* On the one hand, oil refineries and coke ovens use energy to feed the production process. On the other, the return of thermal power stations is rather low: energy escapes into the water through cooling and through chimneys into the air. The total 'losses' of the entire energy sector in the EU between 1973 and 1980 amounted to about 25 per cent of the total consumption of primary energy (OECD, 1987a). But why convert at all if it costs so much energy? The reason is that many processes technically require secondary energy for efficient production and consumption. The primary sources differ widely in the extent to which they are converted into secondary energy. About one-half of all coal is converted, mostly in power stations, with a small proportion in coke factories. Brown coal is converted almost entirely into electricity. Crude oil is fully converted into oil products, of which a portion, in particular fuel oil, is processed further in electric power stations.

Apparently, then, many primary energy sources are ultimately converted into electricity, in spite of the heavy 'losses' incurred. The relative volumes of the various primary energy sources utilised for the generation of electricity have changed substantially over time, as Table 13.2 illustrates.

That the shares differ so much is due to a combination of factors, such as the relative prices of primary energy sources, the technical

Table 13.2   **Percentage shares of energy sources in the consumption of power stations (EU12, calculated on the basis of a conversion in oil equivalent), 1950–90**

	1950	1960	1970	1980	1990
Solid (coal)	71	67	51	47	37
Liquid (oil)	1	7	24	22	11
Gas	—	1	5	7	7
Nuclear	—	1	4	11	36
Hydro	28	24	16	13	9
Total	100	100	100	100	100

Source: OECD, *The Electricity Supply Industry in Western Europe*, various years; CEC, *Panorama*.

appointment of existing power stations and government policy (for instance, stimulation of the use of coal by subsidies).

Production and import

Along with the consumption pattern of energy in Western Europe, the pattern of production and import, and hence the *external dependence*, have greatly changed. The first change came when coal, a predominantly domestic energy source, was replaced by an imported one, oil. More and more coal was imported as well, because the West European mines could not compete with foreign ones. As a result, the dependence coefficient of the EU, defined as the share of net imports in total energy consumption, rose rapidly after the Second World War. From just 1 per cent in 1930, and 7 per cent on the eve of the war, the dependence coefficient had risen to 15 per cent by 1950. From that year on it rose steadily to reach a high in 1973, when two-thirds of all energy consumed in the EU had to be imported. The oil crisis of the early 1970s opened European eyes to the risk of such a development; since then extensive schemes have been carried out to make Europe less dependent on foreign oil, schemes to boost national production as well as reduce consumption. The effects are clearly perceptible in the figures: the external dependence coefficient was down to 42 per cent in 1986. Since then it has gone up again to 48, as a consequence of the fall in imported oil prices (OECD, *Energy Balances*, 1992). Let us look rather more closely at the individual energy sources.

Crude oil The EU's own production, practically negligible in 1950 and only 15 million tons (Mt) in 1970, had risen to 153 Mt a year by 1985. Of that volume, the UK had the lion's share.[5] In fact, in 1985, the EU12 produced 30 per cent of its total oil consumption. By 1990 this had gone down to 23 per cent as the prices of imported oil decreased. By becoming increasingly self-supplying, Western Europe diminishes its total dependence on foreign oil. Moreover it reduces strategic risks by drawing oil from an increasing number of supplying countries. In the early 1960s, four Middle Eastern countries, Iran, Iraq, Kuwait and Saudi Arabia, still accounted for three-quarters of the oil supply to Western Europe. By 1970 their share in European imports had been reduced by half, and this dropped further in the course of the 1970s because new producers, in particular in North and West Africa, but also in Mexico, had joined the traditional Middle Eastern oil suppliers to Europe (OECD, *Oil Statistics*; OECD, 1973). Recently the CEEC have grown in importance (10 per cent of all EU imports). Figure 13.2 gives an idea of the geographical pattern of Western European crude oil imports.

Solid fuels Traditionally Northern Europe produced its own coal and, throughout the 1950–90 period, the largest producer countries in Western Europe were the UK and Germany, with France, Spain and Belgium following at some distance. The production in the rest of Western Europe was negligible in comparison. In the 1950s, no more than about 5 per cent of total demand for coal needed to be imported; in the 1960s, the average percentage was 10, and by 1990, when the consumption of coal had picked up again, the EU12's dependence on imports had risen to some 30 per cent. Most imports came from the USA and Poland. For a long time, coal extracted in EU countries was able to hold its own against oil and imported coal only with the help of supporting measures.

Natural gas The production in the EU has grown to become quite important (particularly in the Netherlands, and later on also in the North Sea (UK)).[6] In Western Europe outside the EU, Norway is another large producer and recently (liquefied) natural gas has begun to be imported (LNG by tanker from North Africa, NG by pipe from Eastern Europe, the latter accounting for 45 per cent of total EU imports).

Other Among the other sources of energy, nuclear is of particular importance. Because uranium can be stocked, the fiction is often maintained that nuclear energy is a domestic source of energy; that uranium has to be imported into Europe is overlooked. As for such alternative primary sources as hydro-power and wind, the EU is by

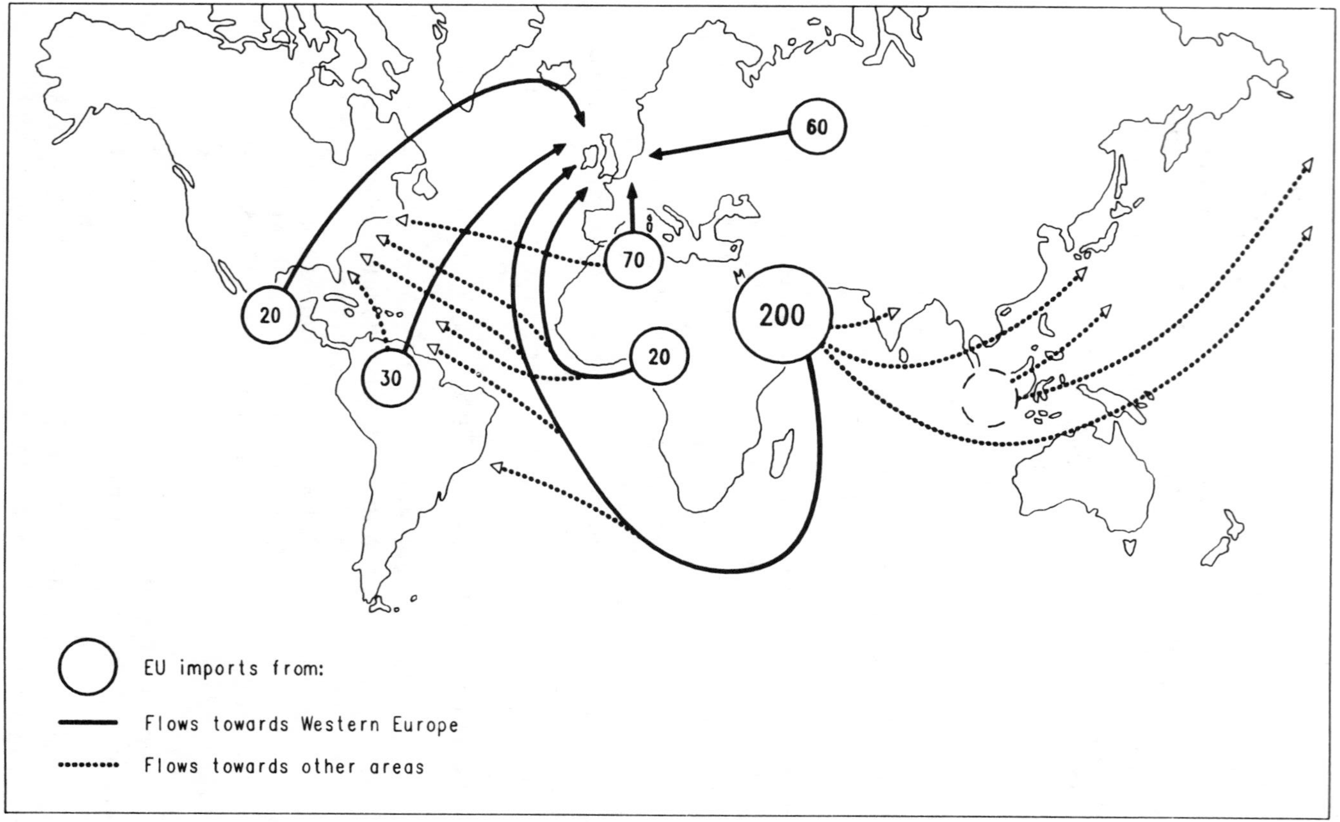

Figure 13.2   Flows of crude oil towards the EU (Mtoe), 1990

definition independent of imports; given their small scale, we need not pay further attention to them here.

Consumption by category

To analyse the consumption pattern[7] we distinguish three main sectors: industry, transport, and household/commerce. The relative position of these consumer categories in total consumption were stable throughout the 1950–90 period (see Table 13.3). Industry is the largest consumer category, with a share of about 40 per cent. It is followed closely by household/commerce, with a share of some 35 per cent. Transport invariably comes in third position, but is coming up fast as a major consumer category.

Table 13.3   Final domestic consumption of energy (including non-energy purposes) in the EU12, by consumer category and secondary energy source (%), 1950–90

	1950	1960	1970	1980	1990
Industry (incl. non-energy)	41	47	47	41	37
Household/commerce	40	35	35	36	34
Transport (incl. bunkers)	19	18	18	23	29
Total	100	100	100	100	100

Sources: OECD (1987g); OECD, *Basic Statistics of Energy, Energy Balances*, various years.

Industry   The iron and steel sector is the largest consumer, accounting for some 10 to 15 per cent of the total sector's 40. Coke and coal (for blast furnaces) are in the lead, but other energy sources, especially electricity, are steadily gaining in importance. A second very important sector is that of chemical products, in particular the petrochemical industry; its share has risen slowly and now accounts for some 12 per cent of the EU's total final energy consumption. By far the largest consumer is the petrochemical industry, which uses mainly oil products and gases. Note that the consumption of industry also comprises non-energetic consumption, for instance of naphtha as a raw material of the petrochemical industry. Non-energy consumption increased significantly as the petrochemical industry grew in importance (Molle and Wever, 1983). The industrial consumption of coal has declined fast since 1960, while that of all other energy forms has been rapidly increasing. This cannot be attributed entirely to the developments in the steel and chemical industries described above, for most sectors of other industry show the same tendency.

Household, commerce   Household consumption ranks first, accounting for some two-thirds of the entire category's consumption in 1990. We do not know much about the structure of this main category in the years before 1975, but from fragmentary data the household group appears always to have represented the body of the entire main category. The development of the various energy forms offers a striking picture: after a rise in the 1950s, coal was practically eliminated in the 1960s, obviously because it was inconvenient to the user. Electricity and gas, on the other hand, have grown fast, as did oil until the decline prompted by the crisis.

Transport   Haulage is by far the largest consumer group, accounting for more than half of the category's total consumption. Moreover its share has steadily increased over time. The demand of the haulage sector is practically entirely for oil products, which is also by far the most important source of energy for air and water transport. Electricity is almost completely and exclusively used for rail transport; coal has lost most of its former important position in shipping and rail transport to oil and electricity.

Case study 1: oil refining

Companies

The European oil market is dominated by a few large multinational companies, some large (state) companies operating mostly on the national markets, and a varying number of smaller companies. The largest European companies are listed by size in Table 13.4.

The various categories of oil firms can be described as follows (Molle and Wever, 1983; Molle, 1992).

Majors   These were formerly called the seven sisters (Sampson, 1977). To this group belonged up to the mid-1970s five American (Exxon, Texaco, Gulf Oil, Mobil Oil and Chevron) and two European companies (Shell and BP). In the turmoil of the oil crisis, two left the European scene: Gulf (operations taken over by KPC) and Chevron. The majors operate on a world scale and show a high degree of vertical integration. This means that they are active at all stages of the oil industry: in the exploration and exploitation of crude oil, the transport of crude and products, the refining and, finally, the marketing of the finished products. They are, moreover, active in such related

Table 13.4   Rank order of European oil companies, 1990

Rank	Company	Country	Sales, in milliard ECU
1	Royal Dutch Shell	NL/UK	81
2	British Petroleum	UK	57
3	ENI	Italy	33
4	Elf	France	28
5	Total	France	19
6	Petrofina	Belgium	14
7	Repsol	Spain	13

Source: The Times 1000.

activities as (petro)chemicals and even in other energy sectors such as nuclear energy or coalmining. The relative position of the seven majors decreased quite a lot in the 1950–90 period: while in 1950 they controlled 65 per cent of total European refinery capacity, in 1990 they were down to about 40 per cent. Among these majors, the American company Exxon and the European companies Shell and BP are by far the greatest in terms of refinery capacity in Western Europe. At the end of the 1960s, at the height of its influence, Shell possessed 23 refineries in 10 European countries; the company controlled about 20 per cent of the total refinery capacity in Western Europe, against some 15 per cent in the 1970s and 1980s. Immediately behind Shell comes the Exxon company, possessing 15 refineries in eight different European countries, with 15 per cent of total European capacity by 1970; by 1980, this figure had gone down to about 11 per cent. BP, the next largest, had 12 refineries in six different European countries, totalling some 10 per cent of Europe's total capacity in the 1980s.

State-controlled European companies   In a deliberate policy to strengthen the national position in the refinery industry with respect to the majors, a number of countries have established state-owned or state-controlled refinery companies. Most of them confine their activities (their refinery activities at least) within the national borders. In France there are the two CFP subsidiaries, Total and Elf/Aquitaine,[8] that together hold a very large share (between 50 and 60 per cent up to 1980) of the total French refining sector. In Italy the dominant company is the ENI, which currently possesses some 20 per cent of total refinery capacity in Italy. The Portuguese national company Petrogal even has a 100 per cent share in the refinery industry of the country. In Spain the semi-national companies are very important. Other countries (Germany, Greece) also have some national or semi-national companies, but their position in the refinery sector is relatively modest.

Independent private companies　Within this group two sub-groups can be distinguished: the Western European companies and the American companies. Within the group of Western European independents we can make a further distinction between some of the larger ones that work internationally (such as Petrofina), some medium-sized companies (like Gelsenberg) and a large number of smaller companies that are mostly active on a local scale only, especially in Western Germany, Italy and the UK. In the course of the post-war period many of these companies ceased to exist, because they stopped production or were taken over by larger companies (state, major or chemical companies). Their market position as well as their resource base are often too weak to stand up to international competition. The refinery operations of the American independents in Western Europe are confined to one or two refineries per company.

Chemical　Many products now based on petroleum feedstock used to be produced from other feedstocks. Starting from their petrochemical base, some of these companies have integrated backwards, participating in or taking over oil refining facilities. Examples are ICI, Montedison and BASF.

National companies from producer countries　The growth of OPEC power since 1973 has caused a profound, worldwide change in the oil industry. The main producer states of the world took control of the majority of world oil and gas reserves. The oil companies of these countries, such as Libya (Tamoil) Kuwait (KPC) and Venezuela (Petroven) strove for increased control of the facilities for processing, distribution, storing and marketing oil products. OPEC states increasingly challenge European producers of refined products by exporting their refinery products to Europe and to the traditional export markets of European producers. Moreover some companies of producer states have moved into Europe with production and distribution facilities; in particular KPC has gained a firm foothold.

Joint ventures　Some refineries are jointly owned by companies belonging to different sub-groups. Examples are the refineries of Rotterdam (BP and Texaco) and Neustadt (Mobil, VEBA, Petroven). Quite a few of these joint ventures have been undertaken by an oil company and a chemical company together. Examples are Erdoelchemie (BP and Bayer) and Rheinische olefinwerke (Shell and BASF).

European integration has had some influence on the company structure, in that it has contributed to a certain concentration of the smaller
producers, but the main driving forces behind the company restructuring were worldwide changes in control over oil reserves and the
wish to obtain national government influence over the sector. In
recent years the competition rules have applied more strictly also to
the state-owned companies; as a consequence the latter are trying to
diversify into other countries and are behaving more as traditional
majors seeking interests abroad (ELF is an example).

Production facilities

Economies of scale play an important role in the refining industry.
Therefore production has been concentrated in a relatively small
number of plants (see Table 13.5). The restructuring process of the
European refining industry has followed a distinct pattern dependent on the different stages of the industry life-cycle (Molle, 1992). The
introductory stage happened shortly after the Second World War.

Table 13.5   Number of refineries by size class and total capacity
of refineries, EU12 (Mt/y), 1950–90

Class (Mt/y)	1950	1960	1970	1980	1990
0.1 – 1.0	61	53	37	18	7
1.1 – 5.0	11	45	64	60	41
5.1 –10.0	—	5	19	57	39
10.1 – 15.0	—	—	6	16	12
15.1 – 20.0	—	—	1	6	2
larger than 20.1	—	—	—	4	1
Total number	72	103	127	161	102
Distillation capacity	41	192	707	1 000	635
Average capacity	0.6	1.8	5.6	6.2	6.3

Source: Molle and Wever (1983), Molle (1992).

The *expansion stage* lasted from the early 1950s up to the first oil crisis
in the mid-1970s. During this period, the total capacity of the refinery
sector in Europe increased rapidly, in line with the strongly increased
demand. Part of that growth was achieved by the expansion of existing refineries, another by the creation of new ones. In oil refining, as
in other industries, growth was attended by a tremendous enlarge-

ment of the scale of plants; Table 13.5 gives an indication. In spite of this increased scale in plant size, there was no spatial concentration of production facilities. Throughout the period 1950–75, markets were indeed growing at an even higher rate than the optimal scale, which permitted refinery activities to orient themselves to national markets and to spread geographically (Molle and Wever, 1983). This orientation to national markets, based on location factors like transport cost, was consolidated by the strategy adopted by several governments to build up their own 'national' oil industries.

The *maturity* stage came suddenly when, in the mid-1970s, the development changed dramatically with the effects of the increase in oil prices, slackening demand and so on. New investment was halted but refineries that had been planned before the events came on stream added to overcapacity (see figures for 1980 in Table 13.5). Only after 1980 was it realised that the fall in demand was of a structural nature and only then were measures taken: many plants were closed altogether, while most others were reduced in capacity. The pattern of these reductions was less influenced by considerations of competition between firms on integrated markets than by the need to adapt local capacity to local demand. As Table 13.5 shows, this implied that most of the smaller refineries were closed; some others were scaled up to reach the minimum efficient size, while many were scaled down to demand, safeguarding their minimum efficient capacity levels.

Like the steel industry, the refinery industry is characterised by very heavy investments, making it difficult to come to a balanced process of capacity adjustments. To improve the situation, the Commission has set up an information exchange with the oil companies, which has functioned satisfactorily. Consequently there has not been much increase in international specialisation and trade in refinery products.

Case study 2: electricity

Actors on the European electricity market

The European market for electric power is practically fragmented along national lines, with only a little exchange among them in terms of products, and without any international integration of firms. The reason is that the manner in which electricity has to be delivered to the customers has favoured local or national monopolies, which are looked upon as a public service rather than a commercial activity. Many of these distribution monopolies have integrated backwards and have created monopolies on the production stage as well. In many countries economies of scale and scope have induced electricity firms to organise on the national level. This is the case, for example, in France (EDF being by far the largest European electricity company), where national companies control the generation, transmission and distribution of electricity. In the UK various companies were created, each controlling parts of the generation and transmission and distribution process. Other member countries show highly diversified patterns as to the organisation of the supply side (Eurostat, several years).

Electricity companies in the EU are grouped into several international organisations. The most important is UCPTE, which groups all but one of the continental countries of the EU, plus Austria, Switzerland and the former Yugoslavia. Denmark is a member of NORDEL, with the other nordic countries. UCPTE countries have an interconnected network, designed for emergencies rather than for regular trading; its capacity is calculated to cope with the need to supply electricity to a country part of whose system has broken down. UCPTE's links with NORDEL have a limited capacity; recently, a link between France and the UK was constructed.

International trade

Electricity consumption has increased very fast in the last few decades. The increase has been achieved by a considerable construction of generation plants and distribution lines in all countries. All the EU member states, in their efforts to be self-sufficient, tend to import primary energy rather than electric power. Indeed the figures of Table 13.6 show that only a small percentage of total electricity production enters international trade. The table also shows that consumption increased fourfold over the 1960–90 period, while exchanges increased three to four times as fast as consumption. However in terms of percentage the share of exchanges in total consumption remains very low, indicating a low degree of integration. Exchange with third countries during this period was limited to some imports.

Table 13.6   Consumption and exchanges of electricity in the EU12, 1960–90

Year	1960	1970	1980	1990
Consumption (TWh)	280	570	880	1130
Exchanges (%)*	2	3	4	7

*   Intra-EU trade as a % of total final consumption.
Source: OECD, *Energy Balance of OECD Countries 1989–1990*, OECD, Paris, 1992.

International exchange of electricity is necessary to overcome several problems.

Long-term   Power stations are, on average, large constructions which take some time to build. The generation capacity of national systems, in particular in the smaller countries, does not match demand, so that electricity has to be imported or exported. Mostly the prices agreed upon in such long-term contracts are indexed to some mix of fuel prices on international markets.

Short-term   Thermal power plants need to be closed down at intervals for maintenance and repair; hydro-power is not constantly available in the same quantities. Trading permits the utilities to economise on the total capacity needed to fulfil a certain level of demand. Prices are usually of the spot type (that is, the price prevailing on the short-term market), depending on the load level, the availability of certain sources of primary energy, and so on.

Very short-term   Technical difficulties like a temporary lack of power, at periods of peak demand, or technical problems of generation or transmission may occur. Such exchanges are not billed but compensated by the recipient helping out the partner at another time; they enable utility companies to economise on standby capacity.

Most exchanges between European countries have been made to cope with the long- and short-term problems; the very short-term difficulties having had but little effect.

   The rationale for the exchange of goods and services is comparative advantage (for theory, see Chapter 5; for clear examples, see Chapters 8 and 12). The rationale for existing electricity trade is the ability to cope with an emergency need, the principle of most governments being national self-sufficiency. The Commission has proposed the liberalisation of electricity markets as part of the completion of the internal market. However very fierce opposition from a vast majority of national governments to the proposals of the Commission has resulted in a continuation of the present position. Consequently intra-European trade in electricity will not yet develop along the lines depicted for goods in previous chapters.

Prices

Market conditions being as described above, it is hardly surprising to find important differences in price among the member countries of the EU. Indeed, when markets are regulated to that extent, inputs (of labour, for instance) are apt to be inefficient. Moreover there is ample scope for setting different prices for different consumer categories (UNIPEDE 1982, 1985). The generally public electricity companies follow different strategies, based on the level of fixed costs of production and distribution and the possibilities of dividing these costs between different categories of users, taking account of market response and industrial and regional policy objectives. The differences among EU countries in the price of electricity for a typical category of household and industrial consumer are quite substantial. Although some relative prices changed considerably in the 1980–90 period, no tendency of convergence to a European price level can be observed, reflecting the industry's lack of integration. One cause of the continuing disparity in electricity prices is that the EU member countries use different fuel mixes to generate electricity. In France almost three-quarters of all electricity is generated in nuclear power stations, while Denmark's power plants are almost exclusively coal-fired. The more expensive producers were those that depended on oil or gas firing. With the completion of the internal market also for this sector, and the increase in trade in electricity that will follow from this, it is likely that the price differences will decrease (see Chapter 16).

Summary and conclusions

- The involvement of the EU with energy is based on three different treaties: ECSC for coal, EAEC for nuclear energy, and the EEC for all other energy products. Gradually a common energy policy has evolved that is largely based on the coordination of member state policies.
- For a long time the dominant energy source was coal. Since the mid-1960s, oil has taken over the lead. Electricity, generated from various primary sources, is becoming ever more important.
- Oil markets have gone through very turbulent times, but the market partners, in particular the multinational oil companies, seem to have responded adequately by changing exploration and exploitation methods (North Sea oil) and adapting and modernising the refining, transport and distribution systems, taking into account the integration of the European market and the linkages with world markets.
- Electricity, on the contrary, is a very fragmented industry. As its importance in energy markets continues to grow, the development of a European view of production and distribution, including pricing, is becoming imperative.

Notes

1   See, for a more complete description, for instance, Weyman-Jones (1986), or Jensen (1983).
2   The extended powers of the EU in the coal sector make this sector highly comparable to agriculture; here, too, there is considerable intervention of public authorities both at the European and at the national level.
3   From its very creation, the OECD has also paid attention to the energy problem. A relatively advanced form of international cooperation, by OECD standards, was initiated after the first oil crisis by the creation of the International Energy Agency. This agency was instructed to draw up an international energy programme; it tries to carry out this programme by coordinating the national policies of the participating states (OECD, various years). The International Energy Agency, however, goes one better: it curtails member states' elbow room by laying down uniform rules of behaviour which all member states are supposed to respect, their conduct being judged regularly, in meetings of government representatives, from detailed reports (for instance, OECD, 1987f). However for energy no more than in other matters does the OECD have authority to enforce the policy agreed upon.
4   To be made comparable, the various energy sources (coal, oil and so on) have all been converted to the energetic content of the dominant one: oil. The unit we have used is Mtoe, which stands for million tons of oil equivalent. The figures for the post-war period should be compared to the historical growth figures of about 1 per cent a year from 1930 to 1950.
5   In addition, some 25 million tons of oil were produced by Norway.
6   For the evolution of the European gas market and its lack of competitiveness, see Golombek *et al.* (1987).
7   Contrary to the OECD definition, we count bunkers in final consumption; the OECD treats this category as exports. The categories are not defined, as in Table 13.1, in terms of primary sources, but in terms of secondary sources (after conversion: 'liquid' comprises all oil products, 'solid' coal, coke and brown coal; 'gas' comprises natural gas as well as coke-oven and refinery gas and so on, and 'electricity' refers to power from nuclear as well as thermal power stations. Final domestic consumption is defined as total domestic production plus imports minus exports and minus the energy sector's own consumption.
8   Elf has a number of refineries abroad, in particular in Germany, which makes it something of a multinational.

14 Services

Introduction

While the European Union has always looked upon services as an essential part of the integration process, it has not in practice devoted much attention to them. In the present chapter we propose to look into the European service sector in some detail. The pattern of this chapter is the same as that of the previous ones.

First we will give a succinct description of the European policy regime. The regulation of the EU had to take into account that the service sector has been subject to considerable national government regulation, springing largely from the desire to protect consumer interest (for instance, minimum standards for the reserves of banks, or qualification standards for medical personnel). Convinced that a socially desirable organisation of quite large segments could not be left to private enterprise, governments have even assumed direct responsibility for production and distribution, especially for services associated with the welfare state (like social security). Other branches (such as medical services) are a combination of public and private effort.

Next we will give a description of the service sector in Europe; we will focus in this chapter on the services that can in principle be traded by private agents, thus excluding the public sector from the discussion. Transport is also left out of the present chapter; because of its special position in the European setting it will be dealt with in a separate chapter.

Finally we will report the results of one case study of integration. The branch selected is insurance. A summary of the findings will complete the chapter.

EU regime

Legislation, adjudication and administration

The Treaty of Rome is fairly brief on services. It reflects awareness of the wide variety in products of the service branches. The general definition of services (Article 60) reads: 'all these activities normally provided for remuneration in so far as they are not governed by the provisions relating to freedom of movement for goods, capital and persons'. They include in particular activities of an industrial or commercial nature and those of craftsmen and professions. For all these activities the treaty stipulates the freedom:

- to provide services (Article 59a): a company of member country A can provide services in member country B without having an office there;
- to set up an establishment (Article 52): companies (or persons) wishing to set up an establishment (that is, a legal entity with, in general, premises, staff and so on) in another member country are free to do so under the same conditions as are laid down for the nationals of the country of establishment.

The substantiation of the freedom to provide services has dragged on for a long time, for two main reasons. One was the difficulty in defining the equivalence of qualifications, another the access to certain markets that were organised by national governments or by private groups sanctioned to organise and protect them.

In the early 1970s several rulings of the Court in principle liberalised almost completely all services connected with agriculture, manufacturing, craft and trade (commerce). There remained, however, quite a few problems regarding the service branches, many of which persisted until 1985, when the programme to complete the internal market in services brought a solution by a combination of three elements (Chapter 7): (1) freedom for cross-border trade in services (liberalisation); (2) mutual recognition of the quality of the home country's control; and (3) minimum sets of European regulation (harmonisation).

Market and structural policy

Apart from its efforts to liberalise intra-Union trade in services, the EU does not pursue a market regulation policy for the service sector. The market for services is indeed 'organised' in much the same way as that for most manufacturing and energy activities (except steel and coal), for which EU institutions have neither responsibility nor power to intervene in prices and quantities. Service markets come under the general rules for competition (see Chapter 16), which are considered sufficient to have European markets function properly. Many service sectors are, however, heavily regulated at the national level, with government influencing important aspects such as access to markets (for example, insurance, medical services) and prices (insurance and so on). The policy pursued by the EC for these sectors in the framework of the programme for the completion of the internal market by 1992 is to let companies working under different sets of rules compete freely, thereby obliging governments to compete with each other in optimal rule setting (see Chapter 16).

Unlike agriculture, manufacturing and energy, the sectors discussed in the preceding chapters, the service sector is not subject to a European structural policy. There are no schemes to encourage innovation, support investments in infrastructure or production equipment, or improve human capital. This is in line with the situation we find back in the individual member countries; the private segment of the service sector is mostly left to fend for itself. There is one very important exception to this and that is telecommunication. The structural policy of the EU uses two instruments: (1) support for innovation via the large-scale technology programmes, and (2) support for infrastructure by the newly established possibility (TEU) for support of trans-European networks.

Neither was there until recently a European external policy to regulate service markets *vis-à-vis* third countries, in stark contrast to the very elaborate schemes operative on goods markets (Chapter 19). Under the impetus of technological change (data transmission) and under pressure from third countries, questions about external trade in services were placed on the agenda of the Uruguay round of GATT for worldwide negotiations[1] and this has finally resulted in an agreement to diminish the protection in trade in many service branches.

Sketch of the sector

Employment and value added by branch

Since the war, the service sector[2] has rapidly advanced to assume the leadership in the total economy of the EU. With increasing productivity and low income elasticities, the shares of the agricultural and manufacturing sectors stagnated first and then dropped, making room for the quickly expanding service sector. One reason why statistics show such a large expansion is that certain functions which had hitherto been carried out within other sectors (cleaning, auditing and so on) have become independent and are thus registered as such. This phenomenon results when technically progressive services break off from manufacturing for economies of scale or organisational advantages.

When the service sector becomes dominant in an economy and many service activities concern the handling of information rather than trade in goods, the terms 'post-industrial' or 'information society' are often used. The EU has entered that stage. Indeed the total service sector that accounted for little over a third of total employment just after the Second World War now accounts for more than two-thirds of employment (and also of GDP) (Tables 14.1 and 14.2). That spectacular growth has been accomplished by a few branches; while the relative position of the construction and transport branches stagnated (the latter will be treated separately in the next chapter), trade, financial services and business and community services were very dynamic. The very fast growth of community services is closely related to the build-up of the welfare state and the ensuing increased involvement of the public sector in society (Saunders and Klau, 1985; Rose *et al.*, 1985).

The breakdown of the service sector into branches reveals some interesting aspects (employment figures). The sector of commerce consists mostly of wholesale and retail trade (14 per cent), the rest being hotels and such. The financial, business service and insurance sector is dominated by banking and insurance (3 per cent), followed by business services (3 per cent) and miscellaneous personal services (1 per cent). The large branch of community services consists of public administration (9 per cent), education (8 per cent), medical (7 per cent) and other (2 per cent). For GDP, the branch composition of these service sectors is in broad lines comparable to that of employment (see Table 14.2).[3]

Table 14.1   **Percentage shares of service sectors in EU12 total employment, 1950–90**

Sector	1950	1960	1970	1980	1990
5 Construction	7	8	8	8	8
6 Commerce	13	14	15	17	19
7 Transport	6	6	6	6	6
8 Finance and business	3	4	5	6	8
9 Community and social	9	12	18	23	27
Total services	38	44	52	60	68

Sources: 1950–70: NEI, Fleur data base; 1970–90: OECD, *Labour Force Statistics*, various years.

Table 14.2   Percentage shares of service sectors in total value added, EU12, 1960–90

Sector	1960	1970	1980	1990
5 Construction	7	7	7	7
6 Trade, restaurants and hotels	13	14	15	16
7 Transport	7	7	6	6
8 Finance and business	5	6	7	9
9 Other	20	24	29	32
Total	52	58	64	70

Sources: OECD, Eurostat, *National Account Statistics*, various years; 1990 some estimates.

Within the service industry there are considerable differences in labour productivity. For repairing, distribution and hotels, for example, productivity levels are below average. In communication, banking and insurance, on the contrary, productivity is high.

Europeanisation or multinationalisation of firms

The list of the largest service firms in the EU (excluding public enterprises like electricity, telecommunications and public and private transport companies) is dominated by trade and finance. For each sub-sector of services, we have indicated in Table 14.3 the biggest firm (by employment), to give an indication of the intersectoral differences.[4]

Generally speaking, service firms have a considerably smaller average size than manufacturing firms. (The 10 largest European manu-

Table 14.3   Service firms, largest by sub-sector, 1990

Name	Country	Branch	Employment (000s)
Tengelmann	Germany	Trade (retail)	167
Crédit Agricole	France	Finance (banking)	74
KPMG	Netherlands	Professional (auditing)	68
Ladbroke	UK	Leisure	52
Bertelsmann	Germany	Media	44

Source: M.W. De Jong (1993b).

facturing firms have three times as many employees as the 10 largest European service firms). The size of firms in certain sub-branches such as professional services (marketing, legal and so on) and leisure are particularly low; concentration and multinationalisation have not yet advanced far in these branches.

Most firms have their home in one of the larger countries of North Western Europe; this is true for all branches. These countries have large internal markets that provided a good basis for early expansion at home and subsequent expansion abroad. Head offices of these firms are mostly in London, Paris and Frankfurt. The Southern European countries are very poorly represented.

Market structures[5]

The markets for services of the EU member countries have long remained sheltered from competition, owing to lack of mobility of services across markets and firms within markets. This situation is due to three factors:

- *Natural determinants of the degree of concentration.* Among these factors we find economies of scale and of scope. For a service like telecommunications, for instance, the cost of a network determines the very high concentration; in other services large numbers of sellers appear on more diversified markets, as with hotels.
- *Barriers to entry.* Many service industries typically incur fixed costs in two types of assets, tangible (such as buildings) and intangible (such as reputation). Sunk costs in the tangible category occur, for example, in telecommunications (networks). Sunk costs in the intangible category consist, for example, in maintaining a good reputation for financial services (banks, insurances).
- *Government regulations.* These are usually divided into two categories: (1) those that affect the structure of the industry (for example, the entry of new firms), and (2) those that impinge upon the conduct of existing firms. Some branches have relatively little of both (construction, for instance), some have much of both (for example, insurance), some are subjected to structural instruments only (for example, distribution).

For a number of service branches we have indicated the scores on these three factors in Table 14.4 (first three columns). From this information we can assess the degree of competition in each branch (last two columns): first the situation that prevailed before the 1992 programme was implemented ('actual' column) and second the situa-

Table 14.4 Market structure in services

| Branch | Determinants | | | Degree of competition | |
	Concentration	Sunk cost	Regulation	Actual	Potential
Construction	low	low	medium	high	high
Distribution	low	low	medium	medium	high
Hotels	low	low	low	high	high
Telecom	high	high	high	low	medium
Banking/ insurance	medium	medium	high	low	medium
Business	low	medium	low	medium	medium

Source: CEC (1993a).

321

tion that is likely to prevail after the effects of the 1992 programme have become apparent ('potential' column).

Table 14.4 clearly indicates the changes that result from the implementation of the programme for the completion of the internal market; low competition becomes medium and medium competition becomes high. This process should lead to a better allocation, that is to the provision of the European consumer with service products that are better adapted to his needs at lower cost. This process is not likely to lead to big changes in the location of production, because of the high degree of proximity between consumers and producers that many services require. However ownership of firms could be absolutely transformed as local service providers become parts of multinational networks. This may be as subsidiaries or via cooperation agreements (licensing, franchising). The latter are often used by branches such as accountancy, consultancy and retailing.

Case study: insurance

National and EU regulation

Within the EU countries, the insurance industry has developed on a national basis, each national sub-market being regulated by a whole array of measures.[6] The only exception to this was the UK industry, which has always been of a highly international nature. The realisation of the common market for services was foreseen by the EEC Treaty by 1970, but this has proved impossible. The Commission has tried to bring about a common European market for insurance services,[7] but for a long time has found it very difficult, given the multitude of national regulations affecting the industry. In these efforts two distinctions were made from the start. One is between life and non-life. This principle of specialisation forbids life insurance companies to do other types of insurance, so as to protect the interests of life policy holders against considerable risks. The other is between freedom of establishment and freedom to provide services abroad.

Freedom of establishment (Articles 52–8) implies the possibility of creating a subsidiary in another member state; non-discrimination requires that such a subsidiary, a broker, or an agent be treated on a level with national companies. In the 1970s, several directives introduced this freedom of establishment (1973 for life, 1979 for non-life). The directives obliged every member state to subject all insurance business, of both local and foreign companies, on its territory to authorisation on the same conditions; as a result, all companies anywhere in the EU have come under supervision. The problem was, however, that this system tended to add to the cost for the insurer (for example, the French authorities, applying French standards, required minimum reserves that had to be franc-dominated and lodged in francs), which added to the costs of the foreign insurer. Subsequent directives have set minimum standards, to inspire mutual confidence in national regulations and to make sure that coverage would be similar (for example, in the motor insurance branch, so as to take away the need for border controls of insurance documents). In 1986, the European Court of Justice confirmed in a case of the Commission against four member states that national restrictions against foreign insurance companies were not acceptable; exceptions could be made, however, if the protection of the consumer so required.

Freedom to provide services (Articles 59–66) means that, for example, a French client can conclude an insurance contract directly with the London office of an English company and is not obliged to do so with a France-based firm. This situation used to be precluded by national regulations. In line with the general sense of Court ruling in other branches of activity, the Commission had proposed several schemes for liberalisation and harmonisation; however, up to the end of the 1980s they had all failed to gain sufficient approval from the Council to reach realisation. The reasons for this are that national regulations were well entrenched, and opposition to further harmonisation and liberalisation was quite fierce (Finsinger *et al.*, 1985). Liberalisation was only half-heartedly supported by insurance companies. Indeed the latter were often well settled behind protecting regulations even in foreign markets. In that situation the German broker Steicher went against the German regulations by arranging for insurance of his German clients directly with non-German insurers. The European Court of Justice, asked to consider the case, ruled in December 1986 in favour of Steicher, considering that corporate clients could very well be left free to choose between products of different companies at home or abroad. The far-reaching implications of that verdict were soon realised, which speeded up the discussions on the proposals for the common market for insurances in the framework of the 1992 programme. A number of directives have been agreed upon. Full freedom of insurance service provision both for the life and non-life markets will be realised as of 1 July 1994 (transition measures for Greece, Spain and Portugal).

The European legislation covers such matters as the formation of an insurance company, the opening of branches and agencies and the subsequent supervision of technical reserves, assets, solvency margins and minimum guarantee funds. Harmonisation of these aspects is important to prevent companies from being pushed by competition into contracts that do not cover the cost of the risks involved. The Commission is counting on a tendency towards spontaneous harmonisation of national regulatory systems as increased international competition of firms implicitly entails competition of the national regulations under which they operate.

The supervision of insurance companies is carried out by national authorities. The coordination of this supervision is an important aspect of European legislation because it is the basis for a double target: (1) to permit a company to do business in several EU countries under a single licence supervised by the authorities of the country where it has its (European) head offices (home country control principle); (2) to afford persons seeking insurance access to the widest possible range of insurance products on offer in the EU (CEC, 1992f; Carter and Dickinson, 1992; Pool, 1990).

Structure of the industry

The insurance business consists of two main branches, 'life' and 'non-life' (motor, fire and so on). The importance of both segments in the total market of the EU has varied over the past decades; now each accounts for about 50 per cent of total business. Insurance is a product for which demand is growing fast; as a result the share of premiums in total GNP increased from 3 per cent in 1960 to 6 per cent in 1990. There is little national variation in the 'non-life' market (gross premium of between 2 and 4 per cent of GDP). On the contrary, national differences in the 'life' market are fairly large (gross premium of between 1 and 6 per cent of GDP) owing to differences in preferences, social security and so on. In the countries with a low coverage, demand for life insurance has grown very fast in the past decades, with double-digit growth rates. Even in mature markets growth outpaced income growth.

Until recently integration had not developed far. The European insurance market used to be segmented into national markets. On each national market concentration tended to be fairly high as a consequence of economies of scale and scope. The largest group typically held a 15 to 25 per cent share in the national market. By the end of the 1980s, the share of national markets accounted for by foreign-controlled companies was very small; for all EC member states it was between 3 and 10 per cent. This small portion was disputed by a few large foreign companies from other EU countries and third countries (notably Switzerland, the USA and Japan) and a large number of medium-sized companies that have started internationalisation). Up to 1985 the lion's share of the insurance market occupied by foreign firms in all EU countries was held by UK firms, some of which got the larger portion of their premium income from foreign operations. In some countries (France, Ireland), a large portion of the business was covered by nationalised companies, but in most countries private firms dominated the market. In all countries, mutual-insurance companies also took a fair share of the market (CEC, 1985c).

The insurance business involves risks, and to spread these is important. Therefore companies will try to attain a certain size. They may also try to achieve economies of scale in marketing, and use their large size as a lever in bargaining with customers and suppliers.[8] In recent years the internationalisation of companies and markets has progressed. There are several reasons for this trend. First, international diversification tends to spread risks. For that reason many companies have started to merge internationally. Whereas in the 1960s the intention of many Western European companies was to acquire a foothold in the USA, they now look increasingly at European markets. As a result, many insurance companies have become multinational firms (MNF) with subsidiaries abroad. Second, such multinationalisation has been stimulated by the demand of MNF, clients of the industry for insurance services, wherever in the world their business is located.[9] Third, the completion of the internal market has entailed a process of restructuring of firms at the European level. Notably in the past few years a very high number of cross-border takeovers and mergers between European companies have been taking place. Only a few of these concerned operations between the large insurance groups. For example, Allianz purchased RAS, the second largest Italian group (and a number of smaller companies in other countries); Groupe Victoire (France) acquired Colonia (Germany) the second largest German firm; Groupe AG (Belgium) merged with AMEV (Netherlands). Recently UAP (France) acquired a major stake in Royal Belge (Belgium), GESA (Sweden) and Sun Life (UK). For the rest, the merger and acquisition operations concerned the takeover of smaller companies by a large foreign company.

This implies that national firms still dominate all home markets and foreign firms continue to compete for smaller segments of these markets. There are indications that the latter share has been increasing as a consequence of price competition and further takeovers. As a result, two changes have occurred. First, the average size of the largest firms has greatly increased, from 3 to 10 million ECU gross premium. Some European firms are now among the world leaders (Japanese and US firms head this list, Allianz rank fifth and UAP tenth). Second, the ranking of the largest EU insurance companies has been profoundly changed (see Table 14.5).

In the future it is likely that a further concentration and internationalisation of firms will occur, as there are still large rationalisation advantages that have not been realised. As a consequence the number of companies is likely to decrease, from the present 4,000 to some 1,500 in the next five years (Dickinson, 1993).[10]

Table 14.5 Largest[a] European insurance companies[b]

Rank	Company	Country	Gross premium (milliard ECU) 1985	1990	Employment (000s) 1990
1	Allianz	FRG	3.1	19	15
2	Union Assurances Paris	France	3.1	15	18
3	Prudential	UK	3.2	10	23
4	Generali	Italy	n.a.	10	n.a.
5	Nationale Nederlanden	NL	2.8	9	18
6	Victoire Colonia	France	n.a.	9	n.a.
7	Royal Insurance Corp.	UK	3.2	8	19
8	Axa	France	n.a.	7	n.a.
9	Ass. Générale France	France	2.0	7	15
10	Commercial Union	UK	3.3	6	20

[a] To choose a reliable measure of size is difficult; we have opted for gross premium. For reasons of comparability with other branches, employment figures are added.

[b] The list is exclusive of some very large reinsurance companies, such as Münchener Re (actually the world's largest specialist reinsurance company). Nor does it include Lloyds, the British firm that occupies a very special place in insurance brokerage. Apart from the companies listed, some Swiss companies are also very active on the EU market (for example, Zurich, Winterthur).

Source: *Europe's Largest Companies*, London, 1985; industry data.

Price differences

The segmentation of markets means that the law of one price does not hold; hence large price differences in insurance can be expected to occur among EU member countries. Such is indeed the case. To illustrate their magnitude, Table 14.6 presents the differences for a standard life (term) insurance policy (BEUC, 1988). They show that in Portugal consumers payed nine times as much for the same product as those in the cheapest country, the UK. Similar differences in prices were found for other categories of insurance (house, motor, fire and liability) (Price Waterhouse, 1988). Assuming that the average of the four countries with the lowest prices would be a fair indication of the average EU price after integration, there is considerable potential for price cuts. The average price cut for all fire insurance categories cited amounted to more than 50 per cent for Italy, 30 per cent for Belgium, Luxemburg and Spain, 25 for France and 10 for Germany.

The causes of the very high prices that obtained in certain countries before the effects of the single market programme began to be felt are generally thought to be lack of competition and inefficiencies due to state regulations. An analysis of the situation in each country

in the mid-1980s (Table 14.6) shows five categories: (1) highly diversified, (2) diversified, (3) competitive, (4) cartel and (5) state-fixed
tariff. The comparison of each country's scores in this categorisation
with the relative prices in Table 14.6 (see right-hand column) confirms that in general high prices did indeed go hand-in-hand with a
lack of competition (BEUC, 1988).

Table 14.6   **Annual premiums (best buy) of a term insurance in**
the EU countries (man of 30, smoker, 10 years' cover,
100,000 ECU) 1985

Country	Strength of Competition	Annual premium in ECU 0 100 200 300 400 500 600 700 800 900 1000
Germany	3	
France	2	
Italy	4	
Netherlands	3	
Belgium	4	
Luxemburg	3	
UK	4	
Denmark	4	
Ireland	1	
Spain	2	
Portugal	5	
Greece	4	

Source: BEUC, *Term Insurance in Europe*, report 51/88, Brussels, 1988.

Summary and conclusions

- The EU had always considered services an essential part of the
  integration process, but paid little attention to it in practice.
  The growing importance of the sector in intra- and extra-EU
  trade has changed that situation, and now policies are being
  worked out for the liberalisation of the internal service market
  as well as for external trade in services.
- Many service firms have up to now been sheltered from international competition by government regulations. For that reason, little multinationalisation of firms has occurred. The sector's low degree of integration is also apparent in the fairly
  high differences in prices among EU countries.
- The case study of insurance, a sector in which economies of

scale are important, shows that both the freedom to provide services in another country and freedom of establishment are now put into practice, leading to a growing interpenetration of markets and multinationalisation of firms.

Notes

1 Indeed the growing importance of services in the economy did not immediately bring about a greater interest among international organisations. For a long time, services were considered an essentially domestic sector hardly in need of international attention. Since the 1970s, however, the awareness has grown that such lack of interest has bred many protectionist measures impeding the internationalisation of service activities (Griffiths, 1975, among others); organisations like GATT now carry the subject on their negotiating agenda. As services are increasingly important to developing countries, UNCTAD (1983) has taken up the issue as well. The OECD has also joined in, focusing on sector-specific studies of trade impediments in services. All these organisations are trying to improve the poor data situation on international trade in services, as an essential first step towards a basis for policy making.

2 Unlike the situation with other sectors of activity, a definition of the service sector is difficult to give. Services are often described as a 'rest sector' encompassing the activities other than primary and secondary. Another approach focuses on the intangible nature of the output, and thus excludes, among other things, construction. Attempts have been made to overcome the problems of definition by adding such criteria as perishability and simultaneity of production and consumption, but, from the literature on the subject, such new criteria have all failed to make a distinction between goods and services, so that the line of severance between the two remains arbitrary. Statistical measurement is poor and hence also the possibility of quantitative analysis of the sector. Within the service sector, sub-sectors of activity are usually distinguished. They include such traditional ones as wholesale and retail trade, but also modern ones, like data services. A wide definition of the sector includes such government services as public administration and defence.

3 Comparisons between the industry figures on GDP and employment need to be made with caution, as the differences between the two tables may be due not only to productivity divergences but also to differences in sector delineation.

4 The service sector is a very mixed bag, and because firms from different service branches are difficult to compare (turnover for commerce, gross premium for insurance, assets for banks and so on) we have opted for employment figures as the best indicator of size.

5 This section is largely taken from CEC (1993).

6 The regulations have been made in the first instance to protect the consumer and to call for a certain prudence in the management of the resources that have been entrusted to the company. Many governments have extended that concern for the consumer into the definition of the product (prescribing certain standard clauses). Many have gone farther and have prescribed prices. It goes as without saying that these measures are easily used for protection against outside competitors. A classification of such protectionist measures can be made, along several lines. OECD (1983a) makes a distinction between establishment and transactions, on the one hand, and between types of different

measure (tax, solvency ratio, public sector and so on), on the other. See also Ingo (1985), Carter and Dickinson (1992).

7 For a more elaborate description of the EU's involvement, see CEC (1985c, Chapter 2); for national systems of some member countries, see Finsinger and Pauly (1986); for the programme see Pool (1990) and for the recent situation CEC (1992f).

8 For an evaluation of economies of scale in the UK insurance industry, see Tapp (1986, p. 56), who finds considerable economies at the lower end of the scale, a very long, practically flat area in the central part, and diseconomies at the upper end.

9 One feature of the non-life insurance market has been the increased centralisation of insurance buying of multinational companies, looking for worldwide coverage of their operations and wanting to establish a contract with one insurance company.

10 A final point to be made is that in recent years banks and insurance companies have increasingly joined forces in companies that go for 'total finance'; the major motor here is economies of scope. This has been made possible by the new 'deregulated' environment.

15 Transport

Introduction

Economic integration implies that each member state specialises in the production of those goods for which it is best equipped in terms of economic, geographic or other conditions. Specialisation within a customs union implies the spatial separation of supply and demand, and hence increased international goods transport. The creation of the common market and the ensuing freedom to provide services, integration of capital markets and free movement of persons (labour), and the progress towards an economic and monetary union with harmonised policies, lead to more and more contacts between workers from different member states, and hence to increased international passenger transport, too. How profitable integration will be depends also on the cost of transport. In that respect, transport costs are not different from customs tariffs or other obstacles to the complete free trade of goods and movement of persons (Zippel, 1985). Logically, therefore, the transport sector should not be overlooked as integration proceeds.

In the following sections of this chapter, the development of the transport sector in the course of the European integration process will be analysed in much the same way as the other economic sectors in previous chapters. The next section will describe the policy regime that the EU has created for the transport sector. Many member states have over a long period pursued very interventionist policies, based partly on the consideration that the transport sector was too vital for the economy to be left to the market forces and partly on the specific characteristics of each mode (regulation of monopolies for railroads, regulation of markets for atomistic supply in road haulage).

Next some significant aspects of the development of the sector such as production capacity, employment and firm size, will be discussed. Finally we will study in separate sections how the integration of two important branches, goods transport (notably by road) and passenger transport (notably by air), has proceeded, specifying the interpenetration of markets, the response of the major companies and so on. A summary of the major findings will complete the chapter.

EU regime

Treaties

The three treaties give different stipulations for transport. The ECSC Treaty is concerned only with preventing the distortion of fair competition by differential tariffs. The transporting of coal and steel is costly, and therefore it was of paramount importance not to have the free market (unhampered by customs tariffs) eroded by differences in transport costs. So rates or other transport conditions that are discriminating by nationality or origin/destination were prohibited (Article 70). For the rest, transport policy was explicitly reserved to the member states. The EAEC Treaty is not very important in transport matters. The EEC Treaty, on the contrary, provides (in its Article 3) for a common transport policy. The principles of such a policy are given in a separate title (IV, Articles 74–84, a privilege shared only with agriculture). The modes of transport are treated differently. Remarkably the transport title as such applies only to the so-called 'inland traffic', namely 'transport by rail, road and inland waterway'. With respect to navigation[1] and aviation, the treaty stipulates merely that 'appropriate provisions may be laid down' (Article 84).

Common rules for international inland transport must be laid down, as well as the conditions under which transport entrepreneurs are admitted to national transport in a member state in which they are not resident (Article 75). This shows that the right of establishment, contrary to the right to provide services, is directly applicable to transport. The rules and conditions referred to must be laid down in the transition period by qualified majority of votes. Unanimity is required in one case, however: the one regarding 'principles of the regulatory system for transport that would be liable to have a serious effect on the standard of living and on employment in certain areas and on the operation of transport facilities' (read: railways). On the other hand, the necessity is recognised to adjust to the economic developments resulting from the creation of the common market. Until common rules were issued (according to Article 75), no member state might take measures that are more damaging to transport companies in other member states than in their own (Article 76).

Markets (that is, prices and conditions) of inland transport are regulated by the treaty in three areas:

- Setting prices (rates). Account should be taken of the economic circumstances of carriers (Article 78) (income policy argument: compare Agriculture).
- Prohibition of discrimination. Applied to transport (Article 79), this principle puts a stop to the practice of cheap tariffs for exports and high ones for imports.[2]
- Equal competition conditions. Member states are forbidden (unless authorised by the Commission) (Article 80) to impose on transport within the Community prices and conditions holding any element of support or protection of manufacturing industry or sectors.

On closer study, the Transport Title of the Treaty of Rome appears to be beset with conflicting principles and vague stipulations as to the way a common transport policy should be achieved. They spring from considerable differences among member states in economic and geographical conditions and in conceptions of transport policy (Button, 1984; Erdmenger, 1981). Some countries (especially Germany and France) saw transport as a public service or as an integral part of the social structure, affecting the distribution of population and shaping the community's social life. They had regulated their transport sector in a very detailed way and considered that government intervention in both markets and structure was the only way to realise the social objectives of their transport policy. Others (The Netherlands and the UK) took a largely commercial view of transport; they considered that the application of market–economic principles was in the best interest of customers (shippers) and society.

Reaching out for a common policy

In the early 1960s, the Commission was striving to establish a common transport market for all inland transport modes, guided by the principles of market economics and inspired by the liberal attitude displayed in the Treaty of Rome with respect to the goods trade (1962 *Memorandum of the Commission*, and 1962 *Action Programme*). It was hoped that a common transport policy, replacing the various national policies, would guarantee fair competition among and within branches of transport, as well as create conditions of equal competition for other sectors in the economy, such as agriculture, manufacturing industry and commerce. In that vein, the *Memorandum* proposed three objectives:

- Removal of obstacles created by transport and impeding the common market for goods and persons. The implementation of

this first objective implied, among other things, the abolition of tariff discrimination for reasons of nationality.
- Integration of the transport market (that is, the intra-EU liberalisation of transport services). In addition, the *Memorandum* proposed quite detailed regulations with respect to market control, namely for tariffs, market access and so on, applicable to both national and international transport (comparable to the market regulations in agriculture).
- Establishment of a European transport system. Obviously that would mean considerable harmonisation. This concerned, first, adjusting the infrastructure to the demands of increased international exchange (frontier-crossing motorways and so on) and also the technical (axle load, carriage length, containers), fiscal (motor-vehicle tax, petrol duty), social (driving hours) and economic (professional requirements) stipulations which would have to be harmonised.

In practice these objectives and principles proved so difficult to realise that the detailed common policy advanced at a snail's pace, and the integrated market for transport services hardly at all (see, for instance, CEC, 1973a). For many years, harmonisation was the first concern, on the consideration that no fair competition would be possible or liberalisation admissible without it. In the second half of the 1970s, the progress of the common transport policy was slowed down even more by the economic recession, the increased concern for the environment, the higher energy costs and the extension of the EU.

Liberalisation by the Court of Justice

Confronted with stagnation, the Commission then proposed new schemes, limiting its own involvement to laying down general principles and emphasising the harmonisation of national measures. The idea of working out a complete European transport system, following the pattern of agriculture, was abandoned. However the new proposals, like the earlier ones, came to nothing because of the Council's indecisiveness. In that situation, in 1982, the European Parliament, always an active promotor of a European transport policy, judged that the Council of Ministers be summoned before the Court of Justice. That this unique procedure was resorted to characterises the regrettable situation that had evolved: 25 years after the founding of the EU, and more than 15 years after the end of the transition period, there was still no EU transport policy worked out.

From the Court's verdict in the 'failure to act' case (13/83, ex Article 175) which Parliament, with the Commission's and the Dutch government's support, had instituted against the Council, we note that the Council:

- is committed to regulate within a reasonable period the liberalisation of frontier-crossing transport within the EU (including transit);
- shall establish the conditions under which entrepreneurs from one member state are permitted to take part in transport in another member state (cabotage);
- may, but is not obliged to, take complementary measures (in practice social, technical, environmental and other harmonisation measures).

The Court thus confirmed the application to the transport sector of the principle of freedom to provide services, but recognised also the special quality of the Treaty's stipulations with respect to transport, and finally established that freedom of transport is not enjoined in the same direct terms as free service traffic in general (Simons, 1986).

The Court left the question of timing open by using the term 'within a reasonable period'. The Commission and the Council have specified the horizon, much in line with the other aspects of the internal market (Chapter 16), as the year 1992.

Market order

In the past, all national governments in Europe became deeply involved in the regulation of transport markets. This has been defended on the grounds of the special characteristics of transport in general and of certain transport modes in particular.

With respect to transport in general, one argument is that, since transportation services cannot be stocked up, capacity tends to be geared to peak demand. Because a large proportion of the costs are fixed, inelastic supply in periods of low demand, combined with a low price-elasticity of demand, could lead to very keen price competition. Governments felt duty bound to prevent such a situation (which is by no means typical of transport alone). Another argument is that transport requires expensive, long-lasting infrastructure for which the government is mostly responsible. Because the construction costs of this infrastructure and their recovery differ widely among transport modes (compare the railways with inland shipping and road traffic), measures are needed to restore a balanced competition. Finally, over the decades, the objectives of transport policy have increasingly become merged with other societal objectives such as cheap transport to backward regions, for certain social groups, and so on and many sectors of transport have so-called 'public service obligations'.

National governments have regulated the markets for the different modes in a variety of ways (see following sections).[3] The EU's efforts towards liberalisation have had only a limited impact. Even at the end of 1992 a large number of situations subsisted where prices, access to the trade and so on were subjected to national restrictions.

All these market-control schemes pushed up the costs for the users of transport services. Companies operating in protected markets were not motivated to increase their productivity, while others were not given scope to develop new initiatives. Such inefficient functioning kept the prices of transport unduly high. If the objectives of the treaty are to be realised after all, national government interventions must be partly harmonised and partly abolished. The experience in countries which have decided to deregulate their transport markets is that service improves and prices drop, without the market being disturbed (Auctores Varii, 1983). In Europe the navigation on the Rhine is the classical example. Economically, therefore, liberalisation of the European transport market is the most desirable solution and one in line with the EU regime for the rest of the economic sectors.

Despite the specific features of transport, the general rules of the treaty with respect to competition conditions apply to all transport modes. This concerns, first and foremost, the right of free establishment; second, the general prohibition of competition-distorting state aids (Articles 92–4); third, the agreements impeding intra-community trade (Article 85); and finally the abuse of a dominant position (Article 86). However, as with other branches, special rules have been laid down for the putting into practice of these general rules in the fields of transport by rail, road, inland shipping, air and seaborne shipping.

For all transport sectors, the EU has established systems of market observation for easy insight into the volume, structure and development of supply and demand; the systems are helpful to market parties in reaching adequate decisions. They vary somewhat as to type of information, frequency, and so on. The co-ordination of the different modes has always been an important object of transport policy. The recovery of infrastructure costs, moreover, poses a difficult economic problem, for different recovery schemes can distort competition between transport modes as well as disturb international trade. Two conditions must be satisfied for the adequate recovery of costs: (1) correct computation of total costs, and (2) correct attribution to users. Levies would have to satisfy two requirements: (1) reflect marginal social costs, and (2) meet the demand of overall budget equality. The computation problem was solved in 1970, when the Council introduced a common system to establish the costs of road, railroad and waterway infrastructure. The attribution problem has not been solved yet. On the basis of the many studies made (see, among others, Allais *et al.*, 1965; Malcor, 1970; Oort, 1975), the Commission has submitted to the Council various proposals for directives; these have not yet been translated into action, however. Coordination of modes implies not only the prices but also the quantity aspect. That means that goods traffic must be able to combine modes, for example rail/truck or truck/barge. The liberalisation of this type of traffic increased greatly in 1990 and new proposals have been worked out.

The outward screening of the EU internal transport market is based to a very limited extent on common European rules; much is still dependent on bilateral deals of member states with third countries.[4] This is the case, for example, for road transport: the bilateral deals concluded by individual member states with third countries make it practically impossible for third country hauliers to offer their services on the EU market. The problem does not occur with rail transport, because any international transport by rail requires the cooperation of nationalised companies with monopoly power. In inland shipping, the Mannheim Act applies only to riverain states of the Rhine, which means in practice that third countries (apart from Switzerland) are banned from services on the Rhine.[5] In civil aviation, national authorities regulate access to their territory for EU and third country companies alike: a common external civil aviation policy has not yet got off the ground. The Commission considers the setting up of a common external policy in transport matters as a cornerstone of its policy. However the progress on this score is limited.

Structural policy

European structural policy in matters of transport has not advanced very far. The policy is concerned with both transport infrastructure (generally in the public domain) and production means (in principle in private hands, in practice also to a large extent in public hands).

The first proposals made by the Commission for intensive coordination of national investments in infrastructure were refused by the Council as an unpermissible intervention of the EU in national autonomy; it accepted only a consultation procedure (Gwilliam *et al.*, 1973). To that end an Infrastructure Committee has been set up (CEC, 1979b). Since the early 1980s the Commission has sought the competence to give financial support to projects of which the execution is an urgent EU interest (see CEC, 1982d, 1982e),[6] because they remove bottlenecks in the networks for international transportation of goods by road, railroad and inland waterways and of information (telecommunication). Examples of such large-scale projects with evident European dimensions are the Channel Tunnel and the very fast trains (TGV) network. Neither the planning nor the financing of such projects were direct tasks for the Commission. However, as far as the latter aspect is concerned, the Commission may, since 1990, contribute its support (Regulations 3359/90).[7] With the Maastricht Treaty the setting up of trans-European networks (Article 129b/d) in the areas of transport, telecommunication and energy has become a EU task. The aim is to promote the interconnection and interoperability of national networks as well as access to such networks.

Policy concerned with the improvement of the production means varies among transport modes. In railroad transport, rolling stock is subject to many national rules, but no relevant EU measures have been taken, nor are there any EU measures to improve the production structure of road transport. To improve access to the European market, certain technical prescriptions as to axle load, brakes, permissible weight and so on have been issued, but even on those points progress has been slow; there are still many impediments to a common structural transport policy. The Commission has taken some perfunctory steps towards a structural policy for inland shipping, more specifically with respect to the scrapping of obsolete ships. Regarding sea and air traffic, the structure-improving programmes that have been developed recently concern measures like the setting up of a European register of ships or the European organisation for air traffic control. Indeed a major problem for the operation of airlines in Europe is the way in which the airspace is managed. In the whole of Western Europe, 54 air traffic control centres are active, working with different computer systems and programming languages. This causes complicated, time-consuming and costly procedures that limit capacity and cause delay. European airlines are now pressing for the setting up of a 'single sky'. (Compare the USA, which, over a much larger area, has 20 centres with one system!)

So in general there is no common policy for improving the production structure in transport comparable to the programmes for the agricultural and industrial sectors.

Sketch of the sector

Importance of the sector

The transport sector is of strategic importance to the EU economy, though relatively modest in terms of wealth creation and employment, accounting throughout the 1950–90 period for a very stable 4 or 5 per cent of GDP and employment (see Table 15.1).

The branches of the sector have developed differently; road transport, now accounting for almost half of employment, has taken the place that rail transport occupied in the 1950s (now some 25 per

Table 15.1 Percentage share of transport sector[a] in total GDP and employment, EU12, 1950–90

	1950	1960	1970	1980	1990
GDP	n.a.	7	7	6	6
Employment	6	6	6	6	6

[a] Including telecommunication, accounting for some 1.5 per cent of GDP and employment.
Sources: Employment: NEI FLEUR data base; OECD, *Labour-Force Statistics*, various years.
GDP: OECD, *National Account Statistics*, various years

cent). The relative importance of water and air transport is less, but the latter is growing very fast.

Production means

The developments of production means reflect the structural changes in European transport. Table 15.2 neatly illustrates the fast rise of road and the decline of railroad transport. The length of the railroad network dropped by 30 per cent and the number of waggons by 60 per cent between 1950 and 1990. On the contrary, the number of lorries increased almost fivefold in the same period. The fast growth of air traffic is also evident, as is the contraction of the European maritime fleets.

The relation between the data for units and for capacity (or production) reveals how much the scale of transport has grown. Such developments can be observed in haulage, rail transport and in river and maritime merchant shipping.

Case study 1: goods transport, haulage

Total volume of inland goods transport

One may expect that, under conditions of integration, transport would develop faster than total economic activity, as goods trade increases faster than production. Figure 15.1 reveals how much total international transport within the EU has grown over a 20-year period. In the long term, total growth of intra-EU inland transport seems to follow that of GDP fairly closely. In making this comparison one should, however, take account of the fast growth of services, activities that do not require much transport. Indeed, compared to industrial production, international transport did grow faster; transport grew by about 3 per cent in the 1970–90 period, against industrial

Table 15.2   **Characteristics of the transport system, EU12, 1950–90**

	1950	1960	1970	1980	1990
Road					
Motorways (000 km)	2	4	13	26	32
Cars owned (millions)	6	20	58	96	129
Cars per thousand population	22	72	194	300	390
Commercial vehicles (millions)	3	5	8	11	15
Railway					
Coaches (thousands)	113	102	79	76	63
Passengers (millions p/km)	n.a.	n.a.	n.a.	208	230
Goods wagons (100 000s)	15	13	11	9	6
Goods (millions t/km)	n.a.	n.a.	n.a.	175	184
Track total (000 km)	163	148	136	129	109
Multitrack, electrified (000 km)	10	18	27	34	38
Inland waterways[a]					
Self-propelled craft (thousands)	n.a.	29	24	18	15
Cap. (million tonnes)	n.a.	12	11	10	10
Dumb and pushed barges (thousands)	n.a.	10	5	3	3
Cap. (million tonnes)	n.a.	5	4	3	3
Sea					
Total fleet (thousands)	n.a.	n.a.	17	18	13
Cap. (million BRT)	n.a.	n.a.	73	121	60
Air[b]					
Aircraft movements (millions)	n.a.	n.a.	n.a.	4	7
Passengers (millions)	n.a.	n.a.	n.a.	277	449
Pipe[c]					
Length in service (000 km)	n.a.	6	11	17	18

[a]   Data indicated for 1960 apply to 1965.
[b]   Within EU and EU with third countries.
[c]   Without Denmark, Ireland, Portugal.
n.a.   No comparable data available.
Sources: UN/ECE, *Annual Bulletin of Transport Statistics for Europe*; Eurostat, *Transport Annual Statistics 1979–1990*, some estimates based on various Eurostat statistics.

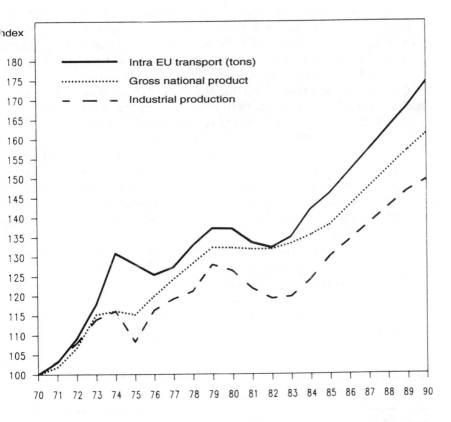

Figure 15.1   Frontier-crossing inland goods transport among EU9 member states,* on the basis of tonnage, 1970–90

* UK, Ireland and Greece excluded.

Sources: *Europe Transport*; Eurostat, *National Accounts*; *Statistical Bulletin, Industrial Production.*

production with an average growth of 2 per cent. Intra-EU international transport has grown (in tons) faster than extra-EU international transport, which confirms the data derived from international trade statistics (Chapter 6).

Road v. other modes of inland goods transport

The relative importance of the various transport modes for goods transport in Europe has undergone important changes over the past 20 years (Table 15.3). The major shift from railroad to road haulage is evident. Before 1960, haulage played only a modest part in goods transport among member states, amounting to less than a fifth of railroad transport (Blonk, 1968). Now, some 35 years later, the roles are reversed: international haulage accounts for several times the tonnage of railroad transport. Internationally (intra-EU) the tonnage carried by road almost equals that of inland shipping. Hauliers account for the greater part of transport growth among member states. In the late 1980s the growth rate of tonnage transported by haulage was 8 per cent, by inland shipping 2 per cent and by railways 1 per cent a year. In ton/km the differences are even more marked; the average distance travelled by trucks rose by 8 per cent a year, for barges it remained unchanged, while it grew only by 1 per cent for railways. These figures reflect the relative retreat of bulk products compared to finished and intermediate goods. Thus road transport has become the most important inland transport sector in the EU. This is even more pronounced if we look at domestic transport; here haulage takes some 90 per cent of all tonnage transported (Eurostat, *Transport Statistics*).

Empirical studies (Voigt, Zachcial and Rath, 1986) suggest that all regulation with regard to prices and quantities affects modal split only marginally, hence liberalisation (deregulation) was the obvious policy choice.

Table 15.3   Inland goods transport (in ton/km) by mode of transport (in percentages), EU12, 1970–90

Mode of transport	1970	1980	1990
Road	50	60	74
Railroad	28	21	13
Inland waterway	14	11	8
Pipeline	8	8	5
Total	100	100	100

Source: 1970–80: CEMT (1985); 1990: Eurostat, various documents.

What has determined this shift in the modal split of goods transport? The significance of the various factors such as price, speed and reliability varies with the nature of the product to be carried. For a low-value bulk good the price comes first, while for high-value finished products speed and reliability prevail. Rail and water transport are eminently suitable for the transporting of homogeneous goods, in large quantities, over long distances, especially if no connecting transport is needed (for example, ores, fuel and metals). Lorries cannot compete with the low costs of that type of transport. Intermediary products and finished manufactures are generally carried in smaller quantities and to more dispersed destinations; here the lorry is most suitable. The latter type of product has an increasing share in the total, owing to the structural changes in the economy. Hence the rise in the share of road haulage.

National and EU regulation

Governments intervene in the haulage industry mostly with the setting of qualitative standards. These are, firstly, derived from social and safety considerations (driving hours, technical check-ups and so on); secondly, from the wish to curb the competitiveness of road haulage with respect to railways; and thirdly, out of concern for the environment and the wish to save energy. Governments intervene also by setting minimum prices and by regulating supply. National road transport used to be reserved for national companies susceptible to national market controls (licensing and permit systems, tariff setting, access restrictions based, for example, on expertise, finance and so on). In some countries, internal long-distance carriage was subject to licensing systems. Neither cabotage nor carrying for third countries was permitted.

The *liberalisation* of the road haulage market in Europe started with international transport. To that end the national regulations on trip permits (quotas) were replaced by a combined EU and bilateral system of trip authorisation with national quotas. That system could never respond adequately to the needs of a market. Many vehicles were forced to return empty.[8] So further liberalisation was undertaken. The number of EU authorisations has been gradually stepped up to become large enough for the transition to a fully free common market for road transport. However that point had not yet been reached by the end of 1992.

Integration has also been realised by *harmonisation*. Regulations have been introduced for the operating conditions of international road transport in the following fields:

- fiscal: exemption from customs duties for 200 litres of fuel in the tanks;
- social rules: mainly concerned with hours of driving and resting and the use of the tachograph;
- admission to the profession: certificates and so on for firms, and a European driving licence;
- safety: periodic inspection of vehicles, speed limits;
- environment: energy consumption, congestion, dangerous materials.

Company response to change

International road haulage is dominated by 'hire and reward' operators; own-account operators take only some 10 per cent of the market. In the domestic markets of a number of EU countries the share of the latter is higher (30 per cent). The supply structure of the industry is dominated by small firms: 80 per cent of the firms have less than 5 vehicles, 10 per cent have 5 to 10 vehicles and another 10 per cent more than 10 vehicles. The average size does, however, grow over time and with it the degree of concentration. A relatively high share of the EU market for road transport is held by companies in the Benelux; this can be explained by the large transport flows that originate in the major North Sea ports.

The deregulation that the EU is carrying through in the framework of the creation of the single market has had a number of effects (Sleuwaegen, 1993). Prices have decreased under the influence of greater efficiency. The modal split has been further changed in favour of the road and away from the railroad. In the future one may expect a company restructuring, with a shake-out of inefficient firms and larger concentration. There will be a drive towards greater efficiency and to reap economies of size (scale, scope, network) made possible by the larger market. Differentiation will be accentuated. One way in which this will manifest itself is in the split between companies that handle only full truck-loads (FTL) and companies that handle less than full truck-loads (LFTL):

- *Full truck-load* firms will tend to specialise (for example, in oil products, containers or flowers). There are some economies of scale to be reaped in the buying and maintenance of trucks; however most will come from the European network with clients and other suppliers. The objective of some firms is to deliver a complete logistic service instead of only transport. For the former task, size is needed, hence many mergers are now being recorded. The latter task can be left to smaller companies (jobbers).
- *Less than full truck-load* companies need to invest heavily in information systems and in additional services, hence a strong concentration is occurring in this segment.

Case study 2: passenger transport by air

Air transport compared to other modes

Passenger transport is an important economic phenomenon. In 1960, the average EU inhabitant spent 8 per cent of his total net income on mobility (purchase and use of car, moped, bicycle and so on, plus train, tram, bus and air tickets). By 1990 the percentage had risen to approximately 14. The choice of mode on international journeys depends largely on distance. The reason for travelling is also relevant (holiday, business, short stay). Passenger transport has grown considerably since the war, as has already been shown by the structural data of Table 15.2. The tremendous growth of passenger traffic is explained by demographic growth, increasing incomes and leisure time, fast-decreasing cost due to increases in productivity (notably air), better services (as to time, destination, luxury and so on) and in particular by the integration of the goods and service markets of the member states. Business traffic has quickly extended as a result of increased commercial contacts. Moreover the greater openness of the market has enhanced tourism. The explosively growing demand could be satisfied thanks to the overall adequate extension of the infrastructure (airports, motorways and so on).

International passenger travel *by land* has grown much faster than national passenger travel. Between 1955 and 1970, the number of international trips by car grew by a factor of eight, while the number of cars rose by slightly less than a factor of three. The growth figures for bus travel are comparable. International passenger traffic by train increased over the 1960–90 period, albeit modestly in comparison with the other traffic modes. The development of international very high speed rail links is likely to change that.

The growth of *air traffic* was spectacular over the 1960–90 period: the total number of passenger kilometres produced by the major European airlines increased twelve-fold. At the end of the 1950s air traffic was still in its growth stage, so that very high growth rates were natural; between 1960 and 1970 the volume increased threefold; international traffic grew faster than domestic flights. Since 1973, the traffic volume in terms of passenger kilometres has slowed down, to some 5 to 7 per cent a year, indicating that the sector is entering the stage of maturity. The growth in the volume produced can be broken down into three elements: more movements; more passengers per aircraft; more kilometres per trip. In the 1970s and 1980s the trip length increased by 1 per cent. The other 4 per cent growth was distributed differently in the two sub-periods. In the 1970s larger aircraft accounted for 3 per cent of increase, extra movement for 1 per cent. In the 1980s the size of aircraft remained stable and the remaining growth was fully realised by more movement (4 per cent).

National and EU regulation

A strictly state-controlled national aviation policy aimed at protecting the national flag-carrier rather than providing optimum service to clients. Governments have a firm grip on the air traffic market, not only through these national air transport companies, but also through airspace control, landing rights and so on. Internationally there is a veritable tangle of multilateral accords (Convention of Chicago) and bilateral agreements governing landing rights, capacity, frequency, routes, tariffs and market sharing (Naveau, 1983). As a result of the protection and the segmentation of markets within the EC, high prices prevailed on all connections.[9]

In the framework of the total programme for the completion of the internal market, the liberalisation of the air traffic market has been undertaken. Progress has been made, first, by gradually liberalising interregional transport (Directive 83/416); next by loosening the market sharing agreements and by restricting intervention in prices, and finally, by improving market access; which means that EU companies are entitled to fly any route within the EU. However fuel-free cabotage will only gradually be realised.

Little integration owing to national regulation

Notwithstanding this very fast growth, the supply structure has changed very little over the past 30 years (see Table 15.4). This could only occur in a situation where the major suppliers were heavily protected against competition. The following three indicators clearly show the extent of segmentation of markets due to considerable protection:

- *The low overall concentration of supply of European air transport.* In 1990, calculated on total world operations, the C_1 index (share of largest company in total operations) = 25 per cent; C_3 (share of nos 1, 2 and 3 companies) = 55 per cent; C_6 = 82 per cent.
- *The stability in participation of companies.* In the 1970–90 period the list showed neither new entrants nor departures, nor were there any mergers between companies on the list (between 1960 and 1970 only two mergers were recorded). Between 1985 and 1990 one merger was made: between British Airways and British Caledonian. Another national merger was concluded recently (since 1990, so not yet shown in Table 15.4) when Air France took over UTA, thereby ensuring its second place in the

rankings. International mergers have up to now failed to be realised (BA/KLM) or are in an embryonic stage (Air France/Sabena; KLM/Swissair/SAS).

• *The stability of the ranking of the major companies.* Indeed from Table 15.4 it can be derived that between 1970 and 1990 two companies did not change places at all; seven changed only one place (of which three returned in 1990 to their 1970 position), while three changed two or three places.

Apart from the companies in the list, there are many more; companies that provide jet services number over 100. Many of the larger charter companies are actually bigger than the smaller flag-carriers in terms of the total number of passenger/kilometres produced. However the overall picture is difficult to get hold of, as many flag-carriers have taken (sometimes majority) stakes in such charter companies.

The EU carriers are not very big by world standards; if companies are compared on the basis of total passengers carried (both domestic

Table 15.4   Total passenger kilometres (1,000 million) on scheduled services (international and domestic) of major international European airlines, 1960–90

Rank	Company	Country	1960	1970	1980	1990
1	British Airways	UK	5.9[a]	15.6	40.1	66.3[b]
2	Air France	France	4.0	10.2	25.4	36.7
3	Lufthansa	FRG	1.3	8.3	21.1	41.9
4	KLM	Netherlands	2.7	5.7	14.1	26.4
5	Alitalia	Italy	1.3	7.8	12.9	22.8
6	Iberia	Spain	0.7	5.5	13.8	22.1
7	SAS	Scandinavia	2.2	5.4	11.0	16.6
8	Olympic	Greece	0.3	2.1	5.1	7.8
9	Sabena	Belgium	1.3	2.4	4.9	7.6
10	TAP	Portugal	0.2	2.3	3.4	6.8
11	UTA	France	0.8[c]	2.0	4.7	6.1
12	Aer Lingus	Ireland	0.4	1.8	2.0	4.2
13	British Caledonian	UK	0.1[d]	0.6	4.0	—
	Total	EU	21.2	69.7	162.5	265.3

[a]   BEA + BOAC.
[b]   Incl. British Caledonian.
[c]   TAI + UAT.
[d]   BUA.
Source: *World Air Transport Statistics*, several years.

and international) many American and Asian airlines take precedence over even the larger European flag carriers.

Company response to change

The recent shift in the EU attitude towards markets has increased competition in passenger transport. Internally this competition comes from other EU suppliers struggling for strategically advantageous positions, but also from high-speed trains. Externally the pressure comes from carriers from third countries that want to integrate their EU operations in a worldwide view. This is bringing about great changes for the companies listed in Table 15.4 that are all of the 'trunk' type, providing full scheduled service at a relatively high price. It also affects two other types of players (not in the table): 'charter'-type companies, that provide low-cost service, and 'commuter' carriers, that operate services between regional airports and between regional and major airports. The reactions of the three groups to further liberalisation, and the effects on the industrial landscape in passenger air transport in Europe, could be as follows (Gialloreto, 1988).

- *Trunk* carriers will have to cut costs and raise productivity to prevent charter and foreign trunk companies from encroaching on their markets. The result may be a more differentiated service level. Of the larger trunk companies, only the better managed will keep their leading positions, while others stand to lose considerable market shares. The smaller ones, to survive in this segment of the air passenger market, will have to align with, or let themselves be absorbed by, larger ones or become regional specialisers. International mergers are needed that, up to now, have been extremely difficult in this industry. As a matter of fact it is not sure whether industrial restructuring will be done on a European basis. As the world market is now a more important determining factor in company strategy (competition on world routes is fierce), worldwide cooperation between carriers is likely to evolve rapidly (after the pattern of world-encompassing companies in manufacturing industry).
- *Charter* companies are likely to meet competition from trunk companies. Some of them may try to enter the trunk market, but, as that has proved a fairly difficult strategy in countries that have already got used to liberal air transport regimes, the effect will be limited.
- *Commuter* companies will increasingly be seen by the large trunk carriers as feeder services to major routes; many independent companies that might have developed into challeng

ers of the majors are likely to be absorbed by, or aligned with, major trunk carriers. As competition intensifies, some new entrants are likely to emerge. However, as the threshold is quite high in civil aviation, the chances of a major upheaval from that type of competition are slight. A set of policies are necessary to make sure that such company responses to deregulation lead to more efficiency and benefits for the consumer (McGowan and Seabright, 1989).

Summary and conclusions

- The European transport market has for a long time been very heavily regulated on a national basis and therefore much fragmented. Rulings of the Court have obliged the Council to work out a common transport policy along the same liberal lines that obtain for the rest of the economy. Liberalisation has been pursued in the framework of the completion of the internal market.
- Goods transport by road has increased much faster than industrial growth. However this growth has not yet gone hand-in-hand with international integration of road haulage firms. Although up to now very few multinational firms have been created, the emergence of a number of large European logistic firms is expected.
- Passenger transport by air has increased very rapidly, but the company structure has until recently remained practically unaltered, evidencing the lack of competition and international integration. In the coming years, liberalisation and worldwide competition are likely to lead to Europe-wide and worldwide mergers and linkages of European companies.

Notes

1 Maritime transport is of critical importance for the EU as well, as a very large share of external goods trade is made by ship. Moreover maritime shipping regulation became particularly important when, with the joining of three new member states (two of them islands!) in 1972, some maritime shipping turned into intra-community transport. The Court has confirmed that sea navigation comes under the general rules of the Treaty. Market control in maritime shipping mostly takes the form of so-called 'shipping-line conferences': associations of shipowners active in the same sailing area, which, in economic terms, are cartels. In the framework of UNCTAD negotiations, the EU was forced not only to accept the existence of such conferences, but also to concede a certain division of the market between developed and developing countries. Admittedly provisos have been made to the effect that the division of cargoes will not be

applied to intra-Community sea traffic and that all EU shipowners will have equal access to EU cargoes to third countries (Hart *et al.*, 1992).

2   Such tariffs were indeed practised by some countries. Just before the Coal and Steel Community was founded, coal produced in Germany was transported at tariffs up to a quarter below those for imported coal. An example of a low tariff for exports is that for French sodium salts, which paid up to two-fifths less for transport than salt destined for the domestic market.

3   The regimes for road and air transport are discussed in the next sections; some major features of the other modes of inland transport are as follows:

Rail. Railways' heavy investment in infrastructure has led to state-owned mo-nopoly enterprises, to a firm hold of governments on the tariff structure, and to railroad companies' obligation to provide transport. The EU has pursued two objectives: (1) a normal price setting in commercial supply and demand situa-tions, and (2) the abolition of subsidies. The harmonisation decision of 1965 commits member states either to reimburse the costs of charges and transport obligations foreign to the trade, or to abolish the obligations. Now governments have to conclude 'public service contracts' with the railway companies. Railway companies are now obliged to be financially independent, and are encouraged to concentrate on the exploitation of the railways (leaving infrastructure to the public sector) and to regroup themselves internationally.

Inland shipping was practically free when the EU was created, thanks largely to the Mannheim Convention, which guarantees free traffic on the Rhine. The economic recession of 1973 inspired associations of shipowners to try and en-force, through a blockade, a rotation scheme for the proportional allocation of freight on the so-called 'north–south' route (Holland, Belgium, France). The system already existed in France and has been introduced in Belgium and the Netherlands. The EU is opposed to such a development, which is at cross-purposes with the Treaty. So far action taken in the framework of the 1992 programme has not resulted in a free market access.

4   Some of the external aspects of the transport market are regulated by interna-tional organisations. Merchant shipping in particular has had the attention of such UN affiliates as ECE, UNCTAD and the International Maritime Organisa-tion, and air transport from the International Air Transport Association. Euro-pean agencies concerned with transport problems are the European Conference of Transport Ministers, the OECD Transport Committee, the European Commit-tee for Civil Aviation and the Central Rhine Shipping Committee.

5   This is still the case; after the opening of the Rhine–Main–Donau canal, ships from Central and Eastern Europe have access, in technical terms, to Western European waters but have as yet no access to Western European markets.

6   Significantly proposals have been made to third countries (Switzerland, Austria and the former Yugoslavia) for the financing of infrastructure (particularly roads and tunnels in their territory as far as is essential to intra-European traffic).

7   This support to infrastructure is based on considerations of transport policy; transport infrastructure in backward regions is supported on regional–economic considerations by the European Regional Development Fund (Chapter 18).

8   In the early 1980s, an estimated 40 per cent of international road haulage had no return cargo at all. Companies often tried to solve the capacity problem by taking care of their own transport, thus avoiding the capacity rules. Around 1980, more than 60 per cent of total haulage capacity in Western Germany, France and Belgium, and about 50 per cent in the Netherlands was thus organ-ised (source: *Eurostat Transport Statistics*, 1981). The percentages apply to total domestic and international transport; for frontier-crossing transport they are considerably lower: an average 20 to 25 per cent for the EU9 in total (*Europa*

Transport). In fact own-account transport is generally even more expensive than professional haulage, because the vehicles are less fully utilised.

9   For a price comparison of Europe and the USA, see, among others, CEC (1979c); more recently Gialloreto (1988) calculated that airline operating costs in Europe were 50 per cent above those in the USA.

PART V
CONDITIONS FOR
BALANCED GROWTH

16 Allocation, Internal Market Policies

Introduction

The main objective of the European Union is to enhance the allocational efficiency of the economies of the member states by removing barriers to the movement of goods, services and production factors. Moreover policies have been agreed upon to make the European market, once created, function properly. In the following sections we will describe in some detail a number of these policies.

Before we go into the specific policy areas, we will first specify some of the basic principles about government intervention in European markets. Next we will describe the EU regime in matters of allocation policies. This has to be consistent with the regimes of member countries. Now national governments have quite different opinions about the best way to devise allocation policies; some have interventionist inclinations, while others favour a laisser-faire approach. The EU has made its own fundamental choices, and has executed major programmes to transform them into practical policy measures. Paramount among these is the 1992 programme on the completion of the internal market.

Competition is the first specific policy area to which we will give attention. The obligation to deal with competition was already enjoined upon the EU by the Treaties of Paris and Rome to prevent private economic actors and national public authorities from cutting up the large European market, thus jeopardising or even cancelling the benefits of integration. Indirect influencing of markets through taxation is the subject of the following section. This applies both to goods and services markets (value added and excise taxes) and production factors (corporate and income taxes). The other side of the coin of indirect influences is subsidies. As these apply rather to production than to products, they are dealt with under competition policy. Regulating market access by defining technical norms and standards for the quality of products is the third major policy instrument by which governments have tried to protect their markets. The policy measures needed to remove such obstacles will be reviewed in a closing policy section.

All these barriers take a heavy toll in welfare from the EU, and their removal has positive welfare effects. Some estimates of these effects will be presented, before a final section in which we present some conclusions and a summary.

Foundations

Theory of market intervention (prices and quantities)

In some cases, market forces are not allowed free play, and governments intervene in product markets either by directly prescribing prices and quantities or by influencing them indirectly. Direct price and/or quantity controls are practised for several reasons.

- Acute scarcity may drive up the prices of products providing for basic needs, which for social reasons must be kept low. Basic economics teaches that, to prevent excess demand in such cases, the quantities need to be controlled as well. Such direct intervention was very common during and just after the Second World War (for example, for food and housing) but has now become the exception rather than the rule.
- Natural monopolies (in electricity distribution, for instance) are inclined to charge too high prices and restrict production. Such potential abuse of market power calls for regulation to keep prices at the level that would prevail under competitive conditions.
- Unstable markets (like the one for agricultural products) may call for intervention; to stabilise prices for producers, governments make use of such instruments as guaranteed prices or selling and purchasing from public stocks.
- Social considerations may lead to the setting of minimum wage levels, compulsory social security contributions and rules about equal pay for men and women in labour markets.
- External effects of the consumption of goods (health and environment, for instance) and the existence of public goods lead in some cases to the fixing of prices (for medical and pharmaceutical products and transport, among others).

The intervention in or regulation of markets has many negative side-effects, and most economists would agree that it should be the exception rather than the rule (see, among others, Breyer, 1984). Moreover the instruments of regulation should be carefully chosen with a view to the objective one wants to attain.

Nowadays intervention rather relies on such indirect instruments as taxes and subsidies. Governments will impose indirect taxes such as excise duties to discourage the consumption of goods with negative external effects (for instance, tobacco and liquor, on account of their harmful effect on health) while subsidising goods with positive externalities (for instance, sport facilities, cultural events and the like). Taxes and subsidies change the (relative) prices of goods.

Differences in national practices of direct intervention distort trade between partners. If prices and quantities are fixed, evidently governments will want to control imports and exports as well. For such elaborate structural intervention schemes as those in operation for agriculture, organisation at the Union level may be inevitable to prevent national compartmentalisation of markets. Indeed different prices can continue to exist side by side only by dint of compensatory import and export duties equivalent to tariffs, or by such quantitative restrictions as import and export controls, both of which are incompatible with the free internal trade that should characterise the Customs Union.

Theory of structural policies

Governments intervene to smooth the continuous restructuring that marks modern economies (Jacquemin and De Jong, 1977), implying the balanced phasing out of old industries and support for the creation of new activities. There are essentially two strands of theoretical foundation for the pursuit of an industrial policy (see, for instance, Odagiri, 1986; Urban, 1983).

The *market-failure theory* states that the perfect-competition model leading to a stable equilibrium does not apply in practice. The reasons are monopolistic behaviour, the existence of public goods, economies of scale, external effects, the cost of gathering information and making adjustments, rigidities, entry barriers and so on (Wolf, 1987). To correct such imperfections and to secure an optimum situation, the government needs to intervene in the market. A classical case in point is the infant industry argument: a firm should be protected (by subsidies, for instance) from its foreign competitors at the first stage of its development, because only in that way can it grow enough to profit from economies of scale and become competitive. The costs of protection in the first period are compensated by the benefits of production reaped at a later stage (creation of private and tax revenue).

The *growth-cycle theory* takes a more dynamic view of the economy. It finds the reason for government intervention in the incapacity of the economic system to pass smoothly and efficiently through the adaptation stages imposed on it by constant structural changes. At the first stage of new products, public intervention may be beneficial because the market is not well informed, the risks are considered too high for the participants, or the socio-economic cost/benefit ratio is greater than one while the private one is not, or not sufficiently (externalities). At the second stage of growing products, disturbances may arise from uncoordinated private decision making (overcapacities); the cost of adjusting capacities to demand levels may be minimised by government intervention. Finally, at the recession stage, the public authorities can steer the sector through the rough waters of capacity reduction.

The quality of the arguments for intervention in the two strands of thought has been severely criticised. One criticism is that the cost of intervention is often overlooked, another that public authorities are generally no better equipped to evaluate future developments than are private decision makers. Many observers (for example, Lindbeck, 1981; Eliasson, 1984) consider the economic record of industrial policy so negative as to make it an empty box.

Structural policies can use various instruments. Aid (subsidy) to investment and aid to innovation (subsidies to R&D) are the most common; other instruments are the reservation of public procurement to certain firms and restructuring allowances to firms in sectors faced with structural overcapacity. The theory of intervention for structural purposes has been developed in particular for the manufacturing sector, but applies also, *mutatis mutandis*, to other sectors (agriculture and services) and factor markets (think, for instance, of programmes for the (re)training of workers who will be needed in certain new industries, or the retraining of workers made redundant in old industries).

Such measures affect the allocative efficiency of the Union economy. Indeed structural subsidies to domestic industry can be recalculated in money values per unit of product, with an effect on importers similar to that of tariffs. For that reason, a common stance towards measures of structural policy aid is an obvious necessity in a customs and in an economic union. Common rules for state aids are the obvious first step; at later stages, common programmes for structural change may become a more efficient solution.

EU regime

The basic principle: a liberalised market

EU member countries have very different traditions of state intervention in markets, be it control of prices and quantities, state responsibility for production and regulation of quality, or vigilance with respect to competition rules. Some countries – France for one – have a more interventionist tradition; others, like Germany, are more of the liberalist type (at least for markets of manufactured goods). However no EU country defends a straightforward laisser-faire regime, nor has any country adopted a system of rigorous central planning.

When the EU was created, to steer some middle course between the two extreme views was the only logical thing to expect. The blend of interventionist and liberalist measures in European policy making varies for different sectors of activity, as the previous chapters have shown. Indeed the ECSC Treaty gave the EU institutions quite considerable powers to intervene in coal and steel markets; the High Authority (now Commission) can influence prices and quantities in the event of a so-called 'manifest crisis', and has the power to control investments and mergers. The EEC Treaty, on the contrary, trusted mainly to market forces for the allocation function; the Commission has no powers for intervention in markets, with two noticeable exceptions: agriculture and transport. The common policy that was elaborated on the basis of the specific treaty principles for the former sector relies very heavily on both quantity and price controls. In the area of transport, many direct influences on price and quantities (quotas) persist, although the EU role is less developed on that score. Together with the coal and steel sector, that leaves three interventionist islands in the predominantly liberalist sea.

Within the general European rules set for the allocation process, national governments are free to prefer a more interventionist or a more liberal approach. There is room for a competition of rules which is supposed to sort out the policy environment that is most conducive to growth.

The practice: persistent segmentation instead of one common market

The underlying principle of the order of the European Union is that decisions as to production, consumption investment, saving and so on have to be left to economic agents and that the public authorities do not intervene in the markets. However, on quite a few points, neither the national governments nor the EU follow that principle, but intervene directly in prices and/or quantities on the markets of goods, services and production factors.

National governments had three major reasons[1] for such intervention:

- The need to comply with technical standards and norms adopted by some countries for environmental reasons or to protect con-

sumers or workers. Related to this are the controls of movements of plants and animals to check whether they come up to
national health standards. In the past the EU has tried to overcome such technical differences by harmonising the national
regulations; that is, by making them so much alike that they no
longer present obstacles to trade. To that end, the Commission
has proposed strings of draft regulations and directives. However very few of them have actually reached the stage of adoption by the Council.

- Different levels of indirect taxation. Goods need to be checked
  to establish the amount of VAT or excise duties to be levied in
  the country of destination.
- Public security measures, giving rise to personal checks at the
  internal borders (illegal immigrants, criminals, terrorists).

The unwillingness of national politicians to give up their elbow
room for electionalist policies, and of national civil servants to adopt
anything else than their own set of rules prevented the actions of the
EU to take these barriers away having effect.[2] As a consequence,
barriers persisted and the liberalisation envisaged by the Treaty of
Rome had not led to the complete abolition of internal borders.

The European Union itself has also contributed to the segmentation of the European Market in national markets:

- The Monetary Compensatory Amounts (see Chapter 11) of the
  Common Agricultural Policy have effectively let the unity of
  the market disintegrate;
- Multi-Fibre Agreement: the insufficiency of the Common External Policy has led to an elaborate system of national quotas
  for so-called 'sensitive' products.

Objective: a single market by 1992

The unity of the market is a basic principle of the EU, whatever the
attitude chosen *vis-à-vis* a particular sector of activity. So much is
clear from many Articles in the Treaty, for instance the ones ordering
the abolition of all customs duties and measures with equivalent
effect by 1970. The obligations with respect to capital went less far,
but the Treaty is again most clear on liberalising the migration of
workers. In defiance of the general principles, many impediments to
the free movement of goods, services, capital and labour persisted
up to the mid-1980s, some of which imply controls at internal borders.

Concern about the negative effect of these barriers to European
growth increased, notably among industrialists who had to stand up

to international competition on world markets. To arouse public interest, Philips' president, Dekker, in 1984 launched his Plan for Europe 1990. Following this impetus the Commission (CEC, 1985d) came up with a white paper containing the bold proposal for a consistent and comprehensive attack on the barriers by doing away with all controls on goods services, capital and persons at the internal borders of the EU by the end of 1992.

The Commission identified all remaining barriers and specified a whole list of measures that had to be taken to realise the 1992 objective. The white paper groups the proposed policy measures under three headings, physical, technical and fiscal barriers.[3] This programme has been endorsed by the Council and was made into a treaty obligation by the adoption of the Single European Act (CEC, 1987a): 'The Community shall adopt measures with the aim of progressively establishing the internal market over a period expiring 31 December 1992. ... The internal market shall comprise an area without internal frontiers in which the free movement of goods, persons, services and capital is ensured in accordance with the provisions of this Treaty' (Article 13 SEA).

The new approach differs from earlier attempts at coping with internal barriers by three distinctive characteristics:

- Complete comprehensiveness: it covers all measures needed to do away with internal frontiers, irrespective of sector of activity, the field of policy and the likely effect on individual member states or groups of society. The rationale for this approach is that the continued presence of any one reason to maintain frontier controls could be enough to keep them intact, thus jeopardising the whole idea and the advantages envisaged.
- A clear timetable: the target set was the end of 1992. This recalls the approach of the Treaty of Rome to the abolition of all tariffs and quotas on internal trade by the end of the transition period.
- A simplified decision-making process: the new rule requires only a qualified majority for decisions on most measures needed to accomplish the internal market, instead of unanimity.

Competition

Some theory

In western industrialised countries, most decisions are left to private economic actors. Market forces (including competition) are allowed to play their role and the price mechanism is largely relied upon to bring about an efficient allocation of resources. However private actors may collude to avoid competition. Indeed Adam Smith wrote, more than 200 years ago, in his famous book, *Wealth of Nations*: 'People of the same trade seldom meet together, even for merriment and diversion, but the conversation ends in a conspiracy against the public or in some contrivance to raise forces.' In these cases, he argues, prosperity is less than with free competition; monopoly spells loss of welfare to consumers. To prevent it, public authorities must take upon themselves to intervene by competition laws and policy (Demsetz, 1982).

The principal theoretical reason for governments to pursue competition policies (see, among others, Shepherd, 1985) is indeed the need to avoid the misallocation resulting from:

- static inefficiency in resource allocation: a firm charging a price above the real (marginal) cost of production (because of monopolist power) keeps production and consumption below the optimum level (with excess profits to the firm and losses to the consumer);
- reduced technical efficiency: firms producing at lowest cost under conditions of competition will begin to operate inefficiently (through overstaffing, higher wages, lack of response to new opportunities, poor management) in sheltered situations;
- dynamic inefficiency: this is an extension of technical inefficiency. To be dynamically efficient requires constant innovation in production and products.

In this way the removal of barriers to competition has similar effects as the removal of barriers to trade, discussed in Chapters 5 and 6.[4] In line with the literature cited there, that on competition indicates that the technical and dynamic efficiency effects are far more important than the static ones (Geroski and Jacquemin, 1985; Pelkmans, 1984).

There are also advocates of limitations to competition, for example, by cartels and monopolies. Cartels, for example, would permit enterprises to finance R&D, while competition would take away the margin that is necessary for making these investments in innovation. Another argument often heard is that one has to beat foreign competition, which can only be done in the long run if a sufficiently large margin is realised on home sales.

The balancing out of arguments pro and con has found its best expression in a school of thinking that advocates the 'workable competition' concept. In this view an authority should be charged with the maintenance of such a workable competition in the various markets. Until recently this task was executed by national authorities.

Their policies differed; some, like the Netherlands, are very lenient towards restrictions, others, like Germany, fairly strict.

In a common market, a set of independent national competition policies is unlikely to be sufficient for establishing a good competition regime in integration areas.[5] Indeed, if two firms in different member states agree to refrain from competing on each other's 'home' market, national competition policy probably cannot do anything against it, since firms do not come under the jurisdiction of states where they are not active; yet such agreements obviously impede the trade between member states. Some form of union competition policy is indeed needed to ensure the fair play of common-market forces.

Basic features of the European regime

The need for a Common European Competition Policy has been recognised right from the start; both the Treaty of Paris (ECSC) and that of Rome (EEC) contain a chapter on it. The powers in matters of competition given to the EU by the ECSC reach further than those bestowed on it by the EEC Treaty. For instance, under the former, companies wanting to merge need the advance approval of the Commission, a stipulation that is unknown in the latter. The European competition policy is complementary to national competition policies; the former regards competition from the angle of inter-state trade, the latter from whatever angle is specific to it. However, as in all other fields, the European competition law prevails in cases where there is a conflict between EU and national laws. (We will follow here the Treaty of Rome regime!)

The objective of the European competition policy is to protect the competitive process and prevent distortions. To that end, different instruments can be used; these are given in Figure 16.1.

We will highlight in the following sections four EU actions that aim to prevent, respectively:

- companies from re-establishing, by means of market-sharing agreements and export bans, less visible but equally effective barriers to trade to replace the customs frontiers that were abolished by the European Common Market for goods and services (Article 85);
- companies that have concentrated economic power from abusing their dominant position in the market and thereby damaging the interests of consumers, competitors or subsidiaries (Article 86);
- state aid from distorting competition by giving unfair advantages to certain firms and occasioning damage to firms in other member states (Articles 92–4);

Problem	Distortion of competition		
	General	Specific	
Action	Harmonisation (Article 95 ff, Article 100 ff)	Competition rules	
Concerning		Private firms or groups	Member states or public enterprises
Forms of distortion and instruments		Cartels (Article 85) Dominant positions (Article 86) Dumping (Article 91) Concentra-tions (Regulations 4064/69)	Anti-discrimination (Article 7) Equivalent measures (Articles 30–36) State monopolies (Article 37) Public enterprises (Article 90) State aids to firms (Articles 92–94)

Figure 16.1   Position and character of EU competition regime (adapted from De Jong, 1993).

- state procurement agencies from discriminating by nationality (Article 37).

Three institutions have in the course of the years developed the fundamental European competition rules: the Council by its legisla tion, the Commission by its administrative practice and the Court by its jurisprudence.

- The Council's role is limited to the issue of regulations and directives on the general application of the rules laid down in the Treaty.
- The Commission has been given the central role. It investigates violations of the rules on its own initiative or upon receiving complaints from member states, companies, private persons or institutions. When the Commission observes an infringement it may order it to be rectified. In many cases such actions end with the company or member state's voluntarily changing its conduct. In other cases, where the Commission finds a com plaint well founded and the company does not change its con duct, the Commission can order changes, and member states are obliged to help the Commission enforce such a ruling. All firms and public institutions are committed to allowing the

officials of the Commission to make any investigations it thinks necessary to gather evidence (CEC, 1985f). The Commission can impose fines, which may amount to tens of millions of ECU.

- The Court deals with appeals from the allegedly infringing company. Since its creation, the European Court has treated a large number of cases, and 'case law' has greatly helped to define competition law (Mathijsen, 1985) and to make clear the interpretation of the three fundamental rules quoted above.

The field of application of EU competition rules is very wide; they apply irrespective of:

- the company's location; so they cover also companies from third countries operating in the EU;[6]
- the legal or proprietary form; which means that government companies (with the exception of public utilities) are subject to EU competition rules too; to identify possible competition distortions, the financial structure of state-owned companies must be transparent;
- the sectors of private economic activity; notwithstanding the differences in market structure, all sectors are now subject to the EU competition policy.[7]

Cartels (company agreements)

The first basic rule for competition (Article 85.1) bans as 'incompatible with the Common Market all agreements between undertakings, decisions by associations of undertakings and concerted practices which may affect trade between Member States and which have as their object or effect the prevention, restriction or distortion of competition within the common market'. Moreover (Article 85.2) any agreement or decision prohibited by the treaty is automatically void.

Since 1962 (Regulation 17), all agreements likely to come under the ban must be notified in advance to the European Commission for examination. After examining the case, the Commission can:

- give a negative clearance, which means that the Commission considers that fair competition is not threatened by the agreement;
- exempt the agreement from the overall ban because its benefits are considered more important than the possible disadvantages of limited competition; such benefits may be the promotion of technical or economic progress and the improvement of production and distribution;

- declare the agreement illegal and order it to be terminated.

The following groups of activities are incompatible with the competition rules of Article 85 (CEC, 1985e):

- market-sharing agreements which create protected markets, dividing the EU into sub-markets that coincide with single member states;
- price-fixing agreements of groups of firms that control a large share of the European market;
- exclusive purchase or supply agreements involving arrangements to buy only from or sell only to specified manufacturers or buyers;
- exchange of company information on cost, production and sales;
- exclusive or selective distribution agreements (the Commission's opposition to any form of restriction of parallel imports has been demonstrated in a number of cases; selective distribution arrangements are sometimes permitted if they improve the quality of the service provided, but discrimination against retailers, especially for their pricing strategies, can be severely punished);
- concerted practices whereby, without a formal agreement, partners align their policies so as to result in practical cooperation.

Exemptions[8] can be given for:

- crises; in view of a reduction of structural overcapacity of a branch, agreements can be made on the phasing out of plants, but complementary agreements that are not strictly necessary for achieving this objective remain forbidden;
- research and development; cooperative research or agreements on specialisations may favour innovation and progress.

Dominant positions

The second basic competition rule (Article 86) reads: 'Any abuse by one or more undertakings of a dominant position within the common market or in a substantial part of it shall be prohibited as incompatible with the common market in so far as it may affect trade between Member States.' Forms of abuse of dominant position include unfair pricing, exclusion or limitation of supply, and discrimination among trade partners. An example of the abuse of a dominant position was given by Hoffman-Laroche, which dominates the world market of vitamins in bulk (market shares of over 80 per cent). The company had passed 'fidelity' contracts with its customers which would give it a permanent position of priority or even of exclusivity as supplier to these customers. The Commission fined Hoffman-Laroche, which thereupon appealed to the European Court. However the Court confirmed the essentials of the Commission's decision, making it clear that the dominant firm may not limit a customer's supply possibilities, nor bar the entry of new suppliers which could put a downward pressure on prices.

To prevent firms acquiring dominant positions, the Commission has intensified its monitoring of mergers.[9] Between 1972 and 1982 the general tendency towards further concentration stopped. Some increase in concentration could be discerned for some branches such as transport and electric engineering; for most other branches the concentration levels in the EU remained about stable. Merger activity during this period stayed at a fairly low level (Figure 16.2). However the perspective of the completion of the internal market has given a big impetus to merger activities. This has been accepted by the Commission because for many growth or high-tech industries (electronics, aerospace, precision engineering and so on) mergers offer real prospects of efficiency gains, and worldwide competition limits the dangers of disadvantages (CEC, 1989).

An analysis of the mergers among the thousand largest firms in the EU between 1973 and 1984 (De Jong, 1993) showed that the majority of mergers were of the horizontal type. The principal

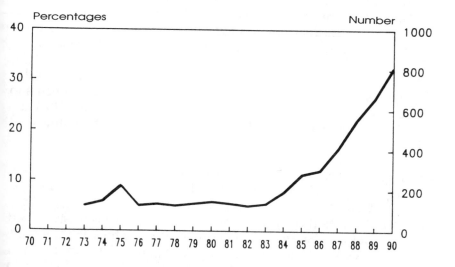

Figure 16.2   Mergers in the EU, 1973–90

Source: De Jong (1993).

motive for such mergers was 'critical mass': to increase efficiency, obtain a better competitive position and spread R&D cost over longer series. Most mergers involved two firms based in the same country and were oriented towards the national market. Increased European integration during this period did not lead to more cross-border European mergers (Lemaitre and Goybet, 1984) because of differences in management strategies, cultural traditions, government intervention and legal practices.

Since 1983 merger and takeover activity has increased very spectacularly. This was largely due to the completion of the internal market, which incited many firms to try to acquire quickly the critical size for effective cost cutting. The composition of mergers changed also. As to branches, mergers involved increasingly firms from service sectors (such as distribution, banking and insurance) that until then were in sheltered markets (NTB). As to nationality, the percentage of cross-border deals rose too. Recently the merger activity has decreased again. The internal market boom being over, it may stabilise at a lower level.

State aid

Aid is given to correct market failures and to attain social objectives by influencing private economic decision making. However it introduces in turn distortions and hence losses to welfare for the domestic and international economy (see CEC, 1991a). To avoid such distortions, the EU in principle forbids state aid. Indeed state aid to firms is incompatible with the Common Market in so far as it distorts trade among member states or damages competing firms (Articles 92–4) (CEC, 1982f).

There has been a continuous debate on the implementation of this rule, state aid being a major instrument for national governments to intervene in the economy. Consequently the Commission has defined the kinds of support that are permissible. As such qualifies aid that aims at:

- regional development; a maximum aid level has been established by the Commission for each problem area; the aid measures have to be public and transparent;
- industrial restructuring; special guidelines have been established for shipbuilding, steel, textiles and synthetic fibres; the Commission insists that such aid be exceptional, limited in duration, and geared directly to the objective of restoring long-term viability to firms or to reducing capacity in declining industries;
- research enabling companies to develop products and compete successfully on the world market;

- environmental improvement ensuring as much as possible the principle 'the polluter pays';
- conservation and development of new indigenous resources of energy.

To permit the Commission to implement this set of rules, plans for such aid must be submitted to the EU for prior approval. Under heavy political pressure, the Commission has been obliged in the past to let many trespassers go unpunished.

Public selling and procurement

Large quantities of products in the EU are sold, not to private firms and individual consumers, but to public procurement offices. The goods bought by the state in its role as a consumer or investor range from food for schoolchildren to nuclear submarines. The total value of public procurement (both government and public enterprise) is estimated (Atkins, 1987) at some 15 per cent of the European gross domestic product. Traditionally procurement is not open to competitive international bidding. Almost invariably, contracts are given to national industries; in 1985, public purchases from foreign suppliers were in the order of magnitude of only 2 per cent in the European countries (Atkins, 1987), much smaller than the import penetration of other sectors of the economy.

This applies in particular to capital equipment for defence, power generation, telecommunication and railways. Large parts of the 'Common Market' are thus screened off from the competitive regime installed by the EC, in spite of the general principles of free movement of goods (Article 30) and services (Article 59), which apply fully to public procurement organisations. Many different government objectives are pursued through public purchase contracts. This has given rise to widely differing national technical standards, unexploited economies of scale in R&D and production, subsidies, and lack of competitiveness on external markets.

In the past, the EU tried to eliminate the discrimination practised by government and semi-government bodies (CEC, 1982g, 1984b). Since 1978 the EU obliges all procurement agencies of central or federal governments (and of lower government layers also) to publish in the *Official Journal* all contracts above a certain minimum amount (Directive 77/62). The procedure must follow certain rules, for example about the criteria by which the contractor will be selected (CEC, 1982g). However analyses carried out by the Commission (for instance, CEC, 1984b) have revealed that these rules were inadequately applied. In 1988, the Council adopted a new directive concerning public works costing over five million ECU. They have to be made public through a new Europe-wide data bank: Tender: Electronic Daily. The directive gives new safeguards to subscriber: against discrimination. Directives for such large sectors as water energy, transport and telecommunications are still lacking.

A similar reasoning applies for the state as a producer (or seller) Obvious cases of infringement by state monopolies (for example, or tobacco) were dealt with in the 1970s (based on Article 37). Many difficulties still exist with the definition of aid to publicly owned enterprises in the form of a capital injection (or a subsidy).

Indirect influence on prices, taxes

Some theory

In the course of time every country has set up an elaborate system o taxation for generating government revenue, and for correcting un desirable effects of the working of markets. The structure, rates, ex emptions and so on of these systems reflect a large number of choice: about the functions of government in allocation, stabilisation and redistribution (Musgrave and Musgrave, 1989). Such systems affec the relative price of goods, labour, capital and so on. In open econo mies these effects are transmitted to partner countries. This limits ir practice the autonomy of nations in tax matters; actually, the mor the economies are integrated the more autonomy is lost.

What would be the best response by both national and EU authori ties to the new situation created by further integration? In line with the principle of subsidiarity, nations should be left with maximum sovereignty and flexibility in arranging their own tax systems. Tha has induced some to favour full competition of rules (no coordina tion, at best some consultation), others to favour harmonisation o even unification of tax rules (Cnossen, 1987). We will indicate the arguments in favour of and those against full competition.

Advantages   The first argument for competition is that it promote: the efficiency of the public sector. Countries will be forced to exam ine critically the quality of the public goods they provide and will try to provide the best service at the lowest cost to the taxpayer. The second argument is that it permits experimentation and quick adjust ment. Different authorities, responsible for the operations of differ ent systems, will react more quickly to new challenges of changes ir external circumstances than large systems and will more easily try out novel approaches that may turn out more effective. The fina argument is that it permits authorities to seek the lowest complianc cost by adapting the system to the exigencies and traditions of the local private sector (Cnossen, 1990).

Disadvantages The first argument is that it may yield a sub-optimal level of public goods because of lack of resources and the difficulty of matching taxes with the marginal benefits of public goods such as health (for example, Gordon, 1983; Zodrow, 1983). The second argument is that competition leads to solutions that frustrate equity. Inter-category equity is jeopardised because the high mobility of capital permits it to flee high tax countries; to avoid this, countries will decrease their tax burden. So competition will result in zero capital taxation in all countries. Consequently the full burden is put on the rather immobile factor, labour. Interjurisdictional equity is put in danger because residents from a low-tax low-public service country may use the public goods of a high-tax high-public service country.

The balancing out of advantages and disadvantages of competition leads to two guidelines for the coordination of taxes in an integration area: (1) only those taxes need be harmonised that cause a real distortion in the process of integration; (2) agreements on minimum levels of taxes should prevent the system evolving to sub-optimal low levels of taxation.

Which taxes should be subjected to harmonisation? The answer to this question differs with the stage of integration (Prest, 1983).

Trade (FTA and CU)   National systems with different levels and structures of indirect taxation (VAT and excise duties) will lead to different prices for consumers in different national markets. That situation may encourage sales of goods from low-tax countries to residents of high-tax countries, at the cost of a loss of government revenue in the latter. To prevent this, national indirect taxation systems are usually complemented by trade controls and border adjustments of taxes. Liberalising trade entails need for adjustment of indirect taxes.

Production factors (CM)   Differences in levels of national direct taxes, such as the corporation tax and the wage (income) tax (including social security), will lead to differences in net income position of the different actors on the capital and labour markets. To prevent both supply (savers and workers) and demand (investors and employers) moving to countries where the net situation is most favourable, border controls are used. Liberalising movements of production factors means that another way has to be found to prevent distortions in allocation. This is most relevant for capital, as it is highly mobile (OECD, 1991).

Policy (EMU)　In moving towards higher forms of integration, more and more taxes (like the income tax) become Union competences. However policy integration can proceed quite far without further harmonisation of taxes (Molle, 1992).

EU regime

The tax policy of the EU has followed the general principles indicated in the previous section. Indeed the EU tax policy has been designed and developed so as to serve the objectives of other policy fields, notably an efficient allocation (Neumark *et al.* 1963). 'It is not a problem of the structure of the tax systems, but a question of the effects and incidence of taxation operated in each country on the processes of integration and economic growth.' In the past, European tax harmonisation served above all to facilitate the functioning of the common market for products (goods and services) and production factors (labour and capital). In the future it will also serve to facilitate the functioning of the emerging economic and monetary union (Puchala, 1984). The EU tax policies have gradually developed with the EU entering higher stages of integration.

Incomplete customs union　In the early 1950s, the workings of the ECSC made it apparent that the differences between member states in sales (turnover) taxes could lead to quite important distortions of the competitive positions of coal and steel producers located in different countries. The report by a study group set up to suggest solutions (Tinbergen, 1953) has actually given the basic principles on which harmonisation of this tax has been based.

Customs union　The Treaty of the EEC, basing itself on the ECSC experience, recognises the necessity of the 'harmonisation of turnover taxes, excise duties and other forms of indirect taxation to the extent that such harmonisation is necessary to ensure the establishment and the functioning of the common market' (Article 99). It forbids the use of such taxes for discriminatory practices (such as high taxes on imported goods, low ones on home-produced goods) (Articles 95–8). Although the major decisions on indirect taxes were made quite quickly, further progress proved slow.

Common market　Even in the early 1960s it was recognised that unharmonised direct taxes could distort the free movement of capital and workers, thus jeopardising the effectiveness of the European Common Market (Article 220). The member states have negotiated the abolition of all double taxation of residents and firms. However, because until recently the EU had not advanced very far towards a fully free market for capital and labour, the problems of direct taxation were considered less urgent than those of indirect taxation, and have accordingly received far less attention.

Internal market   The white paper on the completion of the internal market identified differences in national fiscal regimes as one of the main barriers to free internal movement; it made framework proposals to see them removed (CEC, 1986g). Although much doubt was put on the likelihood of success (fiscal matters needed to be decided with unanimity) the major decisions as to the necessary harmonisation have now all been taken.

Economic and monetary union   The EU's march along the road to an economic and monetary union has not so far necessitated a further integration of the tax systems of the member countries (Brennan and Buchanan, 1980). The Council considers that in the near future the progress towards an EMU will not necessitate harmonisation of other taxes either (Molle, 1993).

Indirect taxes on goods and services: value added tax (VAT)

When the EU was created, member states were operating different systems of sales (turnover) tax. The Neumark report inventoried their advantages and disadvantages. The need for harmonisation of this tax (which accounts for some 25 per cent of total tax receipts in the EU) was quickly accepted by the member states. In the harmonisation process of this tax a series of directives have set up common principles, structures and modalities of application, leaving considerable variation as to rates and specific issues.

Value-added   The different systems of EU countries like the German turnover tax, the UK (wholesale) purchase tax or the French value added tax had certain common features. The French system of taxation at every level of the process, with the possibility of deducting the tax that had been paid already on inputs, had two distinct advantages. One is that it is neutral as to the degree of vertical integration of firms; the second is that it is a self-policing operation; the purchasing firm has an interest in having an invoice from its supplier certifying that the taxes on the inputs have been paid. This system was adopted in the 1970s as the basis for the whole harmonisation process of the VAT in the EU and has been refined since.

Destination   In 1967, the Council adopted the destination principle for taxation, which means that all goods, whether produced domestically or imported, are taxed identically in the country of consumption. Exports leave the country free of tax; the adjustment is made by customs at the border. The elimination of the border controls under the 1992 programme necessitated some changes. One proposal was to transform the system along the lines of any national sytem; exports would have been made at the exporters' tax rate, the VAT adjustment would have been shifted from the borders to the accounting books of taxable persons or firms and a clearing house would add up all the individual international adjustments and settle them with the national tax administration (Cnossen, 1987). This system, already operational for some time in the Benelux, has not been adopted by the EU however. Lack of confidence in the capacity of some member states to guarantee the operativeness of such a EC-wide system has pushed the member states into adopting a different system, that operates without a clearing house. Under that system the exporter sends the goods to another country in the 0 per cent tariff bracket. The importer has to pay the full national VAT to the destination country tax collector. Exporters are obliged to indicate the VAT identification number of the importer to the tax authorities so as to make international checking possible.

Rate categories   The differences between the EU member countries are given in Table 16.1. Most countries have a 'normal' or standard rate for most goods (and services) and a reduced rate for goods that are considered essentials, like food or clothing, or merit goods like cultural services. Some countries apply an increased rate to goods labelled as luxury goods (video-recorders, for instance). The purpose of this differentiation is to achieve some redistribution. Southern member states rely more on (differentiated) VAT, northern countries more on (progressive) income tax for redistribution. The EU has decided to do away with the increased rate and to define precisely which goods fall into each of the two other categories.

Rate levels   There are important differences between EU member states (Table 16.1). The EU has tried to arrive at a diminution of these differences. Initially governments were not very inclined to cooperate. High-rate countries feared that they would not be able to raise equivalent income from other sources if they lowered their VAT rates. Low-rate countries were loth to raise them as they were afraid of inflationary pressures. These attitudes changed with the imperative of the internal market. Indeed, in the years 1986–92, an important 'spontaneous' convergence occurred, as national governments made moves towards EU averages at moments convenient for national political purposes. In this way cuts were made by France and Belgium (abolition of increased rates) the Netherlands and Ireland (decrease of normal rates). On the other hand Germany (reunification)

Table 16.1 VAT (rates and receipts) as a percentage of total GDP and of total tax receipts in member countries of the EU, around 1990

Countries	Year of introduction	Rates (%)			Receipts (%)[a]	
		Standard (normal)	Reduced (essential)	Increased (luxury)	VAT/GDP	VAT/TAX
Germany	1968	14	7	—	6	16
France	1968	18.6	2/7	23	9	20
Italy	1973	19	4/9	38	6	15
Netherlands	1969	18.5	6	—	8	16
Belgium	1971	19	1/6	25/33	7	16
Luxemburg	1970	12	3/6	—	6	14
UK	1973	15	0	—	6	17
Denmark	1967	22	—	—	10	19
Ireland	1972	23	0/10	—	9	21
Spain	1986	12	6	33	6	17
Portugal	1986	17	0/8	30	7	20
Greece	1987	16	3/6	36	9	25
EU minimum	—	15	5	—	—	—

[a] Receipts figures 1988.
Sources: Rates: CEC, Revenue: OECD; rates are as of January 1990 and are tax-exclusive; that is to say, based on selling prices before tax.

and Spain (EMU criteria) have increased their rates. Full unification of the rates is not an objective; as a matter of fact the experience in countries like the USA shows that small differences between the member states do not lead to significant distortions (Pelkmans and Vanheukelen, 1988).[10] The option chosen by the EU is minimum rates (of 5 per cent and 15 per cent) with possible upward national variations (Directive 92/77). This is considered preferable in that it leaves member states free to operate their VAT systems in line with national social and economic policy objectives, albeit within the limits of international competition of systems.

Indirect taxes on goods: excises

Excise taxes are far less important than value added tax to tax revenues of member states. On the other hand, they apply to politically highly sensitive goods which, according to many, have serious negative external effects (alcohol and tobacco on health, petrol on the environment). Excises, like sales taxes, need to be harmonised (Article 99). The systems of excises of the 12 member states had many elements in common, but differed markedly as to the detailed operations (Table 16.2). Harmonisation measures of the EC have focused on two aspects:

- Adopting a common definition of the products that are subject to excises. The establishment of a European list of products subject to excise taxes has resulted in three categories: tobacco products, alcoholic beverages and petroleum products. Excises on other products (for instance on soft drinks in the Netherlands) have been abolished.
- Limiting the variance of the rates applied for each product. The convergence towards a European standard has been very slow for a long time. Recently the 1992 programme suggested a complete unification. However agreeing on a fixed amount in ECU for each product proved impossible to obtain, owing to political resistance on the part of several member countries. The Commission then put forward proposals for minimum rates, coupled for some products with a progressive convergence towards an EU standard.

The situation for each of the three main product categories is as follows. With alcoholic beverages, member states tended to tax imported products more heavily than domestically produced ones, for instance wine versus beer in the UK, whisky versus cognac in France. The Commission in its harmonisation efforts took the view that excise taxes for different products should be based on the rationale of

Table 16.2   Examples of excise taxes (ECU) and importance of excise tax revenue (ETR) in total GDP (percentage) in EU member countries, around 1990

Country	Cigarettes (per 100)	Beer (per litre)	Wine (per litre)	Pure alcohol (per litre)	Premium petrol (per litre)	ETR[a] / GDP
Germany	2.73	0.05	0.20	1.23	0.28	3
France	0.13	0.16	0.03	1.13	0.40	4
Italy	0.18	0.10	0.00	0.23	0.54	4
Netherlands	2.60	0.14	0.35	1.36	0.34	3
Belgium	0.25	0.06	0.34	1.32	0.29	3
Luxemburg	0.17	0.03	0.14	0.89	0.14	4
UK	4.28	0.36	1.37	2.20	0.24	5
Denmark	7.75	0.53	1.61	3.58	0.34	6
Ireland	4.89	0.63	2.58	2.51	0.37	8
Spain	0.07	0.02	0.00	0.38	0.32	4
Portugal	0.22	0.07	0.00	0.22	0.38	9
Greece	0.06	0.09	0.00	0.04	0.15	6
EU minimum	57%	0.19	0.00	0.55	0.29	—

[a]   around 1988.
Source: CEC, Excise tables.

the excise, which is to compensate for negative health effects. Hence the rate should be proportional to the alcohol content. The Court has in many cases ruled against discrimination, considering that all these products were in competition with one another and therefore must be taxed on an equal footing. The option finally chosen is minimum rates for beer and alcohol; for wine the position of the southern countries led to minimum rates of zero (Directives 92/83 and 92/84). For alcohol the minimum rate is to be stepped up gradually to 1.30 ECU; countries that practise a rate higher than this are not allowed to lower it.

For *tobacco* products some headway was made with harmonisation of the excises in the 1980s (Kay and Keene, 1987). The relation with VAT is close: the minimum excise is 57 per cent of the retail price (excluding VAT) of the most common brands (Directive 92/79). For other tobacco products a minimum excise per kilo has been agreed upon (Directive 92/80).

The harmonisation of taxes on *petroleum products* has proceeded very slowly. Member countries operate widely varying combinations of sales, cars, road and fuel taxes to raise money for the covering of the cost of traffic infrastructure and the removal of negative (environmental) effects. From Table 16.2, petrol excises appear to be fairly similar in the EU. For all products (unleaded, diesel and so on) minimum rates have now been set (Directives 92/31 and 92/32).[11]

Direct taxes, labour

The harmonisation of the taxes on the income of the production factor labour (wage tax for dependent workers, personal income taxes, encompassing also independent workers, and social security contributions) has not raised much interest in the EU up to now. This notwithstanding their quantitative importance (more than two-fifths of total tax receipts in the EU). For one thing, as we explained in Chapter 9, the free movement of labour has not created an interpenetration of the labour markets anything like that of the goods market. The completion of the internal market is not going to change this. Hence, tax differences on labour do not cause major distortions of international relations. Furthermore, as these taxes are not levied, controlled or balanced at the internal borders, the Commission does not consider their harmonisation a necessary condition for the completion of the internal market in general and the integration of labour markets in particular, and has not been intent on achieving this.

There is nevertheless reason for public concern as, for migrants and people who work in another country than their country of residence, differences in taxation and different rights to social security cause a lot of private anxiety. For social security contributions (as mentioned in Chapter 9) the EU adopted in 1971 rules (Regulation 1408/7) to avoid discrimination and loss of social security rights. For income tax, things are still at the study stage (McDaniel, 1985).

Direct taxes, capital

The EU member countries operate quite different systems of capital taxation. Paramount among these are the corporate taxes (see Table 16.3). Although they are not very important in quantitative terms (EU average about 1 per cent of total tax receipts) they may cause important distortions, as tax differences are an important determinant in the choice of the country of investment. Distortion may stem from tax incentives, double taxation (by the countries of origin and destination) of income from investment, differential treatment of residents and non-residents and of corporate investments (Segré report, CEC, 1966). For a good functioning of the European capital market, some harmonisation of national tax provisions is needed. In 1967 the Commission proposed its 'Programme on the harmonisation of direct taxes', a uniform corporation tax. These and similar proposals have been rejected by the Council. This resistance to change is not

Table 16.3 Corporate taxes in the EU (rates as of 1985)

Country	Statutory tax rate			Dividend withholding rate		Revenues as percentage of GDP	
	1977	1985	1991	1985	1991	1965	1983
A Imputation system							
Germany	56	63/47	50	5/25	15	2.5	1.9
France	50	50	34	0/25	15	1.8	1.9
Italy	25	41	36	0/30	15	1.9	3.8
Belgium	48	45	39	15	15	1.9	2.7
UK	52	52	35	0/15	15	2.2	4.1
Denmark	37	40	38	15	15	1.4	1.4
Ireland	45	50	10/43	0	—	2.4	1.5
B Other systems							
Netherlands	48	43	35	0/25	15	2.7	2.9
Luxemburg	40	47	37	0/15	15	3.4	7.4
Spain	36	35	35	10/18	15	1.4	1.3
Portugal	36	52/40	36	10/15	15	n.a.	n.a.
Greece	39	49	35	25/42	42	0.4	0.8
European Union	—	—	—			2.1	2.6

Source: Cnossen (1987), Gardner (1992).

379

surprising in view of the complexity of the systems and the fierce opposition of member states to inroads being made into their sovereignty.[12] So hardly any progress was made with harmonisation for a long time. The white paper (CEC, 1985d) has not brought much change; as the corporate tax is not controlled on the internal borders, the elimination of these barriers did not in itself call for further harmonisation.

Table 16.3 shows how widely corporate taxes differ across the EU as to system, rates, dividend withholding rates and so on. This entails important costs to the private sector that has to come to grips with the intricacies of 12 different systems (Devereux and Pearson, 1989). Recently the Commission asked the Ruding Committee (1992) to come up with a proposal for the EU policy on corporate taxes. The report gives ample evidence from the private sector of the important distortions that differences between national systems create. The Committee does not think that fiscal rivalry will remove these and has made a number of proposals for harmonisation:

- *Systems.* Only seven members use the imputation system, which gives shareholders credits for the corporation tax to be 'imputed' to the dividends due to them. Other countries, looking upon the corporation and its shareholders as completely different entities, tax twice (classical system). The Committee does not make a choice as to the best system for the EU but makes proposals for removing the distortions that occur in international transactions.[13]
- *Rates.* The statutory rate varied in 1985 from 35 in Spain to 52 in the UK. Since 1985 the tariffs have converged, while the average has decreased to 40 per cent. The Committee suggest a minimum tariff of 30 per cent.

The Commission has not made its proposals for directives yet and is likely to move slowly in view of the political sensitivity of the matter.

Access to markets, technical barriers

Some theory

Governments wish to limit market access for several reasons.

- Imperfect information makes it hard for consumers to judge the quality of goods and services, and may also spell material losses and risk to health and safety.
- Production and consumption may have external effects in the

shape of costs or benefits to third parties. Environmental damage is a case in point.

To cope with such aspects, governments use various instruments.

- For goods, governments mostly rely on the specification of technical standards and norms with which goods must comply (for instance, safety windshields in cars).
- For services, governments tend to set minimum requirements which key persons in a profession must satisfy (for instance, pharmacists and lawyers). Continuous control of a company's financial soundness is another instrument; such prudential control is applied to financial institutions such as banks, pension funds and insurance companies, to whom the public entrusts large sums of money, sometimes on long-term contracts.
- Governments may reserve certain activities to themselves or to (state) monopolies, thus blocking the entry of other suppliers. Many social services belong to this category, along with, for instance, defence industries.[14]

That a free market cannot be created by simply removing tariffs and quotas will now be clear. Indeed states can effectively use national standards like technical specifications to bar the importation of foreign goods, requirements for qualifications, diplomas and so on to curb the free movement of active persons and services, and prudential control of financial institutions to restrict the movement of capital. They have indeed done so in the past, with different countries having developed different requirements for quality and practices of testing the products' conformation to these requirements. Specified requirements and the ensuing technical trade barriers are often used to protect private interest groups rather than the general public. An example is the telecommunications industry, where the requirements public companies set for the equipment they purchase are such that only domestic firms are likely to comply with them.

Technical trade barriers exist when differing national regulations (specifications of shape, construction or performance laid down or referred to in public law) and/or standards (codifications of shape, quality and so on, voluntarily agreed to) prevent the free movement of goods, or when countries impose duplicative testing and certification procedures on imported goods.

The European Union regime

The European situation has for a long time compelled producers to adapt their products to a number of different sets of national norms and standards. This divides the market and thus costs welfare. For that reason the EU has tried several approaches to do away with the differences.

Law   Technical specifications that are set up as measures of quantitative restriction are prohibited (Article 30). In a number of famous cases, in which the objective of the national regulation was clearly to protect special interest groups in one country rather than the public interest, the European Court has followed that view. The trendsetter was the case of Cassis de Dijon (1979), an alcoholic product not conforming to German liquor standards in that it contained only 18 instead of the prescribed 25 per cent of alcohol. Very recent are the cases against the German *Rheinheitsgebot*, a prescription dating from the 16th century laying down that beer could only be made from certain ingredients, and against the Italian pasta regulation prescribing the use of duram wheat, a type produced only in a small region in Southern Italy. In these cases the Court ruled that a good lawfully produced and marketed in one member country should in principle gain free access to the markets of partner countries. However this does not imply fully free movement in practice, for in the Cassis de Dijon case the Court considered that, in the absence of common European rules, 'mandatory requirements' of public interest may justify national technical obstacles to free movement.

Harmonisation   The 'approximation of such provisions laid down by law, regulation or administrative action in member states as directly affect the functioning of the common market' (Article 100) is a second strategy. Since 1968, when the Commission proposed a general programme of harmonisation, experts of the Commission, national administrators and external institutions have exerted themselves to harmonise the technical standards for a large number of products,[15] with meagre results, however. The standards set cover only a small portion of the products for which some harmonisation is needed, small in particular for the efforts made. The approach has indeed turned out both ineffective and inefficient. Why is the record so poor? For one thing, unanimity in the Council proved difficult to obtain as the experts tended to aim at excessive uniformity and the specification of many technical details. Moreover the procedure was frustrated by the constant stream of new national regulations and the speed of technical progress, often overtaking the work before agreement had been reached. The ministers did nothing to speed·up the long and cumbersome procedure, probably because it was too technical to awaken sufficient political interest. Finally the adoption of a directive still did not solve the problem, many member states showing themselves reluctant to take the measures necessary for implementation.

Mutual recognition and home country control The drawbacks of the above procedures became very apparent at the moment the year 1992 was set as a target for the completion of the internal market. Indeed, in view of the poor record on harmonisation, it appeared well-nigh impossible to get all the necessary work done by the end of 1992 along such traditional lines. So the EU has now adopted a new approach.

Specific features of the new approach

For *goods*, the new approach is based on mutual recognition of, and reference to, standards. Let us indicate briefly its main aspects. The directives implementing the technical harmonisation (according to Article 100) henceforth define only the essential requirements with which products must comply to circulate freely all over the Common Market. They refer to European standards (technical specifications) defined by the competent normalisation organisations, such as CEN, CENELEC and CEPT. Member states are obliged to notify partner countries of, and discuss with them, any plans for new national regulations, in order to circumvent later cumbersome procedures of harmonisation (Article 83/189). All matters are decided on in the Council by qualified majority. (The voting rules of CEN/CENELEC have also been adapted in that sense.) Each member state must give free access to any product manufactured according to the European standards (Article 36); restrictions based on public interest may no longer be invoked.

For *services* the new approach is based on recognition of the quality of control in the home country. The segmentation of service markets is due to national regulations concerning products (insurance products, among others) but also to the prudential control exerted by national authorities on all establishments located in their territory. The Commission has proposed that, in line with the 'Cassis de Dijon' judgements, financial products be accepted in all member states once they are accepted in one member state. Another proposal is to switch to a system of home country control, all member states accepting that the establishments of a multinational company are all supervised by the authorities of the member state in which the head offices are located. Of course this presupposes a minimum standard of surveillance.

The new concept reflects a fundamentally different view of market integration. From a monolithic conception of the EU's integration process in which national legislation and powers are replaced by European powers, the EU has turned to a pluralistic, pragmatic and federalistic conception in which national legislation will not be replaced but framed in a way that respects minimum European requirements (Padoa Schioppa *et al.*, 1987).

Welfare effects

In the early 1980s, a few attempts (for example, Hartley, 1987) were made at quantifying the cost of the remaining non-tariff barriers and formalities at the internal borders of the EC and the other imperfections of the internal market (termed 'cost of non-Europe' by Albert and Ball, 1983). In an attempt to establish a more complete picture of the welfare gains to be obtained by the removal of the remaining obstacles, the European Commission commissioned at the end of the 1980s a series of detailed surveys.[16]

Moreover the Commission has made a major effort to go beyond this sectoral evidence of the cost of non-Europe in order to quantify the overall effects of the completion of the internal market. (Emerson *et al.*, 1988). A distinction is made between three types of effects (see Chapter 5 for theoretical underpinnings).

Border control removal will reduce the cost of administration of both importers and exporters, and the cost of delays for transporters. In economic terms these costs are similar to tariffs that impede trade; their removal lowers prices for consumers of final goods and purchasers of intermediate goods, and releases resources for alternative production. Although highly visible and often cited by entrepreneurs as a major obstacle to trade, their total impact is limited and evaluated at only 0.3 per cent of GDP.

Market entry and competition effects are different for the short term and the long term. The short-term effect is that prices will drop to the level of the most efficient producer in the EU once government procurement is put on a competitive basis and the markets are no longer compartmentalised by technical regulations. The long-term effect is the further reduction of cost through increased competition, enhanced innovation and learning effects. The economic benefits associated with increased competition are considerable (Cecchini, *et al.*, 1988; Emerson *et al.*, 1988; CEC, 1988a); they are estimated at some 4 per cent of GDP, divided about equally between short- and long-term effects.

Economies of scale are another major element. As competition leads industries to restructure, closing down inefficient plants, investing in new plants and expanding output, production will become more efficient. In practice this effect is not always easy to dissociate from the competition effect mentioned earlier. The studies of the cost of non-Europe indicate that in certain branches of the economy there is still ample room for economies of scale, while in many others they seem to have been exploited already to the full. The estimated welfare gain on that score is some 2 per cent of total GDP.

The total welfare gains that can be reaped from the completion of the internal market of the EU may exceed the 6 per cent to which the ffects just discussed add up, provided the right macro-economic policies are carried out. The extra benefits comprise lower unemployment figures, prices and taxes, and an increase in economic growth through the improvement of the EU's international competitive position. Although these long-term growth effects are difficult to measure, one estimate (Baldwin, 1989) suggests that they may be of the same order of magnitude as the one-time effects mentioned earlier.

Summary and conclusions

- The main rationale for the European economic integration is the enhancement of allocational efficiency; the main instrument to achieve it is the liberalisation of markets (negative integration).
- In addition to liberalisation measures, the EU needs to pursue policies of positive integration to create the conditions for the proper functioning of markets; the most important is competition policy.
- The European policies concerning such diverse matters as technical norms, value added tax and government procurement are carried out, not because these matters need harmonisation in their own right, but because they are instrumental in achieving a better allocation of resources and hence more welfare.
- In the 1960s and 1970s the internal market remained incomplete. In the 1980s and early 1990s a new programme succeeded in bringing about the complete abolition of all controls at internal borders on goods, services, workers and capital.
- The welfare effects of this programme are substantial; they have been estimated at some 6 per cent of the EU's GDP. For some sectors, the effects could be achieved only by very thorough restructuring.

Notes

1 A minor reason was the need for basic material for statistics. Although the procedure was greatly simplified by the adoption in 1988 of the so-called 'document unique' (a document containing, in code, all information on value added tax (VAT), transport, customs and so on), it still involves a check on all intra-EU trade in goods and services, which for convenience is made at internal borders.
2 Notably during the years of depression (1974–84), member states' governments were eager to exploit the loopholes in the EU regulations for their short-term interest.

3   This distinction may be convenient for political purposes but it is not very relevant for economic analysis. For that reason we have grouped in this chap ter the discussion of many of these subjects under somewhat different head ings.

4   The same effect can be achieved, of course, by potential competition; when existing suppliers fear that potential new suppliers have easy access to the market, they will set their prices with more care. (This contestable-market theory is elaborated by Baumol *et al.*, 1982.)

5   See, for an introduction to the theory and a review of the competition policies practised by the EU countries (and a comparison with those of the USA and Japan), Shaw and Simpson (1987); and for a popular introduction, CEC (1985e)

6   The external dimension of EU competition policy has recently been enlarged to the European Economic Area (so including EFTA). The new association agree ments with Eastern European countries also contain a section on competition Moreover the Commission has made a cooperation agreement on competition with the US authorities.

7   In the past many branches of the telecommunication, transport, bank and insurance and energy sectors were practically removed from competition policy Deregulation, privatisation and the opening of markets in the framework of the 1992 programme have brought them into EU-wide competition and hence under the EU competition rules.

8   To limit the administrative burden, the Commission has generically exempted from notification some types of agreement considered compatible with the competition rules.

9   Preventive merger control was made possible by the 1990 Merger Regulation A good overview of the foundations of EU merger policy in terms of economic advantages and disadvantages of mergers is given by Jacquemin (1991) and Neven *et al.* (1993); for a broader treatment, see OECD (1984b) and, for the dynamics of the international merger process, Mueller (1980) and Cooke (1988).

10 Tax adjustment for goods crossing the internal EU borders in inter company trade remains necessary also after 1992 to prevent distortions (Guieu and Bon net, 1987). Tax adjustment for goods bought by individuals of high-taxation states in low-taxation states is expected not to cause serious distortions of trade; on the contrary it is expected to keep up the pressure on member states to avoid any new diverging tendencies. For certain activities where this free dom could lead to distortions, as for companies selling directly to the client by mail, special rules have been made.

11 The use of hydrocarbon fuels has a negative impact on the environment. In order to induce more efficient use of fuels, a European tax on CO_2 has been proposed by the Commission. As this might have a negative influence on the competitiveness of the European industry on world markets, the EU has made its introduction dependent on an agreement with the major OECD partners (Pearson and Smith, 1992).

12 This is notwithstanding the relatively limited role that the revenue from corpo rate taxes has in the total revenue of member states; see last two columns of Table 16.3.

13 The external openness of the EC capital markets (Chapter 10) implies that not only EU but also worldwide harmonisation is called for (Giovannini, 1989; OECD, 1991).

14 Access to markets may also be limited as a consequence of firms' behaviour, for instance investment and innovation; this will not lead to static inefficient price setting, however (Van Wittelloostuyn and Maks, 1988).

15 Two main approaches are followed. The first uses the specialised private Euro pean normalisation organisations of CEN and CENELEC (setting standards for

products); the other is used by the EU, which by means of directives 'approximates' technical specifications.

16 The results of these detailed studies have been put together in three volumes: (1) a scientific report (Emerson *et al.*, 1988); (2) a volume containing the executive summaries of the detailed reports (CEC, 1988d); and (3) a more popular book, which became known as the Cecchini *et al.* (1988) Report, after the chairman of the working group.

17 Stabilisation: Towards a Monetary Union

Introduction

The progress along the road from free trade area to full union takes in the station of Economic and Monetary Union (EMU). We recall (Chapter 2) that such a union implies, on the monetary side, either full and irrevocable convertibility of all currencies, coupled with a system of fixed parities (without margins) between the participating currencies, or a single currency. On the economic side, it supposes, apart from policies that sustain the internal market, policies that sustain the monetary union. One implication of this is the need for coherence of the budgetary policies of member states.

The policy integration needed for a monetary union has mostly to do with stabilisation. Stabilisation policies are pursued because adaptation to new circumstances entails cost, sometimes considerable cost (think, for instance, of the retraining of workers and the premature writing off of capital equipment). The purpose of stabilisation policies is to cushion the effects of internal and external shocks to the economy. An example is the intervention of monetary authorities in foreign exchange markets when speculations tend to put these out of alignment with fundamental economic factors. Budgetary policies to soften the effects of the business cycle on economic activity are another example. The latter, however, need to be dovetailed with anti-inflationary policies in order to retain consistency with monetary policy.

European countries are reputed to value stability rather highly (more than, for instance, the USA). As integration of markets erodes the possibility for independent national policies, stabilisation is an important European policy field. We will discuss this below in the following way. First we will go into the theoretical foundations. The main rationale for monetary integration is that it smooths trade and investment in the EU and hence contributes to the efficient allocation of resources. Now, for such relatively small open economies as most

EU member states are, the independent pursuit of stability is very difficult. We will indicate the advantages and disadvantages of different degrees of integration.

Next we will describe the way the EU has gradually developed its economic and monetary integration. We describe the evolution from its hesitant start on a narrow legal basis to the concrete definition of the ambitious goal of the economic and monetary union. Monetary integration is discussed in some detail in the section that follows. We describe subsequently the basic mechanisms of the European Monetary System (EMS), the composition of the European Currency Unit (ECU), and the set-up chosen for the European monetary union with the European Central Bank and so on.

Effective monetary integration imposes a constraint on the setting up of autonomous national macro-economic goals, and rules out divergent national inflation rates. Therefore macro-policy needs to be integrated as well. The forms this is to take in terms of budgetary deficits, government indebtedness and so on to let inflation rates converge sufficiently to make an EMU sustainable are the subjects of the last section.

As usual, we will end the chapter with some brief conclusions.

Some theoretical aspects

The problem: growing interdependence narrows the scope for independent policies

The creation of a customs union and a common market increases the specialisation of the constituent economies and the exchange of goods, services and production factors. As a result, the economies involved become increasingly interdependent, every country being dependent on its partner countries and affected by the developments there.[1] Interdependence has a strong bearing on the degree to which individual governments can influence the economy through budgetary (fiscal) and monetary (exchange rate) policies. For example, a budgetary policy intended to increase output by increased government spending may be ineffective if the additional purchasing power created is spent on imported rather than domestic goods. A monetary policy that restricts the money supply to keep inflation low may be frustrated by price increases of imported goods as a result of wage inflation in the partner (exporting) country. Interdependence of national economies means that developments on the national scale are apt to have spill-over effects in partner countries, each country giving impulses and feeling the impact of impulses in other countries (see Box 17.1, for example).

Box 17.1   The French stimulation plan 1981–83

When the Mitterrand government took office in 1981, it launched an ambitious plan for stimulation of the economy. Several policy measures created an expansion of consumption. The growth rate increased subsequently by 0.2 per cent in 1981 and by 1.8 per cent in 1982. The close links between France and its EU partners resulted in spill-overs of this expansion to other countries. So much of the extra impact on demand and employment was drained away to these countries. Moreover, for domestic policy reasons, Germany pursued policies to cool off its economy. To restore internal and external equilibrium, France was forced to adopt restrictive counter-measures equivalent to a reduction in growth of at least 3 to 4 per cent of GDP. So this experiment (like earlier experiments of France and the UK in the mid-1970s) underlines the incapacity of even large EU countries to pursue isolated policies for stimulation of the economy by reflating demand. The lesson has been costly, as the effect of such independent policies was the opposite of the one intended; instead of providing a boost to growth, the ultimate outcome was a net decline in growth.

This situation imposes severe constraints on domestic macro-economic and monetary policies, constraints that are reflected in the reduced ability to control the instruments of policy (such as the domestic money supply under a regime of fixed exchange rates) and to influence policy targets (such as the level of real output, the level of unemployment and the level of inflation). Now private decision makers in financial markets are very well aware of the reduced effectiveness of policies pursued independently, so public authorities have to make considerable efforts to remain credible. If they fail, private parties will go on responding to expectations of future exchange rates, irrespective of policy intervention, thus doing away completely with whatever room for manoeuvring there was left to the public authorities. This is particularly relevant under the now prevailing conditions of generalised free movements of capital using a technological infrastructure which makes it possible to move considerable sums from one country to another almost instantly. The enormous sums that private traders can now mobilise, compared to the limited means of monetary authorities, reinforces the need for partner countries to cooperate and in this way to regain collectively the control which they had lost individually.

The solution: coordination through institutions

The central element of the solution to the problem of loss of autonomy is, then, policy coordination. This approach finds its theoretical underpinning in game theory (Sachs, 1980; Steinherr, 1984; Buiter and Marston, 1985; Hamada, 1985).[2] The general conclusion of this body of literature is that, in all types of games in which the policy of one country affects (directly or indirectly) the variables making up the other country's welfare function, better results are possible with a cooperative than with a non-cooperative attitude (Fisher, 1987). The important question arises as to why in practice cooperation is the exception rather than the rule. Steinherr (1984) presents the following reasons for limited progress with policy coordination in an EMU:

- *Uncertain relations between objectives and policy.* Players believe in different models of the real world (for instance monetarists versus Keynesians). Even if they agree on one basic model, the quantification of the parameters is very difficult, leaving large error margins. Coordination can be introduced with success only if conceptual problems can largely be eliminated.
- *Absence of compensation mechanisms.* If under coordination country A is not worse off than before, while country B stands to reap large benefits, the scheme is unlikely to be considered a good deal by country A. Better deals may be concluded if side payments are made to countries that lose or gain but little from cooperation. If no mechanisms for such payments exist, cooperation may not be realised. If gains and losses from consecutive games tended to compensate each other, such side payments would not be necessary. However, if there is no institutional stability and hence no guarantee that the game be continued, cooperation is again unlikely to come about.
- *Rank and file.* Players (governments) are constrained not only by other players' strategies, but also by their national parliaments and pressure groups. The need to maintain a balance back home may preclude the choice of the optimum solution in the EMU. Therefore budgetary and income policies may be harder to achieve than monetary policy. The latter is carried out largely by central banks, which in many countries are politically fairly independent.
- *High cost of coordination.* Negotiations can be long-winded, and conditions may change while they are going on. The adoption of compromise objectives and policies, needed because optimum policies are found unfeasible, may incur the highest costs. Indeed welfare functions are very hard to define, and the weigh-

ing of advantages accruing to one group rather than to another meets with conceptual as well as statistical obstacles.

- *Complexity*. Even in a group with a limited number of members and confining its attention to only one or two objectives, the game is already complex. The complexity increases with the number of players (geographical extension) and the number of targets (extension of subjects to deal with). The difficulty increases further with the adding of objectives with different time horizons. So the feasibility of coordination depends critically on the limitation of the number of targets.

We can cite one more reason:

- *Lack of awareness of loss of autonomy*. Countries that have traditionally pursued an independent policy tend to be slow to realise that increased international integration erodes the effectiveness of such policies.

The conclusion that can be drawn from this analysis is that the setting up of institutions and the acceptance of common rules are important conditions for the durability and effectiveness of policy coordination.

Coordination: goals

The principal goals that an EMU should strive for are twofold.

Stability of exchange rates   This first goal is derived from the higher goal of creating the stable conditions for the efficient functioning of markets. The main instrument for arriving at this goal is contained in the very definition of the monetary union: the definitive fixing of the exchange rates with the currencies of all partner countries or the adoption of a single common currency.[3] It is understood that there is full and irrevocable convertibility of currencies, which implies that unlimited foreign exchange is available for all international transactions, be they related to trade, services, capital or remittances (essential for CU and CM). The goal of fully fixed exchange rates is not easy to attain, and therefore intermediate goals have been advocated. In one, the variability of exchange rates is limited to certain target zones around pivot rates. In another, a so-called 'pseudo union' (Corden, 1972b) is established, in which exchange rates are fixed but monetary policies are not fully integrated; there is no union monetary authority, and some doubt persists about the durability of the exchange rates.

Alignment of inflation rates   This second goal is derived from the goal of stable exchange rates; indeed in the long run the exchange rate has to be adapted to changes in the inflation rates between the two countries. So, to keep the former fixed, the latter have to be aligned. The instrument used to arrive at a target rate of inflation for the whole Union is the coordination or unification of monetary and budgetary policies. Obviously, in a complete EMU with only one currency, the money-supply and budgetary policies are agreed upon jointly by partners or decided by Union institutions.[4] In other words, the member states lose all autonomy in that respect. On the way to an EMU, intermediate solutions are likely to be found that gradually reduce the divergence of inflation rates through the coordinated use of policy instruments by member states. During the intermediate stage, governments retain some flexibility as to the degree of compliance with the goal, and as to the mix of instruments used. For the coordination of the latter, target values may be agreed upon for national economic indicators like current account balance, public sector balance, interest rates and so on.

The efficiency of the coordination process (consistent involvement of partners) and the effectiveness of its outcome (credibility in markets) depend critically on the gradual reinforcement of the regulatory and institutional set-up.

Gains and losses

Governments will not give up autonomy in sensitive policy areas to erect an EMU unless they consider the *gains* from integration sufficient to make it worth their while. These gains can be summarised under three heads (Thygesen, 1990; Gros and Thygesen, 1992; de Grauwe, 1992):

- *Efficient goods, service, labour and capital markets.* The basic reason for monetary integration is to relieve traders and investors of transaction costs, that is exchange losses on their international transactions. The second reason is that they take away the uncertainty as to future fluctuation of exchange rates. Indeed uncoordinated policies lead to 'overshooting' in a system of flexible exchange rates, and hence to largely unnecessary fluctuations in trade, production and investment (Dornbusch, 1976). In general stability will increase the volume of international exchanges. This in turn is likely to improve the financial services needed for payments and hence reduce transaction costs even further. The third reason is that the single currency will eliminate significant information cost and price discrimi-

nation that is based on these imperfections. So the better allocation of available resources resulting from these measures will
produce welfare gains.

- *Efficient monetary system.* A MU needs far smaller monetary
  reserves than the group of constituent countries operating individually. For one thing, no stocks need be kept of currencies of
  other MU members; for another, peak demands for the currencies of third countries are unlikely to occur in all member countries at the same time. Intervention in foreign exchange markets by MU authorities is more effective than individual actions because of the increased means and the unity of purpose.
  Finally the easier management of the system will free part of
  the resources now tied up in it (both with the monetary authorities and with the banking system).
- *Faster economic growth.* The growth effects of the increased effectiveness of coordinated budgetary and monetary policies
  are subject to much debate. Some authors consider the dynamic effects to outweigh the static effects discussed earlier
  (among others, Hughes Hallett, 1985).

The *cost* of monetary integration is to be measured in the loss of
production and value added, employment and so on, and stems
from two types of problems:

- *Non-optimal policy mix.* Many governments assume that there is
  in the short run a certain relation between the level of inflation
  and the level of unemployment. Each country that used to
  'choose' independently a combination of these two, is now
  forced to accept a common inflation rate, and hence accept a
  different combination of inflation and unemployment. The costs
  involved depend, of course, on the form of the curve, the discrepancies between independent national targets and the common MU rates, the time period and so on. These costs can be
  reduced if partners take long enough to realise convergence of
  national rates for these two variables so as to realign to the
  Union targets that bring a definite strengthening of confidence
  in the long-run predictability and stability of the price level.
- *Rigidities.* Economies are regularly victims of external shocks.
  Some of these, that affect the whole Union in the same way,
  and others, that are minor and country-specific, will be easily
  accommodated. However a MU constrains domestic policy making in response to major country-specific shocks (as, for example, with a sudden fall in demand for a country's exports or a
  rise in import prices). Adjustment of the exchange rate is no
  longer feasible, so adjustment will have to occur in the real

sector. The cost involved in that adjustment process (for exam
ple, the lay-off of production factors) will depend on the lack o
institutional and social flexibility of the economy.

So the basic cost–benefit assessment of monetary union has to weigh
a set of micro- and macro-economic costs and benefits of very differ
ent sorts. The balance can come out differently for each participan
country, depending on the structure of its economy, its past policies
its institutional arrangements (rigidities) and so on. One feature is
prominent in all this, however: that the cost of monetary integration
in terms of the percentage of welfare (GDP) gets lower, and the
benefits higher, the more open the national economy (in terms o
trade).

Participation

Countries that participate in a customs union, and a fortiori in a
common market, will come to realise that the costs of non-coordi-
nated policies tend to increase. For one thing, the volumes of trade
subject to exchange rate risks have become greater; for another, there
are larger flows of capital, which tend to shy away from exchange
rate risks in so far as they are of a structural nature, but tend to
increase them inasmuch as they are of a speculative nature. These
costs push CU partners and, even more, CM partners, to progress to
an EMU eventually.

This logic is not to be found in the mainstream of literature, however. Here the concept of the Optimum Currency Area (OCA) has
been favoured (Mundell, 1961). The objective is to establish who
should take part in a scheme for monetary integration. To identify
the group of countries likely to form an OCA, different indicators are
used that refer to the stages of integration distinguished earlier (products, production factors and policy). The most popular indicator is
openness of goods markets: pairs of countries with high import or
export figures in respect of their domestic consumption are good
candidates for a monetary union. Next follows the degree of openness to production factors (for example, Ingram, 1973). Finally comes
the degree to which forms of integrated policy with respect to
stabilisation and redistribution are realised (MacDougall, *et al.*, 1977,
Allen, 1983). To some (for example, Hamada, 1985) these indicators
are irrelevant as criteria for EMU membership; to them a monetary
union cannot be sustained without full political unification.

The search for optimality for defining membership of an EMU on
the basis of such criteria as openness to trade, capital and so on has
been severely criticised (by Ishiyama, 1975, among others). For one
thing, the scores on these criteria are often difficult to measure. For

another, which criterion would be best is hard to say; even a combination is of little avail, as we do not know what weights to attach to them. Finally countries may value their independence so highly that the perceived cost of participation outweighs the advantages of integration. There is also a more institutional reason not to follow up the argument of the OCA. To be viable, an EMU must have a fairly strong institutional structure and real powers. Such a structure is unlikely to be created or sustained among countries that have not acquired some experience with the institutional set-up of less difficult forms of integration. This implies that countries already forming a CU or a CM will be the best candidates for participation in an EMU.

The question then becomes a much more pragmatic one: what conditions must be met for CM-partners to realise monetary integration? That depends on the trade-off between the loss of autonomy in certain policy fields and the economic advantages which integration promises, to each member individually and to the union collectively. The loss of political autonomy is not a new phenomenon. We have already seen that countries participating in a customs union waive the right to use tariffs, quotas and other trade instruments *vis-à-vis* their partners, and the right to decide on their own to use such instruments towards third countries. Much in the same way, partners in a common market refrain from using instruments for the control of capital flows to pursue macro-economic objectives. All partners have given up part of their competences because they reckon that the benefits of cooperation outweigh the loss of room for manoeuvre. So the quantification of gains and losses becomes the essential point of analysis for the decision to move towards an EMU.

EU regime

The beginnings: the Treaty of Rome

The Treaty of Rome is not very explicit on the macro-economic and monetary integration of Europe. It does not foresee a Community as an EMU, but rather provides for some embryonic integration on this score, designed to facilitate the proper functioning of the Common Market for goods, services and production factors (Article 105). The general objectives of the EU in matters of economic and monetary policy at its start (Article 104) were to ensure:

- equilibrium of its overall balance of payments;
- confidence in its currency;
- a high level of employment; and

- a stable level of prices.

To attain these objectives, three instruments were to be used:

- coordination of national economic policies (Article 105) par ticularly cyclical policies (Article 103);
- stabilisation of rates of exchange (Article 107.1);
- assistance (in terms of credits) in case of balance of payments problems.

More advanced ideas of an economic and monetary union had beer advocated on several occasions in the 1950s, but gained too little political support to leave a mark in the Rome Treaty.

The role of the European Union in matters of monetary policy is not foreseen by the EEC Treaty but not explicitly forbidden either That is, however, the case for one instrument of macro-economic policy: the EU cannot pursue a budgetary policy (Article 199), as the EU outlays and receipts must be in balance every year. Should the resources of the EU fall short of needs, then member states have to put up the money; the EU cannot, like its member states, raise money by imposing taxes, nor finance spending by loaning on the capita market.[5]

That the Treaty was so cautious in bestowing powers of monetary and economic policy on the EU can in part be explained by the economic conditions of the period: the Bretton Woods system o: fixed exchange rates was functioning smoothly, and the Europear economies were all at a stage of long-term economic growth, so that all attention was given to short- and medium-term policies.

The means: institutions and instruments

The institutional framework provided by the Treaty consisted of sev- eral committees dealing with coordination of different parts of policy making. To promote the coordination of the policies of the member states in the monetary field, a Monetary Committee with advisory status was set up in the 1960s (Article 105). This Committee consisted of representatives of the governments (Ministries of Finance), the na- tional banks and the Commission. Its task was to review the monetary financial and balance-of-payments situation in the member countries and the international payments system. The Committee regularly re- ported its conclusions and suggestions for action to the Commission and the Council. This Committee soon proved inadequate to cope with the upcoming problems, and three more committees were set up

For a smooth-functioning macro-economic policy, a coordination Committee on Short-Term Economic Trends was installed in 1960 ollowed in 1964 by the Committee for Budget Policy and the Medium-Term Economic Policy Committee; all were composed of representatives of the member states and the Commission. Later the three Committees were merged into a new Economic Policy Committee with a view to strengthening the coordination between the various aspects of economic policy (including monetary matters). The work of the former three committees was continued in three new subcommittees.

Because monetary policy is executed in part independently of governments by central banks, the Monetary Committee's activity was not found sufficient, and therefore a Group of Governors of Central Banks was created in 1964. It met regularly in Basle, the headquarters of the Bank for International Settlements, in conjunction with meetings of that bank's Council of Governors. The European Commission participated as an observer. The Group covered topics that are typically the central banks' responsibility, particularly with respect to credits, money and exchange markets. Its members also exchanged information on the most important measures the central banks were taking or planning.

In their many meetings, the various Committees and their working groups have deliberated on very important topics. All that talk has certainly produced a better understanding of one another's motives and constraints, and has thus led to a factual coordination.

The route: controversies between 'economists and monetarists'

Over the past years, an agreement on the ambitious objective of the EMU has been made difficult to reach by the deep-rooted differences in opinion among experts about the best way forward. Although everybody agreed that the benefits of monetary integration increase, and the costs of integration decrease, with increasing interdependence in terms of goods trade (see Figure 17.1), there were differences about the point where the two lines intersect. The main dividing line was between economists and monetarists. They have different conceptions about the balancing of the cost and benefits of the EMU, notably about the cost level of integration (see Figure 17.1).

The *economists* (found in particular among German and Dutch scholars) give priority to the harmonisation of economic policies, and consider results on that score an essential condition for further monetary integration. Their argument is that divergent inflation rates springing from different economic policies and the incapacity to overcome rigidities in the field of wages and immobility of labour will sooner or later lead to exchange rate adaptations. If that option is not open any more, some countries may be forced into a very costly deflation which for internal political reasons they would rather avoid.

The ensuing tensions will almost certainly break up the fragile sys
tems of exchange rate stabilisation agreed upon. The economist
held that the cost curve is far away from the origin (right-hand sid
of Figure 17.1) and hence that the full unification of economic poli
cies must precede full monetary integration.

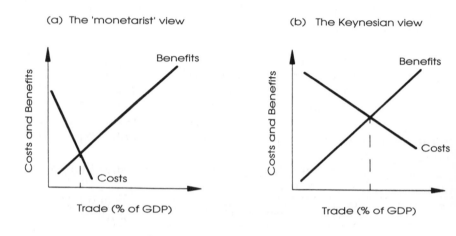

Figure 17.1   Two views of cost and benefits of a monetary union

Source: De Grauwe (1992).

The *monetarists* (chiefly found among the Italians and in earlie
years also among French and Belgians) defend the view that the us
of exchange rates is in the long run ineffective to correct for imbal
ances. In this view (left-hand part of Figure 17.1) the cost curve i
very close to the origin. Monetary integration (fixed exchange rates
controlled liquidity and so on) is the best way to commit nationa
governments to take the necessary measures of economic policy t
curb inflation. Their argument is based on the observation that gov
ernments of high-inflation countries will not start adjusting thei
policies and curb the forces that tend to press inflation upwards
such as politicians (budget policy) and labour unions (wage-cos
inflation), unless forced to do so by fixed exchange rates (for exam
ple, Giavazzi and Pagano, 1986).

The skirmishes between the two schools have flared up with every step taken towards further integration into an EMU. On several occasions there have been cease-fires (as with the EMS), both parties having agreed to the compromise that the two elements need to be gradually integrated in a balanced fashion.

The goal: the Economic and Monetary Union

While European integration was in progress, several proposals for the realisation of an economic and monetary union were made. Experience with the coordination system provided for in the Treaty had shown up severe shortcomings, and further efforts were needed to cope with problems ahead. At The Hague Summit of 1969, the heads of state and government agreed in principle to the creation of an Economic and Monetary Union, and requested the Commission to work out proposals for the successive realisation of its elements.

A blueprint for such a union was the report called 'The Realisation by Stages of the Economic and Monetary Union in the Community', submitted in 1970 by a committee under the chairmanship of Werner. The Werner report, adopted by the Council in 1971, proposed the realisation of the EMU in stages, and presented an ambitious calendar, foreseeing completion in 1980. The Werner plan soon proved an illusion. The monetary disorder of the mid-1970s made it very difficult to obtain adequate political support, and alternative, less ambitious proposals were made (see next section), concentrating on exchange rate stabilisation.

However the cost of the non-Europe soon became apparent both on the micro-economic and the macro-economic level (Albert and Ball, 1983). It was shown repeatedly that, for both small and large EU countries, macro and monetary policies have lost effectiveness. Political sensitivity has made it difficult to accept the obvious conclusion of this state of affairs, that only coherent EU policy making will permit partners to regain collectively the control that they have all lost individually. The growing awareness of the negative effects of the (lack of) macro-economic and monetary cooperation convinced more and more academic, business and political circles that further progress towards the EMU was urgently needed.

In a period when economists were hopelessly divided over the advantages of a system of free-floating exchange rates, on the one hand, and on the best road to monetary stability, on the other (see previous section), a decision was taken by three statesmen (Giscard, Schmidt and Jenkins) to get out of the deadlock. They proposed the European Monetary System (see next section), which has been successfully implemented. As the EMS has some inherent weaknesses, and the advantages of such a scheme fall short of those of full monetary union, a new plan for the realisation of the Economic and Monetary Union was elaborated and unanimously accepted by a committee under the chairmanship of the president of the Commission (Delors Committee, 1989). It was composed of members of the Commission, of the governors of the national central banks and a number of independent experts. It was strongly supported by the business community that had been made painfully aware of the disadvantages of the monetary disorder (AMUE, 1988). The proposal was the basis for the negotiations on the Treaty on the Economic and Monetary Union.

The legal basis: the Maastricht Treaty

The European Council called for an intergovernmental conference that was to prepare for the necessary treaty revisions to set up a complete EMU. This treaty was ratified at the end of 1993. It foresees that the EMU will be realised in three stages.

First stage. All member countries realise the full freedom of capital movements. They strengthen the cooperation between central banks (realised by the end of 1993).

Second stage. A new institution, the European Monetary Institute, will be created. It can be regarded as the precursor of the European Central Bank (ECB). Its main function is to strengthen the cooperation between national central banks. Member states will stimulate the process leading to the independence of their national central banks. They will endeavour to avoid excessive budget deficits. (This stage began in 1994.)

Third stage. Exchange rates between the currencies of the participating countries will be irrevocably fixed. The same holds for the exchange rates of those currencies against the ECU. The ECB will start its operations. It will issue a European currency and will be responsible for monetary policy. Detailed institutional arrangements safeguard its independence and its commitment to price stability.

Between 1997 and 1999 the European Council will decide at what date the EMU will enter into force and which countries meet the criteria of convergence[6] set by the treaty and so can join the Monetary Union. Indeed not all countries need to join at the same time, and some countries have the right not to join at all (UK). Some of the criteria need to be applied strictly, for others some flexibility exists, so it is as yet uncertain when and in what form the EMU will start.

The TEU prescribes in much detail a number of the features of EMU and of the road which will lead there. However it also leaves a large number of questions open. The first important one may be the need for the creation of strong (pre)federal political structures that are able to match economic ambitions (history having shown that monetary unions are stable only under political unions). The second may be the need to increase the means for supporting Union monetary policies (the EU budget being very small!).

Monetary policy: stability of exchange rates

The cornerstone of the exchange rate stabilisation mechanism: the ECU

The stabilisation of the exchange rates of the European currencies is the first step on the road to full monetary unification, which implies the introduction of one currency. While awaiting this single currency, a need has developed for a European monetary unit that does not have all the attributes of a currency. Indeed accepting one of the member states' currencies (German Mark) or a third currency (US dollar) as a vehicle for financial transactions in the EU is hard to defend politically. Therefore several forms of European units of account were developed in the past, all of which proved inadequate for the tasks ahead.

Then the ECU, the European Currency Unit, was created. This is made up of parts of the currencies of all member states and so reflects the whole Community's financial identity. The 'basket' is open and ready to receive the currencies of new members as they join the EU. Each national currency contributes a certain part to the ECU (Table 17.1, first column). The size of the national contributions (0.62 German Mark, 0.09 pound sterling and so on) may appear at first sight rather erratic, but in reality is dependent on a set of criteria. Each contribution or share (in column 1) corresponds to a weight (in column 5); the latter reflects the economic importance of the member state in question, in terms of GDP, share in EC external trade, and so on (see next section). Weights can be changed every five years, the rearrangement being such that the ECU keeps its value on the date of change.[7]

The value of the ECU in terms of member state currencies is calculated daily by the Commission. To illustrate the operation, we have worked out an example in Table 17.1. First the shares (column 1) are divided by the official exchange rates of the EU currencies with respect to a reference currency, in practice the US dollar (September 1993 exchange rates in column 2). The exchange rate of the ECU to the US dollar is obtained by adding up the resulting figures (column 3). Apparently, by the end of 1993, the average value of 1 ECU was 1.2 dollars. To calculate the exchange rate of each currency to the ECU, multiply the values of column 2 by 1.19 (column 3). To permit an easier interpretation of the shares of column 1, they are usually recalculated in terms of percentages, also called the weight of each

Table 17.1   The ECU in relation to the component currencies

	1 Share	2 Exchange rate: 1 $ = [a]	3 1/2	4 Exchange rate: 1 ECU =	5 Weigh
German mark	0.6242	1.6070	0.388	1.91	32.6
French franc	1.3320	5.6470	0.236	6.72	19.8
Italian lira	151.8000	1 547.3730	0.098	1 841.37	8.3
Dutch guilder	0.2198	1.8055	0.122	2.15	10.3
Bel/Lux franc	3.4310	34.4299	0.100	40.97	8.4
UK pound sterling	0.0878	0.6475	0.136	0.77	11.4
Danish krone	0.1976	6.6410	0.030	7.90	2.5
Irish pound	0.0086	0.6915	0.012	0.82	1.0
Spanish peseta	6.8850	128.8800	0.053	153.37	4.5
Portuguese escudo*	1.3930	164.6590	0.009	195.94	0.7
Greek drachma*	1.4400	231.000	0.006	274.89	0.5
Total	1 ECU	=	1.190 $	—	100.0

[a]   as of 10 September 1993.
*   theoretical rate.
Source: CEC.

currency in the ECU (in practice this is done by dividing the value
of column 3 by 1.19; see column 5).

Exchange rate stabilisation

Over the past decades, the EC has worked out several systems to
reduce exchange rate uncertainty among its members. The first ma
jor attempt was the 'Snake' arrangement of April 1972. The widel
varying policy responses of the European countries to the oil crisi
reduced the arrangement to a small group of currencies around the
DM. In 1979, the European Monetary System (EMS) started.[8]

The main aim of the EMS is to create short-term exchange rat
stability in Europe. This is put into practice by an Exchange Rat
Mechanism (ERM). For the currencies that participate in the ERM
reference parities (central or pivot rates) to the ECU are defined
which also define all bilateral exchange rates between these cur
rencies. Together they form a grid of parities. The situation as o
September 1993 is given in Table 17.2. The market value of the cur
rencies changes continuously as a consequence of supply and de
mand conditions. Hence differences between the real rate and the
central rate will occur (compare, for example, the rate of 1.91 DM t
the ECU, from Table 17.1, with the pivot rate of 1.95 DM to the ECU

rom Table 17.2). Now stability is realised by the intervention of monetary authorities on the exchange markets. They have agreed to et the market rate fluctuate only within certain margins. In the past, hese margins were small; for most countries they were fixed at 2.25 per cent above or below the central rate; for Italy, Portugal and Spain hey stood exceptionally at 6 per cent. To take an example: in 1989, he central rate for the FF in Frankfurt was DM 0.298; the permitted luctuations, accordingly, were confined between the upper and lower nargins of DM 0.305 and DM 0.292. In mid-1993, speculation forced nany currencies out of these small margins, and some (like the UK pound) even out of the ERM. In order to make such speculative attacks much more costly for speculators and less costly for the authorities, the margins have temporarily been considerably widened, o some 15 per cent (see Table 17.2). Some have said that with such arge margins one could hardly speak of stabilisation of exchange ates. In practice, however, many countries try to keep much smaller nargins for example, 1 per cent for the DM/Dfl rates, 2–3 per cent or the DM/DKr and DM/FF and 6–10 per cent for most other currencies.

The central banks of the member states are committed to intervene n exchange markets to contain their currencies within these broad nargins. In practice, such intervention starts when the divergence ndicator of the exchange rate from the central rate passes a certain hreshold. In the 1980s this threshold level stood at 0.75 of the margin of 2.25 per cent. Since the 1993 widening of the bands, central banks lo not disclose this threshold value, however, in order to discourage speculation.

The fact that not all EC currencies participate in the exchange rate nechanism (notably not the pound sterling) causes certain complications, as a simple example may illustrate. Assume that the floating of he pound sterling, other currencies remaining stable, results in a lepreciation of, say, 10 per cent. The pound-to-dollar exchange rate changes from 0.6475 to 0.7122, the corresponding value of column 3 of Table 17.1 to 0.123, and the ECU/dollar rate to 1.18, which means a depreciation of the ECU of 1 per cent with respect to the dollar. Although the exchange rates of the other European currencies to the lollar have not changed, the exchange rates of the currencies to the ECU will drop 1 per cent. To keep the ECU value stable and predictable, the EU is in favour of the participation of all currencies in the exchange rate mechanism of the EMS.

The medium-term stabilisation of the exchange rates is done by negotiations on the adaptation of the pivot or central rates. A structurally weak currency, that is a currency steadily valued at, say, around 10 per cent below the pivot rate, may need an adjustment of the central exchange rate. EMS countries have agreed not to proceed

Table 17.2   EMS bilateral central rates and margins of fluctuation (as of September 1993)

EMS intervention rates as of August 1993		Amsterdam in HFL	Frankfurt in DM	Brussels in BFR
HFL 100	S		103.058	2 125.60
	C	100	88.753	1 830.54
	B		76.433	1 576.45
DM 100	S	130.834		2 395.20
	C	112.673	100	2 062.55
	B	97.033		1 775.20
BFR 100	S	6.34340	5.630	
	C	5.46286	4.848	100
	B	4.70454	4.175	
DKR 100	S	34.3002	30.445	627.880
	C	29.5389	26.216	540.723
	B	25.4385	22.575	465.665
FF 100	S	39.0091	34.625	714.030
	C	33.5953	29.816	614.977
	B	28.9381	25.675	529.660
IRL 1	S	3.15450	2.800	57.7445
	C	2.71662	2.411	49.7289
	B	2.33952	2.076	42.8260
PTA 100	S	1.65368	1.468	30.2715
	C	1.42413	1.264	26.0696
	B	1.22644	1.088	22.4510
ESC 100	S	1.32266	1.174	24.212
	C	1.13906	1.011	20.851
	B	0.98094	0.871	17.957
ECU	C	2.19672	1.94964	40.2123

Note: S = Sell; C = Central; B = Buy.
Source: CEC.

Copenhagen in DKR	Paris in FF	Dublin in IRL	Madrid in PTA	Lisbon in ESC
393.105	345.650	42.7439	8 153.70	10 194.30
338.537	297.661	36.8105	7 021.83	8 779.18
291.544	256.350	31.7007	6 047.10	7 560.50
442.968	389.480	48.1696	9 191.20	11 481.10
381.443	335.386	41.4757	7 911.72	9 891.77
328.461	288.810	35.7143	6 812.00	8 517.90
21.4747	18.880	2.33503	445.418	556.89
18.4938	16.261	2.01090	383.589	479.59
15.9266	14.005	1.73176	330.342	413.02
	102.100	12.6261	2 408.50	3 011.20
100	87.926	10.8734	2 074.15	2 593.24
	75.720	9.36403	1 785.20	2 233.30
132.066		14.3599	2 739.30	3 424.80
113.732	100	12.3666	2 358.98	2 949.37
97.943		10.6500	2 031.50	2 540.00
10.6792	9.3895		225.503	276.938
9.1967	8.0863	1	190.755	238.495
7.9201	6.9640		164.276	205.389
5.5985	4.92250	0.60873		145.180
4.8213	4.23911	0.52423	100	125.027
4.1519	3.65050	0.45146		107.670
4.4777	3.93700	0.48688	92.876	
3.8562	3.39056	0.41929	79.983	100
3.3209	2.91990	0.36109	58.850	
7.43679	6.53883	0.80663	154.250	192.854

unilaterally with respect to such exchange rate changes (devaluation or revaluation), but make them subject to negotiations among all EMS partner countries and hence to their approval. The reason is that EMS countries have recognised both the danger of countries competing with one another by successive devaluations and the detrimental effect of sudden exchange rate changes on the interest of partner countries. The revaluations and devaluations of the currencies are chosen in such a way that the value of the ECU in terms of a third currency (such as the dollar) does not change in the operation.

One of the criteria of the TEU for joining the EMU is that a currency has observed the normal fluctuation margins provided for by the exchange rate mechanism of the EMS without severe tensions for at least two years and without devaluing against the currency of any other member state on its own initiative for the same period. If this criterion had had to be applied at the end of 1993, only six currencies would have qualified (Germany, Belgium/Luxemburg, Denmark, France, Netherlands). Three others devalued in 1993 (Spain, Portugal, Ireland), while three others do not participate (Italy, UK, Greece).

Evaluation of the EMS

The EMS was created to establish a zone of stable exchange rates in Europe, with a view to enhancing the efficiency of the internal markets for goods, services and production factors. Let us briefly consider how far those objectives have been realised.

First, stable exchange rates. For several years the system has worked very satisfactorily, producing a fair balance between flexibility (daily variations of exchange rates) and stability (central rates). For the medium term the situation is more complicated. We have to distinguish three periods.

- 1979–83. After a start in a turbulent international environment, realignments were relatively frequent, and some expensive lessons had to be learned (see Box 17.1).
- 1983–6. The number of realignments were few, as the result of more discipline and disinflation. As a consequence, the variability of the EMS currencies among themselves was reduced by almost half. The remaining variability corresponded to the variability of the fundamental determinants of exchange rates (Gros, 1987). This 'within' EMS variability was much smaller than that of a control group of non-EMS currencies (Ungerer *et al.*, 1986). The EMS has contributed to the convergence of inflation rates. Indeed average inflation has decreased and the parity changes have not fully matched the inflation differentials in

EMS countries, which has gained for monetary authorities in inflation-prone countries credibility for their monetary policies, intended to curb price increases (Giavazzi and Pagano, 1986).

- 1987–93. Capital controls were gradually removed. Inflation differentials decreased further, permitting the system to continue without realignments up to 1993. The EMS was thus extremely successful in stabilising exchange rates. However it was less so in terms of convergence. The fundamental values of some currencies got out of line with the central rates, notably the UK pound and the Italian lira, but also the Spanish peseta and the Portuguese escudo. For various political reasons, the authorities of these countries were not prepared to accept a devaluation of their currency. Several rounds of speculation then forced the necessary realignment to be made. The EMS came out of this crisis with less participants, with much broader margins, and with less credibility to force convergence upon national decision makers. Rising unemployment, expanding budget deficits and small political margins of governments made countries adopt policies that were not consistent with the demands of a small margin EMS. In a situation of multiple currencies and mobile capital, divergent policies will inevitably lead to a collapse of fixed parities.

Has the EMS also created the conditions for more efficient markets? This should be reflected in increased intra-union trade and capital movements (increase in migration is not an objective; see Chapter 9).

- *Trade.* Weak support for the thesis that the exchange rate certainty of the EMS has contributed to intra-EU trade comes from empirical econometric research (for example, Cushman, 1983; de Grauwe, 1987). Strong support comes from inquiries among representatives of industry and commerce, which always indicate exchange rate turbulence as a major hindrance to trade (De Lattre, 1985; AMUE, 1988).[9]
- *Capital.* Direct investment flows between EU countries were found to be negatively influenced by exchange rate uncertainty (Molle and Morsink, 1990; Morsink and Molle, 1991).

The EMS is weak in a number of respects. It has a minimal institutional structure. It is not a reserve system. The ECU is not a reserve currency. The European Monetary Institute (EMI) was only an embryo of a European monetary authority, which only handles the credit, accounting and reserve mechanisms of the EMS, its board of governors consisting of the governors of the national central banks, and its technical operations conducted by the Bank of International Settlements in Basle.

Macro policy: the need for convergence of inflation rates

The problem: high and divergent inflation rates

A monetary union cannot be sustained if inflation rates diverge. Indeed, as Figure 17.2 shows, in the long run higher than average inflation rates of EU countries inevitably lead to a corresponding depreciation of their currencies. The opposite is also true.[10] The conclusion is that countries need to bring their inflation rates in line (make them converge) with the inflation rates of their partner coun-

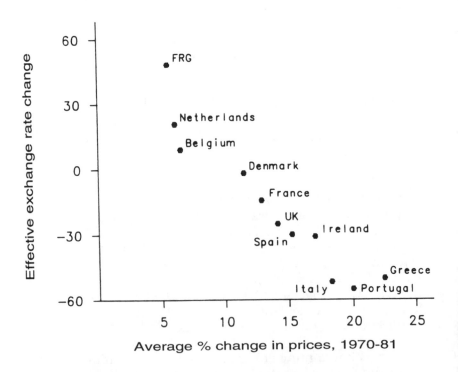

Figure 17.2   Inflation and currency depreciation or appreciation

Source: Cameron (1985).

tries. However this is not enough. Inflation has a certain number of negative economic effects, so low inflation is a desirable policy goal. So the double objective of a group of countries striving for an EMU is to maintain low inflation rates that show only a small divergence from the EU average. These objectives have indeed been taken up by the EU.

Table 17.3   Average annnual inflation rate (GDP price change), by country and period (%)

Country*	1960–72	1973–82	1983–92	1993 (estimates)
Netherlands	5.8	7.1	1.8	2.3
Germany	4.2	4.8	2.8	4.6
Belgium	3.9	7.2	3.7	2.8
Luxemburg	3.7	7.8	3.8	3.7
Denmark	6.3	10.1	4.4	1.0
France	4.6	10.8	4.5	2.5
UK	4.9	14.3	5.5	4.1
Ireland	6.6	14.8	5.5	3.5
Italy	4.9	17.0	7.7	5.2
Spain	6.7	16.1	7.9	5.0
Portugal	3.6	17.8	15.8	6.8
Greece	3.3	17.5	16.9	13.8
EU12	4.8	11.7	5.6	4.2
USA	3.3	7.8	4.0	—
Japan	5.5	7.1	1.8	—

* ranking by the 1983–92 performance.
Source: Eurostat, *National Accounts, Aggregates, 1960–1985*; CEC, *European Economy*, Supplements.

Let us see how the EU countries have performed on these two scores. First, inflation rates of the various EU countries show both increases and decreases (Table 17.3). The economic crisis of 1973 brought about a tremendous increase in overall EU inflation. Since 1983, inflation has been cut back considerably. Many governments have indeed chosen an anti-inflationary policy. Second, inflation rates have shown considerable divergence between EU countries. On the basis of these differences over the whole period 1973–93 we can distinguish three blocs of countries:

- below average rates, inflation-shy countries, mostly in northern Europe;
- about average rates (France, UK, Ireland);
- above average rates, 'inflation-prone' or 'inflation-permissive' countries, all lying in the Mediterranean basin.

What are the causes of inflation and of different inflation rates among countries? An important external factor is the price development of imported goods. Price increases of intermediate goods push up the cost price of home-produced final goods. Price increases of imported consumer goods push up the cost of living and hence wage demands. However there are also internal factors that play important roles. Schematically these internal factors can be grouped in the following three categories (see, for example, Frisch, 1983).

Institutionalist   Trade union action to increase wages beyond the increase in productivity results in a cost push. This mechanism is most effective in countries with a fragmented labour market structure (like Italy). It is least effective in countries with a neocorporatist structure (like The Netherlands), characterised by encompassing organisations on both the employers' and workers' side that involve collective bargaining supervised by the central government (for example, Seidel, 1983; Crouch, 1985).

Monetarist   Price increases result from expansion of the money supply beyond the increase in the total product available (Friedman and Freidman, 1980). This results in general from governments spending more than their income, which is reflected in an increase in the public budget deficit (Cameron, 1985). This largely explains the high inflation in the third group of countries (such as Italy and Greece).

Structuralist   Wage uniformity disregards structural differences, like the dichotomy between a sheltered and an exposed sector in the economy (Maynard and van Ryckeghem, 1976; Magnifico, 1985). In other words, the application of the fairness principle makes every branch and region follow the increase in the most productive part of the economy, notwithstanding differences between sectors (for example, manufacturing v. services) or regions (for example, London v. a provincial town) in the increase in labour productivity.

The average EU inflation rate and the national differences in inflation rates have decreased in recent years, as Table 17.3 shows. The causes of this convergence towards a low inflation average can be found in changes in all three factors cited:

- Trade union power has decreased everywhere, employers' organisations have obtained more flexibility and many governments have tended to withdraw from political exchange in labour markets (Ferner and Hyman, 1992).
- Many countries of Europe that traditionally have had large deficits have adopted fairly strict budgetary policies, sometimes at the cost of considerable unemployment (for example, Spain). On the other hand, a country like the FRG that has always been a model of public finance has had to expand expenditure very considerably so as to cope with the integration of the former GDR.
- More and more branches have come under the pressure of international competition and have come to realise that wage and productivity increases need to be in line in order for them to stay in business. Moreover employers have been rather successful in promoting differentiation and in disregarding claims for economy-wide equality in wage matters.

The EU has decided to create a monetary union. As a monetary union can only be sustained if inflation rates keep in line, a first criterion for joining the EMU should be that the divergence of the inflation rate of a country from the EU average be small. Low inflation being an accepted policy goal, there is a need for taking a measure of good performance as a second criterion. The solution that has been adopted for the practical application of this dual definition of the inflation criterion by the Treaty on European Union is that a member country can only enter the EMU if its inflation rate is below the average rate of the three EU member countries with the lowest inflation plus 1.5 per cent. Had the 1993 situation been chosen as a reference year, the threshold would have been 3.4 per cent. This is a very low rate of inflation if compared to the EU average over the past 25 years. However, as it is only slightly higher than the average of the four countries that performed best over the 1983–93 period, it may very well be a good reference value for the actual decision on EMU membership. This implies that, if the EMU is to start with a significant number of members, many member states will have to make an important effort to lower further their inflation rates.

Government deficit and government debt

In economic terms it might have been sufficient to specify only the inflation criterion for membership of the EMU and leave the type of measures that are needed to come up to that criterion to individual member states. However, in a world of free capital movements, an EMU is only sustainable if the markets are convinced of the firm long-term commitment of the governments of the participating countries to sound principles of public finance. Indicators of this commitment to disciplined behaviour are a small budgetary deficit and a sustainable size of the public debt of the member states. In line therewith, the TEU specifies two more criteria for joining the EMU: no excessive budget deficits and no excessive government debt. The concept of 'excessive' is not easy to translate into numerical values. On the one hand, one should allow governments sufficient flexibility to cope with problems of different nature; on the other, a limitation is necessary as governments will be tempted to use all the available leeway to avoid painful decisions. There is no way of scientifically determining the level at which these two criteria need to be set. So the practical solution chosen in the TEU has been to set early 1990 EU averages as criteria: deficit should not exceed 3 per cent of the GDP and debt should not exceed 60 per cent of GDP.

What would the application of these two criteria imply?[11] For the past and present, the performance of the EU countries on these two criteria (Table 17.4) shows two things:

- the EU as a whole has recently moved away from the targets, as both government spending and government borrowing increased owing to the working of the built-in stabilisers during a recession;
- only very few countries do actually fulfil these two requirements for joining the EMU and a considerable effort is needed during the 1990s to improve the situation.

A national government has limited possibilities of making use of the monetary financing of (excessive) deficits in cases where the national central bank can pursue independently, that is free of government interference, a policy of price stability. Indeed the independence of the German and Dutch central banks is often cited as the reason for the good performance of these countries in matters of controlling inflation. Other countries have now started to give more independence to their national central banks, too, in order to improve the conditions for curbing inflation.

Interest rate levels

The durability of the convergence achieved by the member states and of the participation in the Exchange Rate Mechanism is reflected in the long-term interest rate levels. Indeed these rates are dependent, first, on the expectations of the financial markets as to the future rates of inflation in the country at hand and, next, on the solvency of its government. So a high long-term interest rate may signal a lack of

Table 17.4   Nominal convergence towards EMU criteria, 1985–93

	Deficit (% of GDP)			Debt (% of GDP)			Long-term interest rate (%)		
	1985	1990	1993	1985	1990	1993	1985	1990	1993
Germany	1.2	2.0	4.6	43	44	46	6.9	8.9	7.5
France	2.9	1.5	5.9	46	47	52	10.9	9.9	8.2
Italy	12.6	10.9	10.4	82	98	112	14.3	13.4	12.0
Netherlands	4.8	4.9	3.8	70	79	82	7.3	9.0	7.7
Belgium	9.0	5.8	7.0	120	128	134	10.6	10.1	8.2
Luxemburg	–6.2	0.0	2.0	14	7	8	9.5	8.6	8.0
UK	2.9	1.3	7.7	59	40	53	10.6	11.1	8.6
Denmark	2.0	1.5	4.4	77	67	76	11.6	11.0	10.2
Ireland	11.2	2.5	3.4	108	102	99	12.7	10.1	9.1
Spain	6.9	3.9	4.7	45	45	50	13.4	14.7	12.4
Portugal	10.1	5.5	5.7	71	68	66	25.4	16.8	12.4
Greece	13.6	18.6	13.1	63	95	106	15.8	23.0	21.8
EU	4.9	4.0	6.3	59	60	67	10.6	10.9	9.4

Source: Commission of the European Communities, 'Annual Economic Report for 1993', *European Economy*, no. 54, March 1993; *European Economy*, Supplement A; *Recent economic trends*, nos 6/7, June/July 1993.

policy discipline in the country in question. For that reason the TEU has opted for the divergence of the long-term interest rate as an additional criterion for joining the EMU. In practice this criterion means that, observed over a period of one year before the examination, a member state has had a nominal long-term interest rate on its government bonds that does not exceed by more than two percentage points that of at most the three best performing member states in terms of price stability.

To illustrate the working of the criterion (see Table 17.4) one may take the 1993 situation; the three best performing countries on inflation were Denmark, France and the Netherlands. The average of their long-term interest rates is 8.7, so the threshold value is 10.7. One sees that quite a large number of countries come up to this criterion. Were 1993 values to be applied, only the four Mediterranean countries would not qualify for EMU on this point, as they have to cope with high-risk premia on their long-term bonds, financial markets being concerned about inflation prospects of these countries.

In practice, this criterion may be of limited relevance. Indeed it is unlikely that a member country that fulfils the criteria on inflation, on budget deficits and on government debt will not also fulfil the interest rate criterion, the more so because the margin of 2 per cent is fairly generous.

From EMS to EMU

We recall that the TEU makes the transition to the EMU conditional on five criteria of convergence of national economic performance (Articles 104.c, 109j and adjoint protocols):

- inflation rate not higher than 1.5 per cent above the average of the three countries with the lowest inflation rates;
- long-term interest rate not more than 2 per cent above the rates of the three countries with the lowest inflation rates;
- devaluation of currency not experienced in the two years preceding the entrance into the union;
- budget deficits not in excess of 3 per cent of the GDP;
- government debt not in excess of 60 per cent of the GDP.

The application of the criteria for participation in the EMU to the currently available evidence on convergence performance shows that there are three categories of countries:

- Countries that either fulfil all the criteria or show sufficient convergence to the threshold values for most of the criteria. This group consists of Germany, France, the Benelux and Denmark. Ireland is moving towards joining this group.
- A country that may opt out, but may also qualify for membership, viz. the UK.
- Countries that have rather severe problems in matching most of the criteria of convergence; this group consists of Italy, Spain, Portugal and Greece.

In view of the present economic difficulties it is very unlikely that the third group will be able to reach the target levels of convergence by the end of the century. The road these countries have to go is probably too long and too bumpy to get there in time. Which way the British government is going to decide is difficult to predict, but one cannot discount the possibility of a British opting out. This implies that an EU12-wide Monetary Union is unlikely to be achieved within the time schedule of the TEU. One wonders how the future will then take shape within the legal framework of the TEU. Let us analyse two possible scenarios.

Slow-down   A strict application of the criteria and a poor performance by a number of member states can in principle lead to a postponement of the creation of the MU. In practice this would lead to a prolongation of the second stage. There are important negative aspects to this scenario. First, it is not in the interest of the countries that have already borne the cost of adaptation and now have to wait for the benefits of MU; the unstable institutional environment of the second stage may even lead to extra cost for them. Also the lagging countries will have no incentive to observe more policy discipline if they know that the EMU will anyway not start without them.

Duality Starting the EMU at the date foreseen in the Treaty with only a limited number of members will avoid the disadvantages of the slow-down scenario. It will permit the core group to move on and experiment with the MU and the others to join as soon as they are ready. This has the advantage of flexibility. Countries will tend to speed up the convergence and qualify for membership because they will not want to forgo the benefits of EMU and pay an extra cost in terms of risk premia on interest rates and so on. The main extra disadvantage of this scenario is of a political nature: non-participating countries will not like to be stigmatised as being of secondary rank. The main advantage for these countries is exchange rate flexibility. However the EU as a whole should not favour this, as it may well lead to competitive devaluation, which will put a strain on the working of the internal market.

Overlooking the advantages and disadvantages of both scenarios, the second seems to be the more likely one. This is the more so because several EFTA countries that have applied for EU membership are likely to be able to fulfil the demands for EMU membership together with the core group (for example, Austria and Norway).

Summary and conclusions

- The EU has been slow to develop coordinated (let alone harmonised) stabilisation policies. The recent ratification of the TEU has, however, set the very ambitious target of an Economic and Monetary Union.
- Stable exchange rates are the main objective of European monetary cooperation in view of the welfare gains they bring international traders and investors. The European Monetary System, with its centrepiece the ECU, has for quite some time been successful in bringing about such stability.
- With free capital movement and independent policy making of national governments, it is difficult to maintain the stability of the exchange rates. Therefore national policies need to be con-

strained by European rules in order to maintain the conditions for stability.

- Countries of the EU that want to participate in the setting up of the Monetary Union have to fulfil five criteria: low inflation, no excessive deficits on the public budget, not too heavy a debt burden, a long-term interest rate in line with the rates of the countries with low inflation, and no devaluation of their currency.

- Convergence towards the threshold values of these criteria implies a significant policy effort for virtually all member countries. For some countries, the distance to be bridged is such that it is not certain whether they will be able to join the EMU before the end of the century.

Notes

1   Interdependence is more than openness. An open economy is dependent on the outside world, but small open economies do not necessarily have an impact on the economies of partners. Structural interdependence is notably not the only effect of integration with partner countries. To this needs to be added the effect of openness on the rest of the world. The vulnerability to shocks from outside the group (such as an oil shock) is changed under the influence of group integration, and an effective response will need coordinated action.

2   This approach has supplanted the more traditional approach to monetary integration, which started from the Phillips curve (Fleming, 1971; Corden, 1972b; de Grauwe, 1975). The latter approach was not very well suited, for two reasons; first because the relation does not hold in the long run, and second because the approach does not take into account the policy reactions of other countries. Quite a few authors have tried to develop 'international' macro models (Cooper, 1983). However the fact has gradually become clear that traditional economic modelling is not rich enough to capture the complex interrelationships between private and public economic agents, and in particular the role of expectations and the reactions of other countries.

3   This currency may still take different forms in different countries (Belgian and Luxemburg francs, for instance).

4   Evidently, the exchange rate with all third currencies as well as balance-of-payment questions with the rest of the world will then become matters of common policy, the Union Monetary Authority controlling the pool of exchange reserves.

5   But even if the EU had been authorised to pursue budgetary policies, their effect would have been doubtful with an EU budget amounting to no more than about 1 per cent of total GDP.

6   This type of convergence is also called 'nominal convergence' in opposition to real convergence, which is the reduction of the differences in wealth levels between the member states. The latter is taken up in Chapter 18.

7   The original weights of 1974 were chosen to make the ECU correspond to the Special Drawing Right (SDR) of the IMF (which is also a basket, but of different composition, so that the rates of ECU and SDR have since diverged).

8   For a description of the genesis of the EMS, see Ludlow (1982); for the basic

text see, CEC (1979d) and for an elaborate description, see Gros and Thygesen (1992).

9   Uncertainty in exchange rates has an influence on both imports (sudden increases in production cost through intermediate goods) and exports (sudden fall in a country's competitiveness when its own currency appreciates) (De Lattre, 1985). Next there is the negative influence of floating on the results of foreign investment policy, and, for MNF, the influence on the value of the balance sheet. Although financial markets have responded with different products (forward markets and hedging mechanisms) to cover the risk of floating, short-term exchange rate volatility still entails cost. Moreover, for many risks, coverage is difficult to obtain. This is notably the case for long-run misalignments (Steinherr, 1985). So many firms remain exposed to such financial risk that they prefer exchange rate certainty to floating.

10   These relations remain the same if other OECD countries, including the larger ones, are also taken into account.

11   The criteria for budget deficit and debt can indeed be applied with some room for interpretation. If the development of the indicator is in the right direction and if the reference value is approached, the Council can decide that the conditions are sufficiently met to permit the country in question to join. However at this stage it is not yet decided how this room for interpretation will be used.

18 Redistribution: Cohesion Policies

Introduction

There is a general assumption, if not conviction, among economists and politicians that competitive markets (efficiency) generate considerable inequality. Government intervention is then required to reduce this inequality by redistribution. The EU creates a need for such redistribution on the European scale. Indeed the EU's main objective is to step up efficiency and stimulate economic growth by integrating the markets of goods and production factors and by setting up flanking policies. The structural changes implied (relocation of economic activities, changing composition of sectoral activity) have negative consequences for certain sectors of society. The most vulnerable groups tend to be concentrated, on the one hand, in particular regions or even countries (regional dimension) and, on the other, in particular sectors of the labour force (social dimension).

To reap the benefits of integration, the EU has taken it upon itself to redistribute funds so as to help these groups to adapt to the new situation. It considers that in this way the cohesion of its constituent parts will be improved. EU involvement has developed gradually. In the 1950s and 1960s a hesitant start was made. Real political commitment to a European regional and social policy was achieved at the 1972 Paris Conference of the European Council. In the following 15 years the policies were given shape and substance. With the adoption of the Single European Act (Article 130A), confirmed by the Maastricht Treaty, redistribution has become a firm obligation: 'In order to promote its overall harmonious development, the Community shall develop and pursue its actions leading to the strengthening of its economic and social cohesion.'

Cohesion has no clear definition. It is best understood as *the degree to which disparities in social and economic welfare between different regions or groups within the Community are politically and socially tolerable.* Whether cohesion is achieved is thus largely a political question.

421

However the contribution of economics is in the study of the development of disparities and the possibilities of influencing the system in such a way so as to decrease disparities (NIESR, 1991).

In the following sections we will go into the way the EU has devised its cohesion policies.[1] The chapter is arranged as follows. In a first section we will examine the theoretical foundations. Next we will deal with regional and social policies in successive sections. For both we will follow the same approach, which consists, first, of the assessment of the major problems; second, of the presentation of the objectives of the policy; third, of its gradual development; fourth, of a critical examination of some of its major elements, in particular the Funds; and finally, of an evaluation of its results. The chapter will be rounded off with a brief summary of the major findings.

Some theoretical aspects

Foundations for national intervention

In a free market economy, distribution of income is determined by the demand for and supply of factor services, and hence depends largely on factor endowments. If we look at persons rather than categories (labour, capital and so on), we see that endowments or abilities are unequally distributed among the population. Income from labour being largely determined by the ability to perform highly valued tasks, the resulting distribution of income is likely to be highly unequal among persons and households. Some factors may even end up being unemployed and hence be without any income.

A complex interplay of geographical and economic factors determines the location of people with different endowments and of economic activities with different income-generating capacities and hence the social and regional distribution of welfare. Under some conditions the system tends towards less, under others towards more, disparity. Because the system, when left to its own devices, appears on many occasions to be unable to achieve a good equilibrium, governments have devised policies to bring about a more equal distribution of wealth over persons, categories and regions. Traditionally two reasons for intervention are given.

Efficiency   This argument, of an economic nature, says that measures of regional and social policy help towards the efficient allocation of resources.[2] Total welfare increases, as resources that are badly utilised or not utilised at all will participate (better) in production. Some examples may illustrate this:

- Regional. Unemployed human capital will not be put to work by private investors unless conditions for a profitable operation in that region (for example, in terms of infrastructure) are met. A government programme for such infrastructure removes the obstruction to development.
- Social. A programme for the retraining of workers for taking up jobs in a new industry after being made redundant in an industry that had lost its competitive position will adapt the human capital to new conditions. Private initiative would not have taken this up.

Equity This argument, of a socio-political nature, says that large groups of the population feel that inequality is morally unacceptable. Total welfare would increase if the inequalities between groups and regions were removed. Again we may give some examples:

- Regional. Minimum standards of provision of public goods may be set for all regions (for example, number of hospital beds per inhabitant). The governments' budget then transfers the money to regions that do not have the capacity to generate sufficient revenues themselves.
- Social. Minimum personal income standards may be set. Transfer payments from the most to the least affluent can take the form of detailed schemes of social security: old-age pensions, unemployment benefits, insurance against illness and so on – schemes generally associated with the welfare state. Another way is the definition of basic social rights of workers, including minimum standards for the quality of occupations (safety, health, hours of work, length of paid holidays and so on) and industrial relations (such as collective bargaining, strikes and employee co-management) (Kolvenbach and Hanau, 1988).

The above arguments indicate why government intervention for cohesion purposes is needed. They do not say how much redistribution is needed to obtain the policy goals. To give an answer to that question one needs to make detailed economic calculations, on the one hand, and political trade-offs on the other (Okun, 1975; Padoa-Schioppa *et al.*, 1987).

Foundations for international intervention

The fundamental ideas of different schools of thought on interpersonal redistribution can be adapted to produce the three criteria for the setting up of international redistribution schemes (Findlay, 1982):

Merit   This is an economic concept often used in a utilitarian view of redistribution. It is akin to the efficiency argument. In an international setting its basic idea is that redistribution from richer to poorer states is required up to the point where the gains to union welfare are offset by the losses in economic efficiency incurred by the union as a whole.

Need   This is a moral concept of distributional justice that has a strong tradition, particularly in Marxist-oriented thinking. It is akin to the equity argument. In an international integration context it involves the transfer of resources from rich to poor member states of the union in order to provide the latter with the means for keeping up basic standards of welfare (see, for example, Haack, 1983).

Belonging   This is a legal criterion that restricts the claims for redistribution to participants in schemes of social cooperation for mutual advantage. This has important consequences. Since such schemes coincide traditionally with nation states, claims can be made only by citizens of the specific state involved. Because for participants in economic integration schemes the boundaries of cooperation tend to extend beyond the national framework, it is logical to extend distributional justice to citizens of all member states of the union.[3]

Why are union redistribution policies necessary?

Countries participate in integration schemes because they expect welfare gains from them. However there are also costs involved in progressive integration that may be unevenly distributed. These are different for the various stages of integration.

Customs Union   The internal liberalisation and the development of a common foreign trade policy deprives member states of the trade policy instruments by which they had supported activities of certain social groups or of regionally concentrated industries. In the process of specialisation resources are set free that need to adapt to other occupations. This often entails the loss of expertise, costs of moving and so on. For some countries the benefits may take a long time to materialise, whereas the adjustment costs occur immediately. For others, gains may be quick to come about, while the costs are limited. In other words, costs and benefits may be very unequally distributed among countries.

Common market   The problems are aggravated when the free movement of production factors is introduced, and labour and capital begin to flow to the regions offering the best locations for investment. Now production factors may not always move in such a way as to bring about a better equilibrium. Capital in particular tends to move to those areas that have already secured the best position. Labour may move from low-wage to high-wage countries, but that may entail high social and personal cost. So these movements aggravate the risk of an unbalanced development.

Economic and monetary union   The setting up of an EMU further curtails the instruments available to national states. They are losing, for example, the possibility of influencing the equilibrium with partner countries by exchange rate and monetary policies. In an EMU this requires the moving of production factors (Giersch, 1949; Williamson, 1976; Molle, *et al.*, 1993). Furthermore, with the progress of harmonisation, especially on the industrial and social planes, national instruments lose much of their implicit power to control regional developments.

Countries that find incomes sinking below those of others, and understand they are apt to be losers in the integration game, may be inclined to opt out. Although solidarity with integration schemes is not marked solely by immediate economic gains, for some countries the absence of such gains may become a political factor important enough to inspire compensation schemes.

The effects of integration on regional equilibrium may be both positive and negative. Much depends on the initial situation, the capacity of regions to adapt, the growth effects of integration on all regions and so on (see, among others, Williamson, 1976; Vanhove and Klaassen, 1987, Ch. 6; Molle, 1990).

What form could international redistribution schemes take?

The schemes drawn up in confederations, federations and unitary states for the interregional redistribution of resources differ as to the combination they use of income instruments (tax, social security) and expenditure instruments (grants, programmes) (MacDougall *et al.*, 1977). The highest forms of integration, like federations, will use the income instruments dealing directly with the individual; these are most effective as federal powers over income taxes and social security are substantial and the federal budget represents a considerable portion of GDP. During the lower forms of integration (customs union), redistribution occurs rather through the expenditure instruments involving different layers of government, the reasons are as follows:

- expenditure can be tailored to specific needs (including compensation of negative integration effects);

- governments are generally reluctant to let unions decide or 'internal' redistribution matters;
- the redistributive power of expenditure is greater than that of income instruments.

There are two main ways to handle the redistribution of funds through the union budget (Musgrave and Musgrave, 1989).

General-purpose grants take the form of block payments from the union to a member country. The underlying philosophy is one of needs. These have to be evaluated for each individual state against a standard for public-sector programmes and the capacity of the member state to finance them. The union has no control over the actual use of the funds thus transferred, which thus risk being used in a way not expedient to structural improvement.

Specific-purpose grants, not having the same drawback, are the most common. Here the union decides on the type of programme that should be set up and to which it is prepared to give financial aid. Its inspiration is of the utilitarian type: such grants are considered to lead to optimum welfare in the long run, because they lead to a better allocation of available production factors to whole sections of the economy.

Redistribution schemes should be designed in such a way as to help along (or alternatively to do the least possible harm to) the achievement of the targets of allocation and stabilisation policies. This implies that they must help to create a viable base for future-oriented economic activities. Examples of this type are financial aid programmes for specific social groups, designed to retrain workers who have become redundant because of the structural changes of the economy due to integration. While such schemes are mostly short-term, others are of a structural nature. An example of the latter is a programme for the improvement of the infrastructure in regions that are far below the average level of development, aimed at creating the conditions required for self-sustained regional growth.

The equalisation effect of such policies is illustrated by Figure 18.1. Suppose income growth ($\dot{y}$) is determined completely by increases in production factor availability and productivity, together called p_f. Suppose further that country B is not only a slow-growth but also a low-level income country (OB_1), while country A is not only a fast-growth but also a high-level income country (OA). To make income levels in the Union converge, the curve of country B has to move upwards, with the intercept moving from point OB_1 through OB_2 to OB_3, which is beyond point OA (the structural growth in country A).

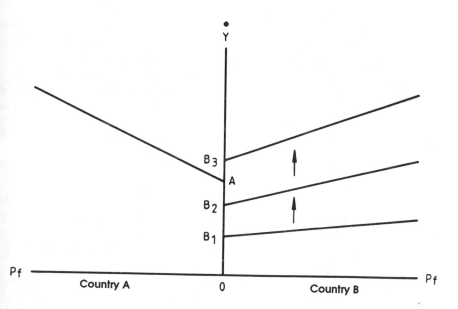

Figure 18.1 Policies for intra-Union balanced growth

Regional disparities and policy

Assessing the regional problems[4]

The European Union shows a considerable diversity in regional situations. For many regions these do not give rise to particular concern at the European level. For others they tend, however, to become particularly difficult, resulting from deficiencies in the infrastructure, production sector, labour force qualifications and so on. These problem regions tend to fall into three types.

Traditionally backward regions These regions have developed hardly any manufacturing or service industry and are still largely oriented to agriculture. Especially in southern member states, agriculture is often not very productive. This type of region is generally characterised by a peripheral situation, a deficient infrastructure, a meagre endowment with business services and a lack of skilled labour with a good industrial and service tradition. Below-average GDP per head is a main indicator of problems here.

Regions of industrial decline   These regions played a leading role at a certain stage of economic development, but have landed in difficul ties as production conditions changed. This type of region is gener ally marked by inadequate infrastructure and serious problems ir old industrial, as well as residential, areas. They often have a highly specialised manpower whose skills are, however, at odds with mod ern requirements. High unemployment is the main indicator of dis tress here.

Regions of rural restructuring   A concentration on agriculture that lacks development potential, a decline of the service sector and long communication distances build up barriers to development in this type of region.

The considerable differences in economic development between mem ber countries, and between the regions of each of these countries have a negative effect on cohesion. To approximate the developmen of cohesion, one can follow over time the development of indicators on the disparity between member countries and regions. Examples are the level of income per capita, the productivity per working person, and the availability and accessibility of environmental goods cultural infrastructure, leisure activities and so on.

The disparity in income per head among the European regions i generally accepted as the key indicator of cohesion. The 10 mos favoured regions in the European Union are three times 'richer' thar the 10 poorest (measured in GDP per head,[5] but also by level o infrastructure, capital endowment and so on). This difference has increased considerably with the southern extension of the Union.

The disparity between all European regions decreased consider ably over the period of analysis (first row of Table 18.1). The causes of this decrease in disparity can be found to a large extent in the decrease in the differences in wealth between countries (rows 2 and 3):

- the movement of capital: direct investment has gone from rich to poor countries (see Chapter 10) and manufacturing plants have moved from central to peripheral areas of the member countries (see Klaassen and Molle, 1982; see also Chapter 10 or direct investment);
- the migration of workers: contrary to that of capital, labou movement was rather centripetal (see Chapter 9);
- the creation of the welfare state: the provision of such welfare services as schools, hospitals, transfer payments and social se curity systems has strengthened the economic base of the less affluent regions (Molle, 1986).

he ranking of European regions by their level of prosperity evi-
lences a remarkable stability. Indeed, throughout the 1950–90 period,
he 'peripheral' regions of Mediterranean countries were always in
he lowest positions, while some urban regions in northern Europe
vere consistently at the top. Only two significant shifts are recorded:
.ll German regions moved strongly upward, and all regions of the
JK and Belgium fell back.

**Table 18.1   Indices[a] of regional disparities of wealth in the EU12,
1950–90**

	1950	1960	1970	1980	1990
disparity among regions	0.124	0.102	0.078	0.066	0.054
disparity among countries	0.095	0.081	0.061	0.054	0.036
2 : 1 (%)	76	79	79	78	66

Theil indices of gross regional product by head of population, based on exchange rates.
ource: Molle *et al.* (1980); Molle (1990), additional estimates.

Assessing the national disparities

he disparity in regional wealth levels is to a large extent determined
>y the disparities that exist between the countries of the EU (row 3 in
[able 18.1). Some member states are particularly poor: GDP per head
evels in Ireland, Greece and Portugal stood at 50–60 per cent of the
:U average in 1990. The underlying factors, such as resources, the
evel of schooling of the labour force, the access to markets and, in
>articular, the social and economic institutional infrastructure, are
1ational rather than regional characteristics. So the improvement of
1ational factors is an important condition for the catching up of the
agging countries and, subsequently, regional cohesion.

The objective of the EU is the *constant improvement of the living and
vorking conditions of the European peoples* and reducing the differences
>etween the various countries. In practical terms this means, first,
he fostering of economic growth for all countries and, second, the
:onvergence of wealth levels among member countries. The EU has
1chieved these two targets (Table 18.2):

Growth   The average for the countries that now make up the EU was
1lmost 3 per cent a year over a 40-year period and more. The pace was

Table 18.2   Average yearly growth rates of GDP (volume) and development of GDP/P (EU12 = 100) for the 12 EU member countries, 1950–93

Country	Growth %			Level (index)			
	1950–73	1973–85	1986–91	1950 ECU	1990 ECU	1990 PPP	1993 PPP
Denmark	3.4	1.7	1.5	153	139	107	107
Germany*	5.6	1.9	3.1	93	128	117	102
Luxemburg	2.5	1.5	5.0	201	125	124	130
France	3.6	1.6	2.8	136	115	112	112
Netherlands	4.4	1.1	2.5	100	102	101	103
Belgium	2.5	1.6	2.9	166	105	105	106
UK	1.8	1.3	2.5	140	93	101	96
Italy	4.2	1.6	2.7	71	103	102	104
Ireland	2.9	2.0	4.0	81	66	68	72
Spain	5.3	1.1	4.2	35	69	75	77
Greece	6.7	1.5	1.6	30	35	47	48
Portugal	4.3	1.3	4.3	35	35	56	58
EU12**	3.9	1.5	2.9	100	100	100	97

PPP = purchasing power parities.
 *   in 1993, including former GDR.
 **   EU excluding former GDR = 100.
Source: OECD, *National Account Statistics*, several years; Eurostat, *National accounts (ESA* Review, several years. National figures on GDP made comparable with exchange rate figures.

different in different periods. First there was a long period of high and stable growth that lasted up to the beginning of the 1970s (first oil crisis). This coincided with the first extension. Next there was a period of adjustment, with low growth; the end of this period coincided with the second extension. Finally there was a period of new dynamism.

Convergence of wealth[6]   Immediately after the Second World War, some of the countries now making up the EU12 were very poor (Portugal Greece and Spain, to a lesser extent Italy, and, compared to the EU9 also Germany) while others (Belgium, Denmark, the UK and France) were relatively well off. Differences in wealth in 1990 were much less than those in 1950. This was due to higher than average growth rates for member countries with an income level below the EU average. On the other hand, growth in the UK was below average (Kaldor 1966; Hudson and Williams, 1986; Boltho, 1982).

To find out why in different countries the output grows at different rates, economists have followed several strands of thought. The four that have received most attention in the European context are the following:

Supply of input   Following the well-known neoclassical production function, growth differs because countries have different inputs of production factors (for example, Denison, 1967). Inputs (sources of growth) can be further differentiated: by labour, total employment, hours worked, age and sex distribution, or education; by capital, investment in machinery, dwellings and international assets. Productivity growth is often derived as a residual (for instance, Chenery *et al.*, 1986); in other models technical progress is traced with the help of such indicators as the progress of knowledge, or the lag in the application of the best practices (Cornwall, 1977; Cripps and Tarling, 1973). A disadvantage of the input approach (which generally explains only half the differences between countries) is that the explanatory factors are themselves in need of explanation. Indeed to state that Germany enjoyed a very high growth rate because it increased its labour force with immigrant labour (see Chapter 9) is unsatisfactory; an explanation is also wanted as to why Germany could increase its output so much in the first place, to the extent that additional labour was needed.

Terms of trade   Countries confronted by high prices on their import markets because of external shocks (oil, for instance) and with lower prices on their export markets because of fierce competition will show lower GDP growth rates than countries in more fortunate circumstances (Bruno, 1984).

Institutions   Individuals and firms with similar interests tend to group together to obtain advantages for themselves at the expense of other groups of society, or of society as a whole (Olson, 1983). By their collective action, special-interest groups reduce overall efficiency and hence aggregate income. Such distributional coalitions also reduce the rate of economic growth because they slow down a society's capacity to adopt new technology and to reallocate resources in response to changing conditions. Moreover they raise the level and complexity of regulation and government intervention in markets, diminishing still more the capacity to adapt. The more a society accumulates special-interest groups and collusions, the lower its rate of growth. The relevance of this theory to the EU is best illustrated with some country situations. The post-war economic miracle of Germany is explained by the fact that the Nazis broke the influence of many special-interest groups, and the allied powers did away

with the influence of many others (large industrial trusts). The slow
growth of the UK, on the other hand, is attributed to that country's
long-term stable evolution, giving rise to a dense network of power
ful special-interest groups, such as trade unions and the upper-class
establishment.[7]

Integration   New competitors challenge the positions created prior
to the integration by special-interest groups. Collusion of firms un
der sanction of the government becomes more difficult, trade union
power in sheltered industries is diminished by competition from
outside, and so on. The access to the EU has had a very clear influ
ence on the relatively high growth figures of France in the 1960–7
period (Hennart, 1983), of Ireland in the 1973–85 period and of Ire
land, Spain and Portugal in recent years (larger than EU average)
(CEC, 1988a).

Policy objectives

The unequal distribution of welfare over regions has obliged both
national and European authorities to intervene. To obtain maximum
effect, the European regional policy is conducted in cooperation with
the member states; indeed EU regional policy is not a substitute for
but a complement to, the national regional policies.
   The main objective of European regional policy is twofold:

*   to improve the situation in existing problem regions. The three
    categories of regions, traditionally backward, industrial restruc
    turing and rural (defined in the previous section) each have a
    specific approach (called, respectively, objective 1, 2 and 5b
    regions) (for example, CEC, 1977; CEC, 1990a);
*   to prevent new regional disparities that could result from struc
    tural changes in the European and world economy. Some of
    these are due to integration, others are the result of the continu
    ous changes that occur in technology, in environment, in social
    values and in world politics.

The arguments for the EU regional policy follow the theoretical ones
we have indicated before:

Efficiency   The economic argument for a European regional policy
has been central in each of the stages of its development. An example
from the crisis period of the late 1970s may be illustrative in this
respect. The lack of alternative activities in 'steel regions', where
substantial cutbacks in employment were necessary, has induced
certain member states to give heavy support to the established in

lustry, to which other member states responded by threatening to :lose their frontiers to these subsidised products. Now that would nean a direct violation of the founding principles of the EU (free narket and international specialisation), so the lack of an effective egional policy to help the regions develop new activities put the /ery functioning of the EU in jeopardy.

Equity The social argument for European regional policy has only ;radually come to the fore. Until the mid-1980s neither the social limension (see, for instance, Vandamme, 1986) nor the public sup->ort for a fiscal contribution to assist regional development in a lifferent EU member country had developed much (CEC, 1980). The :U now puts more emphasis on social and human aspects as neces-;ary complements to purely economic ones; this is in line with the ncreased official and public support for international–interregional ransfer of funds for raising living standards and giving more equal :hances for development of the problem regions (CEC, 1991c).

Gradual development

[he European regional policy has developed gradually under the nfluence of progressive deepening and widening. The major stages :an be described as follows:

- *1955–75*. Regional imbalances were already being debated at the Messina Conference. The fathers of the EU were well aware of the regional problems; this is evident from the preamble of the Treaty of Rome, according to which the member states were 'anxious to reduce the differences existing between the various regions and the backwardness of the less favoured regions'. In spite of warnings by academics (such as Giersch, 1949) that European integration spelled problems for certain regions, the EEC Treaty made no provisions for a European regional policy in the proper sense. However, during the functioning of the Common Market, such problems did indeed arise (for example, with coal and steel regions like Wallonia).
- *1975–85*. The northern enlargement of the EU increased the regional imbalances. The UK, afraid of losing out to its conti- nental competitors, on the one hand, and of an unfavourable distribution of receipts from and payments to the EU budget, on the other, had obtained in the negotiations of accession an assurance that a European regional policy would be set up. This was realised in the second half of the 1970s. Large sums of money were put into a distribution scheme using specific pur- pose grants as the instrument.

- *1985–93.* Two factors caused a further stepping up of the re gional policy efforts. The first was the drive towards more allocative efficiency through the completion of the internal mar ket. The second was the enlargement with three less developed new member states. To improve the economic and social cohe sion in a wider and deeper EU, the resources devoted to redis tribution were doubled, the target groups restricted, the proce dures improved and the instruments refocused (CEC, 1990a).
- *1993–.* Similar factors play a role in the 1990s. Deepening now concerns the setting up of the EMU and coping with interna tional developments like the further decrease of external trade protection (Uruguay round of GATT). To deal with the EMU effect, a cohesion fund was set up (with a gradual shift o specific purpose to general purpose grants). Widening con cerns, first, the integration of the new German *Bundesländer* The extension with EFTA countries does not constitute a major new challenge for EU regional policy, given their relative wealth To deal with these challenges the resources devoted to struc tural adaptation have been stepped up again.

Summarising these developments we may say that the EU set ou without sufficient authority in regional matters, that it has gradually acquired the necessary instruments, and that now the regional ele ment occupies a prominent place among the European policy areas.

Coordination between EU, nation states and regions

All countries in Western Europe have taken up regional policy in the course of the past decades. They have developed a whole panoply o instruments, that can be divided into two groups. The first group applies to people: they concern mainly financial support to persons willing to move house (now practically abandoned everywhere). The second group applies to economic activities. They cover, first, finan cial benefits (loans, grants and so on) meant to encourage locating investment in certain regions, and second, the large category o instruments improving the location conditions in certain regions (roads, ports, industrial sites, training of workers, public utilities innovation and so on) (Yuill *et al.*, 1993).

National governments have gradually learned to take a European view on regional problems. Actually, what from a national point o view may seem a grave problem justifying a substantial money out lay, may seem trifling from the EU point of view. So the first task o the EU was to define the priority regions on the European leve (Figure 18.2). The second task was to prevent governments from outbidding one another with subsidies, which would mean in prac

ice that the richer member states would be able to match any pack-
ge allowed to the poorer ones. The EU has put a ceiling on aid levels
n each type of problem region: that is, high in a very poor region
nd low in relatively prosperous areas.

Because the regional policy of the EU is complementary to that of
he member states, national and EC measures need to be coordi-
ated. Once that need had been recognised, the regional programme
vas introduced as a policy instrument (for example, CEC, 1979c;
EC, 1984d). Its purpose is to give substance to the principle of
artnership by organising the involvement of all competent organi-
ations at the regional, national and European level. There are three
tages in this programming:

- *Development plan.* Submitted by the member state to the Commission, this document sets out the priorities of the regional
  and central authorities in the light of an analysis of the problems.
- *Community support framework.* Drawn up together by the Commission the member state and the region, this document identi-
  fies the areas for priority action, the financial resources and the
  forms of assistance.
- *Operational programmes.* Submitted by a member state to the
  Commission, this document details the concrete activities for
  each priority action in the various regions.

The authorities of the member states and the regions ensure the
mplementation. Monitoring committees in which the regions, mem-
er states and Commission are represented supervise the execution
f the programmes.

For the smooth coordination of more general issues between the
EC and the member states, and as a platform for regular discussions
n priorities, programmes and other matters, other committees have
een installed, consisting of officials of the Commission, the national
overnments of the member states and the EIB. A new Committee of
he Regions with an advisory status was created by the TEU (Article
98 a/c). It will permit the EU to hear directly the opinion of the
ower layers of government.

*The role of the European Regional Development Fund and other structural
unds*

For effective help to regions in distress, the EU must have financial
means. After several attempts the EU obtained in 1975 the necessary
finance with the creation of the European Regional Development
Fund (ERDF).[8] The tasks of the ERDF are to grant subsidies to stimu-

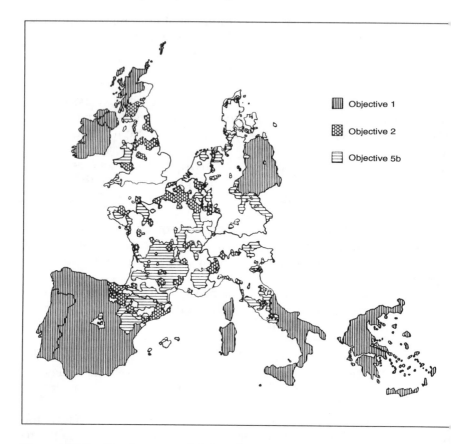

Figure 18.2   Regions qualifying for ERDF aid

late investment and promote innovation in economic activities and
develop the infrastructure in regions designated as European problem areas (see Figure 18.2). Eligible for investment support in these
regions are those activities which are already receiving aid from the
member state in question or one of its agencies; the EU intervention
is indeed meant to complement such aid.

The ERDF works together with three other structural funds, so
termed because their efforts are oriented towards the improvement
of the production environment. These are the European Social Fund
(ESF, see following sections), the Agricultural Fund (EAGGF, Guidance Section; see Chapter 11) and the recently created Fishery Guidance Finance Instrument. The aim is to combine the efforts of these
funds.

The total size of the structural funds devoted to regional development has been gradually stepped up with the increasing needs of the

poorer regions and the increasing accent on cohesion. For the first 10 years (1975–84) it amounted to some 1,000 million ECU a year. In the transition period from 1985 to 1988 it was stepped up to some 5,000 million a year. For the period 1989–93 much larger sums were set aside, some 10,000 million a year. For the period 1994–9 resources will average some 25,000 million ECU a year. The structural funds are fed by the EU budget.

The distribution over regions of the structural funds favours in particular the main problem regions. Objective 1 (traditionally backward) regions receive an average of some 70 per cent of the resources available for only 20 per cent of the EU population (27 per cent since the inclusion of the former GDR). Objective 2 (industrial restructuring) regions and objective 5 (agricultural areas) are rather dispersed geographically; here some 10 per cent of the resources were spent in regions representing some 15 per cent of the EC population. The effect of this is that the financial means of the funds are now attributed in such a way as to strongly favour low-income countries (see Table 18.3).

Table 18.3 Structural funds, 1989–93

Objective		Funds involved	Amount in M/ECU	Population concerned (millions)
Code	Name			
1	Backward	ERDF, ESF, EAGGF	36	70
	ex GDR	ERDF, ESF, EAGGF	3	18
2	Industrial decline	ERDF, ESF	7	56
3/4	Labour market measures	ESF	8	n.a.
5a	Agriculture structures	EAGGF	3	n.a.
5b	Rural areas	EAGGF, ERDF	3	16
	Total		60*	160

* plus some 5 billion ECU for Community initiatives for regional development.

The distribution over the type of project of the funds has changed considerably. In the late 1970s and early 1980s, the bulk (80 per cent) of the resources was used to assist investment in basic economic infrastructure (transport, telecommunications, water energy). Since then, resources devoted to productive investment in industry and

services has increased significantly, and the same holds for project
that improve the business environment and develop human resource
(CEC, 1991a). The accent on various categories differs from countr
to country.

Coordination of EU policies with a regional impact

The different policies of the EU should reinforce each other, or a
least should not be contradictory. This implies two actions. First
while carrying out regional policy (for example, with infrastructur
projects) due account should be taken of such matters as social an
environmental policy objectives; the new regulations for the 1994–
period have made aid conditional on compliance with a number o
such other policy objectives. Second, major European policies shoul
not have an adverse effect on regional equilibrium. For example, th
measures of the agricultural policy, which consumed the lion's shar
of the EU budget, mainly benefited the rich regions (Henry, 1981
Franzmeyer *et al.*, 1991). The EU now tries to assess the probabl
regional impact of its other policies before implementing them. Th
different EU policies (such as trade, energy and technology) hav
different and often contradictory effects. At the end of the 1980s th
combined effects of the major EU policies tended to be more positiv
for the non-assisted areas, and more negative for problem regions o
long standing in southern Europe. Thus the urgency attached by th
EU to the analysis of policy impacts seems justified (Molle an
Cappellin, 1988).

Two elements have dominated the debate on the impact of EL
policies on cohesion. The first is the completion of the internal mar
ket, which, on average, has had no major adverse effects. The secon
is the creation of the EMU, which does entail some new adaptatior
problems for the backward regions (Molle *et al.*, 1993). In order t
fight these a 'Cohesion Fund' was created (of 3 billion ECU a year
that can finance infrastructure developments in the poor Mediterra
nean countries that will face particular problems in fulfilling th
convergence criteria (see Chapter 17).

Some problems come up quite suddenly as the result of EU policy
changes. Take the case of an agreement on the external trade ir
textiles. More openness for third country imports will spell problem
for regions that have specialised in textiles. The EU has the possibil
ity of reacting relatively quickly to such adverse regional develop
ments, including regions other than those listed under objectives 1 t
5. Indeed a certain part of the structural funds is not spent under th
Community Support Frameworks, but is used for so-called 'Commu
nity Initiatives' (some 10 per cent of the total). One programme fron
the EU framework was RETEX, which finances projects that improv

he diversification of textile regions and thereby speed up adaptation
o new circumstances. A whole series of similar sectoral programmes
:xist. Other initiatives help the regions to come up to standards set
>y various EU policies. For instance, the ENVIREG initiative is set up
o assist regions in coming up to European environmental standards.
    This type of programme changes relatively quickly under the in-
luence of new problems. They perform a very important role in the
otal support mechanisms of the EU in the sense that they tend to
leflate political opposition to the EU because of people holding the
:U responsible for important negative effects.

:valuation

Vlany authors have already posed the question as to how effectively
·egional policy helps to realise certain objectives. That question has
wo aspects: a systemic one and an operational one.

- The choice of the EU as to the *system* seems to be a good one.
  Indeed the allotment of aid in the form of specific purpose
  grants in the framework of Community Support Frameworks
  seems to be more efficient than a system that would operate
  with block grants. Moreover the reform of 1989 (with respect to
  the concentration of aid to specific problem areas and so on)
  further improved the procedures and hence the workings of
  the system. Finally the system takes due account of aspects of
  allocational efficiency and policy consistency. Indeed transfers
  were carefully aimed at meeting the objectives (Gordon, 1992).
- The effect of the *operational* efforts in terms of, for example, a
  decrease in regional disparity is not easy to establish. Several
  types of studies have been carried out to find the answer. The
  simplest approach is to measure the effect of regional policy as
  the sum of all employment in activities that have been supported. But the question is how much of that employment
  would have been created anyhow, without support. In the same
  vein one may take the use of equipment supported as a measure of effect (for example, traffic on a motorway). The most
  sophisticated method is to develop a model capable of isolat-
  ing the effects of regional policy from 'normal' development. A
  third approach is to interview the firms concerned, asking them
  how far their choice of location had been influenced by measures of regional aid. The general conclusion from these studies
  is that regional policy measures do not seem to affect the spatial distribution of economic activities in a big way (Uhrig,
  1983; Folmer, 1980; NEI/E&Y, 1992; ECA, 1988).

Even if we cannot pinpoint exactly the effects of regional policy measures, we may give some indicators of the likely impact of the redistribution of funds. Total contribution of structural aid amounted in 1992 to an average 3 per cent of total GDP and 8 per cent of investment in the three poorest member states, Ireland, Greece and Portugal. Somewhat lower percentages obtain for other objective ` and objective 2 and 5 regions. This adds up to a considerable increase in the growth potential of these regions, both in quantitative terms (infrastructure) and in qualitative terms (such as manpower and R&D). Regional aid is supposed to have added an extra percentage point to the growth of these regions and hence to a decrease in disparities at the European level.

Social policy

Assessing the social problems

The EU is confronted by many social problems. *Unemployment* over-shadows all the other social problems in Europe. The development of overall unemployment is shown in Figure 18.3.

It has considerably increased as a consequence of the two crises in the 1970s. Unemployment declined under the impetus of the up-swing related to the completion of the internal market. Since 1990 it has significantly increased again. This overall picture assumes greater significance if we look at some structural differences (Table 18.4) unemployment is particularly concentrated in certain regions and in certain categories.

- *Region.* Unemployment is highest in the periphery of the EU the Mediterranean basin, the British Isles, and the new *Bundesländer.*
- *Category.* Unemployment among women was double that of men. Long-term unemployment is a particularly acute prob-lem; more than half of the EU's unemployed in 1990 had been out of a job for more than one year, one-third for over two years. Women were over-represented in the category of long-term unemployed.

The EU is much less effective in securing employment than both the USA and Japan (see Figure 18.3). To many this is due to the poor functioning of the European labour market, in turn due to too many regulation-based rigidities.

Differences in *the level of social protection* are a second major prob-lem. Over the years the richer countries of the EU have developed an

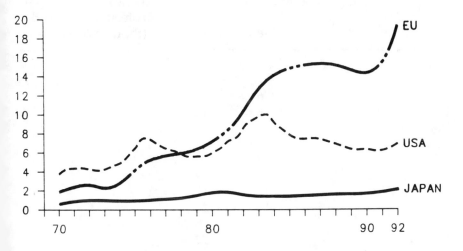

Figure 18.3   Evolution of unemployment (millions), 1970–92

elaborate system of protecting their citizens in general and their
workers in particular against loss of income due to unemployment,
sickness, accidents and so on. Moreover legislation protects workers
against hazards at their workplaces. These systems are much less
well developed in the poorer member countries. (An indication of
the differences in levels is given in Table 18.4.) In the member states
that have high social standards labour cost will be higher than in
states with low standards. This has given rise to the accusation of
social dumping: employment will be lost in the former and won in the
latter because firms faced with losses in market shares will relocate
to low-cost, low-protection locations. Demands for protection against
this social dumping cannot use the instruments that apply to goods
and service markets (free movement), so they advocate countering a
downward pressure upon social conditions by setting for all member
states minimum wage levels, social provisions and health and safety
guarantees.[9]

We will go further into the remedies for these two problems in the
following sections, where it will be seen that the major EU policy
instrument against unemployment is the Social Fund, and against
social dumping the harmonisation of national social security systems.

Table 18.4   Indicators of social disparity in the EU, 1990

	Unemployment (%)			Expenditure on social protection per head (thousands ECU)
	Total	Men	Women	
Germany	5	4	7	4
France	9	7	12	4
Italy	10	6	16	3
Netherlands	8	6	12	4
Belgium	8	5	13	4
Luxemburg	2	1	3	5
UK	6	7	6	3
Denmark	8	7	9	4
Ireland	16	15	17	2
Spain	16	12	24	2
Portugal	5	3	6	1
Greece	8	4	12	1
EU	8	6	11	3

Source: Eurostat.

Gradual development of policy

European social policy is a complement to national social policies developed to attend to such social problems as unemployment, poverty and illness. Social policy is closely associated with, and may even encompass, labour market policy. The objectives of the European Social Policy have changed as the EU has moved into higher stages of integration.

European Coal and Steel Community (1952–8)   The ECSC's activities in the social policy field were inspired mainly by the efficiency argument; the objective was to make the labour force more easily adjustable to the exigencies of the integrated market. Indeed Article 56 of the Treaty of Paris permits the ECSC to provide non-repayable aid towards:

- the payment of tideover allowances to workers;
- the payment of resettlement allowances to workers;
- the financing of vocational training to workers having to change their employment; in 1960 complemented by:
- the payment of allowances to undertakings to enable them to continue paying such of their workers as may have to be tem-

porarily laid off as a result of the undertakings' change of activity.

The equity aspect was given scant attention; Article 46 only authorised the High Authority to obtain the information required to assess the prospects for improving the working conditions and living standards of workers in the industries within its province, and the threats to them.

European Economic Community (beginnings)   The experience of the ECSC proved profitable when the social policy paragraphs of the EEC Treaty were devised. While the countries of Europe were still discussing the need for economic integration, the need for a complementary social policy had already been recognised (ILO, 1956). However the preparatory discussions for the Treaty of Rome did not produce a clear-cut view on such a policy, so that the relevant Treaty articles form rather a mixed bag. For a long time the situation has been characterised by a dichotomy between aims and means. Indeed the aims set are broad and ambitious (Article 117): 'the member states agree upon the need to promote improved working conditions and an improved standard of living for workers, so as to make possible their harmonisation, while the improvement is being maintained'. However the instruments provided are not very specific; the 'improvement is largely to be achieved through the beneficial effects of the Common Market', which has put paid to the hopes of some for a rapid development of a full-dress European Social Policy. The same dichotomy of aims and means is found in Article 118 EEC. The first part of this article states that the Commission's tasks are to promote close cooperation in the social field, particularly in employment, labour law and working conditions, basic and advanced vocational training, social security, prevention of occupational accidents and diseases, occupational hygiene, and the right of association and collective bargaining between employers and workers. The second part of the same article allows very limited means to realise these tasks: the Commission is asked to undertake studies, arrange consultations and so on. The Commission has indeed done so, but, up to the end of the 1980s, with little practical result. Social policy has in practice dealt with two different subjects:

- coordination of social security systems (Article 51) to secure freedom of movement for workers; workers who migrate from one national system of social security to another need protection to safeguard their rights, but that does not necessarily mean that the systems themselves need to be changed; further harmonisation of social security systems may be envisaged (Articles 117–18);

- the Social Fund, which has the task of 'rendering the employment of workers easier and of increasing their geographical and occupational mobility' (Article 123); this was meant to ease the adaptations made necessary by the Common Market.

More activity (1974–85)   As a reaction to the deterioration of the economic situation, the Council agreed in 1974 to an action programme for social policy. Objectives were the improvement of living and work conditions, codetermination of workers and full employment. It proved very difficult to move forwards. At the end of this period some bits and pieces of social legislation had been passed, but the overall situation of a limited practical involvement of the EU in social policy matters had not changed.

Social Charter and Single European Act (1986–92)   The discussion assumed a different perspective when the plans for the single market were set up. There was much concern that the increase in economic efficiency would entail considerable social problems, for two reasons: the adaptation to new circumstances would lead to unemployment, and the erosion of competition from low-wage countries that also have low social protection would lead to an erosion of the high social protection in the richer countries. (In this respect the argument of social dumping was often advanced.) So the Commission, the Parliament and the ESC asked for minimum standards to be applied throughout the EU. As existing international agreements, such as the ILO Convention, proved inadequate, the EU set up its own *Social Charter* of fundamental social rights of workers. This covers aspects such as working conditions, freedom of movement, social protection, collective bargaining, worker participation, health and safety, and so on.[10] The rights listed in the Social Charter are often qualified so as to take account of national practices. Unfortunately the subjects treated are a very mixed bag and do not fall into coherent categories of objectives. That has been one factor explaining why progress on their realisation has been slow. (The other factor being the reluctance of member states to give up their autonomy.)

The Treaty of Maastricht (1993–)   The Social Protocol has considerably broadened the scope of the action of the EU in the social field, ranging from minimum hours of work per day to social security (health and safety requirements and so on). The text has not been accepted by the UK, so the Social Protocol attached to the Treaty is only binding for the other 11 member states. The concern for subsidiarity has meant that the Protocol also expressly excludes certain areas from EU involvement (wages, strikes and so on). An innovation is that the Protocol provides for a direct consultation of the social part ners. This may give a new impetus as the activities of the Economic and Social Committee have never been of much consequence (CEC, 1993b).

Social security

In the debate provoked by the provisions of the Treaty in matters of social security, broadly two views can be distinguished (Holloway, 1981), the 'economic' and the 'social progress', view.

In the *economic view*, the provisions of the Treaty (Articles 117 and 118) demand only that the social security systems be harmonised as far as necessary for the proper functioning of the Common Market. Some understood this to mean that the charge to employers should be to some extent equalised across Europe to prevent distorted competition. Others believed that the differences would be compensated by the exchange rate, their only concern being of a macro-economic nature: since a high proportion of total state expenditure is taken up by social security benefits, the equilibrium among states could be upset if the amounts involved in social security rose too fast. In general economists have suggested that the EU should refrain from any major action.[11]

In the *social progress view* the EU is more than a common market, and has the clear task of enhancing welfare. This view has led to claims from some trade unions demanding harmonisation in the form of upward alignment to the highest level in any member state of the EU, or at least elimination of the gravest shortcomings of the systems in certain member states.[12] Proposals for a redistribution from the rich to poor member countries by means of a European Social Security Fund have been put forward too, but owing to the obvious lack of political support they have not been realised.

The outcome of the debate between economists and social progressists was clear-cut; the economists won. The Commission, which initially had associated itself with the social progress approach, was forced, in 1966, to adopt the economic line advocated by all member states. This line has been followed since. In the period 1965–90 the mere study and exchange of information has entailed some natural harmonisation of the various national systems. One important point in this respect is that the European Social Charter has established that any citizen of the EU is entitled to adequate social protection, including social security; the determination of the level and forms is, however, to be arranged by each member state.

This is in line with the fundamental features of the EU; as a 'prefederation' it does not have the power to use income tax and social security benefits for redistribution purposes. These instruments remain the domain of the member states. So other instruments (specific purpose grants) are used for redistribution (see below) while social security harmonisation is needed for creating the conditions for other policies, on the one hand, and the attainment of objectives of EU social policy, on the other.

European Social Fund

The original objective of the European Social Fund (ESF) (Article 123) is to increase the occupational and geographical mobility of workers in the EU, thus serving both an allocational purpose (to increase the efficiency of the European labour market) and a redistribution purpose. This was to be achieved mainly through vocational retraining and resettlement allowances, but aid could also be granted for the benefit of workers whose employment was reduced or temporarily suspended as a result of conversion (Article 125). The Fund was to be administered by the Commission, assisted by a committee of representatives of governments, trade unions and employers, an arrangement that is still valid. The Treaty allows the Fund to be used for new tasks after the transitional period (Article 126), which indicates considerable foresight on the part of the authors: the tasks of the Fund have indeed been continuously changed under the influence of new political demands and new economic and social circumstances (see Collins, 1983). Four periods can be distinguished.

The *'first' Fund* covers the period of the EU6, from 1958 to 1972. While the Treaty mentioned three purposes, in practice the Fund became almost entirely devoted to enhancing the allocational efficiency of the EU labour market, in other words, occupational mobility. In the period considered, 97 per cent of the Fund's resources went into the financing of vocational training or retraining schemes. Only a minor portion (10 million ECU) of the total amount of 320 million ECU of grants paid in this period were channelled into schemes for resettlement, for the purpose of stimulating geographical mobility. The reasons are not hard to find: the shortages on the labour market were already calling forth large external immigration flows. Nothing was done to encourage reconversion, mostly because member states could not agree on the type of project that would be eligible for aid.

The *'second' Fund* came into operation in 1972 after a major reform and lasted, with major adaptations, until 1983. In this period, its financial scope was gradually increased from some 250 million ECU to 1,500 million ECU. The Fund was able to contribute up to 50 per cent to the training and related costs of programmes for specific target groups. In this period the redistribution objective overtook the allocation objective. Indeed half the Fund's money went to the less developed regions. In that realm, the European Social Fund worked alongside the ERDF, the latter helping to create job opportunities, the ESF

₁elping the labour force to acquire the skills needed for the new jobs. Almost 30 per cent of the grants paid by the ESF were used to improve ₁mployment prospects for young people, because much of the burden ₁f rising unemployment appeared to be shouldered by the young.

The *'third' Fund* came into operation after a major revision in 1983. ₁ts volume was increased to 2,500 million ECU in 1986 (EU12). First ₁riority was given to young people: 75 per cent of the Fund had to be ₁pent on their education, training and initial hiring. In allocation of ₁he Fund's resources, emphasis was placed on the redistribution to- ₁vards the most distressed regions: 45 per cent of total ESF aid ac- ₁rued to the following: all regions of the three poorest countries of ₁he EU (Greece, Portugal and Ireland), the Italian Mezzogiorno, and ₁arge parts of Spain.

The *'fourth' Fund*, since 1988 integrated into the structural funds Agricultural Guidance, Regional and Social), has two main objec- ₁ives, cited as objectives 3 and 4 in Table 18.3. In 1993 these objectives ₁vere merged into one: fighting unemployment, in particular by pro- ₁noting the integration of young people and women into economic ₁ctivity and by reintegration of the long-term unemployed. The re- ₁listribution aspect of the Funds has been much accentuated, as most ₁f the Funds have to be spent in regions that are eligible for aid.

₁valuation

₁rom the preceding sections it can be seen that, up to the end of the ₁980s, European social policy consisted mainly of (1), a set of rules ₁efining the rights of migrant workers to social security benefits, (2) ₁ loose cooperation in the form of exchange of information on other ₁spects of social policy, and (3) a means of redistributing European ₁unds among member countries for the retraining of workers in the ₁oorer regions. The various elements of this stage of European social ₁olicy have drawn mostly unfavourable critiques (Laffan, 1983; ₁teinle, 1988) which argue that, at best, the ESF has served the redis- ₁ribution of European money, but failed to attain any specific Com- ₁nunity objectives (allocation function).

Those who set very high objectives for a European social policy (to ₁emedy the employment situation, remove disparities in welfare ₁mong social groups, all-Europe collective bargaining and agree- ₁nents,[13] full democratisation of the economy – not to speak of more ₁mmaterial aims) look upon the progress made up to now as very ₁imited, and hardly worth attention. On the other hand, those who ₁et their objectives more realistically will conclude that many social ₁mprovements have been realised as the outcome of the spontaneous ₁volution of economic realities, due to the convergence of interests ₁n specific points.

As the internal market is completed (Chapter 16) and the work o:
higher objectives of integration, such as the economic and monetar
union (Chapter 17) advances, the practical conditions for a mor
developed European social policy are likely to establish themselve
gradually, the legal conditions having been provided by the Socia
Protocol of the TEU.

Summary and conclusions

- The most important policies carried out by the EU to improv
  internal cohesion through the redistribution of wealth are re
  gional and social policies. The instruments used for both reflec
  the wish of the EU to make these policies conducive to mor
  allocational efficiency as well.
- Growth rates of GDP have diverged quite a lot in the EU, bui
  as poor countries generally grew faster, GDP levels have con
  verged, which was one cohesion objective. The determinants o
  the differences in growth among countries are as yet insuffi
  ciently known to assess correctly the role of demand and sup
  ply factors and that of increased integration.
- Regional policy's objective is the decrease in disparity. Not
  withstanding a gradual decrease over the past decades, consid
  erable differences in wealth remain. The effect of the Regiona
  Fund on that development is uncertain. The effect of Europea
  integration in general is not solidly documented either, but th
  impression is that the EU has helped to diminish the disparit
  in national wealth, and that is a major determinant of regiona
  disparity.
- Social policy has ambitious objectives, but consists in practic
  mostly of a redistribution of resources through the Europea
  structural funds for the fight against unemployment and th
  harmonisation of a large variety of labour market regulations.
- Evaluations of the effectiveness of both policies are fairly criti
  cal; although the redistribution effect in budgetary terms i
  certain, the contribution to growth and efficiency appears to b
  unsatisfactory.

Notes

1   Cohesion policy aims at decreasing the disparity between regions and socia
    groups. The main instrument for attaining this is redistribution of financia
    resources. The EU has created several Funds to that end. They are calle
    Structural Funds because they stimulate notably the improvement of the eco

nomic structure of problem regions and groups. In that respect one also speaks of structural policies. With the progress of integration and the increase of the size of the funds these policies have increasingly encompassed other issues than those related to redistribution only.

2   In a system where markets do not function perfectly (for example, with little movement of labour) or where important external effects exist (such as underutilisation of public capital) total production and welfare may be enhanced if policy measures remove bottlenecks and barriers.

3   The consequence of such limiting of claims to a well-delimited sub-set of the world, be it the nation or the union, is that international transfers to third countries have more in common with acts of charity than with distributional justice. We have included development policies among the external policies (Chapter 19) as they are considered by the EU as independent policies and not as an external dimension of internal redistribution. The case of the aid to potential member countries in Central and Eastern Europe is on the borderline between the two.

4   From the beginning, the Commission has been active in assessing the regional situation and regional developments in the Community by carrying out or commissioning a number of studies (CEC, 1961, 1964, 1971, 1973b). The main purpose of the reports is to keep the knowledge of the old problems up-to-date and to recognise new problems as soon as they present themselves. They also serve as a foundation for discussions with member states about priorities in regional policy and the changes to be carried through in it. Since the 1980s the Commission has periodically reported on the regional situation in the Community (CEC, 1981b, 1984c, 1987b, 1991c).

5   Turbulence on exchange rate markets does influence disparity figures quite a bit. When the GDP/P figures are calculated with purchasing-power parities instead of exchange rates, they are reduced by about half. Moreover one observes that the decrease in disparity since 1970 is very limited. Another indicator of regional disparity is unemployment. As it appears to be highly concentrated in the same regions that also show a low GDP/P level we have not detailed unemployment here.

6   In the jargon of the European Commission, this is also called 'real convergence' as opposed to 'nominal convergence'. The latter applies to macro-economic indicators like inflation and is relevant in the context of the criteria for joining the EMU (see Chapter 17).

7   Among the attempts at a more rigorous test of the above theory for the EU, we mention the study of Murrell (1983), who compared different industries in the UK and the Federal Republic of Germany. His hypothesis was that special-interest groups are probably most important in old established industries and least in new industries. He found, indeed, that modern British industries held a better position *vis-à-vis* their FRG colleagues than the older ones.

8   For a description of the creation of the Fund, see Talbot (1977), for the restructuring CEC (1981c) and for a review of its performance in the first 10 years the EU brochure (CEC, 1985g). The Single European Act (Article 130) has reinforced the position of the ERDF in the EU institutional framework.

9   There is a parallel with the need for setting up minimum levels of taxation and technical and environmental norms in the single European market; see Chapter 16.

10 All EU member countries except the UK adhere to this document.

11 The only exception, explicitly foreseen by the Treaty, concerns the protection of migrants against the loss of social security rights. We have seen in Chapter 9 that the common market, while not meant to set large flows of migrants in motion, nevertheless led to several millions of migrant workers. The geo-

graphical reallocation of the labour force in Europe would have been an empty phrase without measures to protect migrant workers against the risk of losing social security rights. So the Treaty of Rome commits the EU to coordinating the relevant systems of the member states by:

- removing nationality and residence restrictions;
- deciding that the law of the place of work is applicable;
- organising mechanisms of cooperation among the agencies administering the various schemes in the member states;
- regulating the aggregation and proration of insurance periods in different member countries.

An extensive and detailed system of regulation has been developed by the EU, corroborated by countless decisions of the European Court of Justice. As the details are more interesting to lawyers than to economists, we will not go into them here.

12 This approach of minimum standards has been followed by the International Labour Organisation. Convention no. 102 of that organisation (adopted as early as 1952) commits ratifying states to certain minimum standards for social security systems. For Europe, these standards were raised somewhat in 1964 when the Council of Europe adopted the European Code of Social Security (IEE, 1978).

13 Often claimed by the trade unions. See, for a discussion of their action, Barnovin (1986), ETUI (1992).

19 External Relations

Introduction

Integration schemes need to define rules not only for their internal functioning, but also for their external relations. Owing to the high degree of worldwide economic interdependence, each member country has developed a whole panoply of relations with third countries. The higher the stage of economic integration, the smaller the scope for independent action by member countries. Indeed a matter which has been regulated internally by the Union cannot be treated in external international relations without the participation and consent of the Union (Wellenstein, 1979). In the next section we will go into these fundamental principles and also describe the international institutional setting in which the European regime has evolved.

As the EU is based on a customs union, trade policy will receive ample attention below. Two sections will be devoted to the common external trade policy: the instruments and the specific relations with different groups of trading partners. The EU is developing from a customs union via an economic and monetary union into a political union, which means that other matters than trade are the object of gradual integration and are thus becoming the concern of the common external policy. The final section of this chapter therefore briefly reviews labour and capital movements, international economic and monetary coordination and development aid, and will also touch upon external policies less associated with economic issues, such as foreign and defence policy. Some general conclusions will round off the chapter.

General issues

Dynamics of integration

The setting up of common policies is more efficient than the pursuit of independent policies by member states if the common policy produces better results with less effort than independent ones. This will often be the case in international matters, where the power relations between the various partners determine in part the outcome. The scope of the common external policies is determined by the stage of the integration process.

A *customs union* lays the basis for a common external policy by setting up a common commercial policy. It generally covers both a common external tariff and rules on the common use of non-tariff barriers to prevent member countries using such instruments to obtain supplementary competition advantages for their industry. As international trade in goods and services is welfare-improving, custom unions have an interest in pursuing a policy of openness towards third countries (see, with regard to the better allocation of resources due to trade, and to the disciplining effects of imports competition on domestic supplies, Chapter 5, specifically Figures 5.3 and 5.9). However strategic considerations may nevertheless induce trade blocks to use trade impediments (for example, accepting provisionally some protection for some industries to get sufficient political support for the liberalisation of most other industries' trade).

A *common market* will entail common policies in the fields of labour and capital. For labour, the abolition of internal border controls for workers, and a fortiori for all persons, will induce a common policy for immigration from third countries. It will likewise create a need for the harmonisation of other policies (such as crime prevention and social security). For capital, a similar reasoning applies: the liberalisation of movements between members will imply capital flowing into the whole of the common market through the country that gives the easiest access to capitalists of third countries; a common stance is therefore necessary.

An *economic and monetary union* also brings a need for an extension of the scope of external policy. Let us take just a few examples for illustration. In terms of allocation policies, foreign firms need to know whether they have to comply with the rules on competition and whether they qualify for financial support of technological innovation by one of the EU programmes. The setting up of a monetary union requires a common exchange rate policy, whereas redistribution policies may come into competition with external aid policy, which requires a common policy for the latter.

Financial flows

The importance of the categories of an economic union's external relations can be derived from its balance of payments, which is the financial record of its transactions with the rest of the world. These transactions include current ones concerning merchandise, services and so on, as well as long- and short-term capital transactions. We have rearranged the headings in the statistics of the current account of the European Union to fit the general organisation chosen earlier in this work; the results are given in Table 19.1.

A few brief comments on the results are in order. The first is that the structure of the external transactions has been fairly stable through time. The prominence of merchandise exports is striking; they accounted for about two-thirds of total current transactions. This justifies the considerable attention we will devote in the next sections to the external trade in goods of the EU. Services occupy a modest place in comparison. Among the payments associated with production factors, the returns on capital invested abroad are growing in importance; the payments made by and to the EU for labour (earnings from work and remittances by emigrant workers and so on) are very small in comparison. Next to these current account transactions there are those of the capital account, whose total volume, as a matter of fact, is by far the greater. This justifies an ample discussion of the involvement of the EU in world policies on stabilisation and development.

Table 19.1 Percentage share of categories in total external payments of the EU, average of assets and liabilities,[a] 1970–90

	1970	1980	1990
Merchandise	67	64	59
Services (commercial)	20	19	19
Labour (inc.)	1	1	1
Capital (inc.)	12	16	21
Current account (CA)	100	100	100

[a] Figures of assets being very much like the liability figures for all headings, we have preferred this presentation to the more common one of net figures (assets minus liabilities).

Source: Eurostat, *Balance of Payments, Geographical Breakdown*, various issues; *International Trade in Services EU12, 1980–1989*, Luxemburg, 1993. (Some estimates, as figures from different sources do not always correspond.)

Institutional setting

The process of European integration takes shape in the framework of a rapid globalisation of economic activities. As a consequence there is an increasing need for international institutions to set the policies to accompany these developments. However these have developed to very different degrees according to the subject. Most is done for the basic element of integration, trade, very little for other elements such as macro-economic and monetary policies or allocation policies (Meerhaeghe, 1992).

Trade relations (goods and services) are regulated by GATT, the General Agreement on Tariffs and Trade. All member countries of the EU are contracting parties to the GATT. GATT came into being after the Second World War as a second best option, the International Trade Organisation having failed. At the moment over 100 countries have signed the agreement. Some 30 more apply the provisions de facto. GATT has two main objectives:

- To lay down a set of rules of conduct for international trade. Central to GATT is the principle of non-discrimination; this is enshrined in the so-called 'most-favoured-nation clause'. In the terminology of GATT, it means that any advantage, favour, privilege or immunity affecting tariffs or other trade regulation instruments which is granted to one of the GATT members must immediately be granted to all other members as well.
- To provide a framework for international negotiation. GATT rules say that changes in trade policy, such as the imposition or raising of tariffs, the setting of quotas and so on cannot be decided unilaterally by one national government, but must be subjected to international negotiation. That rules out unilateral increases in protection which might lead to retaliation and tariff wars, and at the same time provides countries prepared to make concessions in the direction of free trade with a lever to obtain similar concessions from other nations (reciprocity). The GATT has engaged the contracting parties in some major rounds of international negotiation, in the course of which substantial reductions of tariffs and other barriers to trade have been realised.[1]

Consultation, conciliation, and dispute settlement are fundamental to GATT's work. Unresolved disputes between signatories are brought before a panel of independent experts for judgement. The GATT has no means, however, to enforce verdicts.

Production factors are much less well covered by international institutions. Some consultation on capital transactions is done by OECD, and was in earlier days in the framework of the IMF. With free capital movements to and from EC countries realised over a wide area, this does not seem to have much relevance any more. For labour markets the ILO has done relevant work on labour market and migration issues.

Policy coordination again has been done in OECD. This organisation has covered the whole range of subjects discussed in this book, from policy coordination for economic sectors to stabilisation. Regular work on worldwide monetary coordination has been done by the IMF, which has the task of monitoring and promoting the stability of the international financial system. Relevant in terms of macro-economic and monetary policy coordination has been the G7, the yearly summit meetings of the heads of government of the seven largest industrialised countries in the world (Hajnal, 1989; Blommestein, 1991).

EU regime

The literature on external economic relations indicates the importance of a regime of openness as most conducive to growth. Indeed the possibility of imports and the rivalry of foreign firms that have made direct investments put the local producers under constant pressure, leading to more dynamism than would occur in a country with a closed economy. The EU practice is meant to be in line with these theoretical recipes.

The preamble of the Treaty of Rome already states the desire to 'contribute by means of a common commercial policy to the progressive abolition of restrictions on international trade'. One major instrument for such a policy is the Common External Tariff (CET). The Treaty (Article 29) gives the following motives:

- the need to promote trade among member states and third countries;
- the possible improvement of the competitive capacity of undertakings;
- the avoidance of competitive distortions in finished-goods markets, related to supplies of raw materials and semi-finished goods;
- the avoidance of serious disturbances in the member states' economies, while ensuring the growth of production and consumption within the EU.

'The common commercial policy (CCP) shall be based on uniform principles' (Article 113). The CCP covers not only tariffs but other trade instruments as well (Court of Justice ruling in 1975). So all

powers regarding changes in tariff rates, conclusion of trade agreements, export policy, the achievement of uniform liberalisation, and
anti-dumping or countervailing duties are within the competence of
the EU institutions. Nevertheless the mixed nature of their economies caused member states to use independently all sorts of instruments on the borderline of trade policy, which has given rise to
lengthy competence battles between the Commission and member
state governments. Over the years a trade policy practice has been
worked out that uses fairly complicated procedures and a very elaborate panoply of instruments (CEC, 1993c).

The extension of EU external relations to other policy areas than
trade has been a source of multiple conflicts between the Council
and the Commission, many of which have been submitted to the
Court. The consequences of the case law of the European Court can
be summarised as follows (Schwarze, 1987):

> The implied powers (of the EU) to conclude treaties with third coun-
> tries does exist when: a) the Community holds the respective internal
> power and b) the treaty is necessary for the attainment of any objec-
> tive recognised by Community law. This concept has become known
> as the principle of parallel powers whereby the Community's treaty
> making powers are congruent with its internal competences in any
> given field.

In practical terms this means that the European external policy has
been extended by new subjects as integration progressed through the
stages we distinguished in Chapter 2 (see also Molle and Van Mourik,
1987; Ward, 1986). In the course of time the Commission has taken
action in such matters as capital transactions and monetary
stabilisation, according to the lines set for trade.

Cooperation in non-economic areas has also gradually established
itself among the 12 member states, first outside the Community legal
framework. The Single Act has attached diplomatic cooperation to
the EC machinery. The Maastricht Treaty has completed this move. It
says (Article 13) that one of the objectives of the European Union is:
'to assert its identity on the international scene in particular through
the implementation of a common foreign and security policy' (see
also title V). The increased weight of the EU implies that it will have
to take increasingly into account the effects of internal policies on
third countries (including agriculture, and also the internal market;
see Borner and Grubel, 1992; Redmond, 1992).

The choice of instruments of external policy integration for the EU
will depend on the advance of internal policy integration. With external policies that are a complement to a clearly defined internal
'union' competence, unification of instruments may be the answer

(for instance, a common external customs tariff for a customs union). In areas where powers are not yet clearly vested in the 'union', for example when countries of a common market strive for some stabilisation of the exchange rates of their currencies internally, the definition of the stance towards third countries will be carried out by consultation or coordination among member countries. The instruments that are used for the reaching of agreement with third countries will depend on the international institutional framework – negotiations in GATT for trade, but consultation and information in G7 for macro policy.

Trade policy: a fan of instruments

Common External Tariff

The Common External Tariff (CET) of the EU was established for each category as the arithmetic average of the tariffs applied by the member states (Article 19.1). Thus the first CET reflected the whole history of the trade relations of all member countries. The EU has effectively worked towards free trade, as the Treaty of Rome had enjoined upon it (in its Article 110), purporting that the EU wishes 'to contribute, in the common interest, to the harmonious development of world trade, the progressive abolition of restrictions on international trade and the lowering of Customs tariffs'.

Some major changes in the CET have been made in the framework of GATT negotiations. The so-called 'Dillon round' of 1960–62 and the subsequent 'Kennedy round' of the mid-1960s cut the tariffs by about half. A further tariff cut of some 30 per cent of the 1978 level was agreed upon during the so-called 'Tokyo round' of the mid-1970s. After the successful completion of the recent Uruguay round, the general level of tariff protection of the EU will be very low, about 2 per cent. For many products the EU tariff is now even nil or negligible. Moreover the dispersion has become very narrow.

In the past, the scope of the reductions was restricted. For one thing, until the recent Uruguay round, the GATT round reductions applied to industrial products only. In the agricultural and service fields the EU remained very protective; indeed substantial tariff and non-tariff barriers exist for most agricultural and service products. For another, for several industrial products of so-called 'sensitive' sectors (like textiles) import barriers continue to prevail, mostly in the form of quotas and voluntary export restraints. 'Sensitive' sectors are composed of low-technology manufacturers, using relatively standardised, labour-intensive production technologies, the very sectors in which LDCs are gaining an increasing comparative advantage. Now work has begun to apply the GATT principles to these sectors too.

Non-tariff barriers

Less visible than tariffs but no less effective as instruments of trade policy are the so-called 'non-tariff barriers' (NTBs). In line with its treaty obligations, the EU tries to free international trade not only from tariffs but also from NTBs such as border formalities, import quotas, administrative and technical regulations, tax laws, aid programmes and discriminate government procurement.

Many NTBs applied to non-EU members date from pre-EU times, when quotas in particular were popular among the present EU member states. Although the Treaty of Rome allows member states to retain such pre-EU quotas on imports from non-member countries, the Commission has been pushing to dispose of them. Its efforts towards liberalisation have been helped by the completion of the internal market, which makes national quotas unpractical as border controls will no longer be permitted. Many of them have been taken away; others have been replaced by EU-wide quotas.

Despite the EU's principles, the use of NTBs by the EU and its member states has been widespread, which means that the EU has taken an active part in the 'new protectionism' (Greenaway, 1983). It is practised in the form of so-called 'voluntary' export restraints (VERs) (by one exporting country) and orderly marketing arrangements (OMAs) (multilateral voluntary restraint agreements). VERs and OMAs exist outside the GATT framework, and are therefore, from a political point of view, more expedient than quotas. Tariff quotas, applied under the GSP (Generalised System of Preferences; see next section), constitute another well-known form of NTB protection. The GSP treatment allows a limited volume of duty-free exports, the excess being subject to customs duties. Many such controls come under the Multi-Fibre Arrangement (MFA), negotiated between the EU and the principal textile-exporting developing countries. The latter have agreed to a voluntary restriction of their textile exports to the EU. In practice, the MFA has deteriorated into a scheme by which the individual EU member countries have fixed the quantities of textile products they will import from each separate exporting country. Recent measures tend to liberalise these bilateral restrictions.

Not only the EU but all major trading countries of the world practise NTB protection. These NTBs can be expressed in a tariff equivalent (Chapter 5). Several studies have empirically measured tariff equivalents (Balassa and Balassa, 1984; Deardorff and Stern, 1981; Whalley, 1985). Their results show a wide variation, not only as to the level of protection for each block (EU, USA, Japan), but even as to their relative positions. The only conclusion warranted from this is that all blocks operated substantial schemes for non-tariff protection.

Protection against unfair trade practices

In their attempts to conquer a new export market, firms sometimes adopt the strategy of first selling at a loss in foreign markets to force local producers out of business, and afterwards raising their prices to very profitable levels. The practice is known as *dumping*. GATT rules allow the importing country to take protective measures against such practices, in particular to impose anti-dumping duties which level off the difference between the selling prices the dumping firm charges in its home and export markets. Other unfair trade practices are used not by private firms but by governments (for example, subsidies to exports). To counteract these, the importing country may impose a countervailing duty to the amount of the subsidy on products given by the exporting country. GATT rules require that such measures be taken only if it can be shown that: (1) imports have increased substantially; (2) there is a substantial price difference between home and export prices of the exporter; and (3) the imports cause material injury to the home producers.

These general rules have inspired the EU anti-dumping regulation (Regulation 2423/88). The procedure is as follows:

- a complaint is lodged by (groups of) firms directly concerned; the regulation indicates in detail what information the Commission requires to judge whether the complaint is justified;
- investigation by the Commission; the Commission verifies the information given by the complaining party (analysis of their accounts) and, if the exporting country is agreeable, sends an investigation team to that country;
- if a dumping margin is found to exist and if injury has been done, the Commission may either accept the exporters' offer to adjust prices and/or subsidies, or, if the adjustment is insufficient, impose an anti-dumping or countervailing duty;
- should the duties have to extend to a longer period than six months, the Council must make them permanent.

Anti-dumping investigations have grown over the past 15 years. However the cases where anti-dumping and countervailing duties have been applied represented only a small percentage of total EU imports (Tharakan, 1988; Messerlin, 1988; CEC, 1993c). So far, most procedures have been concluded by a *'solution à l'amiable'*; that is, by the acceptance of a price undertaking by the producer under pressure from the Commission.

When the EU is faced with a sudden increase in imports, it may take *safeguard measures*. The procedure is much the same as for anti-dumping measures. Safeguard measures are mostly of the surveillance type, which means that importers must apply for licences. The statistics thus obtained allow the EU to follow closely how the imported quantities develop. Licensed imports can still flow into the EU free of quotas or extra duties. More severe safeguard measures are of the quota type. GATT rules preclude discriminating quotas, which means that they cannot be made country-specific. For that reason, the EU has often preferred negotiating VER to having recourse to safeguard quotas.

The above procedures may not be sufficient to make a trading partner change its unfair behaviour. However, if presumed unfair trading practices of third country exporters threaten to disrupt the EU market, quick EU action is taken to warrant the survival of the European firms concerned. The Commission initiates these actions, upon which the Council has to agree within 30 days.

Export promotion and controls

Exports from the EU are essentially unrestricted; some product-related exceptions can be applied to prevent supply shortages of essential goods, for example. Export promotion is often achieved through export credits (soft loans), implying a government subsidy. Other forms of direct export subsidy are also used, as well as indirect ones (subsidies to production, permitting producers to work at lower cost and thus obtain a better export position). The EU has used the instrument very overtly in the case of agriculture (direct subsidy). It has given production subsidies to steel, and accepted or regulated national large-scale subsidies for ships, aeroplanes, arms and other products. The EU has tried to check the efforts of member countries to outbid one another on export markets with finance subsidies. Some alignment has been accomplished, but there remain widely different, detailed national arrangements. By its industrial and competition policy, the EU tries to reduce further such practices. As export promotion is generally considered to fall outside the realm of EU common commercial policy, the Commission has little power to harmonise, let alone unify, this aspect.

Export controls take the form of export quotas or even embargoes. Outside the arms sector, very few export quotas survive.

Liberalisation versus protectionism

There are sound economic arguments for the abolition of all protective measures (Chapter 5). Theoretical analyses (for instance

Greenaway, 1983) have shown that trading partners can obtain a net welfare gain from getting rid of protective measures (see Chapter 8 for the effects of EU trade liberalisation). Empirical analyses of the Tokyo round (for example, Deardorff and Stern, 1981; Whalley, 1985) and of the abolition of the MFA (Koekkoek and Mennes, 1988) and of VERs (Kalantzopoulos, 1986) show that there are mostly positive welfare effects for all partners (EU, USA, LDCs, NICs and so on).

Now, if economic considerations plead so convincingly against the use of protective instruments, why are they so widely used? The reason is that negative effects of protection on welfare in terms of jobs lost are plain to see and directly attributable to trade, while the positive effects are more general and diffuse and hence less visible. That makes it relatively easy to convince policy makers of the need for protection.

In the theoretical analysis of this phenomenon (Caves, 1975; Frey and Schneider, 1984; Baldwin, 1984) protection is demanded by pro-tariff interest groups, which from empirical evidence consist mainly of declining industries using low-technology production techniques, that is, large pools of low-skilled, low-wage labour, and losing out to international competitors. Claims for protection were found to be higher as: (1) the industry is more concentrated corporately or regionally, (2) the historical levels of protection are higher, (3) the industry is better organised, and (4) the macro-economic perform-ance (including the balance of payments) weaker. Export industries and consumers have no interest in protection. However, in contrast to the sectors demanding protection, they tend to be poorly organ-ised and have little influence. Politicians anxious to be re-elected, whatever their ideology, tend to listen more to the slogans of well organised pro-protection pressure groups than to the pleas of anti-protectionists. There is some historical evidence (Borchardt, 1984) that the state will only override the pro-protection interest groups if considerations of international relations carry enough weight.

Empirical work along those lines has confirmed the validity of the arguments (for example, Weiss, 1987).

Trade policy: differentiation by area

A hierarchy of trade relations

EU external trade relations are governed by GATT rules, notably the most-favoured nation (MFN) rule. However there have been factors at work to discriminate in practice between (groups of) countries, so special advantages have been given to specific groups of countries with which the EU wants to retain special relations. This is possible

Table 19.2 The hierarchy of EU trade relations

Countries concerned	Form of relationship	Conditions[a]	Share[b] in EU external trade (%) 1990	Population (millions) 1990
EFTA	Free trade area	MR	25	30
Mediterranean	Mixed[c]	aAMr	10	300
ACP[d]	One-way prefs,[e] special	aAM	4	400
Other third world	Generalised preference	mg[f]	18	3100
US, Japan, etc.	MFN[g]	q[h]	35	400
East European	Association	Mq	8	400

[a] A: covers agricultural trade; M: covers trade in manufacturers; R: reciprocal (that is, partner must offer concessions on EU members' exports); Q: EC imports are controlled by quotas or voluntary export restraints (VERs). Upper-case letters signify full, lower-case partial, application of the measure.

[b] See Table 6.4; 1990 imports and exports divided by two.

[c] Customs unions, free trade areas, reciprocal and non-reciprocal (one-way) tariff preferences.

[d] African, Caribbean and Pacific countries.

[e] One-way (non-reciprocal) preferences: the EC reduces/eliminates its tariffs on imports from the partner country but obtains no reciprocal (reverse) concessions on its exports; generalised preferences apply to all developing countries, special preferences to a selected group.

[f] VERs on NICs' exports, quotas on textiles, tariff quotas/ceilings on other goods.

[g] Most-favoured-nation (MFN) treatment: trade; subject to the (non-discriminatory) tariffs negotiated and bound in GATT.

[h] National quotas on some imports from Japan; some products subject to VERs.

nder the so-called 'enabling clause' of GATT. Table 19.2 gives a
ummary idea of the highly complicated system.[2]

How trade with these country groups has developed has been
hown in Table 6.4. We will evoke the historical backgrounds and
escribe how the EU relates to each layer of trade advantages in the
ext sections.

FTA (other Western Europe)

FTA countries have paralleled the members of the EC in the liber-
lisation of their internal trade in manufacturing goods. In 1966,
ome years ahead of schedule, their free trade area was successfully
stablished. That quick success was helped by the generally good
conomic environment, as well as by the limitation to manufactured
oods only; indeed the agricultural sector was left out entirely. As a
ree trade area, EFTA did not establish a common external tariff. The
roblem of trade deflection, imports tending to pass through the
ountry with the lowest tariff, was solved by a system of rules of
rigin. Goods produced in the area (containing, in value terms, less
han 50 per cent of non-area components) were allowed to move
reely among all member countries.

When at the end of the 1960s the UK and three other EFTA mem-
er countries applied for EU membership, a major problem arose:
rade among former free trade partners risked being greatly dis-
urbed by the trade barriers still remaining between the EU and
FTA. Evidently the relations among the West European countries of
he two groups had to be reformulated. Several factors influenced
he outcome. The first was the general conviction that the introduc-
ion of new trade barriers would be harmful to all concerned, but
articularly to the remaining EFTA members, which are greatly de-
endent on the enlarged EU. Harm could be circumvented only by
nstalling some form of free trade area among all concerned. The
emaining EFTA countries were unable to join the EU for reasons of
oreign policy (neutrality, lack of democracy). A customs union was
ut of the question: the EU clearly stated that it was not prepared to
hare its responsibility for trade matters in the framework of the CCP
vith countries that were not full members. The formula eventually
hosen was that of a large European free trade area, of which the EU
s the core. The EU has negotiated free trade areas on a bilateral basis
vith the individual EFTA countries (of which remain, after the latest
nlargement, Iceland, Norway, Sweden, Finland, Switzerland and
Austria), with largely similar provisions. The remaining EFTA coun-
ries have maintained free trade among themselves on the multilat-
ral basis of the EFTA. In this way, full free trade in manufactured
oods in Western Europe took effect in 1977; as in EFTA, agricultural

goods were excluded from the arrangements. A few additional rule were laid down concerning the incompatibility of state aids an restrictive business practices, to safeguard the proper functioning (the agreements. As a consequence, trade relations between the E and EFTA have intensified throughout the 1960–90 period.

Recently the completion of the internal EU market has pushe EFTA–EU relations into becoming even closer. Most EFTA countrie tended to follow the EU regulations and directives, although the have no formal influence on their elaboration. The EU has conclude a new arrangement with EFTA countries, the European Economi Area (EEA), that has taken effect as of 1994. It achieves, on top of common market for the whole area, the implementation of the *acqu communautaire* by EFTA, with flanking policies in the fields of soci affairs, transport, R&D and environmental protection. The Europea Court of Justice will be competent to settle any disputes according t common rules. EFTA countries stand to reap considerable benefit from this type of relation (Norman, 1989, 1991).

Relations with Mediterranean countries (mixed)

For several reasons, EU trade relations with Mediterranean countrie are of a special nature (Shlaim and Yannopoulos, 1976; Pomfret, 1986 The first is that some North African countries used to have coloni; ties with one of the EU member countries, and wanted to maintai the special trade relations that had been established. Some Europea; countries in the Mediterranean region had applied for EU member ship, and agreements were concluded with them to regulate relation during the waiting time. Yet others wanted to obtain advantages o the EU market similar to those their neighbours had obtained. Th EU gave way to the strong political pressures for preferential treat ment, the form chosen depending on political aspirations, on the on hand, and GATT limitations, on the other. As the GATT rules al lowed such preferential treatment only as the precursor of a genuin free trade area or customs union, many trade agreements betwee; the EU and the Mediterranean countries were made to fit that frame work. When after a while that method proved difficult to continue the EU made efforts to put the agreements on a more uniform basi (Pomfret, 1986). That, together with the second enlargement of th EU with Greece, Spain and Portugal, has simplified the picture enougl for the following classification to be possible:

- *Cooperation agreements* have been concluded with the Maghrel (Morocco, Algeria and Tunisia) and Mashreq (Egypt, Lebanon Jordan and Syria) countries and the former Yugoslavia. Th parts concerned with trade are in the form of a one-way prefer ence scheme, which means that these countries have tariff-free access to the EU market for industrial goods. The EU has settled for an MFN treatment of EU goods on the home markets of these countries. For some sensitive goods, the imports into the EU are limited by quotas or import ceilings. The advantages of the trade agreement with the EU should not be overestimated: for limited quantities these countries already had tariff-free access by their generalised system of preference (GSP) status.

- *Association agreements*, possibly leading to full EU membership, have been concluded with Turkey, Cyprus and Malta. Under these agreements, these countries have obtained tariff-free access to the EU for manufactured goods. As these agreements aspire to a full-fledged customs union, the EU requires in principle full reciprocity. That proved too hard a condition for Cyprus and Malta, so that the next stage of the association has been postponed as far as they are concerned. The same applies to Turkey, for which country progress was moreover blocked by political problems.
- *A free trade agreement*, on the principle of full reciprocity, has been concluded with Israel.

ooking at the overall picture, we observe that the relations with Mediterranean countries are hybrid forms of EFTA and ACP models; indeed many Mediterranean countries, like the ACP, receive aid in various forms from the EU. The Mediterranean countries appear to have been able, in the last 30 years, to increase their share in EC imports considerably, while their share in EU exports has stagnated, which is an indication of their improved position *vis-à-vis* the EU and other countries exporting to the EU (see Table 6.4).

The Lomé Convention (Africa, Caribbean, Pacific)

Right from the start, the EU has taken over the responsibility for easy access of producers of the former French colonies in black Africa to the EU market. After the UK had joined the EU, the schemes were extended to the former British colonies, whose economic structure resembles that of the associated states. The present scheme applies to 9 so-called ACP countries, including practically all countries in sub-Sahara Africa and some few, very small countries scattered across the Caribbean and Pacific areas. The main provisions of the present scheme are tariff preferences, special treatment for products coming under the CAP (Common Agricultural Policy) and development aid to be dealt with in the last section of this chapter).

Tariff preferences are fairly generous for ACP countries; indeed almost their entire exports have access to the EU market free of any tariff or quota. In that sense the ACP countries have a better de≀ than the other developing countries (GSP, see below), which ar sometimes subject to formal and informal quantitative restriction (tariff preference quotas). However access is granted only for good which can be shown to originate for more than 50 per cent of th value added in the country itself, in other ACP countries, or in an El country. The tariff preferences are non-reciprocal; the agreement stipu lates only that the ACP countries grant imports from the EU th same favourable treatment that is allowed to the most favoured de veloped country. ACP exports to the EU of products coming unde the CAP receive, within some quantitative limits, a reduction of th levies which the EU puts on many agricultural imports.

The Lomé agreement has been somewhat disappointing for AC countries, not least because it has failed to prevent their share in th total EC imports falling from 10 to 4 per cent and in EU imports fron non-oil-exporting developing countries from 24 to 12 per cent ove the last 30 years. The 1992 programme does potentially expand th export possibilities of ACP countries. Whether this will happen i very dependent on improvements in trade and internal policies o these countries (Kol, 1992).

Generalised system of preferences (GSP) (Latin America and Asia)

The wish to do something about the problems of developing coun tries in general has been the motive for preferential trade relation with this group of countries. The UNCTAD adagium 'trade instea of aid' has been important in this context. Developing countries par ticipating in world trade face several problems.

- In the developed countries, demand for agricultural product is growing only slowly because of the low income elasticity fo food, while the share of indigenous production is increasin owing to support schemes and increased productivity; worl markets are distorted by dumping and export subsidies to agri cultural production in the developed world. Prices tend to fluc tuate very heavily around a downward trend.
- On non-agricultural commodity markets, a similar situatio prevails: economic growth is now accumulating to the less ma terial and energy-intensive activities. These markets, too, ar highly unstable: prices, and hence export earnings, tend to fluc tuate very much.
- On markets for manufactured products, developing countrie face protective tendencies on the part of developed countries because the very competitiveness of their new industries threat ens the viability of the older sectors in developed countries.

n successive UNCTAD negotiations, the developing countries of outh America and Asia have tried to obtain better prospects of enetrating the markets of developed countries. They have in genral been successful in this strategy, as Table 19.3 shows.

Table 19.3 Market penetration by imports from LDC into the EU (in % of apparent domestic consumption), 1970–90

SIC	Category	1970	1983	1990
1	Food, beverages	4.4	4.5	5.9
2	Textiles, clothing	2.5	9.4	16.6
3	Wood & wood products	1.9	3.8	5.2
4	Paper, publishing	0.1	0.5	0.6
5	Chemical & rubber	0.9	3.3	10.4
6	Non-metallic mineral prod.	0.0	0.5	1.0
7	Basic metals (steel)	5.1	4.6	5.6
8	Metal products (machinery)	0.4	1.8	2.8
9	Other	16.9	41.2	63.9
	Manufacturing	2.2	3.3	6.2

Source: Kol (1987), additional estimates.

The European system of preference (GSP) has the following distinctive features (Hine, 1985; Langhammer and Sapir, 1987).

Status   The GSP is not a uniform world system, applied in the same way by all developed countries; on the contrary, the EU, the USA and others have created their own systems, albeit broadly on the same principles. The EU version of GSP is autonomously granted to a number of beneficiary countries. As it is not an agreement concluded between two or more parties after negotiations, the EU can unilaterally decide to change it or even withdraw it completely.

Instrument   The scheme offers a tariff preference: in general goods coming under the GSP are imported into the EU tariff-free, whereas non-GSP countries face the full Common External Tariff. Access is mostly limited to certain quantities, beyond which the full CET is applied. There is no reciprocity, EU exports to GSP countries receiving MFN treatment.

Product coverage   The GSP is confined to semi-manufactured and manufactured goods. For a list of sensitive goods,[3] it is limited to

sometimes fairly restricted quotas. Moreover some products are com
pletely excluded from the application of the GSP, such as textile:
which are ruled by the Multi-Fibre Arrangement (MFA).[4] On th
other hand, some agricultural products are included. A critical loo
at the product structure reveals that the products that are of mos
interest to GSP countries receive the least benefits; they tend to be th
products from sectors for which the pressure to protect Europeai
production is heaviest.

Countries selected   The GSP is in principle available to all developin;
countries, but the EU has specified those to which it agrees to giv
GSP status. In practice, some countries coming under the GSP, sucl
as ACP and Mediterranean countries, prefer other, more advanta
geous schemes; that leaves Latin American and Asian countries a
the most important beneficiaries.

Discrimination   Although the GSP was initially a non-discriminator
scheme, in practice it has developed into a highly complicated ani
selective arrangement. Indeed the trade advantages are differenti
ated according to the level of development of the country involved.

The evaluation of the total trade record of the EU must make
distinction between sectors. For trade in industrial goods, Table 19.
shows that on average the penetration of LDCs into the EU marke
has improved. For trade in agricultural products, however, the EL
record is rather negative. The CAP has repulsed external supplier
from the EU market and it has thrown its huge agricultural surpluse
on the world market with almost unlimited subsidies. This has drivei
developing countries out of their traditional home and export mar
kets, and caused a steep drop in world market prices, and hence ii
the export earnings of developing countries (see, for instance
Matthews, 1985; IBRD, 1985).

Most favoured nation (MFN) (USA, Japan and others)

There is a group of countries with which the EU has establishec
trade relations on the basis of the most-favoured-nation treatment
To this group belong all non-European industrialised countries
Among these, the USA and Japan take pride of place, while others
like Australia, are less important to the EU. We have already indi
cated that trade among GATT partners has been considerably liberal
ised in successive rounds of tariff reductions.

The trade relations with the *USA* have for a long time been strainec
over the CAP, the Americans arguing that Europe prevents thei
exploiting its advantages to the full, the EU complaining that th

JSA subsidises its farmers with amounts at least equivalent to the rotection given to the EU farmer. In the latest round of discussions n trade, the USA has obtained a fair amount of liberalisation of griculture. It has also brought much pressure to bear on the liberali-ation of trade in services that has resulted in agreements.

The trade relations of the EU with *Japan* are strained for one major eason, namely the considerable deficit on the commercial balance etween the two. While in 1970 the trade balance was still practically 1 equilibrium, now EU exports to Japan cover only 30 per cent of its nports from that country. According to some observers, Japanese xporters owe their success to the protection of their own market, uickly achieving profitability and economies of scale there, and nen invading other markets, including the EU market, with low-cost roducts. Without better access to the Japanese market, many EU ountries are not prepared to give up their protectionist measures gainst the flood of Japanese goods.

Central and Eastern Europe

'he trade relations of the EU with centrally planned countries were f a special nature. Up to the end of the 1980s most of these countries vere not contracting parties to the GATT (Lopandic, 1986). Trade mong Council of Mutual Economic Assistance (CMEA or Comecon) nember countries was conducted in the form of barter, and that is he form which had become dominant in East–West trade as well. As rade was a matter of the state in CMEA countries, most East–West rade was based on bilateral cooperation agreements between indi-'idual EU and Comecon member countries. Consultation between he EU and the CMEA was difficult: the EU has found itself com-elled to set the conditions for imports from Comecon countries nilaterally, in the form of import quotas, which were revised every 'ear, again unilaterally.

Since the political changes that occurred in 1989/90 in these coun-ries, the EU has assumed a new responsibility for them to help the ransition process from a command towards a market-oriented economy nd from absolutism towards representative democracy. Trade rela-ions on a completely new footing (trade and cooperation agreements) ave been elaborated that witness the commitment of the EU to letting hese countries (in particular Poland, Hungary and the Czech Repub-ic) participate directly in the process of market integration with a 'iew to becoming in due time also full members of the EU. The asso-iation agreements define the bilateral relations between each indi-'idual associated country and the EU. They are in parallel with the rogrammes of the EU (notably PHARE) that provide for financial ssistance and resource transfer for development.

Many difficult problems as to specific ('sensitive') products hav regularly to be dealt with; it will take some years for the situation t be clarified and the new distribution of comparative advantages t be sorted out.

Economic analysis of differentiation

The previous sections have shown that the EU has developed a com plicated system of trade relations with (groups of) trading partner: mainly on the assumption of the discriminatory benefits of differer tiated tariffs (and quotas). Many would argue that such discrimina tion can hardly be effective, what with the low level of tariffs, on th one hand, and the uncertain prices and exchange rates involved i international trade, on the other. From the vehemence of the politica debate on changing the clauses of discriminatory arrangements, how ever, the advantages accruing to their beneficiaries do seem to b well worth while. Let us dig somewhat deeper into the question b analysing the results of some empirical studies.

EFTA has benefited from free trade with the EU; the effect of fre trade areas among highly developed countries has been analysed i some depth in Chapter 8 (effects of integration).

Mediterranean countries' preferential access to the EU market ha stimulated their exports, with substantial gains for these countrie (Pomfret, 1986). The EU itself appears to pursue mainly politica objectives; the economic effect of its Mediterranean policy seems t be small. However the GSP countries have suffered from the policy' trade-diversion effects.

ACP. The main effect of the early association agreement has beei to produce windfall gains (due to higher export prices) to exporter in ACP countries of some 2.5 per cent of the 1969 export value. N diversion of EC imports to associated countries could be found (Young 1972). Similar effects were also found for the new countries joinin; the first Lomé convention, that registered small trade-creation ef fects, and even smaller trade-diversion effects (from Latin Americai countries to ACP). On the other hand, the ACP countries have no benefited from the extension of the EU; their losses on EU6 market were hardly offset by their gains on the UK market (Moss, 1982).

GSP. The EU's GSP had led by the mid-1970s to a trade expansioi of some 15 per cent of all eligible exports; trade diversion was sligh (about 2 per cent) (Baldwin and Murray, 1977). The positive effect oi GSP exports was small; in the next period it resulted in welfare gain of some 2 per cent for the beneficiary GSP countries and a loss c about 0.5 per cent for the EU; third countries had lost no welfare a far as the manufacturing sectors were concerned, but about 1 pe cent in agriculture (Davenport, 1986; Langhammer and Sapir, 1987'

The aid equivalent of the tariff preferences was almost negligible as a consequence of the multitude of controls for sensitive products.

Developing countries: these countries have concluded an 'unholy alliance' (Wolf, 1988) with the EU by creating a system of preferential liberalisation and discriminatory protection, which tends to weaken the world's liberal trade system. Both the EU and the developing countries start from the belief that this is beneficial to them. Yet there is evidence (Van Wijnbergen, 1985) that trade intervention not only shifts the terms of trade of LDC adversely, but also leads to higher interest rates. Indeed the protection of the EU *vis-à-vis* LDC countries has considerable negative effects on GDP in both developed and developing countries.

CMEA/CEEC. The proliferation of EU preferential trade agreements with various groups of countries have placed CMEA exporters at an increasing disadvantage as regards market access conditions. However this does not seem to have exerted a restrictive influence on EU–CMEA trade; CMEA exporters appear to have managed to overcome the damaging effects (Yannopoulos, 1985). Now these countries have quickly moved up the hierarchy and in the long run benefits may be expected of the same type as for EFTA.

From trade to foreign policy

Production factors

The EU has been given distinct powers in external trade matters (negotiations with the Commission, treaty with the Council) and the previous sections have given an idea of the complex system that has evolved. There is nothing comparable for the external relations engendered by the Common Market. The competence of the EU and the national governments with respect to production factors (already touched upon in Chapters 9 and 10) are different for labour and capital.

For *labour* the EU resembles a free trade area. There is full freedom of internal movement for EU nationals. External relations with respect to the movement of both workers and non-active persons from third countries are governed by bilateral agreements and conventions that each of the individual member countries has concluded with third countries. That implies that there is no free movement within the EU of nationals of third countries, living or working in another EU member country. Evidently this is becoming a problem now that the controls of the inner frontiers have been abolished, but member states have worked out other administrative rules for controlling residences of non-EU citizens. As these controls cannot be perfect, countries know that they will be confronted with illega immigration. There is significant pressure on the EU to work out common policy towards immigration (permanent stay) and a com mon visa policy (temporary stay), which would bring the EU in lin with the definition of Common Market in this area also. Unlike th situation for trade, there is no institution on the world level that i empowered to deal with migration matters, so the EU is likely t proceed by unilateral rules or bilateral agreements with the mos concerned third countries. The rules that apply now are as follows:

- *European Economic Area.* The EEA Treaty stipulates that th present internal EU rules on freedom of movement will b applicable over the whole EEA area for nationals of all EU an EFTA countries; additional rules for third country nationals.
- *Central and Eastern Europe.* The association agreements betwee the EU and the CEEC liberalise the movement of workers t the extent that this is conditional for the transformation of th CEEC economies (for example, specialists and managers). Fo the rest it is regulated by bilateral agreements.
- *Other.* There is a harmonisation of member states' immigratio policy (both for workers and others) that goes on outside th present EU framework in intergovernmental cooperation; how ever, this has not yet resulted in a common policy, and progres is likely to remain slow.[5]

For capital, external free movement awaits full realisation by th mid-1990s, and in the meantime some EU countries maintain differ ent types of capital controls. Much of the integration in capital mar kets was not achieved by EU countries among themselves (see Chap ter 10), but by individual EU countries with the off-shore capita markets. The efficiency of these markets required that the full liber alisation of the EU capital market be accompanied by a policy o external openness of EU countries 'erga omnes'; that is, free move ment towards partner and third countries alike. Indeed the capita diversion effects of any EU-wide control would have been too costl to be acceptable for countries that had already opened up to the res of the world. The Maastricht Treaty installs such a EU policy o complete openness towards third countries for capital transactions; i foresees, however, some restrictions in the form of safeguard meas ures (see Chapter 10).

Contrary to the situation in goods trade, the EU lacks externa identity with respect to capital movements, which is evident from the fact that the EU as such does not participate in the IMF or th Bank of International Settlements.

Economic and monetary policies

Little progress has been made with the external relations of an economic and monetary union.

- *Allocation* policies are hardly coordinated with third countries. The noteworthy exception is the coordination between the EU and the EFTA in the framework of the 'European Economic Area' on matters regarding the internal market.
- *Redistribution* policies towards third countries are hardly the subject of coordination on the world level either. However the political basis for solidarity has developed to some extent among very close trade partners. Aid to development (LDC) and to transition (CEEC) is an EU matter (see below). A common policy may be more efficient than independent ones, the more so because trade issues are closely related to development issues.
- *Stabilisation* policies, if coordinated internationally, have the same type of advantages as was pointed out for internal EU coordination (Chapter 17). Such global coordination is starting, albeit slowly. The EU involvement in the work of the groups charged with coordinating the macro and monetary policies (the Group of Five (or Seven) largest developed countries) is increasing. The need for coordination and stabilisation of exchange rates on the world scale is most acute for the stabilisation of the key currency, the US dollar. The variations in the $/ECU exchange rate (see Figure 19.1) have been particularly wide over the past 15 years, leading to conflicts between the USA and the EU. Coordination of exchange rate policies is practically limited to the countries of the OECD area, and virtually non-existent with other areas.

Clearly the further development of the EU identity will have to lead to a definition of a common EU policy *vis-à-vis* third countries on all matters that follow from the internal development of the Economic and Monetary Union. It also leads logically to the increased participation of the Commission in the relevant 'negotiations' on behalf of the member states. Given the diversity of third countries, it may be a political necessity to differentiate the EU regime *vis-à-vis* the outside world in a similar way, by groups, as has been done for goods trade.

Aid to development and to transition

The EU and its member states have both a moral obligation and good economic reasons to cooperate to achieve a better distribution of wealth at the world level (legally enshrined in Articles 3k and 227).

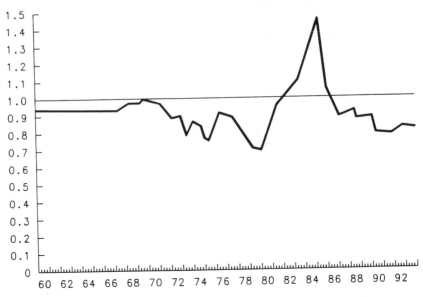

Figure 19.1 $/ECU exchange rate over time

Some theoretical reasons for this involvement of the EU are that the EU is the organisation responsible for commerce; that the gains from international trade may be unevenly distributed among partners; and moreover that the protectionism which the EU maintains on some scores for reasons of internal redistribution may have a negative effect on world equilibrium. The EU ought to compensate for all this with a common policy. Such common policies have been set up for two types of problem areas: aid to developing countries and aid to countries in transition.

Aid to development of third world countries was already foreseen by the Treaty of Rome. Its targets are limited to the associated ACP countries. Abstracting from trade, which was dealt with earlier, and from balance-of-payment aid, which the EU does not give, three types of support mechanism are applied:

- *Investment.* The European Development Fund provides loans and grants to facilitate investment in infrastructure, both of an economic (roads, ports, water) and of a social type (hospitals, schools, information and trade-promotion institutions) and to productive investments in agriculture, mining, industry and energy (Stevens, 1981). Investment is also promoted by loans from the EIB and by the Centre for Industrial Development.[6]
- *Stabilisation of export earnings.* The STABEX mechanism for agri-

cultural and the SYSMIN system for mineral products are simple. If the value of an ACP country's exports to the EU drops by more than a certain minimum percentage, the EU compensates for the loss with a transfer of money. The schemes apply only to products contributing substantially to the country's total export earnings. The schemes give only temporary support, cushioning the first shock rather than compensating losses in the long run. STABEX and SYSMIN transfers represent a special budget line of the EDF.

- *Food aid.* The provision of food to people in areas struck by acute famine is taken from the EU stocks (or surpluses from the farm policy, see Chapter 11). Besides its evident positive humanitarian effects it has also had the negative effect of disrupting the indigenous system of production and commerce, and undoing the efforts of agro-industrial development aid (Eussner, 1986).

The evaluation of the EU development policy produces a mixed picture. In view of the limited value of the trade arrangements for development purposes, the aid programme is looked upon as the centrepiece of the Lomé arrangements. The latter is both cited as an example of good policy and the object of much criticism. In general, EU aid does not seem less effective than other aid schemes (Hewitt, 1984). There are no systematic evaluation studies of the contribution EU aid has made to economic growth in ACP countries and thus to narrowing the wealth gap between them and the EU.

European aid to transition is a recent policy. The major programme is PHARE, an acronym for Poland and Hungary Action for the Restructuring of the Economy; similar programmes exist for the other Central and Eastern European Countries (CEEC). The European Commission implements these PHARE programmes in its role as coordinator of the assistance of 24 western countries. The major contribution to their finances comes from the EU budget. The PHARE programme (as an 'extra-EU' redistribution programme) resembles the set-up chosen for the ERDF ('intra-EU' redistribution programme; see Chapter 18) in that:

- funds are offered as non-reimbursable grants and not in the form of loans;
- projects eligible for support must enhance the process of reform and reconstruction (for example, agriculture, energy, training, environmental protection);
- recipient countries need to propose the relevant programmes for EU support; the EU, however, often provides technical assistance, studies and so on, to set them up.

As the programmes have only recently really come off the ground, it is too early for an evaluation of the effectiveness of the EU policy in this field.

Foreign policy

The European Union has become increasingly aware of two facts: (1) third countries tend to look upon the Union as one political entity also in non-economic matters, and expect a common stand of the member states on a large variety of diplomatic issues (such as apartheid in South Africa, peacekeeping in former Yugoslavia); (2) coordinated foreign policies tend to increase the effectiveness of individual member states' actions (for instance in the fight against terrorism). This led in the 1960s to regular meetings of the Ministers of Foreign Affairs of EU countries regarding diplomatic questions. In the 1970s, the European Political Cooperation (EPC) was created as an intergovernmental 'institution', not linked to the EU framework, and working essentially through information and consultation. The centrepiece of the EPC was the commitment to consultation with partners before adopting final positions or launching national initiatives on all important questions of foreign policy common to EU member countries, and to the joint implementation of actions. Over the years the cooperation has steadily intensified and its scope has continually broadened. The work of the Conference of Ministers was complemented by meetings of the Political Committee (high-ranking civil servants) and expert groups. The dissociation of the EPC from the normal EU institutions was increasingly felt as a problem. This led, first, to the regular participation of the president of the Commission and the Commissioner for External Relations in the EPC conferences. Next, the EPC was formally hooked onto the EU institutional framework by the Single European Act, without changing much its objectives or its intergovernmental features. The Treaty on European Union has brought the still intergovernmental work on foreign policy under the EU umbrella. As external economic and diplomatic issues are closely intertwined the Presidency and the Commission have to ensure the consistency of the two policies.

How important is this common foreign policy in *economic* terms? Two sides of the problem can be distinguished in this regard:

- the use of economic instruments by third countries to pursue non-economic foreign policy objectives may directly affect the European internal market or endanger the security of supplies to the EU. An example was the selective oil embargo of Arab states against some EU countries in the 1970s. Sometimes the

EU uses sanctions (for instance, against South Africa), or imposes export restrictions on strategically important goods;[7]
* progress towards further integration by completing the internal market implies common foreign policy measures. A case in point is the common visa policy for foreign visitors, which has become necessary now that the controls of persons at internal borders have been abolished.

Security (defence) policy

A particularly important matter in the context of a European external policy is defence. The history of this starts right from the birth of the EEC. One of the major objectives envisaged with the creation of the EEC was to contribute to a durable peace; however its pursuit was to be made by economic means, not by military ones. We may bring to mind that, after the failure of the European Defence Community in the 1950s, European defence matters were treated in international bodies such as NATO (North Atlantic Treaty Organisation) and the WEU (Western European Union). All EU12 member states, except neutral Ireland, are members of NATO, in which, moreover, two other West European countries are grouped: Norway and Turkey. The WEU was created by the Treaty of Brussels in 1954 to strengthen peace and security. Its members are the original six EU members plus the UK, Spain and Portugal. Attempts to extend WEU membership to all new EU members and merge its institutional structure with that of the EU have in the past been opposed from two sides. Some of the present members feared that the centrifugal forces resulting from such extension might jeopardise cooperation, difficult enough among the nine present members. On the other hand, in a country like Ireland there is doubt whether its constitution permits WEU membership.

Defence is now an integral part of the competences of the European Union. Like foreign policy it is carried out in an intergovernmental way. The WEU has become an integral part of the development of the EU; the EU will request the WEU to elaborate and implement decisions and actions of the EU which have defence implications (Article 7.4.2. TEU).

Summary and conclusions

* The EU is based on a customs union; in practice its external relations are mostly trade relations. However its progress towards economic and monetary union has drawn other areas, such as immigration, international capital and monetary matters,

into the domain of EU external policy. Moreover the TEU has integrated a number of non-economic elements in a full-dress EU external policy.

- A complicated system of trade advantages, differentiated according to specific groups of countries, has been drawn up. Although this system has some of the economic effects hoped for and has been established for political reasons, it would seem advisable to simplify it considerably.

- The common commercial policy uses a spread of instruments to regulate trade and protect EU industry. However the EU has consistently moved towards greater liberalisation of world trade and, apart from agricultural matters, is fairly open to third country suppliers.

- The external relations implied in the establishment of the Common Market (labour capital) and the Economic and Monetary Union (for example, currency policy) give a growing identity to the EU in matters of foreign policy.

- Foreign and security policies are coordinated with economic external policies. They are the object of intergovernmental cooperation.

Notes

1 Important new subjects discussed in the recent Uruguay round are the regimes for agriculture and services. Subjects treated cover trade-related aspects of intellectual property rights (TRIPS) and trade-related investment measures (TRIMS).

2 The idea of hierarchy, layer, and so on is also found back in the pyramid concept proposed by Mishalani *et al.* (1981). For a more elaborate discussion, see Hine (1985) and Pomfret (1986).

3 For a list of so-called 'sensitive products' (goods whose increased imports would cause serious damage to certain European producers) quotas were set on a national basis, both on the EU (importer) side and on that of the exporters. Davenport (1986) reports that the EU GSP involved some 40,000 different EU-wide and bilateral quotas and ceilings.

4 Although MFA protection was tightened a great deal (quotas specified for individual exporting countries and EC importing countries in the 1970s), no great change of trade flows has resulted from it (Kol, 1987). There was a swift growth of imports from LDCs into the EU, but also of EU exports to the former.

5 On many detailed points, such as visas, passports, asylum seekers and so on some form of coordination has existed for some time on the basis of concerted practices of the national administrations.

6 The principal task of this organisation is to help small and medium-sized firms to establish joint ventures in ACP countries; the EIB can only help to finance profitable projects.

7 For the limited effectiveness of economic sanctions, see Hufbauer and Scott (1985), Van Bergeijk (1987) and Kaempfer and Loewenberg (1992).

PART VI
CONCLUSION

20 Evaluation and Outlook

Introduction

The objective of this book has been to present an economic analysis of the process of European integration. To that end we described in the first part the conceptual basis, the historical roots and the institutional framework of integration. In the next two parts we discussed the theoretical foundations and empirical dynamics of the customs union and common market, respectively, with at their centre the freedom of movement of goods, services, labour and capital. The changes in the organisation of economic activity in the various sectors of the economy under the influence of economic integration occupied the central place in this book. As freedoms cannot flourish nor economic sectors develop unless government creates the proper conditions, a discussion of the policies pursued with these goals in mind complemented the book.

At the end of this analysis of separate segments, a more general view of the dynamics of the whole process of European economic integration seems in order. To measure the progress of integration we will make a distinction between indicators of a more economic nature, such as the share of trade in total GDP, and the more policy-oriented indicators, such as the limitation of power of nation states in different segments of economic policy. As economic integration is to be instrumental to the attainment of higher goals, we will evaluate its contribution to the growth and the distribution of welfare and to a number of non-economic objectives of integration.

The economic integration of Europe is a process of long duration that is far from being completed. In the future, integration will enter new fields and become more intensive in the fields already covered. In the last sections of this chapter we will look ahead. For both deepening (the new areas of competence for the EU) and widening (the geographical extension of the EU) we will sketch the likely developments and their economic impact for a selected range of

issues. A more projective and speculative approach characterises thi
outlook, unlike the rigour with which we have presented the thec
retical and empirical results in all previous parts of the book. A
usual a short summary completes the chapter.

Progress of integration: economic indicators

Quantities

A usual way to measure the progress of integration is by looking a
the evolution of the quantities traded or exchanged. For goods an
services this is done in practice by measuring the extent to which th
production of one country is consumed in another. In much the sam
way, the advance of integration on the markets for production fac
tors can be assessed by the change in the extent to which the labou
and capital of one country are put to work in another. Both indicator
have been employed in the detailed analysis of the preceding chap
ters; Table 20.1 combines the dispersed results.

For *goods and services* the figures leave little room for doubt. B
1990, EU countries had become far more integrated with their par
ners than in 1960 and the same can be said of the integration of th
EU in the world economy. Looking specifically at goods trade, w
observe that the orientation of trade has changed under the influenc
of integration. In 1960 trade in goods was more oriented toward
third countries than to (potential) partner countries, whereas in 199
intra-EU relations largely outweighed the extra-EU ones. For se
vices, intra-EU trade has always been of the same order of magn
tude as extra-EU trade. The increase in internationalisation is ver
visible for both intra- and extra-EU trade; the latter, of course, reflec
the growing importance of the world economy (for example, tran
port, insurance) for EU producers and consumers.

For *labour* the figures indicate that only a small percentage of la
bour in EU countries is of foreign origin, and that this percentage ha
been very stable over the last 30 years. The average percentage shar
of labour from other EU member countries in the total labour force c
the member countries of the EU oscillated within a narrow ban
around 2 per cent between 1960 and 1990. For workers from outsid
the EU, the level is rather low, too; a steep increase in the 1960s wa
followed by a levelling off in recent years. In interpreting this indica
tion of limited integration, one should remember that massive m
gration flows were never an objective of the EU. On the contrary, th
movement of capital to, and the differential growth of, the economie
of poor member countries were intended to keep intra-EU migratio

Table 20.1 Percentage growth of market integration in the EU (goods, services, labour and capital), 1960–90

		1960	1970	1980	1990
Customs unions					
Goods[a]	Intra	5	8	13	17
	Extra	9	10	11	12
Services[a]	Intra	1	2	3	3
	Extra	1	2	2	3
Common market					
Labour[b]	Intra	2	2	2	2
	Extra	1	3	3	3
Capital DI[c]	Intra	n.a.	1	1	2
	Extra	n.a.	1	2	2
Capital income[d]	Intra	n.a.	—	1	2
	Extra	n.a.	1	2	3

[a] Average of imports and exports as a percentage share of GDP.
[b] Non-nationals as a percentage of total labour force.
[c] Direct investment; three-year averages (1970 = average of 1969–70–71); average of imports and exports as a percentage share of Gross Fixed Capital Formation.
[d] Income from investments abroad as a percentage of GDP.
Sources: Goods: Chapter 6; services: Chapter 7, plus some estimates based on balance-of-payments data; labour: Chapter 9; capital: Chapter 10, Matisse (1988), plus some estimates based on balance-of-payments data.

in check (see Chapter 9), while national admittance laws regulated immigration from third countries.

For *capital*, the only way to analyse movements effectively is to break them down by type. The most important category for our purpose is direct investment (DI). Within the EU, foreign direct investment has been fully liberalised since the 1970s. Although its volume increased considerably between 1970 and 1990, its share in total Gross Fixed Capital Formation (GFCF) is still modest. EU countries were less oriented to their partners than to third countries; this is due as much to heavy EU investment activity abroad as to foreign (third country) investment in EU countries. However in recent years the interrelations among EU countries have been developing much faster than those with third countries. Here the effect of the single market is visible. Figures of the quantities exchanged are available for DI but not for other forms of capital movement (Euromarkets).

Another indicator of the integration of capital markets is the income received from investment abroad (both DI and Portfolio). The figures available show a very fast increase for both external and internal EU relations. The increasingly global character of capi tal markets is reflected in the relative importance of the extra-EU relations with respect to the relations among EU countries them selves.

Prices

The progress of integration can also be measured by the convergence of prices for the same goods and services and production factors in the various countries of the EU. However the international comparison of prices is beset with difficulties, both of a methodological and statistical nature. The few figures available are reviewed hereafter (Table 20.2).

Goods   There is a clear convergence of prices for consumer and producer goods in the 1975–85 period. Whether this convergence is entirely attributable to economic integration is not certain. Indeed the integration effect is difficult to isolate from the effects of the many other factors that influence the structure of prices.

Services   The few data available do not suggest any convergence, which is in keeping with the still limited integration of this sector (evidenced in Chapters 7 and 14).

Wages   The price of labour appears to have shown a gradual convergence, but whether that is indeed an integration effect remains highly uncertain at this stage (Chapter 9).

Capital   Prices on the markets for short-term loans have converged. For long-term credit the situation is more involved; here the turbulence of the first oil shock brought a clear divergence; after 1979, however, the prices converged as well. The fact that the figures clearly began to change soon after major measures of liberalisation had been taken suggests that the recent convergence is probably due to integration (Chapter 10).

Progress of integration: policy indicators

Institutions: growth of operations

Looking at the European Union as an organisation, we can measure the progress of integration in several ways, of which we have picked out three. The most obvious indicator is the increase in the *number of members*. Indeed widening has been a distinct feature of the dynam-

Table 20.2   Price convergence for goods, services and production factors, 1965–85

Indicator		1965	1975	1985
Customs union[a]				
Consumer goods	(tax-inclusive)	n.a.	20.5	19.4
	(tax-exclusive)	n.a.	16.3	15.2
Equipment goods	(tax-inclusive)	n.a.	13.7	12.4
	(tax-exclusive)	n.a.	13.7	12.4
Services	(tax-inclusive)	n.a.	27.3	27.2
	(tax-exclusive)	n.a.	n.a.	n.a.
Common market		1963/74	1973/79	1980/86
Labour[b]	wages	n.a.	n.a.	n.a.
Capital[c]	interest rate			
Long-term		0.94	0.81	0.92
Short-term		0.42	0.61	0.71

[a]   Index of dispersion (see Chapters 6 and 7); the lower the indices the higher the integration (source: Emerson *et al.*, 1988).
[b]   See Chapter 9.
[c]   Different indicators taken from studies cited in Chapter 10, note 5. The closer these indicators come to 100, the higher the integration.

ics of the EU. Membership has increased at regular 14-year intervals and by the same number (three). The Benelux, a precursor of the EEC, was created by three countries in 1944; the EEC was created by the original six members in 1958; its first extension came in 1972 when the three northern countries joined, and the second extension with the three Mediterranean countries was realised in 1986.

An indicator of integration that visualises growth, even to the casual observer, is the *number of people* involved in the EU policy-making machinery (input) (Table 20.3). The core of this is formed by the civil servants employed by the Commission and other EU institutions. Their number has rapidly increased; for example, with the Commission, from one to 15 thousand between 1960 and 1990 (in the same period, the total number of civil servants in the countries of the EU12 rose from 4 to 8 million). In the first ring around this core we find national civil servants and politicians. The meetings of the Council of Ministers, of its working parties and of experts of the Commission have become more and more frequent. Finally we cite interest groups. In the 1960–90 period new lobbyist groups were regularly established, and older ones increased their efforts to influence European policy and decision making by extending their membership and consolidating their presence in the centre of EU decision making. The first to be set up were transnational interest groups in the industrial, commercial and professional spheres. From 1965 to 1985, the rate of increase was rather low. From 1985 to 1990 a new upsurge in the growth of lobby groups occurred under the impetus of the single market. Alongside the growth of the traditional ones, many new lobby groups have appeared on the scene (local authorities, extra-EU interest, and so on).

Table 20.3   Growth of activity of those involved in EU operations, 1960–90

Indicator	1960	1970	1980	1990
Permanent civil servants (000s) of Commission[a]	1	5	11	17
Number of lobby organisations[b]	167	309	410	3 000
Official Journal (000 pages)	2	12	26	n.a.
Judgements of the ECJ[c]	n.a.	240	830	1 780

[a] Sources: CEC (1986i), CEC *General Reports, Official Journal* (several years). Own estimates.
[b] In 1990, transnational producer and professional groups were estimated at some 700; new lobby groups at some 2,300; the 3,000 groups totalling some 10,000 lobbyists (Anderson and Eliassen, 1991).
[c] Periods (e.g. 1970 = 1960–69).

A third indicator is the *yearly production of directives and regulations* of the legislature and of judgements by the judicial authorities (output). A cursory analysis of the number of pages of the *Official Journal* and of the number of judgements of the Court between 1960 and 1990 is indicative of the advance of integration (also manifest from the volume of preparatory work that precedes the actual publication: the continuous growth of the total output of expert studies, committee reports, white papers, communications and so on).

Subject matters: the movement to higher stages

There are sound economic as well as political reasons to start economic integration with goods markets (customs union), continue with production factors (common market) and conclude with intensified policy integration (economic and monetary union). In that view, the progress of economic integration in Europe can be measured by the stage it has reached at different points in time. Remember, however, that the stages are not strictly successive in the sense that the lower ones have to be fully realised before the higher ones

:an be tried for. Rather, as remarked earlier (Chapter 2), progress in he higher stages is a condition for the full realisation of the lower ›nes.

The *Customs Union* was to be realised before the end of the 1960s Articles 3a.b). The evidence from internal and external trade in goods ‹Chapters 6, 12 and 19) shows that for large parts of the economy manufactured goods) that objective has indeed been realised quickly. Iowever services and some other sectors have remained protected ʹor a long time (Chapters 7, 14 and 19). For these sectors the CU has ɪlso been implemented in the framework of the 1992 programme see Chapter 16). Apart from relics (such as electrical energy, rail ʹransport and consumer services) this programme is now completed ɪnd hence the CU can for all practical purposes be considered as ʹully realised.

The *Common Market*, implying the abolition of obstacles to the free novement of capital and workers (Article 3c), is an old target. Progress ›n it has been fairly rapid for large parts of both the labour and ʹapital markets (see Chapters 9 and 10). However until recently, ʌarge sections of both remained excluded. For production factors, the ɪ992 programme has set the objective of complete abolition of the ʹemaining frontiers, and this target has also been largely attained. Iere, too, some exceptions persist, such as the fact that the external ʹegime of the labour market has not yet been decided on.

The *Economic and Monetary Union* became an objective of the EU in he 1970s. Before that time, a number of common policies (Articles 3d ›o 3g) had been adopted and the coordination of monetary policy ɪad been prepared. Notably the creation and successful operation of he EMS paved the way for the further integration foreseen by the Maastricht Treaty.

Full Economic Union: in the past, work started on a number of ;ubjects engaging the EU in an even closer integration than that mplied by the CM and the EMU. The EU has penetrated into fields ;uch as environment, culture and education, for which the TEU has ;et the framework for further future developments.

Instruments: the shift of competence from national to European institutions

All progress of integration tends to curb the freedom of action of the member states' policy makers. The more use is made of higher in-;truments from the hierarchy, from information via consultation and ɪarmonisation to uniformity (Chapter 2), the more the autonomy of the member states will be limited and the further integration has ɪpparently progressed. The progress made since the EU came into ɛxistence is indicated in Table 20.4.

Table 20.4   Synoptic view of the development through time[a] of the degree of policy integration[b] by activity area,[c] 1960–90

Field of action	1960	1970	1980	1990
Four freedoms				
goods	U	U	U	U
services	U	U	U	U
labour	U	U	U	U
capital	U*	U*	U*	U
Allocation				
competition	U*	U*	U*	U*
fiscal	C*	H*	H*	H*
technical	C*	H*	H	H
structural	C*	C	C	H
Stabilisation				
monetary	C	C	H*	H*
macro and budgetary	C	C	C	C
growth policy	I	I	C	C
Redistribution				
regional	I	C	H	U*
social	H*	H*	H*	H*
External				
trade: goods	U	U	U	U
trade: services	I	C	H	U
production factors: labour	O*	I*	C	H
production factors: capital	I*	C	H	U
development aid	U*	U*	U*	U*
foreign	O	O	I	C
defence	O	O	O	C
Other				
environment, etc.	O	I	C	H
culture	O	O	I*	C*
home	O	O	O	I
physical planning	O	O	O	I
education	O	O	O	I

[a]   The first column presents the situation at the moment of birth of the EU; the last colum describes the recent situation; the middle columns describe the situation just before th first and second extensions.

[b]   Evidently, each situation is liable to be characterised differently by different observers; w think, however, that the table gives a fair overall picture.

[c]   An asterisk indicates that only part of the policy field is affected by the indicator given; fo that part the highest form is indicated. O means that there was no EC involvement; Information; C: Consultation; H: Harmonisation; and U: Unification.

'or the *four freedoms* – of goods, services, labour and capital – the
situation is clear: from the outset their EEC regimes were fully uni-
orm; in principle the member states ceded from the start all relevant
authority to the EU. An exception was initially made for capital, of
which, until recently, the movements were liberalised only as far as
necessary for the functioning of the Common Market.[1]

Allocation covers policies that aim at the proper functioning of the
common (internal) market, including those that try to improve the
structure of productive activity. Right from the start competition
policy was harmonised, some would say even partly unified. Although the scope of the European competition policy has since been
broadened (services and so on) and the intensity with which it is
pursued stepped up, the situation of the division of competencies
has remained virtually unchanged. For fiscal, technical and related
internal market policies, a timid start with consultation was soon
followed by partial harmonisation efforts (for example, for value
added in fiscal matters). The EU accepted very early responsibility
for a limited part of structural sectoral policy (agriculture, and coal
and steel) but, for most sectors, integrating efforts of industrial policy
have not passed beyond the stage of consultation. In the 1980s some
large-scale European supply-side programmes were implemented
(Esprit, Monitor and so on), for which 'harmonisation' seems to be
an apt description.

For *stabilisation* policies – mostly monetary and macro-economic –
consultation was foreseen right from the start.[2] In the past 30 years,
consultation has intensified but the pattern has remained largely the
same as in 1958. The only form of harmonisation concerned the EMS,
created to stabilise exchange rates.

In *redistribution*, we have distinguished regional and social policies. The EU started in 1958 without a clear idea about regional
policies.[3] By 1973 a consultation procedure (study and so on) had
been put into practice. With the creation of the European Regional
Development Fund (ERDF), national regional policies were subjected
to European harmonisation; with the extension of the scope of the
ERDF, partial unification seems the more adequate characterisation.
For social policies, the situation is different; the European Social
Fund (ESF) was created right at the start of the EU, and there has
been considerable development since. Notwithstanding this extension, we indicate partial harmonisation even for 1990, as some very
important fields, such as social security, remain largely unaffected by
the integration process.

External policies cover a whole array of policies, from trade to defence. The common trade policy (implying uniformity) has been
quickly realised for goods, but for services it has only gradually
come off the ground. External policies for production factors were

absent in the 1960s; some coordination began in the 1970s. Recently common policy for capital was decided on (full external freedom). *A* part of development aid has been uniform right from the beginning but the better part of it remained in national (uncoordinated) hands. In the 1980s some consultation on diplomatic and defence matter was practised (EPC).

Other policies that were non-existent in 1960 have become the objec of EU consultation and harmonisation, cases in point being, respec tively, culture and environment.

Summarising, we find that the use of higher instruments clearly increased over time. Between 1960 and 1990 the number of H score rose from 1 to 7, the number of U from 7 to 10, while the number o uncoordinated areas diminished (O scores going down from 8 to 0), scores from 4 to 3. The progress of policy integration in the EU between periods seemed to have accelerated slightly; 7 scores mov ing up in the 1960–70 period, 9 in the 1970–80 period, and 11 in the 1980–90 period.

Objectives and results

Economic growth and equal distribution

Economic integration is not an end in itself but is pursued to realise faster economic growth, that is, wealth improvement. The income effects of market and policy integration of the EU have been substan tial. We can summarise the various empirical studies, reported on ir the previous chapters, as follows.

For *product markets* the effects have been calculated mostly for manufactured goods, only leaving agriculture, energy and services largely out of account. The static income effects of the free movemen of goods are rather small, somewhere in the order of 1 per cent However the dynamic effects are very important (for example Emerson *et al.*, 1988); the combined effects of better market entry and increased competition, more innovation, learning and economies o scale, amounted to some 6 per cent of GDP.

For *labour markets* the welfare effects spring in particular from the immigration of people from third countries, as migration among EU countries has on the whole been on a low level. The employment o immigrant workers has had a small direct positive effect on tota production and GDP (Askari, 1974). The dynamic effects of labour immigration are not well quantified. Some believe that immigration by removing certain bottlenecks from the economy, has led to a permanently higher growth of GNP; others point out that immigra tion has prevented the economies of the EU from adjusting structur ally to the new world conditions in comparative advantages. The net effect is not quantified.

For *capital markets* the empirical evidence on the welfare effects of integration is very thin, and differs from one sub-market to another. For direct-investment flows attention has been limited to employment effects: these seem invariably positive for the host country, but for the home countries vary from negative (when exports from the home bases are replaced) to positive (when the DI facilitates penetration of a foreign market, thus enhancing activity at home as well) (Buckley and Artisien, 1987).

For *common policies* the situation as regards the welfare effect is very unclear. Although some headway has been made with the study of the efficiency of individual policies, the quantification of the growth and welfare effects of policy integration has received very little attention so far.

A major objective of the EU is to achieve a balanced distribution of this wealth. In other words, the EU strives for a harmonious development of the European economy by reducing the differences in wealth among the various countries and regions. It implies the pursuit of policies leading to higher than average growth rates for low-income countries and regions. The EU has managed to come closer to this objective; indeed a comparison of the growth figures of the individual member countries with the EU average shows that many of the low-income countries in 1950 have grown at a more than average rate, while others that were rich at the outset remained below the average, so that in 1990 there was more equality than in 1950. Although access to the EU is believed to have had a marked influence on the high growth figures of Italy in the 1960s and of Spain and Portugal in more recent years (higher than the EU average: CEC, 1988a) no formal proof of an equalising effect of EU integration has as yet been given.

Beyond economics

Economic integration is also a method for attaining some non-economic objectives. In recent European history (see Chapter 4) two such objectives have been paramount:

- *Peace*. Countries that are very dependent on one another will not enter easily into an armed conflict.
- *Democracy and human rights*. A democratic system of government and respect for fundamental human rights are the conditions for participating in the EU. Attempts to overthrow this order will have little chance of success in an integrated framework.

The three objectives – growth, peace and democracy – have had different weights in the setting up and extension of the institutions that in the past have given form to European integration. The Benelux Economic Union did only pursue economic objectives, the EU strove for both growth and peace, while EFTA's objective was only growth. The first extension of the EU had only an economic target, whereas for the second both the growth and the democracy argument were used. For the future we may extend these lines. The next enlargement of the EU with EFTA countries will again only have an economic objective, whereas for the extension with CEEC all three arguments will be very relevant. Apart from its economic objectives, political scientists agree that the EU has also attained its non-economic objectives.

Each organisation has also defined a number of derived objectives. These can be defined in terms of stages of integration. The gradual stepping-up of the ambitions and development of their realisation over time has been summarised in Table 20.5.

Table 20.5   The process of deepening and widening of European integration

Deepening	Widening				
	1944 Benelux	1958 EU6	1972 EU9	1986 EU12	2000 EU ?
ICM		*	*		
CM				*	*
EU	*			*	*
MU				*	*
PU					*

Looking at the overall process of deepening and widening we may conclude that the EU has needed in the past about 14 years to forge strong links between the members of a group, working towards the attainment of a well-defined objective. This turned out to be the basis on which a new extended group could start work on a higher objective. However, if we analyse the process in rather more depth, we see that there are intermediate steps, too (1952 for the ECSC; 1967 for the first unsuccessful negotiations with the UK; 1981 for the accession of Greece). If at this point of passage from past to future we extend this periodicity, we come up with the prediction that both deepening and widening will proceed. Deepening will lead the EU further on the road to EMU and a political union. Widening will result in a first round of extension between 1993 and 2000 and a second one somewhat further into the next century. We will go into these points in greater detail.

Success factors

From the various strands of literature we have distilled the following general factors that have conditioned in the past the success of progressive integration.

Unity of purpose   The EU started with a limited number of members around the strong axis of France and Germany. The risk of dilution was limited as extensions were few, occurred only after considerable periods of internal strengthening, and new members were only admitted on the condition that they accepted the 'acquis communautaire' of the past and the new objectives for the future.

Limited diversity   Differences in levels of development between the members are not very large by world 'standards'. All EU countries belong, indeed, to the category of (highly) developed countries. As a consequence, one could start without intra-EU financial transfers, always a bone of contention, and continue with a redistribution scheme that kept transfers at a relatively low level.

Safety mechanism against reverse developments   The integration of markets, once achieved, cannot be rejected by a member state. Safeguards are the whole EU legal system and the heavy cost that a breakaway would inflict on business that has organised itself on the assumption of durable and reliable access to markets, complemented by common policies.

Institutional strength   The powers of the EU to make laws on the basis of qualified majority voting that are, moreover, directly applicable in all member states have permitted this 'supranational' organisation to function very effectively and efficiently; it has reduced very significantly the cost of bargaining, that is of reaching cooperative solutions to political problems in areas where national policies have lost effectiveness. So the EU could be successful even in many situations where intergovernmental organisations would have got stuck owing to unwillingness on the part of the national polity and bureaucracy (Moravcsik, 1993).

Operational flexibility   If needed, the EU has permitted exceptions to general rules, for example with longer transition periods for Mediterranean countries to comply with the rules of the internal market or environmental policy. In some cases it has even permitted the opting out of certain members for whole sections of its activity (as with the UK for the social chapter).

Specific accelerations of the process of deepening, like the completion of the internal market, have occurred when the following set of conditions were fulfilled:

- clear-cut objectives that can be easily understood by large sections of society (for example, removal of barriers for the completion of the internal market);
- tangible gains; felt directly by influential interest groups like big business and supported by independent assessments or by academics (as with the studies on the cost of non-Europe for the benefits of the 1992 programme);
- coherent action for realisations, with a timetable and a clear distribution of roles for the various actors (Commission, industry associations and so on; see white paper (CEC, 1985d) and subsequent work programme for '1992').

If these conditions are not all fulfilled, progress may stagnate. An example is the EMU, where the critics question both the gains that can be obtained from the exercise and the best actions that should be taken for the realisation of the objective.

The process of widening has deliberately started from a narrow base. When the EU was created, a number of countries, among them the UK, were in favour of a free trade zone with a large number of participants. For political reasons ('Nous ne voulons pas un arrangement commercial, mais une méthode pour réunir les peuples' from Jean Monnet) a small group of countries opted for a higher degree of integration and strong institutions. The diverging views could not compromise, which resulted finally in two arrangements, the EEC according to the second model and the EFTA on the first model. Of the two, the EU proved to be the more dynamic. Its operation had considerable external effects on other countries (for example, US direct investment deserted UK destinations to favour those in the EU as long as the UK was not a EU member).

Extension came on three conditions: (1) that candidate members became aware that joining meant an excess of economic advantage over cost; (2) that political barriers were taken away (for example lack of democracy and human rights in Mediterranean countries); (3 that there would be a limited strain on the functioning of the EU. Th accession of the six new member countries in two rounds has le each time to an acceleration of the growth of GDP and to largely positive effects for all countries concerned.

Future deepening

Foundations

The past dynamism of the EU, as reflected in the growth of intra-EU trade and investment and the considerable increase in its scope of competences, is poorly explained by economic theory. The most successful concept in this respect is the idea of functionalism. As we explained briefly in Chapter 2, this concept starts from the need to gain competitiveness by using to the full the advantages of economies of scale, dictated by technology. Once markets have been opened, integration spills over into other areas, as one economic function is related to others. For example, common policies are needed as they enhance the effectiveness of market integration.

This economic version of the functionalist interpretation of integration, although capable of explaining the general trend of deepening, is deficient as to the explanation for the differences in pace, the meandering of the path followed and the diversity of forms that European integration has shown in the past. Other branches of economic theory do not help out either; as a matter of fact, economics provides at best the explanation for the starting of a new stage in the process; that is, to show that there are net benefits in setting the next step towards further integration. Most of the explanation is to be found in factors that are the object of study of political science, like the convergence of interests of different member states to look for cooperative solutions in specific policy areas. A projection of the subjects for which such convergence is likely to occur can be done by applying the economic analysis to 'federal' or 'subsidiarity' issues (for example, CEPR, 1993). However whether a cooperative solution on these points will indeed be realised is dependent on 'unpredictable' elements like the relative strengths of lobby groups and the distribution of bargaining power and interest between these lobby groups and the national and the EU institutions.

Consequently the analysis of the past does not provide a clear basis for making the projection of the pattern of deepening in the future. In legal terms the way ahead has for a large part been outlined in the Maastricht Treaty. In practical terms there is still much leeway to make up in the various frameworks outlined. How this will be done is unclear: an analysis of socio-economic factors of change shows that there is a very considerable variety of opinions on the way the EU has to develop its different dimensions; no single leading theme emerges (Jacquemin and Wright, 1993). So, to depict the future deepening we have selected from various sources the elements that are likely to change for each of the main policy areas distinguished earlier (these are presented in the following sections).

Allocation; market policies

The integration of markets, the hard core of European integration, is in need of further development. This need is perceived somewhat differently by the major actors. The *business community* is much in favour of the further move from a single to an integrated market. The latter differs from the former in the sense that it has done away with most of the national differentiation of consumer preferences. This would enable corporations to realise important efficiency gains by exploiting uniform markets even better by making use of economies of scale and so on. It would permit corporations to select optimal internal and external organisational forms; that is, the configuration of their own activities and those of their suppliers as if they were in a market like the USA. To that end, business is in favour of pan-European projects for infrastructure, for R&D and for Eastern Europe, with one exception, the labour market, where the business community is strongly in favour of national responsibility (Jacquemin and Wright, 1993).

From the standpoint of the *public authorities*, in charge of creating the conditions for a good functioning of the internal market, there are other points that it is relevant to develop further:

- *Competition policy.* The role of the EU as a guardian to the fair play of market forces will gain in importance in an integrated market, companies wanting increasingly to have to deal with only one single EU instead of with several national and Union authorities. Moreover there are important issues to be cleared up, such as limitation of state aids and equality of access to corporate control.
- *Intervention in markets.* In the past the number of areas where governments intervened directly in prices and quantities decreased. Some pockets of interventionism still exist, of which agriculture is the main problem, given its important negative effects on consumer wealth, on cohesion, and on external relations.

The challenge for the authorities assumes a much broader dimension if we put allocation policies in the context of the optimal model of European society. On that point, views diverge quite fundamentally. Some advocate a maximum of rivalry, of deregulation and hence of

exibility to gain international economic competitiveness. Others
laim that economic growth is dependent on a harmonious social
evelopment and hence advocate participation, consensus and
tabilisation. Finding a blend of elements that avoid the disadvan-
iges of both views while unleashing the potentialities of both is a
iajor task for the next decade.

tabilisation, the EMU

he stabilisation of exchange rates will be an important target for the
990s. The arguments for a Monetary Union in Europe are very
trong; we recall that the main advantages for the private sector are
ie lowering of transaction costs, the taking away of exchange rate
ncertainty and the avoidance of distortions of competitive situa-
ons that are due to changes in exchange rates triggered by financial
perations but not justified by economic fundamentals. For the pub-
c sector, better for the economy as a whole, the advantage is that the
Ionetary Union precludes competitive devaluations that in the long
:rm have as their only effect that inflation increases, and it saves on
ionetary reserves. The disadvantages are loss of room for manoeu-
ring for the macro (in particular budget) policies of member coun-
·ies. On balance the advantages outweigh the disadvantages, and so
ie EU will continue its efforts to reach its target, the EMU.

The Maastricht Treaty defines the timescale and the route to reach
iat target. The EU may, however, have to adopt a different road, as
ie one laid down in the Maastricht Treaty may be too problematic in
n environment characterised by full freedom of capital movements
ncluding gigantic speculative operations), economic restructuring
:ntailing mass unemployment) and continuous divergence of infla-
onary pressure.

edistribution; towards more cohesion

he European cohesion policies will face a number of new challenges
i the near future (Hall and Van der Wee, 1992). These are on the
:onomic side:

- *EMU*. The further steps towards deepening will undoubtedly
  generate additional pressures for structural adjustment in the
  backward regions. On the one hand, the EMU will have a positive impact in these regions because it will entail lower exchange risks premiums and will enhance the DI flows to these
  countries (Morsink and Molle, 1991). On the other hand, the
  loss of the possibility of adapting the exchange rate, and the
  need for a stricter control on government spending, will make

it more difficult to guide these regional economies smooth
through these new structural adaptations.

- *Central and Eastern Europe.* The opening up of EU market to th
  CEEC (in a perspective of eventual widening) will have fa
  reaching consequences for the present patterns of trade, tou
  ism, technology transfer, direct investment, labour compe
  tiveness and international aid. There is a real possibility th
  the industries of the less well developed regions will be th
  hardest hit by the new industrial specialisation patterns th
  will result. On the other hand, new export opportunities a
  opened up for regions that used to be outside the heartland
  Europe and will be rather centrally located in the extende
  Europe (the new Länder of the FRG and central Italy, for exan
  ple).

The EU faces a number of other problems that put in jeopardy *soci*
cohesion; these include the increasing ageing of the population, ur
employment and immigration. There is a growing need to step u
social infrastructure and to care for the socially disadvantaged group
notably in urban centres. These challenges are of a very diversifie
nature and require different types of answers. One of them is th
continuation of the efforts of the structural policies. Indeed the eval
ation (see Chapter 18) showed that the instruments of the structur
funds were adequate and needed only some adaptations of proc
dure in order to improve their efficiency. In order to combat the
increased problems, measures have been taken for the rest of th
decade that consist of:

- stepping up resources; a new increase in funds has been agree
  to cope with the upsurge in difficulties (by the way, a substa
  tial contribution to this can come from the present EFTA cou
  tries that will become new member countries);
- including more aspects of social policy; for example, the list
  eligible projects has been extended, with health and educatic
  improvement projects in objective 1 regions.

Finally there is need for spatial planning. The conditions for eco
nomic development do often conflict with other objectives, such
the environment, the quality of residential areas and so on. With th
increasing integration there is an increasing need for spatial plannir
at the level of the EU. Most urgent in this respect is the safeguardir
of the coherence of the various actions (for example on transport ar
communication networks) whereby the EU territory needs to be see
as a whole.

External relations: fortress or crossroads?

The European Union was created with two objectives in mind: to establish the conditions for durable peace and to enhance the economic development of Europe. Right from its start it has been aware that promoting integration with non-member countries would serve the same objectives at the world level.

The external *trade* relations of the EU are dominated by its commitment to continue the policy of openness towards third countries. The first implication is that the EU continues to give substance to the agreements that have concluded the latest GATT round and continues to work towards a more liberal trade. For products of agriculture and the service sector, further progress is dependent on political rather than economic arguments. For manufactured goods, the EU must continue its efforts to do away with the remaining protection (so-called 'sensitive' products). The political changes that have occurred in Central and Eastern Europe call for a drastic revision of the trade relations of the EU with these countries. This may involve quite important changes in the patterns of specialisation, not only between the EU and this group of countries, but also between the EU and its other trade partners.

With respect to *production factors*, the EU is not likely to change its policy a great deal. Capital movements will shortly be completely free and require no major further steps. For labour movements, the present situation of nationally regulated and increasingly restricted access is likely to continue in the near future. In some time the logic of the completed market will, however, push towards making uniform the external dimension of the labour market, that means European immigration laws. It is unlikely that the European Union will open up for large-scale external migration. This implies, however, that the EU will intensify its efforts to improve trade possibilities, and step up its development assistance as instruments to alleviate the employment and wage situation in third countries.

For *common economic policies*, however, substantial changes are on the cards for the near future. As the range of matters treated within the EU expands, so does the need to discuss them externally. Likely fields of greater EU activity are:

- international allocation: coordination of technical norms and standards, negotiations on landing rights in civil aviation, telecommunication and so on;
- stabilisation: monetary coordination, some form of EMS for the major world currencies or, less drastic, target zones for exchange rate fluctuations;
- redistribution: expanded EU involvement in development aid.

Common non-economic policies are likely to expand greatly in the future (see below), and so will their external scope, as the EU involves itself in an increasing number of matters such as safety, police and the environment.

So international cooperation between the EU and its partners in the world is likely to intensify in the future in quite a few areas. The present institutions will need to be reinforced to handle these new tasks.[4]

Other areas

A number of policy areas that the EU has only timidly penetrated in the past have come under the competence of the EU. We may cite here environment, social protection, public health, education, culture and the protection of the consumer (Articles 126–129a; 130r–130t). The actions that the EU will take in these fields will be developed in line with the principle of subsidiarity. That means that most of the policy activities in these fields will remain with the national government, and that Union actions will be undertaken where the member countries agree that coordinated action is advantageous. The Commission promotes and supports this cooperation.

The involvement of the EU is likely to differ for the various policy fields cited:

- *Environment.* This will be a full-fledged policy area of the EU, as sustained development has been made into a priority objective of the EU. The already substantial involvement of the EU is likely to develop quickly in the future.
- *Social policy.* Actions may be expected in such diverse areas as social exclusion, poverty and integration of immigrants. (NB: the Social Protocol is only applicable to 11 member states).
- *Education, vocational training and youth.* The action of the EU is geared towards the development of a European dimension, the encouragement of mobility of students, and the teaching of languages.
- *Culture.* EU support will aim notably at the safeguarding of the cultural heritage of European significance and the promotion of European audiovisual products (films, documentaries) in all EU languages.
- *Public health.* Contributing to the prevention of diseases, in particular the major health scourges by promoting research, information and education.
- *Consumer protection.* The EU role is not specified.

The adding of competences, even limited, in all these fields as in the fields of foreign affairs and security, and home and justice affairs, means that the EU institutions will cover almost the complete range of policies usually attributed to (con)federate governments.

Future widening

Foundations

The theory of economic integration is not very explicit on the problem of widening of an existing framework of regional integration. A point of departure is the concept of optimal integration area (OIA). Countries that have reached among themselves a certain degree of exchange, and show a certain degree of convergence of policy, should participate, whereas countries that do not fulfil these criteria should be excluded from participation. One can specify the criteria further for each stage of integration (see Table 20.6).

Table 20.6   Criteria for participation at different stages of integration

Stage	Criteria
Free trade zone	High exchange of goods and services
	Equality of production structure
	Equality of economic order
Common market	Equality on markets for labour and capital (prices and availability)
	Freedom of movement (migration and investment)
	Convergence of policy (e.g. taxes)
Economic union	Effective coordination
	Comparability of institutions
	Transfer payments
Monetary union	Stability of exchange rates
	Similarity of external shocks

The putting into operation of the concept of optimal integration area is not simple. For each stage one is confronted by two problems. The first concerns the relative character of the definitions: one needs to specify what is meant by a high degree of intra-trade, or comparability of policy. If one sets the threshold low, it will mean that many countries will participate; if one sets it high, only a few countries will be accepted to join. The second problem stems from the parallel use of several criteria. It then depends on the weight one attaches to each criterion as to what the end result will be.

Probably a more fundamental criticism is the absence of a dynamic interpretation of the concept. This is very relevant because countries that did not fulfil the criteria at the start have come to do so under the influence of further integration. An example of market integration is the trade that was found to develop among CU partners that had few relations before (for example, Peschel, 1985; Balassa and Bauwens, 1988). Another example in the field of policy integration is exchange rate stabilisation: participating in the EMS facilitated the meeting of criteria (see Chapter 17).

The optimal integration area approach has lost much of its attractiveness because of these flaws. Another approach was needed, and this has been found in a cost–benefit analysis. It suggests that decisions to pass on to a higher form of integration or to enlarge the number of members should be taken on the basis of an assessment of the cost and benefits of the operation for all interested parties. In the end this is not an altogether different approach, as one can translate the discussion on the optimal integration area into a discussion about cost and benefits. For countries that are part of the OIA the benefits will in general outweigh the cost; the opposite is the case for countries that are not part of the OIA. Incidentally, this economic balancing does not fully determine the outcome: many political arguments may come into play and may even overshadow the economic ones in the final decision.

The optimal area for higher stages of integration has been the subject of much debate during the preparation and ratification of the Maastricht Treaty that sets the legal basis for future widening. As a matter of fact it has also permitted some narrowing for certain subjects. For some countries the advantages of moving into a higher stage (an EMU coupled with more redistribution, more social policy and more common foreign and home policies) were evident and they have subscribed to the whole Treaty. Others, like the UK and Denmark, thought that the EU of 12 could not be termed an optimal integration area for this stage and opted out of important parts (EMU and social policy). In between we have a group of countries that want to belong to the first group, but want to take more time over adapting their economy so that it comes up to the criteria. In order to tip the balance of cost and benefits in their favour they have negotiated long transition periods.

EFTA/EEA

In the past a number of non-economic factors such as neutrality have stopped some EFTA countries from becoming EU members. This could not be seen as a grave problem in the 1960s, as the cleavage between the EU and EFTA had forestalled the emergence of an OIA in Western Europe. The first extension of the EU changed this. To avoid major problems, a free trade zone between the EU and remaining EFTA countries was formed. The setting up of the 1992 programme to complete the internal market revived the discussion on the OIA. It appeared that all EFTA countries did indeed fulfil the criteria for participating in the Single Internal Market, as over the years the interwovenness between the two blocks had grown. In fact, the EU and EFTA are by far each other's largest trading partners. Moreover the EU is by far the largest destination of EFTA DI and, for the EU, EFTA DI is more important than those of, for example, the USA and Japan. It comes as no surprise then, that an economic evaluation of the cost and benefits of EFTA participation in the completion of the internal market gave a very positive balance for EFTA and a slightly positive one for the EU (CEPR, 1992).

The political arguments, however, pointed in another direction than rapid membership. On the one hand, the EU feared the institutional sluggishness that might result from an early enlargement. On the other hand, the EFTA countries feared being involved in matters they were not ready for. The solution found was to create the European Economic Area, which permitted the EFTA countries to take part in the internal market without becoming EU members (Tichy, 1992).

The decision as to their future membership will be based on the cost and benefits of subscribing to the Treaty of Maastricht. The main elements to be taken into account are as follows.

Common Market The main advantages for EFTA are in the rationalisation of agriculture, the application of the EU competition rules, and the improvement of their country as a location for economic activity through the credibility of full membership. For the EU the advantages are limited to a somewhat larger bargaining power in the world.

Monetary Union Participation in EMU will imply that the EFTA countries experience the same advantages and disadvantages that we have analysed for the EU countries (see Chapter 17). We may remind here that the EFTA countries do have a good score on the criteria for convergence. All of them being small open economies, the advantages of EMU will make themselves felt earlier for them, than

for large EU countries. For the EU the advantage lies in the reinforc
ment of the system through the cooperation of a number of countri
with a good monetary reputation.

Economic Union   Here the cohesion problem is at the heart of th
debate. The contribution of EFTA countries to the budget of th
enlarged EU will outweigh the expenses to be made in these cour
tries. So EFTA makes a contribution to redistribution. The advantag
for EFTA is that it will have formal influence on the decisions of th
EU in many policy matters, so that its interests will be better saf
guarded.

Political Union   The diversity of the subjects that come under th
heading of the Maastricht Treaty do not make it easy to come to a
overall evaluation. For the EU a disadvantage may be that the dec
sion-making process is slowed down. For the EFTA countries th
main political problem to be solved is, of course, the loss of sove
eignty that membership entails and that limits the independent dec
sion making in the areas where there still exists room for manoeuvr

So, to conclude, the membership of EFTA countries will only brin
small net economic benefits for all parties involved. This conclusio
holds independently of the degree to which one will apply the Treat
of European Union. It makes the decision to join dependent upo
political factors. As a consequence the outcome of the process i
uncertain for each of the candidate members.

Central and Eastern Europe

Until recently the Central and Eastern European Countries (CEEC
were hardly concerned by the integration process in Western Europ
Trade between the EU and the CEEC was limited and other ecc
nomic relations were practically absent. The revolutions of the end c
the 1980s have drastically changed this, and have created the cond
tions for a closer integration in the future. If we look at the criteria fc
the optimal integration area, we have to conclude that the CEE
cannot yet be considered as part of such an area (small trade rela
tions and deficient institutional structures in the CEEC that mak
policy coordination difficult).

   As the EU has in the meantime moved into very high stages c
economic integration, the threshold for most CEEC is very high. Th
will imply that in the future the gradual integration of the CEEC wi
have to follow for good economic reasons the model that in the pa
has been followed for political reasons for the integration of EFT
countries. This model, the gradual participation in ever more aspec

of the integration process without formal membership, has actually been offered to the CEEC by the EU. The alternative model, rapid membership and long transition periods, was demanded by the CEEC, which think that this would be the best way to accelerate growth and change and to safeguard the democratic system. However the EU is very reluctant to chose this model, because the German reunification has shown how high the cost would be in a case where a country that does not belong to the OIA is nevertheless integrated in an accelerated way.

The road the CEEC's must follow in catching up with the integration process in the West is a long one. They have already made some progress towards the first stage; association agreements with a selected number of the CEEC have started the liberalisation of goods trade and created the conditions for EU DI in the CEEC (see Chapter 19). The next stage would be the multilateralisation of the EU/CEEC free trade along the lines of EU/EFTA; this supposes the breaking of strong sectoral interests, both in the CEEC and in the EU. The result would be an enlarged internal market for goods and services encompassing the EEA and the CEEC. Free capital movements might be added in a gradual way; it is likely that freedom of labour movement will be realised only after a considerable reduction of the wealth gap between the EU and the CEEC. Moreover, to fulfil the criteria for an OIA at the internal market level, the CEEC will have to make considerable progress with economic, legal and institutional reform in the CEEC. This, of course, holds a fortiori for the stage of the EMU (CEPR, 1992).

What would be a realistic timetable for the various stages? Critical n this respect is the internal market, with its freedom of movement of persons. The EU wants to preclude large migration flows from CEEC to the present EU. In an internal market that would only be possible where the differences between the richest and the poorest participant do not exceed the ones that exist in the present EU. To arrive at this situation, the CEEC that are now the most developed would have to register over the coming 10 years a growth rate considerably in excess of that of the EU. This is not unrealistic; in the past other countries have demonstrated similar growth rates when catching up. However, to create the conditions for such catching up, the access of the CEEC to the EU markets has to be speeded up and the same is true for the aid to restructuring.

So, for economic reasons, the first CEEC members of the EU may be expected to gain entry only in some 10 years' time. For those early entrants it will be necessary to agree by then on transition periods for those sections of the economy where the EU integration has in the meantime proceeded further (such as the EMU). For the more backward CEEC, longer periods will certainly have to be taken into account before membership becomes feasible. If to some these time periods appear too long, it is worth keeping in mind that the entrance of the southern EU members in the 1980s was only realised some 10 years after their political revolutions too, while in those countries no economic revolution was necessary.

There are political reasons that may upset this timetable, based on economic reasons. One is the need to avoid unrest on the eastern borders of the EU, that may be a recurrent factor if economic growth expectations take too long to be fulfilled. This implies that the EU should prepare itself institutionally for coping with an increased number of difficult issues, with an extended and more diversified group of member countries.

Summary and conclusions

- Integration has made considerable progress in Europe in the post-war years. That is evidenced by many indicators: economic ones, such as the interpenetration of markets and the convergence of prices; and policy ones, such as the fields covered, and the strength of instruments used by EU institutions.
- Integration has reached its objectives: peace and democracy have been safeguarded, and wealth has increased while the distribution of wealth has improved.
- New objectives have been set for future economic integration. After the completion of the internal market, the most important goal will be the gradual build-up of the Economic and Monetary Union. The emergence of a European Union in which increased solidarity leads to considerably more international redistribution and social cohesion seems to be somewhat farther down the road.

Notes

1 Although the freedoms were not immediately implemented, we have considered a U to be the best for 1960; a U also for 1990, notwithstanding some rudiments of national discretion.
2 Article 3g of the EEC treaty refers to coordination, but the standard term 'consultation', describes more adequately the situation that prevailed during this period.
3 Although the EEC Treaty (Article 3c) set regional equilibrium as a common objective (as there was a few of the negative side-effects of EU allocation poli cies), the practice of the formative years of the EC was one of information (se Chapter 18).

4 Tinbergen and Fischer (1987) drew up a plan to reform UN agencies, equipping them to cope with the increasing demand for worldwide coordination. See also in this respect Vosgerau (1989).

ANNEXES

List of Abbreviations

ACP	African, Caribbean and Pacific Countries
BEUC	Bureau Européen des Unions de Consommateurs
BIS	Bank for International Settlements
CAP	Common Agricultural Policy
CCP	Common Commercial Policy
CEC	Commission of the European Communities
CEEC	Central and Eastern European Countries
CEN	Comité Européen de Normalisation
CENELEC	Comité Européen de Normalisation Electronique
CEP	Common Energy Policy
CEPT	Conference Européenne des Postes et Télécommunication
CET	Common External Tariff
CM	Common Market
CMEA	Council of Mutual Economic Assistance (Comecon)
CMU	Capital Market Union
CNIR	Covered Nominal Interest Rate
CU	Customs Union
COREPER	Committee of Permanent Representatives
DI	Direct Investment
EAEC	European Atomic Energy Community (Euratom)
EAGGF	European Agricultural Guidance and Guarantee Fund
EC	European Community
ECA	European Court of Auditors
ECB	European Central Bank
ECE	Economic Commission for Europe
ECJ	European Court of Justice
ECSC	European Coal and Steel Community
ECU	European Currency Unit
EDC	European Defence Community
EDF	European Development Fund
EEA	European Economic Area
EEC	European Economic Community
EFTA	European Free Trade Association
EIB	European Investment Bank
EMCF	European Monetary Co-operation Fund

511

EMI	European Monetary Institute
EMS	European Monetary System
EMU	Economic and Monetary Union
EP	European Parliament
EPC	European Political Community/Co-operation
ERDF	European Regional Development Fund
ERM	Exchange Rate Mechanism
ESC	Economic and Social Committee
ESF	European Social Fund
EU	European Union/Economic Union
FCMA	Free Capital Movement Area
FLMA	Free Labour Movement Area
FPC	Foreign Profit Creation
FPD	Foreign Profit Diversion
FRG	Federal Republic of Germany
FTA	Free Trade Area
FTL	Full Truck-loads
FU	Full Union
GATS	General Agreement on Trade in Services
GATT	General Agreement on Tariffs and Trade
GDP	Gross Domestic Product
GDP/P	Gross Domestic Product per Head of Population
GFCF	Gross Fixed Capital Formation
GJ	Gigajoule
GNP	Gross National Product
GSP	Generalised System of Preference
HFL	Dutch Florin
IBRD	International Bank for Reconstruction and Development (World Bank)
ICM	Incomplete Common Market
ICU	Incomplete Customs Union
IIT	Intra-Industry Trade
ILO	International Labour Organisation
IMF	International Monetary Fund
ISIC	International Standard Industrial Classification
LDC	Less Developed Country
LEC	Labour-Exporting Country
LFTL	Less Than Full Truck-loads
LIC	Labour Importing Country
LMU	Labour Market Union
LPG	Liquefied Petroleum Gas
MCA	Monetary Compensatory Amounts
Mecu	Million ECU
MFA	Multi-Fibre Arrangement
MFN	Most-Favoured-Nation

MNC	Multi National Company
MNF	Multi National Firm
MU	Monetary Union
Mt/y	Million (1 000 000) tons per year
Mtoe	Million (1 000 000) tons of oil equivalent
NATO	North Atlantic Treaty Organisation
NG	Natural Gas
NIC	Newly Industrialising Countries
NORDEL	Nordic Electricity
NTB	Non-Tariff Barriers
OCA	Optimum Currency Area
OECD	Organisation for Economic Co-operation and Development
OIA	Optimal Integration Area
OMA	Orderly Marketing Arrangements
OPEC	Organisation of Petroleum Exporting Countries
PTT	Post Telegraph Telephone
PU	Political Union
QR	Quantitative Restrictions
R & D	Research and Development
RIR	Real Interest Rates
SDR	Special Drawing Right
SEA	Single European Act
SSR	Self Sufficiency Ratio
TEU	Treaty on European Union
TRIMS	Trade-related Investment Measures
TRIPS	Trade-related Intellectual Property Rights
UCPTE	Union for the Coordination of the Production and Transmission of Electric Power
UK	United Kingdom
UNCTAD	United Nations Conference on Trade and Development
UNIDO	United Nations Industrial Development Organisation
UNIR	Uncovered Nominal Interest Rate
UNO	United Nations Organisation
USA	United States of America
VAT	Value-Added Tax
VER	Voluntary Export Restraint
WEU	Western European Union

Bibliography

Adler, M. (1970), 'Specialisation in the European Coal and Steel Community', *Journal of Common Market Studies*, vol. 8, pp. 175–91.

Adler, M. and Dumas, B. (1983), 'International Portfolio Choice and Corporation Finance', *Journal of Finance*, vol. 38.3, pp. 925–84.

Aitken, N.D. (1973), 'The Effect on the EEC and EFTA on European Trade; a Temporal Cross-Section Analysis', *American Economic Review*, vol. 63, pp. 881–91.

Akhtar, A.M. (1986), 'Recent Changes in the Financial Systems; a Perspective on Benefits versus Costs', in D.E. Fair (ed.), *Shifting Frontiers in Financial Markets*, Nijhoff, Dordrecht, pp. 31–41.

Albert, M. and Ball, R. (1983), *Towards European Economic Recovery in the 1980's*, European Parliament Working Documents 1983/84, Luxemburg.

Allais, M., Duquesne de la Vinelle, L., Oort, V.J., Seidenfus, H.S. and del Viscoro, M. (1965), 'Options in Transport Policy', *The EEC Studies*, Transport Series no. 4, Brussels.

Allen, P.R. (1983), 'Policies to Correct Cyclical Imbalance within a Monetary Union', *Journal of Common Market Studies*, vol. 21.3, pp. 313–27.

Alting von Geusau, F.A.M. (ed.) (1975), *Energy in the European Communities*, Sythoff, Leiden.

AMUE (Association for the Monetary Union of Europe) (1988), *European Business and the ECU*; results of a survey carried out by FAITS et OPINIONS among 1036 business leaders in the European Community with the help of the ECU·Banking Association and the European Commission, Paris.

Anarzit, P. d' (1982), *Essai d'une Politique Pétrolière Européenne*, Editions Techniques et Economiques, Paris.

Anderson S. and Eliassen, K. (1991), 'European Community Lobbying', *European Journal of Political Research*, vol. 20, pp. 173–87.

Arge, R. d' (1969), 'Note on Customs Union and Direct Foreign Investment', *Economic Journal*, vol. 79, pp. 324–33.

Artis, M. and Ostry, S. (1986), *International Economic Policy Co-ordination*, RIIA/RKP, London.

Askari, H. (1974), 'The Contribution of Migration to Economic Growth in the EEC', *Economica Internazionale*, vol. 27.2, pp. 341–5.

Atkins (1987), 'The Cost of Non-Europe in Public Sector Procurement', *Research on the Cost of Non-Europe*, vol. 5 part A, CEC, Brussels.

Atkinson, P. and Chouraqui, J. (1985), 'Real Interest Rates and the Prospects for Durable Growth', *OECD Working Paper* no. 21, Paris.

Auberger, B. (1980), 'Quelle Politique Agricole Commune pour Demain?', *Revue du Marché Commun*, vol. 23.241, pp. 519–26.

Aubrey, B. (1984), '100.000 Travailleurs Frontaliers', *Economie et Statistique*, no. 170, pp. 13–23.

Auctores Varii (1983), 'Issues and Experience of Transport Regulation Reform', *International Journal of Transport Economics*, vol. 10.1–2.

515

Ayling, D.E. (1980), *The Internationalisation of Stock Markets; the Trend towards Greater Foreign Borrowing and Lending*, Gower, Aldershot.

Bairoch, P. (1976), *Commerce Extérieur et Développement Economique de l'Europe au XIXᵉ Siècle*, Mouton, Paris.

Balassa, B. (1961), *The Theory of Economic Integration*, Irwin, Homewood, Illinois.

Balassa, B. (1966), 'Tariff Reductions and Trade in Manufactures among Industrial Countries', *American Economic Review*, vol. 56, pp. 466–73.

Balassa, B. (ed.) (1975), *European Economic Integration*, North-Holland/American Elsevier, Amsterdam.

Balassa, B. (1976), 'Types of Economic Integration', in F. Machlup (ed.), *Economic Integration, Worldwide, Regional, Sectoral*, Macmillan, London, pp. 17–31.

Balassa, B. (1977), 'Revealed Comparative Advantage Revisited: an Analysis of Relative Export Shares of the Industrial Countries 1953–1971', *The Manchester School*, pp. 327–44.

Balassa, B. (1986), 'Intra-Industry Trade among Exporters of Manufactured Goods', in D. Greenaway and P.K.M. Tharakan (eds), *Imperfect Competition and International Trade*, Wheatsheaf, Brighton, pp. 108–28.

Balassa, B. and Balassa, C. (1984), 'Industrial Protection in the Developed Countries', *The World Economy*, pp. 179–96.

Balassa, B. and Bauwens, L. (1988), 'The Determinants of Intra European Trade in Manufactured Goods', *European Economic Review*, vol. 32.7, pp. 1421–39.

Baldwin, R. (1989), 'The Growth Effects of 1992', *Economic Policy*, vol. 2, pp. 247–81.

Baldwin, R. and Lyons, R. (1991), 'External Economies and European Integration; the Potential for Self-fulfilling Expectations', in *European Economy*, Special Edition no. 1, 'The Economics of EMU', Background Studies for European Economy no. 44, 'One Market, One Money', pp. 56–75.

Baldwin, R. and Murray, T. (1977), 'MFN Tariff Reductions and Developing Country Trade Benefits under GSP', *Economic Journal*, vol. 87, pp. 30–46.

Baldwin, R.E. (1984), 'Trade Policies in Developed Countries', in R.W. Jones and P.B. Kenen (eds), *Handbook of International Economics*, vol. I, North-Holland, Amsterdam, pp. 571–621.

Bamber, G.J. and Lansbury, R. (1987), *International and Comparative Industrial Relations*, Allen and Unwin, London.

Barnovin, B. (1986), *The European Labour Movement and European Integration*, Graduate Institute of International Studies, Pinter, Geneva/London.

Bartel, R. (1974), 'International Monetary Unions, the 19th Century Experience', *Journal of European Economic History*, vol. 3.3, pp. 689–723.

Batchelor, R. (1982), 'Expectations, Output and Inflation: the European Experience', *European Economic Review*, vol. 17.1, pp. 1–25.

Baumol, W.J., Panzar, J.C. and Willig, R.D. (1982), *Contestable Markets and the Theory of Industry Structure*, Harcourt Brace Jovanovich, San Diego.

Bergeijk, P.A.G., van (1987), *The Determinants of Success and Failure of Economic Sanctions, Some Empirical Results*, Development and Security, Groningen.

Bergh, P. van den et al. (1987), 'Deregulering van de Internationale Financiële Stromen en Valutastelsel', in Auctores Varii, *Sociaal-Economische Deregulering*, 130e Vlaams Economisch Congres, pp. 843–78.

Berghe, L. van den, (1980), *The European Insurance Market; Some Considerations*, Reports and Studies of the International Insurance Seminars, IIS Inc., Paris, pp. 143–56.

Berglas, E. (1979), 'Preferential trading theory: the n commodity case', *Journal of Political Economy*, vol. 87, pp. 315–31.

Bergstrand, J.H. (1983), 'Measurement and Determinants on Intra-Industry International Trade', in P.K.M. Tharakan (ed.), *Intra-Industry Trade: Empirical and Methodological Aspects*, North-Holland, Amsterdam, pp. 201–55.

Bernard, P.J. (ed.) (1978), *Les Travailleurs Etrangers en Europe*, Mouton, The Hague.
BEUC (1982), *Report on Car Prices and Private Imports of Cars in the EC Countries*, BEUC 105892, Brussels.
BEUC (1986), *Car Price Differences in the EEC*, Brussels.
BEUC (1988), *Term Insurance in Europe*, (Report nr. 51/88), Brussels.
BEUC (1989), *EC Study on Car Prices and Progress Towards 1992*, Brussels.
Beuter, R. and Pelkmans, J. (eds) (1986), *Cementing the Internal Market*, EIPA, Maastricht.
Bhagwati, J. (1982), 'Shifting Comparative Advantage, Protectionist Demands, and Policy Response', in J. Bhagwati (ed.), *Import Competition and Response*, University of Chicago Press, Chicago, pp. 153–95.
Bhagwati, J.N. (1987a), 'Trade in Services and the Multilateral Trade Negotiations', *The World Bank Economics Review*, vol. 1.4, pp. 549–69.
Bhagwati, J.N. (1987b), 'International Factor Mobility' in *Essays in International Economic Theory*, vol. 2: (edited by R.C. Feenstra), MIT Press, Cambridge, Massachusetts.
Bhagwati, J.N., Schatz, K.W. and Wong, K. (1984), 'The West German Gastarbeiter System of Immigration', *European Economic Review*, vol. 26, pp. 227–94.
Bianchi, P. and Forlai, L. (1988), 'The European Domestic Appliances Industry 1945–1987', in H.W. de Jong (ed.), *The Structure of European Industry*, 2nd edn, Kluwer, Dordrecht, pp. 269–96.
Bianchi, P. and Forlai, L. (1993), 'The domestic appliance industry; 1945–1991', in H.W. de Jong (ed.), *The Structure of European Industry*, 3rd edn, Kluwer, Dordrecht, pp. 171–202.
Black, J. and Dunning, J.H. (eds) (1982), *International Capital Movements*, Macmillan, London.
Blaise, J., Fouchard, P. and Kahn, P. (1981), *Les Eurocrédits; un Instrument du Système Bancaire pour le Financement International*, Librairies Techniques, Paris.
Blitz, R.C. (1977), 'A Benefit–Cost Analysis of Foreign Workers in West Germany 1957–1973', *Kyklos*, vol. 30, pp. 479–502.
Blommestein, H.J. (ed.) (1991), *The Reality of International Policy Coordination*, North-Holland, Amsterdam.
Blonk, W.A.G. (1968), *Enige Aspecten en Problemen van het Goederenvervoer tussen de Lidstaten van de Europese Economische Gemeenschap, met Name ten Aanzien van de Kwantitatieve Beperkingen en Kwalitatieve Belemmeringen*, Born, Assen.
Boeckhout, I.J. and Molle, W.T.M. (1982), 'Technological Change, Location Patterns and Regional Development', *FAST Occasional Papers* no. 16, EEC, DG XII, Brussels.
Böhning, W.R. (1972), *The Migration of Workers in the UK and the EC*, Oxford University Press, London.
Böhning, W.R. (1979), 'International Migration in Western Europe, Reflections on the Last Five Years', *International Labour Review*, vol. 118.4, pp. 401–15.
Böhning, W.R. (1993), *International Aid as a Means to Reduce the Need for Emigration*, ILO/UNHR, Geneva.
Böhning, W.R. and Maillat, D. (1974), *The Effects of the Employment of Foreign Workers*, OECD, Paris.
Boltho, A. (ed.) (1982), *The European Economy; Growth and Crisis*, Oxford University Press, Oxford.
Bongardt, A. (1993), 'The Automotive Industry; Supply Relations in Context', in H.W. de Jong, (ed.), *The Structure of European Industry*, 3rd edn, Kluwer, Dordrecht, pp. 147–70.
Borchardt, K. (1984), 'Protektionismus im historischen Rückblick', in A. Gutowski (ed.), *Der neue Protektionismus*, Weltarchiv, Hamburg, pp. 17–47.
Bordo, M. and Schwartz, A. (1984), *A Retrospective on the Classical Gold Standard*, NBER, New York.

Borner, S. and Grubel, H. (1992), *The European Community after 1992; Perspectives from the Outsiders*, Macmillan, London.

Bourguignon, F., Gallast-Hamond, G. and Fernet, B. (1977), *Choix Economiques liés aux Migrations Internationales de Main d'oeuvre; le Cas Européen*, OECD, Paris.

Bourrinet, J. (1981), 'L'explication Economique de la Genèse des Communautés Européennes' in D. Lasok et P. Soldatos (eds), *Les Communautés Européennes et Fonctionnement*, Bruylant, Bruxelles, pp. 65–84.

Bouteiller, J. (1971), 'Comparaison de Structure Inter-industrielles de Salaires dans les Pays du Marché Commun', *Annales de l'INSEE*, no. 8, pp. 3–24.

Brennan, G. and Buchanan, J.M. (1980), *The Power to Tax, Analytical Foundations of a Fiscal Constitution*, Cambridge University Press, Cambridge.

Breyer, S. (1984), 'Analysing Regulatory Failure; Mismatches, Less Restrictive Alternatives and Reform', in A.I. Ogus and C.G. Veljanovski (eds), *Readings in the Economics of Law and Regulation*, Clarendon, Oxford, pp. 234–9.

Bröcker, J. (1984), *Interregionaler Handel und ökonomische Integration*, Florentz, Munich.

Brown, A.J. (1985), *World Inflation Since 1950, An International Comparative Study*, Cambridge University Press, Cambridge.

Browne, F.X. (1984), 'The International Transmission of Inflation to a Small Open Economy under Fixed Exchange Rates and Highly Interest-Sensitive Capital Flows', *European Economic Review*, vol. 25, pp. 187–212.

Brugmans, H. (1970), *L'idée Européenne 1920–1970*, De Tempel, Brugge.

Bruno, M., (1984), 'Stagflation in the EC Countries, 1973–1981, a cross-sectional view' in M. Emerson (ed.), *Europe's Stagflation*, Clarendon Press, Oxford, pp. 33–58.

Buchanan, J.M. (1968), *The Demand and Supply of Public Goods*, Rand MacNally, Chicago.

Buckley, P.J. and Artisien, P. (1987), 'Policy issues of intra-EC direct investment; British, French and German multinationals in Greece, Portugal and Spain, with special reference to employment effects', *Journal of Common Market Studies*, vol 26.2, pp. 207–30.

Buckwell, A.E., Harvey, D.R., Thomson, K.T. and Parton, K.A. (1982), *The Cost of the Common Agricultural Policy*, Croom Helm, London.

Buigues, P., Ilkovitl, F. and Lebrun, J.F. (1990), 'The Impact of the Internal Market by Industrial Sector', *European Economy – Social Europe*, Special Edition.

Buiter, W.H. and Marston, R. (eds) (1985), *International Economic Policy Coordination*, Cambridge University Press, Cambridge.

Bulcke, D. van den (1983), 'Multinationale Ondernemingen en Europese Gemeenschap; Impact en Respons', *Maandschrift Economie*, vol. 47, pp. 304–26.

Bulcke, D. van den (1984), 'Decision Making in Multinational Enterprises and the Consultation of Employees; the Proposed Vredeling Directive of the EC Commission', *International Studies of Management and Organisation*, vol. 14.1, pp. 36–61.

Bulmer, S. and Wessels, W. (1986), *The European Council Decision Making in European Politics*, Macmillan, Basingstoke.

Butler, A.D. (1967), 'Labour Cost in the Common Market', *Industrial Economics*, vol 6.2, pp. 166–83.

Button, K.J. (1983), 'Regulation and Coordination of International Road Goods Movements within the European Common Market; an Assessment', *Transportation Journal*, vol. 22.4, pp. 4–16.

Button, K.J. (1984), *Road Haulage Licensing and EC Transport Policy*, Gower, Aldershot.

Buzan, B. (1984), 'Economic Structure and International Security; the limits of the liberal case', *International Organization*, vol. 38, pp. 597–624.

Cairncross, A. (1973), *Control of Long-Term International Capital Movements*, Brookings Institution, Washington.

Cameron, D.R. (1985), 'Does Government Cause Inflation? Taxes, Spending and

Deficits', in L. Lindberg and C.S. Maier (eds), *The Politics of Inflation and Economic Stagnation*, Brookings Institution, Washington, pp. 224–79.

Cantwell, J. and Randaccio, F.S. (1992), 'Intra-Industry Direct Investment in the EC, Oligopolistic Rivalry and Technological Competition', in J. Cantwell (ed.), *Multi-national Investment in Modern Europe*, Edward Elgar, Aldershot, pp. 71–106.

Caramazza, F. (1987), 'International Real Interest Rate Linkages in the 1970s and 1980s', in R. Tremblay (ed.), *Issues in North American Trade and Finance*, North American Economic and Finance Association, vol. 4.1, pp. 123–50.

Carson, M. (1982), 'The Theory of Foreign Direct Investment', in J. Black and J.H. Dunning (eds), *International Capital Movements*, Macmillan, London, pp. 22–58.

Carter, R.L. and Dickinson, G.M. (1992), 'Obstacles to the Liberalisation of Trade in Insurance', *TPRC*, Harvester Wheatsheaf, London/New York.

Casella, A. and B. Frey, (1992), 'Federalism and clubs; towards a theory of overlapping political jurisdictions', *European Economic Review*, vol. 36.2/3, pp. 639–46.

Cassis, Y. (ed.) (1991), *Finance and Financiers in European History 1880–1960*, Cambridge University Press, Cambridge.

Castles, S. and Kosack, G. (1985), *Immigrant Workers and Class Structure in Western Europe*, Oxford University Press, London.

Caves, R. (1982), *Multinational Enterprise and Economic Analysis*, Cambridge University Press, Cambridge.

Caves, R. and Jones, R. (1984), *World Trade and Payments*, 3rd edn Little, Brown, Boston, Massachusetts.

Caves, R.E. (1975), 'Economic Models of Political Choice: Canada's Tariff Structure', *Canadian Journal of Economics*, vol. 9, pp. 278–300.

CEC (1961), *Document de la Conférence sur les Economies Régionales*, vol. II, Brussels.

CEC (1964), *Reports by Groups of Experts on Regional Policy in the European Economic Community*, Brussels.

CEC (1966), *The Development of a European Capital Market*, Segré Report, Brussels.

CEC (1967), *Critère à la Base de la Fixation des Salaires et Problèmes qui y sont liés pour une Politique des Salaires et des Revenus*, Brussels.

CEC (1968), *Mémorandum sur la Réforme de l'Agriculture dans la Communauté Economique Européenne*, Agriculture 1980, COM 68/100e, Luxemburg.

CEC (1969), *A Regional Policy for the Community*, Brussels.

CEC (1970), *De Industriepolitiek van de Gemeenschap*, memorandum van de Commissie aan de Raad, Brussels.

CEC (1971), *Regional Development in the Community: Analytical Survey*, Brussels.

CEC (1972), *La Libre Circulation de la Main-d'oeuvre et les Marchés du Travail dans la CEE*, (DG V), Brussels.

CEC (1973a), Communication from the Commission to the Council on the Development of the Common Transport Policy, COM (73), Brussels.

CEC (1973b), *Report on the Regional Problems in the Enlarged Community;* (Thomson Report), COM 73/550, Brussels.

CEC (1974), *Third Report on Competition Policy*, Brussels.

CEC (1977), 'The Regional Policy of the Community, New Guidelines', *Supplement 2/77 to Bulletin of the European Communities*, Luxemburg.

CEC (1979a), *Etude Comparative des Conditions et Procédures d'Introduction et d'Accès à l'Emploi des Travailleurs de Pays tiers dans les Etats Membres de la Communauté*, Brussels.

CEC (1979b), 'A Transport Network for Europe, Outline of a Policy', *Supplement 8/79 to Bulletin of the European Communities*, Luxemburg.

CEC (1979c), 'Air Transport, A Community Approach', *Supplement 5/79 to Bulletin of the European Communities*, Luxemburg.

CEC (1979d), *The European Monetary System: Commentary Document*, European Economy no. 3, Brussels.

CEC (1979e), 'The Regional Development Programmes', *Regional Policy Series*, no. 17, Brussels.

CEC (1980), *The Europeans and their Regions*, internal EC document DG XXVI no. 9, Brussels.

CEC (1981a), *Energy Strategy to be Adopted by the Community*, Brussels.

CEC (1981b), *The Regions of Europe: First Periodic Report*, Brussels.

CEC (1981c), *Proposal for a Council Regulation Amending the Regulation (EEC), no. 724/75, establishing a European Regional Development Fund*, Brussels.

CEC (1982a), *The Competitiveness of the Community Industry*, Brussels.

CEC (1982b), 'The agricultural policy of the European Community', *European Documentation*, no. 6, Luxemburg.

CEC (1982c), *Review of Member States' Energy Policy Programmes and Progress towards 1990 Objectives*, Brussels.

CEC (1982d), 'Experimenteel Programma betreffende de Vervoersinfrastructuur', COM 82/828 def., Brussels.

CEC (1982e), 'European Transport, Crucial Problems and Research Needs, a Long Term Analysis', *Series FAST* no. 3, Brussels.

CEC (1982f), 'The Community and State Aids to Industry', *European File no. 9*, Brussels.

CEC (1982g), 'Public Supply Contracts in the European Community', *European Documentation*, Luxemburg/Brussels.

CEC (1983a), *Commission Activities and EC Rules for the Automobile Industry 1981–1983*, COM 83/633 final, Brussels.

CEC (1983b), 'Wine in the European Community', *European Documentation* 2/3, Luxemburg.

CEC (1983c), 'The Customs Union', *European Documentation* 6/1983, Luxemburg.

CEC (1984a), 'The European Community's Legal System', *European Documentation* 1984/5, Luxemburg.

CEC (1984b), *Public Supply Contracts, Conclusions and Perspectives*, COM 84/717, Brussels.

CEC (1984c), *The Regions of Europe; Second Periodic Report on the Situation and Socio-economic Evolution of the Regions of the Community*, Brussels.

CEC (1984d), *Les Programmes de Développement Régional de la Deuxième Génération pour la Période 1981–1985*, Collection Documents, Brussels.

CEC (1985a), *Migrants in the European Community*, European File 13.85, Brussels.

CEC (1985b), *The European Community Fisheries Policy*, Luxemburg.

CEC (1985c), *The Insurance Industry in the Countries of the EEC, Structure, Conduct and Performance* (S. Aaronovitch and P. Samson), Documents, Brussels.

CEC (1985d), *Completing the Internal Market*, Cockfield White Paper, Brussels/Luxemburg.

CEC (1985e), 'European Competition Policy', *European File no. 6*, Brussels.

CEC (1985f), 'The European Commission's Powers of Investigation in the Enforcement of Competition Law', *European Documentation*, Luxemburg.

CEC (1985g), *The European Community and its Regions; 10 Years of Community Regional Policy and the ERDF*, Luxemburg.

CEC (1985h), *Main Texts Governing the Regional Policy of the EC*, Collection Documents, Brussels.

CEC (1986a), 'European Act', *Supplement 2/86 to Bulletin of the European Communities*, Luxemburg.

CEC (1986b), 'The ABC of Community Law', *European Documentation* 1986/2, Luxemburg.

CEC (1986c), 'The Court of Justice of the European Community', *European Documentation* 1986/5, Luxemburg.

CEC (1986d), 'The European Communities' Budget', *European Documentation* 1986/1, Luxemburg.

CEC (1986e), *Programme for the Liberalisation of Capital Movements in the Community*, Brussels.

CEC (1986f), *Bulletin of Energy Prices*, Luxemburg.

CEC (1986g), 'The Approximation of European Tax Systems', *European File no. 9*, Brussels.

CEC (1986h), 'The European Monetary System', *European File 15*, Brussels.

CEC (1986i), *Directory of European Community Trade and Professional Associations*, 3rd edn, Brussels.

CEC (1987a), *Treaties Establishing the European Communities*, abridged edn, Luxemburg.

CEC (1987b), *Regional Disparities and the Tasks of Regional Policy in the Enlarged Community* (Third Periodic Report), Brussels.

CEC (1988a), 'The Catching-up Process in Spain and Portugal', *European Economy* Supplement A, no. 10, Brussels/Luxemburg.

CEC (1988b), *Major Results of the Survey of Member States' Energy Policies*, COM 88/174 fin, Brussels.

CEC (1988c), *La Dimension Sociale du Marché Intérieur*, Rapport d'Etape du groupe interservices présidé par M.J. Degimbe, Brussels.

CEC (1988d), 'Research on the "Cost of Non Europe" – Basic Findings', vol. 1; *Basic Studies; Executive Seminaries*, Brussels.

CEC (1988e), 'Europe without frontiers; completing the internal market', *European Documentation* 3/88, Brussels.

CEC (1989), *European Community Research Programmes; France, work programme 1978–1981*, Status 1989, DG XII, Brussels.

CEC (1990a), *Guide to the Reform of the Community's Structural Funds*, OOPEC, Luxemburg.

CEC (1990b), '"One Market, One Money"', an Evaluation of the Potential Benefits and Cost of Forming an Economic and Monetary Union', *European Economy*, no. 44, Brussels/Luxemburg.

CEC (1991a), 'Fair Competition in the Internal Market; Community State Aid Policy', *European Economy* no. 48, pp. 13–114, Brussels/Luxemburg.

CEC (1991b), 'Immigration of Citizens from Third Countries into the Southern Member States of the European Community', *Social Europe*, Supplement 1/91, Brussels/Luxemburg.

CEC (1991c), *The Regions in the 1990's; Fourth periodic report on the social and economic situation and development of the regions of the Community*, OOPEC, Luxemburg.

CEC (1991d), 'European Industrial Policy for the 1990s', *Supplement 3/91 to Bulletin of the European Communities*, Luxemburg.

CEC (1992a), 'The Degree of Openness of the Economies of the Community, the US and Japan', *European Economy*, Supplement A, no. 4, Brussels/Luxemburg.

CEC (1992b), *Social Europe* 2/92, Luxemburg.

CEC (1992c), 'Social Security for Persons Moving within the Community', *Social Europe*, OOPEC, Luxemburg.

CEC (1992d), 'Energy policies and trends in the European Community', *Energy in Europe 20*, OOPEC, Luxemburg.

CEC (1992e), 'Energy policies and trends in the EC; focus on the East', *Energy in Europe 19*, OOPEC, Luxemburg.

CEC (1992f), 'A Common Market for Services', vol. I, *Services Completing the Internal Market*, Brussels.

CEC (1993a), 'Market Services in the Community Economy', *European Economy*, Supplement A, no. 5, pp. 1–11, Luxemburg.

CEC (1993b), *European Social Policy; options for the Union*, (Green Paper), OOPEC, Luxemburg.

CEC (1993c), 'The European Community as a World Trade Partner', *European Economy*, no. 52, Luxemburg.

Cecchini, P. *et al.* (1988), *The European Challenge 1992*, Gower, Aldershot.

CEMT (1985), *Trends in the Transport Sector, 1970–1984*, Paris.

Centi, J.P. (1984), *Intégration Européenne et Concurrence des Monnaies*, Economica, Paris.

CEPR (1992), 'Is Bigger Better? The Economics of EC Enlargement', *MEI* Series 3, London.

CEPR (1993), 'Making Sense of Subsidiarity; How much Centralization for Europe?' *CEPR/MEI4*, London.

CEPS (1986), *The Future of Community Finance*, Centre for European Policy Studies, Brussels.

Chabod, F. (1961), *Storia dell'idea d'Europe*, Laterza, Bari.

Chenery, H. (1960), 'Patterns of Industrial Growth', *American Economic Review*, vol. 50, pp. 624–54.

Chenery, H., Robinson, S. and Syrquin, M. (1986), *Industrialisation and Growth; a Comparative Study*, Oxford University Press, Oxford/New York.

Cheng, L. (1983), 'International Trade and Technology: A Brief Survey of the Recent Literature', *Weltwirtschaftliches Archiv*, vol. 120, pp. 444–69.

Cherif, M. and Ginsburgh, V. (1976), 'Economic Interdependence Among the EEC Countries', *European Economic Review*, vol. 8, pp. 71–86.

Chipman, J.S. (1965/66), 'A Survey of the Theory of International Trade', *Econometrica*, part I, vol. 33.3, pp. 477–519; part II, vol. 33.4, pp. 685–761; part III, vol. 34.1, pp. 18–76.

Cho, D.G., Enu, C.S. and Senbet, L.W. (1986), 'International Arbitrage Pricing Theory: an Empirical Investigation', *Journal of Finance*, vol. 41.2, pp. 313–29.

Claassen, E.-M. and Wyplosz, C. (1982), 'Capital Controls; some Principles and the French Experience', *Annales de l'Insee*, no. 47/48, pp. 237–77.

Clark, C. (1957), *Conditions of Economic Progress*, Macmillan, London.

Clarke, W.M. and Pulay, G. (1978), *The World's Money; How it Works*, Allen and Unwin, London.

Clarotti, P. (1984), 'Progress and Future Development of Establishment and Services in the EC in Relation to Banking', *Journal of Common Market Studies*, vol. 22.3, pp. 199–226.

Clout, H. (1986), *Regional Development in Western Europe*, Wiley, Chichester.

Cnossen, S. (ed.) (1987), *Tax Coordination in the European Community*, Kluwer, Deventer.

Cnossen, S. (1990), 'The Case for Tax Diversity in the European Community', *European Economic Review*, vol. 34, pp. 471–9.

Collins, D. (1983), *The Operations of the European Social Fund*, Croom Helm, London.

Cooke, T.E. (1988), *International Mergers and Acquisitions*, Basil Blackwell, Oxford.

Cooper, R.N. (1983), 'Economic Interdependence and the Coordination of Economic Policies', in R. Jones and P.B. Kenen (eds), *Handbook of International Economics*, North-Holland, New York.

Corden, W.M. (1971), *Theory of Protection*, Clarendon, Oxford.

Corden, W.M. (1972a), 'Economies of Scale and Customs Union Theory', *Journal of Political Economy*, vol. 80.1, pp. 465–75.

Corden, W.M. (1972b), 'Monetary Integration', *Essays in International Finance* no. 93, Princeton University, Princeton NJ.

Corden, W.M. (1974), *Trade Policy and Economic Welfare*, Clarendon, Oxford.

Cornwall, J. (1977), *Modern Capitalism*, Robertson, London.

Council of Europe (1980), *European Migration in the 1980s, Trends and Policies*, Strasbourg.

Council of Europe (1983), *The Situation of Migrant Workers and their Families; Achievements, Problems and Possible Solutions*, Strasbourg.

Cripps, F. and Tarling, R. (1973), *Growth in Advanced Capitalist Economies 1950–1970*, Cambridge University Press, Cambridge.

Crouch, C. (1985), 'Conditions for Trade Union Wage Restraint', in L. Lindberg and Ch.S. Maier (eds), *The Politics of Inflation and Economic Stagnation*, Brookings Institution, Washington, pp. 105–39.

Cushman, D.O. (1983), 'The Effects of Real-Exchange-Rate Risk on International Trade', *Journal of International Economics*, vol. 15, pp. 45–63.

Dam, K.W. (1970), *The GATT: Law and International Economic Organisation*, UCP, London.

Davenport, M. (1986), *Trade Policy, Protectionism and the Third World*, Croom Helm, Beckenham.

Deardorff, A. and Stern, R. (1981), 'A disaggregated model of world production and trade; an estimate of the impact of the Tokyo Round', *Journal of Policy Modelling*.

Delors J. *et al.* (1989), *Report on the Economic and Monetary Union in the European Community*, CEC, Brussels.

Demsetz, H. (1982), *Economic, Legal and Political Dimensions of Competition*, North-Holland, Amsterdam.

Denison, E.F. (1967), *Why Growth Rates Differ*, Brookings Institution, Washington.

Denton, G. (1984), 'Restructuring the EC budget', *Journal of Common Market Studies*, vol. 24.2; pp. 117–40.

Devereux, M. and Pearson, M. (1989), 'Corporate Tax Harmonisation and Economic Efficiency', *Report Series* no. 35, Institute of Fiscal Studies, London.

Dicken, P. (1986), *Global Shift, Industrial Change in a Turbulent World*, Harper and Row, London.

Dickinson, G. (1993), 'Insurance', *European Economy/Social Europe*, no. 3, pp. 183–210.

Dornbusch, R. (1976), 'Expectations and Exchange-Rate Dynamics', *Journal of Political Economy*, vol. 84, pp. 1161–76.

Dornbusch, R. (1980), *Open Economy Macro-Economics*, Basic Books, New York.

Dosi, G. and Soete, L. (1988), 'Technical Change and International Trade', in G. Dosi *et al.* (eds), *Technical Change and Economic Theory*, Pinter, London, pp. 401–31.

Dosser, D. (1966), 'Economic Analysis of Fiscal Harmonisation', in C.S. Shoup (ed.), *Fiscal Harmonisation in Common Markets*, Columbia University Press, New York.

Drabeck, Z. and Greenaway, D. (1984), 'Economic Integration and Inter-Industry Trade, the CMEA and EEC compared', *Kyklos*, vol. 37, pp. 444–69.

Dramais, A. (1977) 'Transmission of Inflationary Pressures between the E.E.C. Members', *European Economic Review*, vol. 9, pp. 21–42.

Druesne, G. and Kremlis, G. (1986), *La Politique de Concurrence de la CEE*, Paris.

Duchêne, F. and Shepherd, G. (eds) (1987), *Managing Industrial Change in Western Europe*, Pinter, London.

Dufey, G. and Giddy, I.H. (1981), *The Evolution of Instruments and Techniques in International Financial Markets*, SUERF, Tilburg.

Duncan, M.G. and Hall, M. (1983), *Proposals for a European Equity Market through Linkage of the Community Stock Exchanges*, CEC, Brussels.

Dunning, J.H. (1979), 'Explaining Changing Patterns of International Production: in Defence of an Eclectic Theory', *Oxford Bulletin of Economics and Statistics*, vol. 41, pp. 269–95.

Dunning, J.H. (1980), 'A note on Intra-Industry Foreign Direct Investment', *Banca Nazionale del Lavoro Quarterly Review*, vol. 34, December.

Dunning, J. and Cantwell, J. (1987), *IRM Directory of Statistics of International Investment and Production*, Macmillan, London.

Durán-Herrera, J.J. (1992), 'Cross Direct Investment and Technological Capability of Spanish Domestic Firms', in J. Cantwell, (ed.), *Multinational Investment in Modern Europe*, Edward Elgar, Aldershot, pp. 214–55.

Duroselle, J.B. (1965), 'L'idea d'Europa nella Storia', *Collana Europa Una*, Edizione Milano Nuova, Milan.

Duroselle, J.B. (1987), 'L'Europe dans l'Historiographie 1815–1914', in A. Rijksbaron *et al.* (eds), *Europe from a Cultural Perspective*, Nijgh en Van Ditmar, The Hague, pp. 31–2.

ECA (1988), *European Fund for Regional Development* (Official Journal, 12 December 1988).

ECJ (1985), *Judgement of the Court of 22 May 1985*, in Case 13/83 European Parliament vs. Council of the European Community.

Edye, D. (1987), *Immigrant Labour and Government Policy*, Gower, Aldershot.

El-Agraa, A.M. (1985), International Economic Integration, in D. Greenaway (ed.), *Current Issues in International Trade, Theory and Policy*, Macmillan, London, pp. 183–207.

El-Agraa, A.M. and Jones, A.J. (1981), *Theory of Customs Unions*, Philip Allan, Oxford.

Eliasson, G. (1984), 'The Micro Foundations of Industrial Policy', in A. Jacquemin (ed.), *European Industry: Public Policy and Corporate Strategy*, CEPS, Clarendon, Oxford, pp. 295–326.

Emerson, M., Aujean, M., Catinat, M., Goybet, P. and Jacquemin, A. (1988), 'The Economics of 1992; an Assessment of the Potential Economic Effects of Completing the Internal Market of the European Community', *European Economy*, no. 35/3, pp. 5–222.

Erdmenger, J. (1981), *The European Community Transport Policy*, Gower, Aldershot.

ESS (1989), *EEC Transport Policy within the Context of the Single Market*, European Study Services, Rixensart.

ETUI (1992), *The European Dimensions of Collective Bargaining after Maastricht*, European Trade Union Institute, Brussels.

Eurostat (1974), *Statistics of Energy*, Special Nr 4, Luxemburg.

Eurostat (1983), *Monthly Bulletin of Foreign Trade*, Special issue 1958–1982, Luxemburg.

Eurostat (1985), *Foreign Population and Foreign Employees in the Community*, Luxemburg.

Eurostat (1987), *Employment and Unemployment*, Theme 3, Series C, Luxemburg.

Eurostat (1992), *International Trade in Services, 1979–1988*, Series 6D, Luxemburg.

Eurostat (several years), *Electricity Prices*, Luxemburg.

Eussner, A. (1986), 'Agro-industrial Cooperation between the EC and ACP Countries', *Journal of Common Market Studies*, vol. 25.1, pp. 51–73.

Eyzenga, W. (1987), 'The Dependence of the Deutsche Bundesbank and De Nederlandsche Bank with Regard to Monetary Policy; a Comparative Analysis', Series: *SUERF Papers on Monetary Policy and Financial Systems*, no. 2, Tilburg.

Faber, M. and Breyer, F. (1980), 'Eine ökonomische Analyse konstitutioneller Aspekte der Europäischen Integration', *Jahrbuch für Sozialwissenschaft*, vol. 31, pp. 213–27.

Farnell, J. and Ellis, J. (1984), *In Search of a Common Fisheries Policy*, Gower, Aldershot.

Feldstein, M. and Horioka, C. (1980), 'Domestic Savings and International Capital Flows', *The Economic Journal*, vol. 90, pp. 314–29.

Ferner, A. and Hyman, R. (eds) (1992), *Industrial Relations in the New Europe*, Blackwell, Oxford.

Findlay, R. (1982), 'International Distributive Justice, a Trade-Theoretic Approach', *Journal of International Economics*, vol. 13, pp. 1–14.

Finsinger, J. and Pauly, M.V. (eds) (1986), *The Economics of Insurance Regulation*, Macmillan, Basingstoke.

Finsinger, J., Hammond, E. and Tapp, J. (1985), *Insurance: Competition on Regulation, a Comparative Study*, The Institute for Fiscal Studies, London.

Fisher, M.R. (1966), *Wage Determination in an Integrating Europe*, Sythoff, Leiden.

Fisher, S. (1987), 'International Macro-Economic Policy Coordination', *NBER Working Paper* no. 2244, NBER, Cambridge, Massachusetts.

Fishwick (1982), *Multinational Companies and Economic Concentration in Europe*, Gower, Aldershot.

Fleming, M. (1971), 'On Exchange Rate Unification', *Economic Journal*, vol. 81, pp. 467–88.

Folmer, H. (1980), *Regional Economic Policy; Measurement of its Effects*, Kluwer, Deventer.

Forte, F. (1977), 'Principles for the Assignment of Public Economic Functions in a Setting of Multi-Layer Government, EC', *Report of the (McDougall) Study Group on the role of Public Finance in European Integration*, vol. II, Collection of Studies of Economics and Finances, Series no. B 13, Brussels.

Francko, L.G. (1976), *The European Multinationals; a Renewed Challenge to American and British Business*, Harper and Row, London.

Frankel, J.A. (1989), 'Quantifying International Capital Mobility in the 1980's', *NBER Working Paper* 2856, NBER, Cambridge, Massachusetts.

Franzmeyer, F. (1982), *Approaches to Industrial Policy within the EC and its Impact on European Integration*, Gower, Aldershot.

Franzmeyer, F., Hrubesch, P., Seidel, B. and Weise, Ch. (1991), *The Regional Impact of Community Policies*, EP, Luxemburg.

Frenkel, J.A. and Goldstein, M. (1986), 'A Guide to Target Zones', *IMF Staff Papers*, vol. 33.4.

Frey, B. (1984), *International Political Economics*, Basil Blackwell, Oxford.

Frey, B. (1985), 'The Political Economy of Protection', in D. Greenaway (ed.), *Current Issues in International Trade*, Macmillan, London, pp. 139–57.

Frey, B. and Schneider, F. (1984), 'International Political Economy, a Rising Field', *Economia Internazionale*, vol. 37.3–4, pp. 308–47.

Friedman, M. (1968), 'The Role of Monetary Policy', *American Economic Review*, vol. 58.1, pp. 1–17.

Friedman, M., and Friedman, R. (1980), *Free to Choose, a Personal Statement*, Harcourt Brace Jovanovich, New York, p. 154.

Fries, T. (1984), 'Uncertainty as a possible rationale for Customs Unions', *Journal of International Economics* vol. 17.3/4, pp. 347–57.

Frisch, H. (1983), 'Theories of Inflation', *Cambridge Surveys of Economic Literature*, Cambridge University Press, Cambridge.

Fukao, M. and Hanazaki, M. (1987), 'Internationalisation of Financial Markets and the Allocation of Capital', *OECD Economic Studies*, no. 8, pp. 35–92.

Gaab, W., Granziol, M.J. and Horner, M. (1986), 'On Some International Parity Conditions: an Empirical Investigation', *European Economic Review*, vol. 30.3, pp. 683–713.

Gardner, E.H. (1992), 'Taxes on capital income; a survey', in G. Kopits (ed.), *Tax Harmonization in the European Community: policy issues and analysis*, IMF occasional paper 94, Washington, pp. 52–71.

Gasiorek, M., Smith, A. and Venables, A. (1992), *1992, Trade and Welfare, a General Equilibrium Model*, Paper for the CEPR Pars Conference on Trade Policies and Trade Flows after 1992.

GATT (1987), *The European Community's External Trade in Services*, Geneva.

Geist, Ch.R. (1979), *Raising International Capital, International Bond Markets and the European Institutions*, Saxon House, Farnborough.

Gerbet, P. (1983), *La Construction de l'Europe*, Imprimerie Nationale, Paris.

Gerloff, W. (1920), *Die Deutsche Zoll- und Handelspolitik von der Gründung des Zollvereins bis zum Frieden von Versailles*, Glöckner, Leipzig.

Geroski, P. and Jacquemin, A. (1984), 'Large Firms in the European Corporate Economy and Industrial Policy in the 1980s', in A. Jacquemin (ed.), *European*

Industry: Public Policy and Corporate Strategy, CEPS, Clarendon, Oxford, pp. 343–67.

Geroski, P. and Jacquemin, A. (1985), 'Industrial Change, Barriers to Mobility and European Industrial Policy', *Economic Policy*, vol. 1.1, pp. 170–218.

Gialloreto, L. (1988), *Strategic Airline Management*, Pitman, London.

Giavazzi, F. and Pagano, M. (1986), 'The Advantages of Tying one's Hands; EMS Discipline and Central Bank Credibility', *European Economic Review*, vol. 28, pp. 1055–82.

Giersch, H. (1949), 'Economic Union between Nations and the Location of Industries', *Review of Economic Studies*, vol. 17, pp. 87–97.

Giersch, H. (1987), *Internal and External Liberalisation for Faster Growth: Economic Papers*, Commission of EC, Brussels.

Giovannini, A. (1989), 'National Tax Systems versus the European Capital Market', *Economic Policy*, pp. 346–86.

Glejser, H. (1972), 'Empirical Evidence on Comparative Cost Theory from the European Common Market Experience', *European Economic Review* vol. 163, pp. 247–59.

Golombek, R., Hoel, M. and Vislie, J. (eds) (1987), *Natural Gas Markets and Contracts,* North-Holland, Amsterdam.

Gomes, L. (1987), *Foreign Trade and the National Economy; Mercantilist and Classical Perspectives*, Macmillan, London.

Gordon, J. (1992), 'An analysis of the EC Structural Funds', in G. Kopits, (ed.), *Tax Harmonization in the European Community: policy issues and analysis*, IMF occasional paper 94, Washington, pp. 92–104.

Gordon, R.H. (1983), 'An Optimal Taxation Approach to Fiscal Federalism', *Quarterly Journal of Economics*, vol. 48.4, pp. 567–86.

Graham, E.M. (1992), 'Direct Investments between the US and the EC, Post 198€ and Pre 1992', in J. Cantwell (ed.), *Multinational Investment in Modern Europe* Edward Elgar, Aldershot, pp. 46–70.

Grauwe, P. de (1975), 'Conditions for Monetary Integration, a Geometric Interpreta tion', *Weltwirtschaftliches Archiv*, vol. 3, pp. 634–44.

Grauwe, P. de (1987), 'International Trade and Economic Growth in the Europeaı Monetary System', *European Economic Review*, vol. 31, pp. 389–98.

Grauwe, P. de (1992), *The Economics of Monetary Integration*, Oxford University Press, Oxford.

Greenaway, D. (1983), *International Trade Policy, from Tariffs to the New Protectionism* Macmillan, London.

Greenaway, D. (1987), 'Intra-Industry Trade, Intra-Firm Trade and European Inte gration; Evidence, Gains and Policy Aspects', *Journal of Common Market Studie:* vol. 26.2, pp. 153–72.

Greenaway, D. and Milner, C. (1986), *The Economics of Intra-Industry Trade*, Bas Blackwell, Oxford.

Gremmen, H. (1985), 'Testing Factor Price Equalisation in the EC: An Alternativ' Approach', *Journal of Common Market Studies*, vol. 23, pp. 277–86.

Griffiths, B. (1975), *Invisible Barriers to Invisible Trade*, Macmillan, London.

Grinols, E.J. (1984), 'A Thorn in the Lion's Paw; Has Britain Paid too much fc Common Market Membership?', *Journal of International Economics*, vol. 16, pɩ 271–93.

Groeben, H. von der (1982), *Aufbaujahre der Europäischen Gemeinschaften*, Nomo Baden-Baden.

Gros, D. (1987), 'On the Volatility of Exchange Rates: a Test of Monetary aո Portfolio Balance Models of Exchange Rate Determination', *Economic Workiɲ Document*, vol. 32, CEPS, Brussels.

Gros, D. (1989), 'Paradigms for the Monetary Union of Europe', *Journal of Comm(Market Studies*, vol. 27.3, pp. 219–30.

Gros, D. and Thygesen, N. (1992), *European Monetary Integration*, Longman, London.

Grubel, H.G. (1974), 'Taxation and the Rates of Return from some US Assets Holdings Abroad', *Journal of Political Economy*, vol. 82, pp. 469–87.

Grubel, H.G. (1981), *International Economics*, Irwin, Homewood, Illinois.

Grubel, H.G. and Lloyd, P. (1975), *Intra-Industry Trade: the Theory and Measurement of International Trade in Differentiated Products*, Macmillan, London.

Gual, J. (1993), 'An Econometric Analysis of Price Differentials in the EEC Automobile Market', *Applied Economics*, vol. 25, pp. 599–607.

Guieu, P. and Bonnet, C. (1987), 'Completion of the Internal Market and Indirect Taxation', *Journal of Common Market Studies*, vol. 25, pp. 209–23.

Gwilliam, K.M., Petriccione, S., Voigt, F. and Zighera, J.A. (1973), 'Criteria for the Coordination of Investments in Transport Infrastructure', *The EEC Studies, Transport Series Nr 3*, Brussels.

Haack, W.G.C.M. (1983), 'The Selectivity of Economic Integration Theories; a Comparison of Some Traditional and Marxist Approaches', *Journal of Common Market Studies*, vol. 21.4, pp. 365–86.

Haaland, J. (1990), 'Assessing the Effects of EC Integration on EFTA Countries; the Position of Norway and Sweden', *Journal of Common Market Studies*, vol. 28.4, pp. 379–400.

Haaland, J. and Norman, V. (1992), *Global Production Effects of European Integration*, Paper for the CEPR Conference Paris.

Haas, E.B. (1958), *The Uniting of Europe; Political, Social and Economic Forces 1950–1957*, Stevens, London.

Hagenaars, A.J.M. (1986), *The Perception of Poverty*, North-Holland, Amsterdam.

Hajnal, P.I. (1989), *The Seven Power Summit*, Documents Kraus, New York.

Hall, G. (ed.) (1986), *European Industrial Policy*, Croom Helm, London.

Hall, R. and van der Wee, D. (1992), 'Community regional policies for the 1990s', *Regional Studies*, vol. 26.4, pp. 399–404.

Hamada, K. (1985), *The Political Economy of International Monetary Interdependence*, Cambridge University Press, Cambridge.

Hammar, T. (1985), *European Immigration Policy*, Cambridge University Press, Cambridge.

Harding, S., Philips, D. and Fogarty, M. (1986), *Contrasting Values in Western Europe, Unity, Diversity and Change*, Macmillan, London.

Harris, S., Swimbank, A. and Wilkinson, G. (1983), *The Food and Farm Policies of the European Community*, Wiley, Chichester.

Hart, P., Ledger, G., Roe, M. and Smith, B. (1992), *Shipping Policy in the European Community*, Avebury, Aldershot.

Hartley, K. (1987), 'Public Procurement and Competitiveness: a Community Market for Military Hardware and Technology?', *Journal of Common Market Studies*, vol. 25, pp. 237–47.

Hartog, F. (1979), *Hoofdlijnen van de Prijstheorie* (Main Lines of Price Theory), Stenfert Kroese, Leiden.

Hawtrey, R. (1947), *The Gold Standard in Theory and Practice*, Longmans, London.

Heidhues, T., Josling, T., Ritson, C. *et al.* (1978), 'Common Prices and Europe's Farm Policy', *Thames Essays*, no. 13, Trade Policy Research Centre, London.

Heijke, J.A.M. and Klaassen, L.H. (1979), 'Human Reactions to Spatial Diversity, Mobility in Regional Labour Markets', in H. Folmer and J. Oosterhaven (eds), *Spatial Inequalities and Regional Development*, Nijhoff, The Hague, pp. 117–30.

Helg, R. and Ranci, P. (1988), 'Economies of Scale and the Integration of the EC, the Case of Italy', in *Research into the Cost of Non-Europe, Basic Findings*, vol. 2, CEC, Luxemburg, pp. 205–85.

Helpman, E. and Krugman, P.R. (1985), *Market Structure and Foreign Trade; Increasing Returns, Imperfect Competition and the International Economy*, Wheatsheaf, Brighton.

Hennart, J.F. (1983), 'The Political Economy of Comparative Growth Rates; the Case of France', in D. Mueller (ed.), *The Political Economy of Growth*, Yale University Press, New Haven, pp. 176–203.

Henry, P. (1981), *Study of the Regional Impact of the Common Agricultural Policy*, CEC, Luxemburg.

Herbst, L. (1986), 'Die Zeitgenössische Integrationstheorie und die Anfänge der Europäischen Einigung 1947–1950', *Vierteljahreshefte für Zeitgeschichte* II, vol. 34, pp. 161–204.

Herman, B. and van Holst, B. (1984), 'International Trade in Services; Some Theoretical and Practical Problems', *Series Occasional Papers and Reprints*, NEI, Rotterdam.

Herman, V. and van Schendelen, M.P.C.M. (eds) (1974), *The European Parliament and the National Parliaments*, Saxon House, Farnborough.

Hewitt, A. (1984), 'The Lomé Conventions: Entering a Second Decade', *Journal of Common Market Studies*, vol. 23.2, pp. 95–115.

Hill, B.E. (1984), *The Common Agricultural Policy; Past, Present and Future*, Methuen, London.

Hill, B.E. and Ingersent, K.A. (1982), *The Economic Analysis of Agriculture*, 2nd edn, Heinemann, London.

Hine, R.C. (1985), *The Political Economy of European Trade*, Wheatsheaf, Brighton.

Hine, R.C. (1992), *The Political Economy of Agricultural Trade*, Edward Elgar, Cheltenham.

Hirsch, S. (1974), 'Hypothesis Regarding Trade Between Developing and Industrial Countries', in H. Giersch (ed.), *The International Division of Labour*, Mohr, Tübingen, pp. 65–82.

Hirsch, S. (1981), 'Peace Making and Economic Interdependence', *The World Economy*, vol. 4, pp. 407–17.

Hirschmann, A.O. (1981), 'Three Uses of Political Economy in Analysing European Integration', in *Essays in Trespassing; Economics to Politics and Beyond*, Cambridge University Press, Cambridge, pp. 266–84.

Hocking, R. (1980), 'Trade in Motorcars between the Major European Producers', *Economic Journal*, vol. 90, pp. 504–19.

Hodges, M. and Wallace, W. (eds) (1981), *Economic Divergence in the EC*, Allen and Unwin, London.

Hodget, G. (1972), *A Social and Economic History of Medieval Europe*, Methuen, London.

Hoffmann, S. (1982), 'Reflections on the Nation State in Western Europe Today', *Journal of Common Market Studies*, vol. 21.1, pp. 21–39.

Hoffmeyer, B. (1982), 'The EEC's Common Agricultural Policy and the ACP States', *Research Report no. 2*, Centre for Development Studies, Copenhagen.

Holland, S. (1980), *Uncommon Market, Capital Class and Power in the European Community*, Macmillan, London.

Holloway, J. (1981), *Social Policy Harmonisation in the European Community*, Gower, Aldershot.

Holtfrerich, C.-L. (1989), 'The Monetary Unification Process in Nineteenth-Century Germany', in M. de Cecco and A. Giovannini (eds), *A European Central Bank?* Cambridge University Press, Cambridge, pp. 216–41.

Hudson, R. and Williams, A. (1986), *The United Kingdom*, Harper and Row, London.

Hufbauer, G.C. (1968), 'The Commodity Composition of Trade in Manufactured Goods', *Conference on Technology and Competition in International Trade*, NBER, New York.

Hufbauer, G.C. (1990), 'An Overview', in G.C. Hufbauer (ed.), *Europe 1992; An American Perspective*, Brookings Institution, Washington.

Hufbauer, G.C. and Scott, J.J. (1985), *Economic Sanctions Reconsidered; History an Current Policy*, Institute for International Economics, Washington.

ughes Hallett, A.J. (1985), 'Autonomy and the Choice of Policy in Asymmetrically Dependent Economies', *Oxford Economic Papers* , no. 38, pp. 516–45.

RD (1985), *World Development Report*, Oxford University Press, New York.

E (1978), *La Charte Sociale Européenne: Dix Années d'Application*, Editions de l'Université, Brussels.

O (1956), *Social Aspects of European Economic Cooperation*, Report by a group of experts, Geneva.

go, W. (1985), 'Barriers to Trade in Banking and Financial Services', *Thames Essays*, no. 41, Trade Policy Research Centre, London.

gram, J.C. (1973), 'The Case for European Monetary Integration', *Essays in International Finance*, no. 98, Princeton University, Princeton NJ.

aacs, G. (1986), *Les Ressources Financières de la Communauté Européenne*, Economica, Paris.

hiyama, Y. (1975), 'The Theory of Optimum Currency Areas, a Survey', *IMF Staff Papers*, vol. 22, pp. 344–83.

cquemin, A. (1979), *Economie Industrielle Européenne; Structures de Marché et Stratégies d'Entreprises*, 2nd edn, Dunod, Paris.

cquemin, A. (1982), 'Imperfect Market Structure and International Trade, Some Recent Research', *Kyklos*, vol. 35, pp. 73–93.

cquemin, A. (1991), *Merger and Competition Policy in the European Community*, Blackwell, Oxford.

cquemin, A. and de Jong, H.W. (1977), *European Industrial Organisation*, Macmillan, London.

cquemin, A. and Sapir, A. (1988), 'European Integration or World Integration?', *Weltwirtschaftliches Archiv*, vol. 124, pp. 127–39.

cquemin, A. and Sapir, A. (1991), 'Europe post-1992; internal and external liberalisation', *American Economic Review*, vol. 81.2, pp. 166–70.

cquemin, A. and Wright, D. (1993), *The European Challenges Post 1992; Shaping Factors, Shaping Actors*, Edward Elgar, Aldershot.

nsen, E. and De Vree, J.K. (1985), *The Ordeal of Unity, the Politics of European Integration 1945–1985*, Prime Press, Bilthoven.

nsen, W.G. (1983), *Energy in Europe 1945–1980*, Fouls, London.

hnson, H.G. (1958), 'The Gains from Freer Trade in Europe, an Estimate', *Manchester School*, vol. 26.3, pp. 247–55.

hnston, R.B. (1983), *The Economics of the Euromarket, History, Theory and Policy*, Macmillan, London.

nes, C.L. and Leydon, K. (1986), 'Developments in Gas and Electricity Prices in the EEC', in P. Odell and J. Daneels (eds), *Gas and Electricity Markets in Europe: Prospects and Policies*, BAEE, Brussels, pp. 8–122.

nes, K. (1984), 'The Political Economy of Voluntary Export Restraint Agreements', *Kyklos*, vol. 37, pp. 82–101.

ng, H.W. de (1981), *Dynamische Markttheorie*, Stenfert Kroese, Leiden.

ng, H.W. de (1987), 'Market Structures in the European Economic Community', in M. Macmillen, D.G. Mayes and P. van Veen (eds), *European Integration and Industry*, Tilburg University Press, Tilburg, pp. 40–89.

ng, H.W. de (1989), 'De Overnamemarkt; Protectie of Vrijhandel?', *ESB*, p. 939.

ng, H.W. de (1993), 'Market Structures in the EEC', in H.W. de Jong (ed.), *The Structure of European Industry*, 3rd edn, Kluwer, Dordrecht, pp. 1–42.

ng, H.W. de (ed.) (1993), *The Structure of European Industry*, 3rd edn, Kluwer, Dordrecht.

ng, M.W. de (1993), 'Service industries; innovation and internationalization', in H.W. de Jong (ed.), *The Structure of European Industry*, 3rd edn, Kluwer, Dordrecht, pp. 337–66.

Kaelble, H. (1986), *Sozialgeschichte der Europäischen Integration, 1880–1980*, Fre Universität, Berlin.

Kaempfer, W.H. and Loewenberg, A.D. (1992), *International Economic Sanctions; Public Choice Approach*, Westview Press, Boulder, Colorado.

Kalantzopoulos, O. (1986), 'The Cost of Voluntary Export Restraints for Select Countries', cited in the World Bank's *World Development Report*, 1987, Oxfo University Press, New York, p. 150.

Kaldor, N. (1966), *The Causes of the Slow Growth of the United Kingdom*, Cambrid University Press, Cambridge.

Kane, D.R. (1982), *The Euro-Dollar Market and the Years of Crisis*, Croom Heli London.

Kapteyn, P.J.G. and Verloren van Themaat, P. (1980), *Inleiding tot het Recht van Europese Gemeenschappen*, Kluwer, Deventer.

Katee, S. (1979), 'De Phillips-curve in Nederland, 1959–1979', *Maandschrift Econom* vol. 43, pp. 484–99.

Kaufman, P.J. (1987), 'The Community Trademark, its Role in Making the Intern Market Effective', *Journal of Common Market Studies*, vol. 25.13, pp. 223–35.

Kay, J. and Keene, M. (1987), 'Alcohol and Tobacco Taxes, Criteria for Harmonis tion', in S. Cnossen (ed.), *Tax Coordination in the European Community*, Kluwe Deventer, pp. 85–112.

Kayser, B. (1972), *Cyclically Determined Homeward Flows of Migrant Workers*, OEC Paris.

Keely, C.B. and Tran, B.N. (1989), 'Remittances from Labour Migration: Evalu tions, Performance and Implications', *International Migration Review*, vol. 23.3, p 500–25.

Kennedy Brenner, C. (1979), *Foreign Workers and Immigration Policy*, OECD/D Paris.

Kenwood, A.G. and Longheed, A.L. (1983), *The Growth of the International Econon 1820–1980, an introductory text*, Allen and Unwin, London.

Keohane, R.O. and Hoffmann, S. (1991), 'Institutional Change in Europe in the 1980' in R.O. Keohane and S. Hoffmann (eds), *The New European Community, Decisi Making and Institutional Change*, Westview Press, Boulder, Colorado, pp. 1–39.

Keynes, J.M. (1936), *The General Theory of Employment, Interest and Money*, Harcou Brace & Co., New York.

Kindleberger, C.P. (1984), *A Financial History of Western Europe*, Allen and Unwi London.

Kindleberger, C.P. (1987), *International Capital Movements*, Cambridge Universi Press, Cambridge.

Kindleberger *et al.* (1979), *Migration, Growth and Development*, OECD, Paris.

Klaassen, L.H. and Drewe, P. (1973), *Migration Policy in Europe*, Saxon House, Far borough.

Klaassen, L.H. and Molle, W.T.M. (eds) (1982), *Industrial Migration and Mobility the European Community*, Gower, Aldershot.

Klein, L. (1985), 'Trade and Sectoral Adjustment Policy Problems', in T. Peeters, Praet and P. Reding (eds), *International Trade and Exchange Rates in the Late Eigh ies*, North-Holland, Amsterdam, pp. 111–30.

Kock, K. (1969), *International Trade Policy and the GATT, 1947–1967*, Almquist ar Wicksell, Stockholm.

Koekkoek, K.A. and Mennes, L.B.M. (1988), 'Some Potential Effects of Liberalisi the Multi-Fibre Arrangement', in L.B.M. Mennes and J. Kol (eds), *European Tra Policies and the Developing World*, Croom Helm, Beckenham, pp. 187–213.

Koekkoek, A., Kuyvenhoven, A. and Molle, W. (1990), 'Europe 1992 and the Dev oping Countries, an Overview', *Journal of Common Market Studies*, vol. 29.2, p 111–31.

Koester, U. (1977), 'The Redistributional Effects of the Common Agricultural Financial System', *European Review of Agricultural Economics*, vol. 4.4, pp. 321–45.

Koester, U. and Tangermann, S. (1976), *Alternative der Agrarpolitik*, Hiltrup, Münster.

Kol, J. (1987), 'Exports from Developing Countries; Some Facts and Scope', *European Economic Review*, vol. 31, pp. 466–74.

Kol, J. (1988), *The Measurement of Intra-Industry Trade*, Erasmus University Press,
Rotterdam.

Kol, J. (1992), *The ACP Countries and the 1992 Programme of the EC*, report to the EC
Commission, EUR, Rotterdam.

Kolvenbach, W. and Hanau, P. (1988), *Handbook on European Employee Co-Management*, Kluwer, Deventer.

Kottis, A. (1985), 'Female/Male Earnings Differentials in the Founder Countries of
the EEC; an Econometric Investigation', *De Economist*, vol. 132.2, pp. 204–23.

Kozma, F. (1982), *Economic Integration and Economic Strategy*, Nijhoff, The Hague.

Krägenau, H. (1987), *Internationale Direktinvestitionen*, IFW, Weltarchiv, Hamburg.

Krauss, H.B. (1979), *The New Protectionism, the Welfare State and International Trade*,
Basil Blackwell, Oxford.

Krauss, L.B. (1968), *European Integration and the US*, Brookings Institution, Washington.

Kreinin, M.E. (1973), 'The Static Effects of EEC Enlargement on Trade Flows', *Southern Economic Journal*, vol. 39, pp. 559–68.

Krugman, P. (1979), 'A Model of Innovation, Technology Transfer, and the World
Distribution of Income', *Journal of Political Economy*, vol. 87, pp 253–67.

Krugman, P. (1986), *Strategic Trade Policy and the New International Economics*, MIT
Press, Cambridge, Mass.

Krugman, P. (1991), *Geography and Trade*, MIT Press, Cambridge, Mass.

Krugman, P. and Obstfeld, M. (1988), *International Economics*, Scott, Foreman and
Co., Glenview.

Kuznets, S. (1966), *Modern Economic Growth; Rates, Structure and Spread*, Yale University Press, New Haven.

Laffan, B. (1983), 'Policy Implementation in the European Community: The European Social Fund as a Case Study', *Journal of Common Market Studies*, vol. 21.4, pp.
389–408.

Lamfalussy, A. (1981), 'Changing Attitudes towards Capital Movements', in F.
Cairncross (ed.), *Changing Perceptions of Economic Policy*, Methuen, London, pp.
194–217.

Lane, J.E. and Ersson, S.O. (1987), *Politics and Society in Western Europe*, Sage, London.

Langhammer, K.J. and Sapir, A. (1987), *Economic Impact of Generalised Tariff Preferences*, TPRC, Gower, Aldershot.

Lannes, X. (1956), 'International Mobility of Manpower in Western Europe' (I + II),
International Labour Review, vol. 73, pp. 1–24 and 135–51.

Lattre, A. de (1985), 'Floating, Uncertainty and the Real Sector', in L. Tsoukalis
(ed.), *The Political Economy of International Money: In Search of a New Order*, Sage,
London, pp. 71–103.

Lebergott, S. (1947), 'Wage Structures', *Review of Economics and Statistics*, vol. 29, pp.
247–85.

Lebon, A. and Falchi, G. (1980), 'New Developments in Intra-European Migration
Since 1974', *International Migration Review*, vol. 14.4, pp. 539–73.

LEI (1987), *Landbouw-Economisch Bericht*, The Hague.

Leigh, M. (1984), *European Integration and the Common Fisheries Policy*, Croom Helm,
Beckenham.

Lemaitre, P. and Goybet, C. (1984), *Multinational Companies in the EEC* (IRM Multinational Report no. 1), John Wiley, Chichester.

Lemmen, J.J.G. and Eijffinger, S.C.W. (1992), 'The Degree of Financial Integration in the European Community', *Research Memo*, FEW 540, Tilburg.

Levi, M. (1981), *International Finance; Financial Management and the International Economy*, McGraw-Hill, New York.

Levi, M. and Sarnet, F. (1970), 'International Diversification of Investment Portfolios', *American Economic Review*, vol. 60, pp. 668–75.

Leyshon, A., Daniels, P.W. and Thrift, N.J. (1987), *Internationalisation of Professional Producer Services; the Case of Large Accountancy Firms*. Working Papers on Producer Services, Universities of Bristol and Liverpool.

Lindbeck, A. (1981), 'Industrial Policy as an Issue of the Economic Environment', *The World Economy*, vol. 4.4.

Lindberg, L.N. and Scheingold, S.A. (1970), *Europe's Would-Be Polity*, Prentice-Hall, Englewood Cliffs, NJ.

Linder, S.B. (1961), *An Essay on Trade and Transformation*, Almquist and Wicksell, Uppsala.

Lindert, P. (1986), *International Economics*, 8th edn, Irwin, Homewood, Illinois.

Linnemann, H. (1966), *An Econometric Study of International Trade Flows*, North-Holland, Amsterdam.

Lipgens, W., Loth, W. and Milward, A. (1982), *A History of European Integration, vol. 1, 1945–1947, The Formation of the European Unity Movement*, Clarendon and Oxford University Press, London and New York.

Lipsey, R.G. (1960), 'The Theory of Customs Unions: a General Survey', *Economic Journal*, vol. 70, pp. 496–513.

Lloyd, P.J. (1982), '3 x 3 Theory of Customs Unions', *Journal of International Economics*, vol. 12, pp. 41–63.

Lloyd, P.J. (1992), 'Regionalisation and World Trade', *OECD Economic Studies*, vol. 18, pp. 7–34.

Locksey, G. and Ward, T. (1979), 'Concentration in Manufacturing in the EC', *Cambridge Journal of Economics*, vol. 3.1, pp. 91–7.

Löffelholz, H.D. von (1992), 'Der Beitrag der Ausländer zum wirtschaftlichen Wohlstand in der BRD', *RWI*, Essen (mimeo).

Long, F. (1980), *The Political Economy of EEC Relations*, Pergamon, Oxford.

Lopandic, D. (1986), 'The European Community and Comecon', *Review of International Affairs*, no. 876, 3, pp. 12–14.

Lucas, N. (1977), *Energy and the European Communities*, Europa Publications, London.

Lucas, N. (1985), *Western European Energy Policies, a Comparative Study*, Oxford University Press, Oxford.

Ludlow, P. (1982), *The Making of the European Monetary System*, Butterworth, London.

Lundberg, L. (1992), 'European Economic Integration and the Nordic Countries Trade', *Journal of Common Market Studies*, vol. 30.2, pp. 157–73.

Lunn, J. (1980), 'Determinants of US investment in the EEC; Further Evidence' *European Economic Review*, vol. 24, pp. 93–101.

MacBean, A.I. and Snowden, P.N. (1981), *International Institutions in Trade and Finance*, George Allen and Unwin, London.

MacDougall, G.D.A. *et al.* (1977), *Report of the Study Group on the Role of Public Finance in European Integration*, CEC, Economy and Finance Series, vol. 1, General Report, Brussels.

Machlup, F. (1977), *A History of Thought on Economic Integration*, Macmillan, London.

MacMillan, M.J. (1982), 'The Economic Effects of International Migration; a Survey' *Journal of Common Market Studies*, vol. 20.3, pp. 245–67.

Magnifico, G. (1985), *Regional Imbalances and National Economic Performance*, Office of Official Publications of the EC, Luxemburg, pp. 85–95.

Maillet, P. (1977), *The Construction of a European Community*, Praeger, New York.

Maillet, P. (1983), *L'Europe à la Recherche de son Avenir Industriel*, Dunod, Paris.

Maillet, P. and Rollet, Ph. (1986), 'L'Insertion de l'Europe dans la Division Internationale du Travail; Appréciations et Suggestions', *Revue du Marché Commun*, no. 299, pp. 371–86.

Malcor, R. (1970), 'Problèmes Posés par l'Application Pratique d'une Tarification pour l'Usage des Infrastructures Routières', *The EEC Studies*, Transport Series no. 2, Brussels.

Mark, N.C. (1985a), 'Some Evidence on the International Inequality of Real Interest Rates', *Journal of International Money and Finance*, vol. 4.2, pp. 189–208.

Mark, N.C. (1985b), 'A Note on International Real Interest Differentials', *Review of Economics and Statistics*, vol. 67.4, pp. 681–4.

Markusen, J.R. (1983), 'Factor Movements and Commodity Trade as Complements', *Journal of International Economics*, vol. 14, pp. 341–56.

Marques-Mendes, A.J. (1986a), 'The Contribution of the European Community to Economic Growth', *Journal of Common Market Studies*, vol. 24.4, pp. 261–77.

Marques-Mendes, A.J. (1986b), *Economic Integration and Growth in Europe*, Croom Helm, London.

Mathias, P. and Davis, J.A. (1991), *Innovation and Technology in Europe; from the Eighteenth Century to the Present Day*, Basil Blackwell, Oxford.

Mathijsen, P.S.R.F. (1985), *A Guide to European Community Law*, 4th edn, Sweet and Maxwell, London.

Matisse, T. (1988), *The European Community's External Trade in Services*, Eurostat, Luxemburg.

Matthews, A. (1985), *The Common Agricultural Policy and the Less Developed Countries*, Gill and Macmillan, Dublin.

Mayes, D. (1978), 'The Effects of Economic Integration on Trade', *Journal of Common Market Studies*, vol. 17.1, pp. 1–25.

Maynard, G. and Ryckeghem, W. van (1976), 'Why Inflation Rates Differ, a Critical Examination of the Structural Hypothesis', in H. Frisch (ed.), *Inflation in Small Countries*, Springer, Berlin. pp. 47–72.

McCorriston, S. and Sheldon, I.M. (1987), 'EC Integration and the Agricultural Supply Industries', in M. Macmillen, D.G. Mayes, and P. van Veen, (eds), *European Integration and Industry*, Tilburg University Press, Tilburg, pp. 119–52.

McDaniel, P.R. (1987), 'Personal Income Taxes; the Treatment of Tax Expenditures', in S. Cnossen (ed.), *Tax Coordination in the European Community*, Kluwer, Deventer, pp. 319–33.

McGowan, F. and Seabright, P. (1989), 'Deregulating European Airlines', *Economic Policy*, vol. 2, pp. 284–344.

McGowan, F. and Trengrove, C. (1986), 'European Aviation; a Common Market?', *Institute of Fiscal Studies*, Report Series no. 23, London.

Meade, J.E. (1955), *The Theory of Customs Unions*, North-Holland, Amsterdam.

Meerhaeghe, M.A.G. van (1980), *A Handbook of International Economic Institutions*, 3rd edn, Martinus Nijhoff, The Hague.

Meerhaeghe, M.A.G. van (ed.) (1992), *Belgium and EC Membership Evaluated*, Pinter, London; St Martin's Press, New York.

Meerssele, P. van de (1971), *De Europese Integratie 1945–1970*, Standaard, Antwerp.

Meester, G. and Strijker, D. (1985), *Het Europees Landbouwbeleid voorbij de Scheidslijn van Zelfvoorziening* (WRR, V46), State Publishing Office, The Hague.

Merlini, C. (ed.) (1984), *Economic Summits and Western Decision Making*, Croom Helm, London.

Messerlin, P.A. (1988), *The EC Anti-Dumping Regulations; a First Economic Appraisal 1980–1985*, Paper presented to the First International Seminar on International Economics, Oxford, August 1988.

Messerlin, P.A. (1992), 'Trade Policies in France', in D. Salvatore, (ed.), *National*

Trade Policies, Handbook of Comparative Economic Policies, vol. 2, Greenwood Press, New York.

Messerlin, P.A. (1993), 'Services in CEC; the European Community as a World Trade Partner', *European Economy*, no. 52, pp. 129–56.

Messerlin, P.A. and Becuwe, S. (1986), 'Intra-Industry Trade in the Long Term; the French Case 1850–1913', in D. Greenaway and P.K.M. Tharakan (eds), *Imperfect Competition and International Trade*, Wheatsheaf, Brighton, pp. 191–216.

Meyer, F.W. and Willgerodt, H. (1956), 'Der Wirtschaftspolitische Aussagewert Internationaler Lohnvergleiche', in *Internationale Lohngefaelle, Wirtschaftspolitische Folgerungen, und Statistische Problematik*, Bundesministerium für Wirtschaftspolitische Zusammenarbeit, Deutscher Bundesverlag, Bonn.

Meyer, G. (1973), *Problems of Trade Policy*, Oxford University Press, London.

Meyer, P.A. (1967), 'Price Discrimination, Regional Loan Rates and the Structure of the Banking Industry', *Journal of Finance*, vol. 22.1, pp. 37–49.

Mihailovic, K. (1976), 'Migration and the Integration of Labour Markets', in F. Machlup (ed.), *Economic Integration, Worldwide Regional Sectoral*, Macmillan, London, pp. 163–186.

Miller, M.H. and Spencer, J.E. (1977), 'The Static Economic Effects of the UK joining the EEC, a General Equilibrium Approach', *Review of Economic Studies*, vol. 44, pp. 71–93.

Mishalani, P. *et al.* (1981), 'The Pyramid of Privilege', in C. Stevens (ed.), *The EEC and the Third World, a Survey I*, Hodder and Stoughton and ODI/IDS, London, pp. 60–82.

Mishan, E.J. (1982), *Introduction to Political Economy*, Hutchinson, London.

Mishkin, F.S. (1984a), 'The Real Interest Rate; a Multicountry Empirical Study', *Canadian Journal of Economics*, vol. 17.2, pp. 283–311.

Mishkin, F.S. (1984b), 'Are Real Interest Rates Equal Across countries, an Empirical Investigation of International Parity Conditions?', *Journal of Finance*, vol. 39.5, pp. 1345–57.

Mitchell, B. (1981), *European Historical Statistics 1750–1975*, (2nd edn), Sythoff/Noordhoff, Alphen a/d Rijn.

Mitrany, D. (1966), *A Working Peace System*, Quadrangle Books, Chicago (reprint from earlier book of 1940s).

Molle, W.T.M., with the assistance of Van Holst, B. and Smit, H. (1980), *Regional Disparity and Economic Development in the European Community*, Saxon House, Farnborough.

Molle, W.T.M. (1983), 'Technological Change and Regional Development in Europe (Theory, Empirics, Policy)', *Papers and Proceedings of the Regional Science Association*, European Congress, pp. 23–38.

Molle, W.T.M. (1986), 'Regional Impact of Welfare State Policies in the European Community', in J.H.P. Paelinck (ed.), *Human Behaviour in Geographical Space*, Gower, Aldershot, pp. 77–90.

Molle, W.T.M. (1990), 'Will the Completion of the Internal Market Lead to Regional Divergence?', in H. Siebert (ed.), *The Completion of the Internal Market*, Institut für Weltwirtschaft, Kiel.

Molle, W.T.M. (1992), 'Oil Refining and Petrochemical Industry', in H.W. de Jong (ed.), *The Structure of European Industry*, 3rd edn, Kluwer, Dordrecht, pp. 41–60.

Molle, W.T.M. (1993), 'Subsidiarité et fiscalité', in P. Maillet (ed.), *Trois défis de Maastricht; Convergence, cohésion et subsidiarité*, L'Harmattan, Paris, pp. 149–66.

Molle, W.T.M. and Cappellin, R. (eds) (1988), *Regional Impact of Community Policies in Europe*, Avebury, Aldershot.

Molle, W.T.M. and Koning, J. de (1991), *Flexibility in the Labour Market: a Quantitative Approach*, in ILO/IILS Discussion Paper DP/31/1991, Geneva.

Molle, W.T.M. and Morsink, R. (1990), 'European Direct Investment in Europe: a

Explanatory Model of Intra-EC Flows', in B. Bürgermeier and J.M. Mucchielli (eds), *Multinationals and Europe 1992*, Routledge, London.

Molle, W.T.M. and van Mourik, A. (1987), 'Economic Means of a Common European Foreign Policy', in J.K. de Vree, P. Coffey and R.H. Lauwaars (eds), *Towards a European Foreign Policy*, Nijhoff, Dordrecht, pp. 165–92.

Molle, W.T.M. and van Mourik, A. (1988), 'International Movements of Labour under Conditions of Economic Integration; the Case of Western Europe', *Journal of Common Market Studies*, vol. 26.3, pp. 317–42.

Molle, W.T.M. and van Mourik, A. (eds) (1989a), *Wage Structures in the European Community, Convergence or Divergence?*, Gower, Aldershot.

Molle, W.T.M. and van Mourik, A. (1989b), 'A Static Explanatory Model of International Labour Migration to and in Western Europe', in I. Gordon and A. Thirlwall (eds), *European Factor Mobility, Trends and Convergences*, Macmillan, London, pp. 30–52.

Molle, W.T.M. and Wever, E. (1983), *Oil Refineries and Petrochemical Industries in Western Europe*, Gower, Aldershot.

Molle, W.T.M., de Koning, J. and Zandvliet, Ch. (1992), 'Can Foreign Aid Reduce East West Migration in Europe; with Special Reference to Poland?', *ILO Working Paper 67*, Geneva.

Molle, W., Sleijpen, O. and Van Heukelen, M. (1993), 'The Impact of an Economic and Monetary Union on Social and Economic Cohesion; Analysis and Ensuing Policy Implications', in K. Gretschmann (ed.), *Economic and Monetary Union; Implications for National Policy Makers*, EIPA, Maastricht, pp. 217–43.

Monnet, J. (1976), *Mémoires*, Fayard, Paris.

Monnier, C. (1983), La Tarification de l'Electricité en France, *Economica*, Paris.

Moravcsik, A. (1993), 'Preferences and Power in the European Community: A Liberal Intergovernmentalist Approach', *Journal of Common Market Studies*, vol. 31, no. 4, pp. 473–24.

Morsink, R. and Molle, W.T.M. (1991), *Direct Investment and Monetary Integration, European Economy*, Special Edition, no. 1, pp. 36–55.

Mortensen, J. (1992), 'The Allocation of Savings in a Liberalised European Capital Market', in A. Steinherr, (ed.), *The New European Financial Market Place*, Longman, London, pp. 208–20.

Moss, J. (1982), *The Lomé Conventions and their Implications for the US*, Westview Press, Boulder, Colorado.

Moulaert, F. and Derykere, Ph. (1982), 'The Employment of Migrant Workers in West Germany and Belgium', *International Migration Quarterly*, vol. 2, pp. 178–97.

Mourik, A. van (1987), 'Testing Factor Price Equalisation in the EC: An Alternative Approach: A Comment', *Journal of Common Market Studies*, vol. 26.1, pp. 79–86.

Mourik, A. van (1989), 'Countries, a Neo-Classical Model of International Wage Differentials', in W. Molle and A. van Mourik (eds), *Wage Differentials in the European Community, Convergence or Divergence?* Gower, Aldershot, pp. 83–103.

Mourik, A. van (1993), *Wages and European Integration*, PhD, RL, Maastricht.

Mueller, C.F. (1980), *The Economics of Labor Migration, a Behavioral Analysis*, Academic Press, New York.

Mueller, D. (1981), 'Competitive Performance and Trade within the EEC, Generalisations from Several Case Studies with Specific Reference to the West German Economy', *Zeitschrift für die Gesamte Staatswissenschaften*, vol. 137.3, pp. 638–63.

Mueller, D.C. (ed.) (1983), *The Political Economy of Growth*, Yale University Press, New Haven.

Mueller, D.C. (ed.) (1980), *The Determinants and Effects of Mergers; an International Comparison*, Oelgeschlager, Cambridge, Massachusetts.

Mueller, D.C. (1989), *Public Choice II*, Cambridge University Press, Cambridge.

Mundell, R.A. (1957), 'International Trade and Factor Mobility', *American Economic Review*, vol. 47.3, pp. 321–35.

Mundell, R.A. (1961), 'A Theory of Optimum Currency Areas', *American Economic Review*, vol. 53, pp. 657–64.

Muntendam, J. (1987), 'Philips in the World, a View of a Multinational on Resource Allocation', in B. van der Knaap and E. Wever (eds), *New Technology and Regional Development*, Croom Helm, London, pp. 136–44.

Murfin, A. (1987), 'Price Discrimination and Tax Differences in the European Motor Industry', in S. Cnossen (ed.), *Tax Coordination in the European Community*, Kluwer, Deventer, pp. 171–95.

Murrell, P. (1983), 'The Comparative Structure of Growth in West Germany and British Manufacturing Industries', in D. Mueller (ed.), *The Political Economy of Growth*, Yale University Press, New Haven, pp. 109–32.

Musgrave, R.A. and Musgrave, P. (1989), *Public Finance in Theory and Practice*, McGraw-Hill, New York.

Myrdal, G. (1956), *An International Economy, Problem and Prospects*, Harper and Bros, New York.

Myrdal, G. (1957), *Economic Theory and Underdeveloped Regions*, Duckworth and Co., London.

Naveau, J. (1983), *L'Europe et le Transport Aérien*, Bruylant, Brussels.

Neary, P. (1987), *Tariffs, Quotas and VER With and Without Internationally Mobile Capital*, Paper to the European Economic Association Conference, Copenhagen.

Neary, P. and Ruane, F.P. (1984), 'International Capital Mobility, Shadow Prices and the Cost of Protection', *Working Paper 32, Centre of Economic Research*, University College Publication, Dublin.

NEI/E&Y (1992), 'New location factors for mobile investment in Europe', *CEC Regional Development Studies*, no. 6, Brussels.

Neumark, F. *et al.* (1963), 'Report of the Fiscal and Financial Committee', *The EEC Reports on Tax Harmonisation*, International Bureau of Fiscal Documentation, Amsterdam.

Neven, D., Nuttall, R. and Seabright, P. (1993), *Merger in Daylight; the Economics and Politics of European Merger Control*, CEPR, London.

NIESR (1991), *A New Strategy for Economic and Social Cohesion after 1992*, London.

Noël, E. (1988), 'Working Together; the Institutions of the European Community' *European Documentation*, Luxemburg.

Nordhaus, W.D. (1972), 'The Worldwide Wage Explosion', *Brookings Papers on Economic Activity*, 2, pp. 431–65.

Norman, V. (1989), 'EFTA and the Internal European market', *Economic Policy*, vol 2, pp. 424–65.

Norman, V. (1991), '1992 and EFTA', in L.A. Winters and A. Venables (eds), *European Integration, Trade and Industry*, Cambridge University Press, Cambridge, pp 120–41.

Oates, W. (1972), *Fiscal Federalism*, Harcourt, New York.

Oberender, P. and Rüter, G. (1993), 'The Steel Industry, a Crisis of Adaptation', in H.W. de Jong (ed.), *The Structure of European Industry*, 3rd edn, Kluwer, Dordrecht, pp. 65–89.

Odagiri, H. (1986), 'Industrial Policy in Theory and Reality', in H.W. de Jong and W.G. Shepherd (eds), *Mainstreams in Industrial Organisation*, Book II, pp. 387–41.

Odell, P. and Rosing, K. (1980), *The Future of Oil, a Simulation Study of the Interrelationship of Resources, Reserves and Use, 1980–2080*, Kogan Page, London.

OECD (1964), *Industrial Statistics 1900–1962*, Paris.

OECD (1965), *Wages and Labour Mobility*, Paris.

OECD (1966), *Energy Policy*, Paris.

OECD (1968), *Capital Market Study*, (five vols), Paris.

OECD (1973), *Oil, the Present Situation and Future Prospects*, Paris.

OECD (1978), *The Migratory Chain*, Paris.

OECD (1979), *International Direct Investment; Policies, Procedures and Practices*, Paris.

OECD (1980), *Controls on International Capital Movements; the Experience with Controls on International Portfolio Operations in Shares and Bonds*, Paris.

OECD (1981a), *International Investment and Multinational Enterprises, Recent International Direct Investment Trends*, Paris.

OECD (1981b), *Regulations Affecting International Banking Operations*, (2 vols), Paris.

OECD (1982a), *Controls on International Capital Movements, the Experience with Controls on International Financial Credits, Loans and Deposits*, Paris.

OECD (1982b), *Code of Liberalisation of Capital Movements*, Paris.

OECD (1982c), *Controls and Impediments Affectinq Inward Direct Investment in OECD Member Countries*, Paris.

OECD (1982d), *World Energy Outlook*, Paris.

OECD (1983a), *International Trade in Services; Insurance: Identification and Analysis of Obstacles*, Paris.

OECD (1983b), *The Implications of Different Means of Agricultural Income Support*, Paris.

OECD (1984a), *International Trade in Services; Banking: Identification and Analysis of Obstacles*, Paris.

OECD (1984b), *Merger Policies and Recent Trends in Mergers*, Paris.

OECD (1985a), 'Relative Wages, Industrial Structure and Employment Performance', *Employment Outlook*, pp. 83–99.

OECD (1985b), *Tourism Policy and International Tourism*, Paris.

OECD (1985c), *Cost and Benefits of Protection*, Paris.

OECD (1986a), *International Trade in Services; Audiovisual Works*, Paris.

OECD (1986b), *SOPEMI; Continuous Reporting System on Migration*, Paris (also 1973–86).

OECD (1987a), 'Science and Technology', *Newsletter* no. 10, Paris.

OECD (1987b), *International Trade in Services; Securities*, Paris.

OECD (1987c), *Recent Trends in International Direct Investment*, Paris.

OECD (1987d), *National Policies and Agricultural Trade*, Paris.

OECD (1987e), *The Cost of Restricting Imports; the Automobile Industry*, Paris.

OECD (1987f), *Energy Policies and Programmes of IEA Countries*, 1986 Review, Paris.

OECD (1987g), *Energy Balances of OECD countries 1970–1985*, Paris.

OECD (1987h), *Taxation in developed countries*, Paris.

OECD (1991), *Taxing Profits in a Global Economy: Domestic and International Issues*, Paris.

OECD (1992), *Trends in International Migration*, SOPEMI, Paris.

OECD (1993), *The Changing Course of International Migration*, Paris.

Okun, A. (1975), *Equality and Efficiency; the Big Trade Off*, Brookings Institution, Washington.

Olson, M. (1965), *The Logic of Collective Action, Public Goods and the Theory of Groups*, Harvard University Press, Cambridge, Massachusetts.

Olson, M. (1983), *The Rise and Decline of Nations (Economic Growth, Stagflation and Social Rigidities)*, Yale University Press, New Haven.

Oort, C.J. (1975), *Study of the Possible Solutions for Allocating the Deficit which may occur in a System of Charging for the Use of Infrastructures Aiming at Budgetary Equilibrium*, CEC, Brussels.

Owen, N. (1983), *Economies of Scale, Competitiveness and Trade Patterns within the European Community*, Clarendon, Oxford.

Ozawa, T. (1992), 'Cross Investments between Japan and the EC. Income Similarity, Technological Congruity and Economics of Scope', in J. Cantwell (ed.), *Multinational Investment in Modern Europe*, Edward Elgar, Aldershot, pp. 13–45.

Padoa-Schioppa, T. *et al.* (1987), *Europe in the 1990's; Efficiency, Stability and Equity; a Strategy for the Evolution of the Economic System of the European Community*, Oxford University Press, Oxford.

Paelinck, J.H.P. and Nijkamp, P. (1975), *Operational Theory and Method in Regional Economics*, Saxon House, Farnborough.

Page, S. (1981), 'The Revival of Protectionism and its Consequences for Europe', *Journal of Common Market Studies*, vol. 20, pp. 17–40.

Palmer, M. and Lambert, J. *et al.* (1968), *European Unity; a Survey of the European Organisations*, PEP, Unwin University Books, London.

Papadimetriou, D.G. (1978), 'European Labour Migration (Consequences for the Countries of Workers' Origin)', *International Studies Quarterly*, vol. 22.3, pp. 377–408.

Pearce, J. (1981), *The Common Agricultural Policy*, Chatham House, London.

Pearson, M. and Smith, S. (1992), *The European Carbon Tax; an Assessment of the European Commission Proposals*, Institute of Fiscal Studies, London.

Pecchioli, R.M. (1983), *The Internationalisation of Banking, the Policy Issues*, OECD, Paris.

Pechman, J.A. (ed.) (1987), 'Comparative Tax Systems; Europe, Canada and Japan', *Tax Analyst*, Arlington, Virginia.

Peeters, T., Praet, P. and Reding, P. (eds) (1985), *International Trade and Exchange Rates in the Late Eighties*, North-Holland, Amsterdam.

Pelkmans, J. (1980), 'Economic Theories of Integration Revisited', *Journal of Common Market Studies*, vol. 18.4, pp. 333–54.

Pelkmans, J. (1982), 'The Assignment of Public Functions in Economic Integration' *Journal of Common Market Studies*, vol. 21.1, pp. 97–121.

Pelkmans, J. (1983), 'European Direct Investments in the European Community' *Journal of European Integration*, vol. 7.1, pp. 41–70.

Pelkmans, J. (1984), *Market Integration in the European Community*, Nijhoff, The Hague

Pelkmans, J. (ed.) (1985), *Can the CAP be Reformed?*, EIPA, Maastricht.

Pelkmans, J. (1986), 'Completing the Internal Market for Industrial Products', CEC Brussels.

Pelkmans, J. (1991), 'Towards Economic Union', in P. Ludlow (ed.), *Setting EC Priorities 1991–92*, CEPS/Brasseys, London.

Pelkmans, J. and Vanheukelen, M. (1988), 'The Internal Markets of North America Fragmentation and Integration in the US and Canada, Research on the "Cost of Non-Europe"', Basic Findings', CEC, vol. 16, Luxemburg.

Pelkmans, J. and Vollebergh, A. (1986), 'The Traditional Approach to Technical Harmonisation: Accomplishments and Deficiencies', in J. Pelkmans and M. Vanheukelen (eds), *Coming to Grips with the Internal Market*, EIPA, Maastricht, pp. 9–30.

Pelkmans, J. and Winters, L.A. (1988), *Europe's Domestic Market*, Routledge, London

Perée, E. and Steinherr, A. (1989), 'Exchange Rate Uncertainty and Foreign Trade *European Economic Review*, vol. 33, pp. 1241–64.

Pertek, J. (1992), 'General Recognition of Diplomas and Free Movement of Professionals', EIPA, Maastricht.

Peschel, K. (1985), 'Spatial Structures in International Trade; an Analysis of Long Term Developments', *Papers of the Regional Science Association*, vol. 58, pp. 97–11

Petit, M. *et al.* (1987), *The Agricultural Policy Formation in the European Communit The Birth of Milk Quotas and the CAP Reform*, Elsevier, Amsterdam.

Petith, H.C. (1977), 'European Integration and the Terms of Trade', *Economic Journa* vol. 87, pp. 262–72.

Petrochilos, G.A. (1989), *Foreign Direct Investment and the Development Proces* Avebury, Aldershot.

Phelps-Brown, H. (1977), *The Inequality of Pay*, Oxford University Press, Oxford.

Philip, A.B. (1978), 'The Integration of Financial Markets in Western Europe', *Journal of Common Market Studies*, vol. 16, pp. 302–22.

Phylaktis, K. and Wood, G.E. (1984), 'An Analytical and Taxonomic Framework for the Study of Exchange Controls', in J. Black and G.S. Dorrance (eds), *Problems of International Finance*, St Martin's Press, New York, pp. 149–66.

Pinder, D. (1983), *Regional Economic Development and Policy; Theory and practice in the EC*, George Allen and Unwin, London.

Pinder, J. (1986), 'The Political Economy of Integration in Europe, Policies and Institutions in East and West', *Journal of Common Market Studies*, vol. 24.1, September, pp. 1–14.

Pirenne, H. (1927), *Les Villes du Moyen-âge*, Lamertin, Brussels.

Poeck, A. van (1980), 'De Belgische Inflatie (1960-1977): Een Interpretatie aan de Hand van de Moderne Phillips-curve', *Maandschrift Economie*, vol. 44.3, pp. 122–40.

Polachek, S.W. (1980), 'Conflict and Trade', *Journal of Conflict Resolution*, vol. 24, pp. 55–78.

Pollard, S. (1974), *European Economic Integration*, Thames and Hudson, London.

Pollard, S. (1981a), *Peaceful Conquest, the Industrialisation of Europe 1760–1970*, Oxford University Press, Oxford.

Pollard, S. (1981b), *The Integration of the European Economy since 1815*, George Allen and Unwin, London.

Pomfret, R. (1986), *Mediterranean Policy of the European Community; a Study of Discrimination in Trade*, Macmillan, London.

Pool, B. (1990), 'The Creation of the Internal Market in Insurance', CEC, Luxemburg.

Pratten, C. (1988), 'A Survey of the Economies of Scale', *Research into the Cost of Non-Europe; Basic Findings*, vol. 2, Luxemburg, pp. 11–165.

Prest, A.R. (1983), 'Fiscal Policy', in P. Coffey, (ed), *Main Economic Policy Areas of the EEC*, 2nd edn, M. Nijhoff, The Hague, pp. 59–90.

Price Waterhouse (1988), 'The Cost of non-Europe in Financial Services', *Research into the Cost of Non-Europe; Basic Findings*, vol. 9, CEC, Brussels.

Priore, H.J. (ed.) (1979), *Unemployment and Inflation; Institutionalists' and Structuralists' Views*, Sharpe, White Plains, New York.

Pryce, R. (1973), *The Politics of the European Community*, Butterworth, London.

Pryor, F. (1972), An International Comparison of Concentration Ratios, *Review of Economics and Statistics*, vol. 54.2, pp. 130–40.

Puchala, D.J. (1984), *Fiscal Harmonisation in the European Communities, National Policies and International Cooperation*, Pinter, London.

Pugliese, E. (1992), 'The New International Migration and Changes in the Labour Market', *Labour* vol. 6.1, pp. 165–79.

Raux, J. (ed.) (1984), *Politique Agricole Commune et Construction Européenne*, Economica, Paris.

Ray, J.E. (1986), 'The OECD "Consensus" on Export Credits', *The World Economy*, vol. 9.3, pp. 1–14.

Reder, M.W. (1962), *Wage Differentials, Theory and Measurement*, Princeton, NJ.

Redmond, J. (ed.) (1992), *The External Relations of the European Community; the International Response to 1992*, St Martin's Press, New York.

Redor, D. (1992), *Wage Inequalities in East and West*, Cambridge University Press, Cambridge/New York.

Resnick, S. and Truman, E. (1975), 'An Empirical Examination of Bilateral Trade in Europe', in B. Balassa (ed.), *European Economic Integration*, North-Holland, Amsterdam, pp. 41–78.

Richardson, J. (1987), *A Subsectoral Approach to Services Trade Theory*, SWF Pergamon, Oxford.

Ricq, C. (1983), 'Frontier Workers in Europe', in M. Anderson, (ed.), *Frontier Regions in Europe*, Frank Cass, London, pp. 98–108.

Riemsdijk, J.F. van (1972), 'A System of Direct Compensation Payments to Farmers as a Means of Reconciling Short Run to Long Run Interests', *European Review of Agricultural Economics*, vol. 1.2, pp. 161–89.

Rijke, R. (1987), *Competition among International Airlines*, Gower, Aldershot.

Rijksbaron, A., Roobol, W.H. and Weisglas, M. (eds) (1987), *Europe from a Cultural Perspective. Historiography and Perceptions*, Nijgh and Van Ditmar, The Hague.

Ritson, C. (ed.) (1978), 'The Lomé Convention and the CAP', *Commonwealth Economic Papers* no. 12, Commonwealth Secretariat, London.

Robson, P. (1988), *The Economics of International Integration*, 3rd edn, Allen and Unwin, London.

Rollet, P. (1984), *Spécialisation Internationale et Intégration Economique et Monétaire dans les Pays CEE*, CREI, Lille.

Rollo, J.M.C. and Warwick K.S. (1979), 'The CAP and Resource Flows among EEC Member States', *Working Paper* no. 27, Government Economic Service, London.

Rose, R. et al., (1985), *Public Employment in Western Nations*, Cambridge University Press, Cambridge.

Rosecrance, R. (1984), *The Rise of the Trading State: Commerce and Conquest in the Modern World*, Basic Books, New York.

Rothwell, R. and Zegveld, W. (1981), *Industrial Innovation and Public Policy; Preparing for the 1980s and 1990s*, Pinter, London.

Ruding, O. et al. (1992), *Conclusions and Recommendations of the Committee of Independent Experts on Company Taxation*, OOPEC, Luxemburg.

Rugman, A.M. (ed.) (1982), *New Theories of the Multinational Enterprise*, Croom Helm, London.

Sachs, J. (1980), 'Wages, Flexible Exchange Rates and Macro-Economic Policy', *Quarterly Journal of Economics*, vol. 94, pp. 731–47.

Salt, J. (1976), 'International Labour Migration, the Geographical Pattern of Demand', in J. Salt and H. Clout (eds), *Migration in Post-War Europe, Geographical Essays*, Oxford University Press, Oxford, pp. 126–67.

Salvatori, D. (1991), 'The Automobile Industry', in D. Mayes (ed.), *The European Challenge, Industry's Response to the 1992 Programme*, Harvester Wheatsheaf, London, pp. 28–90.

Sametz, A.W. (ed.) (1984), *The Emerging Financial Industry*, Lex Books, D.C. Heath, Lexington, Massachusetts.

Sampson, A. (1977), *The Seven Sisters*, Corgi, London.

Sannucci, V. (1989), 'The establishment of a Central Bank; Italy in the nineteenth century' in M. de Cecco and A. Giovannini (eds), *A European Central Bank?* Cambridge University Press, Cambridge, pp. 244–74.

Sapir, A. (1989), 'Does 1992 Come Before or After 1990?; on Regional versus Multilateral Integration', in R. Jones and A.O. Krueger (eds), *The Political Economy of International Trade*, Basil Blackwell, Oxford, pp. 197–222.

Sapir, A. (1992), 'Regional integration in Europe', *The Economic Journal*, vol. 102, pp. 1491–1506.

Sassin, W., Hölzl, A., Hogner, H.H. and Schrattenholzer, L. (1983), *Fuelling Europe i the Future; the Long Term Energy Problem in the EC Countries, Alternative R&D Strategies*, IIASA, Laxenburg.

Saunders, C. and Marsden, D. (1981), *Pay Inequalities in the European Communitie* Butterworths, London.

Saunders, P. and Klau, F. (1985), 'The Role of the Public Sector, Causes and Consequences of the Growth of Government', *OECD Economic Studies*, no. 4, pp. 1–23!

Scaperlanda, A.E. (1967), 'The EEC and US Foreign Investment; Some Empirica Evidence', *Economic Journal*, vol. 77, pp. 22–6.

Scaperlanda, A.E. and Mauer, L.J. (1969), 'The Determinants of US Direct Invesment in the EEC', *American Economic Review*, vol. 59, pp. 558–68.

Schäfers, A. (1987), 'The Luxemburg Patent Convention, the Best Option for the Internal Market', *Journal of Common Market Studies*, vol. 25.3, pp. 193–207.

Schendelen, M.P.C.M. van (1984), 'The European Parliament; Political Influence is more than Legal Powers', *Journal of European Integration*, vol. 8, pp. 59–76.

Schendelen, M.P.C.M. van (1993), *National Public and Private EC Lobbying*, Dartmouth, Aldershot.

Scherer, F. (1974), 'The Determinants of Multi-Plants Operations in Six Nations and Twelve Industries', *Kyklos*, vol. 27.1, pp. 124–39.

Schippers, J.J. and Siegers, J.J. (1986), 'Womens' Relative Wage Rate in the Netherlands, 1950–1983; a Test of Alternative Discrimination Theories', *De Economist*, vol. 134.2, pp. 165–80.

Schmitz, A. (1970), 'The Impact of Trade Blocks on Foreign Direct Investments', *Economic Journal*, vol. 80, pp. 724–31.

Schmitz, A. and Bieri, J. (1972), 'EEC-Tariff and US Direct Investment', *European Economic Review*, vol. 3, pp. 259–70.

Schwalbach, J. (1988), 'Economies of Scale and Intra-Community Trade', in *Research into the Cost of Non-Europe, Basic Findings*, vol. 2, pp. 167–204.

Schwartz, A. and Kooyman, J. (1975), 'Competition and the International Transmission of Inflation', *De Economist*, vol. 123.4, pp. 723–48.

Schwarze, J. (1987), 'Towards a European Foreign Policy; Legal Aspects', in J.K. de Vree, P. Coffey and R.H. Lauwaars (eds), *Towards a European Foreign Policy*, Nijhoff, Dordrecht, pp. 69–97.

Scitovsky, T. (1958), *Economic Theory and Western European Integration*, Allen and Unwin, London.

Scott, N. (1967), *Towards a Framework for Analysing the Cost and Benefits of Labour Migration*, Institute for International Labour Studies, Bulletin, Geneva, February.

Seers, D., Schaffer, B. and Kiljunen, M.L. (1979), *Underdeveloped Europe: Studies in Core–Periphery Relations*, Harvester Press, Hassocks, Sussex.

Seers, D., Vaitsos, C. and Kiljunen, M.L. (1980), *Integration and Unequal Development, The Experience of the EC*, St Martin's Press, New York.

Segré, C. *et al.* (1966), *The Development of a European Capital Market*, CEC, Brussels.

Seidel, B. (1983), *Wage Policy and European Integration*, Gower, Aldershot.

Sellekaerts, W. (1973), 'How Meaningful are Empirical Studies on Trade Creation and Trade Diversion', *Weltwirtschaftliches Archiv*, vol. 109.4, pp. 519–51.

SER (1992), *Migratie, Arbeidsmarkt en Sociale Zekerheid*, Den Haag.

Sexton, J.J., Walsh, B.M., Hannan, D.F. and McMahon, D. (1991), *The Economic and Social Implications of Emigration*, NESC, Dublin.

Sharp, M. (ed.) (1985), *Europe and the New Technologies, Six Case Studies in Innovation and Adjustment*, Pinter, London.

Shaw, R.W. and Simpson, P. (1987), *Competition Policy; Theory and Practice in Western Economies*, Wheatsheaf, Brighton.

Shepherd, G., Duchêne, Fr. and Saunders, Ch. (1983), *Europe's Industries, Public and Private Policies for Change*, Cornell, New York.

Shepherd, W.G. (1985), *Public Policies Towards Business*, 7th edn, Irwin, Homewood, Illinois.

Shlaim, A. and Yannopoulos, G.N. (1976), *The EC and the Mediterranean Countries*, Cambridge University Press, Cambridge.

Siebert, H. (ed.) (1994), *Migration; a Challenge for Europe* (forthcoming).

SIGMA, (1985), *Wirtschaftsstudien der Schweizerischen Rückversicherungsgesellschaft*, Zürich.

Simões, V.C. (1992), 'European Integration and the Pattern of FDI Flows in Portugal', in J. Cantwell (ed.), *Multinational Investment in Modern Europe*, Edward Elgar, Aldershot, pp. 256–97.

Simon, J.L. (1989), *The Economic Consequences of Immigration*, Basil Blackwell, Oxford.

Simons, J. (1986), *Recht en Onrecht in het Europese Vervoerbeleid*, Tjeenk Willink, Zwolle.

Sleuwaegen, L. (1987), 'Multinationals, the European Community and Belgium; Recent Developments', *Journal of Common Market Studies*, Vol. 26.2, pp.255–72.

Sleuwaegen, L. (1993), 'Road Haulage', *European Economy/Social Europe*, no. 3, pp. 211–50.

Sleuwaegen, L. and Yamawaki, H. (1988), 'European Common Market: Structure and Performance', *European Economic Review*, vol. 32, pp. 1451–75.

Smith, A. and Venables, A.J. (1988), 'Completing the Internal Market in the EC, some Industry Simulations', *European Economic Review*, vol. 32, pp. 1501–25.

Söderston, B. (1980), *International Economics*, 2nd edn, Macmillan, London.

Soete, L. (1987), 'The Impact of Technological Innovation on International Trade Patterns: the Evidence Reconsidered', *Research Policy*, pp. 101–30.

Spaak, P.H. *et al.* (1956), *Rapport des Chefs de Délégation aux Ministres des Affaires Etrangères*, Brussels.

Spannent, (1991), 'Direct Investment of the European Community', *Eurostat*, Luxemburg.

Steenbergen, J. (1987), 'Legal Instruments and External Policies of the EC', in J.K. de Vree, P. Coffey and R. H. Lauwaars (eds), *Towards a European Foreign Policy*, Nijhoff, Dordrecht, pp. 109–43.

Steinherr, A. (1984), 'Convergence and Coordination of Macro-Economic Policies: Some Basic Issues', *European Economy*, no. 20, pp. 71–110.

Steinherr, A. (1985), 'Competitiveness and Exchange Rates; some Policy Issues for Europe?', in T. Peeters, P. Praet and P. Reding (eds.), *International Trade and Exchange Rates in the Late Eighties*, North-Holland, Amsterdam, pp. 163–90.

Steinle, W. (1988), 'Social Policy', in W. Molle and R. Cappellin (eds), *Regional Impact of Community Policies in Europe*, Avebury, Aldershot, pp. 108–23.

Stevens, C. (ed.) (1981), *EEC and the Third World; a Survey*, Hodder and Stoughton, London.

Stonham, P. (1982), *Major Stock Markets of Europe*, Gower, Aldershot.

Stonham, P. (1987), *Global Stock Market Reforms*, Gower, Aldershot.

Stopford, J.M. and Baden-Fuller, Ch. (1987), 'Regional Level Competition in a Mature Industry; the Case of European Domestic Appliances', *Journal of Common Market Studies*, vol. 26.2, pp. 173–92.

Strasser, D. (1982), 'The Finances of Europe', *European Perspectives*, Brussels/ Luxemburg.

Strauss, R. (1983), 'Economic Effects of Monetary Compensatory Amounts', *Journal of Common Market Studies*, vol. 21, pp. 261–81.

Strijker, D. and de Veer, J. (1988), 'Agriculture', in W. Molle and R. Cappellin (eds), *Regional Impact of Community Policies in Europe*, Avebury, Aldershot, pp. 23–44.

Struls, A. (ed.) (1979), *Energy Models in the European Community*, IPC Science and Technology Press, Guildford.

Swoboda, A. (ed.) (1976), 'Capital Movements and their Control', in *IUHEI,CEI*, no 3, Sythoff, Leiden.

Talbot, R.B. (1977), 'The European Community's Regional Fund', *Progress in Planning*, vol. 8.3, pp. 183–281.

Tangermann, S. (1984), 'Guarantee Thresholds, a Device for Solving the CAP Surplus Problem?', *European Review of Agricultural Economics*, vol. 11.2, pp. 159–68.

Tapp, J. (1986), 'Regulation of the UK Insurance Industry', in J. Finsinger and J. Pauly (eds), *The Economics of Insurance Regulation*, Macmillan, Basingstoke, pp. 27–64.

Tarditi, S. (1984), 'La Crise de la PAC: un Point de Vue Italien', *Economie Rurale*, vol 163, pp. 28–33.

Teulings, A.W.M. (1984), 'The Internationalisation Squeeze: Double Capital Movement and Job Transfer within Philips Worldwide', *Environment and Planning*, A, vol. 16, pp. 597–614.

Tharakan, P.K.M. (ed.) (1983), *Intra-Industry Trade; Empirical and Methodological Aspects*, North-Holland, Amsterdam.

Tharakan, P.K.M. (1988), 'The Sector/Country Incidence of Anti-Dumping and Countervailing Duty Cases in the EC', in L.B.M. Mennes and J. Kol (eds), *European Trade Policies and the Developing World*, Croom Helm, Beckenham, pp. 94–135.

Thomsen, S. and Nicolaides, Ph. (1991), *The Evolution of Japanese Direct Investments in Europe*, Harvester Wheatsheaf, Brighton.

Thornton, J. (1992), 'Interest Rates in Domestic and Eurocurrency Markets', *Applied Economics*, vol. 24, pp. 1103–5.

Thygesen, N. (1990), 'The Benefits and Costs of Currency Unification', in H. Siebert, (ed.), *The Completion of the Internal Market*, IWW/Mohr, Tübingen, pp. 347–75.

Tichy, G. (1992), 'The European Neutrals', in S. Borner and H. Grubel (eds), *The European Community after 1992. Perspectives from the Outsiders*, Macmillan, London, pp. 165–91.

Tims, W. (1987), 'EC Agricultural Policies and the Developing Countries', in L.B.M. Mennes and J. Kol (eds), *European Trade Policies and the Developing World*, Croom Helm, Beckenham, pp. 135–87.

Tinbergen, J. (1953), *Report on Problems Raised by the Different Turnover Tax Systems Applied within the Common Market*, ECSC, Luxemburg.

Tinbergen, J. (1954), *International Economic Integration*, Elsevier, Amsterdam.

Tinbergen, J. (1959), 'Customs Unions, Influence of their Size on their Effect', *Selected Papers*, North-Holland, Amsterdam, pp. 152–64.

Tinbergen, J. (1962), *Shaping the World Economy; Suggestions for an International Economic Policy*, The 20th Century Fund, New York.

Tinbergen, J. (1991), 'The Velocity of Integration', *De Economist*, vol. 139.1, pp. 1–11.

Tinbergen, J. and Fischer, D. (1987), *Warfare and Welfare, Integrating Security Policy into Socio-Economic Policy*, Wheatsheaf, Brighton.

Tironi, E. (1982), 'Customs Union Theory in the Presence of Foreign Firms', *Oxford, Economic Papers*, vol. 34, pp. 150–71.

Toulemon, R. and Flory, J. (1974), *Une Politique Industrielle pour l'Europe*, PUF, Paris.

Tovias, A. (1978), 'Differential country size as an incentive to the proliferation of trading blocks', *Journal of Common Market Studies*, vol. 16.3, pp. 246–66.

Tovias, A. (1982), 'Testing Factor Price Equalisation in the EEC', *Journal of Common Market Studies*, vol. 20, pp. 165–81.

Tovias, A. (1990), 'The Impact of Liberalising Government Procurement Policies of Individual EC Countries on Trade with Non Members', *Weltwirtschaftliches Archiv* 126.4, pp. 722–36.

Tovias, A. (1991), 'A Survey of the Theory of Economic Integration', *Journal of European Integration*, vol. XV.1, pp. 5–23.

Triffin, R. (1992), 'IMS, International Monetary System or Scandal?', *EPU/EUI Jean Monnet Papers*, Florence.

Tsoukalis, L. (1977), *The Politics and Economics of European Monetary Integration*, Allen and Unwin, London.

Tucker, K. and Sundberg, M. (1988), *International Trade in. Services*, Routledge, London.

Tuma, E.H. (1971), *European Economic History, 10th Century to Present*, Harper and Row, New York.

Twitchett, K.J. (ed.) (1976), *Europe and the World, the External Relations of the Common Market*, Europe Publisher, London.

Uhrig, R. (1983), 'Pour une Nouvelle Politique de Développement Régional en Europe', *Economica*, Paris.

UN (1979), *Labour Supply and Migration in Europe; Demographic Dimensions 1950–1975 and Prospects*, UN/ECE, Geneva.

UN (1980), *Tendencies and Characteristics of International Migration since 1950*, Geneva.

UN/ECE (1967), *Incomes in Postwar Europe: Economic Survey of Europe in 1965*, part 2, Geneva.

UN/ECE (1977), *Intra-European Temporary Migration of Labour, its Consequences for Trade, Investment and Industrial Co-operation*, TRADER 341, Geneva.

UN/ECE (1980), *Economic Role of Women in the ECE Region* (Chapter 4), Geneva.

UN/ECE, (several years) *Annual Bulletin of Electric Energy Statistics for Europe*, Geneva.

UNCTAD (1983), *Protectionism and Structural Adjustment; Production and Trade in Services, Policies and their Underlying Factors bearing upon International Service Transactions*, Geneva.

Ungerer, H. *et al.* (1986), 'The European Monetary System, Recent Developments', *Occasional Paper*, no. 48, IMF, Washington.

UNIPEDE (1982), 'Influence des Prix sur la Consommation d'Electricité', *Rapport du Groupe 60.02*, Brussels.

UNIPEDE (1985), *Compte Rendu d'Activités du Groupe d'Experts pour l'Etude de l'Influence entre Prix et Consommation de l'Electricité*, Athens.

Urban, G. (1983), 'Theoretical Justification for Industrial Policy', in F.G. Adams and C.R. Klein (eds), *Industrial Policies for Growth and Competitiveness: an Economic Perspective*, pp. 21–40.

USDL (1989), 'The Effects of Immigration on the US Economy and Labor Market', in *Migration, Policy and Research*, report 1, Bureau of International Labor Affairs, Washington.

Vandamme, J. (ed.) (1985), *New Dimensions in European Social Policy*, TEPSA, Croom Helm, London.

Vandamme, J. (1986), *Employee Consultation and Information in Multinational Corporations*, Croom Helm, London.

Vanhove, N. and Klaassen, L.H. (1987), *Regional Policy, a European Approach*, 2nd edn, Gower, Aldershot.

Vassille, L. (1989), 'Similarity among Countries; an International Comparison Based on Data from the 1978/79 Survey; and Industries; the Role of Productivity, Skill and Other Factors', in W. Molle and A. van Mourik (eds), *Wage Differentials in the European Community, Convergence or Divergence?*, Gower, Aldershot, pp. 65–83 and 139–63.

Venables, A. (1987), 'Customs Union and Tariff Reform under Imperfect Competition', *European Economic Review*, vol. 31, pp. 103–10.

Verdoorn, P.J. (1952), 'Welke zijn de Achtergronden en Vooruitzichten van de Economische Integratie in Europa en welke Gevolgen zou deze Integratie hebben, met name voor de Welvaart in Nederland?', *Overdruk no. 22*, Centraal Planbureau, The Hague.

Verdoorn, P.J. and Schwartz, A.N.R. (1972), 'Two Alternative Estimates of the Effects of EEC and EFTA on the Pattern of Trade', *European Economic Review*, vol 3.3, pp. 291–335.

Verloop, P.J.P. (ed.) (1988), *Merger Control in the EEC*, Kluwer, Deventer.

Vernon, R. (1966), 'International Investment and International Trade in the Product Cycle', *Quarterly Journal of Economics*, vol. 80, pp. 190–207.

Verrijn Stuart, G.M. *et al.* (1965), 'Europees Kapitaalverkeer en Europese Kapitaalmarkt', *European Monographs*, no. 5, Kluwer, Deventer.

Viaene, J.M. (1982), 'A Customs Union between Spain and the EEC', *European Economic Review*, vol. 18, pp. 345–68.

Viner, J. (1950), *The Customs Union Issue*, Stevens and Sons, London.

Voigt, F., Zachcial, M. and Rath, A. (1986), 'Regulation and Modal Split in the International Freight Transport of the EC', mimeo, University of Bonn, CEC, Brussels.

Völker, E. (1983), 'The Major Instruments of the CCP', in J.H. Bourgeois, *et al.* (eds), *Protectionism and the European Community*, Kluwer, Antwerp, pp. 17–49.

Vosgerau H.J. (1989), *New Institutional Arrangements for the World Economy*, Springer, Berlin.

Waelbroeck, J. (1976), 'Measuring the Degree of Progress of Economic Integration', in F. Machlup, (ed.), *Economic Integration, Worldwide, Regional, Sectoral*, Macmillan, London, pp. 89–99.

Waha, J.P. (1986), 'Intra-European Trade in Electricity', in P. Odell and J. Daneels (eds), *Gas and Electricity Markets in Europe: Prospects and Policies*, BAEE, Brussels, pp. 330–44.

Wallace, H., Wallace, W. and Webb, C. (1983) (eds), *Policy Making in the European Community*, 2nd edn, Wiley, Chichester.

Wallace, W. (1982), 'Europe as a Confederation: the Community and the Nation State', *Journal of Common Market Studies*, vol. 21.1, pp. 57–69.

Ward, E. (1986), 'A European Foreign Policy', *International Affairs*, no. 4, pp. 573–82.

Warneke, S.J. and Suleiman, E.N. (eds) (1975), *Industrial Policies in Western Europe*, Praeger, New York.

Warner, H. (1984), 'EC Social Policy in Practice; Community Action on Behalf of Women and its Impact in the Member States', *Journal of Common Market Studies*, vol. 23.2, pp. 141–67.

Wegner, M. (1989), 'The European Community', in J.A. Pechman (ed.), *The Role of the Economist in Government, an International Perspective*, Harvester/Wheatsheaf, New York/London, pp. 279–99.

Weiss, F.D. (1987), 'A Political Economy of European Community Trade Policy against the LDCs', *European Economic Review*, vol. 31, pp. 457–65.

Wellenstein, E. (1979), '25 Years of European Community External Relations', CEC, *European Documentation* 4/79, Brussels.

Werner, P. *et al.* (1970), 'Report to the Council, Commission on the Realisation by Stages of the Economic and Monetary Union in the Community', *Bulletin of the EC II*, Supplement.

Veyers, G.J. (1982), *Industriepolitiek*, Stenfert Kroese, Leiden/Antwerpen.

Veyman-Jones, T.G. (1986), *Energy in Europe; Issues and Policies*, Methuen, London.

Whalley, J. (1979), 'Uniform Domestic Tax Rates, Trade Distortions and Economic Integration', *Journal of Public Economics*, vol. 11, pp. 213–21 (see also the further debate in *JPE*, December 1981, pp. 379–90).

Whalley, J. (1985), *Trade Liberalisation among Major World Trading Areas*, MIT Press, Cambridge, Massachusetts.

Whichart, O.G. (1981), 'Trends in the US Direct Investment Position Abroad, 1950–1979', US Department of Commerce, *Survey of Current Business*, vol. 61.2, pp. 39–56.

Wijnbergen, S. (1985), 'Interdependence Revisited; a Developing Countries' Perspective on Macro-Economic Management and Trade Policy in the Industrial World', *Economic Policy, a European Forum*, vol. 1.1, pp. 81–137.

Wilke, M. and Wallace, H. (1990), 'Subsidiarity, Approaches to Power Sharing in the EC', *Royal Institute of International Affairs*, Discussion Papers no. 27, London.

Wilkins, M. (1986), 'The History of European Multinationals, a New Look', *The Journal of European Economic History*, vol. 15.3, pp. 483–510.

Williamson, J. (1976), 'The Implication of European Monetary Integration for the Peripheral Areas', in J. Vaizey (ed.), *Economic Sovereignty and Regional Policy*, Gill and Macmillan, Dublin, pp. 105–121.

Williamson, J. and Bottrill, A. (1971), 'The Impact of Customs Unions on Trade in

Manufactures', *Oxford Economic Paper*, vol. 23, pp. 323–51, reprinted in M. Kraus (ed.) (1973), *The Economics of Integration*, Allen and Unwin, London, pp. 118–51.

Williamson, J. and Miller, M.H. (1987), *Targets and Indicators; a Blueprint for the International Coordination of Economic Policy*, Institute for International Economics, Washington DC.

Winsemius, A. (1939), *Economische Aspecten der Internationale Migratie*, Bohn, Haarlem.

Winters, L.A. (1985), 'Separability and the Modelling of International Economic Integration', *European Economic Review*, vol. 27, pp. 335–53.

Wise, M. (1984), *The Common Fisheries Policy of the European Community*, Methuen, London.

Wittelloostuyn, A. van and Maks, J.A.H. (1988), 'Workable Competition and the Common Market', *European Journal of Political Economy*, vol. 16, pp. 1–19.

Wolf, Ch. (1987), 'Market and Non-Market Failures; Comparison and Assessment', *Journal of Public Policy*, vol. 7.1, pp. 43–70.

Wolf, M. (1988), 'An Unholy Alliance: the European Community and Developing Countries in the International Trading System', in L.B.M. Mennes and J. Ko (eds), *European Trade Policies and the Developing World*, Croom Helm, Beckenham pp. 31–57.

Wonnacott, P. and Wonnacott, R. (1981), 'Is Unilateral Tariff Reduction Preferable t a Customs Union? The Curious Case of the Missing Foreign Tariffs', *American Economic Review*, vol. 71, pp. 704–14.

Woolly, P. (1974), 'Integration of Capital Markets', in G. Denton, (ed.), *Economic an Monetary Union in Europe*, Croom Helm, London, pp. 23–55.

WRR (1986), *The Unfinished European Integration*, Netherlands Scientific Council fo Government Policy, The Hague.

Yannopoulos, G.N. (1985), 'The Impact of the European Economic Community o East–West Trade in Europe', *University of Reading Discussion Papers in Economic Series A, no. 165.

Yannopoulos, G.N. (1986), 'Patterns of Response to EC Tariff Preferences; an Em pirical Investigation of Selected non–ACP Associates', *Journal of Common Mark Studies*, vol. 25.1, pp. 14–30.

Yannopoulos, G.N. (1990), 'Foreign Direct Investment and European Integratio the evidence from the formative years of the European Community', *Journal Common Market Studies*, vol. 28.4, pp. 235–57.

Young, C. (1972), 'Association with the EEC; Economic Aspects of the Trade Rel tionship', *Journal of Common Market Studies*, vol. 11, pp. 120–35.

Ypersele, J. van and Koene, J.C. (1985), 'The European Monetary System; Origin Operation and Outlook', *CEC Series European Perspectives*, Luxemburg.

Yuill, D. et al. (1993), *European Regional Incentives 1993–94*, 13th edn, Bowker/Sa London.

Zippel, W. (1985), 'Die Bedeutung einer Harmonisierung der Einzelstaatlich Verkehrspolitiken im Hinblick auf den Integrationsprozess', in F. Voigt and Witte (eds), *Integrationswirkungen von Verkehrssystemen und ihre Bedeutung für EG*, Duncker und Humblot, Berlin, pp. 21–35.

Zodrow, G.R. (1983), *Local Provision of Public Services: the Tiebout Model after Twen five Years*, Academic Press, New York.

Index